THE PHILOSOPHY AND ECONOMICS OF J. M. KEYNES

The Philosophy and Economics of J. M. Keynes

Edited by
Bill Gerrard
University of York
and
John Hillard
University of Leeds

Edward Elgar

Published by
Edward Elgar Publishing Limited
Gower House
Croft Road
Aldershot
Hants GU11 3HR
England

Edward Elgar Publishing Limited
Distributed in the United States by
Ashgate Publishing Company
Old Post Road
Brookfield
Vermont 05036
USA

A CIP catalogue record for this book is available from the British Library

Library of Congress Cataloging-in-Publication Data
The philosophy and economics of J.M. Keynes/edited by Bill Gerrard and John Hillard.
p. cm.
Includes bibliographical references and index.
1. Keynes, John Maynard, 1883–1946. 2. Keynesian economics.
I. Gerrard, Bill. II. Hillard, John, 1946–
HB103.K47P46 1992
330.15'6—dc20 91–37688
CIP

ISBN 1 85278 400 8

Printed and bound in Great Britain by
Billing and Sons Ltd, Worcester

Contents

Figures

Contributors

John Brothwell, School of Business and Economic Studies, University of Leeds, Leeds, UK.

Arthur Brown, School of Business and Economic Studies, University of Leeds, Leeds, UK.

Anna Carabelli, Department of Economics, University of Padua, Padua, Italy.

Victoria Chick, Department of Economics, University College, London, UK.

Amitava Dutt, Department of Economics, University of Notre Dame, Notre Dame, Indiana, USA.

Athol Fitzgibbons, Division of Commerce and Administration, Griffith University, Brisbane, Queensland, Australia.

Bill Gerrard, Department of Economics and Related Studies, University of York, Heslington, York, UK.

John Hillard, School of Business and Economic Studies, University of Leeds, Leeds, UK.

Michael Howard, Department of Economics, University of Waterloo, Waterloo, Ontario, Canada.

John King, Department of Economics, La Trobe University, Bundoora, Victoria, Australia.

Roy J. Rotheim, Skidmore College, Saratoga Springs, New York, USA.

Malcolm Sawyer, School of Business and Economic Studies, University of Leeds, Leeds, UK.

Ted Winslow, Division of Social Science, York University, North York, Ontario, Canada.

Bibliographical note

Throughout this volume all references denoted by CW are to *The Collected Writings of John Maynard Keynes*, published on behalf of the Royal Economic Society by Macmillan and Cambridge University Press and edited by D. E. Moggridge and E. Johnson, 1973–89.

I	*Indian Currency and Finance*
II	*The Economic Consequences of the Peace*
III	*A Revision of the Treaty*
IV	*A Tract on Monetary Reform*
V	*A Treatise on Money, 1 The Pure Theory of Money*
VI	*A Treatise on Money, 2 The Applied Theory of Money*
VII	*The General Theory of Employment, Interest and Money*
VIII	*A Treatise on Probability*
IX	*Essays in Persuasion*
X	*Essays in Biography*
XI	*Economic Articles and Correspondence: Academic*
XII	*Economic Articles and Correspondence: Investment and Editorial*
XIII	*The General Theory and After: Part I, Preparation*
XIV	*The General Theory and After: Part II, Defence and Development*
XV	*Activities 1906–14: India and Cambridge*
XVI	*Activities 1914–19: The Treasury and Versailles*
XVII	*Activities 1920–2: Treaty Revision and Reconstruction*
XVIII	*Activities 1922–32: The End of Reparations*
XIX	*Activities 1922–9: 2 Vols, The Return to Gold and Industrial Policy, I and II*
XX	*Activities 1929–31: Rethinking Employment and Unemployment Policies*
XXI	*Activities 1939–45: World Crises and Policies in Britain and America*
XXII	*Activities 1939–45: Internal War Finance*
XXIII	*Activities 1940–3: External War Finance*
XXIV	*Activities 1944–6: The Transition to Peace*
XXV	*Activities 1940–4: Shaping the Post-War World: The Clearing Union*
XXVI	*Activities 1941–6: Shaping the Post-War World: Bretton Woods and Reparation*

Introduction

This book took shape as a follow-up to the Leeds-based *J.M. Keynes in Retrospect*, edited by John Hillard (Edward Elgar, 1988). Although the present collection remains rooted in Yorkshire, the geographical spread of contributors has been extended to reflect the international dimension of the debate on Keynes. Part I below relates to philosophy and method. Towards the end of the 1980s, the image of Keynes as a philosopher/economist came to prominence and the debate has generated a new Keynesian fundamentalism. A common theme throughout Part I is the role of organic interdependence in the development of Keynes's ideas on method, theory and practice. Part II focuses on Keynes's treatment of the competitive process. Here the contributors explore the connections between the imperfect competition debate of the 1930s and the role of competition in the *General Theory*. Part III presents the work of Keynes as seen through four frames of reference – Keynesian, post-Keynesian, psychoanalytic and Marxist. The overall intention of the collection is to stress the contemporary relevance of Keynes and to promote an interdisciplinary approach which transcends the limitations of orthodox economic perception.

The essays by Anna Carabelli, Victoria Chick, Athol Fitzgibbons, Bill Gerrard and Malcolm Sawyer were presented at the Review of Political Economy conference and a symposium on Keynes held in Malvern, August 1990. We wish to thank the organizers and participants at these events. We acknowledge the financial support given by the SBES Keynes fund, University of Leeds and the Group for Alternative Perspectives, University of York. The essays by John Brothwell, Arthur Brown, John Hillard, Roy J. Rotheim and Ted Winslow were presented at seminars in the School of Business and Economic Studies, University of Leeds. Thanks to Kathy O'Donnell for organizing the seminars. For technical assistance, thanks to Teresa Brier, Joan Camm, Helen Hawksby and Elsie Merrick. Thanks also to Edward Elgar for supporting the project from its inception. Finally the editors wish to dedicate what follows to friends and former colleagues, Rodney Crossley, George Rainnie and Michael Surrey.

Leeds/York

PART I

PHILOSOPHY AND METHOD

1 Organic interdependence and Keynes's choice of units in the *General Theory*[1]

Anna Carabelli

I Introduction

In the *General Theory* Keynes tackles the *negative* task of criticizing classical theory in Chapters 2 and 3. Before moving to the *positive* side of his theory, however, he devotes four chapters to the discussion of the methodological problems. One of these problems is 'the choice of the units of quantity appropriate to the problems of the economic system as a whole' (CW VII: 37). This chapter aims to show how Keynes's choice of units in the *General Theory* reflects his vision of a monetary macroeconomy as a complex system requiring a complex theory. Keynes's choice of units reflects the *object* and the *method* of his investigation. The object is the level and changes in real income and employment resulting from aggregate demand. The method is a way of reasoning to enable Keynes to tackle organic interdependence among the variables of the macro-system without theoretically reducing its complexity.

The discussion below focuses on the problem of organic interdependence, starting with Keynes's refusal to apply the atomic hypothesis to probability in *A Treatise on Probability* (Carabelli, 1985, 1988, 1991a and 1991b). There is a certain consistency in Keynes's thought about organic interdependence, complexity and the choice of units stretching back to 1907, in his early work on probability, in his essay on index numbers and in the various drafts of *A Treatise on Probability*. As will be shown, there are parallels also to be found in the *Tract on Monetary Reform, A Treatise on Money* and the *General Theory*. In the next section, the notion of organic interdependence and its relation to economic theorizing are discussed. There follows an examination of the development of Keynes's ideas on the choice of units up to and including the *General Theory*. In section VI some conclusions are drawn.

II Organic interdependence and economics

For Keynes, a monetary macroeconomy is a system characterized by 'complexity', possessing attributes such as organic interdependence among variables, non-homogeneity through time and space, non-numerical measurability, physical heterogeneity, openness, incompleteness, indivisibility, secondary qualities, contingency and change. Organic interdependence among variables is characterized not by external but by internal relations. Each part of a system characterized by internal relations contains in some way the whole of the system, while the latter is not just a mere sum of its parts. Developments in logic in the 1950s and 1960s demonstrated that internal relations are irreducible to external relations. Contrary to the view of the logical atomists of the early twentieth century, such as Bertrand Russell, neither the logical calculus nor the analytical theory of meaning can be applied to internal relations. In theoretical terms, the choice of the units of quantity appropriate to analyse the economic system as a complex entity is not an easy one.

In the *General Theory*, Keynes argues that the choice of units was one of 'the three perplexities which most impeded my progress in writing this book, so that I could not express myself conveniently until I had found some solution for them' (CW VII: 37). The central concepts involved in the analysis of effective demand are complex and the magnitudes considered by it are themselves complex.[2] These concepts are the volume of real output/income, the volume of real net output, the stock of real capital and the general price level (CW VII: 37). Keynes defines them as 'incommensurable collections of miscellaneous objects' (CW VII: 39). In particular, 'the community's output of goods and services' is 'a non-homogeneous complex which cannot be measured' (CW VII: 38). There is another complex magnitude, that of probability. Keynes considers probability separately in chapters 5 and 12. The problem of probability – though complex – is not confined exclusively to macro-economics.

Complex magnitudes are theoretically vague concepts. Keynes refers to 'the well-known . . . element of vagueness which . . . attends the concept of the general price level' (CW VII: 39). Theoretical vagueness does not mean that these logically indefinable concepts are also vague and ambiguous from an ordinary language point of view or in business practice. In ordinary language their meaning is easily grasped and they can be used for practical purposes. Theoretically, however, they remain 'conundrums . . . of no solution' (CW VII: 39). They raise difficulties which are

> 'purely theoretical' in the sense that they never perplex, or indeed enter in any way into business decisions and have no relevance to the causal sequence of economic events, which are clear cut and determinate in spite of the quantitative indeterminacy of these concepts.' (CW VII: 39)[3]

Complex magnitudes are indefinable in logical terms since the reduction of them to more simple terms is impossible.[4] They cannot be reduced to simple terms without falling into logical fallacies and paradoxes. The fallacy of composition is well known to economists. The reduction of one theory into another has been a common enterprise in the history of science. In physics, various attempts have been made to reduce thermodynamics to statistical mechanics. In economics, the parallel is the theoretical reduction of macroeconomics to microeconomics. This reductionist strategy has involved the search for the micro-foundations of macroeconomics, the aggregation of microeconomics into macroeconomics and an emphasis on disaggregation. But Quine's 'thesis on the irreducibility of theories' (1931, 1960) argues that reducing one theory to another does not necessarily mean that the *reducing* theory explains exactly what the *reduced* theory explains.

Complex magnitudes also possess attributes which belong to different dimensional scales. They are multidimensional magnitudes, inasmuch as they can move simultaneously in more than one direction. This calls for a theory of the units of quantities appropriate to them and it also means having an appropriate theory of measurement.[5] For Keynes, complex magnitudes are theoretically troublesome as far as measurement is concerned. They raise logical 'conundrums' rather than mathematical or statistical difficulties (CW VII: 39). The classical economists had committed logical errors by ignoring this problem: 'the units, in terms of which economists commonly work, are unsatisfactory' (CW VII: 37). Being non-numerical quantitative concepts (CW VII: 40) the quantities of real output, real net output, real capital, aggregate goods and services and the general price level do not exist. Absolute and homogeneous units of measure appropriate to these quantities do not exist either. For this reason Keynes stated that complex concepts 'cannot in themselves provide the material for a quantitative analysis' (CW VII: 39). Thus, the endeavour by classical economists 'to erect a quantitative science' (CW VII: 38) upon these concepts was a logical failure. The outcome was 'a mock precision', as it tried 'to use such partly vague and non-quantitative concepts as the basis of a quantitative analysis' (CW VII: 40).[6]

III Complex magnitudes

There is nothing new in Keynes's approach to complex magnitudes and to their units of quantity and of measure found in the *General Theory*. He had already considered them in at least four of his previous writings. He did this in 1907, in the first version of his dissertation *The Principles of Probability* (later *A Treatise on Probability*) whilst considering the measurement of the relation of probability; in his essay on 'The Method of Index Numbers' while considering the measurement of price level; in his analysis of the price level in the *Tract on Monetary Reform* (1923) and in *A Treatise on Money* (1930).

Probability

In his discussion of the measurement of probability in the first version of the *Principles of Probability* (1907), Keynes considered the contemporary status of the philosophy of measurement and, in particular, of the measurement of relations. His main interest is in the 'philosophy of magnitude', not in the mathematics of magnitude (1907: 119; see also CW VIII: 37). He devotes particular attention to Russell's *Principles of Mathematics* (1903). Keynes's analysis of the measurement of probability as a complex magnitude involves the following: (a) Probability is a relation: 'I have described probability as being a relation whose terms are propositions' (1907: 9).[8] (b) This probability relation is a quantity (1907: 52, CW VIII: 21) or 'magnitude of probability'. Keynes discusses the question raised by Russell as to whether there is any relation having magnitude beside the relation of distance. He answers positively by arguing that probability is a relation similar to Russell's notion of distance. Russell uses this term to cover the relation between different shades of colour or between moments of time, as well as between points of space (1907: 53 fn. +). (c) The probability relation follows Russell's distinction (1903: 181–2) between extensive and intensive magnitudes. Extensive magnitudes are defined as magnitudes which are rendered amenable to numerical measure. In particular the class of relations of distances (relevant to Keynes's relation of probability) and of divisibilities belongs to these magnitudes. All other magnitudes are intensive. For Keynes, the relation of probability, notwithstanding its similarity to Russell's relation of distance, does not belong to extensive magnitudes. In fact he also considers classes of quantities of probabilities relative to propositions for which equal intervals do not exist. He compares the quantity of probability to the quantity measured by specific volume or specific density. Consequently his relations of probability belong, in general, to Russell's intensive rather than extensive magnitudes:

> I think that the classes of quantities, for which equal intervals are in absence of contrary information equally probable, are those which Mr Russell calls 'distances' and 'divisibilities'. 'Intensive' quantities, on the other hand, to which measurement stands in a much less intimate relation, cannot be dealt with in this way. The quantity measured by specific volume or specific density is clearly 'intensive' in the technical sense in which that term is used here. (1907: 119–20)

(d) There are different kinds of magnitudes of the probability relation. Keynes also criticizes Russell's notion of a kind of magnitude. Keynes wants 'a new definition' of this:

> it is upsetting to one's *prima facie* conception of the nature of magnitude. It is necessary to deny Mr Russell's proposition that 'given any magnitude, those

> which are greater or less than that magnitude form a certain definite class, within which any two are one greater and the other less. Such a class is called a *kind* of magnitude' . . . A new definition of a kind of magnitude is required. (1907: 58, emphasis in original; Keynes does not give the page of the quotation but it is from Russell, 1903: 164)

Keynes defends a notion not of a kind but of different kinds of magnitudes of probability. In contrast to Russell he thinks that only if probabilities are of the *same kind* can they be compared in terms of more or less (1907: 58). Therefore comparability of magnitudes of probability relations requires homogeneity in kind. This means that Keynes considers heterogeneity in kind as the general case for probability. Within this general case one can also include those particular decisions (or, better, non-decisions) known as the sophism of Buridan's ass: 'when there is no reason for preferring any one to any others, when there is nothing, as with Buridan's ass, to determine the mind in any one of the several possible directions' (1907: 75).

In these decisions – as well as in those of heterogeneity in kind of probabilities – Keynes holds that it is rational to allow caprice to play a role in the absence of direct judgements of relevance. It is this aspect which gives an element of arbitrariness to these decisions, though they are not considered irrational by Keynes: 'these cases unfortunately comprise the majority of the judgements of probability with which we are in practice concerned. But these cases are not for that reason beyond the pale, or outside the control of our logic' (1907: 125). In the final version of *A Treatise on Probability* this type of arbitrary decision is replaced by the 'for or against the umbrella' dilemma. Again rationality is represented by caprice: 'it will be an arbitrary matter to decide for or against the umbrella' . . . it will be rational to allow caprice to determine us and to waste no time on the debate' (CW VIII: 32).[9]

This general case for probability is important because it is the basis of Keynes's approach to economic decision making in his later writings and especially in the *General Theory*. The following extracts from his letters to Townsend in 1938 show this:

> But that still leaves millions of cases over which one cannot even arrange an order of preference. When all is said and done, there is an arbitrary element in the situation . . . In making a decision we have before us a large number of alternatives, none of which is demonstrably more 'rational' than the others, in the sense that we can arrange in order of merit the sum aggregate of the benefits obtainable from the complete consequences of each. To avoid being in the position of Buridan's ass, we fall back, therefore, and necessarily do so, on motives of another kind, which are not 'rational' in the sense of being concerned with the evaluation of consequences, but are decided by habit, instinct, preference, desire, will, etc. (CW XXIX: 289, 294)[10]

The probability relation is, in general, a non-numerical quantity. Keynes argues that a quantity is not necessarily a number: 'the numerical view of probability is partly traceable to the frequent definition of probability as a number and not as a quantity' (1907: 56). Only probability relations which are of the *same kind* and in the *same unit* of quantity are numerically measurable and therefore numerically comparable (1907: 62). Difficulties in finding a common unit of quantity arise when these quantities of probability are similar to quantities which may, at the same time, be characterized by a collection of attributes, such as a class of qualities rather than by one single quality: 'the comparison of the probability of such propositions as "this book is red", and "this book is blue". By "red" not one single quality is meant, but a class of qualities. The book is to have one out of a class of qualities which we may call "the reds" (1907: 120).

Keynes distinguishes between non-comparable, comparable and numerically comparable (non-ordinable, ordinable and numerically ordinable) probabilities. There are 'three possible degrees of intimacy between the magnitudes of any pair of probabilities. Some cannot be compared at all in this respect; between others the relations of more or less can be established; and others again seem to be capable of numerical measurement in terms of some common unit' (1907: 60–1).[11] This heterogeneity in kind and in the units of quantity depends on a multidimensionality of the magnitude of probability. 'Yet the base units of the different strands (kinds of probability) are not altogether in different dimensions, as, for instance, are those of beauty and goodness' (1907: 65). Later he became more radical as regards economic quantities, speaking of 'things being . . . in different dimensions . . . and capable of variations of degree in more than one mutually incommensurable direction' (CW V: 87–8).[12]

The probability relation has an *intrinsic* quantitative indeterminateness. The impossibility of a numerical measurement of probability is not a product of mental incapacity or lack of knowledge, but arises from the nature of the case itself. This impossibility is 'absolute and inherent in the subject matter' (1907: 65) because there is no determinacy of the units of quantity. These units belong to different kinds of magnitudes:

> they are 'essentially' indeterminate . . . I say 'essentially', because this indeterminacy is not simply relative to our knowledge or to a particular set of premises, but is absolute. We have to do with different kinds of the same species of quantity, whose units are essentially indeterminate in terms of one another . . . The case is not to be compared to that of a real number II and a rational number . . . In these probability scales a new conception of relative indeterminacy of units of magnitude must be introduced. For although we can always express one unit in terms of another to *some* degree of approximation, there are strict limits to this and we cannot increase at will the closeness of the approximation. (1907: 65, emphasis in original)[13]

Probability relations are characterized by a multiplicity of the units of quantity and of measure. Given this quantitative indeterminateness, there exists a multiplicity of units of quantity and of measure of probability relations. This variety of quantity and measure depends on the object under investigation: 'the magnitudes of probability relations must be measured in various units according to the particular case in question, these units being incommensurable among themselves' (1907: 67). Conventional measures which may be applied to complex physical quantities cannot be applied in general to quantities of probabilities. Complex physical quantities (quantities for which there is not a unique unit of quantity) can nonetheless be measured by conventional means. This is done by selecting some other quantity or ratio which, belonging as it does to Russell's class of divisibilities, is characterized by equal intervals among its magnitudes. Conventional measurement imposes a numerical ordinability among complex quantities. Of course the intervals regarded as equal depend upon the initial arbitrary and conventional choice. Keynes thinks that the same cannot in general be achieved for the quantities of probability.[14] Probability is in general a non-numerical magnitude, so that the calculus of probability cannot be applied to it, except in a limited number of cases. Mathematics is relevant to Keynes in its symbolic rather than numerical character: 'the old assumptions, that all quantity is numerical and that all quantitative characteristics are additive, can be no longer sustained. Mathematical reasoning now appears as an aid in its symbolic rather than in its numerical character' (1907: 358–9).

But ordinary language is the most appropriate language for probability, being as it is the most pliable and open. Symbolic and artificial languages require limiting conditions. Also, if probability relations are not extensive magnitudes and cannot be further reduced to external relations, then Russell's extensional logic cannot be applied to such relations nor to the logical calculus. The project of logical atomism of reducing every proposition to atomic ones (Keynes briefly calls this the 'atomic hypothesis') cannot be pursued for probability. His description of probability in the 1921 final version of *A Treatise on Probability* is clear on this point and it also anticipates the often quoted passages on organic interdependence of the 1926 essay on Edgeworth (CW IX: 262) and in his letter to Tyler in 1938 (CW XIV: 286): 'a degree of probability is not composed of some homogeneous material, and is not apparently divisible into parts of like character with one another' (CW VIII: 32). Probability relations are therefore to be considered as internal relations. This is now commonly accepted within the philosophy of language as far as belief and intentional propositions are concerned but it was not the case when Keynes first advanced it in 1907.

What are the implications of this conception of probability as regards Keynes's analysis of economic beliefs and expectations? First, individual beliefs are seen by Keynes as complex magnitudes. Individual psychology is based upon organic hypotheses. Second, individual beliefs (and therefore individual decisions) also depend on theoretical concepts which are complex (that is, concepts which belong to irreducible theories). Macroeconomics is now so widespread and commonly accepted that its concepts influence individual beliefs and therefore micro-decisions. If these concepts are theoretically irreducible to atomic ones, methodological individualism's long-standing hope of reducing macroeconomic concepts to their individual components will remain forever unsatisfied. Methodological individualism is trapped in a vicious circle. It is just as feasible to argue for the macro-foundations of microeconomics. Third, individual beliefs, apart from their internal complexity and their dependence on complex irreducible macro-concepts, further depend upon intersubjective or publicly-held beliefs. Keynes's view of economic beliefs based on internal relations differs both from the traditional view of knowledge as atomistically decentralized, dispersed and subjective, and from that part of modern economics of information which considers knowledge as a commodity characterized by transaction costs. For Keynes, partial knowledge is not homogeneous in kind and, further, it is not subjective and atomistically dispersed. There exist also forms of shared or common knowledge; these are based upon public opinion, conventions and social practices which are the result of societal organizations in which individuals, groups and institutions are organically embedded.

The price level

The second complex magnitude considered by Keynes before the *General Theory* is the price level. In 1905, Keynes wrote an essay for Alfred Marshall on the construction of index numbers of general exchange value. In 1909, he returned to the topic, writing an essay on 'The Method of Index Numbers with Special Reference to the Measurement of General Exchange Value' (CW XI: 49–156). Keynes maintains that the measurement of economic quantities is a task which is carried out prior to the employment of the method of index numbers. He presents his philosophy of measurement of economic quantities in terms of the logical rather than mathematical difficulties in measurement. These difficulties 'depend rather upon reasoning than upon calculation' and postpone 'the mathematical difficulties' (CW XI: 64). There is 'more need for reasoning than for mathematical analysis' (CW XI: 128) in dealing with index numbers. Keynes's philosophy of measurement of economic quantities is in line with that of *The Principles of Probability*. He distinguishes between two classes of economic quantities:

1. quantities which are from the conceptual point of view perfectly definite and capable of measurement but are unmeasurable (CW XI: 52) because of incomplete information or data at the individual's disposal; and
2. quantities which are *in themselves* incapable of measurement.

These quantities may be indefinite, indefinable or theoretically vague from the conceptual point of view. However their theoretical indefiniteness and numerical indeterminateness do not mean that these concepts convey 'only a vague and imprecise idea. Nothing could be more determinate than . . . this concept, although in a limited sense quantitative' (Keynes is referring here to national income as the aggregate of utilities) (CW XI: 53). They are perfectly definite at the ordinary language level.

While the first group of quantities is irrelevant to a discussion of the philosophy of measurement, the second group is not. In the latter, difficulties of measurement arise from the nature of the subject itself, quite apart from an inability to measure them. Keynes thinks that in economics these quantities are numerous. He concentrates on the determination of individual prices, the general price level, the esteem standard and the wages standard.

Individual prices (a) Price is a relation (CW XI: 57, 64–6). A certain sum of money is exchanged for a certain amount of a particular commodity. The relation between money and this commodity is a relation of price. (b) The price relation is a quantity (CW XI: 57) capable of changes in the degree or magnitude of the relation. The notion of kind of magnitude is the same as that advanced in *The Principles of Probability*. There may be two relations of price which have the same magnitude and two others of which one is greater and the other lesser. He points out that different kinds of quantities exist: a ton or a mile for example. Further, there are quantities between which there is an intermediate degree of intimacy (CW XI: 53). The approach is similar to that of quantities of probability; that is, they must be of the same kind: 'a set of quantities are of the same kind when each of the set can be compared in respect of more and less with each of the others' (CW XI: 54). (c) The price relation is a non-numerical quantity. While many relations are capable of measurement, such as the relation of distance, the price relation is not 'in the fullest and strictest sense, numerically measurable'. There cannot be 'two relations of price such that the magnitude of one is x times the magnitude of the other, where x is a number. Strictly, then, relations of price are not measurable' (CW XI: 57). As for probability, Keynes compares the price relation to some physical relation such as the quality of a substance which is constituted by the relation between its mass and the space it fills. This relation is quantitative but not strictly numerical. In his view, a conventional measurement can be given on either of two alternative scales: by the specific volume ratio or by specific density ratio. These ratios measure the *same* physical quantities. But they are two different heterogeneous units and a unique and common absolute unit of measure does not exist. So, in contrast to his view on probability, a conventional measure is allowed for price magnitudes as for physical complex magnitudes. However, in the case of price, one should be particularly careful when dealing with averages of price magnitudes (CW XI: 57–8). Keynes stresses that 'a price ratio . . . is only a conventional measure of the phenomenon of price, useful for most purposes but not fully representative. Not all arithmetic operations performed on price ratios have a corresponding economic interpretation' (CW XI: 69).

He insists that these problems are not 'needless subtleties' but it is important for economic reasoning 'to know exactly in what sense a particular price relation is measurable' (CW XI: 66). All price relations have to be of the same kind, as only in this case the price relations of different commodities can be placed in order in the same series. Secondly, a numerical comparison of particular price relations – and of economic quantities at different times and places – has to be in the same unit. Before numerically comparing economic quantities 'it is essential that we should first measure them in terms of some common unit' (CW XI: 52). Thus 'a set of quantities . . . are in the same *unit* when *numerical* comparison is possible between every pair of the set' (CW XI: 54, emphasis in original). Difficulties in finding a common unit in economics are comparable to physical quantities characterized by a collection of multidimensional attributes, such as colour and shape. Keynes's analogy recalls 'the degree of similarity' used in the *Principles of Probability* to compare degrees of probability: 'a green octavo volume is more like a green folio than a red octavo is, but it would be evidently false to say that it is twice or any other number of times as like' (CW XI: 54). It also parallels the '*different* orders of similarity' characterizing the example of the 'book bound in blue morocco' in the final version of *A Treatise on Probability* (CW VIII: 39, emphasis in original).

The general price level (a) The general price level is a relation like the price relation of a single commodity (CW XI: 64–6). (b) The general price level is a complex relation: 'The *complex* relation of money to the commodities [is] constituted by the fact' of the 'particular price relations' that money possesses with regard to each of the commodities (CW XI: 66, emphasis in original). Another definition of this complex relation is 'an *ensemble* of particular exchange values' (CW XI: 95, emphasis in original). (c) The general price level is a non-numerical quantity. As with individual price relations, it is 'generally incapable of measurement' (CW XI: 95). Thus it is not numerically quantitative: it is a 'false premiss that the *ensemble* of particular price relations is numerically quantitative' (CW XI: 68, emphasis in original). Therefore an absolute and perfect measure of it does not exist: it 'has no real existence' (CW XI: 135). (d) There is an intrinsic numerical indeterminateness of the units of quantities measured by the general price level. It is not the inability to discover a mathematical formula which makes it impossible to find an absolute measure of the exchange value: 'New lines of mathematical investigation' are in this case of no help (CW XI: 135 fn.*). Along these lines, Keynes criticizes the mathematical statistician Walsh:

> His false premiss, that general exchange value must be numerically quantitative, is responsible [for his idea that units are equivalent over periods of time]. If only we are sufficiently ingenious, he thinks, we shall find a formula yielding us an absolute measure of it . . . If there was a perfect measure of general exchange value, Mr Walsh would certainly have found it; but the method of exhaustion is barren, if the object of search has no real existence. (CW XI: 135)

The non-existence of an absolute measure of the general price level, seen as the exchange value of money, means that the 'real' quantities obtained by using it as a standard of measure are indeterminate. What are these quantities? The exchange value standard is related to a specific theory of value. In fact the quantities obtained by using it are the quantities of goods and services purchased in general by a given sum of money. Their physical heterogeneity is the main source of the theoretical conundrums which are behind Keynes's criticism: the numerical quantities relative to collections of heterogeneous goods do not exist. They are ambiguous quantities in themselves because of their intrinsic nature and not owing to an inability to measure them. (e) Fallacies of composition arise in the relationship between individual price and the general price level. The complex relation does not share all the characteristics of the simple price relations of which it is the complex. Properties of the particular price relations cannot be extended to the general level without falling into fallacies of composition: 'while we have a price corresponding to each *particular* exchange value, it is not true, as it is sometimes assumed, that we have a price corresponding to *general* exchange value. General exchange value is a function of particular exchange values, but it does not possess all their properties' (CW XI: 66–7, emphasis in original). Even in the cases where individual price relations are numerical, it does not follow that the complex relation is also numerical: 'a relation determined by several numerically quantitative relations is not necessarily itself one' (CW XI: 72). (f) There is a plurality of price levels. Once the existence of a unique and absolute general exchange price level is denied, a multiplicity of price levels arises. The general exchange value can only be defined as being the exchange value of some specific relevant composite commodity. Only within this definition 'its price is a satisfactory measure as the price of a particular commodity and has the same properties' (CW XI: 95). Instead of the general exchange value, there is therefore a variety of exchange values according to the specific composite commodity chosen. The choice of the representative composite commodity depends upon the specific object under analysis.

The esteem standard The quantities obtained by using the exchange value standard as a measure represent the amount of articles and services purchased in general by a given sum of money. These quantities are ambiguous, given that the units of aggregate commodities and services do not exist. The quantities of utility obtained by 'esteem value' standard represent the amount of utility purchased in general by a given sum of money. This standard forms the basis of the equilibrium theory of value. Keynes applies to these quantities and to their standard unit the same criticism that he applied to the quantities of aggregates of goods obtained by a measure of exchange value.[15] (a) The aggregate of individual utilities is a complex concept: 'there is an aggregate of utilities . . . but not a sum' (CW XI: 60); (b) this aggregate is a non-numerical magnitude.

A measure of the quantity of aggregate utilities does not exist: 'there is no *measure* of the aggregate of individual utilities' (CW XI: 60, emphasis in original). Once more, this has nothing to do with an inability to measure it, but is intrinsic to the nature of the object: 'the measure of the amount of utility which a given sum will purchase is intrinsically and from the nature of the case beyond our reach' (CW XI: 59). Nor is it a function of incomplete information: 'a knowledge of *all* the facts would not enable us to compare numerically' two aggregates of utilities (CW XI: 53, emphasis in original). Hence the laws of addition and multiplication cannot be applied: there is no possibility of 'measuring and applying the formulae of addition to the individuals of the aggregate' (CW XI: 60). This is because quantities of aggregate utility are not of the same kind: they are non-homogeneous. Consequently, there is no common unit of two aggregates of utilities: 'a numerical comparison between two aggregates of utilities would only be possible if each of the utilities were strictly of the same kind and if the laws of arithmetic could be validly applied to their summation. This does not seem to be the case' (CW XI: 54). (c) Theoretical vagueness and numerical quantitative indeterminacy of the aggregate of utility do not mean that the meaning conveyed by this complex concept is vague. The aggregate of utilities enjoyed by a specific set of individuals is thought by Keynes quite determinate at ordinary-language level (CW XI: 53).

The wages standard The other measure of the general value of money considered by Keynes is the cost (or wages) value standard.[16] This is the standard defined in the *General Theory* as the 'essential standard of value' (CW VII: 302). It is 'the money price in a given market of an hour's command' of labour. The units of quantity obtained by this standard are units of labour commanded. They are non-homogeneous in origin but can be made homogeneous by grading the labour into its more distinctive kinds. When dealing with comparison in different places or periods, Keynes further suggests taking the average cost of labour hours actually purchased, with no reference to the heterogeneous kinds of labour or degrees of skill. He considers that this is 'a universal unit of quantity more reasonable than the corresponding units – bulk or weight – in the case of commodities' (CW XI: 60 and fn.*) and he sees 'the individual as a unit of constant importance' (CW XI: 61 fn.*).

IV *A Treatise on Money*

The next stage in the development of Keynes's approach to complex magnitudes is his analysis of the value of money in *A Treatise on Money*. It closely resembles that of his 1909 essay on index numbers. A summing-up of the characteristics of price level shows that it is a mere repetition of the substance of the 1909 argument.[17] (a) The value of money is a complex magnitude. Money is compared to 'many other famous concepts, namely . . . all those which are complex or manifold' (CW V: 88). (b) It is a non-commensurable magnitude:

> It is similar to other complex concepts which are capable of variations of degree in more than one mutually incommensurable direction at the same time . . . The same difficulty arises whenever we ask whether one thing is superior in degree to another *on the whole*, the superiority depending on the resultant of several attributes which are each variable in degree but in a way not commensurable with one another. (CW V: 88, emphasis in original)[18]

(c) There is no absolute measure of the value of money. In line with his 1909 essay, Keynes's criticism of the quantity theory of money is the impossibility of obtaining a unique measure of the value of money. One cannot speak of the general price level both as the value of money in itself and in an absolute sense. This is an explicit criticism of classical economists, lacking in the early essay:

> Classical economists – in particular Cournot, Jevons and Edgeworth – are wrong in holding that the value of money is unique: such ideas (held by Jevons and Edgeworth) . . . are root-and-branch erroneous. The 'errors of observation', the 'faulty shots aimed at a single bull's eye' conception of the index number of prices, Edgeworth's 'objective mean variation of general prices', is the result of a confusion of thought. There is no bull's eye. There is no moving but unique centre, to be called the general price level or the mean objective variation of general prices, round which are scattered the moving price levels of individual things. There are all the various, quite definite, conceptions of price levels of composite commodities appropriate for various purposes and inquiries . . . and many others too. There is nothing else. Jevons was pursuing a mirage. (CW V: 76)

Keynes's denial of the existence of the intrinsic value of money, commonly described 'as the value of *money as such*' or the 'objective mean variation of general prices', strictly follows the lines of his 1909 essay: 'a measure of the "intrinsic value" of money has no separate existence, but is merely one of the currency index numbers' (CW V: 77, emphasis in original). In explicit reference to his 1909 essay, he points out that he has 'long believed that this is a will-o'-the-wisp, a circle squaring expedition which has given an elusive taint' (CW V: 72).

(d) Keynes's rejection of an absolute value of money implies a positive affirmation of the existence of a multiplicity of price levels (incommensurable among themselves). As there is no 'bull's eye', no 'mean objective variation of general prices', no value of money 'as such', what exists 'are all the various, quite definite, conceptions of price levels of composite commodities . . . and many others too' (CW V: 76). Attention has to be paid to the purchasing power of money (or consumption standard), the wholesale standard, the international standard, the currency standard and so on. These are the only 'definite' concepts of the value of money (CW V: 76). The value of money is nothing but 'the price of a composite commodity' (CW V: 71). Given that absolute composite commodities do not exist, a representative one is needed using some criteria of relevance or appropriateness. The choice depends on time, space, purpose and object of inquiry: 'the appropriateness of different composite commodities to different time, places and purposes' (CW V: 71–2; see also 48, 76).

(e) Relative money price levels move in a divergent manner. In their neglect of the plurality of price levels, classical economists made the mistake of thinking that multiple price levels behave equally and tend to move in a convergent manner (CW V: 81). They hold that definite relationships exist between the different price levels (CW V: 79). This is why, in Keynes's view, the classical theory of money neglects the study of the different behaviour of the multiple price levels – a neglect which he finds unacceptable and upon whose criticism the whole analysis of *A Treatise on Money* is articulated. His criticism has not been appreciated by the *Treatise*'s interpreters: 'by overlooking the temporary divergences between price levels which in the long run are likely to move together, [the classical theory of money] assumed away the very facts which it is the task of such theory to investigate' (CW V: 66–7).

(f) The numerical comparison between incommensurable magnitudes represented by price levels relative to different time, space or purposes is theoretically questionable. Keynes questions Fisher's attempt to develop a general formula for a comparison of price levels (CW V: 100–101). (g) The calculus is in general inapplicable. Keynes again stresses the inappropriateness of applying the laws of addition and multiplication and the calculus of probability to the measurement of the value of money (CW V: 72). His constant attention to the *limits* of the application of mathematics to economic material emerges again. (h) There is a difference between physical and economic magnitudes. As regards units of quantities and measure, the extension of the physical science's paradigm to economics is unwarranted.[19] This is the base of the logical fault Keynes attributes to Jevons and Cournot (CW V: 71, 78). The 'kaleidoscope' rather than the mechanical analogy is more appropriate in investigating the value of money. Money does not follow mechanical laws (CW V: 81).

The purchasing power of money

In *A Treatise on Money*, Keynes's discussion of the standard of value in his 1909 essay is repeated and he chooses two particular price levels as specific standards. Keynes's choice depends on the specific *quaesita* raised in this work and is therefore not absolute. The two standards (or units of measure) chosen by him are the purchasing power of money and the labour power of money. The two units of quantity obtained are the consumption unit and the labour unit. For Keynes the neglect of these standards by the classical theory of money is a further reason for its rebuttal:

> they [the forms of the quantity theory] have a further fault, in that the standard . . . is neither the labour standard nor the purchasing power standard . . . This is a serious fault, because it must be the two former standards which are our true *quaesita*. For the labour power of money and the purchasing power of money are fundamental . . . Human effort and human consumption are the ultimate matters from which alone economic transactions are capable of deriving any significance . . . I propose . . . to break away from the traditional method of

> setting out from the total quantity of money irrespective of the purposes on which it is employed. (CW V: 120–1)

The purchasing power of money standard is the inverse of the price level of consumption goods. Keynes calls it the consumption standard (giving rise to the consumption unit). This standard of value is considered by him much more fundamental than both the Fisher standard, based upon the flow concept of monetary transactions, and the Cambridge standard, based upon the stock concept of money balances (CW V: 68–70; see also 199–214). Given that *the* exchange standard no longer exists, these three exchange standards can be considered as non-neutral alternatives. Being non-absolute, the choice of standard has to be justified by the theoretician who uses it. This attempt to match theoretical tools with the object and the material under investigation is one of the main methodological interests in all Keynes's writings. In *A Treatise on Money*, he thinks the consumption standard is most suitable for his object of analysis and gives explicit justification for its uses (CW V: 198).

On this point Keynes also makes a self-criticism of his use of 'consumption units' in his *Tract on Monetary Reform*. There he measured real money balances in terms of these units, without distinguishing the purposes for which cash balances are used. In *A Treatise on Money*, he thinks this way of measuring them is wrong. The units of quantity should correspond to the multiplicity of purposes – something which, in his view, does not happen in the *Tract* (CW V: 199–200). He further criticizes Pigou's choice of the quantities of wheat purchased by the wheat standard (that is, the price of wheat):

> By measuring the quantity of real balances in terms of wheat, Professor Pigou is shirking, rather than solving, the question of the type of price level to which our fundamental equation is intended to lead up. The object of any quantity equation is to discover, not the price of wheat, but . . . the purchasing power of money. But his equation either makes no contribution to this or does so by implying that relative prices are unchangeable, all individual prices and therefore all price levels being fixed in terms of wheat – which is remote from the facts. (CW V: 208; see also 97)

Pigou's choice of the units assumes that relative prices are unchanged. His idea that all price levels are fixed in terms of wheat appears to Keynes as 'remote from the facts'. Keynes's criticism of Pigou had a great influence on his choice of the second standard of value in *A Treatise on Money*: a standard upon which all price levels are, in his opinion, *actually* fixed. This standard is the labour power of money. It is the 'earnings standard which measures the power of money to command units of human effort' (CW V: 49–50). The earnings standard is 'a measure of cost value'. The quantity obtained is the amount of labour which a given sum will purchase by a measure of cost value. The earnings standard of *A Treatise on Money* is the heritage of the 1909 essay's cost (or wages) value standard and provides the wage-unit in the *General Theory*, where Keynes drops the purchasing power standard but maintains the labour power of money.

What is the role of the earnings standard in *A Treatise on Money*? The first component of the *Treatise*'s fundamental equations is represented by this standard. Thus both the price level of consumption goods and of output as a whole are mainly determined by the earnings standard. In consequence, the level of money prices is explained in terms of the earnings standard. On the other hand, changes in the level of money prices are explained either by the second component of the *Treatise*'s fundamental equations or by spontaneous changes in the earnings standard.

Further, the earnings standard is relatively fixed within the period considered by Keynes. This characteristic of the earnings standard is at the root of the divergent behaviour of prices in *A Treatise on Money*. Some prices are relatively fixed or slower to move than others. The economic process is analysed by Keynes as a three-stage process (Hicks, 1967: 191–4). In stage one there is a change in flexible prices (of consumption and investment goods), while rigid prices are taken as fixed. There is no change in output or employment. In stage two, changes in real activity take place. In stage three, changes in rigid prices occur. Rigid prices within the considered period are explained by money contracts which are fixed over periods of time, particularly by money wages (CW V: 83). The existence of money contracts also explains the divergent behaviour of relative money prices: 'there are many kinds of money contracts, money customs and money understandings fixed over periods of time which is a further cause why relative values (i.e. prices) under a monetary regime do not move freely, even in the fairly long run' (CW V: 82). The result is that in *A Treatise on Money* – as in the *General Theory* – all price levels are fixed in terms of money wages.

The price level as a complex magnitude: a monetary analysis

As with the above discussion of probability, comparison will now be made of Keynes's analysis of the method appropriate to price level as a complex magnitude in his 1909 essay and in *A Treatise on Money*. In both cases Keynes's main problem is to match the characteristics of the object under investigation with those of the theory to be applied to it. A complex object needs a complex theory, and probability is the complex object under his investigation in 1907. In 1909 and 1930, it becomes price level. The problem of the choice of the appropriate units of quantity and of measure is the link between these two aspects of theory, that is, object and method.

The key lies in his concept of 'logical independence' (or 'independence for probability' or 'for knowledge' as he also calls it) – first advanced in *The Principles of Probability* (1907) and still present in the final version of *A Treatise on Probability* (1921). This notion of independence is in contrast to physical or material independence.

Keynes uses the concept of independence in his 1909 essay when he deals with the limited application of the calculus of probability to the actual construction of index numbers: 'deviations are "independent" if a knowledge of the magnitude of one of them is no guide whatever to the magnitude of any of the others' (CW XI: 108). He also stresses that:

> This controversy [on index numbers], like so many others in probability, is due to a failure to understand the meaning of 'independence'. The mathematics of the orthodox theory of averages and least squares depend upon the assumption that the observations are 'independent'; but it has been supposed that physical independence is sufficient. In point of fact, the theory requires that the observations shall be independent, in the sense that a knowledge of the result of some does not affect the probability that the others, when known, involve given errors. (CW XI: 155–6)[20]

Keynes holds that money price changes are '*not* strictly independent' (CW XI: 117, emphasis in original). A single isolated price change may not influence (that is, be 'independent for knowledge' from) other individual price changes. At the macro-level, however, money price changes do influence each other.

> One price change is not likely, unless it occurs in a very important commodity, to have very much effect on any other individual price change, so that we can for many purposes assume an approximate independence. But in the aggregate the error may become appreciable . . . The *price* of pepper *is* independent of the price of meat, but the general exchange value of pepper is not independent of the general exchange value of meat. (CW XI: 117–18, emphasis in original)

This interdependence among money price changes does not stem from the mere interdependence among commodities which characterizes the Walrasian economy. This latter case operates within a world of atomic interdependence. In Keynes's theory money itself has a central role to play:

> The general exchange values of different commodities are not strictly independent in the sense required for probability. Any *one* may be approximately independent of any *single* one other; but if we take several, the general exchange value of one of them is extremely dependent on those of the others. (Letter to C.P. Sanger, 23 June 1909, CW XI: 158, emphasis in original)

In *A Treatise on Money*, money cannot be isolated from things and these cannot be isolated from money. Neither does a reality exist with what

Davidson (1983/4: 569) calls the 'axiom of reals'; nor is there a reality where an absolute meaning can be attributed to the value of money. There is organic interdependence between money and commodities, or, more precisely, between the value of money and the relative prices of commodities. Again what underlies this independence is Keynes's concept of 'independence for knowledge': he holds that 'instead of "independence" of relative price changes, there is 'connexity" ' (CW V: 77 and fn. 1; see also 73, 75).[21]

The organic interdependence of money price relations

The continuity of Keynes's approach in these two writings also appears with regard to the role of money. Why does money create such an organic interdependence among the price relations of the economic macro-system? In the 1909 essay on index numbers there is no complete theoretical explanation of this peculiarity of money. The analysis which he was later to develop fully is certainly not yet present. Keynes merely points out that – in contrast to what the classical theory of money asserts – it is difficult to disentangle changes on the side of money from changes on the side of commodities. He emphasizes, however, that a change on the side of money has a 'tendency to disturb the relative exchange values of commodities' (CW XI: 106). When there are changes on the part of money, there 'will also be at work changes on the side of commodities'. The resulting money price changes are a complex result of the organic interplay of both of these influences. This is why 'price changes are *not* strictly independent' (CW XI: 117, emphasis in original). Therefore, 'except in the roughest possible way', the calculus of probability cannot be applied to the measurement of the general price level (CW XI: 119). For the same reason the orthodox assumption of 'a uniform change in a large variety of different objects superimposed upon particular and independent changes' is 'false' or 'unreasonable' (CW XI: 106, 108). These passages contain both an implicit criticism of the quantity theory of money as the full explanation of the general price level, and an explicit criticism of the application of the mathematical calculus of probability to measure the general price level: 'the origin of the method is to be found in the doctrines of the quantity theory of money' (CW XI: 105). The criticism raised against the two theories, here brought together, is based on their common disregard of the problem of the plurality of causes (CW XI: 157).

In *A Treatise on Money*, Keynes's analysis is much better developed. The criticism of classical economists is explicit, as is the criticism of the quantity theory of money which holds that a distinction exists between a real level and a money level; that is, between commodities, on the one hand, and money, on the other. Keynes stresses that there is only one level: a monetary one. Money cannot be isolated from the things coming into contact with it. Being organic, it is not a mere counter and cannot be neutral in its contacts with commodities: 'money, being a mere counter, cannot, it is argued, have any permanent influence on the relative value of the things which are transiently related to it' (CW V: 80). Keynes argues that transient contacts with money have permanent effects. The classical theory's metaphor, based on the dichotomy between transitory and permanent forces, is denied and reversed. Transient money forces rule the roost over permanent ones. Therefore money has real effects. For Keynes money is a non-neutral unit of account, that is, a non-neutral numeraire or counter of the macro-system.[22]

From 1909 onwards, Keynes concentrated attention on investigating why money is the chosen standard of account in a capitalist economy. The variety and multiplicity of price levels is one of the theoretical consequences of the non-neutrality of money. Such thoughts were in Keynes's mind in the 1920s when he wrote about ancient currency and the characteristics of money which influence the behaviour of economic agents.[23] In these writings, Keynes points out two of the characteristics of money: money-of-account and actual money or medium of exchange. It is, however, money-of-account which plays the main role because it is connected with the most important institutional and historical organization of a monetary economy, namely money contracts.

For most important social and economic purposes what matters is the money-of-account: the subject of contract and of customary obligation. The currency reforms which matter are those which change the money-of-account (CW XXVIII: 253; see also Keynes's listed four 'peculiar characteristics of money': 252–3). He underlines that it is 'with the development of contract [that] the conception of money of account . . . makes its entry into human institutions' (CW XXVIII: 226). A pursuit of this characteristic of money and of the implicit criticism of the quantity theory – in its developments through the *Tract on Monetary Reform*, 'The Economic Consequences of Mr Churchill' and *A Treatise on Money* – is also evident in the 1932 table of contents of 'The Monetary Theory of Production' and the distinction between a monetary and a real-wage economy (CW XXIX: 49–54); in the 1933 distinction between cooperative and entrepreneur economy (CW XXIX: 62–3, 66–7) and the triple distinction between a real-exchange, a neutral-monetary and monetary economy (CW XXIX: 67, 77–9, 81).

The non-neutrality of money as a unit of account – a result of its organic role in macroeconomy – in fact explains Keynes's choice of the specific standard of value; that is, his labour power of money (or money wage) standard (CW V: 49–50, 82–3). This reveals the link between money as a unit of account and as a money wage.

V The *General Theory*

In the *General Theory*, Keynes considers macroeconomic concepts as complex (CW VII: 37) and non-numerical (CW VII: 40). Quantities of real output, of real capital, of aggregate goods and services do not exist because of the lack of absolute and homogeneous units of measure. Is a quantitative macro-analysis then impossible?

The answer is yes, if analysis is carried out in real or physical terms. This forms the basis of Keynes's criticism of classical economists. The units of quantities used within the classical scheme are judged by him unsatisfactory (CW VII: 37). His criticism of Marshall's and Pigou's concept of the national dividend, as a measure of the volume of current real output or real income, is based on the difference between measures of physical changes and measures of changes in money values. To measure the volume of real output is obviously different from measuring the value of output or money income. Equally, measuring the net addition to capital equipment raises the same problems. To evaluate new equipment against old is impossible when, because of changes in technique, the two are not identical (CW VII: 38–9). This is the main reason for Keynes's refusal to use physical or real units of quantity in the *General Theory*, a refusal significantly present in Chapter 16 on the nature of capital (CW VII: 214).

The answer is no, if analysis is carried out in terms of money units. This does not raise problems for measurement, money being a homogeneous unit of quantity. For this reason macroeconomics by definition involves monetary analysis. The starting-point must not be real but rather money values. The only appropriate units of quantity in a macroeconomics are necessarily units of money. These are: (a) 'units of quantity' or 'quantities of money-value' (CW VII: 41); (b) quantities which are not physical (CW VII: 214), unlike quantities of commodies and employment (CW VII: 41); (c) quantities which are not produced: 'zero elasticity of production' (CW VII: 231); and (d) 'strictly homogeneous' (unlike physical quantities of output as a whole which are intrinsically non-homogeneous and physical quantities of employment which are not strictly homogeneous) but 'can be made so' (CW VII: 41).

Keynes gives no reasons as to why the units of money are 'strictly homogeneous'. We can advance the hypothesis that money is to economics the equivalent of ordinary language to society. Money is, by convention, the economic ordinary language (Carabelli, 1988: 167–72). Therefore the intrinsic homogeneity of money stems, paradoxically, from its organic nature. Money, as ordinary language, works as a whole, not through its atomic components: this gives rise to complexity. Further, within the established convention, it allows intersubjective, societal and economic communication. Again, this economic language is not absolute and could be changed by monetary reforms. A 'green cheese' – money can substitute a 'moon' – money (CW VII: 235). Equally one can use a 'wage'-money, as Keynes indeed does in the *General Theory*.

Employment as a proxy for the volume of output

If, however, one insists on not using units of money, wanting to analyse, as Keynes does in the *General Theory*, changes in the volume of real output as a whole resulting from changes in effective demand, theoretical 'conundrums' are, save in special cases, inevitable: 'the community's output of goods and services is a non homogeneous complex which cannot be measured . . . except in certain special cases, as for example when all the items of one output are included in the same proportion in another output' (CW VII: 38). For this reason Keynes avoids using the concept of real output as a whole: it is 'not required in this context, since we have no need of an absolute measure of current aggregate output' (CW VII: 40–1).

At this point, two paths are still open to a quantitative macro-analysis. The first is to deflate the value of the output as a whole, using the general price level (or the price level of the output as a whole). This path, however, is equally discounted. Keynes's early studies on the non-existence of *the* general price level forbids his use of this naive escape. In the *General Theory*, he avoids using it (CW VII: 40–41; see also CW XXIX: 73). The second is to use a proxy for the volume of output. For this Keynes uses the quantity of employment. Changes in net real output are proxied by changes in the amount of employment: 'when, for purposes of description or rough comparison, we wish to speak of an increase of output, we must rely on the general presumption that the amount of employment associated with a given capital equipment will be a satisfactory index of the amount of the resultant output' (CW VII: 41). Keynes points out, however, that there is no numerical relation between the volume of output and its proxy (namely the quantity of employment), 'the two being presumed to increase and decrease together, though not in a definite numerical proportion' (CW VII: 41).

This technique of using another numerical quantity as a proxy for a non-numerical quantity is that described by Keynes in his 1909 essay on index numbers: 'if we can find another quantity somewhat similar in its properties to the national income but measurable, this may serve our purpose almost equally well'. This 'would give us an index to something else' (CW XI: 55).[24] Thus, in the *General Theory*, Keynes can speak of the aggregate quantity of employment: 'we can aggregate the N's in a way in which we cannot aggregate the O's, since ΣO is not a numerical quantity' (CW VII: 45). In line with his 1909 analysis, the proxy quantity of employment (labour commanded) is, however, not an original unit of quantity in macroeconomics (it being non-homogeneous in its intrinsic nature and, further, being a derived unit). It is obtained by a process of deflation which starts from money values – already seen to be the only original quantities in macroeconomics. This process fully respects *A Treatise on Money*'s multiplicity of price levels. The standard unit of measure (the wage-unit) used to carry through the deflation of the value of output is not *the* general value of money but only *one* of the specific values of money: *A Treatise on Money*'s labour power of money. This standard provides the institutional and historical link with money seen as the specific unit of account chosen in a capitalist money economy: a 'wage'-money.

This standard of value is the unit of account in which contracts are fixed. It is the unit in which money wages (the most important among contracts fixed in money terms) are stipulated. Keynes's choice of the standard of value is therefore to be connected with his monetary theory of value. As Weintraub (1981/82) forcefully pointed out, we have a price system because we have a money wage system and not vice versa. Keynes's monetary theory of value is a macro-theory because it is based upon money which is *par excellence* a macro-magnitude and because, being macro-magnitudes, money prices are organic complex magnitudes. In sum, in *A Treatise on Money* and in the *General Theory*, Keynes's choice of the standards of value (the units of measure) and of the units of quantity is consonant both to his object of analysis and to his method of investigation.

In *A Treatise on Money*, the object of his analysis is the dynamics of price levels and the fluctuation of real output. In contrast to the standards used by classical economists, Keynes's consumption and labour units 'correspond to the quantities in which we are likely to be interested: the purchasing power of money and the volume of output' (CW V: 210). These quantities are, in his view, the only ones appropriate to his 'real *quaesita*': 'The first advantage is that . . . they [the fundamental equations] do lead up to what are generally our real *quaesita* . . . whereas the alternative methods lead up . . . to various hotchpotch price levels' (CW V: 198). Furthermore the choice of the two standards is also consonant to his method of reasoning capable of dealing with complex magnitudes. In *A Treatise on Money*, the choice of the standards helps to avoid the theoretical difficulties of the complexity of the value of money allowing an expression for the divergent behaviour of the multiple price levels. In the preface to *A Treatise on Money*, Keynes writes:

> I propose a novel means of approach to the fundamental problems of monetary theory. My object has been to find a method which is useful in describing, not merely the characteristics of static equilibrium, but also those of disequilibrium. (CW V: xvii)

For this reason his analysis is meant to be qualitative rather than quantitative:

> Thus when we approach the monetary problem quantitatively, the statistical difficulties which the [fundamental] equations . . . bring to the surface are really latent in any method which we can adopt. In fact the statistical advantages of the other methods only exist so long as we are content with a price level which is by no means the price level we want. The main advantage . . . is for the purposes of qualitative investigation. (CW V: 198)

Equally, in the *General Theory*, Keynes's choice reflects the object and method of his investigation. The object is the level and changes in real income and employment resulting from aggregate demand. The method enables an apprehension of organic interdependence among variables and the complexity of the open macro-system. We can now grasp the full meaning of the passage in Chapter 20:

> There are two reasons why the substitution of the employment function for the ordinary supply curve is consonant with the methods and objects of this book. In the first place, it expresses the relevant facts in terms of the units to which we have decided to restrict ourselves, without introducing any of the units which have a dubious quantitative character. In the second place, it lends itself to the problems of industry and output as a whole. (CW VII: 281)

VI Conclusions

The choice of the standards of value and of the units of quantity in his various writings reflects Keynes's view of the organic interdependence among the variables of the monetary macro-system. This is achieved without theoretically reducing its complexity. Methodologically Keynes is not a reductionist. Thus what is known in the Keynesian literature as the 'problem of aggregation' does not apply to Keynes himself.

Keynes clearly did spend the 20 minutes required to learn the theory of value. He spent years working out a monetary theory of value appropriate to the irreducible complexity of the macroeconomic system. The theory of value and the theory of money are strongly interconnected. his choice of the standards of value reflects his true monetary theory of value. In fact, for Keynes, a macroeconomic system requires money as the necessary standard unit-of-account. Macro-concepts are necessarily monetary magnitudes: real macro-magnitudes do not exist at all. This explains why money plays an essential role in macroeconomics and why macro-analysis should start from monetary magnitudes. It also explains why recent attempts to introduce money in a barter economy or to find microfoundations for macroeconomics have been abortive.

Keynes's monetary theory of value derives from his very early criticism of the quantity theory of money based upon his view that money is a non-neutral unit-of-account. In fact, Keynes raised two criticisms against the quantity theory. The first – present in his early monetary writings up to and including *A Treatise on Money* – concerns the essential role of money as a unit-of-account. Money is a non-neutral standard and has real effects. The multiplicity of price levels is one of the theoretical consequences of this non-neutrality of money. The second is the well-known criticism based on the liquidity preference theory in the *General Theory*. Obviously the first criticism is logically, not just historically, antecedent to the second. Thus Keynes's liquidity preference presupposes his early discussion of money as unit-of-account and his first criticism of the quantity theory. This double criticism has escaped interpreters of Keynes's monetary theory.

Keynes's monetary theory of value and his choice of the units of quantity and of measure are based upon his early approach to probability seen as an organic, complex and incommensurable magnitude. This chapter has shown that it is not probability itself which is the element of continuity between Keynes's early and later writings, but his approach to probability. Method is the element of continuity in Keynes's thought. His and our theoretical and methodological starting-points are once more his writings on probability.

Notes

1. This is part of a larger work on the link between Keynes's approach to probability and his monetary theory of value. I wish to thank Keynes Trustees and King's College, Cambridge for permission to quote from Keynes's manuscripts. Special thanks to John Hillard for help in improving the English.
2. By the term 'general theory', Keynes means a complex and open theory, where assumptions of 'logical independence' among variables are not tacitly introduced at the beginning of the analysis (Carabelli, 1991a).
3. Probability shows similar characteristics. It is logically indefinable, but its meaning can be easily grasped at ordinary language level: 'But that "probability" is, in a sense, indefinable need not trouble us; it is a characteristic which it shares with many of our most necessary and fundamental ideas; and it is not . . . a highly abstract or metaphysical notion, far removed from the normal channels of thought' (Keynes, 1907: 12–13). And further: 'In the case of "probability" the object before the mind is so familiar that the danger of mis-describing its qualities through lack of a definition is less than if it were a highly abstract entity far removed from the normal channels of thought' (CW VIII: 9).
4. The same goes for probability: 'we cannot analyse the probability relation in terms of simpler ideas' (CW VIII: 8).
5. Note that physical heterogeneity is just one aspect of multidimensionality.
6. It is astonishing that this devastating critique of the classical theory and of the attempt

to erect a quantitative science of macroeconomics – save under very restricted conditions – has been totally ignored by economists. If attention were paid to Keynes's critique of measurement and to Chapter 16 of the *General Theory*, the Cambridge controversy (Harcourt, 1972) on the measure of capital would have been unnecessary.

7. Here I use Keynes's manuscript of the 1907 version of *The Principles of Probability* rather than the final 1921 version as it antedates his 1909 essay on index numbers.
8. 'All propositions are true or false, but the knowledge we have of them depends on our circumstances; and while it is often convenient to speak of propositions as certain or probable, this expresses strictly a relationship in which they stand to a *corpus* of knowledge, actual or hypothetical, and not a characteristic of propositions in themselves . . . Let our premises consist of any set of propositions *h*, and our conclusion consist of any set of propositions *a*, then, if a knowledge of *h* justifies a rational belief in *a* of degree α, we say that there is a *probability-relation* of degree α between *a* and *h*' (CW VIII: 3–4).
9. Georgescu-Roegen (1967: 241; see also 209–10) is the only author to have noticed this case's relevance to Keynes's view of probability.
10. I think the neglect of this as a general case for Keynes's probability is at the basis of the misinterpretation of his view of rationality advanced by O'Donnell (1989) and Skidelsky (1991). By their interpretation, Keynes, in *A Treatise on Probability*, would hold a view of strong rationality based on known probabilities, only later to move, in the *General Theory*, to a more radical concept of uncertainty and weak rationality based on unknown probabilities.
11. In the final version of *A Treatise on Probability* Keynes writes of the existence of 'more than one distinct series of probabilities'. He further compares probability to '*different* orders of similarity' (CW VIII: 38–9, emphasis in original). He again clearly distinguishes between numerically ordinable, ordinable and non-ordinable probabilities, where the latter are considered by him as the more general case (CW VIII: 31–2, 36–7, 40–1).
12. On this aspect, Keynes seems to echo Aristotle's criticism of Plato based on the heterogeneity of plural ethical values and on their non-commensurability in *Nichomachean Ethics*, which we know Keynes read in 1906. Plato held that the hallmark of rational choice is the measurement of all alternatives by a single quantitative standard or metric. This was done by supposing a qualitative homogeneity of all the values, that is the Platonic notion of the Single Good. Aristotle, on the contrary, held that this approach renders intractable the problem of choice among heterogeneous alternatives and neglects the qualitative heterogeneity of plural values (for example, beauty and goodness). On this issue see Nussbaum (1985, 1986).
13. This intrinsic indeterminateness is stressed again quite clearly in the final version of *A Treatise on Probability*:

    > It is not the case here that the method of calculation, prescribed by theory, is beyond our powers or too laborious for actual application. *No* method of calculation, however impracticable, has been suggested. Nor have we any *prima facie* indications of the existence of a common unit to which the magnitudes of all probabilities are naturally referrable . . . probabilities do not all belong to a single set of magnitudes measurable in terms of a common unit. (CW VIII: 32–3, emphasis in original; on common unit see also 35–6)

14. The same difficulty arises in the case of nearly all the quantities dealt with by science:

    > There is no unique unit of measurement . . . The ground of the element of arbitrariness in the unit of measurement of most physical quantities is easily explained. The objective quality measured does not really possess numerical quantitativeness, although it may possess some of the properties necessary for numerical quantitativeness . . . In general, the values which it can assume are capable of being ranged in

order of magnitude and, in addition, it will sometimes happen that the series which is thus formed is *continuous*, that is to say, for any two selected values there can be found a value whose order in the series is between the two selected values. But it does not follow from this that there is any meaning in the assertion that one value is twice another value. The relations of continuous order can exist between the terms of a series of values, without the relations of numerical quantitativeness existing at the same time. But we can nevertheless measure the values after a manner which is somewhat arbitrary but which yields results sufficiently satisfactory for many purposes, those, for instance, of mathematical physics, though not for those of probability. This method is to select some other quantity or ratio . . . For instance, the series of values of the quantity measured by a specific volume have this relation . . . to a conventional measurement . . . The intervals which we regard as equal depend upon this arbitrary choice. (Keynes, 1907: 97–8, emphasis in original)

15. An earlier reference in 1905 to the difficulties which the measurement of utility raises for the 'pure theory of economics' can be found in a passage of Keynes's 'Miscellanea Ethica'. Keynes's distinction among qualities is important for his theory of measurement:

    The goodness of a whole is not the sum of the goodness of its parts, nor is the value of a group of individuals necessarily the same as the sum of their values taken separately. This type of difficulty is of very frequent occurrence and is by no means confined to the moral science. The root of it lies in the distinction between those qualities which belong to a whole as a whole and those qualities which it possesses because they belong also to some or all of its parts . . . Most but not all of the qualities dealt with in pure and applied mathematics and capable of exact measurement belong to Class 1 (Class 1: degree of whole = sum of degrees of parts e.g. weight, extension), but the additive property which this class possesses usually requires proof. Class 2 is of no concern in the present issue (Class 2: degree of whole = degree of each part (each part having the quality), e.g. colour, potential of an electrical conductor). In Class 3 the principle of Organic Unities appears (Class 3: whole independent of part, e.g. beauty, utility). The fact that utility belongs to this class leads to difficulties in the pure theory of economics. (Keynes manuscripts: 6.8.1905)

    On Keynes's distinction between primary and secondary qualities, see also note 19 below.
16. Here I am not considering Keynes's distinction between cost and wages value standard and his analysis of the efficiency or productivity of labour.
17. For lack of space I will omit his analysis in *A Tract on Monetary Reform*.
18. In the footnote to this passage Keynes explicitly refers to his early analysis of the measurement of probability and precisely to Chapter III of *A Treatise on Probability*, 'especially pars. 7–16' (CW V: 88 fn 2), exactly where he deals with *non-ordinable* probabilities (CW VIII: 30–9).
19. But remember Keynes's discussion on the limits of the application of the atomic hypothesis within physical science itself in his early writings on probability and also his non-positivist interpretation of Newton's method (see Carabelli, 1988: 100–102, 109). Further a very early reference to the 'mechanical theory' of physical science, with its distinction between primary and secondary qualities – a distinction opposed by Keynes – can be found in his 'Miscellanea Ethica'; 'It is often supposed that in shape, size and motion the objects are like the sensations, and that in colour, taste, smell, heat and cold they are unlike. This is the mechanical theory of the external world' (Keynes manuscripts; 19.9.1905).
20. Compare this with the definition of independence advanced in the *Principles of Probability*:

    My object has been to maintain a distinction between 'causally independent' and

> 'independent for probability'. The distinction is similar to that between *causa essendi* and *causa cognoscendi* . . . The essential relation is that of 'independence for probability'. We wish to know whether one fact throws light *of any kind* on the truth of another . . . Much confusion has arisen from the practice of divorcing the term 'causally independent' from its original and strict sense . . . and of then confusing it with 'independent for probability'. The object of this chapter has been to give a precise meaning . . . and to bring out the distinction between this and the more complete independence required for probability. At the same time the distinctions which have been made show . . . that causal independence is *practically* unimportant in comparison with the – logically – more fundamental property of independence for probability. (1907: 258–9, emphasis in original; see also CW VIII: 182–3, 305–8)

For an analysis for this concept, see Carabelli (1985, 1988).

21. On the role of the concept of independence in Keynes's criticism of the quantity theory of money and of the purchasing power parity in *A Tract on Monetary Reform*, see CW IV: 65, 75, 133–4.
22. Note that this role of money upon which Keynes bases his early criticism of the quantity theory of money (its non-neutrality as a unit of account) is logically prior to that based on liquidity preference later developed, first timidly, in *A Treatise on Money*, and then, fully, in the *General Theory*. His analysis of liquidity preference actually presupposes this early criticism of the quantity theory of money. For example: 'If wage (and contracts) were fixed in terms of wheat, it might be that wheat would acquire some of money's liquidity premium' (CW VII: 233 fn. 1).
23. See also, however, his early 1912–13 lectures on money; his reviews of Fisher, Benedixen, Innes and Hawtrey; his comment on Cannan; his discussion on Indian currency reform (CW XII: Chapter 5, especially 714; CW XI: 378–9, 402, 405, 412, 417–18; CW I and XV).
24. He points out: 'To take a different instance, the closeness of relationship between the different members of one family group is not strictly measurable. But the proportions of common ancestors in the four preceding generations may afford a numerical index which is serviceable to the matter in hand' (CW XI: 55).

References

Carabelli, A. M. (1985), 'Keynes on Cause, Chance and Possibility', in T. Lawson and H. Pesaran (eds), *Keynes's Economics: Methodological Issues*, London: Croom Helm.

Carabelli, A. M. (1988), *On Keynes's Method*, London: Macmillan.

Carabelli, A. M. (1991a), 'The Methodology of the Critique of the Classical Theory: Keynes on Organic Interdependence', in B. W. Bateman and J. B. Davis (eds), *Keynes and Philosophy: Essays on the Origin of Keynes's Thought*, Aldershot: Edward Elgar.

Carabelli, A. M. (1991b), 'Comment', in R. M. O'Donnell (ed.), *Keynes as a Philosopher – Economist*, London: Macmillan.

Davidson, P. (1983/4), 'Reviving Keynes's Revolution', *Journal of Post Keynesian Economics*, **6**, 361–73.

Georgescu-Roegen, N. (1967), *Analytical Economics*, Cambridge: Harvard University Press.

Harcourt, G. C. (1972), *Some Cambridge Controversies in the Theory of Capital*, Cambridge: Cambridge University Press.

Hicks, J. R. (1967), *Critical Essays in Monetary Theory*, Oxford: Clarendon Press.

Keynes, J. M. (1905), 'Miscellanea Ethica', unpublished manuscript, King's College Library, Cambridge.

Keynes, J. M. (1907), 'The Principles of Probability', unpublished manuscript, King's College Library, Cambridge.

Nussbaum, M. (1985), *The Fragility of Goodness*, Cambridge: Cambridge University Press.

Nussbaum, M. (1986), 'The Discernment of Perception: An Aristotelian Conception of Private and Public Rationality', in J. J. Clearly (ed.), *Proceedings of the Boston Area Colloquium in Ancient Philosophy*, vol. 1, Lanham: University Press of America.

O'Donnell, R. M. (1989), *Keynes: Philosophy, Economics and Politics*, London: Macmillan.
Quine, W. V. (1931), *From a Logical Point of View*, New York: Harper & Row.
Quine, W. V. (1960), *Word and Object*, Cambridge: MIT Press.
Russell, B. (1903), *Principles of Mathematics*, London: Unwin.
Skidelsky, R. (1991), 'Keynes's Philosophy of Practice', in R. M. O'Donnell (ed.), *Keynes as a Philosopher–Economist*, London: Macmillan.
Weintraub, S. (1982), 'Hicks on IS–LM: more explanation', *Journal of Post Keynesian Economics*, **4**, 445–52.

2 Interdependence and the Cambridge economic tradition[1]

Roy J. Rotheim

When Marshall recognized the full implications of irreversibility he rejected his mechanical model of growth and called for a biological approach. (Thomas, 1991: 12)

The ghost of Marshall runs like a red thread through the whole of Keynes's theoretical writings. (Clower, 1989: 1680)

I Introduction

Much has been written in recent years on Keynes's philosophy and its impact on his perception of uncertainty (see, for example, Carabelli, 1988; Fitzgibbons, 1988; O'Donnell 1989, 1990). This chapter seeks to move beyond the purely philosophical realm and consider the effect of the economic tradition at Cambridge on Keynes's organicist perspective. Indeed there was an economic environment at Cambridge which may have had as great if not greater influence on Keynes's methodological criticisms than the philosophical environment. The main purpose, then, is to identify the historical antecedents of Keynes's view that meaningful interdependencies created doubt about the orthodox use of supply and demand as a heuristic for understanding and explaining aggregate income and output flows. Those who formulated these ideas all resided at Cambridge. The architect, as one might expect, was Alfred Marshall, who believed that, beyond the static world of the short run, economic phenomena were characterized by interdependencies which questioned the centres of gravity described by the mechanical equilibrium model (Harcourt, 1981). Here questions of an organic interdependence among economic relations came to the surface and threatened to undermine the foundations of traditional economics where equilibrium was determined through the interaction of *uniquely defined* and *independent* supply and demand curves.

It is not clear whether Marshall ever abandoned the mechanical framework or the notion of equilibrium of the forces of supply and demand. Still these methodological and theoretical questions did have a significant influence on the subsequent writings of Arthur Pigou, Piero Sraffa and Maurice Dobb. Pigou flirted with those organic interdependent propositions but he never abandoned the laws of independent supply and demand curves and the concept of economic equilibrium which resulted from that analysis. Sraffa and Dobb, on the other hand, found no difficulty in suggesting that meaningful interdependencies pointed to the vitiation of the principles of a competitive theory of value and distribution mediated by independent supply and demand relations. Keynes's economics was nurtured in this Cambridge tradition which laid the foundations upon which Keynes was able to mount his critique of the 'classical' theory of employment, interest and money.

Before discussing these Cambridge economic influences on Keynes, it is necessary first to outline his methodological critique of what he called classical economics. This will be followed by four sections charting the inception of the views which I consider to constitute this Cambridge tradition, by Marshall, and then Marshall's influence on Pigou, Sraffa and Dobb. The chapter is concluded by a discussion of Keynes's place in the Cambridge economic tradition.

II Keynes's criticism of orthodox equilibrium economics

A distinctive aspect of Keynes's economic analysis, especially in the *General Theory*, was his construction of a theory that was consistent at the level both of the firm and of industry as a whole. This was achieved by valuing aggregate output in terms of a price level constructed from the aggregation of individual money prices which, in turn, were directly related to the money wage rates in those firms. He arrived at this method after rejecting the orthodox metaphor which spoke of an aggregate labour market with a supply and demand curve for labour mediated by a real wage and an aggregate capital market with a supply of savings and a demand for investment mediated by a real rate of interest. Equilibrium in the former reflected the marginal productivity of the labour involved in production relative to labour's valuation of its leisure relative to work, while, in the latter, it reflected the embodied marginal productivity of the capital stock relative to society's valuation of thriftiness versus immediate consumption. In both cases the metaphor embodied a methodological individualism which attributed all decisions to properties unique to those individual entities. Keynes argued, however, that such *markets* were conceptually impossible: an aggregate labour market was a meaningless construct within the logic of the traditional metaphor and at best could only be identified at the unique point of full employment; while an aggregate capital market, in any case, was 'nonsense'.

The reasoning behind his criticism was methodological. It was possible to think of an individual firm where workers and producers could bargain in money terms, which would have no effect on the price of wage goods or demand for that firm's product. However such logic for the individual firm could not be directly expanded to industry as a whole unless certain restrictive assumptions were added. In particular, to consider an aggregate labour market mediated by a real wage, it was necessary to assume that the wage bargain had no effect on either aggregate demand (and therefore supply and income) or the aggregate price level. Then changes in money wages or the price level would not cause a change in the aggregate demand for labour (as opposed to the quantity of labour demanded) or in the price level and, therefore, the real wage other than that which would be predicted by the change in the real wage with a change in money wages if the price of wage goods was not affected by that change in money wages. This logic did not describe an aggregate labour market, only a market in which a given quantity of labour flowed between alternative employments. Unemployment can only occur in a particular sector because there is an excess demand for labour in another sector. There is no concept of *aggregate* unemployment. By means of the orthodox metaphor one could consider, in Keynes's words, 'the direction of employment but not its quantity' (CW VII: vii).

It is of no small significance that Keynes included in his definition of 'the classical economists' not only 'Ricardo and James Mill and their *predecessors* . . . [but also] the *followers* of Ricardo, those, that is to say, who adopted and perfected the theory of the Ricardian economics, including (for example) J. S. Mill, Marshall, Edgeworth and Prof. Pigou' (CW VII: 3, emphasis in original). For, whilst there were clear differences between the theories of these earlier and later economists, what caused them to be lumped together in Keynes's mind is revealed in Chapter 21 of the *General Theory*. There he is concerned with the dichotomies which defined the classical theory's method, language and discourse:

> The division of Economics between the Theory of Value on the one hand and the Theory of Money on the other hand is, I think a false division. The right dichotomy is, I suggest, between the Theory of the Individual Industry or Firm and of the rewards and the distribution between different uses of a *given* quantity of resources on the one hand, and the Theory of Output and Employment *as a whole* on the other hand. (CW VII: 293)

Keynes believed that the former dichotomy was a fair representation of an economy at the point of full employment equilibrium. There increases in the stock of money would affect the general price level because aggregate output was at a maximum. Moreover for a given level of prices there would be a given real wage at that point. General equilibrium would also imply market clearing for labour for each individual firm, also stated in terms of a real wage. It is in this sense that Keynes, in a 1933 draft of the *General Theory*, referred to such an economy as a 'real wage' economy because it was the real wage which was the operative phrase in the equation linking the parts and the whole of the economy (Rotheim, 1981, 1988). However, if it is the general equilibrium solution which defines the unique real wage to which all individuals adapt, then this leads to the false belief that it is the individual markets which are the sole explanatory elements in the general equilibrium solution. This reflects a methodological individualist approach to the macroeconomic problem: we can add up from individual markets where the real wage is determined by independent supply and demand curves to achieve the aggregate labour market solution in real wage/employment space.

But such a conclusion was only valid if the level of aggregate income did not change. Given this assumption, changes in the money wage would have no effect on the aggregate level of output or output prices, and workers would be in control of the real wage with their money wage bargain. Keynes identified the problem as follows:

> In any given industry we have a demand schedule for the product relating the quantities which can be sold to the prices asked; we have a series of supply schedules relating the prices which will be asked for the sale of different quantities on various bases of cost; and these schedules between them lead up to a further schedule which, on the assumption that other costs are unchanged (except as a result of the change in output), gives us the demand schedule for labour in the industry relating the quantity of employment to different levels of wages, the shape of the curve at any point furnishing the elasticity of demand for labour. This conception is transferred without substantial modification to the industry as a whole; and it is supposed, by a parity of reasoning, that we have a demand schedule for labour in industry as a whole relating the quantity of employment to different levels of wages. It is held that it makes no material difference to this argument whether it is in terms of money-wages or real wages. If we are thinking in terms of money-wages, we must, of course, correct for changes in the value of money; but this leaves the general tendency of the argument unchanged, since prices certainly do not change in exact proportion to changes in money-wages. If this is the groundwork of the argument (and, if it is not, I do not know what the groundwork is), surely it is fallacious. For the demand schedules for particular industries can only be constructed on some fixed assumption as to the nature of the demand and supply schedules of other industries and as to the amount of the aggregate effective demand. It is invalid, therefore, to transfer the argument to industry as a whole unless we also transfer our assumption that the aggregate effective demand is fixed. Yet this assumption reduces the argument to an *ignoratio elenchi*. For, whilst no one would wish to deny the proposition that a reduction in money-wages *accompanied by the same aggregate effective demand as before* will be associated with an increase in employment, the precise question at issue is whether the reduction in money-wages will or will not be accompanied by the same aggregate effective demand as before measured in money, or at any rate, by an aggregate effective demand which is not reduced in full proportion to the reduction in money-wages (i.e. which is somewhat greater measured in wage-units). But if the

> classical theory is not allowed to extend by analogy its conclusions in respect of a particular industry to industry as a whole, it is wholly unable to answer the question what effect on employment a reduction in money-wages will have. For it has no method of analysis wherewith to tackle the problem. (CW VII: 258–60, emphasis in original)[2]

If the assumption of fixed aggregate levels of output and prices were dropped, then it becomes impossible to apply the language of the individual to that of industry as a whole. Here the laws of supply and demand for labour in the aggregate have no meaningful relationship to those laws at the level of the individual firm. There is no longer any unique relationship between changes in money wages or the price of wage goods and well-defined, unique aggregate labour supply and demand curves. Keynes saw the breakdown as a result of the factors which underlie the aggregate demand and supply curves for labour not being independent of one another. Thus a change in money wages or the price of wage-goods has an indeterminate effect on the aggregate level of employment. In other words, there is an interdependence among the factors underlying the conditions of supply and demand which preclude the unique definition of an aggregate labour market by which employment in the aggregate is defined.

But what is the 'operative phrase' if we are *not* at the point of full employment equilibrium, if output in the aggregate is fluctuating as the result of the multitude of individual interactions? Then it is the second of the two dichotomies which emerges as relevant; that is, between the individual firm or industry and industry as a whole. Keynes believed that at any point other than the limiting point of full employment, there was an *interdependence* among all firms such that, from the perspective of industry as a whole, effective demand was likely to fluctuate. The discourse of the classical economics based on an aggregate labour market in terms of a real wage emanating from independent supply and demand curves for labour also operating in terms of a real wage was illogical and untenable. In its place he identified a 'money-wage' economy, where labour supply decisions are based on relative money wages, and where these prime costs of production become the basis upon which prices are set by firms relative to their short-term expectations regarding future sales receipts. Because output and pricing decisions are made in money terms, there is a direct link between those decisions and the level of output and prices in the aggregate.

Interdependence through time leads to outcomes which do not mirror the originally posited equilibrium. This was the most telling aspect of Keynes's criticism of classical methodology. As such, the principles of equilibrium economics could not be held as rules of conduct for interdependent economies in time. As Geoffrey Harcourt describes it:

> If a market or an economy were in equilibrium, no question of stability arose – it was as if expectations always were realized. If either were not in equilibrium, then the question of existence did not arise, because the market or the economy evolved under the influence of past and present happenings, and expectations of the future, reacting to any consistencies now present but with no presupposition that they would seek out positions where, once again, they were absent. (1986: 99)

Turning to the classical theory of capital, here the real rate of interest is that price which equates the supply of saving with the demand for capital. Unlike the classical theory of the level of employment which, Keynes believed, was confluent with his own theory at the point of full employment, the classical theory of interest was simply wrong in that it 'involves a formal error' (CW VII: 179; see also Milgate, 1977; Panico, 1987). One of the independent variables of the classical system is the level of aggregate income, while the quantities of savings and investment are the dependent variables for any given rate of interest. Should either the demand curve for capital or the supply curve for savings (the obverse of the demand curve for consumption) shift, then the rate of interest must adjust to change the level of consumption or the quantity of capital demanded; that is, there will be an appropriate movement along the independent supply and demand curves. But, as Keynes observed:

> the assumption that income is constant is inconsistent with the assumption that these two curves can shift independently of one another. If either of them shift, then, in general, income will change; with the result that the whole schematism based on the assumption of a given income breaks down. (CW VII: 179)

Keynes's criticism is again based on the degree to which interdependence among the conditions underlying the supply of savings and the demand for capital precludes the possibility of a unique equilibrium. Any individual may change her savings or purchase of capital goods out of a given amount of her income and it may be possible to construct a supply of savings or demand for capital schedule for that individual which is independent of the level of income. In the aggregate, however, a change in either schedule will change the level of income and thus change the position of either or both curves.

In 1935, Harrod went to great lengths to persuade Keynes that his theory of the rate of interest (liquidity preference) was conformable to the classical theory under certain circumstances (in the same way that Keynes agreed that his theory of aggregate employment converged to the classical theory at the point of full employment). Here, however, he could not accept Harrod's attempts at a reconciliation. The classical system was simply, in Keynes's words, a nonsense theory: 'I make a great distinction between the classical theory of employment, which does make perfect sense and works all right on certain special assumptions, and the classical theory of the rate of interest which makes no sense on any assumptions whatever' (CW XIII: 557). Consider also Keynes's discussion of Harrod's analogy to the supply and demand curves for German lessons:

> You say quite correctly that the price of the lesson equates the propensity to give German lessons with the marginal efficiency of German lessons. In the case you have chosen price does play that function. But suppose that whenever the price of a German lesson went down the demand schedule also shifted its position; the whole thing would have no meaning. You get your point of equilibrium because the demand and supply schedules for German lessons do not shift their position whenever the price changes. If for any price whenever the demand and supply schedules shifted so that they intersected at the point in question, clearly they would not be determined by the price. Now it is the characteristic of the demand and supply schedules for savings that they have this unfortunate characteristic. In truth there are no such things as these schedules. They are completely bogus. (CW XIII: 550–1)

Moreover, since any flow of investment generates its equivalent flow of savings, it is impossible to conceive of an aggregate capital market along classical lines:

> The analogy with the demand and supply for a commodity at a given price is a false analogy. For whereas it is perfectly easy to name a price at which the supply and the demand for a commodity would be unequal, it is impossible to name a rate of interest at which the amount of saving and the amount of investment could be unequal. (CW XIV: 476)

The remainder of this chapter will sketch the development of economic thought and analysis that led up to Keynes's rejection of the orthodox theory of value and distribution as separate from the theory of money and prices. For, as Keynes said in the opening chapter to the *General Theory*:

> I shall argue that the postulates of the classical theory are applicable to a special case only and not to the general case, the situation which it assumes being a limiting point of the possible positions of equilibrium. Moreover, the characteristics of the special case assumed by the classical theory happen not to be those of the economic society in which we actually live, with the result that its teaching is misleading and disastrous if we attempt to apply it to the facts of experience. (CW VII: 3)

Our story starts with Alfred Marshall.

III Marshall's mechanical and biological analogies

Keynes, in his memorial to Alfred Marshall, recognized that 'the explicit introduction of the element of time as the factor in economic analysis is mainly due to Marshall . . . Nevertheless, this is the quarter in which, in my opinion, the Marshall analysis is least complete and satisfactory, and where there remains most to do' (CW X: 206–7). In fact Marshall did not handle the element of time very well in the *Principles*, for it was clear to him that its introduction had unwieldy implications for the primary mechanism of analysis, the notion of the equilibrium (centres of gravity) of supply and demand. Still, in the *Principles*, Marshall was uncomfortable with questions of the 'fixity' of economic relations over time, both in terms of the changes in objective circumstances that occurred and in terms of the ability of economic models to apply the simplified terminology of supply and demand.

Brinley Thomas (1991) argues that Marshall in the *Principles* only went so far as to employ biological analogies but not biological analysis: 'there are sound reasons for concluding that Marshall was for the most part indulging in analogies or figures of speech' (Thomas, 1991: 8). Marshall still felt that his mechanical method could approximate the methods of economic analysis. Currie and Steedman (1990: 11–12) confirm this view:

> Irreversibilities in time and qualitative changes in both individuals and institutions indeed feature prominently in 'Marshall's conception of economic change as "organic growth" ' . . . Yet . . . within the *Principles*, Marshall did not come even within sight of the 'Mecca of the economist'. The *Principles* constitute 'a volume on Foundations' . . . and if there are ample warnings of the limitations to mechanical analogies and equilibrium, the brute fact remains that the *Principles* does not provide any general demonstration of the nature and of the results of an alternative reasoning; there are but hints. The 'higher stages of our work' and 'the high theme of economic progress' lie beyond the *Principles*.

There is plenty of evidence in the *Principles* that Marshall was terribly uneasy about the blanket use of static models. We can identify two effects of Marshall's uneasiness with the standard theory of supply and demand. The first relates to situations where time changes the objective circumstances by which the supply and demand functions are established. Technology and tastes are capable of changes over time which cause a reconsideration of the conclusions that emerge from the static bases of such relationships. Secondly, there is the unique situation where the objective circumstances themselves are not independent of each other. These are occurrences, however, that are not necessarily time-dependent.

Marshall tried to reconcile the mechanical with the biological analogies in Book V of the *Principles*, where he identifies four periods: market period, short period, long run and the secular period. In V.II he characterizes the temporary equilibrium of demand supply in the market period in terms of the 'higgling and bargaining' of the market. In the short period, Marshall assumes that expected market price is the inducement for resources to flow in and out of certain manufactures. However, as the long period is approached, Marshall recognizes that 'the value of a thing [its normal price] tends in the long run to correspond to its cost of production' (1920: 348). In this case 'the term normal being taken to refer to a long period of time, the normal price . . . would decrease with an increase in demand' (ibid.: 371). Decreasing normal price occurs because of increasing returns, which can be internal and external to firms, but also because increased demand over long periods of time cause new technologies to become a part of the industry which results in irrevocable reductions in long-period normal price.

Marshall has created something of a fiction by the employment of his statical edifice. And, as he observed, everything is not so smooth with the passage of time:

> for indeed the demand and supply schedules do not in practice remain unchanged for a long time together, but are constantly being changed; and every change in them alters the equilibrium amount and the equilibrium price, and thus gives new positions to the centres about which the amount and the price tend to oscillate. These considerations point to the great importance of the element of time in relation to demand and supply. (Ibid.: 346–7)

In these cases all change is exogenous, the result of changes in the conditions of either supply or demand. It is the passage of time, rather than some truly organic interdependence which is the compelling force behind Marshall's framework. Marshall does recognize, however, that the phenomenon of increasing returns potentially undermines the statical theory, because of the internal and external economies which it creates:

> The statical theory of equilibrium is therefore not wholly applicable to commodities which obey the law of increasing returns . . . In long periods both the internal and the external economies of production on a large scale have time to develop themselves. The marginal supply price is not the expenses of production of any particular bale of goods; but it is the whole expenses . . . of a marginal increment in the aggregate process of production and marketing. (Ibid.: 501–2)

Marshall leaves the whole issue in a very murky state by clouding the confluence between individual firm decisions and consequences in the aggregate. While not identifying the interdependencies that occur from the internal and external economies resulting from increasing returns in the long run, they cry out for articulation as an alternative metaphor to the statical one to which he devoted so much energy. At the end of the chapter on increasing returns (V.XII) Marshall comes full circle, returning to the biological metaphor which he always believed was the fundamental mode for understanding economic analysis:

> The theory of stable equilibrium of normal demand and supply helps indeed to give definiteness to our ideas; and in its elementary stages it does not diverge from the actual facts of life, so far as to prevent its giving a fairly trustworthy picture of the chief methods of action of the strongest and most persistent group of economic forces. But when pushed to its more remote and intricate logical consequences, it slips away from the conditions of real life. In fact we are here verging on the high theme of economic progress; and here therefore it is especially needful to remember that economic problems are imperfectly presented when they are treated as problems of statical equilibrium, and not of organic growth. For though the statical treatment alone can give us definiteness and precision of thought, and is therefore a necessary introduction to a more philosophic treatment of society as an organism, it is yet only an introduction. (Ibid.: 461)

Finally there was one instance at least in which Marshall had serious doubts about the efficacy of the laws of supply and demand to yield a unique and meaningful centre of gravity. This was the specification of the supply curve for labour. For an equilibrium to be established in the market period for a commodity it was a critical assumption for Marshall that the individual's marginal utility for commodities declined the more she purchased. This declining marginal utility was the factor which in conjunction with the fluctuating market price eventually led to the equilibrium. However he made the further assumption that no amount of purchase affected an individual's marginal utility of money. His justification for this assumption was that, in normal circumstances, purchasing something for one's own consumption constituted a small portion of one's total expenditures: 'when a person buys anything for his own consumption, he generally spends on it a small part of his total resources; while when he buys it for the purposes of trade, he looks to re-selling it, and therefore his potential resources are not diminished. In either case there is no appreciable change in his willingness to part with money' (ibid.: 335). This caveat is critical because, if one's marginal utility of money changed with each expenditure of money, then each person's demand curve for commodities would shift with every change in the price. The determinateness of market equilibrium would then be somewhat problematic.

Marshall then made the startling admission that, while the exceptions are rare and unimportant in markets for commodities:

> in markets for labour they are frequent and important. When a workman is in fear of hunger, his need of money [its marginal utility to him] is very great; and, if at starting, he gets the worst of the bargaining, and is employed at low wages, it remains great, and he may go on selling his labour at a low rate. This is all the more probable because, while the advantage in bargaining is likely to be pretty well distributed between the two sides of a market for commodities, it is more

> often on the side of the buyers than on that of the sellers in a market for labour. (Ibid.: 335–6)

Marshall makes very little of this, other than to caution against considering labour as a commodity like any other commodity. Indeed he pays no more attention to the rather significant methodological point that a movement along a curve can cause that curve to shift. We will see below that this 'pregnant observation' by Marshall was put to good use by Maurice Dobb in the latter's criticism of the orthodox theory of distribution.

When Marshall first took up economics, his goal was to include only those principles which could be included under the guise of mathematical principles. With the working-out of the *Principles* in the latter part of the nineteenth century, Marshall became more confounded with problems associated with time, irreversibility, the notion of marginalism and the supply curve (Thomas, 1991: 10). For example, in his Inaugural Lecture at Cambridge in 1885, Marshall stated:

> The change that has been made in the point of view of Economics by the present generation is due to the discovery that man himself is in a great measure a creature of circumstances and changes with them. The chief fault in English economists at the beginning of the century was not that they ignored history and statistics, but that they regarded man as so to speak a constant quantity, and gave themselves little trouble to study his variations. They therefore attributed to the force of supply and demand a much more mechanical and regular action than they actually have. Their most vital fault was that they did not see how liable to change are the habits and institutions of industry. (Quoted in Keynes, CW X: 196)

In 1898, Marshall published an article in the *Economic Journal* in which he attempted to address, head on, the irritating questions of statics and dynamics. Marshall distinguishes between the dynamics of physics and that of the biological sciences. In the case of physics, dynamics includes statics: 'to get the statical solution from the dynamical all that is needed is to make the relative velocities of the thing under study equal to zero and thus reduce them to relative rest' (1898: 37–8). Marshall found the static method quite appealing as it 'is simpler than the dynamical; it may afford useful preparation and training for the more difficult dynamical solution; and it may be the first step towards a provisional and partial solution in problems so complex that a complete dynamical solution is beyond our attainment' (ibid.).

The appeal of such static analysis is that it readily conforms with an atomistic approach to the study of physical phenomena. Indeed Marshall notes the benefits that Mill, for example, saw in this application of physical statics to the atomistic economic method. He cites Mill with reference to the principle of the Composition of Forces: 'when the mind applies this principle it performs a simple act of addition. It adds the separate effect of one force to the separate effect of the other, and puts down the sum of these separate effects as the joint effect' (Mill, cited in Marshall, 1898). The movement from physical statics to dynamics is not simply a matter of positing the variable to change over time. When variables interact, Marshall observed, there are *organic* changes which make the mathematical modelling of such problems unobtainable: 'when a force moves the thing on which it acts, it thereby changes the force which that thing afterwards exercises' (1898: 38).

Such a methodology would remain viable so long as the individual parts do not add up to a whole which itself is varying and affecting the ability of those parts to move. However Marshall warns that 'mechanical analogies ought, therefore, not to be abandoned hastily on the ground that economic events react upon the conditions by which they are produced; so that future events cannot happen under exactly the same conditions as they did' (ibid.: 317). The example he offers is one of a pendulum on a flat surface swinging along a constant path suddenly being upset if the surface is inclined. Then 'the vibration of the pendulum may make it [the clock] slide downwards towards a final catastrophe'. Here one of the conditions has changed and the result has been altered. But that is not to say that such a catastrophe would not have occurred if the plane upon which the clock rested remained horizontal. For something to be seen *organically*, then, to warrant a biological rather than a physical analogy, required a change 'in the character of the forces at work' (ibid.). In other words, biological analogies are relevant when parts and whole interact to a degree that some meaningful or organic progress (or retrogress) occurs.

From these considerations Marshall concludes that the device of physical statics offers a useful starting-point for 'earlier stages of economic reasoning'. However, because of the organic nature of economic processes, the dynamical processes of physics should be abandoned in favour of more biological conceptions:

> The catastrophes of mechanics are caused by changes in the quantity and not in the character of the forces at work: whereas in life their character changes also. 'Progress' or 'evolution,' industrial and social, is not mere increase and decrease. It is organic growth, chastened and confined and occasionally reversed by decay of innumerable factors, each of which influences and is influenced by those around it; and every such mutual influence varies with the stages which the respective factors have already reached in their growth. In this vital respect all sciences of life are akin to one another, and are unlike physical sciences. And therefore in the later stages of economics, when we are approaching nearly to the conditions of life, biological analogies are to be preferred to mechanical, other things being equal. (1898: 42–3)

Marshall never fully abandoned the laws of supply and demand leading to a centre of gravity, despite his dissatisfaction with the purely static analysis as matters carry out over longer time periods: 'the balance, or equilibrium, of demand and supply obtains ever more of this biological tone in the more advanced stages of economies' (1898: 318). Brinley Thomas contends, however, that, by the end of the nineteenth century, Marshall's views radically changed in the direction of organicism; so much so that he was prevented, not by numerous diversions and weak health, as he claimed, but by philosophical/methodological barriers, from writing the second volume of the *Principles*. Marshall realized by the end of the century that he had to abandon the mechanical metaphor that he used as the foundation of Volume I and switch over to an economic biological foundation for Volume II, 'a task for his successors not for him' (Thomas, 1991: 12).

To sum up, it was the factor of time, rather than organic interdependence, which dictated the metaphysical foundations for Marshall's choice of physical versus biological analogies to economics. The laws of supply and demand and the idea of a centre of gravity, or equilibrium, held a principal role in Marshall's economics. He obviously did not feel that the organic interdependence of the laws of supply and demand were so overwhelming that the ultimate independence of those two curves would be vitiated, at least in the first volume of the *Principles*: 'economic biology remained promise rather than substance' (Thomas, 1991: 11). And, of course, by minimizing the importance of the interdependencies, he was able to perpetuate a tradition which held the principle of equilibrium as its metaphysical foundation. Bharadwaj observed that: 'Marshall, while he was acutely aware of the difficulties posed by irreversibilities and "the element of time" in the case of increasing returns, nevertheless tried to present them only as "limitations" which qualified the results' (1972: 44).

Still, by raising the question, Marshall opened up a line of inquiry that intrigued, and in some sense, significantly affected the direction that economics was to take at Cambridge. Some, like Pigou, following Marshall's lead, also considered these questions of time and interdependence, and, like Marshall, rejected them as unimportant to the mainstream of economic theory. Others, notably Sraffa and Dobb, were not so easily deterred and used those methods and questions as the bases for rejecting orthodox theories of value and distribution. Indeed, by laying out the respective arguments put forth by Sraffa and Dobb, we shall see how they followed from the Marshallian tradition and the direct influence their methodological critiques had on Keynes's own critique of the logic of orthodox economics.

IV Pigou's flirtation with the problem of interdependence and aggregation

In 1913, Pigou made his first attempt at addressing the question of aggregate unemployment (Pigou, 1913a). In addition to coining the phrase 'involuntary unemployment', Pigou saw unemployment in the aggregate as the result not of a fall in the demand for labour but rather of the inability of the real wage to adjust after demand had declined.[3] Real wages were sticky downwards because of what he called a 'wages policy' which reflected intransigence on the part of labour to accept a lower wage in the light of the fall in the aggregate demand for labour. The methodology employed by Pigou was to posit independent aggregate supply and demand curves for labour which equilibrated aggregate employment through fluctuations in the aggregate real wage. Positing such curves requires that they be somehow built up from individual supply and demand curves. Otherwise the metaphor at the aggregate level possesses no analytical foundation. This relationship between the individual firm and industry as a whole seems to have been on Pigou's mind at a number of junctures in the development of his thought, appearing in print first in 1913 (Pigou, 1913b), at the same time that his book was published, and again in 1933 with the publication of his *Theory of Unemployment*.

In the latter work Pigou shows how it is possible first to derive the real-wage elasticity of demand for labour for a firm, and then to consider the same notion for labour in the aggregate. Pigou elaborates at some length on the problems that arise as a result of interdependencies during the aggregation process. And, while others might have been deterred from making the analogy from the individual firm to industry as a whole, Pigou in unabashed style simply *assumes* the existence of a demand curve for labour for industry as a whole and proceeds to attempt an estimate of the real-wage elasticity of demand for that function as well.

Pigou's first attempt at tackling the interdependence/aggregation problem, like those by Sraffa and Dobb, which will be cited below, was published in the *Economic Journal* while Keynes was editor. Moreover, although Pigou 'looked upon his early work as being "merely supplementary" to that of Marshall' (Bharadwaj, 1972: 32), I think that, in the case of his 1913 *Economic Journal* article, his motivation may not have been so benign. It is possible that he needed to state, in print, his own justification for embracing the concept of aggregate functions (in his book) despite the fact that aggregation from individual supply and demand curves was a suspicious endeavour. In the article 'The Interdependence of Different Sources of Demand and Supply in a Market' (1913b), Pigou examined the conditions under which aggregate supply and demand curves could be identified as being the result of the sum of individual demand and supply curves.

On the demand side, Pigou is influenced to a large extent by Veblen's idea of conspicuous consumption (but without attribution). Pigou distinguishes between commodities 'that are desired wholly for the direct satisfaction yielded by them, and not at all for the indirect satisfaction which their possession contributes through our thirst for reputation or distinction' (1913b: 19). According to Pigou, aggregation is possible in the former case, though not in the latter. With regard to supply, aggregation can occur 'in respect of agriculture and the extractive industries' where 'the role of "external economies" is unimportant' (ibid.). Even in the case of the latter, aggregation might be possible in instances 'which relate to disturbances of equilibrium so small that the aggregate output or consumption of the commodity affected is not greatly changed' (ibid.: 19–20). Pigou believed that, even in cases where interdependencies between the individual and the aggregate were pervasive, it would still be possible to depict aggregate supply and demand curves. However he added, 'the demand (or supply) schedules of the separate sources that make up the market cannot be so represented, and cannot be simply added together to constitute the aggregated demand (or supply) schedule' (ibid.: 21). As such Pigou observed that the independence assumption was violated and aggregation became next to impossible.

Why Pigou permitted himself to use aggregate relationships which were based on micro-entities even though it was impossible to map the latter onto the former is simply a curiosity. Perhaps he suffered from a sort of Ricardian Vice in formulating theory which prevented him from recognizing the illogical nature of the theory that he was espousing. Such a vice did not plague the likes of Sraffa and Dobb. Relying to a large degree on the heretical passages in Marshall (and also on their background in Marx), these two were able to hold up the orthodox theory of value and distribution as illogical and therefore scientifically unrelated to the conclusions touted by that theory. First to Sraffa.

V Sraffa and the interdependence of supply and demand

In his 1926 *Economic Journal* article, Piero Sraffa argued that the theory of competitive equilibrium ran counter to the laws of decreasing and increasing returns. He also focused on the untenability of meaningful independence of supply and demand curves under such conditions. As such, how could it be said that relative prices were *determined* by the intersection of independent supply and demand curves? It is worth citing his response at length:

The really serious difficulties make their appearance when it is considered to what extent the supply curves based on the laws of returns satisfy the conditions necessary to enable them to be employed in the study of the equilibrium value of single commodities produced under competitive conditions. This point of view assumes that the conditions of production and the demand for a commodity can be considered, in respect to small variations, as being practically independent, both in regard to each other and in relation to the supply and demand of all other commodities. It is well known that such an assumption would not be illegitimate merely because the independence may not be absolutely perfect, as, in fact, it never can be; and a slight degree of interdependence may be overlooked without disadvantage if it applies to quantities of the second order of smalls, as would be the case if the effect (for example, an increase of cost) of a variation in the industry which we propose to isolate were to react partially on the price of the products of other industries, and this latter effect were to influence the demand for the product of the first industry. But, of course, it is a very different matter, and the assumption becomes illegitimate, when a variation in the quantity produced by the industry under consideration sets up a force which acts directly, not merely upon its own costs, but also upon the costs of other industries; in such a case the conditions of the 'particular equilibrium' which it was intended to isolate are upset, and it is no longer possible, without contradiction, to neglect collateral effects.

It unfortunately happens that it is precisely into this latter category that the applications of the laws of returns fall, in the great majority of cases. As regards diminishing returns, in fact, if in the production of a particular commodity a considerable part of a factor is employed, the total amount of which is fixed or can be increased only at a more than proportional cost, a small increase in the production of the commodity will necessitate a more intense utilisation of that factor, and this will affect in the same manner the cost of the commodity in question and the cost of the other commodities into the production of which that factor enters; and since commodities into the production of which a common special factor enters are frequently, to a certain extent, substitutes for one another (for example, various kinds of agricultural produce), the modification in their price will not be without appreciable effects upon demand in the industry concerned. If we next take an industry which employs only a small part of the 'constant factor' (which appears more appropriate for the study of the particular equilibrium of a single industry), we find that a (small) increase in its production is generally met much more by drawing 'marginal doses' of the constant factor from other industries than by intensifying its own utilisation of it; thus the increase in cost will be practically negligible, and anyhow it will still operate in a like degree upon all the industries of the group. Excluding these cases, and excluding – if we take a point of view embracing long periods – the numerous cases in which the quantity of a means of production may be regarded as being only temporarily fixed in respect to an unexpected demand, very little remains: the imposing structure of diminishing returns is available only for the study of that minute class of commodities in the production of which the whole of a factor of production is employed. Here, of course, by 'a commodity' is to be understood an article in regard to which it is possible to construct, or at least to conceive, a demand schedule which is tolerably homogeneous and independent of the conditions of supply, and not, as is frequently

> implied, a collection of diverse articles, such as agricultural products or ironware. (Sraffa, 1926: 538–9)

Sraffa also rules out increasing returns as being compatible with competitive conditions, since internal economies 'are most seldom to be met with' and external economies create interdependencies which disrupt the uniqueness of the competitive equilibrium. Consequently the only 'normal' case under competitive conditions is one of constant cost. And thus, as Sraffa so clearly articulated it in his contribution to the 'Symposium on Increasing Returns and the Representative Firm' in 1930: 'Marshall's theory cannot be interpreted in a way which makes it logically self-consistent and at the same time, reconciles it with the facts it sets out to explain [so that] Marshall's theory . . . should be discarded' (1930: 93).

Sraffa solved the problem of the inconsistency of the assumption of competitive conditions with respect to the laws of returns and the interdependence of individual supply and demand schedules by assuming that each firm operated as if it were a monopolist.[4] Writers at the time focused almost exclusively on the market conditions question and left to one side the much more damaging criticism concerning the inability of the interaction of supply and demand to determine relative prices. Geoffrey Harcourt, for example, made the following observation about Joan Robinson: 'In writing *The Economics of Imperfect Competition*, Joan Robinson developed her ideas from Sraffa's "pregnant suggestion" that each firm was its own little monopolist in a nevertheless competitive environment but she virtually ignored the message of his argument that it was, except for some minor, empirically unimportant, exceptions, inadmissible in competitive theory to assume that supply and demand curves were independent of each other' (1986: 98–9). Likewise Richard Kahn, in his retrospective lectures on *The Making of Keynes' General Theory*, concurs with Harcourt when he states that 'the section of particular interest to Cambridge economists was that on increasing returns' (1984: 23).

Keynes, on the other hand, paid virtually no attention to the debate on increasing returns, at least in print, although as editor of the *Economic Journal* he wrote a brief introduction to the 1930 Symposium. Instead his focus was upon the question of the interdependence of supply and demand curves and the bearing that had on the competitive solution to the laws of value. But more on this later. While most of the discipline became attracted to Sraffa's focus on the untenability of competitive conditions, which led to his contribution being folded back into the mainstream, one writer at least picked up the more damaging aspect of Sraffa's article, that of the question of meaningful interdependence and the orthodox theory of value. That writer was Maurice Dobb.

VI Dobb's critique of orthodox wage theory

Three years after Sraffa's 1926 article, Keynes, as editor of the *Economic Journal*, published a piece by Maurice Dobb, "A Sceptical View of the Theory of Wages" which continued Sraffa's criticism of the orthodox theory of value, this time directed towards the theory of distribution. Like Sraffa, Dobb was a proponent of the Ricardian/Marxian theory of value which saw little role for the interaction of supply and demand in the determination of the value of reproducible commodities.[5] In this article Dobb borrows Marshall's questioning of the invariance of the marginal utility of money with respect to labour supply decisions and couples it with Sraffa's focus on the interdependence of conditions of supply and demand for outputs. He shows that the concept of an aggregate supply curve for labour, independent of the aggregate demand curve for labour, is untenable. This result vitiated the traditional theory of distribution which held that each factor of production received a return equal to the value of its marginal contribution to aggregate output. And it implied that economic theory does not allow for an aggregated labour market where the real wage is determined in exactly the same manner as any other price determined by the laws of supply and demand.

Dobb questioned the independence of the supply and demand curves for factors of production upon which the marginal productivity theory rested. In this context, Dobb defines 'independence . . . to mean that a change in [the supply or demand curves], through its effect on the price of labour or on any other prices, does not thereby produce a change in the other' (Dobb, 1929: 509). He cites the long quotation from Sraffa, above, on the interdependence of conditions of supply and demand, and attributes his own train of thought as being influenced by that perspective. He then repeats Marshall's idea (literally, but without attribution) that

> In the majority of cases . . . where a commodity occupies only a small part of the total supply of the factors of production, while the money spent on it represents only a small part of the total income of the consumers who buy it, reactions of this kind are regarded as being sufficiently small as to be negligible. They are relegated to the category of the 'second order of small quantities'. The prices of the factors of production on the one hand, and the marginal utility of income to consumers on the other hand, are regarded as being virtually unaffected by the terms of this particular act of exchange; and the assumption of independence, though not precisely true, is held to be true with a sufficient degree of approximation to satisfy both logic and expediency. (1929: 510)

If the theory of the labour market is subsumed in the theory of the determination of exchange value, as orthodoxy assumed, then a corollary to this theory of the labour market would be that 'the aggregate demand for labour . . . is positively correlated with the profit received by the investing class . . . In other words, the demand for labour is . . . *elastic*; . . . every cheapening of the cost of labour must *increase* aggregate wage-earnings and so benefit capitalists and labourers alike' (ibid., emphasis in original).[6]

Dobb, however, doubted this parallel between the labour market and all other commodity markets. He drew this directly from Marshall's concern, that unlike the purchase of any other commodity which normally constituted a small portion of one's income, the wage bargain determined the bulk of a worker's income: 'In our case of labour an equilibrium cannot be postulated because labour is not one among many alternative objects of sale and purchase, but is the sole object of exchange in this particular sphere' (ibid.: 513). Thus changes in the wage would cause significant modifications in the marginal utility of income for the workers. Consequently 'a change in the price of labour in either direction is likely to produce a change in the supply-price of labour of a similar kind, thereby creating a tendency for any fall in wages to become cumulative' (ibid.: 512). Dobb cites Marshall saying that 'while "equilibrium has been attained, it is not *the* equilibrium, but *an* accidental equilibrium . . . it would be an arbitrary equilibrium" ' (ibid., emphasis in original).[7] He did not hold the same objection to the demand for labour curve contending rather that 'the conception of a demand-curve for labour as independent of the price of labour is still regarded as approximately correct, even while the independence of the supply-curve may be relegated to the limbo of discarded doctrine' (ibid.: 513).

But the matter does not end there, because Dobb then raises the question about the demand curve for labour being real wage-elastic. What is the meaning of such a proposition if a change in the wage shifts the demand for labour curve? At first glance, there is no reason why the demand curve for labour should be affected by changes in wages. But Dobb observes that, when wages rise and the profit share falls, the marginal utility of income to capitalists rises, because their flow of income may not be enough to sustain their conventional style of living. In this instance their savings rate may fall and there will be less money available to act as a fund for wages. As a result, the demand for labour curve will fall (see Keynes, CW XIII: 392). Dobb then asserts that, although it is reasonable to accept an independent supply and demand curve at the individual level, so long as competitive conditions prevail, it is unreasonable to accept this assumption of independence for industry as a whole. Any change in the price of labour, in the aggregate, changes distribution, and, through its effect on the marginal utility of income, changes the supply and demand curves for labour. The resultant equilibrium is thus indeterminate.

Finally he puts his methodological criticism of the theory of distribution in the context of the theory of value:

> It may well be that just as a determinate equilibrium for wages can only be postulated for particular sectional wage-rates, so a determinate equilibrium can only be postulated for particular commodities in isolation. In this latter case . . . the postulate of an equilibrium is rendered adequate on the assumption that any reaction of the price on the marginal utility of income to buyer and seller is so small as to be negligible. The price of one commodity is, therefore, determinate on the assumption that the prices of all other commodities remain constant. As we pass to more important commodities, such as bread in the consumption of the poor, or to larger *groups* of commodities . . . this assumption progressively breaks down. (1929: 517–18, emphasis in original)

Moreover, in the longer period, where aggregate income is changing, Dobb contends that the interdependence of supply and demand vitiates the idea of labour market equilibrium where fluctuations in the wage balance out the independent forces of supply and demand:

> The conception of an independent demand-curve for labour, equally with that of an independent supply-curve, definitely seems to break down. Neither the 'will to work' nor the 'will to save' are independent of subjective valuations of income by the parties concerned and of conventional standards; and these in turn are not independent of the way in which income has been distributed by the wage-bargains of the immediate past. To postulate an equilibrium level of wages, relative to which any existing rates can be declared to be 'too high' or 'too low', is to stride [*sic*] a system of assumptions which can be made consistent neither with one another nor with the facts. (Ibid.: 516)

Dobb concluded that aggregate income distribution was not the result of factors receiving a reward equal to their net contribution to the value of output, but rather the historical outcome of tradition, custom and, of course, a class struggle. By showing that the theory of distribution could not be subsumed under the theory of exchange value, he was able to resuscitate the Marxian idea of profit as a category emanating from exploitation in the process of production. Questions of utility and disutility, if they are to have any bearing in economics at all, would have to come subsequent to a theory of distribution, not contemporaneously, as the orthodox theory assumed:

> What meaning is there in speaking of a determinate point of intersection of two curves when one curve cannot move without producing a related movement in the other? The matter appears to be further complicated when we are regarding an economic system in which persons who enjoy utilities in consumption partly constitute a distinct class from the persons who suffer the disutilities of production. Under one set of conditions the worker will equate a loaf of bread to a day's labour, under other circumstances to the labour of an hour. If one is to

> speak of a general equilibrium where utility and disutility equate at the margin, one must *assume* a certain relationship between a worker's loaf and his labour, which is itself the result of an indeterminate bargain. Had a different bargain, or a different scale of production, been arrived at previously, a different relation between utility and disutility and a different equilibrium might have been established. And it is in this sense that the solution of the problem of distribution is logically prior to the solution of the problem of value. (Ibid.: 518–19, emphasis in original)

The political implications of Dobb's article provoked a rejoinder from Hicks (1930) in defence of the competitive labour market (the existence of which Dobb denied): 'competition does tend to abolish the exploitation of labour, but it is very slow about it. It is quite slow enough for some interference to be desirable, but what kind of interference is altogether another question' (Hicks, 1930: 146). What stands out the most from Dobb's conclusions is that there is no sound theoretical foundation for explaining unemployment in terms of wages that are too high once the link between wages and productivity has been broken. Nor is the demand for labour real wage-elastic, since the interdependence between conditions of supply and demand makes the effects of a cut in wages indeterminate. Keynes did not warm up to the former conclusion at first, but the latter one was so evident to his susceptibilities that they became a cornerstone of his writings on employment policy over the next five years.

VII Keynes and the Cambridge economic tradition

Keynes's criticism of orthodox economics, as was indicated in Section II, was directed at what he believed to be a misapplication of the metaphor of the laws of supply and demand to the particular questions that they tried to address: an aggregate labour market in terms of a real wage and an aggregate capital market in terms of a real rate of interest. He wanted to consider when it was appropriate to employ the traditional metaphor of supply and demand mediated by a price, and those when it was not. He did *not* reject the laws of supply and demand or the idea of a centre of gravity towards which those relations might gravitate (see Harcourt, 1981; Rotheim, 1990). This is a critical point because, towards the latter stages of the drafting of the *General Theory*. Roy Harrod became worried as he caught glimpses of what Keynes was actually saying. His reaction, in a letter to Keynes on 1 August 1935, was most poignant:

> You may wonder why I lay such stress on a point that merely concerns formal proof rather than the conclusions reached. I am thinking of the effectiveness of your work. Its effectiveness is diminished if you try to eradicate very deep-rooted habits of thought *unnecessarily*. One of these is the supply and demand analysis. I am not merely thinking of the aged and fossilised, but of the younger generation who have been thinking perhaps only for a few years but very hard

> about these topics. It is doing great violence to their fundamental groundwork of thought, if you tell them that two independent demand and supply functions won't jointly determine price and quantity. Tell them that there may be more than one solution. Tell them that we don't know the supply function. Tell them that the *ceteris paribus* clause is inadmissible and that we can discover more important functional relationships governing price and quantity in this case which render the s. and d. analysis nugatory. But don't impugn that analysis itself. (CW XIII: 534, emphasis in original)

Keynes, however, was not rejecting the metaphor of supply and demand or the notion of centres of gravity as formal structures of analysis. He only rejected them in the traditional approach because the use to which they were put was blatantly illogical. Harrod could not grasp Keynes's subtle distinction between a criticism of supply and demand in general and the criticism of the 'classical' utilization of that method. Keynes noted to Harrod that 'my own firm conviction is that your mind is still half in the classical world, and that you ought to be accusing me, not of bad manners, but of faulty theory' (CW XIII: 551).

From 1930, Keynes began to address questions of employment in terms of the organic interdependent method which we have called the Cambridge economic tradition.[9] His lectures in the United States in 1931, his essay on 'The Great Slump of 1930', the early draft chapter of the *General Theory* which he tentatively called 'The Effects of Changes in the Rate of Earnings', the strong criticism lodged against Pigou's *Theory of Unemployment* and Chapters 2, 19 and the appendix to Chapter 19 in the final version of the *General Theory*, are all examples of Keynes's discomfort with the orthodox notion of an aggregate labour market with independent supply and demand curves mediated by a real wage. These many examples of Keynes's critical mind-frame also attest to the strong influence that Dobb's 1929 *Economic Journal* article had on Keynes's overall perspective. For Dobb, the interdependencies among the relations which constituted the supply and demand curves for labour were seen to occur because of the effect that changes in price variables had on 'subjective valuations of income by the parties concerned and of conventional standards' (1929: 516). For Keynes, such interdependencies occurred as the result both of subjective and of objective circumstances. The subjective circumstances embodied Keynes's psychological propensities, the state of long-term expectations, liquidity preference and the attention that individuals and groups paid to what he called 'conventional' behaviour. The objective factors, which helped to provide the basis for reactions in the subjective factors (such as the convention of labour bargaining in terms of money wages because they had no control of the real wage), centred around the organic interdependent effects that changes in specific variables, such as money wages and the money rate of interest, had on aggregate income and the price of wage-goods. Workers accepted the convention of bargaining in terms of money wages because they could not possibly know what effect their wage-bargains would have on aggregate demand and the price of wage-goods.

When considered in this light, questions such as the effect that a reduction in the real wage (through a reduction in the money wage) would have on aggregate employment, as seen in terms of the real-wage elasticity of demand for labour (which was the metaphor embraced by Pigou), become non-questions at the hand of both Dobb and Keynes. Assessing Keynes's criticism of the orthodox theory of an aggregate labour market, it is clear that it marked a significant improvement on the foundation laid by Dobb. Keynes's response to the effect a fall in money wages had on aggregate demand for output, and therefore the aggregate demand for labour, was more sophisticated than Dobb's focus on the effect these changes had on psychological attitudes toward work and savings. For Keynes it becomes clear that the real wage comes in as a by-product of changes in the level of employment and not the opposite. No longer could he think in terms of a real wage elasticity of the demand for labour. But that was only a matter of degree, not of substance. For the basic framework in which Keynes was able to repudiate wage-cuts as a remedy for unemployment came from a tradition at Cambridge at least as far back as Marshall, culminating in the exemplary heuristic so clearly laid out by Dobb in his 'A Sceptical View on the Theory of Wages'.

Moreover the Cambridge economic tradition caused Keynes to reject the marginal productivity theory of distribution that so dominated orthodox theory and policy (see Rotheim, 1990). For example, Keynes in an article written in 1930 on 'The Question of High Wages' observed that:

> there is a growing scepticism abroad as to the psychological and theoretical validity of the orthodox theory of value which leads others to dispute that there is any natural level of wages at all, or at any rate, one that is rigidly fixed; . . . Limits there are, no doubt, this school of thought would admit; but there is a fairly wide margin, they would maintain, within which the determining factor is, not so much what used to be called economic law, as social and political habits and practices, and the trend of public opinion. (CW XX: 5)

Keynes identifies two perspectives on this 'scepticism', one of which is attributed to Dobb's 1929 *Economic Journal* article. Among Keynes's comments, all of which are laudatory, is the following:

> The second type of critic makes a much more fundamental attack on the old theory. He questions altogether the rigidity of what economists call the theory of distribution. This theory flows from two sets of assumptions: The first is that

> the supply of a given factor of production responds in a very sensitive way to the absolute reward offered to it; and the other is that there is a possibility of substitution between the factors of production depending upon the relative rewards offered to them . . . The new theory attacks the rigidity of the solution offered on the basis of these assumptions. It would not dispute that such considerations fix limits within which the actual situation must lie, but it contends that these limits are somewhat wide, and that within them the situation is determined first and foremost by historical influences as gradually modified by contemporary social and political forces.
>
> There is a large arbitrary element in the relative rates of remuneration, and factors of production get what they do, not because in any strict economic sense they precisely earn it, but because past events have led to these rates being customary and usual. So there is nothing sacrosanct about them. If the working class have the political and bargaining power to get a larger share of the product of industry than formerly, well, that is a new historical fact; historical evolution is this time on their side. The business men will have to get less, and that is all there is to it. (CW XX: 6–7)

Keynes sought to question the immediate concusions of what he called the 'high wage' advocates, because, when they were seen from an international perspective, one could still go a long way in explaining relative global unemployment by the degree to which wages were too high. In fact the same perspective can be found just one month later in a radio conversation that Keynes had with Sir Josiah Stamp on the unemployment situation. Keynes noted that, while a great deal of the unemployment could be attributed to economic fluctuations, he maintained that another major cause of unemployment was

> the existence of the dole [which] undoubtedly diminishes the pressure on the individual man to accept a rate of wages or a kind of employment which is not just what he wants or what he is used to. In the old days the pressure on the unemployed was to get back somehow or other into employment, and if that was so today surely it would have more effect on the prevailing rate of wages than it has today, so that the power of industry to absorb would be much greater than we have experienced. I cannot help feeling that we must partly attribute to the dole the extraordinary fact . . . that, in spite of the fall in prices, and the fall in the cost of living, and the heavy unemployment, wages have practically not fallen at all since 1924. (CW XX: 318–19)

Keynes seems to be saying that unemployment persists to a large degree because wages are too high. However he also observed that, even though wages might be too high, and might be considered as a cause of unemployment in Britain, 'I do not think, any more than you [Stamp] do, that it is practicable to reduce wages, whether they are too high or not' (ibid.: 322). So it is fair to say that in 1930, Keynes was still half in the classical world, in that he chose to see unemployment as explicable by relatively high wages. On the other hand, he disavowed the use of wage cutting as a remedy for that unemployment on the grounds that it would reduce aggregate demand for wage-goods and therefore aggregate demand for labour in both the wage-goods and the producer-goods markets and, to the degree that they caused prices to fall, would cause the real value of debt to rise, resulting in increased bankruptcies and lower demand for labour. In addition the high wage explanation of unemployment must, by definition coexist with marginal productivity theory of distribution. But Keynes was already questioning that theory as well. One of those sign-posts is already evident in 1930:

> Now I am not here concerned to defend the orthodox analysis and the orthodox hypotheses against these attacks. To a large extent I sympathise with the attacks. I think there is a great deal in what the critics say. I believe that the best working theories of the future will own these assailants as their parents. All those, who want to improve economic theory and to make a contribution to it, ought to pay a great deal of attention to what Mr Dobb . . . and others are saying. (CW XX: 7–8)

Keynes's total rejection of the orthodox analysis was yet to occur. And even in the *General Theory* it was couched in vague language and obscured in 'sundry observations' so as to slip by most readers. But it is there, and the roots of that dissent are clearly situated in the discussion of organic interdependence within 'the Cambridge economic tradition'.

Notes

1. Earlier versions of this chapter were presented to the ESRC Post-Keynesian Economics Study Group at University College, London and the Kress Society, Harvard University. Special thanks to Nahid Aslanbeigui and John Hillard.
2. Keynes reveals this methodological criticism of orthodoxy in a letter to Daniel Macmillan in 1932, in response to a request to review Hicks's *Theory of Wages*. Keynes suggests that he is too unsympathetic to give the book a fair review and comments:

   > The book seems to me to assume that prices are fixed independently of wages, so that whatever happens to money wages may be assumed to happen, more or less to the same extent, to real wages. This assumption may be legitimate when one is dealing merely with equilibrium, but after the first chapter the author is avowedly dealing with disequilibrium, and such problems as unemployment. For these problems his method of approach seems to me, as I have said, quite hopeless. But then I should say much the same about a good deal of Pigou's treatment of this subject. (CW XII: 861–2)

3. This assessment of Pigou may be too harsh, as he did say in his first book on the topic:

   > If, for all grades of workpeople, the average wage rates over fairly long periods – not the wage rates prevailing at particular moments – were determined by the free play of competitive forces, *unemployment would only be possible in so far as the demand for labour of the different grades is subject to fluctuations*. Apart from fluctuations there could not exist any unemployment whatever. (1913a: 51–2, emphasis added)

   I am grateful to Nahid Aslanbeigui for this reference.

4. Eatwell and Panico (1987) contend that Sraffa had in mind two routes by which these inconsistencies could be mitigated, the first being the employment of a general equilibrium solution and the other being the abandonment of the assumption of perfect competition. This assertion has been the source of some recent controversy (see Panico, 1991 and Samuelson, 1991; also Steedman, 1988).
5. See Ricardo (1820) Chapters I and XXX, and Marx (1867). Dobb and Sraffa were colleagues at Cambridge in the late 1920s in what was then a very small department. Sraffa's critique of the orthodox theory of distribution, published in *The Production Of Commodities By Means Of Commodities* (1960), was actually written in the late 1920s (see Eatwell and Panico, 1987) and was probably shared with Dobb (as with Keynes) at that time. We can infer that from a piece written by Dobb in 1931 ('An Introduction to Economics') where he discusses what became an essential theme of Sraffa's introduction to their joint edition of Ricardo's *Principles* published in 1950. Dobb notes his indebtedness to Sraffa.
6. This question of the real-wage elasticity of the demand for labour was paramount in the traditional theory of the labour market. At the time when Dobb was writing this article, the primary source on the subject would have been Pigou's *Industrial Fluctuations* (1927b).
7. In fact Dobb went so far as to call the outcome 'indeterminate' in the sense of Edgeworth and Marshall. This prompted a rather misguided response by Hicks (1930). See also the rejoinder by Dobb (1931b).
8. It is certainly not difficult to include Kahn's analysis of the multiplier as falling within the organic interdependent method (see Brown-Collier, 1985). Perhaps the inability of neoclassical economists to embrace the concept of the multiplier is an inability to embrace an organic interdependent method which stands in opposition to an equilibrium method of analysis. For, if the idea of an employment multiplier is accepted as the mode by which the flow of output expands and contracts, then such heuristics as saving creating its own investment (mediated through movements in a real rate of interest) and a real wage adjusting the supply of and demand for labour in the aggregate make very little sense.

References

Bharadwaj, K. (1972), 'Marshall on Pigou's *Wealth and Welfare*', *Economica*, **153**, 32–46.

Brown-Collier, E. K. (1985), 'Keynes's View of an Organic Universe: The Implications', *Review of Social Economy*, **43**, 14–23.

Carabelli, A. (1988), *On Keynes's Method*, London: Macmillan.

Clower, R. W. (1989), Review of R. Dimand's *The Origins of the Keynesian Revolution*, *Journal of Economic Literature*, **27**, 1679–80.

Currie, M. and I. Steedman (1990), *Wrestling With Time*, Michigan: University of Michigan Press.

Dobb, M. (1929), 'A Sceptical View of the Theory of Wages', *Economic Journal*, **39**, 506–19.

Dobb, M. (1931a), 'An Introduction to Economics', in W. Rose (ed.), *An Outline of Modern Knowledge*, London: Gollancz.

Dobb, M. (1931b), 'A Note Concerning Mr J. R. Hicks on the Indeterminateness of Wages', *Economic Journal*, **41**, 143–5.

Eatwell, J. and C. Panico (1987), 'Piero Sraffa (1898–1983)', in *The New Palgrave Dictionary of Economics*, London: Macmillan.

Fitzgibbons, A. (1988), *Keynes's Vision: A New Political Economy*, Oxford: Clarendon Press.

Harcourt, G. C. (1981), 'Marshall, Sraffa and Keynes: Incompatible Bedfellows?', *Eastern Economic Journal*, **7**, 39–50.

Harcourt, G. C. (1986), 'On the Influence of Piero Sraffa on the Contribution of Joan Robinson to Economic Theory', *Economic Journal*, (Suppl.), **96**, 96–108.

Hicks, J. R. (1930), 'The Indeterminateness of Wages', *Economic Journal*, **40**, 215–31.

Kahn, R. F. (1984), *The Making of Keynes' General Theory*, Cambridge: Cambridge University Press.

Marshall, A. (1898), 'Distribution and Exchange', *Economic Journal*, **8**, 37–59.
Marshall, A. (1920), *Principles of Economics*, London: Macmillan.
Marx, K. (1867), *Capital: Vol I*, (1949) trans. D. Torr, London: Allen & Unwin.
Milgate, M. (1977), 'Keynes on the "Classical" Theory of Interest', *Cambridge Journal of Economics*', **1**, 307–15.
O'Donnell, R. M. (1989), *Keynes: Philosophy, Economics and Politics*, London: Macmillan.
O'Donnell, R. M. (1990), 'An Overview of Probability, Expectations, Uncertainty and Rationality in Keynes's Conceptual Framework', *Review of Political Economy*.
Panico, C. (1987), 'The Evolution of Keynes's Thought on the Rate of Interest', *Contributions to Political Economy*, **6**, 53–71.
Panico, C. (1991), 'Some Notes on Marshallian Supply Functions', *Economic Journal*, **101**, 557–9.
Pigou, A. C. (1913a), *Unemployment*, London: Williams and Northgate.
Pigou, A. C. (1913b), 'The Interdependence of Different Sources of Demand and Supply in a Market', *Economic Journal*, **23**, 19–24.
Pigou, A. C. (1927), *Industrial Fluctuations*, London: Macmillan.
Pigou, A. C. (1933), *Theory of Unemployment*, London: Macmillan.
Ricardo, D. (1820), *On the Principles of Political Economy and Taxation*, London: Murray.
Rotheim, R. J. (1981), 'Keynes's "Monetary Theory of Value" (1933)', *Journal of Post Keynesian Economics*, **3**, 568–85.
Rotheim, R. J. (1988), 'Keynes and the Language of Probability and Uncertainty', *Journal of Post Keynesian Economics*, **11**, 83–99.
Rotheim, R. J. (1990), 'Keynes and the Marginal Productivity Theory of Distribution', paper delivered at the ROPE conference, Malvern (August).
Samuelson, P. A. (1991), 'Sraffa's Other Leg', *Economic Journal*, **101**, 570–73.
Sraffa, P. (1926), 'The Laws of Returns Under Competitive Conditions', *Economic Journal*, **36**, 535–60.
Sraffa, P. (1930), 'Symposium on "Increasing Returns and the Representative Firm: a Criticism and Reply', *Economic Journal*, **40**, 89–93.
Steedman, I. (1988), 'Sraffian Interdependence and Partial Equilibrium Analysis', *Cambridge Journal of Economics*, **12**, 85–95.
Thomas, B. (1991), 'Alfred Marshall on Economic Biology', *Review of Political Economy*.

3 Keynes, orthodoxy and uncertainty[1]

John Hillard

Standard economics, by opposing the idea that the economic process may consist of something more than a jig-saw puzzle with all its elements given, has identified itself with dogmatism. (Georgescu-Roegen, 1966: 104)

It is rather as though the teachers of physics had ignored the quantum theory and had gone on, year after year, teaching precisely those radiation laws which the quantum theory had been brought in to replace. And teaching them with that special insistence which strains the voices of the priests of a dying religion. (Snow, 1964: 84)

A host of columbines and pathics
Who show by mathematics
In their defence
That wealth and poverty are merely
Mental pictures, so that clearly
Every tramp's a landlord really
In mind events.

(W. H. Auden)

I Introduction

It is commonly accepted that Keynes's two main achievements were his articulation of the principle of effective demand and his identification of the behavioural implications of irreducible uncertainty. The former was successfully incorporated into the mechanical equilibrium framework. The latter, which comprised the non-Euclidean component of the holistic theory of effective demand outlined in the *General Theory*, was quietly ignored. In the so-called Keynesian era, classical economics remained firmly attached to its ultra-rationalist foundations and, ultimately, in the form of New Classical economics, it re-emerged 'as if' Keynes had never happened. Beyond the restricted scope of orthodox perception, however, economists have begun to take seriously the implications of uncertainty for their approach to method, theory and practice. This chapter explores the impact of Keynes's philosophical background upon his economic perception.[2].

It will be argued that Keynes's endeavour to articulate a practical theory of the future still represents an unanswered, revolutionary challenge to the integrity of the equilibrium framework. Keynes's discussion of the decision problems associated with reasonable behaviour in an uncertain environment forced him to confront the ontological and epistemological foundations of equilibrium theory. In the next section, the organizing principles which underlie the equilibrium habit of mind are detailed to provide the benchmark against which Keynes's critique can be explored. Then Keynes's methodological stance is investigated, with attention devoted to his rejection of the 'homogeneity postulate' (CW XIV: 109) and his reaction to 'the awkward fact' (CW XIV: 114) of uncertainty. Section IV assesses the contemporary relevance of Keynes's vision and, finally, some implications are drawn for the development of the Post-Keynesian project.

II Orthodoxy and uncertainty

Notwithstanding the power of the argument, the citadel of equilibrium economics has remained impervious to the heretical onslaught of the twentieth century. The reasons for the resilience of equilibrium economics constitute a topic beyond the scope of this discussion. For present purposes, I will focus on the emergence and development of equilibrium economics as an element within the rationalist tradition of western intellectual thought. To anticipate the argument, economic man is the natural heir of rationalism, which has a lineage stretching back to Greek antiquity and probably beyond. From Plato onwards, rationalist philosophers have sought the basic principles underlying intelligible order and have struggled to mirror the world with a formal theory in the mind. They have tried to represent the world as a system of objective principles which, 'like the truths of geometry, could be defended in rational argument and used to explain nature and justify actions' (Dreyfus and Dreyfus, 1986: 2). The rationalist mode of thought is underlined by a faith in the attainability of complete, consistent and, above all, certain knowledge.

This vision of absolute perfection is manifested by forming representations which can be reduced to primitive elements (or rational first principles) and then reformed into complex combinations of those elements. Objective laws are derived by the isolation of basic elements, which, in rule-like combinations, enable the explanation of the whole. Theory is designed to specify the relationship between context-free elements in terms of abstract principles. The successful application of such theory in classical physics promoted the belief that a set of context-free elements and relations between those elements could be formulated to account for the order within any domain. It was presumed that even the most complex of processes were reducible to an association of known elementary units acting in a predictable manner as a result of the forces acting between them. The method of Cartesian reductionism in the world of classical mechanics was taken as the appropriate exemplar for the study of economic phenomena (Bramhall, 1986). Most important, the advent of marginalism marked the acceptance of the idea that the goal of economic science was to supply law-like generalizations which did not differ in their logical form from those applicable to natural phenomena in general (Mirowski, 1989).

The procedure of applying rules to basic features and defining the world as a totality of logically independent atomic facts thus provided the ontological basis of orthodox equilibrium economics. The translation simply involved the discovery of the 'atoms' of which the economy is composed and the 'forces' which act upon them. The project consisted of decomposing the economic domain into its ultimate units; the relationship between these units was then analysed using a simple behavioural rule and, finally, the units were reconstituted into the whole. In short, the aim was to create 'a complete analytical system encapsulating economic relationships deduced from axioms depicting a universal pattern of individual behaviour exemplified by some form of "economic man" ' (Dow, 1985: 50–51). Economic man (or his equivalent in the aggregate) furnishes the natural law foundation upon which equilibrium theory is fabricated. The complete sanctity of the individual unit forms the context-free element of the theoretical system, which then relates to other such units by the operation of a formal optimization rule.

The application of atomistic individualism to the study of economic phenomena permitted the construction of a generalized account in which individuals are characterized as self-regarding and well-informed in the calculated choices required by their rationality. The theoretical structure was predicated on a faith in the 'coherent rationality' of the 'optimising agent whose actions are determined by applying to the natural givens of [its] situation (endowments, technologies, future states of nature), preference functions that are naturally given' (Loasby, 1989: 191). The prescription for rationality was the logical consistency of an individual's conduct in applying deduction from given premises. The argument was so constructed that, if the premises are true, then the conclusion must also be true. The analytical coherence of the expected utility-maximization approach derived from the insistence that economic behaviour 'can and does proceed by reason and calculation based on sufficient data' (Shackle, 1974: iii) so that, in deciding upon a course of action, the individual is able to undertake a total evaluation of all the possible alternatives:

> The economist's chief model of man has, on the one hand, needs and tastes, and on the other, exact, complete and infallible knowledge of the degree to which any pattern of disposal of his resources would satisfy each of those desires. His intellectual attainments are mathematical only: he can integrate the small increments of want-satisfaction which are yielded by small increments of any

> one resource devoted to the satisfaction of one want. In this way he arrives at a total of satisfactions of all kinds, and this total is maximized. (Shackle, 1966: 123)

It is taken for granted that, through the application of fully-informed reason, the individual can assess all possible outcomes of potential actions and their probable likelihood and carry out the appropriate expectational calculation. In sum, economic agents operate within a static order where the whole derives its meaning from the independent parts of which it is composed: 'the combined All of the social whole is the secondary result of a joining of prior units, the pre-formed Ones who are presumably capable of making contracts *before* their social juncture is established' (Ogilvy, 1977: 61). The only way to prevent the stability conditions of equilibrium from being rendered indeterminate is to confine the theory to 'deducing conclusions about maximising under certainty from a fundamental assumption of adequate knowledge' (Hutchison, 1978: 206). In other words, the entire theoretical schema rests on the precondition that, 'although the future cannot be known, at least its possible events and outcomes can be corralled into probability distributions whose parameters can be uniquely determined' (Vickers, 1989: 170).

In the equilibrium framework uncertainty corresponds to a situation of numerically measurable probabilistic knowledge: 'individuals possess measurable knowledge of all possible courses of action and passively optimise some accepted objective on the basis of something like mathematical expectations' (Lawson, 1990: 12). Whatever uncertainty exists within the mind/brain of the decision maker and/or the economic environment is finessed 'by providing individuals with the most sophisticated learning features and probability adjustment processes [so that] the uncertainty is removed and encapsulated in an innocuous "error" term' (Bianchi, 1990: 151). Uncertainty is transmuted into calculable risk by positing that the relevant variables can be expressed randomly in the form of subjectively designated probability distributions, the parameters of which are assumed to be known. The economic agent is perceived as an information-processing device programmed to maximize subjective expected utility, in an environment where a clearly-defined probability distribution can be ascertained about the consequences of action.

The axioms of individual behaviour have to be defined in this way so as to depict a system wherein equilibrium solutions, however temporary, are nonetheless attainable. The result is 'the supposedly unique pattern of exchanges to which the consent of all market participants could be obtained if every one of them, with his given endowment of resources, had a complete perception of the entire array of possible patterns of exchange'

(Shackle, 1988: 213). Without the specification that 'theory be exclusively constructed within a closed, formal framework, deriving theorems from a set of axioms delineating rational individual behaviour' (Dow, 1985: 68–9), the deterministic certainty conferred by the law and principles of the equilibrium method is absolutely meaningless. The equilibrium outcome, as befits a theory following the analogy of a physics modelled for an absolute space, an absolute time and an absolute determinism for nature, occurs within a timeless setting where the complete consistency of the agents' plans before any actions are undertaken guarantees the equality of decisions and realizations. As Hutchison (1978: 209) pointed out in the 1930s:

> An analysis of a world with uncertainty in it, and particularly an analysis which takes into account the factor of money, cannot start from the same assumption of 'rational' conduct as that applicable to a world without uncertainty – the kind of world within which, consciously and explicitly or not, the bulk of pure economic theory from Ricardo onwards appears to have been concerned.

In effect, decisions not based on a *conscious* deduction from explicit premises, or taken in a situation where fully specified and complete evidence is absent, cannot be accommodated within the equilibrium framework. The rationalist mode of thought demands the absolute certainty of proof, so that human conduct must be motivated solely by logic. Its 'all or nothing' approach, based on a strict demarcation between the quantifiable (rational) elements and non-quantifiable (irrational) factors, has enabled the scientific pretensions of the discipline to be upheld. The reductionist imperative dictates economic perception, thereby encouraging a habit of mind that it is sufficient to erect a structure of explanation upon a collection of coupled linear differential equations that correspond to interacting elements. The outcome is a total dependence upon calculative thinking and a denial of the relevance of less formalizable powers of the mind to the process of decision making.

This degeneration of reason into mere calculation sets an artificial limit on what is to be regarded as rational behaviour. But also the prerogative of a consistent reductionist basis for constructing theory ultimately restricts the scope of enquiry to what can be deterministically derived within the confines of its closed system of logic. Such an outlook ignores Heisenberg's warning (1958: 157) that

> when we represent a group of connections by a closed and coherent set of concepts, axioms, definitions and laws which is in turn represented by a mathematical scheme, we have, in fact, isolated and idealised this group of connections with the purpose of clarification. But even if complete clarity has been

> achieved this way, it is not known how accurately the set of concepts describes reality.

While Heisenberg was referring specifically to the conduct of the 'hard' sciences, this is equally relevant to equilibrium economics. The striking difference between the two activities, of course, is that economic orthodoxy is based on an *a priori* judgement about the omniscient agent. The character of *homo economicus* remains inviolate in the process of aggregation and 'investigation proceeds in one direction only; the macro is explained by the micro, the parts explain the whole' (Hodgson, 1988: 67). Economic man is purely Cartesian, in that 'each unit of economic matter is and remains independent of any other unit, meeting those other units in purely external relations analogous with push and pull. Their inner constitution as revealed in action directives and explanations is not to be affected by such encounters' (Lowe, 1965: 105–6).

The ' "sacred proposition" ' (Wiles 1983: 70) about the self-contained autonomy of the individual unit pervades the entire structure of economic explanation. As Harry Johnson put it: 'the central concept of economics is that of a system by which the resources of an economy are allocated in production, distribution and exchange by the interactions of decisions of individual economic units in an interrelated network of markets' (1968: 6). But, as Roy J. Rotheim has pointed out (1988: 85–6), the orthodox argument involves a circularity because, whereas in appearance it is the parts which determine the whole, in fact the individual units can only be defined in terms of the whole of which they are a part:

> if the premises are taken to be immutable, then there must already exist a reality which, itself, must be conceived as immutable. The nature of the atomistic system is such that there must be, by definition, a pre-ordained reality. Thus the premises are not truly *a priori* but already embody their own conclusions. The reality is implied within the premises and the conclusion dictates the method.

In Lakatosian terms, the atomistic individual is, unambiguously, the 'hard core' of the orthodox research programme 'which by (implicit) methodological decree, [is] for the present not to be tested' (Loasby, 1984: 403). Economic orthodoxy is thereby protected by an impregnable immunizing stratagem. The emphasis on allocative efficiency restricts the scope of economic science to relations of exchange, with the production process hidden away inside the 'black box' and with the question of distribution left on the sidelines. Immanent criticism is both impossible and futile because of the enforcement of a collective identity that is invariant across those who profess equilibrium economics. Not only is the orthodox world-view programmed by the axiom of the atomistic individual, but also equilibrium theory has been safeguarded by academic tradition embodied as

> the whole institutional apparatus of a normal scientific community – controlling as it does the training and socialisation of recruits, access to research facilities and channels of communication and publication, and the distribution of rewards. [This apparatus] . . . is geared towards keeping the science within the bounds set by the ruling paradigms and thus preventing the energies of scientists from being dissipated by their engaging in interminable disputes over basic assumptions, or tackling insoluble problems or engaging in debates with 'deviants' who do not accept the rules of the game. (King, 1971: 28)

In the post-Keynesian world, the obsessional fixation on micro-foundations showed the lengths to which the Pharisees were willing to travel in their effort to defeat the Keynesian rebellion. The process reached its apotheosis with the New Classical resurgence. The message from Chicago was loud and clear. For reasons of disciplinary coherence, a total adherence was demanded to 'the essential postulates (a) that markets clear and (b) that agents act in their own self-interest' (Lucas and Sargent, 1981: 304). The mission impossible of voluntaristic individualism required the production of robust and tractable models of continuous market clearing. Imbued with 'a remarkable optimism about the explanation of social phenomena in terms of individuals' (Hodgson, 1988: 54), the New Classicals proceeded to stretch the logic of atomism to its limit. The intellectual task was made less onerous, however, by allowing the qualifying postulate that 'labour supply and demand are always in equilibrium, no matter what the official statistics of unemployment say. The level of unemployment is natural – all those wanting employment at the current wage rate are employed' (Simon, 1984: 49).

As a conditioned reflex to the logical gauntlet thrown down by the proponents of the 'strong' version of New Classical economics, the New Keynesians then journeyed a bridge too far in trying to combine rational expectations logic with the fact of non-market clearing. In the event, the non-robustness of the coefficients derived from New Keynesian models heralded a pyrrhic victory for the New Classicals. At the very least, however, the New Keynesians have shown that an equilibrium outcome is dependent critically on the assumption of market clearing, not of agent rationality. Nevertheless such 'Keynesian' models perpetuate the Anglo-American view that Keynes's message centred on short-term rigidities which subvert the operation of individual economic rationality. The present theoretical impasse, with each side better able to criticize the other than to progress on its own behalf, exhibits an intellectual exhaustion derived from attempting to solve puzzles where the axiom of the atomistic individual of necessity dictates the shape of the final outcome.

The atomistic, rationalist and reductionist elements of economic orthodoxy thus combine to insulate equilibrium economics from phenomenal change:

> Economics ignores facts as irrelevant, bases its constructs on axioms arrived at *a priori*, or 'plucked from the air', from which deductions are made and an imaginary edifice created. It inhabits a world of purely economic phenomena, of universal validity yet, or because of this, without history; therefore subject to mathematical treatment, its variables and constants unaffected by the passage of time. Man and society are stripped of their attributes as if they could exist without psychological, political, legal or historical dimensions. Thus verification is both impossible and regarded as unnecessary. In effect, then, orthodox economics becomes a matter of faith and, *ipso facto*, immune to criticism. (Routh, 1989: 25–6)

The orthodox economists' predilection for imposing order on reality in this manner indicates 'the triumph of the quest for certainty over the quest for wisdom' (Rorty, 1980: 16). But as Peter Wiles argues

> there is no such thing as a 'proposition that neither can nor need be proved' unless, of course, it is a definition. 'Axiom', in the sense that Aristotle gave the word, is a vicious attempt to straddle the divide between fact and definition. An economics built upon it is a house that, however handsome and commodious, is built upon the sand. It is not scientific to say, 'I forbid you to argue about my assumptions'. (Wiles, 1983: 85)

III Keynes

Keynes had been variously described as a pragmatist (Dillard, 1946), an empiricist (Littleboy, 1983), a rationalist (Hodgson, 1985) and 'a critical but constructive rationalist' (O'Donnell, 1989: 93). While such packaging is a convenient means of introducing an element of certainty into the proceedings, it first presupposes a common acceptance of the meaning of such terms. Secondly, it is precisely because Keynes is difficult, if not impossible, to classify along conventional lines that makes the study of his work an exciting enterprise. The endeavour to reduce the Keynesian corpus to manageable proportions by the use of classificatory labels has imposed a false coherence upon his work. Instead of identifying himself with particular lines of commentary, he addressed intellectual and practical problems using what seemed to him to be the most appropriate approach for the task in hand. Keynes adopted a habit of mind in approaching the subject-matter of economics which was profoundly different from the canonical stereotype. He was fundamentally opposed to the application of the mechanical model of the natural sciences to the material of economics. He insisted that economic phenomena cannot be reduced to the status of physical objects obeying mechanical laws. The 'scientists' of equilibrium economics were certainly able to construct a rigorous theory based on rational maximization from an individual to the economy as the determinate outcome of the motivations and actions of those individuals. Yet 'its tacit assumptions are seldom or never satisfied, with the result that it cannot solve the economic problems of the actual world' (CW VII : 378).

Before outlining Keynes's criticism of received doctrine, it is worth identifying those features of 'the simplified world' (CW XIV: 107) of equilibrium economics that were untenable to him. In 'The End of Laissez-Faire' he outlined 'the unreal assumptions' which underlay 'the conclusion that individuals acting independently will produce the greatest aggregate wealth'. The unreality of equilibrium economics derived from two sources. The first related to the question of ontology: it was presupposed that 'the processes of production and consumption are in no way organic'. Secondly, there existed a problem of epistemology: the belief in 'a sufficient foreknowledge of conditions and requirements and adequate opportunities of obtaining this foreknowledge' (CW IX: 284). The debate over whether Keynes was an atomist and/or an organicist has provoked a considerable literature. In its bare essentials, the question here is but a recomposed version of an age-old dilemma given meaning only through the either/or imperative of dualistic reason. Western thought is divided into two distinct sets of

> ontological premises embedded in the assumptions made about the nature of individuals. An atomist social ontology is usually associated with the premise that essential aspects of human character and motivation are independent of social relations and hence immutable. In contrast, an organicist ontology assumes the essential traits of character are the product of these relations and hence variable with changes in them. (Winslow, 1989: 1174)

In tracing the relationship between the methodological position adopted in *A Treatise on Probability* and his subsequent work in the domain of economics, Anna Carabelli (1988) presents a convincing case in favour of Keynes's adoption of an organicist perspective. Keynes stressed that economic material possesses the attributes of 'complexity', making it 'not immediately susceptible to analytical tools' (Carabelli, 1988: 151). 'Complexity' derived from the material being 'capable of variations of degree in more than one mutually incommensurable direction at the same time' (CW V: 88). In a word, Keynes's objection was that the economic material lacks the *precision* necessary to justify 'the inductive claims with reference to the future' (CW XIV: 316) which are derived from the hypothetical canons of the orthodox schema. The Cartesian mechanical analogy of classical economics breaks down operationally when 'the system is in a state of constant flux because the structural relationships described by the form and the parameters of equations change through time' (Leontief, 1971: 3). In the face of 'the apparent lack of any degree of uniformity in the environment' (CW XIV: 316), it was unacceptable to Keynes to predicate economic analysis upon the assumption that it consisted of 'the action of independent atomic factors . . . on material constant and homogeneous through time' (ibid.: 286).

Orthodox thinkers shy away from the idea of a non-atomistic individual, even though an holistic outlook does not imply the disappearance of the individual. Keynes's reference to Paley's dictum that, 'although we speak of communities as sentient beings . . . nothing really exists or feels but *individuals*' (quoted in O'Donnell, 1989: 128) is compatible with individuals operating within *a system of interdependence*. Every relationship within the system is more than and different from the sum of the individual elements: 'the real issue is whether or not the parts function merely because of their inherent qualities, after taking in inputs (information etc.) from outside, or whether there is a more complex web of determination where parts are partially constituted in their relations with the whole' (Hodgson, 1988: 69). Or as Roy J. Rotheim (1989/90: 318–19, 323) emphasizes, in response to the atomistic interpretation of Davis (1989):

> Keynes understood . . . the economic process in terms of recursive interdependencies between wholes and parts. Organic processes, then, [do] not require explanation at the level of the whole. Instead, they require explanation of the process by which parts and wholes interact and redefine each other in the course of those interactions . . . For Keynes, individualism is an organic individualism. The individual's very nature is moulded by the social context in which she exists and in which she attempts to make decisions.

Keynes's proposed synthesis, the principle of 'organic unity through time', was designed as an alternative to equilibrium theory, which was unable to handle 'the state of affairs as a whole [which] cannot be usefully analysed into parts' (CW X: 436). His holistic vision necessitated 'a distinction between a logic relative to the individual, to his motivations and actions, and a logic relative to the collectivity as a whole' (Carabelli, 1988: 213). His denial of the atomistic ontology underlying equilibrium theory and his use of an holistic approach to analyse the economic system brought into focus the relationship between uncertainty and economic behaviour. Given that it was no longer possible to uphold a symmetry between the past and future, as is assumed within the mechanical universe of equilibrium theory, the prominent question became 'foreknowledge' and its relation to decision making.

In transcending the limitations imposed by the 'assumption of a definite and calculable future' (CW XIV: 107) and taking on board 'the indefinite character of actual expectations' (ibid.: 106), Keynes became increasingly dubious about his adherence to the equilibrium mode of thought. In 1926, he traced the genesis of the total irrelevance of equilibrium economics to the end of the nineteenth century:

> Mill, Jevons, the Marshall of the late 'seventies and early 'eighties *believed* the utilitarian psychology and laid the foundations of the subject on this belief. The later Marshall and the later Edgeworth and many of the later generation have not fully believed; but we still trust the superstructure without exploring too fully the soundness of the original foundations. (CW X: 260)

In 1937 he summed up as follows:

> At any given time facts and expectations were assumed to be given a definite and calculable form; and risks, of which, though admitted, not much notice was taken, were supposed to be capable of an exact actuarial computation . . . It was, I think, an ingredient of the complacency of the nineteenth century that, in their reflections of human behaviour, they accepted an extraordinary contraption of the Benthamite School, by which all possible consequences of alternative courses of action were supposed to have attached to them, first a number expressing their comparative advantage, and secondly another number expressing the probability of their following from the course of action in question; so that in multiplying together the numbers attached to all the possible consequences of a given action and adding the results, we could discover what to do. In this way a mythical system of probable knowledge was employed to reduce the future to the same calculable status as the present. *No one has ever acted on this theory*. But even today I believe our thought is sometimes influenced by some such pseudo-rationalist notions. (CW XIV: 112, 124; emphasis added)

Nevertheless

> as living human beings, we are forced to act. Peace and comfort of mind require that we should hide from ourselves how little we foresee. Yet we must be guided by some hypothesis. We tend therefore to substitute for the knowledge which is unattainable certain conventions, the chief of which is to assume, contrary to all likelihood, that the future will resemble the past . . . We fall back, therefore, and necessarily do so, on motives of another kind, which are not rational in the sense of being concerned with the evaluation of consequences, but are decided by habit, instinct, preference, desire, will, etc. (CW XIV: 124; CW XXIX: 294)

For Keynes uncertainty is an absence of probabilistic knowledge. He argued that, instead of acting like an automaton employing the decision rules of probabilistic risk to calculate the costs and benefits of a course of action, the decision maker possesses neither the imagination nor the knowledge to act like economic man. The crux of the argument revolves around the premise of the perfectly informed optimizer. The expected utility-maximization approach allocates a probability to a prediction on the basis of past or present information and on a hypothesis about its future trajectory. But the existence of uncertainty robs the hypothesis upon which the probability is founded of any rational justification. If rational action needs probable knowledge and probable knowledge does not exist, then nor does rational action itself.

In such circumstances, 'our decisions to do something positive, the full consequences of which will be drawn out over many days to come, can only be taken as a result of animal spirits – of a spontaneous urge to action rather than inaction, and not as the outcome of a weighted average of quantitative benefits multiplied by quantitative benefits' (CW VII: 161; see Dow and Dow, 1985). In other words, uncertainty in the mind of the decision maker (and, it should be added, in the economic environment) means that 'there is no scientific basis on which to form any calculable probability whatever' (CW XIV: 114). As Douglas Vickers (1989: 170–71) concludes:

> the preponderance of economic decisions are unique decisions. They take place at unique points in the unidirectional flow of historic time, and they are made by decision-makers who possess unique information, hopes, attitudes, and an entire range of epistemological baggage. But if, for these reasons, economic outcomes are also to be regarded as unique events, unanchored to stable density functions and defining non-distributional, rather than distributional, variables, no meaning can possibly attach to the averaging of such variables or the manipulation of them to define, for example, their variance or dispersion characteristics. For what meaning can possibly attach to the variance of unique observations of unique variables at unique points in time?

It is not primarily a question of 'bounded' rationality but relates to the problem of decision making in situations of genuine uncertainty where the decision maker is ill-informed (or more likely ignorant) about the effects of current actions. Nor does it concern routine modes of behaviour, such as following habitual consumption patterns. It is the crucial decision, like investment expenditure, to which unpredictable consequences are attached (Runde, 1990).

In terms of application, George Shackle (1989: 55–6) has described Keynes's treatment of uncertainty as akin to a split personality which is manifested clearly in the dualistic structure of the *General Theory*:

> . . . one personality is oblivious of time-to-come and is concerned essentially only with comparisons of economic measurables that can be observed at one and the same moment. The other personality bursts out suddenly in Chapter 12 where the meaning of time-to-come, with its content of takings-place [*sic*] not

> yet in being, and not inferable from the present, appears as the *General Theory*'s real and vital theme.

Keynes thus employed two approaches in putting across his argument in the *General Theory*. The first accepted the homogeneity postulate, and here Keynes presented the principle of effective demand as a 'static' pedagogical device to demonstrate logically that unemployment in a monetary production economy was something more than a short-run disequilibrium phenomenon (Kregel, 1976). He derived the functional relationships needed to operationalize the theory of effective demand, independent of changes in expectations. As he put it: 'the main point is to distinguish the forces determining the position of equilibrium from the technique of trial and error by means of which the entrepreneur discovers where the position is' (CW XIV: 182). In this exercise, the conventions for coping with uncertainty were operative throughout, but, in the long period, the economy could still settle at an under-full employment equilibrium.

But also Keynes knew that, over calendar time, 'the actual course of events is more complicated . . . for the state of expectations is liable to continual change' (CW VII: 50). In reality all relationships are bound to change over time as a result of the non-achievement of plans and unintended consequences of actions. This necessitated 'a theory of a system in which changing views about the future are capable of influencing the present situation' (CW XIV: 293). Such a 'dynamic' perspective, wherein expectational propensities change through time, encompassed the fragility of conventions by covering the non-realization of short-period expectations and autonomous changes in expectations. The path of shifting equilibrium tracks the decision maker through historical time, in contrast to the static equilibrium framework where the functions are only definable for a given state of expectations. Of necessity, a degree of indeterminacy has to be admitted because there can be no guaranteed uniform relationship between a set of events and the subsequent state of expectations. As Paul Davidson and Jan Kregel (1981: 141, 143) conclude:

> In Keynes's paradigm, the indefinite character of actual expectations [is] the free autonomous variable which governs everything else rather than being governed by everything else . . . Keynes envisioned his real world model as one of shifting equilibrium, a world of continuous movement without the necessity for the plans of the economic agents to ever be reconciled.

In presenting a realist explanation of the decision-making process in the monetary production economy, Keynes argued that human behaviour was not explicable in terms of optimality derived from a global perspective. In moving beyond 'a world in which risk exists without uncertainty'

(CW XXIX: 258), he broke from the dismal creed and exploded the myth of economic man.

IV The relevance of Keynes's vision

In the build-up to the publication of the *General Theory*, Keynes came across the following quotation from Hume: ' 'Tis not reason which is the guide of life, but custom. That alone determines the mind, in all instances, to suppose the future conformable to the past. However easy this step may seem, reason would never, to whole eternity, be able to make it' (quoted in Carabelli, 1988: 300, n. 8). This raises the question of Hume's influence on Keynes. The latter's initial venture into philosophy was strongly motivated by a desire to solve the conundrum set by the 'Master'. Hume's critique of the inductive method was that causation cannot be founded on *any a priori* premise. Keynes accepted Hume's case against induction that statements about the future cannot be logically inferred from statements about the past without the indefensible 'medium' of perfect foresight. He understood also Hume's dictum that logic says nothing because its process and results are equivalent. *A Treatise on Probability* aimed to provide a rational basis for inductive inference, where a conclusion is made only probable, not certain, by its premises.

Keynes's study of probability as the concern 'with the general theory of arguments from premises which are reasonable but not certain' (CW VIII: 106) exposed the scientism of the equilibrium method where the problem of knowledge was assumed away. Outside the realm of atomic uniformity:

> there might well be quite different laws for wholes of different degrees of complexity, and laws of connection between complexes which could not be stated in terms of laws connecting individual parts. In this case natural law would be organic and not, as it is generally supposed, atomic. If every configuration of the universe were subject to a separate and independent law, or if very small differences between bodies . . . led to their obeying quite different laws, prediction would be impossible and the inductive method useless. (CW VIII: 260, 277.)

Keynes's investigation of the potential of rationally grounded induction involved 'ordinary powers of reasoning and limited knowledge and not the logic of choice prescribed by general equilibrium theory in which ultra-powerful intellects make decisions in the relevant informationally complete environments' (O'Donnell, 1989: 162). He viewed 'rationality as practical and contingent' (Carabelli, 1988: 236) rather than being narrowly defined in terms of mere calculation. He argued that, because 'consequences enter into the rational calculation' (CW XXIX: 162), complete exactitude is impossible: 'as soon as one is dealing with the influence of expectations and of transitory experience, one is, in the nature of things, outside the realm of the formally exact' (CW XIV: 2). The process of reasoning was not after all completely analysable.

Whilst not becoming a total sceptic, Keynes perceived the limitations of atomic uniformity which implicitly permeated the equilibrium mind-set. He came to the conclusion that rationality is best defined as practical wisdom or reasonableness, as opposed to the reason of economic rationality. For Keynes, then, a rational belief is one for which there is some justification, not one reliant totally on a dedicated calculating machine. If the individual is not characterized as ultimately rational, the reasonableness of a set of beliefs is related to their adequacy in coping with the problem of everyday existence. Above all the reasonableness of a belief does not imply an economically rational reason for holding it. In confronting 'our actual psychology and ways of behaving and deciding' (CW XII: 433) Keynes, in effect, stepped outside the equilibrium framework, where 'there is always full employment, and where doubt and fluctuations of confidence are ruled out' (CW XIV: 107). He then proceeded 'to reverse completely the positivist application of the Newtonian method of physical science to economics' (Carabelli, 1988: 213).

Returning to the current debate, much confusion has been generated by the wholesale tendency to conflate rationality and reason. For example, Rod O'Donnell (1989) distinguishes between what he calls 'strong' and 'weak' rationality. 'Strong' rationality is defined by O'Donnell in orthodox terms as being associated 'with complete information and mathematical computability' (O'Donnell, 1989: 253). 'Weak' rationality 'operates in some region lying between pure logic and mere psychology' (ibid.: 147) when agents 'fall back on other behavioural patterns *without losing their rational dispositions*' (249; emphasis added). In this way 'behaviour is not without its core of rationality when viewed from within the informational environment in which agents are irretrievably embedded' (ibid.: 254). O'Donnell's dichotomy thus permits the retention of traditional economic rationality on the grounds that 'when reason has arrived at its limits, arbitrary or conventional behaviour will be *consistent* with, and not opposed to reason, (ibid.: 59; emphasis in original). This interpretation is based on the starting-point of the economically rational agent, who, in the face of irreducible uncertainty, 'is obliged to resort . . . to devices taking on some of the characteristics of purely psychological responses' (ibid.: 261). This is but a revamp of the discredited principle of indifference, which claims that probabilistic knowledge can be produced by reason in the absence of reasons.

To extend the argument, and moving beyond the tunnel vision of rationalism, I will now sketch an alternative basis for human understanding. If knowledge is not grounded in principles and theories but upon everyday experience, then understanding is 'a skill akin to knowing how to find one's way about in the world, rather than knowing a lot of facts and rules for relating them' (Dreyfus and Dreyfus, 1988: 4). According to this account, human beings behave intelligently without having recourse to a theory of the world, and 'when we try to find the ultimate context-free, purpose-free elements we are in effect trying to free aspects of our experience of just that pragmatic organisation which makes it possible to use them intelligently in coping with everyday experience' (ibid.: 26–7). Far from being based on rational first principles, an individual's theories and actions are *rationalized* against the rather imprecise background of cultural tradition. Knowledge is gained through habits of mind established through effective coping. In these circumstances, decisions are made without conscious analytical decomposition and recombination. Whereas rationalists rely upon rule-guided 'knowing that', common sense thinkers are more interested in the evolution of experience-based 'know-how'.

Dreyfus and Dreyfus (1988: 28–9) equate know-how with intuition:

> [It is] neither wild guessing nor supernatural inspiration, but the sort of ability we all use all the time as we go about our everyday tasks. [It is] the understanding that effortlessly occurs upon seeing similarity with previous experiences [or] the ability to use patterns without decomposing them into component features. Intuition is the product of deep situational involvement and recognition of similarity.

The process of holistic similarity recognition implies that the human brain/mind is more than an inference machine. The labyrinth of the nervous system can integrate more variables than the scanning process of conscious attention. So there is more to intelligence than calculative rationality and 'the mind works from an intuition that experience suggests is rational' (Fitzgibbons, 1988: 14). These insights resonate with Keynes's description of 'practical intuition' (CW VII: 249) and his perception of 'the hidden element of direct judgement' (CW VIII: 69). Such practical reason expresses the mind/brain's capability of 'direct knowledge about empirical entities which goes beyond a mere expression of our understanding and sensation of them' (CW VIII: 292).

The rationalist response to such claims is to posit the existence of unconscious computational mechanisms on the grounds that any alternative is essentially anti-scientific. Of course, given 'the quasi-religious philosophical prejudice against holism' (Dreyfus and Dreyfus, 1988: 23), this whole issue is more a matter of faith than reason. To be sure, the rhetoric of economic orthodoxy, with its categories, concepts and distinctions, is a perceptual vantage point structured by the language it uses as its communicative instrument. The atomistic ontology of equilibrium economics is an intrinsic feature of that language. At the end of the day, the veracity or otherwise of the axiom of the rational and maximizing agent cannot be resolved by weight of evidence alone (Hodgson, 1988: Chapter 4). What appears at first sight to be an arcane exercise in the history of economic thought in fact 'mentions the unmentionable' of equilibrium habits of mind. Indeed the mere broaching of the fallibility of atomism as the basis for economic science shows the potential for an act of negation which, for understandable reasons, its practitioners refuse to contemplate.

V Concluding remarks

The underlying vision of equilibrium economics is atomistic, certain and determinate. As a Cambridge rationalist, Keynes was drawn to the polar opposite view of the world as holistic, uncertain and indeterminate. In synthesis, Keynes viewed the future as a combination of certain and uncertain elements which remains at odds with the dominant predictionist creed (Simon, 1990). The rationalist response to uncertainty has been simply to deny its existence: 'the whole of chapter 12 of the *General Theory* gives arguments and insights which we have not refuted but ignored' (Hahn, 1990: 234; see also Patinkin, 1991). The logic of economic rationality dismisses Keynes's treatment of uncertainty in a changing monetary economy as being beyond the analytical pale. The fact of uncertainty poses unanswerable questions for orthodoxy because it stands at the opposite pole to economic man's absolutely certain outlook on the world. Yet, if 'the hypothesis of a calculable future leads to a wrong interpretation of the principles of behaviour' (XIV: 122), then Keynes proposed a qualitatively different kind of reasoning from that of certainty equivalence. His critique of the pseudo-rational premises of equilibrium economics was directed at the unquestionable 'hard core' of the discipline. In facing up to fundamental uncertainty, he invalidated economic man as being based on the flimsiest of human logic.

Keynes's broad consideration of the *cognitive* aspects of human behaviour was underlined in 1937 and 1938 as being central to the generality of the *General Theory*. Although the economic majority may 'regard the heresies of Keynes as small (albeit important) heresies' (Simon, 1984: 36), a post-modernist reading suggests that Keynes's heresy was more global than local (Amariglio, 1990). In brief, Keynes's timeless contribution was his rejection of the timelessness of the equilibrium mode of thought. The Second World War brought the academic debate to an abrupt halt just as J. R. Hicks's *Value and Capital* (1939) appeared on the scene. As Arthur Brown (1988: 37) reflects, Hicks could 'hardly be accused of underemphasising expectations, except in the rather important matter of shrugging off their uncertainty'. To be fair, John Hicks (1977: vii) did subsequently suspend his disbelief in fundamental uncertainty and, in the true spirit of Keynes, stated: 'One must assume that people in one's model do not know what is going to happen, and know that they do not know what is going to happen. As in history!'

Keynes's struggle for emancipation from the 'old ideas' remains a positive exemplar for those who perceive that the New Classical reaction is but a more sophisticated and elaborate rendering of the self-same dogma which Keynes tried to lay to rest. His contemporary relevance lies in his escape from the tenacious grip of free-market ideology. In the 1990s, as it dawns that the supply-side transformation of the last decade was a miracle achieved largely through marketing hype, the practical task is still dominated by the need to reconstitute the relationship between 'the Agenda and non-Agenda of the state' (CW IX: 288).

> As for our thoughts, our rationalisms, our logics and our deductions and so on, it can be said with absolute certainty that cats and dogs and monkeys cannot make a rocket fly to the moon or weave artificial dress materials out of the by-products of petroleum. But as we sit in the ruins of this variety of intelligence it is hard to give it much value: I suppose we are under-valuing it now as we over-valued it then. It will have to find a place: I believe a pretty low place at that. (Lessing, 1976: 74)

> The power of reason must be sought not in the rules that reason dictates to our imagination but in the ability to free ourselves from any kind of rules to which we have been conditioned through experience and tradition. (Reichenbach, 1951: 141)

Emancipate yourselves from mental slavery
None but ourselves can free our minds
(Bob Marley)[3]

Notes

1. Earlier versions of this chapter were presented at Vanderbilt University, Nashville, February/June/July 1988 and at a School of Business and Economic Studies Workshop, Leeds, March 1990. Thanks to the participants at these events, especially Clive Bell, J. S. Butler, Bill Damon, Robert W. Rich and William O. Thweatt. Many thanks to Frank, Jennie, Maria, Rob, staff and friends at the Commodore Hotel, Music City USA for helping in the production of *We're just a bunch of economists* (WRVU 91 ROCK ©1988). Thanks also to Anna Carabelli, Bill Gerrard, Keith Glaister, Tony Lawson, Roy J. Rotheim and Jochen Runde for good discussion; and to Kevin Keasey, John King, Peter Nolan, Jerry Ravetz and Malcolm Sawyer for constructive comments on earlier drafts. Finally, thanks to Teresa & Co. for invaluable assistance in the preparation of the manuscript. With good memories, this essay is dedicated to P. W. S. Andrews, Kath Burt and Dale Hannah.
2. Important recent articles include Davidson (1982/3), Shackle (1983), Loasby (1984), Brown-Collier (1985), Lawson (1985, 1987, 1988), Brown-Collier and Bausor (1988), Rotheim (1988), de Carvalho (1988), Winslow (1989) and Dow (1990). Books include Chick (1983), Coddington (1983), Wiles and Routh (1984) (eds), Lawson and Pesaran (1985) (eds), Carabelli (1988), Fitzgibbons (1988) and O'Donnell (1989).
3. 'Redemption Song', 11: *LEGEND*. (1980/1991) © Bob Marley Music Ltd.

References

Amariglio, J. (1990), 'Economics as a Postmodern Discourse', in W. Samuels (ed.), *Economics as Discourse*, New York: Kluwer Academic Publishers.

Bianchi, M. (1990), 'The Unsatisfactoriness of Satisficing: from Bounded Rationality to Innovative Rationality', *Review of Political Economy*, **2**, 149–67.

Bramhall, D. F. (1986), 'Economics and Cartesian Science', in S. W. Helburn and D. F. Bramhall (eds), *Marx, Schumpeter, Keynes: A Centenary Celebration of Dissent*, New York: M. E. Sharpe.

Brown, A. J. (1988), 'A Worm's Eye View of the Keynesian Revolution', in J. V. Hillard (ed.), *J. M. Keynes in Retrospect*, Upleadon/Brookfield: Edward Elgar.

Brown-Collier, E. K. (1985), 'Keynes' View of an Organic Universe: The Implications', *Review of Social Economy*, **43**, 14–23.

Brown-Collier, E. K. and R. Bausor (1988), 'The Epistemological Foundations of the *General Theory*', *Scottish Journal of Political Economy*, **35**, 227–41.

Carabelli, A. M. (1988), *On Keynes's Method*, London: Macmillan.

de Carvalho, J. F. C. (1988/9), 'Keynes on Probability, Uncertainty and Decision-making', *Journal of Post Keynesian Economics*, **11**, 66–81.

Chick, V. (1983), *Macroeconomics After Keynes*, Oxford: Philip Allan.

Coddington, A. (1983), *Keynesian Economics: The Search for First Principles*, London: Allen & Unwin.

Davidson, P. (1982/3); 'Rational Expectations: A Fallacious Foundation for Studying Crucial Decision-making Processes', *Journal of Post Keynesian Economics*, **5**, 182–98.

Davidson, P. and J. A. Kregel (1981), 'Keynes's Paradigm: A Theoretical Framework for Monetary Analysis', in E. S. Nell (ed.), *Growth, Profits and Property*, New York: Cambridge University Press.

Davis, J. B. (1989), 'Keynes and Organicism', *Journal of Post Keynesian Economics*, **12**, 308–15.

Dillard, D. (1946), 'The Pragmatic Basis of Keynes's Political Economy', *Journal of Economic History*, **6**, 121–52.

Dow, S. C. (1985), *Macroeconomic Thought: A Methodological Approach*, Oxford: Blackwell.

Dow, S. C. (1990), 'Beyond Dualism', *Cambridge Journal of Economics*, **14**, 143–57.

Dow, S. C. and A. Dow (1985), 'Animal Spirits and Rationality', in T. Lawson and H. Pesaran (eds), *Keynes's Economics: Methodological Issues*, London: Croom Helm.

Dreyfus, H. L. and S. E. Dreyfus (1986), *Mind over Machine*, New York: Macmillan.

Dreyfus, H. L. and S. E. Dreyfus (1988), 'Making a Mind Versus Modeling the Brain:

Artificial Intelligence Back at the Branchpoint', in S. R. Graubard (ed.), *The Artificial Intelligence Debate*, Cambridge: MIT Press.
Fitzgibbons, A. (1988), *Keynes's Vision: A New Political Economy*, Oxford: Clarendon Press.
Georgescu-Roegen, N. (1966), *Analytical Economics: Issues and Problems*, Cambridge: Harvard University Press.
Hahn, F. H. (1990), 'Expectations' in J. D. Hey and D. Winch (eds), *A Century of Economics*, Oxford: Basil Blackwell.
Heisenberg, W. (1958), *Physics and Philosophy*, New York: Harper.
Hicks, J. R. (1939), *Value and Capital*, Oxford: Clarendon Press.
Hicks, J. R. (1977), *Economic Perspectives*, Oxford: Clarendon Press.
Hodgson, G. M. (1985), 'Persuasion, Expectations and the Limits to Keynes', in T. Lawson and H. Pesaran (eds), *Keynes's Economics. Methodological Issues*, London: Croom Helm.
Hodgson, G. M. (1988), *Economics and Institutions*, Cambridge: Polity.
Hutchinson, T. W. (1978), *On Revolutions and Progress in Economic Knowledge*, Cambridge: Cambridge University Press.
Johnson, H. G. (1968), *The Economic Approach to Social Questions*, London: Weidenfeld & Nicolson.
King, M. D. (1971), 'Reason, Tradition and the Progressiveness of Science', *History and Theory*, **10**, 3–32.
Kregel, J. A. (1976), 'Economic Methodology in the Face of Uncertainty: The Modelling Methods of Keynes and the Post-Keynesians', *Economic Journal*, **86**, 209–25.
Lawson, T. (1985), 'Uncertainty and Economic Analysis', *Economic Journal*, **95**, 909–27.
Lawson, T. (1987), 'The Relative/Absolute Nature of Knowledge and Economic Analysis', *Economic Journal*, **97**, 951–70.
Lawson, T. (1988), 'Probability and Uncertainty in Economic Analysis', *Journal of Post Keynesian Economics*, **11**, 38–65.
Lawson, T. (1990), 'Keynes and the Analysis of Rational Behaviour', University of Cambridge (mimeo).
Lawson, T. and H. Pesaran (1985) (eds), *Keynes's Economics: Methodological Issues*, London: Croom Helm.
Leontief, W. (1971), 'Theoretical Assumptions and Non-observed Facts', *American Economic Review*, **61**, 1–7.
Lessing, D. (1976), *Memoirs of a Survivor*, London: Paladin.
Littleboy, B. (1983), 'Keynes and Economic Man', La Trobe University (mimeo).
Loasby, B. J. (1984), 'On Scientific Method', *Journal of Post Keynesian Economics*, **6**, 394–410.
Loasby, B. J. (1989), *The Mind and Method of the Economist*, Aldershot: Edward Elgar.
Lowe, A. (1965), *On Economic Knowledge*, New York: Harper & Row.
Lucas, R. E. and T. J. S. Sargent (1981), *Rational Expectations and Econometric Practice*, London: Allen & Unwin.
Mirowski, P. (1989), *More Heat Than Light: Economics as Social Physics, Physics as Nature's Economics*, Cambridge: Cambridge University Press.
O'Donnell, R. M. (1989), *Keynes: Philosophy, Economics and Politics*, London: Macmillan.
Ogilvy, J. (1977), *Many Dimensional Man*, New York: Oxford University Press.
Patinkin, D. (1991), 'On Different Interpretations of the *General Theory*', *Journal of Monetary Economics*, **26**, 205–43.
Reichenbach, H. (1951), *The Rise of Scientific Philosophy*, Berkeley: University of California Press.
Rorty, R. (1980), *Philosophy and the Mirror of Nature*, Oxford: Basil Blackwell.
Rotheim, R. J. (1988), 'Keynes and the Language of Probability and Uncertainty', *Journal of Post Keynesian Economics*, **11**, 83–99.
Rotheim, R. J. (1989/90), 'Organicism and the Role of the Individual in Keynes' Thought', *Journal of Post Keynesian Economics*, **12**, 316–26.
Routh, G. (1989), *The Origin of Economic Ideas*, London: Macmillan.
Runde, J. (1990), 'Keynesian Uncertainty and the Instability of Beliefs', University of Cambridge (mimeo).

Shackle, G. L. S. (1966), *The Nature of Economic Thought*, Cambridge: Cambridge University Press.
Shackle, G. L. S. (1974), *Keynesian Kaleidics*, Edinburgh: Edinburgh University Press.
Shackle, G. L. S. (1983), 'The Romantic Mountain and the Classical Lake', *Journal of Post Keynesian Economics*, **6**, 241–51.
Shackle, G. L. S. (1988), *Business, Time and Thought*, Basingstoke: Macmillan.
Shackle, G. L. S. (1989), 'What did the *General Theory* do?', in J. Pheby (ed.), *New Directions in Post-Keynesian Economics*, Aldershot/Brookfield: Edward Elgar.
Simon, H. A. (1984), 'On the Behavioural and Rational Foundations of Economic Analysis', *Journal of Economic Behaviour and Organisation*, **5**, 35–55.
Simon, H. A. (1990), 'Prediction and Prescription in Systems Modeling', *Operations Research*, **38**, 7–14.
Snow, C. P. (1964), *The Two Cultures and A Second Look*, Cambridge: Cambridge University Press.
Vickers, D. (1989), 'The Money Capital Constraint and Decisions in the Firm', in J. A. Kregel (ed.), *Inflation and Income Distribution in Capitalist Crisis*, London: Macmillan.
Wiles, P. (1983), 'Ideology, Methodology, and Neoclassical Economics', in A. S. Eichner (ed.), *Why Economics is Not Yet a Science*, New York: Macmillan.
Wiles, P. and G. Routh (1984) (eds), *Economics in Disarray*, London: Macmillan.
Winslow, E. G. (1989), 'Organic Interdependence, Uncertainty and Economic Analysis', *Economic Journal*, **99**, 1173–82.

4 From *A Treatise on Probability* to the *General Theory*: continuity or change in Keynes's thought?

Bill Gerrard

I Introduction

An important strand in post-Keynesian thought is that of Keynesian fundamentalism, a term coined by Coddington to describe 'those who have seen Keynes's work as a frontal assault on the whole reductionist programme' (1976: 1259). The principal exponents of this approach have been George Shackle and Joan Robinson. They see the core of Keynes's critique of orthodox economics as contained in Chapter 12 of the *General Theory* as well as the subsequent *Quarterly Journal of Economics* 1937 article. Fundamentalists interpret these writings as a thoroughgoing attack on neoclassical economics for its failure to deal adequately with the nature of human decision making in the face of uncertainty. The fundamentalists stress the importance of expectations and ignorance and the need to replace static equilibrium analysis with a truly dynamic analysis of movement through historical time.

The orthodox reaction to Keynesian fundamentalism has been almost entirely dismissive. Coddington (1976; 1982) is typical. He argues that the fundamentalists give emphasis to an aspect of Keynes's thought which was merely a ground-clearing exercise (1976: 1271), Keynes's forays into the area of uncertainty being nothing more than 'an opportunistic but mild flirtation with subjectivism' (1982: 487). As well as criticizing the interpretative merits of Keynesian fundamentalism, Coddington rejects the seemingly nihilistic consequences for economic theory and its applicability if one adopts the fundamentalist position. For Coddington fundamentalism is a step onto the slippery slope of subjectivism which drives a wedge between behaviour and circumstance and hence, taken to its logical conclusion, implies that economic theorizing is impossible.

While there is some validity in the nihilistic charge against Keynesian fundamentalism, Coddington's dismissal of Keynes's concern with uncertainty as a merely passing phase is clearly at odds with the evidence. Keynes's interest in probability and related issues spanned over thirty years from his undergraduate days onwards, culminating in 1921 in the publication of *A Treatise on Probability* (hereafter referred to as the

Treatise). It is this long-term aspect of Keynes's thought on probability that has given rise recently to the emergence of a 'new' Keynesian fundamentalism. The new fundamentalists such as O'Donnell (1989), Carabelli (1988), Lawson (1985) and Fitzgibbons (1988) view Keynes as a philosopher–economist. They seek to provide a rational reconstruction of Keynes's early philosophical thought and to show the links with his later economic thought. In so doing the new fundamentalists refute both the interpretative and nihilistic criticisms levelled at the 'old' Keynesian fundamentalism. In particular Keynes's thought is portrayed as a constructive attempt to analyse decision making under uncertainty. Keynes may have been a sceptic but his was a practical, not a nihilistic, scepticism always concerned with the task of constructive analysis.

The emergence of the new Keynesian fundamentalism has been characterized by a good deal of controversy, much of which has centred on what O'Donnell calls the continuity thesis. The key question in the new fundamentalist research programme has been whether or not there is a continuity between Keynes's early philosophical thought up to the *Treatise* and his subsequent writings, especially the *General Theory*. A number of contributors to the debate have argued that Keynes's philosophical thought changed radically after the *Treatise*. The aim of this chapter is to provide an account of the development of Keynes's philosophical thought. It is suggested that there is both continuity and change in Keynes's thought. In particular it is argued that Keynes's later thought encompassed his early thought as Keynes became more concerned with practical, rather than purely speculative, aspects of decision making.

The structure of the chapter is as follows. Section II outlines the origins of Keynes's theory of probability. Section III provides an account of the main elements of the *Treatise*. Section IV considers the evidence on whether or not Keynes changed his views after the *Treatise*. An encompassing interpretation of Keynes's thought is developed. Section V considers the alternative interpretations of Keynes's post-*Treatise* thought. Section VI offers some critical comments on the debate by way of conclusion.

II Keynes's early philosophical thought

The origins of the *Treatise* are to be found in Keynes's reaction to Moore's *Principia Ethica* which was published in October 1903 at the beginning of Keynes's second year at the University of Cambridge. Keynes produced two critiques of *Principia Ethica*. The first, entitled 'Ethics in Relation to Conduct', was read to the Apostles on 23 January 1904. The second, entitled 'Miscellanea Ethica', comprises a set of notes compiled between July and September 1905. Probability emerged as a central theme in

Keynes's critique of Moore. His interest in probability was further developed as a fellowship dissertation between September 1906 and December 1907. This dissertation was revised and resubmitted in 1908. It was worked up into *A Treatise on Probability* in the period 1910/11 but was not published as such until 1921.

Moore's *Principia Ethica* focused on two questions: what objects are good in themselves and what actions ought to be performed? In 'Miscellanea Ethica' Keynes termed the first of these as the area of speculative ethics and the second as that of practical ethics. With regard to the question of speculative ethics Moore argued that goodness is a property of objects. Goodness is indefinable and known by intuition. On the question of practical ethics Moore adopted a position of rule utilitarianism, recommending the following of well-established rules. Moore believed that well-established rules represented the accumulated knowledge of which courses of action would lead to the greatest total good in the majority of cases. It was an argument, as Bateman (1988) has pointed out, which can be seen as an early form of the expected utility model using a frequency notion of probability. Keynes's critique of Moore turned on this issue.

Moore was the principal intellectual influence on the Apostles but the *Principia Ethica* caused a degree of consternation, for two main reasons. Firstly, Moore's concern for action was in stark contrast to the Apostles' concern for contemplation, for being good rather than doing good. Second, Moore's advocacy of rule following went against the Apostles' rejection of established social conventions. As Keynes stated in his later autobiographical essay, 'My Early Beliefs', the Apostles accepted Moore's religion but not his morals. It was this conflict which moved Keynes to provide a detailed rebuttal of Moore's morals, that is, his practical ethics.

Keynes's paper, 'Ethics in Relation to Conduct', contained his critique of Moore's practical ethics. This paper was written in conjunction with his study of probability as part of the mathematics tripos. Keynes criticized Moore's implicit use of the frequency theory of probability. He proposed instead that probability be treated as a degree of belief. Judgements of probable outcome are made on the basis of available evidence. Since more evidence is available relatively for a specific case rather the general case, Keynes argued against general rule following, proposing instead that each situation be evaluated on a case-by-case basis. This constituted a position of act utilitarianism. It invoked an early form of the notion of the weight of evidence. This went against Moore who repudiated any departure from well-established rules on the grounds that one can only know that a rule is best in the majority of cases; one cannot know when a specific case warrants a departure from the rules. Keynes, on the other hand, did not believe that there is sufficient evidence to justify general rule following.

Moore conceded the argument to Keynes. In his *Ethics*, published in 1912, Moore adopted act utilitarianism and treated probability as a degree of belief.

A key feature of Keynes's early thought is the tension between speculative and practical concerns. The early Keynes emphasizes the speculative but his critique of Moore pointed towards an alternative practical ethics. This tension generated an internal dynamic of change and development within Keynes's thought. As a consequence it seems inappropriate to describe Keynes's early thought as either a single, fully coherent, set of beliefs or as unintentionally consistent. Much sterile debate is generated by trying to fit Keynes into some neat philosophical pigeon-hole. Keynes's early thought was neither a unitary nor a fixed set of beliefs. His early thought was just that, early.

III *A Treatise on Probability*

The central theme of the *Treatise* is induction. Keynes sought to formalize the inductive method and to provide a justification for its use. In so doing, he tried to generalize (or encompass) the orthodox approaches to both probability and logic. With regard to the former, Keynes attempted to move the theory of probability beyond the frequency approach and the concern for numerical probabilities. He also sought to generalize logic by extending it beyond its traditional focus on conclusive argument and taking logic into the realm of non-conclusive argument. To these ends, Keynes proposed a logical theory of probability.

There are four dimensions to Keynes's logical theory of probability. Each of these dimensions has a primary emphasis but allowance is made for alternative approaches having some relevance. First, Keynes viewed probability as epistemic in nature rather than aleatory. Probability is a degree of belief, a feature of knowledge, not a feature of the world itself. Keynes rejected the frequency theory, an aleatory approach, as the appropriate basis for a general theory of probability. Relative frequency data are only one special type of evidence from which degrees of beliefs may be inferred.

A second dimension of Keynes's probability theory is that it is objectivist. Probabilities are logical relations beyond human caprice. A validly inferred probability has the same status as the proposition that $1 + 1 = 2$. But Keynes did allow for subjectivist influences in his concern for unknown probabilities as the result of individuals having inadequate evidence or lacking sufficient powers of reasoning.

Thirdly, Keynes proposed that probabilities are largely non-numerical and may be non-comparable. He considered numerical probabilities as a special case, given too much significance because of the opportunities afforded for mathematical manipulation. Probability is a qualitative notion that is only partially amenable to quantification.

The final dimension is the rationalist nature of Keynes's approach to probability. Probabilities are known by intuition and logical deduction. Keynes acknowledged the role of observation in providing evidence but such empiricist aspects of the problem are dominated in the *Treatise* by Keynes's concern with the logical issue of inferring degrees of belief, given the available evidence. The *Treatise* abstracts from the empiricist concern with the process whereby the evidence is acquired.

The starting-point of Keynes's theory is the probability argument

$$p = a/h$$

where p represents the probability of some proposition, a, on the basis of the available evidence, h. This probability is interpreted by Keynes as the degree of belief it is rational to hold in a proposition, given the available evidence. Thus Keynes can be said to have a concept of rational probabilities in which the rationality of any probability is determined *ex ante* by the logical validity of the deductions drawn from the available evidence. The rationality of a probability judgement is not determined *ex post* in the light of actual outcomes.

An important element in Keynes's theory is the notion of the weight of an argument which refers to the amount of available evidence used in a probability argument. The weight of an argument, V, is increased if there is additional evidence, h_1, made available. This is stated algebraically by Keynes as

$$V(a/hh_1) > V(a/h)$$

provided that the additional evidence, h_1, is not irrelevant.

Keynes's concern with the logical aspects of probability to the exclusion of more empirically orientated matters is clearly apparent in his assumptions about the premises of the probability argument. He assumes that the premises are either direct knowledge or indirect knowledge which has been logically deduced from direct knowledge. All direct knowledge is assumed to be true. By implication, all the premises of the probability argument are assumed to be true. Thus Keynes abstracted his analysis from any problem of uncertainty arising from the doubtful status of the premises themselves.

Keynes identified two types of inductive argument: universal arguments concerning relations that hold in all cases, and statistical arguments concerning relations that hold only in a proportion of cases. An inductive argument is seen to consist of two elements: analogy and pure induction. Analogy is the likeness of observed instances, whereas pure induction is the number of instances. Analogy is positive (if instances are similar) or negative (if instances are dissimilar). It is only an increase in negative analogy that may lead to an increase in probability. The accumulation of identical observations (same positive analogy with no new negative analogy) leaves the probability of the proposition unchanged in the event of new observations. This process of revision requires that an initial non-zero probability be known *a priori*.

According to Keynes the validity of the inductive process depends on the assumption of limited independent variety. This is the assumption that only a finite number of characteristics are relevant to the proposition under investigation. This requires that the natural law be atomic; that is, the system consists of legal atoms exercising separate, independent and invariable effects. If the system is not atomic there cannot be limited independent variety. Thus Keynes argued that the inductive method is not valid if the system is organic in such a way that the laws of connection between complexes cannot be stated in terms of laws connecting individual parts. He believed the assumption of limited independent variety is plausible on the basis of experience. Thus the inductive method is justified but not conclusively so since the justification is based not on purely logical grounds but on the facts of experience.

The *Treatise* exemplifies Keynes's encompassing approach to established systems of thought. His approach involves three stages: (a) exposing to scrutiny the tacit assumptions underlying an established theory; (b) showing the restrictive nature of these assumptions; and (c) encompassing the established theory within a more general theory based on a less restrictive set of assumptions. In the *Treatise*, he attempted to encompass both the frequency theory of probability and conclusive logic. Keynes also tried to encompass various oppositional philosophical positions, at least implicitly. He retained a multiplicity of beliefs which he sought to reconcile by delineating the limits to their relevance. Keynes neither wholly accepted nor wholly rejected a number of philosophical positions. He transcended the 'either/or' dualism that is so characteristic of traditional philosophical debates. It is therefore inappropriate to ask if Keynes was a rationalist or an empiricist, a subjectivist or an objectivist and so on.

The *Treatise* should not be seen as a unitary set of beliefs. Furthermore it does not provide an analysis of human decision making under uncertainty. The *Treatise* considers the logical aspects of probability in the context of premises assumed to consist entirely of true knowledge. This assumption severely restricts the relevance of the *Treatise*. In particular Keynes is not providing an account of rational behaviour in circumstances of vague knowledge when the premises themselves are uncertain. Thus Keynes's analysis of behaviour under uncertainty in the *General Theory* cannot be understood solely by reference to the *Treatise*. The two analyses relate to two different domains of application. It follows, therefore, that the link between the *Treatise* and the *General Theory* necessarily involved development and change in Keynes's thought.

There has been little substantial disagreement between the new Keynesian fundamentalists over the main elements of the *Treatise*. Differences have emerged primarily with regard to the issue of whether or not Keynes altered his views on probability after the publication of the *Treatise*. In other words the debate has focused not on the meaning of the *Treatise* but rather on Keynes's own subsequent evaluation of its significance.

IV Beyond the *Treatise:* continuity or change?

The 'continuity-or-change?' debate has focused on two principal issues. First, did Keynes retain his logical theory of probability after the *Treatise*? Secondly, did Keynes continue to believe that the inductive method is only applicable if the system under investigation can be assumed to be atomic in nature? The textual evidence is very limited. After the publication of the *Treatise* in 1921 the vast proportion of Keynes's writings were in economics. There was very little in the way of philosophical writings. Hence much of the evidence concerning Keynes's later philosophical thought is indirect, inferred from his economic writings. The direct textual evidence on Keynes's later philosophical thought is obtained from four sources: the biographical essay on Edgeworth published in 1926, a letter to Urban, the German translator of the *Treatise*, also written in 1926, a review of Ramsey's *Foundation of Mathematics* in 1931 and finally Keynes's autobiographical essay, 'My Early Beliefs', which was read to the Bloomsbury Group in 1938.

In the biographical essay on Edgeworth, Keynes considered the validity of the atomic hypothesis for the study of human behaviour.

> The atomic hypothesis which has worked so splendidly in physics breaks down in psychics. We are faced at every turn with the problems of organic unity, of discreteness, of discontinuity – the whole is not equal to the sum of the parts, comparisons of quantity fail us, small changes produce large effects, the assumptions of a uniform and homogeneous continuum are not satisfied. Thus the results of Mathematical Psychics turn out to be derivative, not fundamental, indexes, not measurements, first approximations at the best; and fallible indexes, dubious approximations at that, with much doubt added as to what, if anything, they are indexes or approximations of. (CW X: 262)

Thus Keynes considered the atomic hypothesis as appropriate to the natural world but not for the social world. Yet the assumption of an organicist social ontology would rule out the use of the inductive method in the social sciences if Keynes retained the position he adopted in the *Treatise*.

The letter to Urban, who was translating the *Treatise* into German, indicates Keynes' dissatisfaction with the *Treatise* and his belief that the logical theory of probability will be superseded by a revised form of frequency theory.

> It have not thought about the subject very deeply in recent times. But as time goes on I myself feel that there is a great deal in the book which is unsatisfactory, and, indeed I felt this even when I was writing it. It was published as it stood because it seemed to me that it would help on the subject that I should do so more effectively that if I was to try to make further refinements and revisions which might quite likely prove beyond my capacity. I believe that the ultimate theory of the subject may differ very considerably from mine. But I still think that the problems as I have posed them may be the right starting point for further research.
>
> Amongst those students in England for whose opinion I feel most respect I find a marked reluctance against finally abandoning some variant of the frequency theory. They admit my criticisms hold good on existing versions, and they are not yet ready to prepare a version which can resist them. But they maintain all the same that they have a strong instinct that some kind of frequency theory will be found in the end to be more fundamental to the whole conception of Probability than I have yet allowed. I shall not be surprised if they prove right. I suspect, however, that the first step forward will have to come through progress being made with the partly psychological subject of vague knowledge, and that further developments in a strictly logical field must wait for a clear distinction between logical probability proper and the theory of what I have called vague knowledge. (Keynes to F.M. Urban, 15 May 1926, as cited in Winslow, 1989a: 5)

This letter points to one perceived inadequacy of the *Treatise*, namely its failure to deal with the problem of vague knowledge.

The review of Ramsey's *Foundations of Mathematics* contains Keynes's reply to Ramsey's criticisms of the *Treatise*. Ramsey rejected the notion of probability as an objective relation. For Ramsey probability is a subjective assessment made by individuals. Furthermore, through the use of a betting method, these subjective probabilities could be measured in numerical terms. Ramsey's critique of Keynes provided the basis of the subjective expected utility model. Keynes accepted part of Ramsey's critique but not its central propositions. What Keynes took from Ramsey was the distinction between formal logic and human logic.

> Thus he was led to consider 'human logic' as distinguished from 'formal logic'. Formal logic is concerned with nothing but the rules of consistent thought. But in addition to this we have certain 'useful mental habits' for handling the material with which we are supplied by our perceptions and by our memory

> and perhaps in other ways, and so arriving at or towards truth; and the analysis of such habits is also a sort of logic. The application of these ideas to the logic of probability is very fruitful. Ramsey argues, as against the view which I had put forward, that probability is concerned not with objective relations between propositions but (in some sense) with degrees of belief, and he succeeds in showing that the calculus of probabilities simply amounts to a set of rules for ensuring that the system of degrees of belief which we hold shall be a *consistent* system. Thus the calculus of probabilities belongs to formal logic. But the basis of our degrees of beliefs – or the *a priori* probabilities, as they used to called – is part of human outfit, perhaps given us merely by natural selection, analogous to our perceptions and our memories rather than to formal logic. So far I yield to Ramsey – I think he is right. But in attempting to distinguish 'rational' degrees of belief from belief in general he was not yet, I think, quite successful. It is not getting to the bottom of the principle of induction merely to say that it is a useful mental habit. Yet in attempting to distinguish a 'human' logic from formal logic on the one hand and descriptive psychology on the other, Ramsey may have been pointing the way to the next field of study when formal logic has been put into good order and its highly limited scope properly defined. (CW X: 338–9)

There is no textual evidence that Keynes accepted either of Ramsey's two central propositions that probabilities are subjective and numerical.

Keynes's autobiographical essay, 'My Early Beliefs', provides a general statement on Keynes's own evaluation of his early philosophical thought. Keynes remained wedded to the essential features of his early beliefs but came to see their limitations. In particular he came to regard his early beliefs as excessively scholastic, embodying too rational a view of human nature and too dogmatic a treatment of experience.

How are these texts to be interpreted? The main theme which emerges in Keynes's later writing is his increasing concern for the status of the premises. The reference to the importance of vague knowledge reflects Keynes's increasing concern with situations in which the premises themselves are uncertain. He also indicates that probability cannot be understood solely in terms of logical relations but is in part a psychological matter. The review of Ramsey reiterates the limitations of a purely formal logical approach to probability. There is a need to move beyond formal logic into the field of human logic. Formal logic can deal with the issue of consistency between degrees of belief but cannot explain the basis of those degrees of belief.

Keynes did not only seek to encompass his logical theory of probability. He also encompassed his atomistic ontology within a more general organicist ontology. In so doing Keynes repudiated his earlier view, expressed in the *Treatise*, that organicism is incompatible with induction. An atomic system is one in which the parts are separate and independent entities which act in an invariant manner. An organic system is one in which the nature and behaviour of the parts is context-dependent; the whole affects the parts and vice versa. The analysis of organic systems requires the use of temporary independence assumptions. The context is assumed to be fixed in nature in order to allow attention to be focused on particular aspects of the system. These independence assumptions are subsequently relaxed. An atomic system can be regarded as a special case in which the context has no significant effect on the nature and behaviour of the constituent parts. The essay on Edgeworth indicates that Keynes believed an organicist ontology to be the most appropriate for dealing with human and social phenomena. This can be viewed as a recognition of the inherent practical rather than the purely speculative. This is the central message of 'My Early Beliefs'. It is also evidenced by the emphasis that Keynes placed on economics, particularly matters of policy. This is not to say that Keynes came to deny the usefulness of abstract theory. Rather he placed increasing stress on the need to develop theories with appropriate regard to practical realities.

To this end Keynes sought to encompass the logical theory of probability within a more general theory of human behaviour under uncertainty. He tried to extend his analysis beyond the restrictive domain of the *Treatise*. Carvalho (1988/9) describes this change in emphasis as a move from a concern with the problems of probability to that of the problems of uncertainty. Probability and uncertainty are complementary concepts. Probability relates to the logical relationship between premises and implications. Uncertainty relates to the empirical relationship between the premises and the real world. The *Treatise* deals with the former and this accounts for its predominantly rationalistic outlook. The problem of uncertainty is assumed away in the *Treatise* by treating the premises of a probability argument as true knowledge. The move from the *Treatise* to the *General Theory* was a move from a theory of logical or speculative rationality to a theory of practical rationality. The theory of practical rationality encompasses the theory of speculative rationality.

Both the letter to Urban and the review of Ramsey can be interpreted as supporting evidence of this change in orientation in Keynes's thought. The letter to Urban signals Keynes's dissatisfaction with the limited relevance of the *Treatise*. The belief that some revised form of frequency theory will provide a more general theory of probability is a recognition of the need to consider the empirical limitations of analytical methods in the human and social sciences. Analysis, by its very nature, is atomistic, seeking to construct laws of connection between the constituent parts of a system. Organicism does not preclude analysis but highlights its limitations. This is the position Keynes seems to have adopted by 1926.

Keynes's adoption of an organicist social ontology, after all, went hand-in-hand with his attempt to develop economic analysis.

Thus the development of Keynes's thought involved the encompassing of his own early beliefs within a more general system of beliefs. Keynes's thought is characterized by a dialectical process of change in which he attempted to reconcile seemingly oppositional philosophical positions by defining the limits to their relevance. The *General Theory* emerged as the product of a long struggle of escape from the restrictions of established economic theory as well as those of Keynes's own earlier thought. Keynes sought to encompass classical economic theory. He defined the limits to its relevance. Classical theory deals with the explanation of frictional and voluntary unemployment. Keynes constructed a more general theory to explain involuntary unemployment. This also involved encompassing his own established economic theories. *A Treatise on Money* concerned price adjustment rather than fluctuations in output and employment. Keynes also encompassed his logical theory of probability developed in *A Treatise on Probability* within a more general and practical theory of human behaviour under uncertainty. The *General Theory* is, in part, a theory of practical rationality. The main elements of such a theory are sketched out: the relevant time horizon (short-term or long-term), the usual practice of assuming the future to be like the existing situation unless there is specific reason for believing otherwise, the importance of the confidence with which a forecast is held, the recognition that action does not depend on calculation alone and the role of conventional behaviour. Such concerns lie beyond the *Treatise* which deals with speculative rationality, the formal logical aspect of inference in the case of non-conclusive arguments. In order to consider matters of practical rationality, Keynes had to move beyond the *Treatise*. In this sense Keynes's post-*Treatise* thought did involve change but that change was one of transcending the limitations to the relevance of his earlier thought and not a mere denial of his earlier thought. The development of Keynes's thought seems best described as a process of dynamic continuity. The essential aspects of his early beliefs were retained but encompassed within a more general framework.

V Beyond the *Treatise:* alternative interpretations

A number of different interpretations have been offered of Keynes's philosophical thought after the *Treatise* with regard to probability and the appropriateness and necessity of atomism. Turning first to Keynes's later views on probability, there are at least three different interpretations. O'Donnell (1989; 1990) has proposed the continuity thesis, arguing that Keynes retained the logical theory of probability. O'Donnell describes the relationship between the *Treatise* and the *General Theory* using the 'two dimension, two domain' model. In both the *Treatise* and the *General Theory*, O'Donnell identifies two different dimensions to the decision-making process and two different domains within which decisions are made. In the *Treatise* the two dimensions of the decision-making process are probability and weight. This distinction is paralleled in the *General Theory* in the distinction drawn between expectation and confidence. O'Donnell argues that there is a direct correspondence between the two analyses. Likewise in the *Treatise* there are two domains: the determinate and the indeterminate. Corresponding directly to this in the *General Theory* is the distinction drawn between short-term and long-term expectations.

O'Donnell characterizes the determinate domain of the *Treatise* and the short-term domain of the *General Theory* as both being instances of strong rationality. The indeterminate domain of the *Treatise* and the long-term domain of the *General Theory* are both viewed as instances of weak rationality. O'Donnell argues that Keynes's thought became increasingly focused on decision making under indeterminate conditions after the *Treatise*, culminating in the analysis of the investment decision in the *General Theory*. The letter to Urban and the review of Ramsey are interpreted as evidence of Keynes's growing concern with the problem of weak rationality. O'Donnell dismisses Keynes's remarks about the need to move to a revised form of frequency theory. These remarks are viewed as an expression of lessening confidence in the face of Ramsey's criticisms. This loss of confidence is seen as being caused by Keynes's concentration on other matters and is not to be construed as a repudiation of the logical theory.

O'Donnell's interpretation underplays the restrictive nature of the *Treatise*. While there is clearly a direct correspondence between the two dimensions of the *Treatise* and the *General Theory*, it is much more problematic if the same can be said with regard to the domains of the respective analyses. It seems more appropriate to treat the *Treatise* and the *General Theory* as having very different domains of application. This can explain Keynes's subsequent recognition of the likely need to move towards some revised form of frequency theory. O'Donnell merely dismisses this 'surrender' as 'entirely misleading', a rather unconvincing interpretative ploy (1990: 64). Acceptance of a revised frequency theory need not entail rejection of the logical theory. O'Donnell does not seem to recognize the inherent limitations to the *Treatise*. This is particularly evident in O'Donnell's interpretation of uncertainty in the terms of the *Treatise* as low-weight, non-numerical probabilities, or non-comparable probabilities. While these are all important aspects of uncertainty they do not encompass the vagueness of knowledge arising from the uncertain status of the premises themselves.

An alternative interpretation is provided by Winslow (1986; 1989a; 1989b) who argues that Keynes retained an objectivist approach but moved from a logical theory to a frequency theory. The letter to Urban is interpreted as evidence of the switch to a frequency theory but Winslow provides no explanation of the reasons for this change in Keynes's views. The review of Ramsey is read as a statement that the study of degrees of belief is now considered as the subject of human, not formal, logic but these degrees of belief are still objective. The latter proposition is not actually stated by Keynes and seems at odds with his increased concern with the implications of vague knowledge.

The third interpretation is Bateman's 'two changes' thesis. Bateman (1987, 1990) interprets the review of Ramsey as evidence of Keynes's change to a subjective epistemic (logical) theory of probability. Bateman argues that Keynes subsequently changed his approach again, moving to a dualistic position in which an aleatory (frequency) theory is appropriate in the natural sciences but an epistemic theory is appropriate in the social sciences. Yet there is no textual evidence to support Bateman's claim that Keynes embraced a thoroughgoing subjectivism in the light of Ramsey's criticisms. Indeed Keynes specifically criticized Ramsey for failing adequately to distinguish between rational degrees of belief and belief in general. As for the subsequent adoption of a dualistic position on probability this could be supported by Keynes's dualistic position on atomism and organicism as set out in the essay on Edgeworth. However Bateman rejects such a linkage by denying that Keynes adopted an organicist social ontology (see below).

The second principal issue in the 'continuity-or-change' debate is whether or not Keynes changed his views on the appropriateness and necessity of assuming that the system under investigation is atomistic. The majority of commentators have interpreted the essay on Edgeworth as evidence of Keynes's adoption of an organicist social ontology and, by implication, his rejection of the view in the *Treatise* that organicism and induction are incompatible. The organicist nature of Keynes's later thought was originally pointed out by Gruchy (1948) and has been presented more recently by Brown-Collier (1985), Carabelli (1988), Hamouda and Smithin (1988), Rotheim (1989/90) and Winslow (1986; 1989a; 1989b). The latter two writers have added particular slants to the organicist interpretation. Rotheim distinguishes between the Hegelian notion of organicism and the much more restrictive principle of organic unity found in Moore's *Principia Ethica.* Rotheim argues that Keynes's conception of an organic system in the *Treatise* is consistent with Moore's principle of organic unity but that subsequently he adopted a more Hegelian viewpoint as found in the writings of Marshall. Winslow (1989a; 1989b) finds parallels between Keynes's move towards an organicist social ontology and Whitehead's later thought. Whitehead developed the method of nested hierarchies as a means of analysing organic systems. This method is akin to Keynes's use of temporary independence assumptions in the *General Theory*. There is, however, no direct evidence of Whitehead's influence on Keynes. Indeed Whitehead left Cambridge in 1910 for Imperial College, London and subsequently moved to Harvard in 1924. There appears to have been no contact between Keynes and Whitehead after 1910. The relationship between their thinking on organicism seems best described as parallel but independent.

The organicist interpretation of Keynes's later thought is rejected by Bateman (1989) and Davis (1989a; 1989b) who argue that Keynes retained an atomistic ontology throughout his life. They interpret the passage from the essay on Edgeworth not as a criticism of atomism *per se* but rather the particular use of it made by Edgeworth. Bateman argues that Keynes was in fact criticizing Edgeworth's frequency approach to probability while Davis views Keynes's target as Edgeworth's attachment to Benthamite utilitarianism. Both of these interpretations involve rather convoluted and unconvincing readings of the essay on Edgeworth. Bateman's rejection of the organicist interpretation is somewhat surprising since such an interpretation would complement his contention that Keynes eventually adopted a dualistic approach to probability. An atomistic natural ontology but organicist social ontology would be consistent with the use of frequency theory in the natural sciences but not in the social sciences. The rejection of the organicist interpretation by Bateman and Davis is based on the view that an organicist social ontology would deny the appropriateness of analysing the behaviour of individuals. As Rotheim (1989/90) points out, Bateman and Davis consider organicism as assigning priority to the whole, as in Moore's principle of organic unity. But this is not the only alternative to atomism. A more Hegelian notion of organicism would not preclude consideration of the behaviour of individuals within the system and would reconcile Keynes's ontological views expressed in the essay on Edgeworth with the mode of analysis used in the *General Theory*.

A middle position in this debate is taken by O'Donnell (1989) who argues that Keynes entertained both atomism and organicism, with the choice between them being open-ended and context-specific. O'Donnell rejects an attempt to portray Keynes as embracing an all-pervading organicism. This view runs counter to the encompassing interpretation developed here. O'Donnell portrays Keynes as becoming increasingly eclectic.

This interpretation underplays the transcendental qualities of Keynes's later thought.

VI Some concluding thoughts

The new Keynesian fundamentalism has done much to shed light on the philosophical foundations of Keynes's economics. However there has been a good deal of sterile debate generated by trying to fit Keynes into some particular philosophical straitjacket. The whole debate is infested by a plague of '-isms'. The appearance of division may mask an underlying, if hardly recognized, agreement between many of the commentators. Is there any essential difference between what Bateman and Davis mean by 'subjectivism', what Winslow means by 'human logic', what Carvalho means by 'uncertainty' and what O'Donnell means by 'weak rationality'? Are not all of these commentators just saying in different ways that Keynes sought to develop a more practical theory of rationality and needed to move beyond the *Treatise* to do so?

Within the debate the notion of continuity has been particularly elusive, meaning different things to different people. The 'strong' version of the continuity thesis is that Keynes retained his early philosophical beliefs without any substantive change. The 'weaker' version of the continuity thesis is that Keynes only retained some aspects of his early philosophy. O'Donnell's position seems nearest to the 'strong' end of the spectrum but he allows for some change, namely Keynes's increased concern with the problem of weak rationality. The whole debate is set in very linear terms: continuity or discontinuity. The encompassing interpretation attempts to overcome this 'either/or' dualism by recognizing an essential continuity in Keynes's thought, but in the context of radical change as Keynes sought to generalize the practical relevance of his belief system. The continuity in Keynes's thought is a dynamic continuity.

The debate highlights two problems of interpretation. Firstly, most of the commentators treat consistency with the textual evidence as some form of objective test criterion in the assessment of alternative interpretations. But the continued existence of alternative interpretations, each claimed to be consistent with the textual evidence, demonstrates the inevitable underdetermination of the process of interpretation. A particular interpretation may reveal more about the hidden agenda of the interpreter than about Keynes. In the 'continuity-or-change' debate interpreters may just be revealing their own value-judgements as to what Keynes should or should not have retained of his early beliefs.

Another problem with the debate so far is its emphasis on the task of interpretation. This is the natural order of things, but there is an urgent need to move towards the task of application. Keynes's analysis should be considered with regard to its relevance to the development of models of economic behaviour. Ultimately the significance of Keynes's thought lies in its applicability, not in its being Keynes's thought. Keynes's early speculative beliefs need to be approached in the same practical way that Keynes himself subsequently did.

Note

I am grateful to John Hillard and the participants in the departmental seminars at the universities of Exeter and Hull for many useful comments on an early draft of this chapter. The usual disclaimer applies.

References

Bateman, B. W. (1987), 'Keynes's Changing Conception of Probability', *Economics and Philosophy*, **3**, 97–120.

Bateman, B. W. (1988), 'G. E. Moore and J. M. Keynes: A Missing Chapter in the History of the Expected Utility Model', *American Economic Review*, **78**, 1098–1106.

Bateman, B. W. (1989), ' "Human Logic" and Keynes's Economics: A Comment', *Eastern Economic Journal*, **15**, 63–7

Bateman, B. W. (1990), 'The Elusive Logical Relation: An Essay on Change and Continuity in Keynes's Thought', in D. E. Moggridge (ed.), *Perspectives on the History of Economic Thought, Vol.IV: Keynes, Macroeconomics and Method*, Aldershot: Edward Elgar.

Brown-Collier, E. K. (1985), 'Keynes' View of an Organic Universe: The Implications', *Review of Social Economy*, **43**, 14–23.

Carabelli, A. (1988), *On Keynes's Method*, London: Macmillan.

de Carvalho, F. J. C. (1988/9), 'Keynes on Probability, Uncertainty and Decision-making', *Journal of Post Keynesian Economics*, **11**, 66–81.

Coddington, A. (1976), 'Keynesian Economics: The Search for First Principles', *Journal of Economic Literature*, **14**, 1258–73.

Coddington, A. (1982), 'Deficient Foresight: A Troublesome Theme in Keynesian Economics', *American Economic Review*, **72**, 480–7.

Davis, J. B. (1989a), 'Keynes and Organicism', *Journal of Post Keynesian Economics*, **12**, 308–15.

Davis, J. B. (1989b), 'Keynes on Atomism and Organicism', *Economic Journal*, **99**, 1159–72.

Fitzgibbons, A. (1988), *Keynes's Vision: A New Political Economy*, Oxford: Clarendon Press.

Gruchy, A. G. (1948), 'The Philosophical Basis of the New Keynesian Economics', *Ethics*, **58**, 235–44.

Hamouda, O. F. and J. N. Smithin (1988), 'Some Remarks on "Uncertainty and Economic Analysis" ', *Economic Journal*, **98**, 159–64.

Lawson, T. (1985), 'Uncertainty and Economic Analysis', *Economic Journal*, **95**, 909–27.

O'Donnell, R. M. (1989), *Keynes: Philosophy, Economics and Politics*, London: Macmillan.

O'Donnell, R. M. (1990), 'Continuity in Keynes's Conception of Probability', in D. E. Moggridge (ed.), *Perspectives on the History of Economic Thought, Vol.IV: Keynes, Macroeconomics and Method*, Aldershot: Edward Elgar.

Rotheim, R. (1989/90), 'Organicism and the Role of the Individual in Keynes' Thought', *Journal of Post Keynesian Economics*, **12**, 316–26.

Winslow, E. G. (1986), ' "Human Logic" and Keynes's Economics', *Eastern Economic Journal*, **12**, 413–30.

Winslow, E. G. (1989a), 'Organic Interdependence, Induction and Probability', paper presented to the ROPE Conference, Malvern.

Winslow, E. G. (1989b), 'Organic Interdependence, Uncertainty and Economic Analysis', *Economic Journal*, **99**, 1173–82.

5 The political economy of new Keynesian fundamentalism

Athol Fitzgibbons

I Introduction

The new Keynesian fundamentalism is a name given to a field of study which analyses what Keynes historically said and distinguishes his ideas from the Keynesian systems which were subsequently perpetrated in his name. It takes a particular interest in Keynes's philosophy, partly because of the intrinsic interest of that subject, and partly because of the light which it throws upon theoretical macroeconomics. In addition Keynes's philosophy reveals much about his approach to economic policy, which is the object of this chapter.

Without representing that there is unanimity in the field it seems generally agreed that it is possible to connect Keynes's early writings on moral and political philosophy to his *Treatise on Probability* and *The Economic Consequences of the Peace*. It is further possible to relate these intermediate writings to the *General Theory* and Keynes's other later works. It might be expected that the philosophy of probability would underlie the economics of uncertainty, but the links between Keynes's writings are more general and pervasive. Keynesian fundamentalism has been cross-referencing Keynes's writings on economics, politics and philosophy and discovering a pattern which was not previously suspected.

Keynes's stature has gained from this extended scrutiny, which has confirmed him as one of the few great economist–philosophers. He was one of the few thinkers – Smith and Marx are the others – who developed a new philosophy to address the economic problems of his time. The *General Theory* is the fruit of an integrated system of thought, incorporating morals, scientific method and a utopian political vision.

But, as we have come to appreciate the depth of Keynes's thought, the gulf between the Keynesians and Keynes with respect to both theory and policy has become more apparent. All Keynesians owe a debt to Keynes because of his refutation of Say's Law that supply creates its own demand, but major differences remain. One reason of course is that Keynes addressed the economic problems and aspirations of the 1920s and 1930s, whereas the Keynesians tried to solve economic problems which emerged after the Second World War. But, from our point of view, the important differences are with respect to political orientation and method. The major schools of Keynesian economics – the neoclassical Keynesian synthesis, post-Keynesianism, and the New Keynesian economics – manifest ideological and instrumentalist tendencies which Keynes opposed explicitly and throughout his life.

Possibly for this reason 'Keynesian fundamentalism' was originally coined as a term of abuse, and not long ago there were warnings that any close investigation of Keynes's original ideas would be futile and anti-scientific. However it was never explained why Keynes and Keynes alone should be excluded from the processes of scholarly study, and fortunately the intellectual taboo was eventually broken as the significance of Keynes's writings on morals and the *Treatise on Probability* became apparent.

The early writings, meaning Keynes's unpublished essays on moral and political philosophy written over the period 1904–14, rounded out an emerging picture. There are doubtless problems with the exegesis of these early works, and it would be exaggerated to claim that Keynes had an intellectually constant position over the whole of his life. But in the same way that Marx's early writings have provided additional insight into his values, and Smith's lectures on *Rhetoric and Belles Lettres*, discovered in 1969, have given very valuable insights into the Smithian method of analysis, so Keynes's *Treatise on Probability* and early writings help to reveal an enlarged system which with hindsight we can see was always there.

Keynesian fundamentalism was not originally motivated by political or policy considerations, and most of its literature has been at an abstract methodological level, where such problems seem very remote. Nevertheless the reason why the exegesis of Keynes has needed a special label is that a clearer understanding of his system has policy implications, particularly at a time when Keynesian macroeconomics is in disarray and there is a general drift towards economic pragmatism without anyone being able to enunciate what that means.

Keynes's own doctrine was more logical in its criticism of classical economics, and more flexible with regard to policy, than Keynesianism conveys. Many of the complaints about the Keynesian system – the arbitrariness of assuming wage-price rigidities, money illusion, the problems of fine tuning the economy and so on – do not apply to Keynes's original formulation. This does not mean that we should displace all Keynesian theories with another more 'authentic' one, if only because there is probably no such thing as a definitive and original Keynesian economics. He was able to go through a long process of intellectual evolution mainly because he was not committed at the usual ideological and theoretical levels. 'When I am wrong sir, I change my mind. What do you do?' Our interest lies in the prior way of thinking which generated Keynes's economic theories, as much as in the theories themselves.

II Keynes and rational expectations

The motto of the old Keynesian fundamentalism, which built on the work of G. L. S. Shackle, was uncertainty. The influence of Shackle has been strong and pervasive, to the extent that it is now widely believed that Keynes lacked a theory of rational action. Since Keynes vacated the field of rational behaviour, another common argument goes, the only theoretical way forward is the theory of 'rational expectations' and the new classical economics.

The new fundamentalism recognizes that Keynes emphasized two aspects of every practical decision, uncertainty and judgement. Shackle's work correctly emphasized that Keynes rejected the mechanical world-view and was a valuable corrective at a time when the narrow IS–LM system was in the ascendant, but nihilism is an impossible philosophy for anyone engaged in practical affairs. Keynes did not subscribe to it because he was orientated towards practical action. He believed that the complex and shifting nature of economic phenomena would defeat any attempt to find the absolute truth, but he investigated what might constitute *reasonable* grounds for reaching a decision.

He defined probability in a general way which included both uncertainty and risk. The major theme of Keynes's *Treatise on Probability* was that there was a role for rational judgement despite the uncertainty of practical affairs.

> Its object [of the *Treatise on Probability*] has been to emphasise the existence of *a logical relation between two sets of propositions* in cases where it is not possible to argue demonstratively from one to the other. (CW VIII: 9, emphasis in original)

Keynes admitted that, under conditions of uncertainty, which covered the general and usual case in life, it was not normally possible to draw strictly scientific conclusions. Nevertheless he called his theory the *logical* theory of probability, to indicate that conclusions which could be drawn in uncertain situations could be rational in a meaningful sense. He conceded that there is an irreducible element of art in the judgement of facts and values, but he argued at length that this art drew upon analogies which could be good or bad.

It might seem very pedestrian to conclude that there was a logic to judgement, especially given the abstruse arguments which the *Treatise on Probability* mounted to reach it. Nevertheless it was by no means an empty conclusion, as can be seen by comparing the *Treatise* with our new classical economics. Keynes rejected the 'frequency theory of probability', which is a cousin to the modern theory of rational expectations. He demonstrated that the axiomatic condition required for the frequency theory (the principle of non-sufficient reason, now the assumption that the residuals of expectations are randomly distributed around a norm) was so restrictive that it could not be relied upon except in artificially structured situations.

> But it was not long before more sceptical persons began to suspect that this [frequency] theory proved too much. Its calculations, it is true, were constructed from the data of experience, but the more simple and the less complex the experience the better satisfied was the theory. What was required was not a wide experience or detailed information, but a completeness of symmetry in the little information there might be. It seemed to follow from the . . . doctrine that the primary qualification for one who would be well informed was an equally balanced ignorance. (CW VIII: 92)

The common belief that Keynes's radical theory of uncertainty excluded rational behaviour is wrong. In fact the *Treatise on Probability* attacked David Hume's philosophical nihilism, which went to the effect that reality is too complex to be seriously understood. Translated into economic terms, Hume's theory was much the same as the radical theory of uncertainty which G. L. S. Shackle later attributed to Keynes himself. Steering between the extremes of statistical superficiality and of philosophical nihilism, Keynes argued that it was logical to understand probable and uncertain situations in terms of common sense.

The *General Theory* applied the schemata in the *Treatise*. It described a situation in which (with apologies for the solecism) investors typically tried to rely upon 'rational expectations' within a context of financial conventions. However, Keynes's theory went, the climate of uncertainty could only justify an investment philosophy of constructive impulses, which meant judgement. The *General Theory* concluded that investors' misconceived attempts to follow the theory of rational expectations had led to financial instability and ultimately to the Depression.

Keynes developed a different type of rational expectations theory to the new classical economics. New classical economists believe that it is not possible to be rational if there is uncertainty; they conclude that uncertainty should be assumed away. However Keynes's conclusion was that, since there is uncertainty, rationality had to be given a wider definition. His theory was more realistic, though less quantitative, than the new classical system.

III The intellectual origins of Keynes's philosophy

Contrary to common opinion Keynes was not a superficial philosophical amateur. He had highly-developed powers of philosophic analysis, and ranged widely over the world of thought. However the particular focus of his attention was the Age of Reason, and Keynes has made contributions to our understanding of some of the strongest influences upon that period, Isaac Newton, David Hume and Edmund Burke.

Keynes's biographical essay on Newton changed scholarly perceptions of Newton's orientation. Keynes's attempt to write a substantive critique of Hume was thwarted; but there are many scattered comments on that philosopher throughout Keynes's works. There are also various comments and the long undergraduate essay on Burke, who was the great recidivist from the Age of Reason.

The eighteenth-century Age of Reason was a great intellectual watershed of western thought, when the modern world emerged. During this period the mechanical world-view took root and economic science was born, but at the same time the moderns were cut off from a long tradition of thought, Newton, Burke and Hume were three of the four most influential British minds which influenced the Age. It is unfortunate that, in all the 30 volumes of Keynes's *Collected Writings*, there are almost no substantive references to the fourth great figure, Adam Smith, economist and philosopher, admirer of Newton, and the friend of Burke and Hume. Some unpublished correspondence of Keynes's revolving around W. R. Scott's book, *Adam Smith as Student and Professor*, reveals that Keynes was vitally interested in Smith, but we have only a few lines in the last essay that Keynes wrote shortly before his death.

The brilliance of Newtonian physics seemed to demonstrate that the world could be explained along strictly instrumentalist lines. But Keynes argued, in his elegant and influential essay, that Newton was by no means the mechanist that the Age of Reason had believed him to be. Despite his formidable ability to express his imaginative powers in mathematical form, Newton's mind was intense, insightful and creative:

> In the eighteenth century and since, Newton came to be thought of as the first and greatest of the modern age of scientists, a rationalist, one who taught us to think on the lines of cold and untinctured reason. I do not see him in this light . . . Newton was the first of the age of reason. He was the last of the magicians, the last of the Babylonians and Sumerians, the last great mind which looked out on the visible and intellectual world with the same eyes as those who began to build our intellectual inheritance rather less than 10,000 years ago. (CW X: 363–4)

The actual person who set out to establish a mechanical system of *social* science, and the real antagonist in Keynes's *Treatise on Probability*, was

David Hume. Hume first made the distinction between positive and normative knowledge, which we now accept as easily as breathing, to tear down the old religious structures of Europe, and replace them with a new emphasis on liberalism and economic growth. But, having excluded intuitive knowledge, and replaced it with an utterly mechanical system, Hume had been forced to conclude that all we ever know is theoretical, and that our knowledge of reality can have no foundation.

> Hume stands for the plain man against the sophisms of metaphysicians and theologians. Yet such scepticism goes too far. The judgements of probability, upon which we depend for almost all our beliefs in matters of experience, are more than [what Hume called] 'lively imaginations'. (Abridged from CW VII: 56)

Keynes conceded that Hume had been the 'master' of the theory of knowledge. But Hume's excessive scepticism, which overlooked the logic possibilities in probable knowledge, seemed to make the new values and ideals as irrational as the old. Keynes attacked Hume's mechanical view, which he regarded as reductionist. He believed that a deeper theory of knowledge, with roots in pre-enlightenment thought, could provide liberalism with a more logical foundation.

Burke's errors were the opposite to those of Hume. Keynes regarded Burke's criticisms of the Age of Reason as correct in principle, but wrong in the way that the principles were applied. Burke had thought of society as a complex organic unity, and had said that a political philosophy would necessarily be arbitrary and illogical if it lacked a moral or religious foundation. But Burke had not understood the significance of economic growth, and the justification it could provide, even within his own framework of thought, to equalitarian and liberal values. Burke

> did not ask whether the large ideas, which the revolutionaries set up as their watchwords, might not have an enobling influence upon men who had lived on the husks of feudalism . . . They preached what was not logical . . . He should have seen in the new evangel the fruitful germs of some of the principles which he himself held dear. (Quoted in Fitzgibbons, 1988: 61–2)

Keynes's philosophy was meant to avoid the reductionism associated with classical economics, without being seduced by the regressiveness of traditional thought.

IV An extended process of reason

It is therefore a misrepresentation to say that Keynes's politics arose out of sympathies for big government and the socialist state. In some ways his policy was indeed very radical, but in some ways much more conservative than has been understood.

If we try to analyse his position on the usual political spectrum it seems very paradoxical, because over time Keynes's politics shifted to the right while his economics went to the left. It is possible to portray a very left-wing Keynes by combining his early politics and his late economics; for example, Joan Robinson did this when she combined the *General Theory* with the 'The End of Laissez-Faire'. It is also possible to present an extremely right-wing Keynes by combining his *Tract on Monetary Reform* with the social conservatism in his autobiographical essay, 'My Early Beliefs'. It would be more accurate, however, to say that Keynes was not on the conventional political spectrum.

His political philosophy was strictly not an ideological doctrine at all, but a way of thinking which would facilitate practical action. Its absolutes were a commitment to the processes of analysis and reason, and a probably excessive faith that they would prevail in public life. 'Clear thinking' would therefore solve all problems, because if policy mistakes were made they could be recognized and a different course taken.

This extended process of reason went well beyond the boundaries of technical economics. The technocratic idea of Keynes-neutrality, according to which the economist coordinates the economy after the political policy maker has imposed his irrational objectives, was virtually the opposite of the historical truth. In Keynes's system of thought the ends of policy were subject to logical analysis, and macroeconomic policy was supposed to contribute to a moral goal.

In accordance with his activist philosophy Keynes rejected Hume's distinction between positive and normative judgements in favour of a general account of judgement which would cover both the positive and normative sides. The difference between values and facts may be basic to modern science, but the rules of science are not the rules of action; and it was the latter, the question of what should be done, that Keynes had in mind. In life it is as likely that poverty will warp the psyche as that an increase in the money supply will reduce the rate of interest; but according to the strict principles of science the first statement has no meaning, whereas the second might well be right. Keynes accepted the first proposition as largely correct, and was tentative about the second.

Keynes did not reject the scientific outlook because he was unfamiliar with it, and in fact his father, J. N. Keynes, had written a book which argued that the positive/normative distinction should be observed. But according to Keynes economics was necessarily a moral science; we judge facts as we judge values, with only part of the evidence available to us but with a more general schemata in mind.

So, despite his opposition to Christianity, Keynes's morality was spiritual rather than utilitarian. He conceived of a realm of freedom in some future time when economic problems could be less pressing, and morality would not need to be so materialistic and purposive. Keynes's emphasis on low rates of interest and economic growth should be regarded as part of a plan to advance this long-run goal.

However his liberal and equalitarian values were intermediate rather than final goods. Consequently the problem which preoccupies us, namely the best economic system, he regarded as a technical issue:

> The fiercest contests [about socialism] and the most deeply felt division of opinion are likely to be waged in the coming years not around technical questions, where the arguments on either side are mainly economic, but around those which, for want of better words, may be called psychological, or perhaps moral. (CW IX: 293)

Keynes's policy principles were elitist, as any system based on judgement rather than strictly demonstrable science must be. They were not essentially anti-democratic, though he did become suspicious of the democratic process, which fell a long way below 'truth as a method'. The form of state which he advocated most consistently was a laissez-faire democracy supervised by an elite which recognized the rules of practical wisdom and was committed to a moral goal.

V How Keynes understood economic policy

As Allan Meltzer has emphasized, Keynes was not the author of the policy of functional finance, or fine tuning, which was only devised after the Second World War. The Keynesian system in that period became highly mechanistic, and commonly portrayed the economy as a motor car which only needs to be steered. As Abba Lerner put it:

> You look into the [classical economists'] car and before you can control yourself you cry out 'Why there's no steering wheel!'

There is no analogy between the economy and a machine anywhere in the 30 volumes of Keynes's *Collected Writings*, if only because an economics of uncertainty cannot be expressed in strictly mechanical terms. However this is a long way from the full story, and Meltzer is wrong to go to the opposite extreme and portray Keynes as a form of classical economist.

To capture how Keynes understood economic policy it is necessary to change the metaphor and get the policy maker out of the car. The policy maker is no longer driving a new car down an American freeway, but is riding across rough country on a potentially refractory bull. There are some improvised reins, and if the policy maker pulls to the left the animal might turn in that direction. However he might also turn right, or stop in his tracks, or try to throw the rider off, because the creature we are describing is an organic unity propelled by motives which no one fully understands.

Keynes's approach to macroeconomic management was a generalization of what the organic metaphor suggests. A theoretical analysis of the economic situation was essential if the policy maker was to isolate the broad lines of causation and put the detail in perspective. Nevertheless the world was always changing, and sometimes by a great deal; and everything depended upon judgement, which was an imperfect combination of logic and art. Keynes also pointed out, in the *Treatise on Probability*, that, since there was never enough information to reach a formally correct conclusion, the right process of analysis might lead to the wrong decision.

He preferred to avoid theoretical complexities because they could never match all the complexity of life; and he thought it was advisable to avoid being committed to a particular theory, thereby precluding a different approach if something went wrong. His own appreciation of the *General Theory* was expressed in admirably tentative terms:

> I am more attached to the comparatively simple fundamental ideas which underlie my theory than to the particular forms in which I have embodied them, and I have no desire that the latter should be crystallised at the present stage of the debate. (CW XIV: 11)

It is a very dubious way of thinking and, despite the long intellectual pedigree behind it, it is the way which most people use to resolve practical problems. It does imply the tool box approach to economics instead of a grand and universal theory, but it is a way of thinking which is pragmatic, systematic and ultimately orientated to values.

Keynes's system should not be made less specific than it really was. In particular it was the original schemata which justified the welfare state and the pursuit of full employment. Today, however, the obvious macroeconomic question is whether it is possible to reject Say's Law and classical economics, but without necessarily becoming committed to the theoretical and ideological baggage, including Phillips curves and wage-price controls, which is typically associated with Keynes. The answer is, that is just what Keynes did himself.

Reference

Fitzgibbons, A. (1988), *Keynes's Vision: A New Political Economy*, Oxford: Clarendon Press.

PART II

COMPETITION

6 The relationship between Keynes's macroeconomic analysis and theories of imperfect competition[1]

Malcolm Sawyer

I Introduction

Whilst Keynes's *General Theory* and most of Keynesian economics have been based on some form of atomistic competition, there have often been suggestions lurking of the involvement of imperfect competition. These suggestions have ranged from the use of some aspects of imperfect competition to justify an assumption of price rigidity through to the argument that the economics of Keynes requires imperfect competition as part of its micro-foundations. This chapter specifically addresses the questions of whether the macroeconomic analysis of Keynes requires imperfect competition as part of its microeconomic foundations and whether Keynes would have been well-advised to have used imperfect competition rather than atomistic competition as the industrial structure. The term 'imperfect competition' will be used to signify those theories which conclude that price diverges from marginal cost, for reasons of fewness of numbers and/or from product differentiation. The term 'perfect competition' is used to signify the case where there are large numbers of firms which are essentially price-takers. The industrial structure assumed by Keynes is described as polypolistic or atomistic competition. This has some but not all of the features of perfect competition for, as Chick (1983) argues, 'Keynes's representative firm is an anomaly from the point of view of established thinking: it is a small "polypolistic" or atomistic firm which operates under uncertainty and therefore is not a price taker'. Robinson (1976) also argues that 'Keynes did not accept the "perfect competition" of the textbooks, but some vague old-fashioned notion of competition that he never formulated explicitly'.

II Keynes and theories of imperfect competition

It is clear that the *General Theory* did not draw upon any notions of imperfect competition in the sense defined above. There is reference to the degree of competition (but not degree of monopoly) being taken as given (CW VII: 245), which contains the suggestion that it is not necessarily atomistic competition which is assumed. However the equality of price and marginal cost and of real wage and marginal productivity of labour strongly suggests that atomistic competition is assumed.

From the perspective of this chapter, there are two crucial aspects of the way in which Keynes modelled the production side of the economy. First, production and prices adjust rapidly to changes in demand for ' "the degree of competition" which Keynes took for granted approximated Marshallian assumptions of sufficient competition in most markets to guarantee quick responses by sellers to shifts in the demand for their products' (Lekachman, 1977). The second is that there is a positive relationship between price and output produced (and the obverse of that, a negative relationship between real wage and employment). In effect a situation of monopoly in which production adjusted rapidly to changes in demand (which is the way monopoly is generally modelled) and where prices and production were positively related (which is not necessarily the case) would mimic the situation of polypolistic competition as portrayed by Keynes.

At much the same time as Keynes was developing the *General Theory*, there was much activity on theories of imperfect competition, to some degree in response to the difficulties over perfect competition raised by Sraffa (1926). Keynes began work on what became the *General Theory* soon after completion of the *Treatise on Money* (CW V, VI) so the first half of the 1930s can be seen as the period of development of the *General Theory*, Chamberlin submitted his thesis in April 1927, and it was published in 1933 (as Chamberlin, 1933). Joan Robinson also published her *Economics of Imperfect Competition* in 1933, and she was a key member of the famous circus who were closely involved in debates with Keynes over the *General Theory*. Richard Kahn's fellowship dissertation (submitted in 1929, and now published as Kahn, 1989) had been concerned with the role of imperfect competition. Kahn is often given a particularly important role in the development of the *General Theory* and Schumpeter suggested that his 'share in the historic achievement cannot have fallen very far short of co-authorship' (Schumpeter, 1954: 1172). Kahn dismissed that suggestion as 'clearly absurd', and described his role thus: 'I relieved the solitude and provided, by being on the spot, a more rapid method of discussion than correspondence by post' (Kahn, 1984: 178).

The intellectual environment against which Keynes was working suggests that at a minimum the retention of an atomistic competitive framework was a deliberate decision by Keynes and generally thought by him and the members of the circus (especially Kahn and Robinson) to be unnecessary for his key propositions.[2] Collard (1990) notes that 'neither of the main progenitors of the "revolutions" in macroeconomics and microeconomics in the 1930s, Robinson and Keynes, had any doubt that the revolutions were totally separate ones'. The broad line of argument of this chapter is that the revolutions were indeed quite separate, but that, whilst the crucial propositions of Keynes did not require imperfect competition, his arguments could have been strengthened by its use.

Ohlin (in Keynes, CW XIV) provided an early statement of the view that Keynes should have used imperfect competition rather than atomistic competition in his analysis. He was concerned with an issue to which we return below, namely the relationship between real wages and employment, and argued that employment could increase without any reduction in real wages. He identified the contrary view with 'perfect' competition (inverted commas as used by Ohlin), and continued by saying that 'in this as in some other respects Keynes does not seem to me to have been radical enough in freeing himself from the conventional assumptions. When reading his book one sometimes wonders whether he never discussed imperfect competition with Mrs Robinson' (CW XIV: 196). Keynes replied in some puzzlement to this, when he wrote that he had 'not been able to make out here what you [Ohlin] are driving at. The reference to imperfect competition is very perplexing. I cannot see how on earth it comes in. Mrs Robinson, I may mention, read my proofs without discovering any connection' (CW XIV: 190). A few years earlier, Robinson had argued that 'there is no natural tendency even under competition to maintain full employment, which depends upon the level of saving and of investment. We are here only concerned to discuss an economic system in equilibrium, and we must suppose that both under competition and under monopoly the conditions necessary to full employment are maintained'; and in a footnote that, 'if there was full employment under competition, in equilibrium conditions, there will be full employment under the monopolists' (Robinson, 1933: 310).

There did appear to be a potential complementarity between imperfect competition (most clearly in Chamberlin's *Theory of Monopolistic Competition*) and Keynes's *General Theory*. The theory of monopolistic competition predicted excess capacity as a long-term feature and that firms were essentially demand-constrained rather than cost-constrained (in the sense that each firm would willingly produce more if they could sell at the prevailing price). These features find echoes in Keynes's analysis, where the level of economic activity is constrained by the level of aggregate demand rather than by aggregate supply. However at another level there is a conflict. In the analysis of Chamberlin, it is the actions of the firms (and in particular entrants in each industry) in pursuit of profits which lead to the tangency solution between the perceived demand curve and the average cost curve. There is no particular reason to think that the wages and profits which arise would lead to expenditure which would be equal to the output produced (at the ruling prices). This can also be expressed as saying that the extent of excess capacity cannot be determined by both the level of aggregate demand and the interaction of firms. Further a permanent increase in aggregate demand would lead to entry rather than a fall in the degree of capacity underutilization in the approach of Chamberlin.

The interchange between Keynes (as editor of the *Economic Journal*) and Joan Robinson (CW XII: 829–36) over a paper submitted by Kalecki (which was rejected by Keynes but published as Kalecki, 1941) illustrates that the central ideas of imperfect competition had not become ingrained in the thinking of Keynes. Kalecki had assumed that firms operated subjected to excess capacity in the long period, to which Keynes reacted by asking, 'is it not rather odd when dealing with "long-run problems" to start with the assumption that all firms are always working below capacity?' (CW XII: 829). Joan Robinson replied to the effect that under-capacity working was 'part of the usual bag of tricks of Imperfect Competition theory' (830) and produced the now standard diagram for the 'tangency solution' of imperfect competition with free entry exhibiting excess capacity in equilibrium. Keynes's response was to claim to be 'still innocent enough to be bewildered by the idea that the assumption of all firms always working below capacity is consistent with "a long run problem" ' (830–1).

The original formulation of theories of imperfect competition focused on questions such as product differentiation, excess capacity (notably in Chamberlin, 1933) and exploitation (payment to a factor below marginal product, which featured particularly in Robinson, 1933).[3] Whilst the relationship between price and marginal cost was explored there was no suggestion of price rigidity (see, for example, Robinson, 1933: Chapter 4) though there was recognition that a decrease in the level of demand could lead to a rise in price (Robinson, 1933: 72–4). The treatment of imperfect competition took on a rather different perspective in the second half of the 1930s, as compared with the first half, and price rigidity came to the fore. This change of direction can be identified with Means (1935; 1936). The celebrated kinked demand curve approach (Sweezy, 1939) was explicitly concerned with explaining price rigidity in the context of differentiated oligopoly. Hall and Hitch (1939) was distinct in many respects, such as being built on empirical observation and generally rejecting profit maximization. For our purposes, the important aspect is that prices were seen as a (relatively) constant mark-up over average direct costs. With average direct costs viewed as approximately constant with respect to output, this suggests that price is constant (relative to average costs) in the face of variations in demand. By a differerent route, Kalecki (1938) arrived at a similar conclusion (for further discussion see Sawyer, 1992).

However most theorizing in macroeconomics continued to assume (at least implicitly) atomistic competition, but departing from Keynes by assuming price rigidity. This came to the fore with the reinterpretation of Keynesian economics and the temporary equilibrium school. In the context of atomistic competition, they are correct to argue that there will be elements of trading out of equilibrium (simply because prices cannot adjust instantaneously in an economy without a Walrasian auctioneer), but the general assumption that there is rapid quantity adjustment is unappealing when applied to a production (rather than an exchange) economy. Our argument is that the causes and implications of price inflexibility are quite different under imperfect competition as compared with perfect competition. Under the latter, price inflexibility is either imposed or arises as an approximation to incomplete price adjustment (cf. Leijonhufvud, 1968), whereas in the former it arises either from the deliberate decisions of producers or from a delay in adjusting prices because of the costs of doing so. In a situation of perfect competition, price inflexibility is generally associated with a difference between (notional) demand and supply, with the actual trade being set by the short side of the market. In contrast, under imperfect competition (as argued below) the producers generally supply whatever is demanded at the price which they have set (or at least not changed) and there is an adjustment of supply to demand.

III Interpretation of the *General Theory*

This section outlines an interpretation of the parts of Keynes's *General Theory* relevant to this chapter. Although our main concern is with the output side, we begin on the labour side. The terminology of the labour market is avoided on the grounds that a major aspect of the approach of Keynes is that the determination of real wages does not occur in the way envisaged by a neoclassical labour market analysis (cf. Davidson, 1983a; 1983b). Specifically, real wages are *not* viewed as determined by the interaction of demand and supply of labour. It will be seen below that this point is reinforced when imperfect competition is used to characterize the output side.

In Chapter 2 of the *General Theory*, Keynes argued for the rejection of the 'second classical postulate', namely that real wage is equated with marginal disutility of labour: in other words, some workers are forced off their supply curve. But he argued for the continued acceptance of the first postulate, namely the equality between real wage and the marginal product of labour. This implies, in the context of atomistic competition, a negative relationship between real wage and employment. Keynes's response to the empirical doubts cast on the negative sign of that relationship by Dunlop and Tarshis is discussed below.

Keynes clearly argued that workers cannot set real wages: 'There may exist no expedient by which labour as a whole can reduce its *real* wage to a given figure by making revised *money* bargains with entrepreneurs . . . We shall endeavour to show that primarily it is certain other forces which determine the general level of real wages' (CW VII: 13, emphasis in original).

In Chapter 21, Keynes clearly postulated flexible prices, and indeed in some respects prices that adjust instantaneously. Firms equate price with marginal cost by adjustment of price. 'Keynes' treatment of the labor demand function implies that the market for current output is clearing. The *General Theory* seems perfectly consistent on this point, Keynes implies throughout that prices, as contrasted with wages, adjust instantaneously, to bring the quantity demanded into line with the quantity supplied, the latter being fixed in the short run' (Grossman, 1972). 'Indeed there is little doubt that Keynes regarded product prices as highly flexible – he frequently insisted in the *General Theory* that the real wage varied inversely with the level of employment in the short-run (which, given the assumption of a relatively stable *money* wage, implies flexible product prices)' (Brothwell, 1975).

The equality of the real product wage and the marginal productivity of labour clearly implies that price equals wage divided by marginal product of labour. The money wage *w* is set by bargaining (individual or collective) by workers and employers. The marginal product of labour (*mpl*) depends on the volume of employment, which itself is set by the level of aggregate demand. The setting of price leads to the equality between real wage and *mpl*, though this equality has a quite different interpretation from the equality of neoclassical economics between the same variables. The direction of causation in the neoclassical analysis runs (at the level of the firm) from real wage (which is externally set so far as the firm is concerned) to the level of employment, whilst in the analysis of Keynes the direction of causation is essentially reversed (cf. Brothwell, 1988). Further, in the analysis of Keynes, the real wage is effectively set by the producers through their setting of price, and not set in the labour market by the interaction of the demand and supply of labour.

This view of Keynes's *General Theory* can be portrayed as follows. Money wages are set in the labour sector, but the level of money wages is of little direct relevance for the level of employment (reflected in the use of the wage unit as the numeraire).

Chapter 19 analyses the effects of a change in money wages which work through the level of aggregate demand and expectations. The level of employment is closely based on the level of economic activity, which itself is set by the level of aggregate demand. The level of employment determines the marginal productivity of labour, and the equality between real wage and marginal productivity of labour is brought about by price changes. The labour sector is unable to influence the real wage, and in a number of respects is irrelevant for the macroeconomy.

In his review of the *General Theory*, Kalecki gave his own presentation of what he saw to be its key ideas.[4] From the perspective of this chapter, two elements of presentation are particularly relevant, though much of Kalecki's review was a critique of Keynes's approach to investment. The first notable element was the use of a monopoly model where the equilibrium position for the representative firm of marginal value added curve had to be such as to ensure that the volume of profits forthcoming (at the output where marginal value added and marginal cost were equal) matched the volume of capitalists' expenditure (assuming that workers spent all their wage income).

The second element was Kalecki's focus on Keynes's use of the wage-unit as the numeraire: 'This way of accounting for the value of commodities has a deeper significance, because Keynes, in a subsequent part of his theory, shows that a movement of wages induces a proportional movement of prices'. Further, despite some deficiencies in his argument, 'Keynes's statement, that the nominal wage magnitude does not influence, at least directly, the determination of short-period equilibrium, seems correct' (Targetti and Kinda-Hass, 1982). In a footnote Kalecki added that he had also shown the independence of production from the movement of nominal wages in Kalecki (1933).

IV Imperfect competition

There are numerous theories of imperfect competition, incorporating different views on the underlying industrial structure and on the objectives of the firms involved. However there is the common feature that it is possible to derive a non-causal relationship between real wage and employment (though this relationship cannot be unambiguously signed). A firm faces demand and cost conditions, and is envisaged to make interrelated decisions on price, quantity of output and use of inputs. As a result of those decisions, a real product wage is offered by the firm, along with a particular volume of employment, with the expectation of making a particular level of sales. As the level of demand facing a firm is varied, its decisions on price (and thereby on real product wage) and employment (in addition to output, of course) vary in response. Thus a relationship between real product wage and employment can be mapped out, and one such is given in Figure 6.1 by the curve labelled '*p*-curve'. Variations in

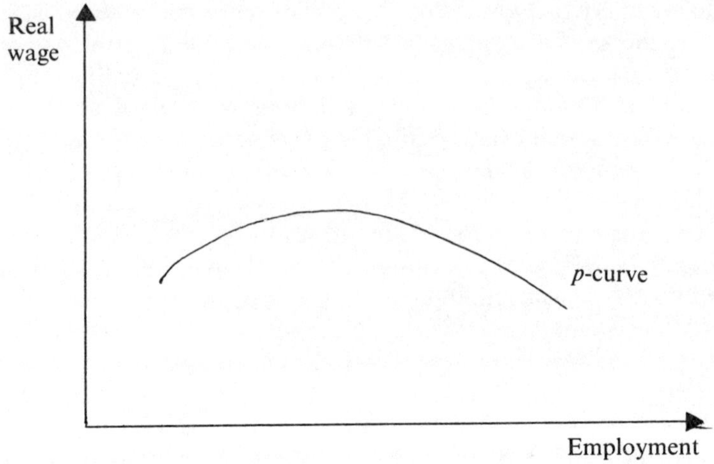

Figure 6.1 The p-*curve*

non-labour costs would shift the curve (for example, higher non-labour costs would shift the curve downwards). Movements along the curve would be generated by variations in the level of demand facing the firm (whether brought about by variations in aggregate demand or by changes in the prices of other products). The slope of the *p*-curve is not restricted to being negative. A positive slope could occur, for example, under profit-maximizing oligopoly from either increasing marginal product of labour or from the degree of monopoly varying negatively with the level of demand. A formal derivation for the case of a monopolist is given in the Appendix.

The status of the relationship between real wage and employment under imperfect competition is essentially the same as that derived by Keynes under atomistic competition. In neither case is there an implication that the relationship corresponds to a demand for labour function, in the sense that the real product wage is not parametric, and to which the firm responds in terms of its employment decision. Firms respond to the demand which they face by deciding price and output (and thereby employment). Movements along the real wage/employment relationship occur through variations in the level of demand facing the firm. A firm could only move along the curve in the absence of the relevant demand variation at the expense of their own objectives, such as profits.

It should be noted that most models of imperfect competition do not involve any notion of price rigidity. Indeed, in most respects, the situation is the exact opposite, namely that it is (implicitly) assumed that prices are speedily adjusted as required. Any constancy of price in the face of demand changes arises from the decisions of firms as to what is in their best interests. This constancy is endogenous rather than exogenous, and particularly important is the intention of firms to meet the demand forthcoming at any price set. There will generally be mistakes over the expectations of demand and difficulties of adjusting production to meet demand, which are assumed to be absorbed by stock changes.

The evidence that prices are cost-determined with little influence from demand has been cited (for example, Malinvaud, 1977) in support of price rigidity. However that evidence can be interpreted as saying that firms adjust prices in the face of cost changes. The equations often relate to quarter-to-quarter price changes, and would not make sense unless firms adjusted prices fairly frequently (that is, more than once a quarter). To say that prices do not respond significantly to variations in demand (whether level or rate of change) is not the same as saying that prices are rigid.

The key feature of imperfect competition in the context of macroeconomic analysis is not that prices are rigid (or even constant), but rather that the pricing decisions of firms set the real product wage. This exactly parallels the approach of Keynes in our interpretation above. In both cases, money wages are used as a key element on which prices are based. In effect, producers have the last call in the determination of the real (product) wage. Clearly Keynes felt that he did not need any assumption of imperfect competition to derive this result, though he did require that output prices adjust rapidly. Keynes did not discuss the process by which prices change, though it is implicit that producers (and not a Walrasian auctioneer) vary prices in line with marginal costs, and that producers have no significant market power.

In many representations of Keynesian economics, perfect competition is used, and as such presents continuing difficulties. The first is that at the level of the individual firm, a variation in the level of aggregate demand can only be exhibited as a variation in price. Simply, when the demand curve facing a firm is horizontal, changes in the level of aggregate demand cannot be represented by other than a vertical shift which is identical with the effect of a price variation. In contrast, in the case of imperfect competition, the demand curve facing a firm has to be positioned by reference to the general level of demand (as well as factors such as other prices) and variations in that level of demand cause the demand curve facing the firm to shift.

The second (and related) difficulty is that the marginal product of labour curve (which is mapped into the demand for labour curve) has an unchanging position (with respect to aggregate demand changes). A variation in the level of aggregate demand has to be shown as leading to a variation in output and employment, and then a move along the marginal product of labour curve through a variation in the real wage to maintain its equality with the marginal product of labour. Thus there is no simple way to represent aggregate demand changes in perfect competition at the level of the firm. The route developed by Patinkin (1965) was for firms to be forced off their (notional) demand for labour curves by an inability to sell the output which would be produced by the employment of labour as indicated by the demand for labour curve. In contrast, in the representation of imperfect competition above, firms are not forced off the *p*-curve but rather move along the *p*-curve as the level of aggregate demand varies. The difficulties of portraying aggregate demand effects on the perfectly competitive firm have added to the apparent problems of deriving a Keynesian macroeconomics with microeconomic foundations.

Two interrelated features of the approach of Keynes derived in the circumstances of polypolistic competition, which are in our view misunderstood when placed in the context of perfect competition and which could be more readily derived from considerations of imperfect competition. The first of these features is that the labour sector and production sector (and, though outside the scope of this chapter, also the financial sector) operate in different ways. Specifically the labour sector is able to set money wages but the production sector sets relative prices and real wages.

The second feature is that the relationship between the real wage and employment is a non-causal one, with the real wage set by producers. There is, though, the difference, further explored below, that under imperfect competition that relationship may be positive or negative.

The early writing of Kahn on imperfect competition (now published in Kahn, 1989) is significant since, as indicated above, Kahn was a major influence on Keynes. There are two aspects of Kahn (1989) which are particularly relevant for our discussion. The first is that his analysis of imperfect competition was set against the background of a general depression and he argued that 'it is however just when the theory of perfect competition appears to break down, namely during a period of slump, that a slight degree of imperfection may have far-reaching effects. Short-time working is no longer the mystery that it was before . . . A substantial improvement in the perfection of the market, while of little consequence to a prosperous industry, would often be devastating in its effects on a depressed industry' (Kahn, 1989: 87). The second is that the cost curves which producers typically face are of an inverted L-shape; that is, constant variable costs up to full capacity. Cost curves of this form clearly pose considerable difficulties for the sustainability of perfect competition. Further, such cost curves would ease the problems (discussed below) of explaining the cyclical movements of real wages, since they do not create any presumption that real wages move countercyclically.

An important, though little discussed, point arising from Kahn (1989) is that perfect competition is incompatible with the general excess capacity observed in a depression. Under perfect competition the level of output of a firm is such that marginal cost is equal to price, provided that price is above average variable cost. Thus, in a depression (reflected in a low price), firms where price is below minimum average variable cost close down whilst the remainder produce with marginal cost above average variable cost, and hence it should be observed that some firms close down and the remainder operate without excess capacity (and with rising average costs).[5] Clearly this assumes that there are variations in the cost conditions of firms, and it also undermines the usefulness of the use of the 'representative' firm. In contrast, under imperfect competition, firms suffer from a fall in demand during a depression but generally remain in business operating with excess capacity (though some may go out of business).

V Real wages and employment

The relationship between real wages and employment suggested by Keynes can be summarized by his conjecture that,

> in the case of changes in the general level of wages, it will be found, I think, that the change in real wages associated with a change in money wages, so far from being usually in the same direction, is almost always in the opposite direction ... This is because, in the short period, falling money wages and rising real wages are each, for independent reasons, likely to accompany decreasing employment; labour being readier to accept wage-cuts when employment is falling off, yet real wages inevitably rising in the same circumstances on account of the increasing marginal return to a given capital equipment when output is diminished. (CW VII: 10)

The empirical work of Dunlop (1938) and Tarshis (1939) cast doubt on Keynes's proposition.[6] Dunlop suggested that the English experience was that 'increase in wage rates have usually been associated with increased real wage rates, while decreases in wage rates have equally often been associated with a rise or fall in real wage rates'. Also 'wage rates have risen or fallen (almost equally often) at relatively low levels of unemployment. While *changes* in employment are more closely associated with changes in wage rates, important deviations remain. There seems to be no simple relation – and especially of a causal nature – adequate to summarize the two movements without very wide margins of error' (1938: 432). He gave a number of reasons as to why Keynes's expectations had not been fulfilled, of which two are notable for our purposes. The first was that 'the extent to which cost curves are rising, except at the very peak of the boom, has probably been over-emphasised'. The second was that 'removing Mr. Keynes' assumption of perfect competition is more significant' and Dunlop argued that the degree of monopoly tends to rise in the slump, thereby reducing real wages.

Tarshis (1939) concluded that empirically 'there is a rather high direct or positive association between changes in money wages and changes in real wages'. It is interesting to note that he argued that Keynes's contrary predictions were based on three assumptions which were not realistic, of which the two relevant here are rising marginal costs and the constancy of degree of competition over the trade cycle. But these arguments were directed towards the relationship between the movements of real wages and those of money wages. Similar findings have been found subsequently, and many would regard the absence of a negative real wage/employment relationship as a stylized fact (see Michie, 1987: Chapter 3).

Whilst Keynes had 'always regarded decreasing physical returns in the short period as one of the very few incontrovertible propositions of our miserable subject!' (CW XIV: 190), there is a sense in which diminishing returns were not an integral part of the *General Theory*. Indeed it could be argued that a rejection of diminishing returns and the associated negative relationship between real wages and employment would have enhanced his approach, though in order to do so he would have had to invoke imperfect competition. The derivation of a non-negative relationship between real wages and employment would surely have helped to reinforce the rejection of the real wage/employment relationship as a demand for labour curve. If we follow Brothwell (1988) in seeing Keynes's acceptance of the first classical postulate (equality between marginal product of labour and the real wage) as opening the way for the neoclassical synthesis, then the use by Keynes of imperfect competition rather than perfect competition might have had a profound effect on the evolution of macroeconomic analysis.

Keynes (CW VII: 401) indicated that the generally positive relationship between real wages and output/employment found by Dunlop, Tarshis and others would have strengthened rather than weakened his argument, and 'it would be possible to simplify considerably the more complicated version of my fundamental explanation which I have expounded in my "General Theory" ', and in a footnote indicated that Chapter 2 would be in most need of revision (a task which was not carried through as far as we are aware). Keynes argued that a positive relationship between real wages and employment strengthens the case for effective demand being the cause of employment variations, and considerably weakens the case for those who argue that public investment and similar policies 'produced their

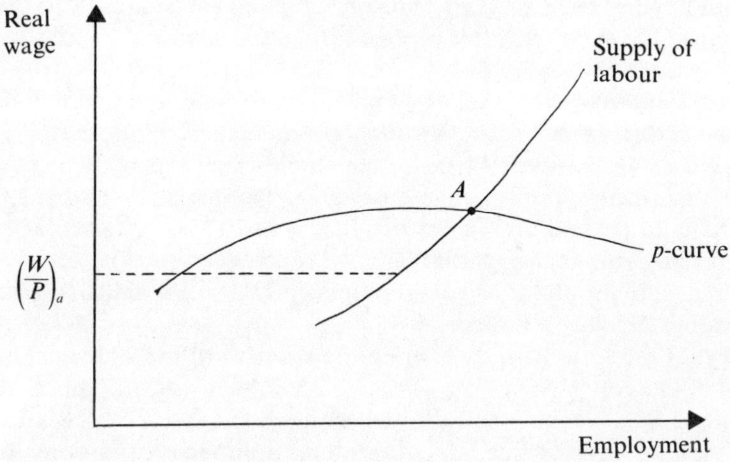

Figure 6.2 Employment and unemployment under imperfect competition

effects by deceiving, so to speak, the working class into accepting a lower real wage, effecting by this means the same favourable influence on employment which . . . would have resulted from a more direct attack on real wages . . .' (CW VII: 401). Finally, Keynes said that he was 'comforted by the fact that their [Dunlop, Tarshis and Kalecki] conclusions tend to confirm the idea that the causes of short-period fluctuations are to be found in changes in the demand for labour, and not in changes in its real-supply price' (CW VII: 411).

The use of imperfect competition in the produce market undermines the notion of the real wages and employment being determined by a labour market operating according to Walrasian principles. The real wage/employment relationship (the *p*-curve in Figure 6.1) derived from the producer's decision making does not have the status of a demand for labour curve. If the *p*-curve is given the status of a demand for labour curve, and many have committed such an error, then there are possibilities of instability in the labour market. The aggregate real wage/employment relationship, based on the corresponding firm-level relationship would have the same status, but there is little we can say about its shape. For simplicity its shape is taken to be an inverted U-shape, though more complex shapes would tend to reinforce our conclusions. In Figure 6.2 an aggregate *p*-curve is combined with a supply-of-labour curve, and it can be seen that, at a real wage of $(w/p)_a$, there may be excess supply of labour but the real wage is below the 'equilibrium' level. The use of imperfect competition strengthens the view that the labour sector cannot be treated like a market with well-defined demand and supply schedules, with real wages responding to excess demand. It can be noted as an aside that the inverted U-shaped 'demand' schedule is not restricted to labour but could apply to any input.

In this approach the level of employment in equilibrium would depend on the industrial structure through the influence of the latter on the position of the *p*-curve.[7] In each such equilibrium, unemployment would appear to be voluntary, though the degree of employment and unemployment would depend on the industrial structure. This analysis, of course, ignores any role for aggregate demand, and there is no reason to think that the 'equilibrium' levels of employment real wages could be sustained in aggregate demand terms.

Keynes raised some questions on the strength of the statistical conclusions of Dunlop and Tarshis, and suggested that a suitable generalization would be that, 'for fluctuations within the range which has been usual in the periods investigated which seldom approach conditions of full employment, short-period changes in real wages are usually so small compared with the changes in other factors that we shall not often go far wrong if we treat real wages as substantially constant in the short period . . .' (CW VII: 403). Further Keynes pointed out that the sign of the relationship between real wages and employment (as that between average cost and output) is likely to depend on the average level of employment and output over the relevant data period. However this was rather different in tone from his earlier view, expressed in an interchange with Ohlin, that 'employment never did fall materially without a rise in the real hourly wage. Is not this one of the best established of statistical conclusions?' (CW XIV: 190). Ohlin responded by saying that he had 'talked this matter over with some Americans who know a lot about facts and they agree that in a recovery from a severe depression employment often grows without any fall in the real wage' (CW XIV: 201).

Thus, in response to the empirical work on real and money wages mentioned above, Keynes acknowledged the possible role of imperfect competition. Further there is some indication (for example, in the quotations used above), that Keynes saw imperfect competition as strengthening his approach, but not fundamental to it.

VI Should Keynes have used imperfect competition?

It is well known that Walrasian general equilibrium analysis rests on perfect competitive assumptions and leads to an outcome of full employment. The 'imperfectionist' approach (Eatwell and Milgate, 1983) seeks to identify some features of the real world which are absent from general equilibrium analysis and argues that such features are the cause of unemployment in the real world. A particular example of this is the case of imperfect competition, where the terminology rather suggests an imperfectionist interpretation:

> Keynes was quite explicit about all of these [Keynesian market failures] except the fifth [imperfections of competition]. Kaldor makes that last one, imperfect competition, the sole genesis of macroeconomic difficulties. Pure competition implies full employment equilibrium, he says, while imperfect competition implies Keynesian macroeconomics. He therefore blames Keynes for failing to see, or at least to say clearly, that his *General Theory* requires microfoundations encompassing increasing returns to scale and consequently monopoly, oligopoly, or monopolistic competition. (Tobin, 1983)

Weitzman (1982) sought to argue that imperfect competition (arising from the presence of increasing returns to scale) was the underlying reason for the occurrence of unemployment. There was no suggestion in the original article that his analysis was closely linked with that of Keynes. Nevertheless some have seen his analysis as providing important microeconomic underpinnings for Keynes

> that 'money wage flexibility is not capable of maintaining full employment'. However the argument leading up to this conclusion is by no means as decisive and clear-cut as the conclusion itself and no doubt Keynes would have been very grateful for Mr Weitzman's support had it been available to him – the more so since the latter's argument (unlike Keynes's) relates to *real* wages and not merely to money wages. (Kaldor, 1983)[8]

The interest generated by Weitzman (1982) revived the question as to whether Keynes would have been well advised to have based his analysis on imperfect competition rather than on atomistic competition. The thrust of our argument (elaborated in Sawyer, 1990/91) is that a shift from atomistic competition in the output sector to imperfect competition would not in itself lead from a full employment outcome to one of unemployment of labour. In terms of Figure 6.2, variations in the degree of competition would lead to shifts in the *p*-curve. But, in each case, the intersection between the *p*-curve and the supply of labour curve would provide a position of full employment. It should be noted, though, that there is no guarantee, in any of these cases, that such an outcome could be sustained in terms of aggregate demand. Economies with an imperfect competitive structure would behave in many ways which are different from economies with a perfect competitive structure (at least according to our theories, since there must be substantial doubts as to whether a perfectly competitive economy has ever been observed). In particular, we would expect that the distribution of income, decisions on savings and on investment would be different (under imperfect competition as compared with perfect competition). The equality between *ex ante* savings and investment would still determine the level of economic activity (a point made by Robinson, 1933: Chapter 27) and the nature of the industrial structure would only influence that level through its impact on savings and investment decisions – not through price/output decisions. Further, as argued above, the modelling of the labour sector is different since, under imperfect competition, it can no longer be argued that the real wage/employment relationship is a negative causal one.

When seeking to answer the question of whether Keynes would have been well advised to have used imperfect competition rather than perfect competition, it is necessary to ask what Keynes's purpose was. It can be argued that he sought to show that unemployment would arise even with atomistic competition.

> Even though the small firm is no longer the dominant market form, it is well that Keynes took it as his model, for in doing so he met the neoclassical theory on its own ground. Only the assumption of perfect knowledge was changed. Those who wish to claim greater realism for the theory by introducing monopolistic elements into it do not seem to recognise that by doing so they undermine the power of Keynes's argument: Keynes showed that, even *taking the assumption* of neoclassical analysis, he could produce non-neoclassical results. Monopoly elements then strengthen the argument but the argument does not depend on them. (Chick, 1983, emphasis in original)

This line of argument suggests that Keynes did not think that imperfect competition was in any sense intrinsic to his explanation of unemployment and, further, that Keynes was concerned with establishing some theoretical proposition (that is, that unemployment can occur under atomistic competition) rather than with the development of an analysis based on realistic assumptions.

It can be further argued that the essence of Keynes's 'message' for economic policy was the role of aggregate demand in the determination of the level of economic activity. There are, of course, many other themes in the *General Theory*. The role of aggregate demand, the focus on quantity adjustment to bring planned savings and planned investment into equality and so on arise in a monetary/financial economy but not in a barter economy. Thus it is important whether an economy is a monetary or a barter one but for some purposes it may not matter whether the economy is atomistic or imperfect competitive.[9] However, as indicated above, the nature of the industrial structure is of relevance for issues such as the sign of the real wage/employment relation, and the distribution of output between firms. Industrial structure, including that of the financial sector, would also be seen to be relevant for the determination of investment and savings.

The approach of Keynes was subject to considerable simplification and misrepresentation; in connection with this chapter the misrepresentation of particular relevance concerns price and wage rigidity. In the second half of the 1930s, theories of imperfect competition were relatively novel, and there is clearly a strong possibility that Keynes's underemployment equilibrium would have been represented in arising from imperfect competition, rather than from a lack of effective demand.

> Why did Keynes not exploit the microeconomic revolution fomented in this very town [Cambridge] by his own colleagues and disciples in the same years he was revolutionizing macroeconomics? That certainly is a puzzle, as Kaldor says. To try to win the game on the other side's home field and with their book of rules was a mistake. But faithful neoclassicals on both sides of the Atlantic had no compunctions dismissing imperfect competition from microeconomic theory, as a trivial exception proving the rule of pure competition. They probably would not have found Keynes's macroeconomics any more appealing if he had based it on imperfect competition. (Tobin, 1983)

Some support for Tobin's view is provided by the way in which Kalecki's macroeconomic analysis was generally ignored by mainstream economists. As noted in note 9, Kalecki's initial macroeconomic analysis implicitly assumed 'free competition'. However the work of Kalecki available in English from the late 1930s onwards was firmly based on imperfect competition.

VII Concluding remarks

The general line of argument of this chapter has been that Keynes did not use and did not need to use any notions of imperfect competition to derive his major conclusions on the causes of unemployment. We have argued that some of his conclusions can be more easily derived in the context of imperfect competition than in that of atomistic competition. In particular, the idea that there are significant differences between the output sector and the labour sector, with the output price effectively settling the real wage, can now be seen as readily derived from theories of imperfect competition, whereas the corresponding derivation for perfect competition has not found widespread appeal. Further, as suggested by Kahn, imperfect competition is required to explain why firms work with excess capacity during recession (rather than the reduction in output being met by some firms closing and others operating above capacity). Finally, as indicated above, when the levels of output and employment are viewed as essentially determined by the equality between *ex ante* savings and investment, then the industrial structure is relevant (for the levels of employment) only in so far as it influences savings and investment. A recent statement of an emerging conventional wisdom is that 'it has come to be accepted that it is impossible to explain the constraints that give rise to

Keynesian macro results without recourse to theories of imperfect or monopolistic competition' (Collard, 1990). The line of argument of this chapter is to reject that conventional wisdom, but to suggest that Keynes's theory would have been much enhanced by the use of imperfect competition.

Notes

1. I am grateful to Philip Arestis, Victoria Chick and Bill Gerrard for comments and discussion. This chapter was presented as a paper at the Review of Political Economy conference August 1990, and I have benefited from comments made by participants there.
2. This suggestion could be seen as a rationalist reconstruction of history. Marris (1991) suggests that Keynes's lack of use of imperfect competition arose for other motives, such as jealousy.
3. Chamberlin and Robinson are regarded here as the originators of theories of imperfect competition. Cournot, Bertrand and others pre-date them, particularly in discussion of oligopoly. However, for our purposes, it is the interest generated by Chamberlin, Robinson *et alia* in the early 1930s which is particularly relevant.
4. Kalecki's review of the *General Theory* has been translated into English with a commentary as Targetti and Kinda-Hass (1982) and reprinted in Osiatynski (1990).
5. 'The importance of the dissertation rests largely on the analysis of the influence of imperfection of the market on the manner in which, at a time of depression, an industry's output is distributed between the individual firms. I opened Chapter 7 by asking why most of the firms in the cotton-spinning industry, in which the degree of competition was regarded as high, work short-time, instead of those enjoying the lowest prime costs working to capacity. While the obvious answer is "imperfection of the market", until 1930 it was seldom given' (Kahn, 1989: xx).
6. For discussion between Dunlop and Keynes see CW XXIX: 282–8, and for a recent discussion see Michie (1987).
7. The usual static analysis would suggest that the *p*-curve shifts to the left as the degree of monopoly rises, leading to lower real wages and employment. But such analysis assumes that the cost and demand conditions facing the producers are unchanged, whereas it is expected that both cost and demand conditions depend on the industrial structure.
8. See *Journal of Post Keynesian Economics*, 1985 for a critical symposium on Weitzman (1982); see also Sawyer (1992).
9. Kalecki, in his essay of 1933 (published in full in English for the first time in Osiatynski, 1990), which many have seen as anticipating some of the key insights of Keynes, 'tacitly assumed that free competition rules unhindered in our economic system'. In the last two pages of the essay he considered the difference between a partially cartelized system and a free competition one. Kalecki modelled cartels as imposing a constant profit margin, and likely to exacerbate the extent of fluctuations in output and employment. But, as Osiatynski says in his editorial notes, Kalecki did not view the 'mechanism of the business cycle' as being different under cartelization (as compared with free competition).

References

Brothwell, J. F. (1975), 'A Simple Keynesian Response to Leijonhufvud', *Bulletin of Economic Research*, **27**, 3–21.

Brothwell, J. F. (1988), 'The *General Theory* After Fifty Years: Why Are We Not All Keynesians Now?' in J. V. Hillard (ed.), *J. M. Keynes in Retrospect*, Aldershot: Edward Elgar.

Chamberlin, E. (1933), *The Theory of Monopolistic Competition*, Cambridge, Mass.: Harvard University Press.

Chick, V. (1983), *Macroeconomics After Keynes*, Oxford: Philip Allan.

Collard, D. (1990), 'Unemployment', in J. Creedy (ed.), *Foundations of Economic Thought*, Oxford: Basil Blackwell.

Davidson, P. (1983a), 'The Dubious Labour Market Analysis in Meltzer's Restatement', *Journal of Economic Literature,* **21**, 52–6.

Davidson, P. (1983b), 'The Marginal Product Curve is Not the Demand for Labor Curve and Lucas's Labor Supply Function is Not the Supply Curve for Labor in the Real World', *Journal of Post Keynesian Economics*, **6**, 105–17.

Dunlop, J. (1938), 'The Movement of Real and Money Wage Rates', *Economic Journal*, **48**, 413–34.

Eatwell, J. and M. Milgate (1983) (eds), *Keynes's Economics and the Theory of Value and Distribution*, London: Duckworth.

Grossman, H. (1972), 'Was Keynes a Keynesian?', *Journal of Economic Literature*, **10**, 26–30.

Hall, R. and C. Hitch (1939), 'Price Theory and Business Behaviour', *Oxford Economic Papers,* **2**, 12–33. (Reprinted in Sawyer, 1988).

Kahn, R. (1984), *The Making of Keynes' General Theory*, Cambridge: Cambridge University Press.

Kahn, R. (1989), *The Economics of the Short Period*, London: Macmillan.

Kaldor, N. (1983), 'Keynesian Economics After Fifty Years', in D. Worswick and J. Trevithick (eds), *Keynes and the Modern World*, Cambridge: Cambridge University Press.

Kalecki, M. (1933), *Proba Teorii Koniunktury*, Warsaw Institute of Research on Business Cycles and Prices (English version appears as Chapter 1 of Kalecki, 1971).

Kalecki, M. (1938), 'The Determinants of Distribution of the National Income', *Econometrica*, **6**, 97–112.

Kalecki, M. (1941), 'A Theorem on Technical Progress', *Review of Economic Studies*, **8**, 178–84.

Kalecki, M. (1971), *Selected Essays on the Dynamics of the Capitalist Economy*, 1933–70, Cambridge: Cambridge University Press.

Leijonhufvud, A. (1968), *On Keynesian Economics and the Economics of Keynes: A Study in Monetary Theory*, London: Oxford University Press.

Lekachman, R. (1977), 'The Radical Keynes', in R. Skidelsky (ed.), *The End of the Keynesian Era*, London: Macmillan.

Malinvaud, E. (1977), *The Theory of Unemployment Reconsidered*, Oxford: Basil Blackwell.

Marris, R. (1991), *Reconstructing Keynesian Economics with Imperfect Competition*, Aldershot: Edward Elgar.

Means, G. C. (1935), 'Industrial Prices and Their Relative Flexibility', Washington: US Senate Document 13, 74th Congress, 1st Session.

Means, G. C. (1936), 'Notes on Inflexible Prices', *American Economic Review* (Suppl.), **26**, 23–35.

Michie, J. (1987), *Wages in the Business Cycle: An Empirical and Methodological Analysis*, London: Frances Pinter.

Osiatynski, J. (1990) (ed.), *Collected Works of Michal Kalecki, vol. 1 Capitalism: Business Cycles and Full Employment*, Oxford: Clarendon Press.

Patinkin, D. (1965), *Money, Interest and Power: An Integration of Monetary and Value Theory*, Evanston, Illinois: Row Peterson.

Robinson, J. (1933), *The Economics of Imperfect Competition*, London: Macmillan.

Robinson, J. (1976), 'Michal Kalecki: A Neglected Prophet', *New York Review of Books*, 4 March 1976.

Sawyer, M. (1988) (ed.), *Post Keynesian Economics*, Aldershot: Edward Elgar.

Sawyer, M. (1990/91), 'On Imperfect Competition and Unemployment', in A. del Monte (ed.), *Recent Developments in the Theory of Industrial Organization*, London: Macmillan.

Sawyer, M. (1992), 'On the Relationship Between the Origins of Post Keynesian Pricing Theory and Macroeconomics', in P. Arestis and V. Chick (eds), *Recent Developments in Post Keynesian Economics*, Aldershot: Edward Elgar.

Schumpeter, J. (1954), *History of Economic Analysis*, London: Allen & Unwin.

Sraffa, P. (1926), 'The Laws of Returns Under Competitive Conditions', *Economic Journal*, **36**, 535–50.
Sweezy, P. (1939), 'Conditions of Demand Under Oligopoly', *Journal of Political Economy*, **47**, 568–73.
Targetti, F. and B. Kinda-Hass (1982), 'Kalecki's Review of Keynes' *General Theory*', *Australian Economic Papers*, **21**, 244–60.
Tarshis, L. (1939), 'Changes in Real and Money Wages', *Economic Journal*, **49**, 150–4.
Tobin, J. (1983), 'Comment', in D. Worswick and J. Trevithick (eds), *Keynes and the Mordern World*, Cambridge: Cambridge University Press.
Weitzman, M. (1982), 'Increasing Returns and the Foundations of Unemployment Theory', *Economic Journal*, **92**, 781–809.
Worswick, D. and J. Trevithick (1983) (eds), *Keynes and the Modern World*, Cambridge: Cambridge University Press.

Appendix: Derivation of the *p*-curve for the case of monopoly

Let the demand facing a monopolist be $Q^d = (p/r)^{-k}D^b$ where p is the price of output of monopolist, r is an index of substitutes and D is a measure of real level of aggregate demand. The production function is taken for convenience as homothetic transformation of a Cobb–Douglas function, so that $Q^s = f(L^c M^{1-c})$ where L is a measure of labour input, M of material input. The price of material input is m and wage of labour is w. The decision variables for the firm are taken as L and M, with p and Q derivable as a consequence of decisions on L and M. The relationship between L and M is given by:

$$M = ((1-c)w/cm)\cdot L \qquad (6A.1)$$

It is then possible to derive the equation for labour demand in terms of exogenous variables (w, m, r and D) as:

$$(k-1/k)\cdot D^{b/k}\cdot c\cdot f(X)\cdot f'(X)^{-1/k}\cdot((1-c)w/cm)^{(1-c)} = (w/r) \qquad (6A.2)$$

where $X = L((1-c)w/cm)^{1-c}$

There are numerous ways of expressing the employment decision which involves endogenous variables, and we require one which involves the real product wage, which is:

$$(k-1/k), f'(X)\cdot c\cdot((1-c)w/cm)^{(1-c)} = w/p \qquad (6A.3)$$

The implied relationship between real product wage and labour employment in (6A.3) can be positive or negative, depending upon the sign of the second derivative of f. The relationship is illustrated in Figure 6.1 with the curve labelled *p*-curve (drawn for a specific value of w/m).

It can be seen from (6A.2) that the employment (and, behind that, output) decision depends on price of substitutes (r) and the level of aggregate demand. But in this example the employment decision is uniquely linked with the real product wage of the firm.

It would be a complex aggregation problem to move from (6A.3) to the comparable aggregate relationship (as drawn in Figure 6.1). Apart from the non-linearities involved in (6A.3), there is also the complication of the interdependence of prices across industries. Informally we can argue as follows. For given real aggregate demand, money wages and input prices, consider an equilibrium set of output prices. Those output prices will then set workers' real wages as well as each firm's real product wage. At the same time as those prices are established, output and employment will also be established. The relationship between real wage and employment is then reflected as the *p*-curve in Figure 6.1.

In this appendix the simplest case of a monopoly has been taken. However the case for oligopoly is essentially similar.

7 Keynes, market forms and competition[1]

Amitava Dutt

I Introduction

What did Keynes assume in the *General Theory* regarding market form in developing his theory of unemployment equilibrium in the short period? What should he have assumed? These are questions that continue to be discussed and hotly debated in the literature on Keynes. One view is that he assumed perfect competition to stay as close as possible to neoclassical (or, as Keynes called it, classical) theory. Another view is that his notion of competition was a Marshallian one or one that introduced sales constraints for firms, and quite different from the standard neoclassical notion of perfect competition. Yet another is that, even though Keynes was not quite aware of it, it is necessary to assume imperfect competition to have a consistent theory of unemployment equilibrium.

The purpose of this chapter is to discuss the nature of market form assumed by Keynes, to show that his formal analysis in the *General Theory* was a form of competition quite close to – but not the same as – neoclassical perfect competition, and to appraise critically some alternative views on Keynes's method in this regard.

There are at least three reasons for examining the question of market form in the *General Theory*. First, it is a worthwhile task to assess the relative merits of the large variety of conflicting views on this controversial subject. Second, the question is connected to the issue as to whether Keynes's theory was truly revolutionary, since his predecessors already realized that unemployment could exist in the presence of market imperfections:[2] if for Keynes unemployment is due to imperfect competition there is little theoretically new in the *General Theory*, and that presumably makes it less important. Finally, and of greatest importance, it is worth knowing whether the existence of unemployment in market economies is explained by market imperfections which can in principle be removed, or if it is connected with the more fundamental aspects of capitalism which are intrinsic to it.

The rest of this chapter proceeds as follows. Section II discusses the evidence on what market form Keynes assumed in the *General Theory*, by examining the statements made by Keynes in the book and in later discussions. Section III discusses the question of the consistency of Keynes's theory with some form of competition and shows that a notion of competition consistent with Keynes's theory which is close to, but not the same as, perfect competition, can be made precise. Section IV critically discusses some influential alternative views on the market form in Keynes's theory. The chapter ends with a brief summary of conclusions.

II Keynes on market forms

In his summary of the general theory of employment in Chapter 18 of the *General Theory* Keynes writes that 'we take as given . . . the degree of competition' (CW VII: 245) and this is repeated in the preface to the French edition (CW VII: xxxiv). These statements suggest that he was assuming *any given* degree of competition, and not a particular degree, perfect or otherwise.

Elsewhere in the book he is a little more explicit. First, when he discusses the first postulate of the 'classical' theory of employment he states it, in italics, as 'The wage is equal to the marginal product of labour'. While he criticizes the second classical postulate, he states that 'we shall maintain the first postulate as heretofore, subject only to the same qualifications as in the classical theory' (CW VII: 17). He adds, however, that this is 'subject . . . to the qualification that the equality may be disturbed, in accordance with certain principles, if competition and market are imperfect' (CW VII: 5). Second, in presenting the theory of effective demand in Chapter 3, Keynes does not use any particular assumption on market form, but states that 'the marginal productivity of labour . . . determines the real wage' (CW VII: 29). While there is no statement that the real wage is equal to the marginal product of labour, in the absence of a statement of other determinants it would not be outlandish to infer that this is in fact what Keynes implies. Third, in presenting the algebra of the employment function in Chapter 20 Keynes writes down some equations 'provided we can assume that the price is equal to the marginal cost' (CW VII: 283). In all these cases it appears that he is stating conditions that are relevant for a price-taking world of perfect competition, but adding that the conditions have to be modified if market imperfections are introduced.

It seems fair to conclude that Keynes probably had some type of perfectly competitive market form in mind when developing the formal structure of his analysis, but thought that his theory was consistent with imperfectly competitive market forms as well.[3] An important implication of this is that the theory of effective demand does not *require* that competition be imperfect; it is quite consistent with perfect competition at least in the sense that firms are price-takers.

That Keynes did not think that imperfect competition was essential to his theory of unemployment equilibrium is also revealed by some later discussions. Ohlin wrote, in an unpublished article, regarding the relationship between the real wage and marginal product, that Keynes had not been 'radical enough in freeing himself from the conventional assumptions. When reading this book one sometimes wonders whether he never discussed imperfect competition with Mrs. Robinson' (CW XIV: 196). In response, Keynes writes, 'I have not been able to make out here what you are driving at. The reference to imperfect competition is very perplexing. I cannot see how on earth it comes in. Mrs. Robinson, I may mention, read my proofs without discovering any connection' (CW XIV: 190). Later on Keynes retracted his earlier views and came to re-evaluate the importance of imperfect competition after the demonstration by Dunlop (1938) and Tarshis (1939) and others that the real wage moved in a procyclical manner, unlike the anticyclical manner that the real wage–marginal product equality implied (see Kregel, 1985). However this has no bearing on the question as to whether Keynes thought that perfect competition in the sense of price-taking behaviour was inconsistent with his *General Theory* analysis. Kaldor (1983: 14) writes, albeit critically, that 'it would be an exaggeration to say that Keynes even then showed full awareness of the critical importance of increasing returns and imperfect competition to his general theory of employment'. He continues that 'Joan Robinson . . . tried to interest Keynes in imperfect competition for many years, and its relevance to the problem of the insufficiency of effective demand – but she never succeeded.'

Though Keynes does not provide any reason as to why he was not emphasizing the role of imperfect competition, and in fact probably had the perfectly competitive model in mind, it is not difficult to speculate why he chose to do this. If his objective in the book was to establish the existence of unemployment equilibrium, and convince economists trained in the neoclassical tradition of this, it was tactically wise for him to develop an analysis which departed as little as possible from the neoclassical model of perfect competition.[4] An alternative view – that Keynes did not know much about imperfect competition – must be rejected, since he was aware of the work of Sraffa, Shove and Kahn in this area, and was also a reader, for Macmillan, for Robinson's *The Economics of Imperfect Competition*.[5]

There are, however, some obvious objections to the argument that Keynes's approach was consistent with perfect competition. First, Keynes appears to believe that economic agents – including producing firms – are surrounded by pervasive uncertainty. Keynes assumes not only that firms do not have knowledge of markets in the future, when they will be selling output produced using capital invested at present, but that they do not know the market price at which they will sell their current output before they plan how much to produce. Keynes thus views firms as making decisions in historical time in which the future in unknown (see Chick, 1983). All this suggests that Keynes is departing from one of the standard prerequisites of perfect competition, namely perfect knowledge or perfect information. Moreover, since firms do not know the market price when they decide how much to produce, they cannot be 'price-takers', another notion connected with perfect competition (Chick, 1983). Second, Keynes writes that 'short-term expectations' refer to the 'expectations as to the cost of output on various possible scales and expectations as to the sale-proceeds of this output' (CW VII: 47, see also 24). This suggests that Keynes believes that individual firms can guess how much they will earn from their sales, which appears to contradict the requirement of perfect competition that firms must expect to sell any amount that they want to.

III Keynes and competition

We have argued that Keynes believed that his analysis of unemployment equilibrium did not require any form of market imperfection, but that his theory departed in some obvious way from the neoclassical assumption of perfect competition. This section will explore what notion of competition Keynes may have had in mind, and examine whether his analysis of unemployment equilibrium is consistent with that notion. To do so we first examine the meaning of perfect competition, then present our interpretation of Keynes's theory of unemployment, and finally discuss how Keynes's notion of competition departed from perfect competition.

Perfect competition

As Stigler (1957) has argued, it is difficult – if not impossible – to give a complete listing of necessary and sufficient conditions for the existence of perfect competition. Nevertheless a perusal of current textbooks on neo-classical microeconomic theory suggests that the conditions implicit in the notion of perfect competition are as follows:

1. 'Small' buyers and sellers in the sense that each expects to be able to buy or sell *any* amount it wants to at the going market price.
2. Homogeneity of products in the sense that all consumers regard the product sold in the market to be the same.
3. Perfect information.
4. Perfect mobility of all resources, buyers and sellers.
5. Absence of collusion.

These conditions have two important and separate implications. First, individual firms act as price-takers. Second, competitive equilibrium implies that normal profits are driven to zero. Robinson (1934) points out a number of problems with the second implication but, fortunately for us, it is relevant only for the Marshallian long period, in which firms can change their stocks of capital and enter and exit industries, where Keynes confines his attention to the Marshallian short period, in which firms take as given their stocks of capital. Since Keynes does not require such a stringent notion of competition, it would seem that his theory would require a less stringent list of conditions than those listed above. However all these conditions are still required for the first implication; it is only that each one of the conditions becomes less restrictive. For instance, while we can dispense with the requirement that firms be perfectly mobile between industries and that capital be perfectly mobile between uses (since such mobility only occurs in the long period), as we shall see, we still require consumers to be perfectly mobile as between firms.

Regarding the first implication – with which we are concerned here – it needs to be emphasized that the firm is *choosing* to be a price-taker, and that it is doing so because of the five conditions stated above, and because it maximizes its profits.[6] Condition (3) implies that the firm knows the market price. The firm will not, acting individually – which is guaranteed by condition (5) – wish to charge a higher price than the market price, because by condition (3) buyers will know that it is doing so, by condition (2) they would rather buy from some other firm selling at the market price, and by condition (4) these buyers would actually move to the other firms. The firm will not also charge a price lower than the market price because by condition (1) it expects to sell all it wants to at the going price, so that it would not be profit-maximizing to charge a lower price.

This implication has some further implications. First, profit-maximizing firms will set their real wage equal to the marginal product of labour (assuming additionally that production functions are neoclassical) and that price will be equal to marginal cost. Second, firms will not hold unintended inventories. This follows from the fact that firms will sell all that they intended to sell when they made their sales and production decisions, since their expectation that they can sell all they want to at the going price makes it irrational (in the sense of not being profit-maximizing) for them not to sell everything. The price will adjust to clear the market.[7]

An interpretation of Keynes's analysis

In the *General Theory* Keynes appears to adhere to some of these implications – such as assuming that the real wage equals the marginal product of labour – but departs from other aspects of competition, for example, by introducing uncertainty. To obtain a clear idea of what exactly Keynes was assuming we first present an interpretation of the relevant aspects of Keynes's theory of effective demand.

To rule out aggregation problems (which are separate from the problem of market structure) assume that all firms in the economy are identical, so that we can think in terms of a representative firm. This firm has a production function given by

$$Y = F(N) \tag{7.1}$$

where Y is output, N is labour employed, and where technology and the stock of capital is assumed to be given since we confine our attention to the short period.

The firm expects to sell all it can at the going market price, but does not know what this price will be after it makes its production and employment plans and is ready to sell. Keynes assumes that the firm forms short-period expectations regarding this price; we denote this by P_e. We may then derive the curve which denotes the sales proceeds that the firm expects to get for each level of employment it offers. Since it expects to sell all it produces, the expected proceeds as a function of employment are

$$E(N) = P_e F(N) \tag{7.2}$$

which is fixed for a given level of short-period expectations.[8] Keynes calls it the aggregate demand function: 'let D be the proceeds which entrepreneurs expect to receive from the employment of N men, the relationship between D and N being written D = f(N), which can be called the *aggregate demand function*' (CW VII: 25, emphasis in original). Since Keynes refers to a different function by the same name, we will call this the expected proceeds function, and its curve, the expected proceeds curve.

The firm also maximizes profits in the short period in making its employment plan. Keynes introduces the aggregate supply function using this assumption, which shows the sales proceeds just necessary to make the firm offer a certain amount of employment. If the firm faces a given price, P, and a given wage, W, then the profit-maximizing firm would choose to employ labour up to the point at which

$$W/P = F'(N) \tag{7.3}$$

where $F' \equiv dF/dN$. Thus the proceeds which would be just sufficient to make the firm employ a particular level of employment, N, is

$$Z(N) = PY = WF(N)/F'(N) \tag{7.4}$$

which we interpret to be Keynes's aggregate supply function.[9]

For any given price expectation (and hence an expected proceeds curve), the intersection of the expected proceeds and aggregate supply curves will determine the amount of labour that the firms will hire. From (7.2) and (7.4) it can be checked that this point satisfies the condition

$$W/P_e = F'(N) \tag{7.5}$$

which is the condition that the firm maximizes expected profits, given P_e, W and the production function.

There is no guarantee, of course, that the firm's short-period expectations will be realized once it has employed this amount of labour and produced a certain amount of output. Keynes is not very clear on what exactly happens after production takes place, although he does say that actual sales depend on the amount of demand from households and firms in the form of consumption and investment demand. Consumption demand rises with the level of employment, while investment demand depends on the firm's long-period expectations. Given long-period expectations, as long as actual demand responds to price we can find the price which will clear the market, assuming that firms wish to sell all that they produce (so that they plan to hold no inventories) and the price varies to clear the market.[10] This price, which depends on consumption and investment behaviour and the level of output produced by firms (given their short-period expectations), will in general be different from P_e. In the next 'period' the firm will revise its expectations, and ultimately, short-period equilibrium will be determined when the actual P will be equal to P_e, where the firm not only maximizes profits given its expected price and sell its entire output, but its short-period expectations are also realized. Note that in this equilibrium the real wage is equal to the marginal product of labour, since (7.5) is satisfied, and also $P = P_e$. Further, since the supply of labour may be higher than the resulting amount of employment, the short-period equilibrium position may be one with unemployment.[11]

Keynes's notion of competition

From this interpretation of Keynes's theory we can distil the assumptions about market structure Keynes was implicitly making, assuming ours to be a correct interpretation. We may proceed by discussing the *minimum* amendments to the five postulates of perfect competition enumerated above. We find that there is nothing in Keynes's discussion which makes him contradict postulates (1), (2), (4) and (5), at least in their less restrictive forms required for short-period analysis which were required to ensure that firms were price-takers. However Keynes cannot be assuming price-taking behaviour in the usual sense since, at the time that producers make their production plans, they do not know the product price, simply because the product market has not yet opened, and the firms do not know the future. Thus Keynes is clearly departing from postulate (3). However the departure is very limited in extent: firms do not have perfect knowledge of the future (what we call temporal information), but they continue to have perfect knowledge of the present (what we call spatial information). Regarding the future, they form short- and long-period expectations, short-period expectations about the price which will prevail when their product will be marketed, and long-period expectations regarding issues relevant for their investment decision. What is important for our purposes is to note that in making their production plans the firms expect that they will be able to sell all that they want to at the going price when they enter the market and, because this price is not known, they form an expectation about it. It should be noted that, since the market does clear through price variations, they do end up selling everything that they produced and wished to sell at the market price; thus there is nothing to make them want to change their assumption that they can sell all that they want to at the going market price. The only 'mistake' they may possibly see themselves making is in estimating the market price, an estimate which they can subsequently revise in the route to short-period equilibrium. The firms are thus price-takers in the sense that they 'take' their expected price. This is what guarantees that given the money wage they will be profit-maximizing and choosing the level of employment according to equation (7.5) (which guarantees real wage–marginal product equality in short-period equilibrium). This 'minimal' departure from the standard notion of perfect competition, jettisoning only the assumption of temporal perfect competition, is enough to obtain a model consistent with Keynes's analysis. We may refer to this notion of competition as 'pure competition', following Chamberlin (1933), who states that the former

> is a much simpler and less inclusive concept than 'perfect' competition, for the latter may be interpreted to involve perfection in many other respects than in the absence of monopoly. It may imply, for instance, an absence of friction in the sense of an ideal fluidity or mobility of factors such that adjustments to changing conditions which actually involve time are accomplished instantaneously in theory. It may imply perfect knowledge of the future and the consequent absence of uncertainty. (1933: 6).

In confining attention to the short period, Keynes was abstracting from the mobility of capital goods, and he was certainly emphasizing the presence of uncertainty regarding the future.

It should be noted that, if we depart from any one of conditions (1), (2), (4) and (5), or assume away spatial (as opposed to temporal) perfect information, then the marginal product–real wage equality may no longer be valid. If we depart from (1) the firm will have an incentive to want to reduce the price below the market to want to sell more; if we depart from (2) the firm can charge a price higher than the market price and still sell; if we depart from (4) consumers will not be able to move between firms, creating monopoly elements; and if we depart from (5) firms can collude and affect the market price. Further, departing from perfect spatial information will imply that consumers do not have full knowledge of the prices charged by firms at a point in time, and thus an individual firm can raise its price and still sell with some consumers not knowing that the price is higher than that of other firms.

IV Some alternative views

We have argued that Keynes's theory of unemployment equilibrium is consistent with the assumption of pure competition which implies that firms can expect to sell any amount they wish at the price they expect to prevail and moreover, that this was the assumption presumably made by Keynes in the development of his formal theory. This view is quite consistent with the view that Keynes's theory can be recast assuming some notion of imperfect competition,[12] and in fact this is quite in accordance with Keynes's own assumption of a given degree of competition.

In contradiction to this view, however, a number of writers have argued that Keynes introduced, or should have introduced, sales constraints into his analysis, or assumed some different form of competition such as the Marshallian one, or that Keynes's theory is internally consistent if and only if market imperfections are introduced. In this section we critically discuss these views.

Sales constraints

Several interpreters of Keynes have taken the view that the theory of effective demand necessarily implies that firms face sales constraints so that they cannot sell all that they want to at a given price or expected price. Of these, some have accepted that Keynes assumed price-taking behaviour or perfect competition of some form and also introduced sales constraints, while others have argued that by introducing sales constraints Keynes much have departed from price-taking behaviour.

Those in the first category have assumed that even with some notion of perfect competition – or at least price-taking behaviour – firms make guesses regarding how much they can sell. Parrinello (1980/1) and Torr (1981), while assuming that expected price equals marginal cost when firms maximize profits (thereby assuming price-taking behaviour),[13] also assume that when firms form their expectations of sales proceeds they take their *value* of sales to be given. Wells (1962), while explicitly assuming perfect competition, appears to believe that if a firm sells more it expects to obtain a lower price. Finally a recent model by Fazzari (1986) assumes that firms are atomistic price-takers but, because a given amount of aggregate demand is randomly distributed among firms, they have an expected distribution of demand, denoted by a probability density function. The level of production and employment of firms is then shown to depend on a parameter representing the firms' expected demand distribution.

These writers, who believe that perfectly competitive firms make guesses about markets, are being inconsistent. Price-taking behaviour makes sense only if firms can expect to sell all that they want to; otherwise firms will not choose to be price-takers and attempt to sell more by reducing their price. It follows that – and here we should refer to pure competition to be exact – the only expectations that they can form is about the market price, and none about their sales. It is therefore incorrect to assume that perfectly competitive firms will have expectations about the total value of sales – either given expectations or probability distributions of expectations.[14]

Turning now to those who have argued that Keynes did not assume perfect (or pure) competition because he introduced sales constraints, consider the recent example of Torr (1988), who writes:

> Under perfect competition it is generally assumed that producers believe that they can sell everything that they produce. This raises the question of whether Keynes employed such an assumption. Keynes's decision to populate the *General Theory* with a large number of small firms was an attempt to concede as much as possible to the opposition – if he had employed a small number of large firms, it could always have been claimed that involuntary unemployment was a result of monopolistic elements. On the other hand, could Keynes have presumed – in the midst of the depression – that firms could sell everything that they produced? Keynes accordingly populated the *General Theory* with a large number of small firms, but the principle of effective demand hardly suggests that firms have unlimited sales opportunities . . . A brickmaker is unlikely to believe that he can sell all the bricks he can produce if the most recently realized results have indicated otherwise. When history enters the picture, it becomes difficult to argue that entrepreneurs have no knowledge of the business cycle. (69–70)

Torr allows the firms to engage in inter-firm guesswork whereby they take into account that, when they increase employment, other firms will also increase their employment, and to make forecasts of sales based on the expectations of changes in total employment (and markets). In terms of our terminology, Torr is not only implying that Keynes's theory is not consistent with perfect competition but also that it is inconsistent with pure competition.

The error here lies in saying that firms with effective demand problems cannot be purely competitive. In the analysis of Section III above firms were assumed to believe that they could sell any amount they wanted to, and the economy still ended up at an unemployment equilibrium. Pure competition does not imply that firms will sell an infinite amount; it only implies that at the going market price they *expect* to sell any amount they want to. Nor does it imply that at *any* price they can expect to sell any amount they want to; merely that at the *going* price they can do so. Thus, in recessions, Keynesian competition implies that firms will expect the market price to be low. Thus market conditions can enter the calculations of firms, but they can only enter into the formation of their short-period expectations regarding what the price will be.

Marshallian competition

It has frequently been observed that Keynes was following Marshall's method, for example in dealing with periods and therefore giving a role to historical processes, and in his treatment of demand and supply.[15] But it has also been argued (see Clower, 1989; Wulwick, 1989) that Keynes was following Marshall's notion of competition, which is different from the standard notion of perfect or even pure competition.

This is a difficult claim to examine because Marshall was extremely imprecise in defining competition. Stigler (1957) writes that 'Marshall's exposition [of competition] was almost as informal and unsystematic as Smith's in this area'. Samuelson (1967) is even more critical:

> The ambiguities of Alfred Marshall paralyzed [sic] the best brains in the Anglo-Saxon branch of our profession for three decades . . . Because of his unwillingness to make sharp distinctions between perfect and less-than-perfect competition, Marshall managed to set back the clock on both competitive theory and on the theory of monopoly . . . Marshall was so afraid of being unrealistic that he merely ends up being fuzzy and confusing – and confused. (109–11)

Marshall (1890: 94) defines a 'perfect market' to be 'a district, small or large, in which there are many buyers and many sellers all so keenly on the alert and so well acquainted with one another's affairs that the price of a commodity is always practically the same for the whole district'. In a market with 'free competition' no dealer is driven to 'taking a lower or paying a higher price than others are doing' (ibid.: 284). As Reisman (1986) shows,[16] Marshall was aware of four conditions implicit in the notion of this perfect market: 'the commodities referred to are always the same quality' (Marshall, 1890: 95); 'perfect knowledge of the state of the market' (ibid.: 448); mobility and transportability (ibid.: 273); and 'there is no close combination among dealers on either side' (ibid.: 284).[17]

Nevertheless Shirai (1968) has compared subsequent editions of the *Principles* to show how Marshall had a growing tendency to 'list his ship to the more realistic and vaguer side'. Most significantly he drops reference to the 'perfect market' in a key description of market structure; Shirai points out that Marshall was perhaps groping towards the notion that initially buyers and sellers are bound by custom and inertness, and perfect knowledge required of perfect markets takes time for its diffusion. Another example of imprecision is that when trade is slack Marshall believes that each firm has an incentive to increase its output and/or to reduce its price to undersell other firms, but that they do not, either because they wish to avoid 'incurring odium from other producers for spoiling the common market' (1890: 380, 412), or because of 'formal or informal agreement with other producers' (ibid.: 311). The firms' incentives to cut prices, and their reasons for not doing so, all appear to contradict Marshall's notion of perfect or free markets.[18]

Having noted Marshall's imprecision, let us turn to Clower's (1989) argument that Keynes's theory of aggregate employment followed closely Marshall's theory of pricing in competitive markets, and employed a notion of competition quite different from the price-taking behaviour of Walrasian perfect competition. Clower cites Whitaker (1975: 125) approvingly: 'Marshall's conception of competition was from the first a qualified one akin to monopolistic competition'. He then argues (convincingly) that Keynes adapted Marshall's notions of supply and demand price, and developed a notion of equilibrium using Marshall's theory of output adjustment in response to a gap between demand and supply price. In Keynes's approach quantity can be treated as the independent variable, and for each quantity we need to compare Keynes's aggregate supply (or Marshall's supply price at that quantity times the quantity) and aggregate demand (or Marshall's demand price at that quantity times the quantity); then quantity can be assumed to adjust to the gap between aggregate demand and supply. Clower shows that this story is quite different from the Walrasian (which takes the price to be the independent variable) and Hicksian (which takes price to be fixed and assumes that short-period sales are limited by aggregate demand) approaches. Comparing Keynes and the Walrasian approach, for instance, he writes that the 'Walrasian interpretation fails to conform with Keynes' argument mainly because it presumes that output adjustments are driven by market-determined prices rather than by the competitive jostling of independent profit-seeking, *market making* firms' (144, emphasis added).[19]

We agree with Clower's Marshallian interpretation of Keynes's theory; in fact our interpretation is also Marshallian in treating output as the independent variable in the short period. We also agree with Clower that Marshall's notion of competition was not the same as the modern notion of perfect competition: as discussed above, Marshall was somewhat imprecise in defining his notion of competition and, indeed, one can find aspects of modern monopolistic competition in some of his notions of competition.[20] What we disagree with, however, is the implication that Keynes – accepting Clower's Marshallian interpretation – is inconsistent with purely competitive behaviour in the sense in which we have defined it. Clower does not discuss how output – the independent variable – is arrived at in any moment of time. In our interpretation it is chosen by maximizing firms given their expectation of the market price, who expect that they can sell everything they want to at the going price. Of course, unless their short-period expectations accidentally happen to be realized, the firms do not produce to maximize profits at the actual market price; thus the market does not operate in a standard Walrasian manner with actual price always equal to marginal cost or actual real wage equal to marginal product of labour. But this does not mean that Keynes (and Marshall, at least where he is also explicit in stating that output is produced in the market period according to expected price[21]) is necessarily departing from the notion of price-taking behaviour, only that they are introducing time and the temporal lack of knowledge. When firms form expectations they are not setting the price, but merely making their best guess about the market price. The firms do not 'make markets' and they are not monopolistic competitors; if they did these things equilibrium would not be consistent with the real wage equal to marginal product as it was in Keynes's theory.

Increasing returns and imperfect competition

Some interpreters have argued that, to be internally consistent, Keynes's theory *requires* the existence of imperfections in competition. In an influential paper Weitzman (1982) has argued that

> with perfect divisibility, when unemployed factor units are all going about their business spontaneously employing themselves or being employed, the economy will automatically break out of unemployment. While the simple story of supply creating its own demand can be told in a closed barter economy, I do not see the existence of money, savings, investment or international trade *per se* invalidating the basic proposition that a logical inference of strict constant returns to scale and perfect competition is full employment . . . There is a sense therefore in which the natural habitat of effective demand macroeconomics is a monopolistically competitive micro-economy. Analogously, perfect competition and classical macroeconomics are natural counterparts. (793, 801)

No less a Keynesian than Kaldor has endorsed this view, quoting the above approvingly. Kaldor (1983) writes that under conditions of constant returns to scale which (in the absence of institutional monopolies) create perfect competition,

> the 'free play of economic forces' will necessarily . . . establish (and maintain) a state of full employment. . . . Once the artificial assumption of pure (or perfect) competition is abandoned, a Walrasian equilibrium with market-clearing prices in every market becomes a mirage, not in any way descriptive as a 'first approximation' of the conditions obtaining in the real world. (12–13).

Kaldor goes on to argue that Keynes was not aware of this inexorable link between unemployment equilibrium and imperfect competition and, had he been aware of it, much needless controversy over Keynesian economics would have been avoided.

Weitzman's (1982) argument is that, unless the economy has increasing returns and imperfect competition, it would tend to a position of full employment because unemployed workers could set up their own firms with very small amounts of capital. He develops a model of monopolistic competition and increasing returns which admits of unemployment equilibrium because unemployed workers cannot set up their own firms because of high start-up costs, because no new firms will want to enter the market because profits are zero, and because existing firms will not want to expand output, fearing that they would push down their price and no longer maximize their profits. Weitzman also shows that a fall in the money wage does not result in a rise in the level of employment.

While Weitzman's model is a most ingenious one, and may be a correct explanation of unemployment in some situations, in our opinion it does not show that Keynesian unemployment requires departures from pure competition. Three comments may be made in this regard. First, Weitzman attaches much importance to the entry of new firms, which are issues relevant to the long period, ignored in Keynes's short-period analysis. Thus one cannot argue that Keynes's theory was based on entry barriers, since the short period, by definition, is one in which entry cannot occur. But to put it this way implies that Keynes's theory is that involuntary unemployment is valid only for the short period; in the long period the entry of firms will drive the economy to full employment. If we believe that Keynes's unemployment has nothing to do with short-period frictions, the question of the entry of firms must be squarely faced.

Second, Weitzman invokes entry barriers to rule out the possibility that unemployed workers can become firms. The notion of perfect mobility which is a part of the notion of perfect competition is usually taken to denote that consumers can move between different goods, resources can move between different uses and firms can move between different sectors. The notion that consumers and workers can become firms is not generally used, and this is perhaps related to the fact that in neoclassical economics the firm is generally treated as a black box, without any theory explaining its existence. Keynes's theory does require that unemployed workers cannot start their own firms, but this does not depart from the usual notion of perfect mobility.[22] If one interprets perfect mobility to allow for all consumers to start their own firms, the departure Keynes requires is again a minimal one – and does not interfere with the other aspects of perfect mobility. We merely need to impose the condition that production cannot be run on a very small scale, but we may continue to assume constant returns to scale in the relevant range at which firms usually produce.[23]

Third, it may be argued that Weitzman's model has nothing to do with Keynes's theory of effective demand. Weitzman completely adheres to Say's Law: all income is consumed in his model. The reason that the economy is trapped at unemployment is that firms do not wish to expand output because by so doing they would drive their price down (because they do not believe that they can sell any amount they wish to at the going price). Clearly such a model with Say's Law is an inappropriate vehicle for showing that Keynes's theory requires imperfect competition. Keynes does not need it because he is opposed to Say's Law: all output does not create its own demand. Whereas in Weitzman's model, if the economy could be forced to produce at any level of output, this level of output can be sold, in Keynes's theory this is not the case since if output were higher than the equilibrium level it would shrink back to that level. In Keynes's theory firms are not deterred from producing more because they fear they will reduce their price, but because they are maximizing profits at the existing market price.[24]

Imperfect competition and limits to investment

A similar view – that imperfect competition is necessary for Keynes's unemployment equilibrium – has been put forward by Sardoni (1987, 1990), but using a different argument. Sardoni argues that Keynes believed that unemployment equilibrium was consistent with perfect competition, but that he was mistaken in this belief. He follows Kalecki (1982), arguing that under perfect competition nothing limits investment demand by firms to a level which causes unemployment. Keynes believed that, given the rate of interest, the demand for investment would be limited by the rising supply price of capital and investment expanded. The criticism is made that perfectly competitive firms will take the price of capital goods to be given, and push investment to the full employment level. Sardoni also considers an *ex post* interpretation of Keynes's theory, according to which the actual expansion of investment raises the price of capital goods, which would then limit investment spending. But here he agrees with Kalecki (1982), saying that this rise in the price of capital goods will also raise the general price level, raise firm's expectations and provide a further impetus to investment expenditure. Thus, Sardoni concludes, the only consistent (and also realistic) theory of unemployment requires imperfections in competition; some sort of financial constraint is required for limiting investment, '*à la* Kalecki'.

While Kalecki's theory of demand-determined output based on mark-up pricing and constant prime costs is certainly a powerful and important one, this particular critique of Keynes's theory, in our opinion, is not convincing. This issue did not surface in our earlier discussion because we assumed that investment was given, but, confronted with this critique, we need to explore why investment can be assumed to be given below its full employment level.[25]

Keynes believed that individual firms would have a limited demand for investment goods, given their long-period expectations and the interest rate. This is not only because of the rising supply price of capital goods, but also because of the falling expected returns from successively less profitable investment outlets. This latter reason, however, is overlooked by Sardoni. In addition, even if one overlooks this reason, it is not clear why in the *ex post* version a rise in the price of capital goods should raise expected future prices (and long-period expectations) sufficiently to drive the economy to full employment. Sardoni does not explain why, but merely cites Kalecki's statement that all that is required for reaching full employment is that expectations of future prices improve to some extent. But, since a rise in the price of capital goods deters further investment, and a rise in expectations of future prices (presumably affecting what Keynes called long-period expectations) encourages investment, what is required for investment to keep rising is that the latter effect dominates the former. While this *may* happen, it need not. Thus we must again reject the view that imperfect competition is *necessary* for unemployment equilibrium.

V Conclusion

This chapter has argued that Keynes believed that his analysis was compatible with any given degree of competition. We have argued that his analysis is compatible with pure competition, and it is most likely that this is the assumption he had in mind in developing his argument in the *General Theory*. We have argued that alternative interpretations of Keynes which see some form of deviation from pure competition, and which argue that imperfect competition is necessary for unemployment equilibrium, are erroneous, given the structure of Keynesian theory. Thus unemployment equilibrium exists in capitalist economies owing to more fundamental factors than market imperfections which are in principle removable.[26]

These conclusions, however, are subject to two caveats. First, the issue that has been discussed in this chapter is the compatibility of Keynes's theory of unemployment equilibrium with pure competition, and not whether pure competition is an appropriate assumption for analysing capitalist economies. On grounds of realism the assumption may be quite unacceptable. As we have seen Keynes came re-evaluate his views on imperfect competition in connection with the empirical relation between real wages and productivity, but this is related to whether pure competition is realistic, and not relevant to the question as to whether unemployment equilibrium is theoretically caused by market imperfections. Second, it is well known that there are problems with the notion of pure competition relating to the compatibility of price-taking behaviour and the dynamic adjustment of prices in the absence of the fictitious auctioneer (Arrow, 1959) and we have swept these issues under the rug to examine the question of the compatibility of Keynes's unemployment equilibrium and pure competition.

Notes

1. I am grateful to Victoria Chick for drawing my attention to some of the questions examined in this chapter, and for her many comments and suggestions. I am also grateful to Geoff Harcourt for discussions. I am alone responsible for any remaining errors.
2. On this issue, see Darity (1984/5). That imperfect competition could lead to unemployment was recognized by Pigou (1920), one of the main contemporary figures amongst Keynes's 'classical' economists. Robbins (1934) also emphasized this point. As Leijonhufvud (1968: 53, n.7) writes, 'emphasis on "monopolistic elements" puts the analytical diagnosis of depressions back to its pre-Keynesian stage'.
3. This conclusion is the same as that arrived by Kregel (1985) and Harcourt (1987), among others.
4. This interpretation follows Kregel (1985), Darity (1984/5) and Harcourt (1987: 13). As we have already mentioned, that unemployment could occur with imperfect competition was well known at the time and Keynes must have been aware of this, having read Pigou. If his theory was to be considered novel it would be tactically unwise to introduce imperfect competition into his analysis.
5. See Harcourt (1987).
6. This is perhaps why Knight (1921: 76–7) adds rationality to his list of conditions for perfect competition. We prefer to think of it as a separate assumption, since it says nothing of the market, but is an assumption regarding the behaviour of agents.
7. This price adjustment story is of course problematic, since it is not clear who adjusts the price; buyers and sellers cannot, since they behave as price-takers. We abstract from this problem by assuming that there is a benevolent and omniscient auctioneer who finds the market-clearing price.
8. This interpretation follows Casarosa (1981) and Dutt (1987).
9. This is quite standard among interpreters of this curve. See Dutt and Amadeo (1990) for references.
10. For a specific example which shows how price is determined, see Dutt (1987). The

model developed there assumes that investment is fixed in real terms, workers who receive a fixed money wage consume all their income, and profit-recipients either do not consume or consume an amount fixed in real terms. Given expected price the firm produces as discussed above in the text, and corresponding to that level of output and employment the price varies to clear the market.

11. Our entire analysis has assumed that the money wage is given. This follows Keynes. It should not be taken to imply, however, that unemployment is due to wage rigidity. Keynes (CW VII: Chapter 19) argues convincingly why money wage flexibility may not take the economy to full employment. See Dutt (1986/7) for a discussion.
12. This has been done by several writers: for instance, Tarshis (1979) and Chick (1983: Chapter 5) have used the neoclassical theory of monopoly, and Weintraub (1958) a mark-up pricing model.
13. See Torr (1981: 337). Parrinello (1980/1: 66) assumes 'sufficiently' strong competition, but takes it to imply that when firms maximize profits, price (expected?) equals marginal cost.
14. Fazzari's (1986) model is very much in the tradition of fix-price disequilibrium models of the Malinvaud variety which suffer from the same inconsistency between price-taking behaviour and the presence of sales constraints; see Dutt (1987) for a discussion. Fazzari's model also appears to be far removed from Keynes's analysis since, unlike Keynes's first classical postulate, the real wage is less than the marginal product of labour and, more importantly, the model implies the full employment of labour unless, in addition to sales constraints, wage rigidity is introduced into the analysis.
15. See, for example, Harcourt (1981; 1987) and Clower (1989).
16. The page references and quotations are taken from Reisman (1986).
17. Note that Marshall has referred to four of the conditions for perfect competition mentioned in Section III. He only omits the first one.
18. Kaldor had a similar view of Marshall's theory of competition, but he assessed it to be enlightening rather than ambiguous. See Kaldor's comments in Harcourt (1987: 93–4).
19. Leijonhufvud (1974), earlier on, distinguished between Marshallian and Walrasian notions of competition, and a critique similar to that following can be made of his work. Leijonhufvud also argues that Keynesian firms face sales constraints, which is in contradiction with our reading of Keynes. See also Wulwick (1989).
20. See Reisman (1986).
21. See Marshall (1890: 281) who points out that today's stock of grain depends on what was sown at a previous date and 'that, in its turn, was largely influenced by the farmers' guesses as to the price which they would get for it this year' (quoted in Reisman, 1986: Chapter 3).
22. As Darity (1984/5) argues, however, there is nothing inconsistent with Keynes's theory and the fact that unemployed workers can start their own work and be *underemployed*, in Joan Robinson's sense.
23. Alternatively we could assume that the unemployed workers could have access to less productive lines of activity, but that they would still be considered to be involuntarily unemployed since they were underemployed or disguisedly unemployed (see Darity, 1984/5).
24. In Weitzman's model a cut in wages does not raise demand since it reduces consumer income, which represents to monopolistically competitive firms a reduction in the incomes of their consumers. In Keynes's theory the cut in wages will not clear the labour market because of a variety of different effects on aggregate demand, including the distribution of wealth between different groups, the distribution of income and uncertainty (see CW VII: Chapter 19). Had Weitzman introduced an investment function into his model he would have had to invoke some of these ideas to show why a money wage cut does not raise the level of employment.
25. Sardoni (1986) argues, as we have earlier that, given investment, Keynes's theory is consistent with what we call pure competition.
26. It may be argued that, in the absence of imperfections, neoclassical general equilibrium theory shows that no unemployment can exist in equilibrium so that in this sense

unemployment equilibrium is due to imperfections. This notion of imperfection tautologically defines imperfections in terms of general equilibrium theory, and does not distinguish between different types of imperfections. In our analysis we distinguish between imperfections implying deviations from pure competition due to monopolies and other types of 'imperfections' – such as uncertainty – which are more fundamental. Even imperfections due to natural monopolies could be removed by government regulation, but the same is not true for pervasive uncertainty.

References

Arrow, K. J. (1959), 'Toward a Theory of Price Adjustment', in M. Abramovitz *et al.* (eds), *The Allocation of Economic Resources*, Stanford: Stanford University Press.

Casarosa, C. (1981), 'The Microfoundations of Keynes's Aggregate Supply and Expected Demand Analysis', *Economic Journal*, **91**, 188–94.

Chamberlin, E. H. (1933), *The Theory of Monopolistic Competition*, Cambridge, Mass.: Harvard University Press.

Chick, V. (1983), *Macroeconomics After Keynes*, Cambridge, Mass.: MIT Press.

Clower, R. W. (1989), 'Keynes's *General Theory*: The Marshall Connection', in D. A. Walker (ed.), *Perspectives on the History of Economic Thought, Vol. II*, Aldershot: Edward Elgar.

Darity, W. A. Jr. (1984/5), 'On Involuntary Unemployment and Increasing Returns', *Journal of Post Keynesian Economics*, **7**, 363–72.

Dunlop, J. G. (1938), 'The Movement of Real and Money Wage Rates', *Economic Journal*, **48**, 413–34.

Dutt, A. K. (1987), 'Keynes with a Perfectly Competitive Goods Market', *Australian Economic Papers*, **26**, 275–93.

Dutt, A. K. and E. J. Amadeo (1990), *Keynes's Third Alternative? The Neo-Ricardian Keynesians and the Post Keynesians*, Upleadon: Edward Elgar.

Fazzari, S. (1986), 'Sales Expectations and Demand-Constrained Firms: A New View of the Microfoundations of Aggregate Supply', unpublished, Washington University.

Harcourt, G. C. (1981), 'Marshall, Sraffa and Keynes: Incompatible Bedfellows?', *Eastern Economic Journal*, **7**, 39–50.

Harcourt, G. C. (ed.) (1985), *Keynes and His Contemporaries*, London: Macmillan.

Harcourt, G. C. (1987), 'Theoretical Methods and Unfinished Business', in D. A. Reese (ed.) *The Legacy of Keynes*, San Francisco: Harper & Row.

Kaldor, N. (1983), 'Keynesian Economics After Fifty Years', in D. Worswick and J. Trevithick (1983), *Keynes and the Modern World*, Cambridge: Cambridge University Press.

Kalecki, M. (1982), 'Some Remarks on Keynes's Theory', *Australian Economic Papers*, **21**, 245–53.

Knight, F. H. (1921), *Risk, Uncertainty and Profit*, 1971 edn, Chicago: Chicago University Press.

Kregel, J. (1985), 'Harrod and Keynes: Increasing Returns, the Theory of Employment and Dynamic Economics', in G. C. Harcourt (ed.), *Keynes and His Contemporaries*, London: Macmillan.

Leijonhufvud, A. (1968), *On Keynesian Economics and the Economics of Keynes. A Study in Monetary Theory*, Oxford: Oxford University Press.

Leijonhufvud, A. (1974), 'Keynes' Employment Function', *History of Political Economy*, **6** 164–70.

Marshall, A. (1890), *Principles of Economics*, London: Macmillan.

Parrinello, S. (1980/1), 'The Price Level Implicit in Keynes' Point of Effective Demand', *Journal of Post Keynesian Economics*, **3**, 63–78.

Pigou, A. C. (1920), *The Economics of Welfare*, London: Macmillan.

Reisman, D. (1986), *The Economics of Alfred Marshall*, London: Macmillan.

Robbins, L. (1934), *The Great Depression*, London: Macmillan.

Robinson, J. (1934), 'What is Perfect Competition?', *Quarterly Journal of Economics*, **49**, 104–20.

Samuelson, P. (1967), 'The Monopolistic Competition Revolution', in R, E. Kuenne (ed.) *Monopolistic Competition Theories: Studies in Impact*, London: Wiley.

Sardoni, C. (1986), *Marx and Keynes on Economic Recession. The Theory of Unemployment and Effective Demand*, New York: New York University Press.

Sardoni, C. (1990), 'Effective Demand and Market Forms: A Comment', unpublished, University of Rome.

Shirai, T. (1968), 'Alfred Marshall on Free Competition', *Ozaka Economic Papers*, **16**, 11–15.

Stigler, G. J. (1957), 'Perfect Competition, Historically Contemplated', *Journal of Political Economy*, **65**, 1–17.

Tarshis, L. (1939), 'Changes in Real and Money Wages', *Economic Journal*, **49**, 150–4.

Tarshis, L. (1979), 'The Aggregate Supply Function in Keynes's *General Theory*', in M. J. Boskin (ed.), *Economics and Human Welfare*, New York and London: Academic Press.

Torr, C. (1981), 'Microfoundations of Keynes's Point of Effective Demand', *South African Journal of Economics*, **49**, 334–48.

Torr, C. (1988), *Equilibrium, Expectations and Information. A Study of the General Theory and Modern Classical Economics*, Cambridge: Polity Press.

Weintraub, S. (1958), *An Approach to the Theory of Income Distribution*, Philadelphia: Chilton.

Weitzman, M. (1982), 'Increasing Returns and the Foundations of Unemployment Theory', *Economic Journal*, **92**, 781–809.

Wells, P. J. (1962), 'Aggregate Supply and Demand: An Explanation of Chapter III of the *General Theory*', *Canadian Journal of Economics and Political Science*, **28**, 585–90.

Whitaker, J. K. (1975), *The Early Economic Writings of Alfred Marshall, 1867–1890, Vol. 1*, New York: Free Press.

Worswick, G. N. D. and J. Trevithick (eds) (1983), *Keynes and the Modern World*, Cambridge: Cambridge University Press.

Wulwick, N. (1989), 'Review of Marx and Keynes on Economic Recession', *Economics and Philosophy*, **5**, 109–18.

8 The small firm under uncertainty: a puzzle of the *General Theory*[1]

Victoria Chick

It is fairly widely agreed that in the *General Theory* Keynes used the conventions of perfect competition – the equality of the wage to marginal product and of price to marginal cost – yet for many the conclusions of the *General Theory* are incompatible with that market form. The central problem is this: perfectly competitive industries are populated by very many firms, each of them relatively small and having a negligible influence on the market. Therefore each firm can sell all it likes. How can there be persistent unemployment if firms can sell all they want to sell?

It is the purpose of this chapter to show, first, that, even within the theory of perfect competition, the small firm is demand-constrained and cannot sell an indefinitely large amount.[2] Second, the received canon of perfect competition imposes much more than properties which follow only from firm size. In particular, as is well known, the established theory of perfect competition imposes the assumption of perfect foresight. By contrast, in the *General Theory*, producers are uncertain of the demand they face. Therefore, even though their individual influence on price is negligible, small firms cannot be price-takers in what has become the accepted sense.

By doubting the received theory of perfect competition, we have uncovered principles which unify the theories of firms in concentrated and atomistic industries. We conclude that, once the question of uncertainty is addressed, the *General Theory* is compatible with any or all market structures.

The chapter proceeds as follows. In the first section we clarify what Keynes *did* assume about market form. Then in Section II we prepare the ground for the proposition that the *General Theory* is compatible with *any* market form by first unbundling the assumptions normally associated together in the market form called perfect competition, distinguishing those which follow only from the number of firms in the industry from other, associated assumptions. In particular, price-taking, as generally understood, can and shall be divorced from a market form which retains the central feature of perfect competition, namely the existence of many firms in the industry. It is shown that even a perfectly certain small firm cannot sell an indefinitely large amount at the going price. This is the crucial issue, for compatibility with the Principle of Effective Demand depends on firms' demands being determined by aggregate demand. To keep the argument focused on this issue, we deal only with the most elementary, textbook expressions of the theory of the firm.

The standard theory of perfect competition embodies perfect certainty and is timeless. We argue that it is this feature which makes the theory incompatible with the *General Theory* model. But, in so far as the elementary theory of oligopoly and monopoly is based on the same static method as perfect competition, the *General Theory* is also incompatible with them. The theory of the firm compatible with the *General Theory* is that of the firm under uncertainty, whatever the size of the individual representative firm.

To distinguish the small firm under uncertainty from perfect competition as usually understood, we call this form 'polypoly' (as in Chick, 1983). This usage falls into line with other nomenclature derived from the number of firms in the industry: monopoly, oligopoly, polypoly. Examination, in Section III, of the profit-maximizing behaviour of the polypolistic firm under uncertainty reveals that its formulation of a price–quantity strategy at least in principle shares one element with the (uncertain) oligopolistic or even monopolistic firm: as stressed by Keynes, all producers must first forecast industry and macroeconomic demand, to which their own demand is subject. The implications, for the demand facing an individual firm, of these forecasts of industry and aggregate demand will depend critically, in polypoly and oligopoly alike, on whether other firms are expected to react in a similar way or not. The monopolist, of course, has only his own firm to consider. We end by emphasizing the unity of the theory of the firm across market forms.

We deal in this chapter only with the theory of production, not with the theory of investment. The role of investment demand in generating new income and employment is, of course, central to the *General Theory*. But investment demand fulfils that role only when the capital goods industries produce to meet that demand. Thus the theory of production is fundamental, and the propositions in this chapter apply to all industries which produce for market sale. (Many capital goods are produced to order.)

I Market form in the *General Theory*

In my book on the *General Theory* (Chick, 1983) I supported a widely-held view that Keynes assumed small firms. I argued in favour of this choice on the grounds, by no means unique to me, that by making this choice Keynes minimized the difference between himself and his classical opponents – a useful strategy if one's aim is to show just exactly what is the critical difference. On the other hand I have always maintained that, whatever Keynes's own assumption, the *General Theory* is, in broad outline, compatible with any market form, though imperfect competition would complicate its mathematical expression.

However, on reading the relevant passages of the *General Theory* again, for what must be the eightieth time, in preparation for this chapter, I see the first aspect of my position differently. Those who have argued that Keynes did not assume perfect competition have appealed to his statement that he would 'take . . . as given the degree of competition' (CW VII: 245). But there is further evidence that he did not plump for any single form.

There are four other passages where the matter of market form arises. All of them are ambiguous; the first two make it clear that he is keeping his options open. The first classical postulate is stated thus: 'The wage is equal to the marginal product of labour . . . subject, however, to the qualification that the equality may be disturbed . . . *if* competition and markets are imperfect' (CW VII: 5, emphasis added). And, on page 283, a price equation is defined: '*provided* we can assume that the price is equal to the marginal prime cost . . .' (emphasis added).

Particularly in the context of Keynes's theory of prices, mathematical convenience is sufficient reason for working with the properties of small firms. In Chapter 19, however, elements of the standard theory of the small firm are challenged. First, it is asserted that the Principle of Effective Demand holds even for small firms, and the relevance of the marginal product of labour is questioned:

> In any given industry we have a demand schedule for the product relating the quantities which can be sold to the prices asked; we have a series of supply schedules relating the prices which will be asked for the sale of different quantities . . . and these schedules between them lead up to a further schedule which, on the assumption that other costs are unchanged (except as a result of a change in output), gives us the demand schedule for labour . . . This conception is then transferred without substantial modification to industry as a whole . . . If this is the groundwork of the arguments . . . surely it is fallacious . . . unless we also transfer our assumption that the aggregate effective demand is fixed. (CW VII: 258)

Second, the belief that expansion is possible at unchanged prices is shown to be incorrect, again because of the Principle of Effective Demand:

> the individual entrepreneur, seeing his own costs reduced, will overlook at the outset the repercussions on the demand for his product and will act on the assumption that he will be able to sell at a profit a larger output than before. [They will succeed] only if . . . [the *mpc*] is equal to unity. (CW VII: 261)

The first two passages challenge the accepted wisdom that, by using $p =$

mc and *w* = *mpl*, Keynes was assuming small firms as a necesary part of the structure of the *General Theory*. Rather he appears to be using the assumption of the small firm merely provisionally. The last two passages indicate a stronger attachment to the small firm, but hardly to perfect competition, for the last passage asserts the macroeconomic perspective, within which it is shown that small firms cannot sell all they want at the going price (an aspect of price-taking) whatever they may believe. We conclude that, while Keynes leans towards the small firm as his model, he never commits himself fully even to polypoly, still less to perfect competition as we know it today.

It must never be forgotten that we are evaluating Keynes's notion of competition after a long period of refinement and extension of Walrasian economics. Not only Keynes, but also Marshall, have been reinterpreted from a Walrasian perspective. That perspective is always prepared to sacrifice relevance for logical consistency. We proceed in Section II to challenge even that consistency.

II Unbundling perfect competition

Perfect competition entails a number of assumptions, the logical priority of which is rarely made explicit:

1. there are many sellers;
2. there are many buyers;
3. the product is uniform;
4. the buyers are perfectly informed about prices at any point of time;
5. the buyers have no customer loyalty but will seek the cheapest supplier (perfect mobility);
6. there is no collusion;
7. no firm can substantially influence the price by its actions;
8. all firms charge the same price;
9. the price is given by the market; and
10. firms can sell all they want at the market price.

It will be immediately apparent that assumptions (2)–(6) have nothing to do with the number of firms in the industry. Thus in our later discussion they may be freely altered. For the moment they are retained. They imply that no supplier can set a price above the market price and hope to retain any custom. A firm whose price is below the market price can expect to face the whole of market demand, which of course it does not have the capacity to meet. Thus the small firm loses if it deviates from market price in either direction. So it is concluded that they *do not* deviate: they are said to *take* the market price, despite the implausibility of the model which ensures this behaviour. To this model we now turn.

Price-taking in conventional microeconomics

There is a story about price-taking and there is a theory of price-taking. There is nothing in general wrong with the storytelling mode, except that it may obscure the theory's methodology and, in this case, make the theory more convincing than it really is.

The story is that pressure from buyers of a uniform good and inability of an individual firm to influence price will lead to a uniform price. The theory predicts that this is the market price; that is, the price determined by the intersection of market supply and demand. The story is plausible. The theory is less so, for how are the firms to get to know the market price? How, indeed, is the market price to be determined?

The theory enjoins one to determine price by confronting the market demand curve with the market supply curve. There seems to be no difficulties with the market demand curve: it is simply the aggregate of individual buyers' demand curves, however these come to be known or estimated. But the market supply curve requires information from firms, who are supposed to predicate their actions on the price taken from the market.

How are firms to get this information? By common consent the dominant form of business in the West in the twentieth century is production for market sale: that is, production decisions are made *before* the markets which they will address have occurred. Also by common consent the *General Theory* is based on the recognition of this fact: demand is uncertain and must be forecast, over a short span for production and over a longer period for investment. Whatever our theory of the firm, if it is to stand as a micro-foundation for the *General Theory* it must be compatible with this fundamental assumption of the *General Theory*.

How can firms take prices from markets which lie in the future? The short answer, of course, is that they cannot. The long answer may also be interesting. In terms of the modern theory of perfect competition, there can be no knowledge of the market price without full knowledge of firms' supply decisions and no supply decisions without knowledge of the market price. Without the firms' supply curves the position of the market supply curve is unknown and without the market supply curve the market price cannot be determined.

One could reply in defence of the theory that it is static, timeless. If there is no time, it makes no sense to ask for one piece of information before another, and the above complaint is dismissed. The firms' supplies and the market price are simultaneously determined. But then in what sense do firms 'take' prices? There is a conflict between story and theory here. (As said above, the story is more plausible and serves to disguise the methodology.)

Or alternatively one could appeal to the fact that this is an equilibrium theory and, since equilibrium repeats itself, firms take prices from *yesterday*'s markets, knowing that tomorrow's prices will be the same. We then go into infinite regress, searching for the ultimate yesterday. This is what led Joan Robinson to argue that static equilibria were states one could not get into unless one had been in them since the Fall of Man. Worse, once one is in the equilibrium one must stay there forever, unless one can go back to the Fall of Man and start again. The theory reduces to the equilibrium solution only: the disequilibrium points which give supply and demand curves their length have no real part to play, since the theory is incapable of dealing with change in historical time.

Infinitely elastic demand in conventional theory

A corollary of price-taking is that firms can sell any amount without affecting the price. This is said to follow from assumptions (1) and (7). One could even argue, very sensibly, that this corollary *defines* the small firm; from this perspective, the small firm has something special about it, rather in the same way as infinity is a special number (or set of numbers). A further corollary is that the demand curve facing the small firm is infinitely elastic. Let us look at these propositions more closely.

The market supply curve is the aggregate of firms' supply curves; these indicate each firm's profit-maximizing output for each potential price. Each potential price indicates a hypothesized level of demand as it impinges on the firm. Thus the market supply curve indicates that each firm has reached the limit of its willingness to produce, given the price: even if all the demand were to flow to one firm, that firm would have no more to sell. It is not profit-maximizing for the firm to produce more.

Let us be more precise. Assume a large number of identical firms, each of which has an equal share of demand. These are represented in Figure 8.1 by Firms 1, 2 and 3. (It is realized that there needs to be only one representative firm, but the visual image may be helpful.)

The usual procedure is to argue that the industry demand and supply curves determine the market price P_0, which then determines the position of an infinitely-elastic demand curve for each firm at that price.

Let us for the moment accept without question that the demand curve facing each firm is flat at the price determined by the market supply and demand. Then, at the market-clearing price of P_0, Firm 1 will produce Q_{10}, Firm 2 will produce Q_{20} and Firm 3 will produce Q_{30}. The sum of these quantities gives a point Q_0 on the market supply curve at P_0. But since P_0 is the market-clearing price, it also equals market demand, Q_0. Thus

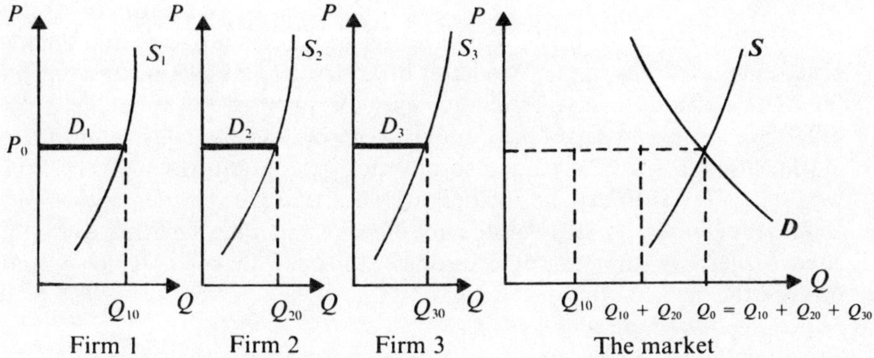

Figure 8.1 *The market supply curve*

$$Q_0 = Q_{10} + Q_{20} + Q_{30}:$$

the share of market demand for each firm at the market-clearing price is truncated at the point of intersection with each firm's profit-maximizing supply at the market-clearing price. If the theorist intends to indicate the actual demand facing each firm, the extension of each firm's demand curve beyond the intersection with their supply curves at the going price is simply incorrect. (He can, of course, sell more by *lowering* the price, but that is a separate issue.)

This conclusion is very much at variance with the spirit if not the letter of the proposition that the small firm 'can sell all it likes at the going price'. This property is inferred from the horizontal demand curve and/or from the assumption that, however much the firm put on the market, it will not affect the price. The capacity of demand to absorb any supply is not questioned.

The happy state of the firm's 'being able to sell all it likes' is contrasted, in fix-price theory, with the situation in which the firm is 'demand-constrained', when it cannot 'sell all it likes'. But this is a completely false dichotomy: in the perfect competition model, the firm can indeed always sell all it likes, but what it *likes* is the quantity given by the intersection of its marginal cost curve with the price. Price represents demand, but even if, therefore, the demand curve is horizontal up to a point, at that point, where $p = mc$, it is truncated. The firm is demand-constrained, even with perfect knowledge of the market-clearing price.

The extended horizontal demand curve could be interpreted as representing what each firm *thinks* it can sell (the perceived demand curve) but not only do we, as theorists, know that this perception is an illusion (this is what Keynes was saying in the passage quoted above, on page 261 of the *General Theory*); plainly this is an illusion which has no place in a theory based on perfect foresight. The habit of drawing a flat curve extending as far as one cares to draw it cannot even be justified by appealing to a difference between what a firm thinks it can do and the constraint of the market, for the curve is truncated at exactly the point at which the firm would decide not to expand further, even if it thought that demand would extend indefinitely.[3] (This point is not inconsistent with Keynes's example cited earlier, for that example begins with a fall in costs, which *would* prompt the firm to attempt to expand.)

Price-taking and the construction of firms' supply curves

It is widely believed that only for perfectly competitive firms can supply curves be drawn. This is supposed to derive from the 'fact' of price-taking and the option of 'selling as much as firms would like', of 'not being demand-constrained'. Since we have shown that perfectly competitive firms are always demand-constrained and cannot know the market price when making production plans without reducing the theory to a single equilibrium outcome, the fact that the belief is false is just as well.

All that is needed in order to draw supply curves is the concept of hypothetical demand: levels of demand to consider quite apart from what might actually be forming in 'the market' or in the minds of those actually thinking of buying the goods in question. Then one can ask how much it would be optimal to supply if demand gave rise to such-and-such a price, *assuming* that there will be enough demand; the assumption does not have to be true.

Even where demand constraints are easily perceived by market participants, most obviously by a monopolist, a supply *point* can be derived for every demand situation, and the strategies pertaining to similar situations, such as those resulting from parallel shifts in demand, can be linked together as a supply curve. This procedure is no different from that followed in deriving the small firm's supply curve: what is one doing if not tracing the implications of parallel shifts in hypothetical levels of demand?

The objection that supply curves exist for small firms but not for oligopolists or monopolists, because the latter *set* prices, will be addressed in Section III. First the matter of the elasticity of the small firm's demand curve must be looked at afresh. The reader will have noticed that the phrase 'horizontal demand curve' has been used in preference to 'infinitely-elastic demand curve'. There is a reason for this choice which will be apparent later.

Elasticity and size of firm

We have demonstrated that price-taking, as exposited in the theory of the perfectly-competitive firm, is neither logical nor empirically relevant. It therefore cannot provide a rationale for the flat demand curve associated with the small firm. But the good news is that there is no need for the assumption of price-taking to be able to derive the elasticity of a small firm's demand. Indeed, the argument should be turned around: for an industry of similar-sized firms (strictly, identical firms) the elasticity of a firm's demand curve depends on the number of firms in the industry.

Stigler (1966) demonstrated this years ago, by showing the effect on the individual firm's elasticity of a gradual increase in the number of firms in the industry. In a numerical example he drew a continuum of demand curves for two firms, ten firms, 50 firms. His purpose was to show how quickly the curve flattens out, but an alternative lesson can be drawn: that the size of the firm relative to the industry, rather than price-taking, is the explanation of elastic firm demand curves. His general proof follows.

Let the output of r firms by Q and that of the $(r + 1)^{th}$ firm be q. The market demand curve will be

$$Q + q = f(p)$$

so

$$dq/dp = f'(p) - dQ/dp$$

and

$$(dq/dp)(p/q) = [pf'(p)]/[Q + q] \cdot [Q + q)/q] - (dQ/dp)(p/Q)(Q/q)$$

or

$$\eta_{qp} = [(Q + q)/q]\ \eta_{Q+q,p} - (Q/q)\ \eta_{Qp}$$

where the first elasticity is that of the output of the $(r + 1)^{th}$ firm, the second is the market price elasticity, and the third is the elasticity of supply of the r firms.

If we take $Q = rq$, we have

$$\eta_{qp} = (r + 1)\ \eta_{Q+q,p} - r\ \eta_{Qp}$$

There are two features of Stigler's demonstration which should be noted. First, the supply elasticities of other firms enter into the determination of the nth firm's demand. This is a property of the perfect competition model which we have learned from the neo-Walrasians. It has unpleasant implications for any attempt to formulate rigorous microfoundations; identical firms are the only obvious escape. Second, demand is assumed to be shared equally amongst firms. This point is not essential here but is of interest in the next section.

The small firm in Stigler is remarkably free of the excess baggage perfect competition is normally made to carry. He does not even assert that the small firm's demand curve is infinitely elastic, only that its elasticity is large in comparison to the elasticity of the market demand curve. Monopoly, oligopoly and polypoly are all part of a continuum in this respect. This is heartening, since it can unify post-Keynesians who at present divide between the 'minimal difference from the classics' school and the 'realists', who prefer oligopoly.

If price-taking is not a necessary assumption, all features of the small firm which appear in the *General Theory* can be retained and the troublesome assumption of price-taking can be restricted to models of perfect foresight for those who like that sort of thing. We have no need of it. What we do need is a unified theory of firms under uncertainty. The rest of this chapter will make some tentative steps in this direction.

III The firm under uncertainty

It has been argued that

1. all firms, however small, are demand-constrained;
2. no firm is a price-taker in the sense embodied in the modern theory of perfect competition;
3. supply curves can be drawn for any firm; and
4. the elasticity of a firm's demand depends on the market demand curve, other firms' supply elasticities and the firm's size.

These conclusions point to a unity in the theory of the firm, away from the sharp distinctions to which we are accustomed.

In the framework of the *General Theory*, all firms are uncertain of the demand they face. As explained in Section II, this is owing to the simple fact of production for market sale: production and hiring decisions must be made in advance of offer for sale and knowledge of market demand. At least price expectations, perhaps even price-setting decisions, must also be made in advance of the market. The weight of conventional theory notwithstanding, the small firm is no exception to this.[4]

In Chapter 5 of the *General Theory* Keynes offers two choices of adjustment to an incorrect assessment of demand: the price can change to clear the market or firms can absorb the shock through changes in stocks. These two options are allied to assumptions of firms' attitude to prices at the beginning of the production period. Either firms decide a quantity strategy and expect a price but allow the market to set it or, expecting a level of demand, they set both price and quantity. The first of these options is explored by Dutt in this volume. Although we cannot take the matter very far here, we explore the second option.

In addition to the above, certain Keynesian propositions are taken for granted:

1. in the short period, supply conditions (the capital stock, technology) are given;
2. production always takes place in the short period; therefore the problem for producers is variations in demand;
3. price is an indication of demand; expected price is determined by expected demand, given what is known about supply; in the case of polypoly, firms are not concerned with what others supply; and
4. the demand for the product of an industry depends on aggregate demand and the industrial distribution of demand.

The small firm under uncertainty

The 'correct' price is that which, if simultaneously charged by all firms, would exactly clear the market. In the price-taking story, charging more or less than the 'correct' price looks highly irrational. But since the price is 'known' there is no reason to do other than accept it. Under uncertainty, however, (a) a price must be set without the 'correct' price being known; (b) the price could well be set 'too high' or 'too low' by accident; and (c) others may do the same.

Figure 8.2 illustrates a market-clearing position for an industry of many identical small firms. Demand is shared equally between them. S_i is the supply curve of one such firm. Bold capitals, ***SS*** and ***DD***, indicate the aggregate of firms' supply curves and the market demand curve, respectively.[5]

Assumptions (2)–(6) (Section II) imply that, if a supplier sets a price above the market price, his demand will fall to zero. If he sets a price below the market price, his demand, at least in principle, will equal the whole of the industry's demand. This proposition of course assumes that this producer acts alone in both cases, and that the rest of the industry has chosen the 'right' price. The result is traced out in Figure 8.2 as a bold line labelled *dd*, following the vertical axis down to P_0 where it becomes horizontal; it is then truncated at $(1/n)\ Q_0$ (where Q_0 is industry demand at

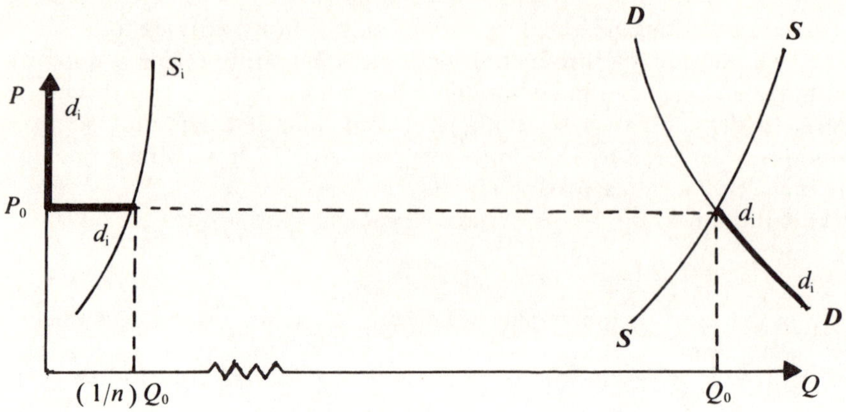

Figure 8.2 Market-clearing in an industry with many identical small firms

the market-clearing price, P_0) and resumes at the far side of the figure, coinciding with the market demand curve below P_0.

By contrast, suppose all firms choose the same price but it is not the 'correct' (market-clearing) price. Then the demand curve they face is $DD = 1/n{\cdot}\boldsymbol{DD}$, not just at P_0 but over the full range of prices.

There is something reminiscent of oligopoly here: we have distinguished the result when one firm acts alone from the result when all act together. The choice of notation for the demand curves is not an accident. The assumption which leads to the discontinuity of *dd* is neither price-taking nor the smallness of the firm but, rather, the uniformity of output and mobility and perfect information of consumers.

Let us return to Stigler's proof. Recall that he assumed equality of market shares. Thus what he determined was the elasticity of *DD*, the equal market shares curve. The demand of a small firm is, just because that firm is small, close to the vertical axis. Now we know that *any* demand curve, whatever its slope, is infinitely elastic at its intersection with the *y* axis, just because *Q* is zero. Even the demand curve of a monopolist is infinitely elastic at this point. Thus Stigler does not demonstrate that the demand curve facing a small firm is a horizontal line; such a curve is compatible with his demonstration but does not follow from it. The small firm makes a small amount of output, that is all.

Matters become even worse if one defines 'small' as being of measure zero, for then the demand curve is not a line, but a point, infinitely close to the *y* axis. The horizontal demand curve to which we are all so accustomed is justified neither by the theory nor by the story of the small firm. The

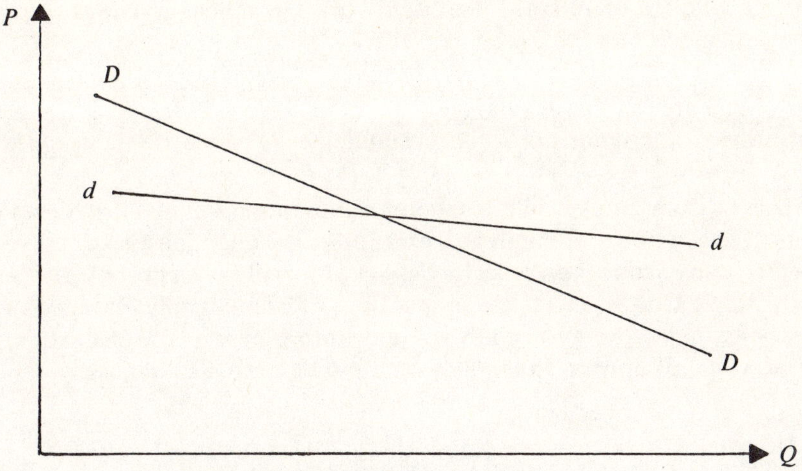

Figure 8.3 The kinked demand curve

correct rationale for the horizontal portion of *dd* is that the whole area behind *DD* constitutes demand. There is an infinitely dense set of such lines; we have just drawn the one for the current market price. Thus if the market price should fall, firms find themselves facing a new 'market price line' (the old 'horizontal demand curve'), truncated to the right of the old market price line. The locus of truncation points is *DD*.

We have not entered into the question of how that market price is determined. Turning our attention to oligopoly we see that, although the distinguishing feature of oligopoly is supposed to be that firms set prices, how they do so is, in the elementary theory, a mystery.

Oligopoly

In textbook oligopoly theory based on the kinked demand curve, there is a *DD* curve which describes what will happen if others in the industry follow and a *dd* curve which portrays what will happen if the firm acts alone, as in Figure 8.3. Notice that no reason is given for the point of cross-over: the market price. It is simply the prevailing price. The purpose of Figure 8.3 is only to explain why the oligopolist does not readily change price. This firm is every bit as much a price-taker, in the sense of being assumed to 'know' the market price, as is the perfectly competitive firm!

Part of the oligopoly story, of course, is product differentiation: it is said that without it, and/or customer loyalty, there can be no possibility of charging different prices. If we follow the logic of differentiating between industries only on the basis of the number of the firms each contains, we should see what oligopoly looks like with all the relevant assumptions of perfect competition retained: that is, (2)–(6). The other surviving assumptions are modified as follows:

1a. there are few sellers; and
8a. firms' output decisions will substantially alter price, by virtue of (1a).

These assumptions would result in a figure of market and firm demand indistinguishable from Figure 8.2, except that the oligopolist's *DD* curve is further away from the vertical axis; hence it will be less elastic for any given slope. Conversely, if the assumptions of product differentiation and customer loyalty were to be incorporated into polypoly, the discontinuity of *dd* would disappear. Polypoly would look exactly like oligopoly.

Monopoly

In monopoly there is no problem of what your rivals will do: the *dd*, *DD* and ***DD*** curves coincide. The only questions for the monopolist are the level of aggregate demand and how much of that will be directed to his product. Uncertainty concerns these factors alone.

IV Conclusion

The firm and market form

We have argued that all firms, however small, are demand-constrained, that none are price-takers in the sense embodied in the modern theory of perfect competition, that supply curves can be drawn for any firm, and that the elasticity of demand a firm faces depends on its size and whether it acts alone or in concert with others in the industry. These conclusions point to a unity in the theory of the firm.

The essence of distinctions of market form is, we argue, not whether the firm is price-making or price-taking, but what account must be taken of others in the industry. Thus those who argue, in contrast to the neoclassics, that monopoly is the archetypal market form are, in my view, mistaken, for it by necessity leaves out a factor crucial to the other two market forms: firm interdependence. Among standard models, oligopoly is the most general.

*Consistency of market forms with the **General Theory***

The perfectly competitive firm in standard microeconomics is certain of its market; the market-clearing price is known to all participants before production decisions are made. This implies that the theory is Equilibrium

Theory, with only one solution: demand cannot fluctuate and give rise to changes in price. There is an equilibrium price known and charged by all.

The *General Theory* cannot have such a market structure as its microfoundations, for in the *General Theory* firms are uncertain of demand and demand may fluctuate. It is this methodological difference, rather than the implications of a horizontal demand curve, which makes the *General Theory* incompatible with perfect competition, for we have shown that even the perfectly certain small firm is demand-constrained and thus compatible with the Principle of Effective Demand.

However we have argued that the certainty aspect of perfect competition can be stripped away, leaving a market form, here called polypoly, comprising a large number of small firms, and that this market form is completely compatible with the *General Theory*. One can approach the question of the small firm under uncertainty in at least two ways. One is to retain the assumption of price-taking but restrict it to taking the price at the point of market sale. This is a coherent story (Dutt, Chapter 7 of this volume) and can be combined with an adjustment mechanism which ensures convergence to the 'correct' price. Alternatively, if one evaluates market forms only by the number of firms in the industry, they become very similar. It is shown here that how producers obtain knowledge of the market price and of the supply responses of others is as much a mystery in textbook oligopoly theory as it is in the standard theory of perfect competition, though the theory of rational conjectures has made strides here.

Notes

1. The author wishes to thank Philip Arestis, Amitava Dutt, Bill Gerrard, John van Reenen and Peter Skott for helpful comments. They are not responsible for the end-product.
2. What I mean by 'demand-constrained' conforms to ordinary English usage. There is another usage, in which firms are only demand-constrained if prevented from selling the profit-maximizing quantity.
3. The perfect-competition outcome is 'on the cusp' between two situations: genuine rationing, in which the firm wants to expand sales but is not able to, and the circumstance of demand being to the right of the supply curve, when a firm is able to increase output, but does not want to. One might say that, in the latter case, the firm was 'supply-constrained', though since the supply curve is generated by the firm it is stretching language a bit. The perfectly-competitive firm is, however, objectively constrained from further market penetration, and the term 'demand-constrained' should apply.
4. Just how deep-rooted is the association of the small firm with price taking is demonstrated in Arrow's famous article (1959) on the question of how prices change in perfect competition: when, in this exploration, the managers of small firms are given the responsibility for changing prices – for *someone* must do it – the firm is then said to possess a 'degree of monopoly'. We do not agree with this description.

   Arrow's question, while it would have been legitimate in the present framework, is, of course, misguided in the context of perfect competition. In perfect competition prices cannot change, because perfect competition is an equilibrium theory. See the end of the sub-section on price-taking in conventional microeconomics, above.
5. The industry or market demand curve is, in turn, dependent on aggregate demand.

References

Arrow, K. J. (1959), 'Toward a Theory of Price Adjustment', in M. Abramovitz *et al.* (eds), *The Allocation of Economic Resources*, Stanford: Stanford University Press.
Chick, V. (1983), *Macroeconomics after Keynes*, Oxford: Philip Allan.
Stigler, G. J. (1966), *The Theory of Price*, 3rd edn, London: Macmillan.

PART III

PERSPECTIVES ON KEYNES

9 Keynes and the quantity theory of money

Arthur Brown

1 What Keynes inherited

In the preface to the French edition of the *General Theory*, Keynes states, 'the following analysis registers my final escape from the confusion of the Quantity Theory, which had once entangled me' (CW VII: xxxiv). This chapter aims first to remind the reader of what the Quantity Theory was, as Keynes inherited it. There follows a discussion of what Keynes did to it, both before and in the liberating *General Theory*. Then it is instructive to see how his modification or rebuttal has survived experiences of a further 50 years and, finally, some conclusions are drawn.

At its simplest, the Quantity Theory may be taken as the proposition that the unit value of money, its unit purchasing power over a representative bundle of commodities, tends to vary negatively with the size of the stock of money. So long as money meant gold or silver, its value would settle into equilibrium where the amounts of labour and other factors needed to produce a unit of it were equal to those required to produce a money unit's worth of anything else. That the *demand* for money is related to the value of the transaction for which it is required – by implication in a somewhat inelastic way – is a notion going back at least to Sir William Petty in the seventeenth century. By the time Keynes first learned his economics, it had been taken up by Marshall and become the basis of the Cambridge 'cash balance' approach. Marshall's starting-point was the proposition that 'in every state of society there is some fraction of their income that people find it worthwhile to keep in the form of currency', so that, other things being equal, a change in the supply of currency would result in an equiproportionate rise in the price level – demand was not for a particular quantity of currency as such, but for a particular amount of real purchasing power in monetary form.

The doctrine that Keynes inherited included not only the comparative static form of the Quantity Theory – the proportionality, *ceteris paribus*, of the price level to the stock of money in equilibrium – but also two related items, concerned with the process by which change in money stock affected prices, and the operational significance of the Theory. The process of monetary influence on prices was perfectly clear in the case of a money supply consisting entirely of gold or silver. If, say, a new source of the precious metal was discovered, the people who dug it up either had it minted or sold it to others who did so. More money thus appeared and was spent on other goods and services, raising their prices – something like proportionately if the supply of them was fixed, rather more if non-gold output was reduced by the diversion of labour to gold-digging. There had been studies of the spreading waves of price increase following gold discoveries. But Marshall was clear that matters were far more complicated than they seemed. The ratio of the stock of gold to the aggregate of monetary payments could be, and had been, highly variable. Marshall, who was also aware of the advance of bank deposits to predominance among the media of exchange, provided an account in more modern terms; Keynes believed him to be the only economist to have done so.

This account, however, if characteristically cautious, was also uncharacteristically vague. The trouble was that, while the arrival of additional gold in the banks was seen as likely to make bankers more willing to lend, it was not clear that borrowers would be more willing to borrow unless interest rates fell – and interest rates were believed to be constrained by a necessary relation to the rate of profit in business. Marshall tried to escape this difficulty by suggesting that news of an influx of gold would make businessmen expect higher prices. In response they would increase their borrowings in order to make speculative or precautionary purchases of, for instance, materials or equipment; but his main emphasis was on the tendency of the gold influx to produce a temporary fall in discount rate, a 'wave on the surface', not sufficient to violate the essential equality between the interest and profit rates, but enough to stimulate borrowing for speculative purposes. He also suggested that the new gold would 'bide its time' until the next increase (not explained, but taken as a practical probability of economic life) in speculative sentiment, when it would permit a greater expansion of credit and of speculative buying than would have been possible without it.

As for the operational significance of the Quantity Theory, the chief point was that the direction of causation was taken as being from money stock to price level, not the reverse. For the world as a whole, gold discoveries and banking systems which economized the monetary use of gold raised prices. At national levels uncontrolled issues of paper currency had done likewise. Some of these causes were seen as being within the control of policy, some not. For a single country, acquisitions of gold, either from domestic production of through an external surplus on current account, would tend to raise domestic prices. This process was self-limiting because higher prices would eliminate the surplus or lead to a deficit on current account. The gold standard system was self-regulating; so long as the convertibility of currencies into gold was maintained, the purchasing power of a unit of gold could nowhere move far from its marginal cost of production in terms of other internationally tradeable goods and services. And output everywhere was supposed to be limited only by factor supplies; money supply had nothing to do with it, except perhaps in a very short run in which economists were not greatly interested.

How did Keynes modify this body of doctrine? We can trace his attitude towards it through three main landmarks: his *Tract on Monetary Reform* (1923), the *Treatise on Money* (1930) and the *General Theory* (1936).

II Keynes's modifications – up to the *General Theory*

In the *Tract*, Keynes's discussion of the Quantity Theory was on broadly Marshallian lines. His equation of exchange, however, explicitly took account of the public's demand for current banking accounts, as well as for cash (as Fisher and Pigou had already done). With regard to the simple presumption of proportionality between the cash stock and prices, Keynes maintained the Marshallian scepticism, though on rather different grounds – variation in demand for liquidity rather than changes in 'the methods of doing business'. He noted that, in the downswing of 1920–2, the public's increased real demand for both cash and bank deposits had 'had more to do than the deflation of "cash" had with the fall of prices'. Hence his emphasis was on the need for active management of the money stock if the price level was to be kept stable, because of the substantial cyclical changes in the public's demand for real money balances. He had already conceded that a doubling of the cash supply might well lead *in the long run* to a price level twice as high as it would otherwise have been, but this evoked the qualification which is probably the most famous of all his dicta: '*In the long run* we are all dead. Economists set themselves too easy, too useless a task if in tempestuous seasons they can only tell us that when the storm is long past the ocean is flat again' (CW IV: 65, emphasis in original). The 'tempestuous season' since 1914 had begun to undermine his contentment with the long-run, comparative static, equilibrium methods of nineteenth-century economic theory.

The *Treatise on Money* of 1930 was not only a much more substantial work than the *Tract*; it had been written over six years during which unemployment in the United Kingdom had remained substantially higher than could be regarded as normal by pre-war standards, and there was a pervasive feeling that the economy was not working properly. Keynes had already, in 1929, endorsed the Liberal programme of public works as a remedy for unemployment. Nevertheless the *Treatise* is not a book about unemployment; it is primarily about the price level and how it is changed. He says at the beginning of Chapter 10:

> The fundamental problem of Monetary Theory is not merely to establish identities or statistical equations relating (e.g.) the turnover of monetary instruments to the turnover of things traded for money. The real problem of such a Theory is to treat the problem dynamically, analysing the different elements involved in such a manner as to exhibit the causal process by which the price-level is determined, and the method of transition from one equilibrium to another. The forms of the Quantity Theory, however, on which we have all been brought up . . . are but ill adapted for this purpose. (CW V: 120)

The key to his approach was the division of the national product into two parts, cost of production (including 'normal' rewards to capital and entrepreneurship) and the residue, positive or negative, which Keynes called 'profits'. George Shackle later pointed out that this amounted to much the same thing as distinguishing between the levels of income (and of its components) which were *expected* when planning decisions were taken and those departures from the expected which came as surprises in the event – thus incorporating the distinction between *ex ante* and *ex post* magnitudes which subsequently proved so fruitful in Myrdal's hands.

Dividing these two elements of the national product – cost of production and profits – by some measure of the real (constant price) level of output yields the simplest form of Keynes's fundamental equation: price per unit of total output is normal cost of production per unit *plus* (positive or negative) profit per unit. This simple operation leads to a distinction between the two possible immediate sources of change in the price level. On the one hand there are changes in the money costs necessary to call forth the required factors of production, and changes in those factors' physical productivities. In the language of a later time this could be exemplified by 'cost push'. On the other hand there are changes in the amount of 'profits' per unit of output, largely associated later with 'demand pull' or its negative version. Changes from the former Keynes called 'incomes' inflation of deflation. To changes from the latter source he gave the prefix 'profit'.

'Profits' are the excess of value of output over its cost of production. Subtract the cost of production of consumption from each of the two last-named magnitudes and one arrives at the identity of 'profits' with the excess of investment over savings – since on Keynes's definitions investment (the net increment of capital) includes profits, and savings do not. So far as the second right-hand term of the fundamental equation is concerned, therefore, the condition of price equilibrium, that profits in the Keynesian sense should be zero, requires savings and investment (also in his sense) to be equal – or, in Myrdal's terms, that they should be equal *ex ante*. How can the relation between savings and investment most conveniently be adjusted? Keynes's answer is by the rate of interest, changes in which may be presumed to affect them in opposite directions. He acknowledges that he is here following in the footsteps of Wicksell, for whom there was a 'natural' rate of interest which preserved a constant price level; and from which the ruling, market rate could, at least temporarily, diverge.

What about Marshall's insistence, with which Keynes had previously concurred, that the interest rate was constrained by a necessary equality with the rate of profit in business? No more is heard of it. Perhaps Keynes would have said, if challenged, that such a constraint operated only on the average over long periods, and that he was discussing short-period dynamics. But, in effect, as Shackle points out, he had already invented liquidity preference, without giving it a name. In the crucial Chapter 10 of the *Treatise*, he points to the function of the interest rate on securities (and of the rate paid by banks on deposits) in reconciling investors to the necessity of holding the stocks of savings deposits and of securities which are in existence. An alternative theory of interest was thus already in his mind.

Liberated from the necessary equality of (long-term) interest with the rate of profit on business capital, he could acknowledge that a lowering of short-term interest rates, typically through the action of the Bank of England in lowering the Bank Rate, will tend to lower all interest rates. The value of investment goods will thus be raised, and virtually all kinds of investment rise relatively to saving. The price level is immediately raised by the action of the second term on the right-hand side of the fundamental equation – profits per unit of output are raised. But there is a further effect; the increased pressure of demand for factors of production raises *their* prices, so that the first term on that side of the equation – cost of production per unit of output – is also raised, though the process may take some time because of the stickiness of labour markets. In addition to such 'induced' changes in factor prices, Keynes recognized that there may also be what appear as 'spontaneous' changes, in fact due to causes 'including e.g. the powers and activities of Trade Unions'.

Where does the quantity of money come into this picture? The increased borrowing stimulated by reduced interest rates is in part borrowing from banks, so that new deposits are created. The higher level of money income and money transactions following higher investment means that larger total money balances are demanded for transactions purposes. These considerations, by themselves, suggest a rise in the stock of money more or less *pari passu* with that of money income. But there is more to it than that. One of the main points of the *Treatise* is that money is held for other purposes besides the carrying out of transactions. The extent to which accumulated savings are held in bank deposits rather than as securities will vary with the 'state of bearishness' of the public, roughly what Keynes was later to call their 'liquidity preference', and bearishness may vary widely, especially over the course of the trade cycle.

Thus, while Keynes devoted a chapter to the analysis and comparison of the various forms of the 'quantity equation', the quantity of money does not really occupy the centre of his stage. The relation between that quantity and the price level is seen as a complex one and, in any case, he is most interested in the processes through which price levels can be changed by the monetary authorities. A constant (or regularly increasing) supply of money is not the recipe for stability because of changes in bearishness. The key lies in the possibility of controlling the level of investment, as circumstances require (his old *Tract* point), to which he comes, as 'the crux of the whole matter', in Chapter 37.

In the circumstances of the time he was naturally more concerned with the Central Bank's ability to stimulate investment rather than to check it. He was sceptical of the governability of investment in working capital through short-term rates, which is implicit in Hawtrey's writings, mainly because such investment is very sensitive to volatile expectations about prices. He had greater hope for the influence of Central Banks (or, at least, the Bank of England) through the effect which the general liquidity of the banking system exerts on lending to the 'unsatisfied fringe' of borrowers, in whose cases the banks' assessment of risks rather than the interest the customer can afford is the limiting factor. He attaches some weight also to the direct influence which the bank can exert, in either direction, on issue houses and underwriters. But it is the long-term interest rate, especially in relation to borrowing for investment in such long-lived assets as new buildings and utilities, to which he attributes the greatest potential influence. He admits that Bank Rate changes, though real, are somewhat muted, and pins his hopes for a more effective control on much more vigorous use of open market operations than had yet become respectable – in effect, on the purchase or sale of securities by the Central Bank in whatever quantities might be required to offset the excessive temporary bullishness or bearishness of the public, and to bring the long-term market rate of interest into harmony with the natural rate, at which savings and investment would be equal. All that said, he admits that, for any national economy, not only can 'spontaneous' variations in internal factor prices prove harder to counter, but 'no Central Bank which is a member of an international system . . . can expect to preserve the stability of its price level if it is acting in isolation and is not assisted by corresponding action on the part of other Central Banks'.

In the *Treatise*, therefore, Keynes cast doubt on the accuracy of the Quantity Theory, at least as a short-term guide to the appropriateness of the money supply, with his insistence on the scale and variability of 'bearishness' as a motive for holding money, giving firmer substance to qualifications that Marshall would have recognized. It was perhaps more important that he took it out of the limelight by concentrating on the dynamics of change in the price level, and pointed out that such changes, so far as the national economy is concerned, may come from changes in monetary conditions, but also from changes in world prices of internationally traded goods, from changes in propensities to save or invest, or from industrial and labour market changes which affect the level of efficiency wages.

III The General Theory and after

Just as the *Treatise* is a book about the price level, the *General Theory* is essentially about the level of activity, and what it has to say about the price level is mainly drawn together in Chapter 21. The fundamental equations of the *Treatise* have gone, their second term sunk by the decision to define savings and investment in *ex post* social accounting terms, so that they become identical. Emphasis falls on the ghost of the first term, appearing as the ratio of factor prices to productivity. In the short term, the level of utilization of capacity, virtually the central variable of the book, affects both of these. Productivity is affected negatively, though this is hardly represented as a major source of price variation. Factor prices are affected because their *sensitivity* to total expenditure varies with factor utilization. In a simplified world they would be completely insensitive so long as any of the relevant factor was unemployed; when a factor was fully employed its price would move (or at least rise) in proportion to total expenditure on it. But, in the real world, wages, in particular, are less simple; they tend to rise before full employment is reached:

> Since each group of workers will gain, *ceteris paribus*, by a rise in its own wages, there is naturally for all groups a pressure in this direction, which entrepreneurs will be more ready to meet when they are doing better business. [But] in actual experience the wage unit does not change continuously in response to every small change in effective demand, but discontinuously. These points of discontinuity are determined by the psychology of the workers and by the policies of employers and Trade Unions . . . They have, moreover, a good deal of historical importance, but they do not readily lend themselves to historical generalisations. (CW VII: 301)

The special role of factor prices, already established in the *Treatise*, is thus elaborated, at least so far as wages are concerned.

More generally, the key importance of interest rate, asserted in the *Treatise*, is further clarified. In partnership with the schedule of the marginal efficiency of capital it regulates investment, which, in turn, through the multiplier, regulates total expenditure. Interest is itself controlled, in a given state of liquidity preference (or bearishness) by the supply of money. The *General Theory* might, therefore, be said to contain a 'Quantity of Money Theory' of expenditure, the major qualifications to which would have to be that it holds only given constant shapes and positions of the schedules of marginal efficiency of capital, propensity to consume and liquidity preference. Keynes's emphasis was on the mobility and uncertainty of the marginal efficiency of capital, as it might present itself to entrepreneurs, and of the liquidity preference schedule. In addition to the uncertainty and variability of the relation between money stock and national expenditure which is thus implied, there remains the uncertainty between national expenditure and price level, given that the volume of output has now become a variable. In consequence changes in expenditure may affect price level and output in various ratios to one another, from unity to zero.

There is little evidence that Keynes's views relevant to the Quantity Theory changed substantially after 1937. In *How to Pay for the War* he said nothing about the stock of money, except that a government in control of the banking system will have no difficulty in obtaining the money needed to buy that part of the national product that it requires. The Quantity Theory remained in the shadows for three reasons. First, expenditure was, at least under wartime conditions, largely controllable without resort to monetary restrictions. Secondly, low interest rates were thought important for keeping down the long-term cost of government borrowing, and finally, after the war, there was widespread fear of a 1921-type depression, which might have longer-lasting adverse effects on confidence. Keynes's influence strengthened all three of these reasons. His fears of a high interest bill on the national debt, as liable to impose an intolerable social and economic burden on those who were not rentiers, had featured prominently in the *Tract*. More recently he had come to mistrust the use of high rates of interest as short-term regulators of activity. He feared that, if those rates established a reputation for volatility, their average levels would become too high to be consistent with high levels of activity, once the temporary post-war backlogs of demand had disappeared. The Quantity Theory could hardly have provided a practical guide to policy in the conditions of that time. The wartime (and early post-war) economy, with its reliance upon direct controls, was essentially a 'disequilibrium system' involving the high ratio of debt to income and high liquidity mentioned above.

Keynes emphasized that money is not only a medium of exchange but also an asset, and therefore a medium of speculation. He also established the place of interest in the demand function for it. But the fundamental point was elaborated in Chapter 21 of the *General Theory*:

> So long as economists are concerned with what is called the Theory of Value, they have been accustomed to teach that prices are governed by the conditions of supply and demand . . . But when they pass in Volume II, or more often in a separate treatise, to the Theory of Money and Prices, we hear no more of these homely but intelligible concepts, but move into a world where prices are governed by the quantity of money . . . One of the objects of the foregoing chapters has been to escape from this double life and to bring the theory of prices as a whole back to close contact with the theory of value . . . As soon as we pass to the problem of what determines output and employment as a whole, we require the complete theory of a monetary economy. (CW VII: 292)

The substance and emphasis of economic writing depend, naturally enough, on what economists are worried about. Keynes's hard words about the Quantity Theory, which I quoted at the beginning of this chapter, derived from his concern about unemployment and the level of activity, on which it throws no light, whereas he had devised a theory of the level of activity in which the quantity of money plays a substantial part. When, subsequently, the war and full employment made him worry about the price level, the control of money supply was not the prime instrument chosen for dealing with it. And, for some time after the war, fear of a depression existed alongside the fear and experience of inflation. Thus the Quantity Theory, in addition to the modifications and qualifications which Keynes's work added to it, was, to use an expressive Yorkshire word, 'sided'. Experience of persistent inflation in the 1960s and 1970s combined with a freedom from major depressions rescued it from that condition, raising questions which are now examined.

IV The quantity theory as an aid to policy

The main source of interest in the Quantity Theory has never been theoretical curiosity. Behind the discussion has always lain the question: is the price level controllable by operating on the supply of money? Keynes, in the *Treatise*, gave a cautious positive answer. He thought complete success was unattainable, necessitating great sensitivity and flexibility, but that the banking system should at least try harder. Money supply had a part to play in the crucial business of regulating the amount of investment, but budgetary and perhaps other measures were also needed. All these measures together should make it possible to avoid deflation or what was later to be called 'demand pull' inflation. But, also, changes outside central control (especially wages) might prevent the achievement of high employment with a steady price level.

The controllability of price level through money supply can be broken down into a number of subsidiary questions:

1. Can we specify the definition of the money supply?
2. Is the relation between the money supply and total expenditure constant over the trade cycle and in the longer term?
3. By what mechanism does the money supply affect expenditure? Does it work through interest rates, as Keynes believed? And how strongly?
4. How important are sources of change in expenditure other than domestic monetary ones?
5. How are changes in expenditure divided between real output and prices?
6. Is the money supply controllable?

What counts as money?

Keynes had few doubts about what should count as money for discussing the Quantity Theory; the money supply equalled bank deposits plus notes and coin in the hands of the public. Since, in the *General Theory*, the key quality of money, after its liquidity, was the absence of interest on holdings of it, he might have wished to exclude deposit accounts, giving a definition approximating to our M1 rather than M2 or M3, but he is there concerned with theory rather than statistical application, and (167: fn) he claims the right to draw the line between 'money' and 'debt' at any point that is convenient.

That matters are not so simple now can be gathered from the history of monetary policy since the mid-1970s. The perils of aiming to target monetary growth were foreshadowed by the Radcliffe Committee (1959) in that, from the point of view of the holder, any short-dated debt of high quality is a close substitute for money, in the sense that it has nearly as great an effect on decisions to spend as would possession of money to the same value. Any relation existing, *ceteris paribus*, between the quantity of money (on a given definition) and expenditure is liable to be upset by changes in the holdings of assets which fall outside that definition of money. The practical consequence is that the monetary authorities have been driven to formulating a number of different definitions (and publishing the corresponding statistics), ranging currently from M0 (notes, coin and Bank of England deposits) to M5 (private-sector non-bank holdings of notes, coin, sterling deposits with banks and building societies, National Savings Bank accounts, Premium Bonds and certain National Savings instruments).

A spectrum of substitutes for 'money', in the *General Theory* sense of cash and interestless bank deposits, give rise to problems of selecting the appropriate money supply variable, but, also, institutional changes have broadened the range of such substitutes. In recent years, the expectations aroused by two generations of continuous inflation and increased competition between financial institutions have meant that the interestless current account deposit has lost ground to equally liquid but interest-bearing rivals. These institutional changes complicate the empirical testing and practical application of the Quantity Theory. The creation of new close substitutes for whatever is regarded for the moment as 'money' raises problems for authorities' ability to control the total money stock, a point examined later in this section.

Is the velocity of circulation constant?

Setting aside the difficulties of identifying what should count as the monetary stock and defining it as M3, is the ratio of that stock to the price level, or to total expenditure, in fact constant over time? Nobody has posited a constant ratio between money and prices in anything but a fairly short run because, throughout modern times in countries advanced enough to provide the required statistics, growth of the real volume of output (usually accompanied by growth of population) has been substantial over anything but quite short periods. This creates a presumption that increasing quantities of money are needed to maintain a given price level. It is, therefore, at the ratio of money to nominal income (or expenditure) that one looks. Keynes did not believe this ratio (often referred to as the 'Cambridge k') or its inverse, the income velocity of circulation of money, to be constant, at least over the trade cycle. The ratio varied with changes in 'bearishness', later described as shifts of the liquidity preference schedule, or changes in interest rates which would cause movements *along* that schedule. For the longer run, Keynes stressed that 'the . . . relationship between the national income and the quantity of money will depend on liquidity preferences'. He was not inclined to place any bets on the longer-run constancy or inconstancy which those preferences might be expected to show.

As for the short-run, or business-cycle behaviour of velocity, Keynes's expectations were justified. If short-term variability is measured by standard deviation of year-to-year percentage changes, then, between the early 1950s and 1979, velocity was more variable than money supply in France, Germany, Japan and immensely more so in India (Brown, 1985). In Italy, the United States and the United Kingdom its variability fell below that of money supply by less than one-sixth. Velocity of circulation, according to this short-term criterion, was decidedly the more variable of these two magnitudes in the United Kingdom, especially in the 1920s and 1930s.

In the countries with more flighty velocity, correlations of changes in money stock with those in expenditure are low, at least for the post-war period. With the exception of Italy, correlations between changes in money stock and those in velocity were generally negative in the short term. In France, Germany, Japan and Italy it was the velocity variations that proved to be better correlated (negatively) with expenditure changes, indeed, significantly so; whereas in the United States the closer relation involved the money stock. Velocity seems to have been considerably better correlated with expenditure than money stock was in the United Kingdom, both in the generation before 1914 and between the two world wars, though not in more recent times. In the short term, therefore, not only is velocity not sufficiently stable to be treated as constant in the face of changes in money supply, but its variations seem to play a greater part than those of money stock in the process of adjustment to alterations in expenditure, the United States providing, in the last generation or two, the major exception.

The chief exponents of the Quantity Theory in recent years, Professor Milton Friedman and his associates, have not sought to stress the constancy of velocity in the short run. Friedman's formal position in his 1956 essay, 'The Quantity Theory – A Restatement', was that the demand for money could be expressed as a function of a reasonably small number of variables – interest rates, prices, real income, rate of change of prices (a proxy for expectations of further changes) and the ratio of human to non-human forms of wealth – and that this function is stable. This may be described as being half in the spirit of Keynes and wholly in the spirit of those who sought to interpret the *General Theory* in a mechanistic way. Such an approach underrates Keynes's emphasis on unavoidable ignorance of the future as a motive for money holding, with its corollary that the relevant demand function is unlikely to be easily specifiable in terms of measurable magnitudes.

Later the estimation of demand functions for money became a substantial industry, which suffered from the operation of the econometric version of Sod's Law – whenever an apparently stable relation is discovered, it at once ceases to apply. A recent study (Hall *et al.*, 1989) states, 'Perhaps the most striking conclusion we reach is that in no case does the simple text book set of variables prove to be adequate. To practitioners this is not surprising, of course, as it is simply another way of saying that models based on this set of variables are inadequate and will be found to be structurally unstable.' Institutional innovations (introduction of new types of account, credit cards and so on) which take time to become effective and wealth effects from changes in stock exchange values are among the disturbing factors which have to be taken into account. These matters operating on the attitudes of money holders, even if identifiable after the event, are largely unpredictable before it. Keynes's stress on the unknown character of the future was not misplaced; it does not mean that one should not try to forecast the future from the experience of the past, only that one should expect a substantial failure rate. This is a view to which modern chaos theory has added respectability in many departments of knowledge.

Friedman and his associates were not content, in practice, with substituting stable money demand functions for stable velocities of circulation. They also investigated the stability of velocity. In their monumental *Monetary Trends in the United States and the United Kingdom* (1982) Friedman and Schwartz commit themselves to the judgement that: 'The simplest of quantity theories, which supposes that the ratio of nominal money to nominal income is a constant aside from independent random errors in money and income ... turns out to be an impressive first approximation ...' This, however, relates not to variations taken directly from series of annual figures, but to those between averages computed over whole phases (rising or descending) of 'reference cycles', the average length of such phases being two or three years. Most cyclical variation – that between peaks and troughs – is thus deliberately eliminated. This procedure seems to throw the baby out with the bath-water.

At the practical level of monetary policy, most discussion has been directed to such questions as how to prevent an inflationary boom which, if unchecked, would be expected to blow itself out in two or three years, or how to arrest a dive into depression from which, without a policy change, recovery might be expected to begin after a similar interval. There are, of course, decisions which are at least intended to be of longer-term significance – whether to return to the Gold Standard (in 1925), to sign the Bretton Woods Agreement or to join the European Monetary System – but most monetary steering activity is concerned with the urgent need to keep the chariot of state out of the roadside ditches. The long run, as Keynes plainly saw, is a succession of short runs. And the monetarist doctrine that all would be well, and short-term problems would cease to exist, if one kept the growth of money supply steady and in line with the trend of real output capacity founders precisely on the rock of fluctuations in non-transactional demand for money to which Keynes drew attention.

Even on the basis of averages for cycle phases the constancy of average velocity seems to be less impressive than the above quotation from Friedman and Schwartz suggests. Setting aside the long-term *trends* (as the authors themselves point out, velocity in the United States fell by nearly two-thirds in a century) British velocity almost doubled between the cycle phases centred on 1949 and 1970. It also rose by about 30 per cent between the descending phase of 1973–5 and that of 1979–83, probably because of the rise of substitutes for M3. Between the irregular assaults of institutional change and the short-term fluctuations of sentiment, the velocity of circulation is battered into something a good way from constancy.

Does the money supply affect expenditure through the interest rate?
Those who are impressed by what they see as the empirical constancy of velocity sometimes take the view that anything that reduces the stock of money will reduce expenditure. If they believe, further, that prices are generally highly market-sensitive, this suggests to them that changing interest rates will, by affecting the demand for money, operate more or less directly on the price level, with little effect on real output. This is the view which inspired monetary targeting in the United Kingdom in the 1970s (Fforde, 1983). Keynes's view was different. One of his major contentions was that the Bank Rate, which Montague Norman, for instance, had seen as primarily an instrument for safeguarding monetary reserves by influencing the international flow of funds, was also, through its influence on domestic interest rates generally, a major influence on domestic investment and employment. It was not long, however, before some doubt began to be thrown on the efficiency of interest rates in this latter connection. Within a couple of years of the publication of the *General Theory*, the Oxford Economists' Research Group had suggested that most entrepreneurs find interest rate changes a minor matter in comparison with alterations in the outlook for costs, sales and prices; that much investment in even fixed capital is intended to have a short pay-off period; and that, where this is not so, the returns in the more distant years carry such an aura of uncertainty that the rate at which they are discounted for time does not make much difference to their present value.

More recently the influence of interest rates on investment has been widely investigated in the course of general economic modelling. The OECD (1982) surveyed the evidence from models in seven leading countries, on residential and non-residential fixed investment, stock-building and expenditure on consumers' durable goods. Only in the United States did it find significant effects on all those categories. Nowhere else was there any effect on stockbuilding; Canada was the only other country showing a significant effect on consumers' durables; but four countries out of seven showed significant effects on private non-residential fixed capital, and all seven showed it on residential building. This is broadly in accordance with theoretical expectations; the longer and safer the investment, the greater the effect of interest rate. A survey of the United Kingdom economic models by W. W. Easton (1985) presents a not dissimilar picture, with residential building the only category for which all four models that distinguished it, attributed a significant influence to interest rates – though a majority of the models gave interest rates some power also over stock-building and purchases of durable goods.

A still more recent National Institute study (Fisher *et al.*, 1989) shows that short-term interest rate changes operate directly on housebuilding, with an elasticity of about one-third; the effects on other categories of investment are less powerful and less well agreed. The effects detected on consumers' spending were smaller still proportionately but, because this expenditure is so large, very considerable absolutely. The great increase in consumers' use of credit since Keynes's time must be held responsible for much of this effect. Altogether, short-term interest rate changes seemed, in the four relevant models, to operate directly on real gross domestic product (GDP) with an elasticity of anything from a tenth to a thirtieth. That is not the end of the story; there would be indirect effects, one of the most important being that which works through alterations in the exchange rate which interest rate changes may be expected to produce. In full simulations including all the repercussions which the respective models encompassed, the maximum effect of the hypothetical interest rate changes, attained after intervals of two or three years, amounted to between a half per cent and one per cent change in income for a one percentage point change in short-term interest (an elasticity, at the interest rate levels of the later 1980s, of a tenth or a twentieth). The same simulations, however, suggest changes of zero to four per cent in general price levels, so that the elasticity of nominal expenditure with respect to short-term interest rates could, on this evidence, be anything between a twentieth and a half, with the corollary that the increase in expenditure may, or may not, be a matter more of price than of output – a question to which we shall return later.

All this suggests a fairly high degree of uncertainty about the effect of interest rate changes on expenditure, including some uncertainty as to whether their effects are mainly exercised directly through real domestic spending, the resultant price changes, or changes in foreign exchange rates which would impinge on expenditure through both price levels and external competitiveness. The general impression is that the elasticity of *real* expenditure is rather low.

As mentioned earlier, Keynes in the *Treatise* put some emphasis on the influence upon investment (and so on expenditure generally) of changes in banks' assessments of borrowers' creditworthiness, as opposed to changes in the interest rates they charged. It is possible that such changes have been generally parallel to those in interest rates, so that their effects will have been in some degree included in the econometric estimates of the influence of the latter. Otherwise the influence of the banking system on expenditure, especially through the strategically important channel of 'finance', may be considerably greater than estimated elasticities of the interest rate imply. More important to the present discussion is that variations in credit rationing to the 'unsatisfied fringe of borrowers' constitute an alternative to the interest rate mechanism for regulating the money supply, which some close observers, including Keynes himself, and more recently, Dow and Saville (in their *Critique of Monetary Policy*, 1988), believe to be an important one.

The remaining part of the question at the head of this section is whether it is through changes in money supply that the authorities regulate interest rates, as Keynes, in general, supposed. In so far as their instrument is open market operations, they work directly on non-bank holdings of money by exchanging that money for other assets (or vice versa). On the other hand, changes in interest rates play an essential part in such operations in that some alteration in the money prices of non-monetary assets is necessary to induce the public to participate in the transaction. Like the administrative use of the interest rate to increase or restrict borrowing from the banks, these operations amount to moving the non-bank public along its liquidity preference schedule. Dow and Saville argue that administrative changes in the key interest rates (Bank Rate, Minimum Lending Rate) have a rather different mode of operation. They are signals about official attitudes and intentions, and thus clues to the future, eagerly grasped by markets which are short of positive expectations and rich in what Shackle called 'areas of zero potential surprise' – in short, that within limits these changes can move the liquidity preference schedule of the market bodily. This seems to be an essentially Keynesian notion, even though the eye of faith is needed to see more than a hint of it in the famous Chapter 12 of the *General Theory*.

Sources of change in expenditure other than domestic monetary ones

So much for the processes by which domestic monetary changes may affect expenditure. It is, however, plain that other matters can affect it. In any single national economy, for instance, changes in the world prices of internationally traded goods – and especially of those materials the prices of which are highly flexible – are largely 'autonomous' from that economy's point of view. Keynes did not make much of this in his two major works of the 1930s. In 1938, however, stimulated by government preparations for the stockpiling of strategic commodities, he produced his British Association paper on the general advantages of a wider stockpiling scheme, among which some moderation of price fluctuations was included; and subsequently, from 1941 onwards, he was active in devising buffer stock schemes, first in connection with his Clearing Union plans, later separately. He would hardly have been surprised at the way in which the Korean commodity price boom of 1950–1 or the oil shocks of 1973 and 1979–80 promoted general price increases in the industrial countries, largely through the mechanism of the price–wage spiral, the working of which he had outlined in *How to Pay for the War*. Nor, I think, in view of his reference in the *Treatise* to the 'power and activities of Trade Unions', would he have been surprised at the inflationary effects in most of the leading industrial countries of the wage explosion of the later 1960s, which seems to have owed more to the political and social temper of the time than to any identifiable economic cause.

Can one diagnose the nature of the various shocks that affect expenditure? My own study (1985) was based on observations of four sets of symptoms, regarded as indicating different kinds of 'impulses', positive or negative. First, there are the domestic *monetary* impulses, characterized by change in the rate of growth of the money supply and simultaneous change of the rate of growth of velocity in the opposite direction; preferably with interest rates, and/or their rates of change, moving in the same direction as velocity, to indicate that whatever velocity has done is not the result purely of a change in liquidity preference. Secondly, there are *expenditure* impulses, in which the growth rate of final expenditure changes, with the accompaniment of a change in the same direction in the profit ratio, to suggest that it was, indeed, on the side of final expenditure, not cost of production, that the episode originated. Thirdly, there are *wage* impulses, changes in the rate of growth of wage rates coupled with opposite changes in the profit ratio, to suggest that what happened to wages was a result of change on the side of labour supply, not of demand. And finally, for a national economy, impulses from the main non-labour input costs can be represented by any substantial changes in the (suitably weighted) rate of increase of *import prices*.

This exercise, based on changes between one year and the next, in the main OECD countries between 1951 and 1979, yielded a number of suggestions. First, monetary impulses, diagnosed from changes in money growth and in velocity alone, are, indeed, fairly frequent, occurring in any given country, on average, once in rather less than two years; but their suggestions of an easing or tightening of monetary conditions are contradicted, in about a fifth of the cases, by what happens to interest rates, indicating that changes in liquidity preference rather than in money supply were predominant in these instances; while the indications in some other cases were ambiguous, so that clear cases of monetary impulse occurred typically about once in three years. Impulses of the three other kinds distinguished above each occurred with something not very different from this frequency.

To what extent do the monetary impulses appear to be the causes of changes in nominal expenditure or of wage changes? (They can hardly be at all direct causes of changes in import prices.) For the six biggest OECD economies taken together, there does seem to have been a significant tendency for a positive monetary impulse to be followed in the next year by accelerating expenditure – the corresponding relation of negative monetary impulses with decelerating expenditure is not significant. There was quite a strong tendency for monetary impulses to be *negatively* associated with wage impulses of the same sign, and virtually no connection between monetary impulses and the occurrence, or non-occurrence, of wage impulses in the following year or the year after that.

On the face of it, therefore, increased monetary ease seems to have had some effect on expenditure, but not at all directly on wage inflation. Monetary stringency tended to coincide with periods of wage inflation, import price inflation, and rising inflation generally, which apparently prompted it, and its effects on them were more diffuse, or, at least, less clearly apparent. Import-price and wage shocks have to be treated as independent, in at least the first instance, of a country's monetary policy, though they may impinge upon it. Since, together, they have been (in the three post-war decades, at least) more numerous than impulses from change in the domestic monetary situation, it is not surprising that whatever impact the monetary changes have had in the short run on expenditure and prices has been blurred.

The division of demand pressure between output and prices

In what proportions a change in expenditure divides itself between changes in output and in prices is a crucial question for anyone seeking empirical support for the *General Theory* against the doctrines that preceded it or the New Classical doctrine that has followed. It is also important in relation to the Quantity Theory in that, if change in the quantity of money acts on quantities of goods and services rather than their prices, that constitutes a departure from at least the strongest version of the Theory, and one which may have important policy implications.

Old classical doctrine dealt with a long run in which factors of production were fully employed and output independent of what happened to the price level. Keynes, in his later works, concentrated on a shorter run in which prices are not very sensitive to expenditure so long as factors are unemployed, and carry the main weight of increasing expenditure only when bottlenecks develop in the productive process – reductions in expenditure tending to manifest themselves more through output than through price. Of course, in the really long run ('in which we are all dead') few people would deny that the change in output will owe more to the change in the supplies of factors of production (including technical know-how) than to change in nominal expenditure – the net change in the percentage of available factors unemployed will be a minor influence – though some (including Keynes) would argue that the general level of inflationary or deflationary pressure over such a long period can make a considerable difference to the rate of accumulation of capital and perhaps (in a given country) to the growth of population, mostly through the effect of demand pressure or its opposite on net immigration or emigration.

I return to the shorter run to which monetary and other policies are more directly geared, if only for the reason that vision more than, say, five years ahead is cloudy indeed. Have we empirical confirmation of the Keynesian expectation that increases of expenditure in conditions of general unemployment, and perhaps all reductions of expenditure, would act on output rather than prices in at least the first instance? This question would be easy to answer if aggregate demand curves (plotted on axes of output and price) moved up and down in accordance with changes in entrepreneurial mood, external trade conditions or macroeconomic policy, while the corresponding aggregate supply curves obligingly remained stationary. The latter condition, however, is far from being fulfilled. My own study of the period 1950–79 shows a general tendency, especially over the later years, for inflation to fall as real output growth rises and vice versa, suggesting a predominance of cost-push inflation (upward shifts of the aggregate supply curve), probably inimical to growth in itself, and tending to stimulate contractionary policy. In some countries and sub-periods, however, (such as the United States 1952–67, Japan 1960–9, Canada 1952–64, Germany 1955–69) there was a pattern of relatively large fluctuations in growth rates slightly leading much smaller ones in rates of inflation – output apparently much more sensitive than prices to fluctuations in aggregate demand. Elsewhere, and later in the countries just mentioned, the story seems to be of successive major cost-pushes from import prices or wages, each followed by a fall in growth rate.

My study dealt with times of generally high employment and nearly continuous inflation and output growth. Major depressions, however, give plenty of evidence that output as well as the price level is sensitive to nominal demand. British real GDP fell some 6 per cent below its (peak to peak) trend in the depression of the 1880s, 10 per cent below in the 1890s and the 1930s; that of the United States fell about 7 per cent below in the 1870s, nearly 14 per cent below in the 1890s, more than 30 per cent below in the 1930s. In the 1980s, United Kingdom real GDP fell 8 per cent below the (logarithmic) 1979–89 trend, and nearly 19 per cent below the extrapolated trend of 1950–73. In the depression of the 1930s, both United Kingdom and United States outputs fell (from their peaks, not relatively to trend) by about the same percentages as those by which the respective GDP deflators fell; in the succeeding recoveries the percentage increases in output were in both cases (from the rising trends of population and technical knowledge) very much greater than those of prices.

It is hardly necessary to remind the reader that the British depression of the 1980s, which reduced absolute nominal expenditure by 3 per cent in two years, did not manage to make the general price level fall at all; it in fact rose faster than before, under the combined influence of accelerations in wage and import price inflations, though the harder times can claim some of the credit for reducing its increase (not its absolute level) later, after expenditure and output had started to recover. The upshot is that real output is, indeed, sensitive to nominal expenditure in at least the short or medium run, appropriate for consideration of the usual approximately four- and eight-year trade cycles, except for increases at high levels of capacity utilization. This sensitivity, however, is frequently masked by impulses which are not easily relatable to the immediate influence of expenditure or activity levels, especially those in a single country. Keynes's picture of output as the main beneficiary of increased expenditure up to the point of full employment, price the sole beneficiary after that, is a large simplification, but it contains the truth that output is influenced by expenditure in the short run to an extent which is of great importance for economic welfare.

Is the money supply readily controllable?

I have already mentioned that the *operational* importance attributed to the Quantity Theory depends mainly on the belief that the supply of money can be manipulated. Keynes shared this belief both in the *Treatise* and in the *General Theory*. When control of the money supply began to be advocated by the Monetarist school as a preventive of inflation, however, difficulties – such as likely resort to substitutes for whatever is officially defined and controlled as 'money' – were pointed out by, for instance, Nicholas Kaldor. After more than a decade of widespread attempts to effect such control these difficulties have been elaborated by Christopher Dow and Iain Saville (1988), basing their arguments largely on their own experience in the Bank of England.

At first sight, Central Banks have three possible methods of controlling the money supply at their disposal. Given that the deposit banks can be relied upon to keep their total liabilities at a fixed multiple of their reserves, which include deposits at the Central Bank, the latter can operate on the total of those liabilities – effectively the money supply – by buying or selling securities in exchange for deposits with it. Alternatively it can operate on interest rates, especially those at which the deposit banks lend to their clients, so as to influence the total amount of borrowing from those banks. The third method is direct quantitative control, exercised either through instructions (or effective hints) about the lending to be done, through ability to alter at least the maximum permissible ratio of the deposit banks' liabilities to their deposits with the Central Bank, or by requiring them to place specified non-operational deposits with it.

Dow and Saville point out that the power of the first method is limited by the Central Banks' relative smallness, and that of their operations; the assets of the Bank of England, Banking Department, are only about a fiftieth, and the operational Bank of England reserves of the deposit banks only about a thousandth, of M3. The deposit banks derive their liquidity mainly from their holdings of currency (several times as large as their operational Bank of England reserves) and of money at call and short notice, several times larger, again. Individual banks also hold large balances with each other. That the Bank stands ready to come to the rescue, by way of the Discount Market, if there *is* a liquidity crisis in the deposit banks is, of course, a fact of crucial importance for the stability of the financial system, but hardly evidence of its power to control the money supply in general; it rather points to a limitation of its power to act restrictively without provoking a widespread collapse of credit.

In fact such operations as 'driving the market into the Bank' have been seen more as means of making the Bank's lending rate effective than as measures of quantitative control in themselves, and the Bank's power to move the whole spectrum of interest rates merely by announcing a change in that lending rate has long been recognized as out of proportion to the buying and selling power which it commands – or at least that which it actually uses. Dow and Saville explain this convincingly by arguing, in line with the Keynesian 'boot-strap' doctrine, that market interest rates are highly sensitive to views about their future, which (like most views about the future) are largely conventional constructs derived from indistinct perceptions in a cloud of ignorance. In such cases, anything as solid as an indication of official intentions – or something that others in the market are thought likely to take as such as indication – will have substantial effects in shifting the demand curves for assets. Within limits, therefore, the monetary authorities can make interest rates what they like, but only within limits. If the authorities' prescriptions, or indications, come too much into conflict with other forces in the market, they will cease to be effective, and unless the authorities bow to the inevitable gracefully, they will lose the credibility on which depends their ability to influence rates in the future. In so far as Central Banks *do* influence the monetary situation, they are alleged to do so mainly by operating on interest rates directly, shifting liquidity preference schedules, not, as Keynes, at least in the

General Theory, suggested, by altering the supply so as to move the markets along those schedules.

Dow and Saville share my earlier reservations about the effect of interest rates on investment but allow that, given time, some effect is likely to be produced at least on longer-term capital formation. This effect, of course, operates on expenditure, and perhaps prices, by suggestion, *not* through the quantity of money. They also point out that shifts of the total spectrum of interest rates may not have much effect on the desired holdings of that deposit money (nowadays much the greater part) on which the holders receive interest, and that a rise in interest rates will have only a once-for-all effect on desired holdings of non-interest-bearing money, which will be of limited use if there is a continuing pressure for money holdings to rise.

The third class of Central Bank possibilities, involving more or less direct interference with the deposit banks' lending (or ability to lend), comes up most against the difficulty that the authorities' list of those banks, or, indeed, of any class of institutions selected at a particular time as performing bank-like functions, is likely to become out of date if the control to which they are subjected results in excess demand for loans which other institutions can be created or adapted to satisfy. What Marshall called 'the methods of doing business' evolve to satisfy demands for money or its close substitutes. This does not mean that control is impossible; only that to have a continuing effect it has to be flexible and probably of widening scope. The various British episodes of credit control, most of them operating by sterilizing parts of the reserves of the deposit banks, have had at least temporary successes. But in inflationary conditions they have also promoted the rise of banking functions outside the controlled area. The same would apply to any other quantitative controls, including specification of reserve ratios coupled with open market operations on the reserve base.

Dow and Saville maintain that the chain of causation runs from prices to money supply, rather than in the opposite direction. Banks' lending is governed in the first place by their perceptions and expectations concerning the incomes, and the value of the assets, of their clients, which means that it tends to be stimulated by increases, depressed by falls, in the general price level and to move in general with nominal national income. This behaviour arises because individual banks are in competition not only with each other but also with non-bank sources of funds and with foreign banks. For reasons touched upon above, the amount of influence which the Central Bank can exert over their lending, though not negligible, is limited. If there is a wage explosion, or a rise in prices of imported materials, banks will be under pressure to finance an increase in working capital and will know that, short of a substantial depression (which the authorities have mostly been anxious to avoid), prices and sales of final output will be adequate to make their loans safe. If wages or import prices fall, the demand for loans will also generally fall.

I do not subscribe to the proposition that prices *always* lead the dance; the evidence which I have quoted concerning different kinds of inflationary or deflationary 'impulses' still allows an important place for changes in monetary conditions. There is some evidence that these have had expenditure effects but it is clear that, within a given country, in recent decades, changes in prices or expenditure largely independent of the domestic monetary situation *often* led the way. The most important question is to what extent Central Banks can control the supply of money, in the face of whatever changes occur in the demand for it, and, at least so far as the United Kingdom is concerned, the analysis of Dow and Saville is convincing. The authorities have only a limited ability to influence the level of interest rates, they cannot make people hold more money than they want to at any given rate, and their power of limiting the money stock by restrictions on lending by 'banks' can succeed in anything but the fairly short run and at the cost of calling into existence a supply of money substitutes. In these circumstances, control of the money supply can hardly earn its keep as the prime instrument of macroeconomic policy. Control of interest rate levels (by suggestion) is more practicable, within limits, and Dow and Saville suggest that its main operation may be through international capital movements, the rate of exchange and the balance of trade, rather than through domestic capital formation. If so, it looks as if Montague Norman had a better case against Keynes than most people have supposed.

V Conclusion

This discussion has involved two kinds of question, one academic, about how the system works, the other practical, about how to make it deliver particular results. Keynes was interested in both. Take the academic side first. He inherited a doctrine which, largely because it was concerned with comparisons of states before and after a hypothetical change, with plenty of time for the dust to settle, was able to consider the volume of output as independent of the money supply, which impinged simply on the price level. Such debate as there had been of *processes* by which a change in money supply might work had been conditioned by the supposition that the rate of interest always equated the flows of planned saving and planned investment, and was thus always equal to the rate of return on capital. By stages he arrived at his 'general' theory that the market rate of interest governed the flow of investment, the interest rate was itself governed by the supplies of, and the demand for, money and non-monetary assets, and was relieved of pressure to equate planned saving and investment by the automatic change in total expenditure – and in real output – which would result from their inequality. That real output responded to change in expenditure followed from the imperfect flexibility of prices; Friedman much later pointed out that Keynes had reversed the 'classical' assumption that prices are more flexible than outputs. Prices, for Keynes, depended on the level of utilization of plant and on the efficiency wage, and money wages, although under full employment they were sensitive (upwards, at least) to demand pressure, were otherwise marked by a mixture of inertia and dependence on the vagaries of bilateral bargaining.

This picture of the economy was clearly inconsistent with the dichotomy between money-governing-price and factor-supplies-governing-output which formed the philosophical basis of the Quantity Theory. Moreover, along with the Keynesian perception of bearishness or liquidity preference as a volatile component of the public's tastes, it also discouraged expectations of finding that approximate constancy of the velocity of circulation of money which the Theory, in its simpler forms, was taken to imply. From there, Keynes advanced to his theory of underemployment equilibrium, which, if one allows that high unemployment *eventually* lowers money wages, and thus raises the real value of money and net financial assets, depends ultimately on the 'liquidity trap'. In the absence of much empirical evidence for that 'trap', underemployment equilibrium has been probably the most controversial feature of the *General Theory*. The most fruitful approach to *long-lasting* underemployment, or stagnation, may well be through Harrod's dynamics; but for my present purpose the *theory* of underemployment equilibrium is something of an optional extra to the basic Keynesian insight into the dynamics of underemployment. Disequilibrium may last quite long enough to be of major importance if equilibrating processes are slow.

There are other features of Keynes's theoretical picture relevant to the Quantity Theory that require some qualification or amendment, some because the world has changed rather than because he was wrong about the world of his day. He may have overdone the role of interest rates as a controller of domestic capital formation, in his time and since. The growth of consumer's credit may have made his playing-down of the interest rate's effect on personal saving out of date; certainly the 1970s and 1980s have revealed other, more powerful influences on the propensity to save. Attempts at monetary targeting have revealed how difficult it is, especially in combination with attempts to liberalize financial institutions. Also such attempts have shown that Central Banks' powers are exercised, and limited, in ways which Keynes did, indeed, illuminate in his discussions of liquidity preference and of long-term expectations, but not simply by operating with a fixed liquidity preference schedule. The demand function for money, which incorporates that schedule (and is central to the more conservative of Friedman's restatements of the Quantity Theory) has proved elusive, partly because financial institutions have evolved and the criteria for identifying what counts as money have become clouded. And, in writing about a closed economy, Keynes neglected the effects of world supply and demand mismatches (and of changing degrees of monopoly) on the 'flex-price' international markets, and their repercussions on the sort of economy with which he was concerned.

On the positive side, Keynes was clearly right about the persistence, and importance, of what Pigou called 'lapses from full employment'. The interest rate does not equalize planned saving and planned investment without a lot of help from the changes in total expenditure which are the first result of their inequality. The determination of prices in advanced countries being sensitive to changes in costs of production has been confirmed by many studies. Money wages have been resistant to econometric explanation; what has become clear is that they do not move in a rapid and orderly manner to clear the labour market. In the *General Theory*, Keynes was wise to assume that he could take them as exogenous, correct about how they would behave, without appropriate controls, under wartime full employment, and amply justified in worrying about what would happen to them under high and steady employment in peacetime.

Friedman accused Keynes of having no theory of the general level of prices, such as he (Friedman) believed the Quantity Theory to provide. But Keynes was aware that, in the real world, even if the quantity of money 'explains' prices (which it cannot do without taking for granted a number of other matters, equally in need of explanation) one still has to ask, what 'explains' the quantity of money? The only short answer is: 'History'. Beyond that, the answer is a complex one, some of the main elements of which, as they have revealed themselves in the post-war period, Keynes at least foreshadowed.

This brings us from the academic to the practical side of the matter. To justify picking out one variable as uniquely explanatory in a complex, interrelated system, the usual, practical, argument is that it is uniquely controllable. Both Keynes and most of the monetarist writers assumed this about the quantity of money. Experience in the last 20 years cast grave doubt on this assumption. The authorities have some control over *expenditure* through budgetary and fiscal policy and through their influence over interest rates, which may work as much through the foreign balance as through domestic spending. The consequential changes in money holdings are secondary. The expenditure changes (as Keynes insisted) involve employment changes, except when they are pushing against a full employment ceiling.

The claim of the Quantity Theory to be the main illuminator of policy relating to the price level needs to be dropped. The interest in it over the past generation has been primarily motivated by the desire to control inflation, and for that one needs to look at the roots from which inflation springs, which are multiple, and call for different treatments. Demand-pull inflation (which monetarists tend to think the only kind) requires that expenditure be kept within the limits of prospective output valued at initial prices – not too hard nationally, but needing to be undertaken also on something approaching a world scale because of the flexible-price international markets. Cost-push inflation, is essentially wage-push and OPEC-push (and the like) and calls for treatment through the institutions of the markets concerned. What we have certainly learned is that controlling demand to a level substantially lower than the checking of demand-pull inflation alone would require has produced only an incomplete solution at a high cost in unemployment and lost growth. Whereas wage costs, the exchange rate and total nominal expenditure are directly relevant variables upon which policy may operate with varying degrees of difficulty, the money supply is vaguer as a concept, less directly relevant and no easier for policy to manipulate. Keynes's suspicion of the Theory has been justified by further experience, even if for reasons which are only partly related to those that he presented.

References

Brown, A. J. (1985), *World Inflation Since 1950:An International Comparative Study*, Cambridge: Cambridge University Press.

Dow, J. C. R. and I. Saville (1988), *A Critique of Monetary Policy:Theory and British Experience*, Oxford: Clarendon Press.

Easton, W. W. (1985), 'The Importance of Interest Rates in Five Macroeconomic Models', Bank of England Discussion Paper, no. 24.

Fforde, J. S. (1983), 'Setting Monetary Objectives', *Bank of England Quarterly Bulletin* **23**, 200–208.

Fisher, P. G. *et al.* (1989), 'Comparative Properties of Models of the UK Economy', *National Institute Economic Review*, **129**, 200–8.

Friedman, M. (1956), 'The Quantity Theory: A Restatement', in *Studies in the Quantity Theory of Money*, Chicago: University of Chicago Press.

Friedman, M. and A. Schwartz (1982), *Monetary Trends in the United States and the United Kingdom*, Chicago: University of Chicago Press.

Hall, S. G. *et al.* (1989), 'The Long-run Determination of the UK Monetary Aggregates', Bank of England Discussion Paper, no. 41.

OECD (1982), *Budgetary Financing and Monetary Control*, Paris: OECD.

10 Extending the *General Theory* into the medium run

John Brothwell

I Keynes's monetary production economy

A major weakness of Keynes's *General Theory* is that it is a short (single)-period model which analyses a temporary (usually unemployment) equilibrium level of output for a given state of entrepreneurial expectations. But what happens in the next period and the period after that? The neoclassical theory purports to explain that such short-period unemployment is due to temporary market imperfections, but insists that the system, given flexible prices and substitution between goods in consumption and factors in production, will soon converge on the full employment (natural rate of unemployment) growth path. If, as Keynes believed (and as should be patently obvious) unemployment persists even in the long period, then a post-Keynesian theory of accumulation is required to explain why there is likely to be an effective demand problem in the longer run. The *General Theory* must be extended over a succession of short periods into at least the medium run. To do this, however, also involves (a) understanding the fundamental difference between Keynes's system and the neoclassical system, in particular the different conceptions of equilibrium in the two systems; and (b) providing Keynes's system with satisfactory micro-foundations in the form of a realistic theory of the firm and, therefore, of pricing (value) and distribution (Brothwell, 1987).

The economics of Keynes is fundamentally different from orthodox neoclassical theory. Keynes's theory is an attempt to break away completely from the typical marginalist scheme of Walrasian general equilibrium, which has no relevance to real world economies. Keynes's macrotheory is, therefore, wholly separate from the 'Keynesian economics' of the neoclassical synthesis–American textbook (bastard) Keynesianism and the New Keynesian economics – all of which are much closer to monetarism and the higher lunacies of the New Classical Macroeconomics than they are to Keynes, because they are all based upon the Walrasian general equilibrium system, a system in which there is no room for time, change, uncertainty and money. The central message of the *General Theory* is that, to understand the forces which determine changes in the scale of output and employment as a whole, it is first necessary to understand that the real world we inhabit is a dynamic, *monetary production* economy – what Keynes (CW XXIX: 76–83) called a 'money-wage or entrepreneur economy' to distinguish it from what he called a 'real-wage or co-operative economy' in which Say's Law always holds true – moving irreversibly through calendar (historic) time from an unchangeable past to a necessarily uncertain future; uncertain because it has yet to be created and is certain to be different! The decisions of firms regarding the level of employment they will offer, and the amount of investment they wish to undertake, are all guided by their *expectations of demand* in the near or more distant future. Firms are demand-constrained, not resource-constrained. But, in the words of Joan Robinson (1979): 'As soon as the uncertainty of the expectations that guide economic behaviour is admitted, equilibrium drops out of the argument and history takes its place.' Thus, in Keynes's model, short-period equilibrium is a very different concept from the neoclassical general equilibrium in which flexible prices rapidly adjust to clear all markets including the factor markets.

In Keynes, equilibrium simply means that, in aggregate, firms have guessed correctly what the level of output over the period should be; they have produced and sold just the amount of consumer goods and services and capital goods which they expected to sell. Thus, if the state of short-term expectations governing the *supplies* of all goods (both current and capital) and the state of long-term expectations governing the *demand* for capital goods remain unchanged, employment will remain unchanged. This is a very limited concept of equilibrium – so limited that it hardly warrants the term – as Joan Robinson suggests. It is at most a 'quasi', temporary equilibrium, which will change if expectations change (as they are almost certain to do) and contains the seeds of its own destruction as net investment (necessary to maintain aggregate demand) adjusts the capital stock to the level appropriate to the equilibrium level of output and, therefore, ceases. There is no suggestion that all markets should clear; 'equilibrium' has come about as a result of output adjustments rather than price adjustments. The economy (like the firms) is demand-constrained rather than resource-constrained: though the goods market is clearing in aggregate, the labour market is likely to be in a state of excess supply (involuntary unemployment) and firms are likely to be operating below capacity. As Goodwin (1988) puts it, 'the *differencia specifica* of capitalism is that employment is not determined by the wishes or desires of the workers, but by employers'.

The fact that the economy is moving irreversibly through time towards an *unknowable* future explains some crucial features of a real-world monetary production economy. Production processes take time and hence the decision to organize production in a particular way must occur earlier in time than the outcome. In an uncertain environment, the outcome is more or less unpredictable and fallible humans therefore evolve an institutional framework to reduce uncertainty as much as possible – in particular, a system of fixed forward money contracts. Such fixed money contracts (of which the money wage contract is the most common) are an essential adjunct of organizing time-consuming production processes, as Davidson has often emphasized: 'In the absence of money contracts limiting nominal liabilities and controlling expected cash flows, it is unlikely that entrepreneurs, facing a statistically unpredictable and unknowable future, would undertake large-scale, long-lived, complex production processes' (1988: 171). Thus the prices of newly produced (and reproducible) goods are anchored to labour costs which are fixed over the contract period. A monetary production economy could not operate without the degree of price stability provided by a system of money wage and forward contracts: the value of money must be reasonably stable if money is to fulfil its key functions of a medium of exchange and hence a liquid store of value – a refuge from uncertainty and a means of carrying *uncommitted* purchasing power through time. It follows that the general equilibrium system of perfectly flexible prices is in essence a non-monetary system, a world of certainty in which any commodity can act as the numeraire, but *not* as money since money is not required! Money has no function in such a world; it is neutral.[1] Shackle sums it up in his inimitable way: 'For the effects which Keynes is concerned with, in the character and scale they take in our world, the explanation must be sought, as he sought it, in both the finally inescapable uncertainty of things and in the dependence of our system on money' (1967: 137); and, in one short sentence: 'Unemployment arises from the preference of liquidity over enterprise' (Shackle, 1983).

II Liquidity versus enterprise

In the world of reality, Say's Law does not hold because, from time to time, entrepreneurs will prefer financial investment to real investment and everything hinges, in the end, on the relationship between the rate of interest and the expected rate of profit – Keynes's marginal efficiency of capital. That is why, again in Shackle's words: 'The liquidity-preference theory . . . stands as Keynes's most unalienable piece of original economic thought' (1967: 145). The irony is that Keynes's liquidity-preference theory is 'neoclassical' in that it is a 'flex-price' analysis of *stockholding*, the one field in which the assumption of flexible prices holds good because time-consuming production is not involved! Here, as Shackle puts it, 'Keynes had dramatically illuminated and thrown into relief a method by no means new but currently neglected, the attribution to stocks (in this case, of money or bonds) and their owners' valuations of them, of a life of their own' (ibid.). It is of the essence of the liquidity-preference theory that stocks (not flows) are in command and therefore flexible prices exist. Thus, in this case, demand (marginal valuation in the minds of holders) determines price – the rate of interest – a purely monetary phenomenon grounded in uncertainty, *for which there is no counterpart in the neoclassical system.* The rate of interest in a monetary production economy, depending upon expectations of its own future, is subjective, indeterminate and a highly conventional phenomenon. In Keynes's own words: 'its actual value is largely governed by the prevailing view as to what its value is expected to be. *Any* level of interest which is accepted with sufficient conviction as *likely* to be durable *will* be durable; subject, of course, in a changing society to fluctuations for all kinds of reasons round the expected normal' (CW VII: 203).

In the neoclassical system, the rate of interest is a real phenomenon, equilibrating the demand for capital goods (dependent upon the marginal product of capital) with the supply of savings (dependent upon the marginal rate of time preference). In Keynes's model (and the real world) investment determines saving, via changes in the national income, and *there is no counterpart to the marginal product of capital.* The demand for capital goods depends upon the marginal efficiency of capital – the expected rate of profit (rate of return) on an investment project – compared with the rate of interest the entrepreneur could obtain from financial investment. Only if the gap between these rates is large enough will entrepreneurs undertake the considerable hazards of real investment: and Keynes's marginal efficiency of capital concept has no connection with the marginal product of capital – the return to a process of capital *deepening*.[2] In Keynes's marginal efficiency of capital argument, if a fall in the rate of interest induces real investment, the entrepreneur expands his whole production process (plant, machinery, labour and other inputs). This has nothing to do with substitution between capital and labour and marginal productivity; there is no reason to assume a change in technique. The fall in the rate of interest raises the demand price of capital, relative to the supply price, just as does an improvement in the flow of expected returns. Both lead to capital *widening*, an expansion of capacity with fixed factor proportions. Thus Keynes's marginal efficiency of capital theory of investment is easily reconcilable with accelerator theories of investment – an expected rise in demand induces investment, in both fixed equipment and inventories. Of course, if by the time the entrepreneur is planning his investment project technical progress has evolved an improved (lower cost) method of production, the entrepreneur will change to the new technique. The new technique is likely to be labour-saving, in the sense that it is likely to be more mechanized, with a higher capital–labour ratio, but there may well be little change in capital intensity of production as measured by the capital–output ratio.

Confusion between the money, or nominal market, rate of interest (the rate of return on rentier capital determined by liquidity-preference), the expected rate of profit from real investment (Keynes's marginal efficiency of capital) and the neoclassical marginal product of capital often arises. This confusion is further compounded when the monetarist concept of the real rate of interest (the money rate of interest less the rate of inflation) is brought into the argument.[3] Mills and Wood (1988), for example, use a sophisticated econometric analysis to test whether the neoclassical (Robertsonian) theory of the interest rate is a real phenomenon determined by the real factors of saving and investment, or the Keynesian liqudity-preference theory is correct. The test is whether, over a period, the 'real rate of interest' is permanently susceptible to the influence of monetary policy. Since Mills and Wood wrongly assume that the 'real rate of interest' in neoclassical theory is simply the nominal rate, corrected for inflation, rather than the marginal product of capital, it is difficult to see how their analysis throws any light at all on the merits of the two theories. Again Goodhart (1989) has tried to rehabilitate the neoclassical theory of the interest rate without apprehending that the theory applies only within the context of a non-monetary general equilibrium system, and has no relevance to a real-world monetary production economy.

III The irrelevance of marginal productivity theory

Pasinetti (1981) argues convincingly that the marginalist scheme of general equilibrium applies only to a pure exchange economy. In such an economy, individuals with given stocks (endowments) exchange them until a Pareto optimum allocation is attained. Given flexible prices, the economic problem investigated is that of finding the vector of equilibrium prices which brings about, through exchange, an optimum allocation of the given stocks. (This may be compared directly with the pricing and exchange of existing financial assets in liquidity-preference theory, as pointed out above.) Pasinetti argues that it is legitimate to apply the method of constrained optimization to this (relatively minor) case, but not to extend the principle to all economic problems. In particular it is wrong to apply it to time-consuming production processes, thereby neglecting the vital distinction between scarce commodities and produced commodities, the supply of which may be perfectly elastic over time. But, as Pasinetti explains, the neoclassical marginalists accomplished the trick of applying the constrained optimization principle to production by introducing marginal productivity theory. As long as the time period is so short that technology is fixed and one or more of the factors of production is fixed, diminishing marginal productivity will ensure rising marginal costs, limiting output and the size of firms and keeping goods scarce (as in the simple fixed endowments model).[4] Of course, in reality, production coefficients tend to be fixed and the bulk of products are reproducible under constant returns or even increasing returns in the long run, especially with technical progress. The whole marginal productivity model of varying factor proportions, and the substitution of one factor for another, changing technique within a given state of technology in response to changing factor prices, is extremely artificial. It reaches its ultimate absurdity in the concept of the aggregate production function, 'jelly capital' and the marginal productivity theory of income distribution, now completely discredited as a result of the assaults of Joan Robinson and the outcome of the Cambridge Capital Controversy.

However Keynes never managed to make the necessary complete break with marginal productivity theory. He wrote the *General Theory* to overthrow the neoclassical theory of employment but failed to realize that the neoclassical theories of employment, pricing and distribution are inseparable and need to be discarded *in toto* (Brothwell, 1988). Thus, despite the fact that Keynes's theory of employment completely rejects the notion of a neoclassical labour market determining employment and the real wage, by accepting the first classical postulate (the wage is equal to the marginal product of labour) he appeared to be accepting the marginal productivity theory of factor prices and income distribution, with its implication that the marginal productivity of labour curve is the demand curve for labour at the macro-level – so paving the way to the neoclassical resurgence. Thus, in extending and building on Keynes, post-Keynesians must reject marginal productivity theory and supply a different theory of pricing and the distribution of income, a theory appropriate to a monetary production economy.

IV The *General Theory* in the longer run

Having described the nature of Keynes's single-period unemployment equilibrium, arising from the preference of liquidity over enterprise in a monetary production economy, it is necessary to consider how the system moves from period to period. Why does the preference of liquidity over enterprise persist? Why is there likely to be an effective demand problem in the long run? This question was partially answered by Harrod (1939). Starting from the fairly obvious position that, in an economy with positive net investment, the only possible equilibrium is a moving, dynamic equilibrium of steady growth, Harrod set out some of the necessary conditions for such a 'golden age' path to be attained, thereby demonstrating that a real-world economy would never achieve dynamic equilibrium.[5] Harrod showed that there is a notional equilibrium growth path, the warranted path, which, if it is expected by entrepreneurs in aggregate, so that they gear their investment plans to it, will be achieved. Thus, starting from full capacity output, demand, output and the capital stock will all grow in step at this warranted rate.[6] However this possible growth path is almost certain to be unstable, depending as it does on the unstable interaction of the multiplier and accelerator. Indeed Harrod suggested that therein lay the root cause of the trade cycle. On top of this, this unstable, notional, demand growth path would not provide full employment growth unless the rate of growth of demand, output and capital stock along it equalled the rate of growth of the labour force and its productivity allowed by technical progress – the natural rate of growth. In other words, full employment growth requires an economy's natural rate of growth to equal its warranted rate of growth and, since these growth rates depend upon variables which are largely independent of each other, such an outcome would be purely fortuitous. Harrod, like Keynes, believed the normal lot of an advanced capitalist economy in peacetime would be for the warranted rate (depending on the propensity to save) to exceed the natural rate (depending on technical progress and therefore governing investment opportunities) with consequent chronic demand deficiency and unemployment. Booms would be short-lived, while depressions would be of long duration with only weak growth on average.[7]

However the trouble goes much deeper than this, for several reasons. Even if entrepreneurs seize *all* the investment opportunities which technical progress makes available, if the warranted rate of growth exceeds the natural rate planned savings will exceed planned investment and demand will be inadequate. But it is extremely unlikely that all potentially profitable investment projects will be implemented, for technical progress, the ultimate engine of growth, is also one of the fundamental sources of change and therefore of uncertainty. Technical progress changes the whole structure of the economy, leading to new products and new processes which entrepreneurs, pursuing greater profits, must endeavour to seek out and invest in before their competitors do (and without knowing the plans of their competitors). Overall, technical progress will be labour-augmenting, raising output per head. But it is likely that labour productivity will grow at different rates in different lines of production. Hence relative costs will change and so relative prices and the price structure will change. More importantly, the structure of demand will continually change. As the productivity of labour increases and real per capita incomes rise, the increments of demand will cluster in succession around different goods (Pasinetti, 1981). Demand determines output and the actual output of each product will follow a non-steady growth path of its own. Also, of course, new products and modifications of old ones will be introduced continually. Competition takes the form of a process of creative destruction (Schumpeter, 1957) as entrepreneurs pursue higher rates of return by investing in new products, new methods of production, transport and communication, new markets and new forms of industrial organization, rendering the existing ones obsolescent. No wonder that Keynes, in the famous Chapter 12 of the *General Theory*, when considering the long-term expectations governing the investment intentions of entrepreneurs, emphasized the importance of 'animal spirits' and 'spontaneous optimism' in the face of the 'dark forces of time and ignorance'. A preference of liquidity over enterprise will often be tempting.

But will the behaviour of the financial system make it too tempting? Harrod's model, like nearly all the other growth models, neglects the financial sector. Harrod is solely concerned, one might say, with shifts of the IS curve over time; but what about shifts of the LM curve? Any theory of the growth of a *monetary*, production economy must consider the growth of the stocks of financial assets – money, near-money, bills, bonds and equities, as well as the growth of the real capital stock.[8] The behaviour of the rate of interest and the structure of interest rates will depend upon the growth of the supply of the various financial assets (of different degrees of liquidity) compared with the growth of the demand for them. Even though post-Keynesians stress the degree of endogeneity of the money supply, it is not satisfactory to assume that the money supply somehow simply adjusts, because the method by which it adjusts may be crucial to the whole growth process. Davidson (1968) points out that the increases in investment in the growth process must be financed and re-emphasizes the significance of Keynes's 'finance motive'. Firms must obtain the finance before the increase in spending can take place. They will require the money not only for expenditure on investment in fixed equipment and inventories but also for the increase in working capital required to expand output. The money must be obtained either by reducing their portfolio holdings of non-money financial assets (which Davidson terms 'placements') or issuing new placements. If they sell such placements to the banks then the money supply is increased, but any sold to the non-bank public will mean some fall in their price (rise in the rate of interest). Thus the finance of a rise in investment affects both the total supply of financial assets and the composition as between money and placements. There will also be a rise in the demand for money and placements. The demand for money will rise as the value of transactions (income) rises and there is likely to be a rise in the asset (speculative) demand as the total size of portfolios of financial assets increases as a result of net saving. It is therefore at the level of financing investment projects that the money supply plays an essential role in stimulating economic growth in a monetary production economy, rather than at the level of portfolio balances. It is vital that the investment necessary for full employment growth is not restrained by a lack of finance on reasonable terms: the monetary authorities must ensure that the desire for liquidity does not inhibit enterprise.

What the above discussion of the long-run behaviour of a monetary production economy amounts to is that there is no long-run, natural, full employment, growth path, waiting to be attained as a result of the forces of competition and the operation of the market mechanism. The fact that a statistical trend can be fitted to past data must not delude us into thinking that, thereby, we have discovered such a path; it is a purely notional concept. The long-run growth path has yet to be created by man's ingenuity, embodied in the investment projects of profit-seeking, competitive, innovating entrepreneurs. The economic system is not a self-equilibrating mechanism but a cumulatively unfolding process.

V The 'medium run'

Nevertheless if investment, the key determinant of the level of employment in the short period, is to be explained, it is necessary to look beyond the short period into at least the 'medium run', into the period(s) when the expected returns from the investment projects now being undertaken will be received. The period of the 'economic life' of the projects, the focus of Keynes's long-term expectations, must be considered. In other words, it is impossible to analyse Keynes's short period satisfactorily in isolation from later periods; if there is net investment in *this* period it must be because, in aggregate, entrepreneurs expect greater demand and output to justify it in *later* periods. What the capital goods firms expect to produce and sell in this period (their short-term expectations) depends upon what firms in aggregate expect to produce and sell in the future (their long-term expectations). But what did Keynes think the likely course of the economy would be through time? He made no attempt to link his short periods together in a definite sequence. He rejected the closed dynamic systems of Harrod, Hicks and Kalecki, which reduce the investment function to a mechanical version of the accelerator theory; instead he emphasized the significance of psychology, the state of expectations, 'animal spirits', confidence and the vagaries of the economic climate in the determination of the marginal efficiency of capital.

There are only two places in the *General Theory* where Keynes considers the 'medium run' – the move from one temporary equilibrium to another as the state of expectations changes: the final section of Chapter 18 and Chapter 22 ('Notes on the Trade Cycle'). In Chapter 18, Keynes summarizes his theory; output and employment are determined by:

> (1) the three fundamental psychological factors, namely, the psychological propensity to consume, the psychological attitude to liquidity and the psychological expectation of future yield from capital assets, (2) the wage-unit as determined by the bargains reached between employers and employed, and (3) the quantity of money as determined by the action of the central bank. (CW VII: 246–7)

However 'there is not one of the above factors which is not liable to change without much warning and sometimes substantially. Hence the extreme complexity of the actual course of events.' (Ibid.: 249)

Shackle has always emphasized the 'kaleidic' sequence of events as the kind of system in which we actually live moves into the future:

> When economic theory elects to bring in imperfect competition and to recognise uncertainty, there is an end of the meaning of general equilibrium. Economics thereafter is the description, piece by piece, of a collection of fragments. These fragments may fit together into a brilliant, arrestingly suggestive mosaic, but they do not compose a pattern of unique inevitable order. One vital aspect of the process of theoretical innovation is its destructive aspect. (1967: 295)

Is the system then chaotic? Is Keynes's theory nihilistic? No, says Keynes, there are certain features which limit instability:

> In particular, it is an outstanding characteristic of the economic system in which we live that, whilst it is subject to severe fluctuations in respect of output and employment, it is not violently unstable . . . Full, or even approximately full, employment is of rare and short-lived occurrence. Fluctuations may start briskly but seem to wear themselves out before they have proceeded to great extremes, and an intermediate situation which is neither desperate nor satisfactory is our normal lot. (CW VII: 249)

The stabilizing factors, according to Keynes are (a) the multiplier is not much greater than unity and consumption is sustained in the slump by social security payments; (b) when the marginal efficiency of capital or the rate of interest changes the change in the rate of investment is likely to be moderate; (c) money wage changes are moderate, though this is a condition of the stability of prices rather than of employment; and (d) changes in the rate of investment tend to reverse themselves in due course and the rate of investment is also limited in boom periods by the capacity of the capital goods industries.

We can add to these stabilizing elements the various institutional and social factors which contribute to stability by helping agents to cope with uncertainty: wage contracts, debt contracts, supply agreements, administered prices, trading agreements, informal rules and customs, habits, routines and conventions. These would be regarded as 'market imperfections' from the viewpoint of general equilibrium theory but, in reality, enable an actual economy to operate more effectively. Nevertheless the system, left to its own devices, is likely to follow a fluctuating path in the medium run, as Keynes explains in the chapter, 'Notes on the Trade Cycle'. He argues that (a) the main cause of the cycle is fluctuations in the marginal efficiency of capital, owing to the volatility of expected future yields of capital goods, reinforced from time to time by adverse shifts in the state of liquidity preference and, perhaps, in the propensity to consume; (b) full employment is reached only at the peak of strong booms which end in 'crisis', precipitated by a collapse of the marginal efficiency of capital, then a rise in liquidity-preference and interest rates, which may make the slump very intractable; also, a serious fall in the marginal efficiency of capital tends to affect adversely the propensity to consume via a collapse of Stock Exchange prices; and (c) the duration and intensity of the slump will be greatly affected by the need to absorb surplus inventories and reduce working capital as output declines; on the other hand, after the recovery has begun, both factors will be favourable to investment.

Keynes goes on to offer advice for dealing with the trade cycle in one of the few passages in the *General Theory* concerned with economic policy. He emphasizes that the cure for the boom is not a high rate of interest but a lower rate, to enable it to be prolonged: 'The right remedy for the trade cycle is not to be found in abolishing booms and thus keeping us permanently in a semi-slump; but in abolishing slumps and thus keeping us permanently in a quasi-boom' (CW VII: 322). It is clear that Keynes believed that the main danger facing a monetary production economy was inadequate effective demand (not surprising at the time he was writing) and that both fiscal and monetary policies should be used to promote investment and consumption together: 'For it is unlikely that full employment can be maintained, whatever we may do about investment, with the existing propensity to consume. There is room, therefore, for both policies to operate together' (ibid.: 325). In sum, Keynes's view of the likely course of the economy through time is consistent with Goodwin's (1953, 1955) theory: the economy grows unsteadily, driven by random, disequilibrating Schumpeterian bursts of innovatory investment, followed by lapses into recession. The boom generates the trend in a process of continual disequilibrium.[9]

VI Microeconomic foundations

There has been much criticism of Keynes's model of income determination because of its supposed lack of micro-foundations. Certainly the IS/LM version lacks micro-foundations and therefore cannot explain supply-side phenomena – costs, prices and inflation. But such criticism of Keynes's *General Theory* is unwarranted. Keynes did provide microfoundations in Chapter 3 ('The Principle of Effective Demand') and Chapter 5 ('Expectation as Determining Output and Employment'). He shows how the behaviour of each individual firm in deciding how much employment to offer in the coming short period (the period during which decisions once made cannot be altered) is determined by its short-term expectations 'as to the cost of output on various possible scales and expectations as to the sale-proceeds of this output', the entrepreneur endeavouring to fix the amount of employment at the level which maximizes expected profit. Keynes states at the beginning of Chapter 18 that his theory is unaffected by changes in the degree of competition but, ill-advisedly (Sawyer, 1992), assumes an industrial structure of many small, highly-competitive firms, operating with Marshallian U-shaped cost curves – what has been termed 'atomistic' or 'polypolistic' competition. These firms are demand-constrained, not resource-constrained, since output is limited by 'expected proceeds', as argued above; they are operating in conditions of uncertainty, far removed from the textbook conditions of perfect competition. Nevertheless this is yet another instance of Keynes's failure to make the necessary complete break with neoclassical marginal productivity theory, thereby weakening his assault upon orthodox economics. It is unfortunate that Keynes did not take into consideration the advances in microeconomics and the theory of the firm made by his colleagues in Cambridge when constructing his *General Theory*. It is much more convincing to base the aggregate expected proceeds curve on the micro-foundation of demand-constrained, price-making, oligopolistic firms; there is no doubt that the macroeconomics of Keynes and oligopolistic competition complement each other, just as perfect competition is integral with the Walrasian general equilibrium system.

Accordingly marginal productivity theory must be discarded in favour of a realistic approach to the theory of the firm, price and income distribution. The 'representative' firm operates in an oligopoly market, with constant average variable (equal to marginal) costs up to capacity and output limited by demand (see Figure 10.1 below). Price is set by a mark-up on average variable cost; the typical firm adjusts output rather than price in the face of unanticipated changes in demand; prices are related to costs and only change if costs change significantly. The firm attempts to obtain a mark-up sufficient to cover its average fixed costs at the expected output plus a 'satisfactory' profit margin. It is a 'profit satisficer' because it does not have sufficient information about demand conditions to maximize profits. Also it is much more concerned with *growth* of profits than immediate maximum profits. The firm's mark-up (degree of monopoly) will depend upon its market power, but this in turn depends upon the expected behaviour of its competitors and the strength of demand for its

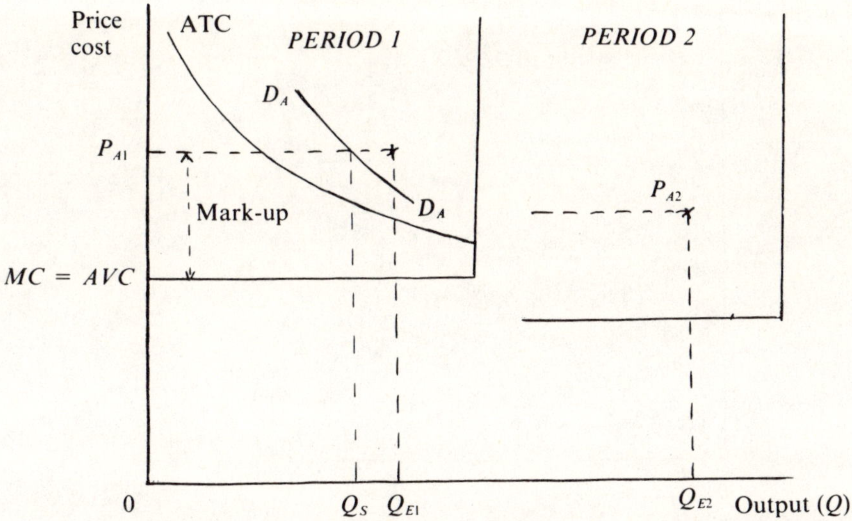

Figure 10.1 *Price and output for the representative firm in the medium term*

product(s) as indicated by whether demand is growing: the determination of the mark-up involves a dynamic element. If the firm (entrepreneur) expects demand to expand significantly in the coming period(s) it is likely (a) to set a higher mark-up and (b) to decide upon, and begin to implement, an investment plan to increase capacity to supply the increased demand expected in future periods. Any increased profits obtained in this period will help to finance such investment expenditure. The pricing and investment decisions of the firm are closely related; both the price mark-up (rate of profit) and the investment decision are linked to the expected growth of demand.[10]

The firm will, of course, take advantage of any improvements in technology in its investment plans and may well decide that investment to produce new products is best carried out in conditions of buoyant demand. Again we see that the firm in the medium run is much more concerned with the growth of profits, resulting from the growth of sales at a particular profit margin, than with absolute profit maximization if a dynamic view is taken.

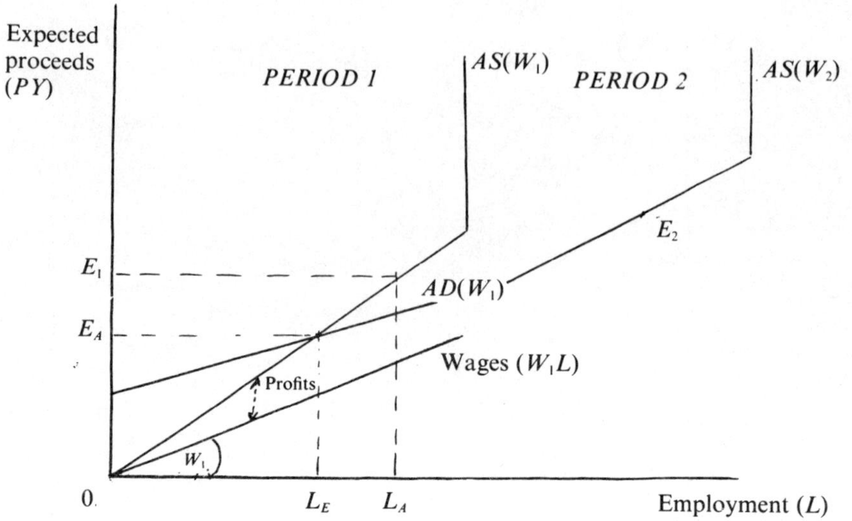

Figure 10.2 Macro outcomes in the medium term

Thus at both the micro-level of the firm and the macro-level it is impossible to analyse Keynes's short period adequately in isolation from later periods. The *General Theory* must be extended into the medium run, and a succession of periods considered, fully to comprehend Keynes's 'method of analysing the economic behaviour of the present under the influence of changing ideas about the future'. This is illustrated in Figure 10.1, which shows the situation at the level of the 'representative' firm. The entrepreneur must estimate as best he can the mark-up and administered price which will provide satisfactory profits at normal utilization of capacity in the expected demand conditions. His expected output (sales) is Q_{E1} at price P_{A1}, giving expected proceeds of P_{A1} Q_{E1}. He will therefore employ the labour necessary to produce Q_{E1}. If he expects demand and proceeds in the future (period 2) to grow to P_{A2} Q_{E2} he starts to implement investment plans in period 1 to have the capacity installed by the time period 2 arrives. It is assumed in the figure that the new plant will have lower average variable costs.

Figure 10.2 shows what is happening at the macro-level. The money wage, determined outside the model, is W_1 in period 1. *AS* (W_1) is the aggregate supply curve which Keynes defines as 'the expectation of proceeds of a given amount of employment which will just make it worth the while of the entrepreneurs to give that employment' (CW VII: 24). It is drawn on the assumption of constant returns up to capacity (full employment) output and a constant distribution of income between wages and profits (constant degree of monopoly). Keynes's theory certainly has micro-foundations; it is grounded in the output (supply) decisions of individual entrepreneurs, dependent upon the state of technology, factor costs and short-run expected sales. In Figure 10.2, if aggregate expected proceeds are E_1, then L_A will be employed and E_1 money income generated. The crucial question is, will the output be sold and the expected proceeds realized? Will aggregate demand be sufficient? In the simple two-sector case, will investment match savings? As the figure indicates, only if expected demand in period 2 (E_2) generates sufficient investment in period 1 will this be so. In this example, entrepreneurs were overoptimistic, demand was less than expected, D_AD_A in Figure 10.1 with sales of Q_S (not Q_{E1}) and AD (W_1) in Figure 10.2, so that actual proceeds (E_A) were less than expected (E_1) with an unanticipated build-up of stocks. The actual outcome in period 1 is likely to affect (in this case adversely) both short-run and longer-run expectations held in period 2, with consequences for the further course of the economy, as discussed in the previous section.

VII Growth, profits and the functional distribution of income

If marginal productivity theory must be rejected, and the rate of profit on capital is not the marginal product of capital, what does determine profits, the rate of profit and the distribution of income between profits and wage? Investment is Keynes's *causa causans* but entrepreneurs must be induced to undertake the hazards of real investment by the expectation of the profits to be obtained from expanding markets; and the ultimate source of expanding markets (growth) is labour-saving technical progress – the result of human imagination and ingenuity. Thus the factors which determine Harrod's natural rate of growth, growth of the labour force and its productivity, are the ultimate source of profits. As Pasinetti states:

> Labour emerges ... as the only ultimate factor of production. And it is interesting that, in a growing economic system, this does imply a rate of profit. Contrary to what traditional economics has maintained for a long time, it is not the 'productivity of capital', or of any commodity, that turns out to be the *raison d'être* of a rate of profit. It is the growth, and the increasing productivity, of labour! (1981: 133)

A high natural (potential) growth rate offers the opportunity for entrepreneurs to profit from real investment. As long as the investment plans are not frustrated by financial considerations – as long as the expected rate of profit from real investment (marginal efficiency of capital) well exceeds the rate of interest obtainable from financial investment and enterprise overcomes the preference for liquidity – actual investment will generate actual profits, with a likely feedback on expected profits and investment in the next period. In the simple two-sector case, assuming savings entirely from profits:

$$I = S = s_c P, \text{ therefore}$$
$$I/K = s_c\, P/K \text{ and}$$
$$I/Y = s_c\, P/Y$$

where I = investment, S = savings, s_c = propensity to save out of profits by capitalists, P = profits, K = value of capital, I/K = rate of growth of capital and output, P/K = rate of profit on capital, Y = income, I/Y = share of investment in income, P/Y = profits share.

Thus the chain of causation from the natural growth rate (G_n) to the rate of profit on capital and the share of profits in income can be shown symbolically:

$$G_n \quad (P/_K)\text{expected} > r \qquad \begin{matrix} (I/K)\text{actual} = s_c\,(P/Y)\text{actual} \\ (I/Y)\text{actual} = s_c\,(P/Y)\text{actual} \end{matrix}$$

The rate of profit is determined fundamentally not by the quantity of capital (or its productivity) but by the natural rate of growth. The higher the natural growth rate, in particular the higher the rate of technical progress, the greater the expected rate of profit and therefore the greater the gap opened up between the marginal efficiency of capital and the rate of interest (r). The greater this gap, the greater will be the actual rate of accumulation and the actual rate of profit, the share of investment in income and the profits share. It would be expected, then, that the rate of profit on capital and the share of profits in income would be higher in innovatory boom periods and in the more dynamic, rapidly growing, technologically advanced economies.

Thus our theory of income distribution is, not surprisingly, an amalgam of Kalecki's short-run 'degree of monopoly' theory (1954) and Kaldor's long-run, full-employment theory, incorporated in his growth model (1960). Kaldor's distribution mechanism serves to equate an economy's natural and warranted rates of growth, enabling it to achieve steady growth at full employment on average in the long run. Any change in the investment share of full employment income is accommodated by a change in profits share; investment determines saving through changes in profits share and Say's Law holds in the long run. But Kaldor admits that in the short run profit margins (and the degree of monopoly) are much less flexible and changes in investment will change income in accordance with multiplier theory. An actual economy will experience cyclical movements from period to period, as already explained. Kaldor's stabilizing income distribution mechanism will operate, but only to a very limited extent in the medium run. Profit margins and the profits share will increase somewhat during booms and contract during recessions, as argued above, reducing the amplitude of the cycle but not eliminating it.

VIII Policy implications

The implications of the above for economic policy are obviously the opposite of the policy irrelevancy conclusions of the New Classical Macroeconomics. Although the future course of the economy is impossible to predict with any accuracy, major disequilibria will occur almost certainly and require correction; the economy is *not* self-equilibrating to full employment in the short or the longer run. The primary task of econometric analysis is continually to adjust the coefficients in 'Keynes-based' econometric models, updating them to allow for the structural changes occurring in the economy and capturing as far as possible the effects of changing expectations on the major psychological functional relationships. The models can then be used to make conditional predictions for a year or two ahead. We do not have sufficient knowledge to 'fine-tune' the economy, but we should be able to limit deviations from a high employment growth path by a judicious combination of fiscal and monetary policies. The only way to combine such a high employment policy with low inflation is to set up permanent institutions to monitor and control the behaviour of the general level of money wages and prices. This is just one example of the need for government intervention in any market in which social and private costs and benefits greatly diverge. There will be considerable scope for the government to carry out (or assist the private sector to carry out) long-term investment in the infrastructure and high risk projects. 'The duty of ordering the current volume of investment cannot safely be left in private hands' (CW VII: 320). But, above all, there must be very substantial government investment in human capital – expenditure on health, education and training to improve the quality of labour, the ultimate factor of production and source of wealth.

So there is still a role for economists to play, even though it is a more humble one (perhaps on a level with dentists?). Or perhaps economists are more like meteorologists, only able with their computer models to predict (somewhat inaccurately) a short period ahead, but with the advantage over meteorologists that they are able to do at least something to improve the economic weather.

Notes

1. The 'Pigou Effect', real balance effect, argument, so often used to attack the concept of an unemployment equilibrium, purports to show that, if money wages and prices were flexible, the system would adjust to full employment. But this is tantamount to saying, 'Let's assume that the economy is a *non-monetary* economy'!
2. There are indications in the *General Theory* that Keynes himself was not clear about this distinction. At certain points he seems to be thinking in terms of an aggregate production function with declining marginal product of capital as the capital stock grows, in a given state of technology. See, for example, his discussion of a state of 'full investment' on p. 324 and his argument on pp. 375–6 that, since the demand for capital is strictly limited, 'it would not be difficult to increase the stock of capital up to a point where its marginal efficiency had fallen to a very low figure, leading to the euthanasia of the rentier'.
3. Monetarists argue that high nominal market rates of interest can be interpreted as due to the public's average expectation of high future rates of inflation. But, as Keynes (CW VII: 142), Harrod (1971) and Davidson (1988) show, a fully anticipated expectation of a change in the rate of inflation cannot affect the nominal rate of interest, though an increase in uncertainty about the future rate of inflation can affect the nominal rate of interest by inducing a greater demand for liquidity.
4. 'The Marginalists have eliminated from their analysis all the relevant features of the production process in order to maintain intact the model they have built for the problem of optimum allocation of scarce goods' (Pasinetti, 1981: 16).
5. Cf. the common defence of static general equilibrium theory – that it was never meant to be realistic or positively useful but shows how far the real world departs from it!
6. $G_W = s/v$ where G_W = warranted rate of growth, s = average = marginal savings ratio, v = marginal = average capital-output ratio.
7. If, on the other hand, the natural rate exceeded the warranted rate there would be chronic excess demand and 'secular exhilaration' – continual inflation and growing unemployment, owing to lack of capital to equip the growing labour force. Harrod thought this was typical of developing countries.
8. Cf. the macroeconomics textbooks' incorrect treatment of the government budget constraint, in which the shifting of both LM and IS curves owing to changes in the stocks of financial assets over time (resulting from an unbalanced budget) is analysed without considering the impact of the changes in the real capital stock and output which are occurring during the same period.
9. Although trend and cycle can be separated statistically, it is illegitimate to separate them, both in theory and practice. Technical progress and growth of the labour force determine the *potential* growth path but this can only be *realized* by embodying the innovations in new capital equipment. Goodwin emphasizes the organic connection between cycle and trend by assuming that all actual growth in the full employment (capacity) ceiling occurs only during booms, when capital is being accumulated to equip with the newest techniques the expanded labour force. In each upswing the economy goes higher than it did previously, but it does not swing back lower than previously because of the nature of the cost structure. In the boom, agents become involved in 'fixed' outlays which cannot be reduced very easily in the downturn. Firms must continue to make fixed interest payments, try to maintain stable dividends and continue to pay the salaries of an expanded managerial, maintenance, sales and research staff. Consumers draw on savings rather than accept a reduced standard of living. Such fixed outlays, together with social security payments to the unemployed, in effect 'ratchet up' the consumption function. The economy surges upward and plunges down, but it does not go back to its old low. There is no 'progress' during the

depression: it all occurs during the boom, or at least is 'realized' during the boom. The cycle and trend are indissolubly fused together.

10. Harcourt and Kenyon (1976) examine the relationship between the pricing decision and the investment decision of an oligopoly firm but lay more emphasis on the need to finance investment expenditure than on the strength and growth of demand in determining the firm's profit margin.

References

Brothwell, J. F. (1987), 'On the Nature and Use of the Marginal Physical Product in Post Keynesian Economics: A Comment', *Journal of Post Keynesian Economics*, **9**, 496–501.

Brothwell, J. F. (1988), 'The General Theory After Fifty Years', in J. V. Hillard (ed.) *J. M. Keynes in Retrospect*, Aldershot: Edward Elgar.

Davidson, P. (1968), 'Money, Portfolio Balance, Capital Accumulation and Economic Growth', *Econometrica*, **36**, 297–320.

Davidson, P. (1988), 'A Post-Keynesian View of Theories and Causes for High Real Interest Rates', in P. Arestis (ed.), *Post-Keynesian Monetary Economics*, Aldershot: Edward Elgar.

Goodhart, C. (1989), 'Keynes and Monetarism', in R. Hill (ed.), *Keynes, Money and Monetarism*, London: Macmillan.

Goodwin, R. (1953), 'The Problem of Trend and Cycle', *Yorkshire Bulletin of Economic and Social Research*, **5**, 89–97.

Goodwin, R. (1955), 'A Model of Cyclical Growth', in E. Lundberg (ed.), *The Business Cycle in the Post-War World*, London: Macmillan.

Goodwin, R. (1988), 'My Life and Times in the Shadow of Keynes', in O. F. Hamouda and J. N. Smithin (eds), *Keynes and Public Policy after Fifty Years Vol 1: Economics and Policy*, Aldershot: Edward Elgar.

Harcourt, G. C. and P. Kenyon (1976), 'Pricing and the Investment Decision', *Kyklos*, **29**, 449–77.

Harrod, R. F. (1939), 'An Essay in Dynamic Theory', *Economic Journal*, **49**, 14–33.

Harrod, R. F. (1971), 'Discussion Paper', in G. Clayton *et al.* (eds), *Monetary Theory and Policy in the 1970s*, Oxford: Oxford University Press.

Kaldor, N. (1960), 'A Model of Economic Growth', in *Essays on Economic Stability and Growth*, London: Duckworth.

Kalecki, M. (1954), *Theory of Economic Dynamics*, London: Allen & Unwin.

Mills, T. C. and G. E. Wood (1988), 'Interest Rates and the Conduct of Monetary Policy', in W. Eltis and P. Sinclair (eds), *Keynes and Economic Policy*, London: Macmillan.

Pasinetti, L. L. (1981), *Structural Change in Economic Growth*, Cambridge: Cambridge University Press.

Robinson, J. (1979), 'History versus Equilibrium', in *Collected Economic Papers, Vol. 5*, Oxford: Basil Blackwell.

Sawyer, M. C. (1992), 'The Relationship between Keynes's Macroeconomic Analysis and Theories of Imperfect Competition', this volume, Chapter 6.

Schumpeter, J. A. (1957), *Capitalism, Socialism and Democracy*, London: Allen & Unwin.

Shackle, G. L. S. (1967), *The Years of High Theory*, Cambridge: Cambridge University Press.

Shackle, G. L. S. (1983), 'Levels of Simplicity in Keynes's Theory of Money and Employment', *The South African Journal of Economics*, **51**, 357–67.

11 Psychoanalysis and Keynes's account of the psychology of the trade cycle

Ted Winslow

I Introduction

According to Keynes, it is primarily cyclical fluctuations in investment which cause cyclical fluctuations in output and employment (CW XIV: 118–19). Cyclical fluctuations in investment are in turn the product of cycles of optimistic and pessimistic 'psychological expectations of future yield from capital-assets'. Elsewhere (1989, 1992), I have attempted to show that Keynes regards these expectations as normally irrational. This chapter attempts to demonstrate that his account of the cyclical behaviour of expectations as 'waves of irrational psychology' (CW VII: 162) and of other psychological characteristics of the trade cycle are consistent with the psychoanalytic theory of the anal-sadistic character. In Section II, that element of psychoanalytic theory which is relevant to Keynes's account of the psychological characteristics of the trade cycle is examined. Section III then points to correspondences between this theory and Keynes's account.

II The psychology of the business world

In 'The End of Laissez-Faire' (CW X: 293), Keynes claims that the essential characteristic of capitalism is its 'dependence upon an intense appeal to the money-making and money-loving instincts of individuals as the main motive force of the economic machine'. In the *General Theory* (CW VII: 374), he links money making and private wealth to other motives which he calls 'dangerous human proclivities'. These are proclivities which 'can be canalised into comparatively harmless channels by the existence of opportunities for money-making and private wealth, [and] which, if they cannot be satisfied in this way, may find their outlet in cruelty, the reckless pursuit of personal power and authority, and other forms of self-aggrandisement'. This description of business motivation closely matches the psychoanalytic theory of the anal-sadistic character (see Winslow, 1986), a theory with which Keynes was acquainted (CW VI: 258–9). This section of the chapter begins with a brief recapitulation of this theory as it is found in the works cited by Keynes in *A Treatise on Money*. It then examines two other aspects of psychoanalytic theory which are utilised in Section III's discussion of Keynes's treatment of the psychology of the trade cycle. These are Abraham's elaboration of the original theory, an elaboration which ties it to obsessional neurosis and manic-depressive psychosis, and Freud's theory of mass psychology, a theory which, in combination with the theory of anal-sadism, points to a basis for the formation of business psychological groups (in Freud's sense of this term).

The anal-sadistic character

Psychoanalysis derives adult character traits from the repression in childhood of sexual and aggressive drives. These repressed interests resurface in adult character as what Freud calls sublimations and reaction-formations. Because constitutional predispositions and patterns of repression differ from child to child, adult traits vary. On the other hand, because patterns of repression are often similar across a given culture, particular traits can become typical. The typical complex of adult traits in the expression of the complex of repressed interests produced by the usual pattern of repression. The typical traits of what Keynes calls an entrepreneur economy are those of Freud's anal-sadistic character.[1] These traits are parsimony, obstinacy, excessive orderliness and an irrational interest in money. All are sublimations of and reaction-formations to childhood anal eroticism and aggressiveness. For example, the irrational interest in money is a sublimation of the child's initially very positive attitude to its own excrement. Freud claims that money is unconsciously identified with, and therefore a symbol of, excrement. Excessive orderliness is both a sublimation of aggressiveness and a reaction-formation to anal eroticism.[2] An irrational interest in economizing, saving, collecting and waiting is an expression of the childhood interest in maximizing the pleasure obtainable from defecation by postponing it as long as possible. Obstinacy derives from the wish to pursue this interest free from outside interference.

The childhood environment most likely to lead to the dominance of these traits is found in a particular kind of authoritarian and patriarchal family. This family creates the repressive context in which what Freud calls the Oedipus complex will normally be resolved by regression to the anal-sadistic stage of development. It is this regression, combined with repression of the interests dominant in the anal-sadistic stage, that produces the adult character dominated by anal-sadistic traits. Psychoanalysis also associates the anal-sadistic stage with two illnesses: manic-depressive psychosis and obsessional neurosis.

Anal-sadism, manic-depressive psychosis and obsessional neurosis

Freud himself pointed to connections between anal-sadistic interests and these illnesses. Karl Abraham provided an elaboration of these connections which, as we shall see, further links psychoanalysis to Keynes's account of the psychology of the trade cycle.[3] Abraham (1927: 423) claims that melancholic and obsessional characters are very similar. In both cases the individuals involved display pronounced anal character traits in the periods when they are relatively free of the symptoms which define their illnesses. On the basis of this and other evidence, he argues that manic-depressive psychosis and obsessional neurosis are connected in an essential way to the anal-sadistic phase of childhood development; they are extreme versions of the anal-sadistic character. It follows from the psychoanalytic understanding of mental phenomena that extremes provide insight into the nature of the normal. Manic-depressive and obsessional features will be found in the anal-sadistic character even where there is no neurosis or psychosis (categories whose boundaries are in any event imprecise because of the continuum connecting normality and illness).

Abraham (1927: 425–8) divides the anal-sadistic stage into two sub-stages: early and late. In the early part of the stage anal eroticism takes the form primarily of a desire to obtain pleasure from evacuation, sadism the form of a desire to destroy the object. In the later part, anal eroticism takes the form primarily of a desire to obtain pleasure from retention, sadism the form of a desire to control the object. The erotic component can also be expressed as a relation to objects. Hence the earlier phase is associated with a desire to lose and destroy the object; the later with a desire to retain and control it. Like the anal-sadistic character itself, manic-depressive psychosis and obsessional neurosis are the product of what Freud calls 'regression'. The manic-depressive has regressed to the earlier part of the stage; the obsessive to the later part. The characteristics associated with each sub-phase are found, however, in all three personality types (1927: 431). In addition, all share the traits expressive of the stage as a whole: strong sadism and a pronounced tendency to treat all objects, human and non-human, as property. 'In marked cases of anal character-formation almost all relationships in life are brought into the category of having (holding fast) and giving, that is, of proprietorship' (1927: 382).

The three types also share an extremely harsh super-ego. In Freud's theory, this is a structure in the mind formed through the operation of the defence mechanism that he calls 'identification'. It is the source, among other things, of conscience, the inner critic and controller of the desires of the ego. By identification is meant the modelling of the ego and the ego ideal on a figure of authority, usually the parent of the same sex. It is undertaken as a defence against the dangers to which the ego is exposed by the complex of desires which Freud called the Oedipus complex. Regression to the anal-sadistic stage serves the same function. As pointed out above, the latter defence is particularly likely to be employed in just those circumstances which will, through the operation of identification, produce an extremely harsh super-ego, circumstances associated with a cruel, harsh and authoritarian father. The harshness produced by taking this as the model for the super-ego is accentuated by the stronger sadism which comes to be present in all structures of the mind as a result of regression to the anal-sadistic stage.

This super-ego is closely connected to the characteristic features of the three personalities. Mania, for example, is the outcome of throwing off the super-ego. This explains 'the carefree and unrestrained cheerfulness, the increased feeling of self-importance, the removal of inhibitions, the careless gaiety, the tendency to reckless and aggressive conduct, and the overestimation of "knowledge and power" ' typical of mania (Abraham, 1927: 150–51 and 470–76). Depression, on the other hand, is associated with a strengthening of the super-ego. This may result, for example, from object loss (as we shall see, the object need not be human). This causes all object ties to be broken off; libido returns, so to speak, from these objects to the ego and the super-ego. This strengthens the super-ego and produces the feelings and behaviour characteristic of clinical depression, including extreme, perhaps suicidal, feelings of guilt, worthlessness and pessimism; irrational feelings of impoverishment; and compulsive hoarding. These feelings can be expressed in several ways, one of which is 'organ speech'. Mania is likely to be accompanied by diarrhoea, depression by constipation. Section III, I will attempt to show that this description of mania and depression corresponds closely to Keynes's description of the psychology of economic booms and depressions.

As we shall now see, the tendency to episodes of mania and depression normally present in the anal-sadistic character is strengthened by membership of what Freud calls a psychological group.

Psychological groups

A group is psychological in Freud's sense when it is bounded together by emotional ties which have an unconscious origin in repressed sexual and aggressive instincts. For example, the tie binding what Freud calls a primary group is the outcome of each member substituting the same leader for the super-ego. Since this requires similarity between the leader and the super-ego these individuals must have similar super-egos. As pointed out above, the super-ego is the product of identification, the original form of emotional tie with an object. This is the wish to become like another individual or group of individuals, 'to mould a person's own ego after the fashion of the one that has been taken as a model' (Freud, 1985: 135). In the circumstances which lead to the formation of the super-ego or ego ideal, identification is a defence mechanism employed in association with others to resolve the Oedipus complex. By identifying with his father the little boy both converts his murderous impulses toward his father into affection and realizes in fantasy his wish to copulate with his mother. This enables him to escape the dangers to which he perceived himself exposed by these desires. This defensive measure against particular early forms of the sexual and aggressive instincts creates the basis for the formation of psychological groups.

The desire to become like the father takes the form of the super-ego. The ego itself will also take on characteristics of the father, partly as a consequence of identification, but also as a result of pressures exerted by the super-ego. Normally the super-ego and the ego are in less than perfect harmony. Conflict is particularly likely in the case of anal-sadistic personalities. The results of identification depend on the characteristics of the father. The similarities between individual egos and super-egos which provide the basis for the identification which creates a psychological group are, therefore, themselves the result of earlier identifications with similar fathers. As noted above, personalities rooted in anal-sadism tend to be the product of harsh and tyrannical fathers. Identification here produces a harsh and tyrannical super-ego; that is, a super-ego in conflict with the ego. As we shall see, this provides one of the main incentives for such individuals to unite in psychological groups.

Identification can also occur in adulthood. Freud (1959b: 40) claims that

> it may arise with any new perception of a common quality shared with some other person who is not an object of the sexual instinct. The more important this common quality is, the more successful may this partial identification become, and it may thus represent the beginning of a new tie.

Here we have the basis for the formation of psychological groups. The resolution of the Oedipus complex also creates sexual impulsions which are inhibited in their aim. These provide a basis for another kind of emotional tie between members of a group, an object tie (Freud, 1985: 141–2 and 146–7). As Freud understands them, both types of tie ultimately have a sexual basis. This is what he means when he claims 'that love relationships (or, to use a more neutral expression, emotional ties) . . . constitute the essence of the group mind' (1985: 120).

The basis for identification between individuals can be either identification with the same leader or 'a common interest in an object, or a similar emotional bias' (1959b: 16). Alone or in combination these common elements enable the individuals concerned to identify themselves with one another in their ego and form a psychological group (1973: 99). Though there are business leaders, the common element likely to prove most important in the formation of business psychological groups is the shared love of money, money making and power.

The process of identification which binds the individual to the group alters the individual's own psychology. He resigns those sublimations and reaction-formations which are distinctively his own and takes on those common to the other members of the group. He also gives up his super-ego and substitutes for it identification with the group. The emotional aspect of mental life is strengthened, the rational aspect weakened, the degree to which this occurs depending on the extent to which the group itself has acquired organizational structure and in this way secondarily acquired the characteristics of an individual (1959b: 48). The substitution of the group for the super-ego has the effect of generating great pressure on the individual to keep his beliefs and opinions in conformity with the beliefs and opinions of the other members of the group. This is the basis of the extreme openness of members of a psychological group to reciprocal influence, to what Freud calls 'suggestion'.

This provides an irrational anchor for belief. Suggestion generates 'a conviction which is not based upon perception and reasoning but upon an erotic tie' (1959b: 59–60). It is 'influence without adequate logical foundation' (1959b: 22). It is another instance of ideas which have their source in what Keynes, in *A Treatise on Probability*, calls 'pure instinct or irrational associations of ideas (acquired or inherited)'.[4] In his 1937 *Quarterly Journal of Economics* article, 'The General Theory of Employment', Keynes, in his account of the third convention on which he claims individuals base their long-term expectations, defines a conventional judgement in terms which closely match Freud's account of the operation of suggestion in a psychological group:

> Knowing that our own individual judgement is worthless, we endeavour to fall back on the judgement of the rest of the world which is perhaps better informed. That is, we endeavour to conform with the behaviour of the majority or the average. The psychology of a society of individuals each of whom is endeavouring to copy the others leads to what we may strictly term a *conventional* judgement. (Keynes CW XIV: 114, emphasis in original)

Identification explains how psychological groups are formed. It does not, however, explain why they are formed. Freud points in answer to the benefits which such groups confer on their members. Three are particularly relevant to the formation of business psychological groups: (a) the pleasure made possible by escaping from the renunciations and limitations imposed by the super-ego; (b) the elimination of feelings of inferiority and of the inhibitions such feelings place on action; and (c) relief from the anxiety which would otherwise accompany a situation of danger.

For Freud, the process of individual development is a constant struggle between what he calls the pleasure and reality principles. Even in the best circumstances, the reality principle does not achieve complete dominance over the pleasure principle. For example, in earliest infancy recognition of a 'changing external world' disturbs the individual in her enjoyment, in accordance with the pleasure principle, of the 'absolutely self-sufficient narcissism' which characterizes this period when no differentiation has yet occurred between self and other (1959b: 62–3). Consequently the recognition is given only reluctantly and normally incompletely. One sign of this is that we periodically, in our sleep, revert from such recognition 'to our former condition of absence of stimulation and avoidance of objects'. The incompleteness of recognition provides a justification for Keynes's claim that 'the idea of the future being different from the present is so repugnant to our conventional modes of thought and behaviour that we, most of us, offer a great resistance to acting on it in practice' (CW VII: 125).

The conflict between these principles also generates a permanent conflict between the ego and the super-ego. The super-ego represents the demands of external reality. The ego must mediate between these demands and those of the instincts which are constantly pressing for direct satisfaction. Freud claims:

> this separation of the ego ideal from the ego cannot be borne for long either, and has to be temporarily undone. In all renunciations and limitations imposed upon the ego a periodical infringement of the prohibition is the rule; this indeed is shown by festivals, which in origin are nothing less or more than excesses provided by law and which owe their cheerful character to the release which they bring. The ego ideal comprises the sum of all the limitations in which the ego has to acquiesce, and for that reason the abrogation of the ideal would necessarily be a magnificent festival for the ego, which might then once again feel satisfied with itself. (1959b: 63)

Membership in a leaderless psychological group substitutes the identification with the other members of the group for the ego ideal. Even here the inhibitions of the super-ego may be replaced by other inhibitions resulting, for example, from the organizational structure of the group. (In groups with strong leaders, the inhibitions imposed by the super-ego are replaced by those imposed by the leader.) It will be much easier, however, for the members of the group to escape from these inhibitions and realize 'a magnificent festival for the ego'. Group membership will therefore strengthen whatever tendency to mania is already present. For the reasons given above, the tendency to mania is particularly strong in the anal-sadistic character. Moreover the benefit available from abrogation of the ego ideal is here much greater than normal because of the super-ego's harsh and tyrannical character.

While membership in a group weakens the individual's capacity for independent action, it also provides means by which the will can be strengthened. In this and other ways, it facilitates action. The means are found in the openness to reciprocal influence, to suggestion, created by group membership. In a group, Freud claims,

> an individual's private emotional impulses and intellectual acts are too weak to come to anything by themselves and are entirely dependent for this on being reinforced by being repeated in a similar way in the other members of the group. We are reminded of how many of these phenomena of dependence are part of the normal constitution of human society, of how little originality and personal courage are to be found in it, of how much every individual is ruled by those attitudes of the group mind which exhibit themselves in such forms as racial characteristics, class prejudices, public opinion, etc. (1959b: 49)

Openness to suggestion also facilitates action by providing a means for alleviating the sort of anxiety to which Keynes points in explaining the use of forecasting conventions. Suggestion, as we saw above, provides an alternative basis for belief. Consequently, where no rational basis exists and where, in addition, consciousness of this produces incapacitating anxiety, suggestion provides a means whereby this consciousness can be suppressed and the anxiety avoided. For reasons which will now be examined, consciousness of what Keynes calls fundamental uncertainty is quite likely to produce incapacitating anxiety in an anal-sadistic character.

Freud (1959a: 138–9) claims that the feeling of anxiety is a reproduction of the unpleasurable, uncontrollable stimulation experienced during birth. A similar feeling arises whenever an infant's needs go unmet. When it is discovered that non-fulfilment of need coincides with the absence of the mother, the feeling starts to arise whenever such absence threatens. The danger of loss of the object is treated as identical to the danger of unpleasurable and uncontrollable stimulation. What consciousness takes to be a danger of loss of the mother is then further transformed. At one stage in this process it is identified with the danger of castration. Castration represents loss of the mother because in the unconscious the penis is a means of reuniting with the mother through copulation with someone unconsciously identified with her (1959a: 138–9).

The anal-sadistic character is the product of regression to the anal-sadistic stage and of repression of the interests dominant in that stage. This gives increased importance to another set of unconscious equivalents: money, excrement and penis (173: 133–4). Regression and repression make the danger of losing money unconsciously equivalent to the danger of castration. Through these unconscious associations, consciousness of the former danger can produce incapacitating anxiety. This can readily be connected to Keynes's account of the relation between anxiety and fundamental uncertainty. Consciousness of fundamental uncertainty is consciousness of the danger of losing money. For this reason, 'peace and comfort of mind require that we should hide from ourselves how little we foresee' (CW XIV 124). Membership in a psychological group provides a means of doing this. Suggestion provides an irrational basis for belief which enables members to suppress their consciousness of fundamental uncertainty.

We turn now to an examination of the consistency of this psychoanalytic view of 'the uncontrollable and disobedient psychology of the business world' (CW VII: 317) with Keynes's account of the psychological characteristics of the trade cycle.

III Psychological characteristics of the trade cycle

Freud's psychology of groups in combination with Abraham's account of manic-depressive illness enables us to provide a psychoanalytic interpretation of the various psychological elements to which Keynes directs attention in his account of the trade cycle (CW VII: Chapter 22). We will examine characteristics of each of the three phases of the cycle: the boom, the crisis and the slump.

The boom

As described above, the escape from the limitations of the super-ego and the openness to suggestion made possible by membership of a psychological group increase the possibility of mania-condition in which 'the ego and the ego ideal [are] fused together, so that the person, in a mood of triumph and self-satisfaction, disturbed by no self-criticism, can enjoy the abolition of his inhibitions, his feelings of consideration for others, and his self-reproaches' (Freud, 1959b: 64). Goodman (1969: 48 and 70–71) claims that this accurately describes the psychological condition of the participants in a bull market in stocks.[5] Keynes's description of the final phase of a boom points to psychological characteristics similar to those of mania. This phase is characterized by unjustified optimism about the profitability of present investment (CW VII: 315). The boom is based on 'illusions':

> It is an essential characteristic of the boom that investments which will in fact yield, say, 2 per cent in conditions of full employment are made in the expectation of a yield of, say, 6 per cent, and are valued accordingly . . . a boom is a situation in which over-optimism triumphs over a rate of interest which, in a cooler light, would be seen to be excessive. (Ibid.: 321–2)

In *A Treatise on Money* he claims that the boom is associated with 'an atmosphere of buoyancy, exhilaration and freedom from economic cares', an atmosphere conducive to the production of great literature. Shakespeare's

> active career chanced to fall at the date of dates, when any level-headed person in England disposed to make money could hardly help doing so. 1575 to 1620 were the palmy days of profit – one of the greatest 'bull' movements ever known until modern days in the United States (with some bad years, of course, due to harvests, plague, commercial crises and chances of war – 1587, 1596, 1603) – Shakespeare being eleven years old in 1575 and dying in 1616. I offer as a thesis for examination by those who like rash generalisations, that by far the larger proportion of the world's greatest writers and artists have flourished in the atmosphere of buoyancy, exhilaration and the freedom from economic cares felt by the governing class, which is engendered by profit inflations. (CW VI: 137)

The crisis

Keynes claims that an adequate theory of the business cycle must be able to explain crisis:

> There is, however, another characteristic of what we call the trade cycle which our explanation must cover if it is to be adequate; namely, the phenomenon of *crisis* – the fact that the substitution of a downward for an upward tendency often takes place suddenly and violently, whereas there is, as a rule, no such sharp turning-point when an upward is substituted for a downward tendency. (CW VII: 314, emphasis in original)

This is explained by the psychoanalytic theory of panic in a psychological group. Freud distinguishes between two types of panic. The first results from the breakdown of the libidinal ties that constitute a group. This is brought on by loss of the object. The paradigm case is provided by the army whose leader is killed:

> A hint to the same effect, that the essence of a group lies in the libidinal ties existing in it, is also to be found in the phenomenon of panic, which is best studied in military groups. A panic arises if a group of that kind becomes disintegrated. Its characteristics are that none of the orders given by superiors are any longer listened to, and that each individual is only solicitous on his own account, and without any consideration for the rest. The mutual ties have ceased to exist, and a gigantic and senseless fear is set free . . . If an individual in panic fear begins to be solicitous only on his own account, he bears witness in so doing to the fact that the emotional ties, which have hitherto made the danger seem small to him, have ceased to exist.Now that he is by himself in facing the danger, he may surely think it greater. The fact is, therefore, that panic fear presupposes a relaxation in the libidinal structure of the group and reacts to that relaxation in a justifiable manner. (Freud, 1959b: 28)

The second results from suggestion. Fear aroused in one individual by a real or imagined danger can be amplified into panic by the reciprocal influence of members of a group on each other.

There are neurotic and realistic elements in the fear associated with both types of panic. In the first case, the panic ensuing upon the breakdown of libidinal ties, although much of the perceived danger is imaginary, some is realistic. In the example offered by Freud, the danger actually is greater because the individual is now alone in facing it. In the case of a business group, the breakdown of the ties destroys the psychological basis of the third convention which had enabled individuals to forget the real dangers they faced. These will, therefore, be forced back into consciousness. In the second case, panic resulting from an increase in the common danger, openness to reciprocal influence exaggerates the fear far beyond what is reasonable. The two types can be combined in some circumstances.

Such circumstances are very likely to characterize what Keynes refers to as a trade cycle *crisis*. The panic may start out as a response to an increased danger, real or imaginary. This is amplified by contagion. Panic, however, will lead to a drop in the money value of financial and real assets. In the business group love of money and of money making substitutes for a common tie to a leader. Here, therefore, the object loss corresponding to the death of a leader is the loss of money. For this reason money losses destroy the emotional ties of the group and so lead to panic of the second type.

Keynes's account of the crisis points to both types of panic. Once doubts begin to arise about the reliability of estimates of prospective yield, they can quickly be amplified into panic by suggestion. 'The forces of disillusion may suddenly impose a new conventional basis of valuation' (CW XIV: 115). In the boom, the estimates of prospective yield upon which decisions were based were over-optimistic. Consequently evidence will eventually come to light that the marginal efficiency is much lower than has been believed.

> The disillusion comes because doubts suddenly arise concerning the reliability of the prospective yield, perhaps because the current yield shows signs of falling off, as the stock of newly produced durable goods steadily increases. If current costs of production are thought to be higher than they will be later on, that will be a further reason for a fall in the marginal efficiency of capital. (CW VI: 317)

Moreover speculators play an important role in the stock market. On Keynes's definition, a speculator is a person engaged in forecasting the psychology of the market, in 'aping unreason proleptically'. At some point in the boom, speculators will foresee a downturn and by acting in anticipation of it cause the prices of stocks to cease climbing as rapidly as they had and perhaps even to fall.

This initial panic, whatever its cause, will bring about financial losses which destroy the emotional ties of the group. This, together with the actual present losses on investments, restores consciousness of what is now perceived as an extreme danger, if not certainty, of object loss. This produces anxiety: 'A collapse in the marginal efficiency of capital' is accompanied by 'dismay and uncertainty as to the future' (CW VII: 316). For the psychological reasons explored below, this is associated with an increase in the propensity to hoard. This adds to the forces causing a devaluation of non-money assets:

> It is of the nature of organised investment markets, under the influence of purchasers largely ignorant of what they are buying and of speculators who are more concerned with forecasting the next shift of market sentiment than with a reasonable estimate of the future yield of capital-assets, that, when disillusion falls upon an over-optimistic and over-bought market, it should fall with sudden and even catastrophic force. (CW VII: 315–16)

The slump

The collapse into slump brings with it extreme pessimism, the counterpart of the excessive optimism of mania:

> When the disillusion comes, [the over-optimism of the boom] is replaced by a contrary 'error of pessimism', with the result that investments, which would in fact yield 2 per cent in conditions of full employment, are expected to yield less than nothing. We reach a condition where there is a shortage of houses, but where nevertheless no one can afford to live in the houses that there are. (CW VII: 321–2)

Keynes (CW VII: 151) claims a stock market crash itself exerts a very depressing effect on the marginal efficiency of capital. Extreme pessimism, feelings of inferiority and weakness of will are, as pointed out above, characteristic of clinical depression. Part of the explanation is found in the loss of group ties and the restoration of the harsh and tyrannical super-ego which accompanies this. As we shall see, the consequences of this are accentuated by the general cutting of libidinal ties to external objects which accompanies loss of the object. It is this accentuation that produces the characteristic feelings of clinical depression.

In both *A Treatise on Money* and the *General Theory*, Keynes associates pessimistic expectations with what he calls feelings of ' "psychological" poverty'. In the *Treatise* he points to both as consequences of the 1929 crash:

> The pessimism and the atmosphere of disappointment which the stock-market

> collapse engendered reduced enterprise and lowered the natural-rate of interest; while the 'psychological' poverty which the collapse of paper values brought with it probably increased saving. (CW VI: 176)

The association is also alluded to in the *General Theory*:

> Unfortunately a serious fall in the marginal efficiency of capital also tends to affect adversely the propensity to consume. For it involves a severe decline in the market value of stock exchange equities. Now, on the class who take an active interest in their stock exchange investments, especially if they are employing borrowed funds, this naturally exerts a very depressing influence. These people are, perhaps, even more influenced in their readiness to spend by rises and falls in their investments than by the state of their incomes. (CW VII: 319)

Psychological poverty is a feeling engendered by the collapse in the paper values of bonds and shares. Because it causes the wealth-owning class to increase its saving out of a given income, Keynes claims 'it should be classified amongst the major factors capable of causing short-period changes in the propensity to consume' (CW VII: 93). In the *Treatise* (CW VI: 176–7) he claims that such behaviour is irrational.

In his original discussion of depression, Freud claimed that feelings of impoverishment were one of its invariable features: 'In the clinical picture of melancholia dissatisfaction with the self on moral grounds is far the most outstanding feature; the self-criticism much less frequently concerns itself with bodily infirmity, ugliness, weakness, social inferiority; among these latter ills that the patient dreads or asseverates, the thought of poverty alone has a favoured position' (1925: 157–8) Further on he provides the following hint as to where one might find the source of this dread of poverty: 'We may expect to find the derivation of that one striking feature of melancholia, the manifestations of dread of poverty, in anal eroticism, torn out of its context and altered by regression' (1925: 163).

The reaction to loss of money of a personality with a tendency to depression is likely to be withdrawal of libido from the world back into the ego. The attempt to attach libido to an external object has failed. 'Incapable of making a lasting and positive application of his libido, the patient unconsciously seeks seclusion from the world' (Abraham, 1927: 147). This reaction explains 'feelings of impoverishment':

> Certain features commonly present in states of depression become comprehensible if we accept the well-founded conclusions of psycho-analytic experience. Take, for instance, the frequent ideas of impoverishment. The patient complains, let us say, that he and his family are exposed to starvation. If a pecuniary loss has actually preceded the onset of his illness, he will assert that

> he cannot possibly endure the blow and that he is completely ruined. These strange ideas, which often entirely dominate the patient's thoughts, are explicable from the identification of libido and money – of sexual and pecuniary 'power' – with which we are so familiar. The patient's libido has disappeared from the world, as it were. Whereas other people can invest their libido in the objects of the external world he has no such capital to expend. His feeling of poverty springs from a repressed perception of his own incapacity to love. (Ibid.: 148)

Psychological poverty is an aspect of a general inhibition of object-love which characterizes the anal-sadistic personality. As Keynes says of two business men in H. G. Wells's *The World of William Clissold*: 'Clissold and his brother Dickon, the advertising expert, flutter about the world seeking for something to which they can attach their abundant *libido*. But they have not found it. They would so like to be apostles. But they cannot. They remain business men' (CW X: 320, emphasis in original). The change from boom to depression is also accompanied by a change in the propensity to hoard. The collapse, including the collapse of the conventions, generates anxiety. Keynes directly associates this aspect with an increased propensity to hoard: 'The dismay and uncertainty as to the future which accompanies a collapse in the marginal efficiency of capital naturally precipitates a sharp increase in liquidity-preference' (CW VII: 316). He claims that 'a financial crisis or crisis of liquidation' of this kind occurred in the United States in 1932, 'when scarcely anyone could be induced to part with holdings of money on any reasonable terms' (CW VII: 207–8).

Keynes (CW XIV: 116) claims that the possession of actual money is able to 'lull this disquietude, partly on reasonable and partly on instinctive grounds'. This is made possible by 'a feeling about money [which] is itself conventional or instinctive [but which] operates . . . at a deeper level of our motivation'. Elsewhere (1986: 571–5) we have attempted to explain this in terms of the psychoanalytic theory of regression. As pointed out in Section II, an increased propensity to hoard is a characteristic feature of psychological depression. In listing the 'several reasons, which taken in combination are of compelling force, why in an economy of the type to which we are accustomed it is very probable that the money-rate of interest will often prove reluctant to decline adequately' (CW VII: 233), Keynes points to the factors leading to an increased propensity to hoard in a slump as 'the most fundamental consideration in this context', namely 'the characteristics of money which satisfy liquidity preference. For, in certain circumstances as will often occur, these will cause the rate of interest to be insensitive, particularly below a certain figure, even to a substantial increase in the quantity of money in proportion to other forms of wealth' (CW VII: 233). In *A Treatise on Money*, Keynes makes use of what from the perspective of the preceding discussion is a particularly interesting analogy to explain what happens when remedies proposed for the trade cycle fail to take account of time lags:

> A change-over in the type of production from investment-goods to consumption-goods (or *vice versa*) does not, on account of the period occupied by the process of production, produce its results in the market until after an appreciable time has elapsed. Thus, as we have seen, the price-stimulus to a change-over is apt to be continued until some time after the necessary steps have been taken. The result is that the remedy is overdone. It is as though the family were to go on giving a child successive doses of castor-oil every ten minutes until the first dose had done its work. Or – to take a better parallel – it is as though different members of the family were to give successive doses to the child, each in ignorance of the doses given by the others. The child will be very ill. Bismuth will then be administered on the same principle. Scientists will announce that children are subject to a diarrhoea–constipation cycle, due, they will add, to the weather, or, failing that, to alternations of optimism and pessimism amongst the members of the family. If the time taken by the first dose to act is constant, they will discover that the cycle is a true one with a constant period. Perhaps they will suggest that the remedy is to be found in giving the child bismuth when it is constipated and castor-oil at the other extreme. But more probably the parents will divide into bismuth and castor-oil parties, one of which, impressed by the horrors of diarrhoea, will renounce castor-oil, and the other, moved by the depression of constipation, will abjure bismuth. Thus it is not easy to keep to the middle path of continuous health. (CW VI: 200, emphasis in original)

Recovery from the slump will take considerable time – typically three to five years according to Keynes. The main requirement is recovery of the marginal efficiency of capital. A rise in the marginal efficiency will have to await a 'sufficiently obvious scarcity' of capital and the absorption of surplus stocks (CW VII: 318). On the psychological side, the recovery from depression and the re-establishment of emotional ties to the external world, including those that bind together a psychological group, will also take time. This may then be followed, in a collective as in an individual context, by a fairly long 'free interval' in which expectations are neither manic nor melancholic, but are in any event insufficient, on their own, to raise investment to the level required for full employment. Periods of manic boom and deep slump will be interrupted by fairly long periods of relative stability. As Keynes says (CW VII: 162), everything does not depend on 'waves of irrational psychology'.

Trade cycle policy

Keynes also points to irrational elements in trade cycle policy proposals and in the arguments offered in their support. For example, he once described the policy of using high interest rates to check the boom in its early stages as 'sadistic puritanism'.[6] He says this in disagreeing with D. H. Robertson's defence of the policy as something other than 'sadistic barbarism'. He explicitly claims (CW XIII: 238) that an understanding of the foundations of this policy proposal must be sought in psycho- rather than economic analysis.

Robertson's defence is found in a 1931 review of *A Treatise on Money*. In the *Treatise* (CW V: 246) Keynes describes advocates of the policy as 'puritans of finance, sometimes extreme individualists'. Their claim that real wealth grows faster in a depression than in a boom is, he claims, a screen for the real source of the 'gloomy satisfaction' they get from 'the speculative and business losses, the low prices, and the high real wages, accompanied, however, by unemployment, which characterise the typical depression'. The real source is satisfaction of an unconscious wish for punishment arising out of the unconscious guilt ('suppressed reactions against the distastefulness of capitalism') produced by the relatively unrestricted pursuit of the vulgar passions that fuel a boom.

Also in 1931, in his Harris Foundation lectures, 'An Economic Analysis of Unemployment', Keynes, having denied (CW XIII: 347–8) that the boom from 1925 to 1929 had, as advocates of the doctrine of 'forced saving' were claiming, produced serious over-expansion and misdirection of investment (see also CW VII: 320–4), went on to claim that:

> it seems an extraordinary imbecility that this wonderful outburst of productive energy should be the prelude to impoverishment and depression. Some austere and puritanical souls regard it both as an inevitable and a desirable nemesis on so much over-expansion, as they call it; a nemesis on man's speculative spirit. It would, they feel, be a victory of the mammon of unrighteousness if so much prosperity was not subsequently balanced by universal bankruptcy. We need, they say, what they politely call a 'prolonged liquidation' to put us right. The liquidation, they tell us, is not yet complete. But in time it will be. And when sufficient time has elapsed for the completion of the liquidation, all will be well with us again. (CW XIII: 349)

This criticism of 'the austere view', which sees high rates of interest as an appropriate way to check the boom, is repeated in the *General Theory* (CW VII: 326–9).[7] He claims it is 'extraordinary' that this school of thought should exist. Only Robertson's defence is treated as possessing any merit, and it is a 'counsel of desperation and despair'. Other arguments are said to be founded entirely in 'confusion of mind'. This is said, in particular, of the view that the boom is the product of forced saving brought on by an excessive increase in the money supply reducing interest rates below the desirable level (ibid.: 328–9; see also the discussion of Hayek on 79–81). This argument and the policy of holding the money supply constant to which it points are described elsewhere in the *General*

Theory (CW XIV: 183) as equivalent to the wild duck's propensity when wounded to dive down to the bottom of the marsh and bite 'fast hold of the weed and tangle and all the rubbish that is down there'. In 'Alternative Theories of the Rate of Interest', Keynes connects the confusion of mind involved with an irrational association of ideas; he claims there is a 'deep seated obsession associating idle balances . . . with some aspect of current savings' (CW XIV: 214).

IV Summary and conclusion

Whatever the psychology on which it is based, Keynes's account of the trade cycle does give a significant role to irrationality. Irrational waves of optimism and pessimism, irrational feelings of poverty and irrational changes in the propensity to hoard all play significant roles in this account. I have suggested that his treatment of this irrationality is consistent with the theory of irrationality found in psychoanalysis, specifically with the psychoanalytic theories of anal-sadism and group psychology. The psychological characteristics Keynes attributes to the boom are similar to mania. Mania is the product of the effect of psychological group membership on the predispositions of the anal-sadistic personality. The characteristics of the crisis and collapse are similar to the reactions of this personality to loss, reactions amplified by the effects of group psychology. Finally the psychology of the slump is similar to the psychology of clinical depression.

Keynes once looked forward to a time when we would be able 'to inquire more curiously' into the nature of the 'intense unsatisfied purposiveness' of those who 'blindly pursue wealth'. Then, he claimed, we would

> be able to afford to dare to assess the money-motive at its true value. The love of money as a possession – as distinguished from the love of money as a means to the enjoyments and realities of life – will be recognized for what it is, a somewhat disgusting morbidity, one of those semi-criminal, semi-pathological propensities which one hands over with a shudder to the specialists in mental disease. (CW IX: 329)

Notes

1. The essential references, particularly for an account to be used in interpreting Keynes, are, as noted above, found in Keynes's footnote reference to the 'Freudian theory of the love of money' in *A Treatise on Money* (CW VI: 258–9). These are Freud (1977), Jones (1961a and 1961b) and Ferenczi (1956). The theory has also been used by others as a basis for explaining economic phenomena. See, in particular, Fromm (1970), Brown (1985) and Goodman (1969). Brown and Goodman point to similarities between the Freudian theory and Keynes's economics.
2. This linkage of a conscious interest or attitude to more than one unconscious repressed interest is what Freud refers to as 'overdetermination'. It is found in all the anal-sadistic traits.
3. Abraham was an important influence on the psychoanalyst associates and members of

Bloomsbury. He analysed Alix Strachey in Berlin from 1924 to 1925 (see Kendrick and Meisel, 1985). Strachey and Douglas Bryan subsequently translated his work into English. Abraham also influenced the Bloomsbury analysts indirectly through his influence on Melanie Klein. James and Alix Strachey arranged Klein's first visit to England in 1925. On this visit she delivered the set of lectures which formed the basis for her book *The Psychoanalysis of Children*.

4. Freud explicitly points to an inherited 'archaic heritage' which he claims provides a basis independent of contemporary circumstances for the formation of psychological groups. The archaic heritage is the basis for an irrational association of ideas. For example, fathers, independent of whether they themselves are 'paramount and dangerous personalities', awaken in their children 'the idea of a paramount and dangerous personality, towards whom only a passive–masochistic attitude is possible' (1959b: 54–5 and 75).
5. In *The Roaring '80s* (1990), Goodman points to Ben Graham's *Security Analysis* (1934) as an approach to speculation (in Keynes's sense) based on a view of the psychology of the market as manic-depressive: according to Graham, 'following the market is like having a manic-depressive partner. Sometimes Mr. Market becomes so giddy he will ignore all reality and offer you outrageous sums of money for your part of the business. When Mr. Market is manic, you should sell him your part. Sometimes Mr. Market falls into despair, seeing no end of problems, and he will offer you his share of the business at a discount that would be silly. So you buy it. In between, you keep your bat on your shoulder' (1990: 230). See Kindleberger (1989: 4) for evidence supporting the thesis that 'speculative excess, referred to concisely as a mania ['irrational by definition'], and revulsion from such excess in the form of a crisis, crash, or panic can be shown to be, if not inevitable, at least historically common'.
6. In a section of *The Economic Consequences of the Peace* entitled 'The Psychology of Society', Keynes claims that, in the nineteenth century, saving and accumulating became the focus for 'all those instincts of puritanism which in other ages has withdrawn itself from the world and has neglected the arts of production as well as those of enjoyment.' The sadistic aspect of these instincts is pointed to by his additional claim that 'the new rich preferred the power which investment gave them to the pleasures of immediate consumption' (CW II: II–12).
7. Keynes repeatedly warned against the policy. In a January 1937 series of articles in *The Times*, he claimed that 'if we play with dear money on the ground that it is "healthy" or "natural", then I have no doubt that the inevitable slump will ensue. We must avoid it, therefore, as we would hell-fire.'

References

Abraham, K. (1927), *Selected Papers on Psychoanalysis*, London: The Hogarth Press and The Institute of Psychoanalysis.

Brown, N. O. (1985), *Life Against Death: The Psychoanalytic Meaning of History*, Middletown, Connecticut: Wesleyan University Press.

Ferenczi, S. (1956), 'The Ontogenesis of Interest in Money', in *Sex in Psycho-Analysis (Contributions to Psycho-Analysis)*, New York: Dover.

Freud, S. (1925), 'Some Character-types Met with in Psycho-analytic Work (1915)', in *Collected Papers, vol. IV*, London: The Hogarth Press and The Institute of Psychoanalysis.

Freud, S. (1959a), 'Inhibitions, Symptoms and Anxiety', in *The Standard Edition of the Complete Psychological Works of Sigmund Freud, vol. XX*, London: The Hogarth Press and the Institute of Psychoanalysis.

Freud, S. (1959b), *Group Psychology and the Analysis of the Ego*, New York: W. W. Norton & Company, Inc.

Freud, S. (1973), *New Introductory Lectures on Psychoanalysis, vol. 2*, Harmondsworth: Penguin Books.

Freud, S. (1977), 'Character and Anal Erotism', in *On Sexuality*, Harmondsworth: Penguin Books.

Freud, S. (1985), 'Group Psychology and the Analysis of the Ego', in *Civilisation, Society and*

Religion, Group Psychology, Civilisation and its Discontents and Other Works, Harmondsworth: Penguin Books.

Fromm, E. (1970), 'Psychoanalytic Characterology and its Relevance for Social Psychology', in *The Crisis in Psychoanalysis*, Greenwich, Connecticut: Fawcett Publications, Inc.

Goodman, G. W. (1969), *The Money Game*, New York: Dell Publishing Co.

Goodman, G. W. (1990), *The Roaring '80s*, New York: Viking Penguin.

Graham, B. (1934), *Security Analysis: Principles and Technique*, New York: McGraw-Hill.

Jones, E. (1961a), 'The Theory of Symbolism', in *Papers on Psychoanalysis*, New York: Beacon Press Paperback.

Jones, E. (1961b) 'Anal-erotic Character Traits', in *Papers on Psychoanalysis*, 5th rev. edn, New York: Beacon Press Paperback.

Kendrick, W. and P. Meisel (1985) (eds) *Bloomsbury/Freud: The Letters of James and Alix Strachey 1924–1925*, New York: Basic Books, Inc.

Kindleberger, C. P. (1989), *Manias, Panics, and Crashes: A History of Financial Crises*, New York: Basic Books, Inc.

Winslow, E. G. (1986), 'Keynes and Freud: Psychoanalysis and Keynes's Account of the "Animal Spirits" of Capitalism', *Social Research*, **53**, 549–78.

Winslow, E. G. (1989), 'Organic Interdependence, Uncertainty and Economic Analysis', *Economic Journal*, **99**, 1173–82.

Winslow, E. G. (1992), 'Keynes on Rationality', in B. Gerrard (ed.), *The Economics of Rationality*, London: Routledge.

12 Keynes, Marx and political economy

Michael Howard and John King

I Marxist and Keynesian perspectives

Neither Marxism nor Keynesianism can be identified today with a single perspective. Each system of thought has been subject to diverse interpretations and reconstructions. Samuelson's representation of Keynes's insights within the 'neoclassical synthesis' (Samuelson, 1955), for example, is very different from the microfoundational approach adopted by Hahn (1984), which in turn bears little resemblance to Shackle's Keynesianism (Shackle, 1967). The various strands of post-Keynesian thought are different again (see Harcourt, 1985). On the other hand, Althusser's Marxism (1967) and the humanistic concerns emphasized by Thompson (1978), are poles apart and both depart significantly from the account of historical materialism favoured by Cohen (1978). Indeed so great has become the variation within each school of thought that some theorists who claim to be Marxists or Keynesians are in fact closer to a neoclassical vision of the world, which was rejected by both Keynes and Marx, than to any of the distinct viewpoints of the founders of each type of political economy (Howard and King, 1989c; 1991: Chapter 17).

Nevertheless it remains generally true that virtually all forms of Marxism have a more ambitious concern than any version of Keynesianism. In particular, Marxists have usually retained allegiance to a conception of human emancipation which extends well beyond the modified liberalism or social democracy to which Keynesians typically remain attached (Howard and King, 1985: Chapter 2). Although the historical record of Marxist endeavours to realize the 'ideal' has been a series of catastrophic failures, the belief that liberation requires the transcendence of the welfare state and mixed economy is still evident in most modern forms of Marxism. Keynes had views on the 'good society' that went beyond managed capitalism, and so too have some radical Keynesians (O'Donnell, 1989). However, for the most part, these ideas are ill-defined and are not integrated into the theory of the functioning of existing economic structures, as are the views of Marxists.

Even if the focus of comparison is limited to more narrowly defined matters of political economy, Marxist theory encompasses problems that Keynesians have not usually considered. The materialist conception of history attempts to explain the organization and dynamics of modes of production in general, whereas Keynesians have most often limited their concern to understanding the coordination failures arising from effective demand deficiencies in market economies. This substantive difference is also associated with contrasting methodologies. While Keynesians have shown some sensitivity to the importance of institutions, they have not conceptualized economic behaviour in sociological terms as Marxists have consistently attempted to do. Consequently a subjective voluntarism plays a far greater role in Keynesian economics than in Marxist theory, which remains far more attached to objectivism. Not surprisingly, mainstream versions of Keynesianism lie within a supply and demand tradition of economics, whereas Marxism is part of the surplus tradition, which relegates decisions and choices to the level of structurally determined variables (Dobb, 1973).

So far as the operation of the capitalist mode of production is concerned, differences between Keynesians and Marxists are also clearly evident. The 'contradictions of capitalism' include, but are not exhausted by, effective demand failures. Marx believed that equilibrium growth paths on which there is full capacity utilization would exhibit rising unemployment of labour power as well as a falling rate of profit. Some of his arguments are now widely recognized as erroneous, but Marxist economists have remained convinced that capitalism can malfunction in the sphere of production quite independently of problems arising in the sphere of exchange. The attention of Keynesians, however, is limited to the sphere of circulation.

In addition Marxist theorists have been more concerned than have Keynesians with the analysis of the transformation of economic relations within capitalism. The very dynamism of this mode of production repeatedly generates the need for 'restructuring' which Marxists have sometimes designated as successive 'regimes of accumulation' (Lipietz, 1986). And it is in terms of this idea that they have understood the practical significance of Keynesian economics. While there is no complete unity of view on the matter. Marxist economists have tended to regard Keynesianism as a system designed to contain class conflict within bounds that facilitate the continued growth of the capitalist mode of production (Przeworski, 1985; Negri, 1988). Marxist theorists, therefore, have treated Keynes's ideas not only as important in their own right, but also as part of the reality which their analysis seeks to explain. For their part, Keynesians have shown much less interest in understanding Marx, and they certainly have no special theory of their own with which to explain Marxism.

II Anticipations of Keynesian ideas in Marxist economics

Despite Keynes's formidable intellect and reputation as a polymath, he was an ignoramus when it came to Marxist theory, and totally out of sympathy with what he took to be its political project (Howard and King, 1991: Chapter 5). Even with regard to matters of crisis theory, Keynes attributed to Marx positions he did not hold – in particular, an adherence to Say's Law. In fact Marx was a sharp, and sometimes perceptive, critic of the view that 'supply creates its own demand'. Although not fully aware of the analytical issues involved, he implicitly recognized how dependent Say's Law was on what are now known as notional or Walrasian supplies and demands, and he formulated an alternative conception involving quantity constraints on sales from which Say's Law no longer follows (Howard and King, 1985: 110–12, 209–14).

There are also many other anticipations of Keynesian propositions in Marx's economics. Like Keynes, Marx stressed that a monetary economy functioned very differently from a system of barter, and he sought to characterize crises in terms of sharp increases in the demand for money, or the 'universal equivalent'. Marx always conceived crises as involving deficiencies in effective demand. The volatility of investment expenditures is given special importance in his work; there is an intuitive understanding of multiplier processes, and a clear recognition of the complex problems involved in explaining cyclical growth, together with a valiant attempt to tackle them (Howard and King, 1985: Part IV). Furthermore, prior to the publication of the *General Theory*, the dominant theory of crisis to which Marxist economists adhered was an underconsumptionism that bore a striking resemblance to the ideas of some early Keynesians, and in no way contradicted Keynes's own views (CW IX: 358–73; VII: 377).

Marx identified various causes of crises. First, he appealed to his theory of the falling rate of profit, which was based on the presumption of a bias towards labour-saving technical change, so that ultimately the rise in the capital–labour ratio would outstrip the increase in surplus per worker, and the rate of profit would fall even with a constant wage.[1] Although the theory was formulated independently of any deficiency in effective demand, Marx nevertheless recognized that a declining capability of the economy to *produce* a surplus could result in an inability to *realize* potential profits as capitalists cut back on investment expenditure (Howard and King, 1985: 200–205, 215–16). Beginning with the critique of Tugan-Baranovsky in the 1890s, it is now generally accepted that the profit rate can fall as a result of technical change in the face of a constant wage only if capitalists adopt techniques according to criteria other than maximum profitability. In consequence most Marxist economists have accepted that Marx was mistaken, and his law of the falling rate of profit is not law at all

(Howard and King, 1989a; 1989c: Chapters 9, 10; 1991: Chapter 7). However, as we indicate in Section IV below, many Marxists have retained the more general proposition that difficulties in the production of surplus can underpin realization crises.

Second, Marx himself argues for exactly this proposition independently of any reference to his theory of the falling rate of profit. He claims that 'over-accumulation' in an investment boom can so deplete the 'reserve army of unemployed' that wage increases cut into profits to the point of sharply curtailing capital expenditures, so bringing about a realization crisis (Howard and King, 1985: 215–16; Sweezy, 1942: Chapter 9). The shelving of investment plans, however, is but a particular example of 'disproportions' between different sectors of production, which underpin contractionary multiplier processes. And it is the manifold possibilities for disproportionality arising from the 'anarchy of production' that constitutes the third basis for crises in Marx's view. In general, he was not impressed with the ability of a price system to bring about a transfer of resources smoothly, believing instead that reductions in quantities produced would become cumulative once they were underway on a significant scale, whatever the impetus (Howard and King, 1985: 181–93, 217–18).

Fourth, Marx pointed to the possibility of crises arising from underconsumption (Howard and King, 1985: 216–18). It is by no means clear what mechanism he had in mind, but Joan Robinson's interpretation is consistent with his many comments in this context, and with their reading by successive generations of Marxists:

> Marx intended to work out a theory on some such lines as this: consumption by the workers is limited by their poverty, while consumption by the capitalists is limited by the greed for capital which causes them to accumulate wealth rather than enjoy luxury. The demand for consumption goods . . . is thus restricted. But if the output of the consumption-good industries is limited by the market, the demand for capital goods . . . is in turn restricted, for the . . . capital of the consumption-good industries will not expand fast enough to absorb the potential output of the capital-good industries. Thus the distribution of income between wages and surplus is such as to set up a chronic tendency for a lack of balance between the two groups of industries. (Robinson, 1942: 49)

Prior to the Second World War, all four theories of crisis were used by Marxists, but it was the underconsumptionist strand which proved to be dominant. Only Henryk Grossmann, in 1929, claimed that Marx's theory of the falling rate of profit was central to comprehending the contradictions of capitalist development, but Grossmann failed to gain an immediate following, and was sharply criticized by other Marxist economists (Howard and King, 1988; 1989c: Chapter 16). The idea of over-accumulation proved to be more popular – most notably with Otto Bauer

– although it too represented a minority viewpoint. Bauer himself, as well as Karl Kautsky, Rosa Luxemburg, Eugene Varga, Nikolai Bukharin, Leon Trotsky and Vladimir Lenin, all maintained allegiance to some form of underconsumptionism (Howard and King, 1989c; 1991).

The importance of disproportionalities was stressed by Rudolf Hilferding and Mikhail Tugan-Baranovsky, and Tugan used the idea to mount an important critique against underconsumptionism. He argued that, providing sectoral proportions were maintained, profitable accumulation could continue irrespective of the magnitude of consumption expenditure. Moreover Tugan believed that actual capitalist development involved an increasing relative size of the capital goods industries because of labour-saving innovations. Thus accumulation was primarily and increasingly 'the production of machines for the production of machines'. Absurd as this conclusion seemed from the viewpoint of human values – and he readily admitted this element of absurdity – Tugan believed that consumption demand posed no constraint on growth, since under capitalist conditions investments were governed by profitability, which could be sustained by further investments (Howard and King, 1989a; 1989c: Chapters 9, 10).

Tugan aimed his critique of underconsumptionism primarily against non-Marxist theories of secular stagnation. However he recognized the dominance of underconsumptionist ideas among Marxist economists, who used them to explain cyclical crises, and he included their theories in his attack on underconsumptionism. The weaknesses of his own position were twofold: Tugan failed to formulate a coherent notion of effective demand to sustain his own explanation of cycles, and he provided no account of the determinants of investment to show that consumption expenditure was as irrelevant in practice as it might be shown to be in theory. It is however true that the self-same limitations were evident in all Marxist analyses of crises between 1883 and 1936 – there was no clear notion of effective demand, nor any systematic theory of investment (Howard and King, 1990a; 1991: Chapter 1; Kalecki, 1971 : 146–55). These lacunae provided the two principal ways in which Keynesian theory could be used to strengthen Marxist economies.

III Initial reactions to the *General Theory*

The *General Theory* was the first systematic and comprehensive expression of the view that mass unemployment could be the normal outcome of an unregulated capitalist economy to emerge from the pen of a respected and hitherto mainstream economist. As such its appearance was a major event which Marxist theorists could not ignore. However, for the greater part, their initial responses failed to appreciate the significance of the book, either for the further development of 'organized capitalism' or as a crucially important buttress for Marxist economic theory. The incorporation of Keynesian ideas into Marxism had to await the experience of the 'long boom' of the post-war years, and even then there was resistance on grounds similar to those voiced by Marxists in the 1930s.

Marxist reviewers of the *General Theory* frequently pointed to the analytical similarities between Marx and Keynes. Both theorists recognized the importance of crises; both could be interpreted as underconsumptionists; and they agreed on the monetary determination of interest rates. In addition Keynes's concept of wage units was thought to parallel Marx's labour values, and the marginal efficiency of capital schedule was compared to the theory of the falling rate of profit. On the other hand, Keynes was severely criticized for his inability to break with the subjectivism characteristic of neoclassical theory, his concentration upon the surface phenomena of exchange and the consequent neglect of production, and for misplaced confidence in the bourgeois political process (Howard and King, 1991: Chapter 5). It was these alleged deficiencies that allowed Marxists to underestimate the significance of Keynes's work, and they have continued to be used in criticism of Keynes by some Marxist economists ever since.

Some of this was undoubtedly wrong. Any relation between Keynes's wage units and Marx's labour values is purely formal, and the Marxists seem not to have appreciated that Keynes placed far more importance on shifts in the marginal efficiency of capital schedule than on movements along it. In any event the concept relates to a much shorter time dimension than Marx's theory of the falling rate of profit. These weaknesses in Marxist views of Keynes arose in large part from their failure to see that Keynesian economics originally pertained to the short period, in which both the capital stock and technology were unchanging. Criticism of Keynes's failure to break decisively with neoclassical theory and the subjectivism of his analysis was more soundly based. Nevertheless Marxists failed to recognize that a structuralist approach to economic theory ought to incorporate a microeconomic component in which the actions of agents are specified consistently with the materialist determinants of their decisions (Howard and King, 1989b; 1991: Chapter 17).

However there were also real insights into the nature of Keynesianism. Keynes's economics focused squarely upon circulation. The structure of production and the labour process were ignored, with the implication that the supply side was passive. In addition, there were important strands of utopianism in Keynes's *Weltanschauung* (O'Donnell, 1989: Part III) and, as Emil Lederer argued, a 'rational analysis as such is not a force . . . The ideas put forward by Keynes would entail a revolution in power and property, but we can hardly believe that mankind will accept a new economic and social set-up by persuasion' (1936: 437). Lederer underestimated the transformative potential of capitalism, as did Marxists generally, but he was correct in so far as his comments presumed that ideas are impotent unless based on interests. By contrast, Keynes saw the class struggle as nothing more than a 'frightful muddle' (CW IX: xviii) and failed to see that a Keynesian regime of accumulation might prevail only in specific historical conditions which would be transitory.

IV Keynesian Marxism

A Keynesian regime of accumulation held sway in advanced capitalist countries for the quarter-century following the Second World War. During this period, Keynes's ideas began to be married to those of Marxism through the work of Michal Kalecki, Joan Robinson, Paul Sweezy and Paul Baran. It is now widely recognized that Kalecki formulated independently a version of Keynesianism devoid of the neoclassical residues evident in the *General Theory*. This explains why it has been his system of thought, rather than the concepts of Keynes, which have been dominant in Keynesian Marxism. The basic equation of Kalecki's system is a class-specific expression of the equality between aggregate income and aggregate expenditure:

$$\text{Wages} + \text{Profits} = \text{Workers' Consumption} + \text{Capitalists' Consumption} + \text{Investment} \qquad (12.1)$$

This differs from the normal Keynesian income–expenditure equation by distinguishing explicitly the incomes, and the expenditures, of workers and capitalists. It is a fairly close approximation to the truth to assume that workers consume the whole of their wage incomes, as any saving done during their working lives (for example via pension funds) is offset by dis-saving after retirement. Hence (12.1) can be simplified to

$$\text{Profits} = \text{Capitalists' Consumption} + \text{Investment} \qquad (12.2)$$

This is similar to Keynes's celebrated 'widow's cruse' model of total profits (CW V: 139), in which capitalists' incomes are determined by their expenditure, and in particular (since little stress is placed upon their consumption) by their investment expenditure. Hence capitalists' investment decisions set a maximum limit, in the aggregate, to their profits, independently of the production of surplus.

State expenditure can also be taken into account, on Kalecki's argument, so long as some assumption is made concerning the incidence of taxation. On the supposition that workers bear none of the burden, (12.2) can be rewritten as

$$\text{Net Profits} + \text{Taxes} = \text{Capitalists' Consumption} + \text{Investment} + \text{Government Expenditure}, \quad (12.3)$$

or

$$\text{Net Profits} = \text{Capitalists' Consumption} + \text{Investment} + (\text{Government Expenditure } \textit{minus} \text{ Taxes}). \quad (12.3a)$$

Thus, where effective demand would otherwise be inadequate, a budget deficit will increase net profits and encourage the production of surplus.

Because Kaleckians abstract from the production process, they generally fail to recognize the limitations of their equations. In particular, if for some reason sufficient surplus cannot be produced to sustain the level of profitability specified by equations (12.1), (12.2), (12.3) and (12.3a), then the expenditure plans of the state or of capitalists will be frustrated. Subject to this very important qualification, to which we return later in this section, Kaleckian economics does provide the basis for an integration of Marxist and Keynesian theory in which the realization of surplus depends on the level of effective demand.[2]

Joan Robinson began to study Marx's economics in the 1930s, but her early articles share some of the misunderstandings of Marxism exhibited by Keynes himself. However, by the early 1940s, she had reached a more accurate appreciation of Marx's crisis theory. In her *Essay on Marxian Economics* (Robinson, 1942) she remained sharply critical of Marxist value theory and of the theory of the falling rate of profit, but recognized that Marx had anticipated the ideas of the *General Theory*. The conclusion of the book defined her attitude for the next four decades: 'Marx was mainly concerned with long-run dynamic analysis, and this field is still largely untilled . . . however imperfectly he worked out the details . . . [Marx] . . . set himself the task of discovering the law of motion of capitalism, and if there is any hope of progress in economics at all, it must be in using academic methods to solve the problems posed by Marx (1942: 95). By 'academic methods', Robinson meant those of Keynesian economics, and she was later to describe her work as a 'generalisation of the *General Theory*' by incorporating the theory of effective demand into long-period analysis, which had been Marx's primary concern (Robinson, 1965:5; 1977: 1325).

In reaching these conclusions Joan Robinson was influenced by Michal Kalecki, and her admiration for his analysis of effective demand strengthened after 1945, particularly in her magnum opus, *The Accumulation of Capital* (Robinson, 1956). Here, and in many other works, she analysed various forms of equilibrium growth paths in terms of five key variables: capitalist expenditure decisions, rates of growth of labour power and technical change, the level of money wages and the price policy of firms (or the size of the mark-up). In Robinson's view, though, the focus on equilibrium was primarily methodological; as with Marx in his treatment of the reproduction schemata, the properties of equilibria were investigated to reveal their fragility, and thereby to demonstrate the manifold sources of instability and malfunction in capitalist economies (Howard, 1979: Chapter 6).

Joan Robinson's concentration upon long-period equilibria also reflected her concern with undermining the hegemony of neoclassical theory. From the very beginning she emphasized that Keynesian ideas brought into question the whole structure of that theory (although she also recognized that this was not Keynes's own belief). To support this position, Robinson felt impelled to engage neoclassical theory on its own terrain of equilibria, to provide an alternative analysis of the puzzles there thrown up, and to highlight the logical and substantive limitations of mainstream analysis. But, from her viewpoint, the positive significance of propositions about long-run equilibrium positions is distinctly limited. Capitalist economies rarely even approximate the requirements for equilibrium, so that the treatment of specific historical conjunctures and practical economic problems must be in terms of short-period relations.

Both in the investigation of the properties of equilibrium growth paths and in the critique of neoclassical theory, Robinson was immensely influenced by Piero Sraffa's work, which sought to rehabilitate classical and Marxist value theory on a new, rigorous foundation. *The Production of Commodities by Means of Commodities* (Sraffa, 1960) provided theorems that conclusively undermined the logical coherence of the Clarkian theory of capital productivity and the Austrian analysis of capitalistic production, which had been the principal vehicles for the neoclassical understanding of accumulation (Howard, 1983). Furthermore Sraffa's treatment of valuation neatly complemented Robinson's analysis of growth. On the one hand, the 'openness' of the systems of commodity pricing in Sraffa's book could be 'closed' through determining the profit rate on Robinsonian lines (Howard, 1983). On the other hand, once Sraffa's models were supplemented by the assumption of constant returns to scale, they generated prices for all goods appropriate to equilibrium growth paths. Not surprisingly the Keynesian–Kaleckian reconstruction of the Marxist project which Joan Robinson had first outlined in 1942 received great reinforcement from Sraffa.

However there were limits beyond which Robinson would not venture. When Sraffians sought to subordinate Keynes to Sraffa's predilection for classical methodology, and to use propositions derived from comparisons of different equilibria in arguments about historical causation, she restated her position very forcefully. Long-period equilibria were artificial constructions designed for limited purposes of clarification and critique; they could play only a marginal role in 'realistic' analysis, which must take its main cue from short-period theory (Robinson, 1979).

The reconstruction of Marxist economics on Keynesian lines by Paul Sweezy and Paul Baran is a spirited attempt to break through the disciplined restraint of Robinson's methodology and the abstract formalism of Sraffian theory, and instead to outline the principal 'law of motion' governing advanced capitalism. *Monopoly Capital* (Baran and Sweezy, 1966) has been the single most important work of American Marxism, and in conjunction with Baran's earlier *Political Economy of Growth* (1957) and Sweezy's *Theory of Capitalist Development* (1942) sought to depict the central contradictions of world capitalist accumulation. It is therefore considerably more ambitious than anything provided by those forms of British Marxism which sought to come to terms with the Keynesian Revolution.

Like Robinson, Sweezy was (briefly) a Keynesian before falling under the sway of Marx. Much more than for Robinson, however, it was Marxism that became dominant in Sweezy's work. In consequence he placed far more stress on monopoly and imperialism, and the influence of Marxists other than Marx – notably Hilferding, Bauer and Lenin – is clearly evident. Nevertheless the key factor in Sweezy's analysis is underconsumption and the basic elements of Keynesian effective demand analysis play an indispensable role.

Despite these differences, the essentials of Baran's and Sweezy's idea can be understood in terms of Robinson's economics. The monopolization of advanced capitalism, and more especially that in the American economy, raises the mark-up on costs of production, which has a secular tendency to rise further with technical change. Thus the potential surplus grows continuously and the share of socially useful (as opposed to wasteful) consumption contracts. As a result lower levels of output and smaller employments are associated with any given level of capitalists' expenditures, as underconsumption works towards stagnation. According to Baran and Sweezy, this has so far been offset only by powerful counteracting forces: military expenditures, sales promotion and wasteful product variation figure most prominently in their analysis, which then proceeds to document how each of these factors tend to decline in significance, while stagnation comes to predominate (Howard and King, 1991: Chapter 6).

Robinson's economics is, of course, in no way tied to this interpretation, and the limitations of Baran's and Sweezy's thesis have been increasingly appreciated in the last two decades (Howard and King, 1989c: Chapter 6). In Western Europe an alternative tradition of monopoly capital theory has, however, proved more enduring. This school, represented by writers such as Keith Cowling and Malcolm Sawyer, offers an analysis which is much more rigorous than that of Baran and Sweezy, but also less obviously informed by a conception of historical materialism. For this reason it is more appropriately characterized as post-Keynesian than Marxist in character, although by the very nature of Keynesian Marxism the exact line of division is open to debate.[3] Only in one respect did the ideas of *Monopoly Capital* have a more permanent impact upon Marxist economics in the advanced West. This was the treatment of armaments expenditure as a force maintaining effective demand and realizing the surplus.

The notion that militarism can stabilize capitalism has in fact a long history in Marxism. Both Karl Kautsky and Rosa Luxemburg recognized that military expenditure could work to offset underconsumptionism (Howard and King, 1989c: Chapters 5, 6; 1991: Chapter 8). Joan Robinson, in commenting upon Luxemburg's economics, also noted that from a Keynesian perspective armaments expenditure has a distinct advantage compared with investment, since it 'creates no further problem by increasing productive capacity (not to mention the huge new investment opportunities created by reconstruction after the capitalist nations have turned their weapons against each other)' (Robinson, 1951: 27–8). The empirical evidence in favour of the hypothesis that military spending has stabilized effective demand in the post-war years is, however, weak, as several Marxists have shown (Howard and King, 1991: Chapter 8). Also influential in Marxist circles is a different mechanism, suggested by Marx's theory of the falling rate of profit. In this context, weapons production is seen to alter the sectoral distribution of capital accumulation in such a way as to retard the decline in the rate of profit that would otherwise occur. The analysis relies on a crucial proposition: capital diverted into militarism has no effect on profitability in the wider economy. The value analysis of Ricardo, Bortkiewicz and Sraffa, as well as that of Marx, can be used to support this proposition. But the argument itself is deeply suspect, because the idea that the arms economy has acted to inhibit crises by precluding a fall in the rate of profit rests upon an argument of Marx that has been known to be false for nearly a century (see Section II above) (Howard and King, 1989a; 1989c: Chapters 9, 10; 1991: Chapter 7).

The real significance of this form of Marxist economics lies elsewhere. Appeals to the 'falling rate of profit', whether or not associated with the analysis of arms expenditure, represent a fundamentalist reaction to Keynesian Marxism. Prior to the 1960s, Marx's theory of the falling rate of profit had been politely ignored by the orthodox Marxists in their explanation of crises; the overwhelming majority endorsed some form of underconsumptionism. It was this that facilitated the integration of Keynesianism into Marxism, and the dilution of a specifically Marxist conception of crisis. Coupled with the association of social democracy and Keynesianism, the fear among Marxists of class compromise no doubt acted to encourage product differentiation (Yaffe, 1973; Mattick, 1971; Pilling, 1986). However, there is a rational kernel to the fundamentalists' concerns. Keynesian Marxists generally take for granted the possibility of *producing* sufficient surplus to preserve a rate of profit which is adequate for continued accumulation. They concentrate instead upon the problems which may arise from the demand side in realizing the surplus as profit. But, quite apart from the materialist conception of history which maintains that production is the primary sphere, the labour process in a class-stratified society promises no such convenient concentration of problems in circulation.

Fundamentalist Marxists have not simply remained content to highlight the Keynesian abstraction from production. Increasingly since the 1960s they have argued, albeit in different ways and often independently of Marx's theory of the falling rate of profit, that to see deficient demand as the principal factor in crises is to mistake symptom for cause. Rather, they maintain, it was the inability to produce sufficient surplus that resulted in the end of the long boom in the early 1970s and the jettisoning of Keynesian ideas by governments in the West. Since production is the core of the economy, large state expenditures may intensify the problem of inadequate surplus. The public sphere is by and large non-capitalist, producing no surplus of its own, so that its activities constitute a dissipation of the surplus which is produced by productive labour in capitalist labour processes. State intervention reduces the amount of surplus available to capital and serves to intensify the chief cause of crises. Keynesian economics is not simply wrong; it is the reverse of the truth (Howard and King, 1990b; 1991: Chapter 16).

From a Keynesian perspective this argument seems to share the Ricardian fallacy which Keynes denounced in Marx himself, and which in recent years has been confidently proclaimed by monetarists, new classicals and neo-Austrians. In actual fact this is not so. The anti-Keynesian Marxists are under no logical imperative to deny the possibility of deficient effective demand. Their arguments require only that the problems of profitability originate in the sphere of production. They can accept that the resulting cut-back in investment reduces effective demand, which is an important factor in generalizing and deepening the crisis. However an implication of this position is that Keynesian policy cannot alleviate the problem in the long run and that a Keynesian regime of accumulation was but a transitory stage in the development of capitalism.

V Conclusion

Keynesian Marxism is not yet moribund, but it has been seriously challenged in recent years by Marxists who have rehabilitated the importance of the sphere of production relative to that of circulation in the understanding of crises. One element of this argument rests upon Marx's theory of the falling rate of profit, and is therefore of dubious importance. But other theories are much sounder, because they point to alternative mechanisms which inhibit the production of surplus. Moreover they imply that a Keynesian regime of accumulation can intensify, rather than alleviate, the problem. In this respect, if no other, developments in Marxist theory have been part of the great wave of anti-Keynesianism that has swept through advanced capitalism since the late 1960s.

Simultaneously Marxist theorists have highlighted another set of forces which constrain Keynesian policy, irrespective of the validity of the underlying theory. Over the course of the previous four decades, and especially in the 1980s, the universalizing tendency of capitalist relations, which was repeatedly stressed by Marx (Avineri, 1968), has greatly reduced the barriers to the globalization of production and circulation. One effect of this have been to undermine the power of nation-states to implement policies directed towards their own territorial economies, and no supranational organizations have yet emerged which could replace them on a grander scale. Consequently the presumption of Keynesian economics that there exist institutions capable of sustaining a Keynesian regime of accumulation is less and less believable (Lash and Urry, 1987; Harris, 1986).

Notes

1. Marx states the law of the falling rate of profit in terms of the categories of his value theory. Here, and elsewhere, we have expressed Marx's argument in more conventional terminology.
2. Kaldor (1956: 81) maintains that the view of capitalists' incomes being the result of their expenditure decisions rather than the other way around is 'perhaps the most important difference between "Keynesian" and "pre-Keynesian" habit of thought'. For a discussion of the wider relationship between Kalecki and Marx, see Sawyer (1985: Chapter 8).
3. Some post-Keynesians, such as Eichner, Kaldor and Weintraub, were distant from or openly hostile to Marxism. Even Kalecki, who was closer to Marx than any other prominent post-Keynesian, differed sharply from him on many questions. See Sawyer (1985: Chapter 8).

References

Althusser, L. (1967), *For Marx*, Harmondsworth: Penguin.
Avineri, S. (1968), *The Social and Political Thought of Karl Marx*, Cambridge: Cambridge University Press.
Baran, P. A. (1957), *The Political Economy of Growth*, New York: Monthly Review.
Baran, P. A. and P. M. Sweezy (1966), *Monopoly Capital*, New York: Monthly Review.
Cohen, G. A. (1978), *Karl Marx's Theory of History: A Defence*, Oxford: Oxford University Press.
Dobb, M. H. (1973), *Theories of Value and Distribution Since Adam Smith*, Cambridge: Cambridge University Press.
Hahn, F. A. (1984), *Equilibrium and Macroeconomics*, Oxford: Basil Blackwell.
Harcourt, G. C. (1985), 'Post-Keynesianism: Quite Wrong and/or Nothing New?', in P. Arestis and T. Skouras (eds), *Post-Keynesian Economic Theory*, Brighton, Sussex: Wheatsheaf.
Harris, N. (1986), *The End of The Third World*, Harmondsworth: Penguin.
Howard, M. C. (1979), *Modern Theories of Income Distribution*, London: Macmillan.
Howard, M. C. (1983), *Profits in Economic Theory*, London: Macmillan.
Howard, M. C. and J. E. King (1985), *The Political Economy of Marx*, Harlow: Longman.
Howard, M. C. and J. E. King (1988), 'Henryk Grossman and the Breakdown of Capitalism', *Science and Society*, **52**, 290–309.
Howard, M. C. and J. E. King (1989a), 'Russian Revisionism and the Development of Marxian Political Economy in the Early Twentieth Century', *Studies of Soviet Thought*, **37**, 15–37.
Howard, M. C. and J. E. King (1989b), 'The Rational Choice Marxism of John Roemer: A Critique', *Review of Social Economy*, **47**, 392–414.
Howard, M. C. and J. E. King (1989c), *A History of Marxian Economics: Volume I, 1883–1929*, London: Macmillan and Princeton, NJ: Princeton University Press.
Howard, M. C. and J. E. King (1990a), 'Marxian Economics and the Great Depression', *History of Political Economy*, **22**, 46–62.
Howard, M. C. and J. E. King (1990b), 'The "Second Slump": Marxian Theories of Crisis after 1973', *Review of Political Economy*, **2**, 267–91.
Howard, M. C. and J. E. King (1991), *A History of Marxian Economies: Vol. II, 1929–1990*, London: Macmillan and Princeton, NJ: Princeton University Press.
Kaldor, N. (1956), 'Alternative Theories of Distribution', *Review of Economic Studies*, **23**, 83–100.
Kalecki, M. (1971), *Selected Essays on the Dynamics of the Capitalist Economy, 1933–70*, Cambridge: Cambridge University Press.
Lash, S. and J. Urry (1987), *The End of Organised Capitalism*, Cambridge: Polity Press.
Lederer, E. (1936), 'Commentary on Keynes', *Social Research*, **3**, 478–87.
Lipietz, A. (1986), 'Behind the Crisis: The Exhaustion of a Regime of Accumulation; a "Regulation School" Perspective on some French Empirical Works', *Review of Radical Political Economics*, **18**, 13–32.
Mattick, P. (1971), *Marx and Keynes: The Limits of the Mixed Economy*, London: Merlin.
Negri, T. (1988), *Revolution Retrieved: Writings on Marx, Keynes, Capitalist Crisis and New Social Subjects, 1967–83*, London: Red Notes.
O'Donnell, R. M. (1989), *Keynes: Philosophy, Economics and Politics*, London: Macmillan.
Pilling, G. (1986), *The Crisis of Keynesian Economics*, London: Croom Helm.
Przeworski, A. (1985), *Capitalism and Social Democracy*, Cambridge: Cambridge University Press.
Robinson, J. (1942), *An Essay on Marxian Economics*, 2nd edn, 1966, London: Macmillan.
Robinson, J. (1951), 'Introduction', to R. Luxemburg, *The Accumulation of Capital*, London: Routledge.
Robinson, J. (1956), *The Accumulation of Capital*, London: Macmillan.
Robinson, J. (1965), *Collected Economics Papers: Volume II*, Oxford: Blackwell.
Robinson, J. (1977), 'What Are the Questions?, *Journal of Economic Literature*, **15**, 1318–39.

Robinson, J. (1979), 'Garegnani on Effective Demand', *Cambridge Journal of Economics*, **3**, 179–80.
Samuelson, P. A. (1955), *Economics*, 3rd edn, New York: McGraw-Hill.
Sawyer, M. C. (1985), *The Economics of Michal Kalecki*, London: Macmillan.
Shackle, G. L. S. (1967), *The Years of High Theory*, Cambridge: Cambridge University Press.
Sraffa, P. (1960), *The Production of Commodities by Means of Commodities*, Cambridge: Cambridge University Press.
Sweezy, P. M. (1942), *The Theory of Capitalist Development*, New York: Monthly Review.
Thompson, E. P. (1978), *The Poverty of Theory and Other Essays*, New York: Monthly Review.
Yaffe, D. S. (1973), 'The Marxian Theory of Crisis, Capital and the State', *Economy and Society*, **2**, 286–332.

Name index

Subject index

Foundations of Engineering Mechanics

Shorr

Springer

Berlin
Heidelberg
New York
Hong Kong
London
Milan
Paris
Tokyo

B. F. Shorr

The Wave Finite Element Method

With 164 Figures

Springer

Series Editors:
V. I. Babitsky
Department of Mechanical Engineering
Loughborough University
Loughborough LE11 3TU, Leicestershire
United Kingdom

J. Wittenburg
Institut für Technische Mechanik
Universität Karlsruhe (TH)
Kaiserstraße 12
76128 Karlsruhe
Germany

Author:
B. F. Shorr
Central Institute of Aviation
Motors (CIAM)
Aviamornaya str. 2, 111250
Moscow
Russian Federation

ISBN 3-540-41638-2 Springer-Verlag Berlin Heidelberg New York

Cataloging-in-Publication Data applied for
Bibliographic information published by Die Deutsche Bibliothek.
Die Deutsche Bibliothek lists this publication in the Deutsche Nationalbibliografie;
detailed bibliographic data is available in the Internet at <http://dnb.ddb.de>.

Springer-Verlag is a part of Springer Science+Business Media

springeronline.com

Printed in Germany

Typesetting: Camera-ready copy by translator
Cover-design: de'blik, Berlin
Printed on acid-free paper 62 / 3020 hu - 5 4 3 2 1 0

Preface

Computational mechanics, as a science employed for the numerical modeling of processes in nature and engineering, has over the last few decades developed two strands. The first concerns the putting of more and more powerful software packages into computational practice, using increasingly high-performance computers with increasingly large memory. The traditional finite element and finite difference approaches are still prevalent.

Over the years however, researchers have met with new problems; their solutions on the basis of traditional methods are at best difficult and at worst impossible to obtain. Such problems provided a powerful impetus in the development of the second strand, resulting in the development of essentially new approaches for numerical modeling, for example meshless methods, "molecular" dynamics, neuron networks. The current state of the art formed the basis of many papers presented at the Fifth World Congress on Computational Mechanics, Vienna 2002.

It is within the framework of the second strand that this book has been written.

The book concerns the problem of numerical finite element analysis of non-stationary dynamic processes in solids, using a novel 'wave' approach. The method is able to take into account strong discontinuities of stress, deformation, and velocity wave fronts, as well as finite wave propagation speeds. Such phenomena are particularly important within problems for which the time-scale is the same order as that of the time taken for a wave to propagate over the system; for instance, within explosions, shocks, seismic waves and structures with rapidly varying mass or stiffness.

The investigations were begun by the author in the mid 1970's at the Central Institute of Aviation Engines (Moscow). The first results relating to 1-D problems were presented in a number of reports and journal papers. The methodology was applied to analysis of numerous engineering problems and generalized in a monograph by Shorr B.F and Mel'nikova G.V. "Calculation of Mechanical Systems Using the Method of Direct Mathematical Modelling", 1988. However, all these publication, and other up until 1995, were in Russian and remain little known to western professionals.

In the last few years the 'wave' approach has been refined and extended to multi-dimensional processes, allowing a number of new solutions for unsteady problems in solids to be found. In this book the wave finite element method (WFEM) is systematically presented for the first time.

The book is designated for researchers, lecturers, post-graduates, and final year under-graduate students interested in problems of numerical modeling of non-stationary dynamic processes in deformable bodies and continua, as well as general problems of computational mechanics. Engineers and researchers, engaged in the design and analysis of machines and structures in which shock, vibro-impact and other unsteady dynamic processes play an important role may well find the book beneficial to their own research. The author believes that acquaintance with the method can be also of utility to specialists in design of electrical circuits and liquid currents in pipelines.

The author expresses deep gratitude to Prof. V.Babitsky, under which initiative the English edition of the book was carried out and which valuable councils the author repeatedly used, Prof. G.Rogerson, whose aid in 'polishing' the English of the book was very appreciated, and Dr. D.Merkle and the staff of Springer-Verlag for assistance in preparation and publication of the book. The author is also grateful to Prof. Ju.Kaplunov for useful discussion of a number of aspects of this work and to colleagues who have rendered help in realization of some numerical computations.

And finally, I am externally grateful to my wife and colleague Dr. G.Mel'nikova, without whose daily help and support this book would never have been ready for publication.

Boris Shorr, Moscow

Contents

Introduction

Many dynamic processes in machines, structures, and various deformable continua posses a highly expressed unsteady (non-stationary) character. To such processes belong, for example:

- explosive, shock, and vibro-impact loading;
- propagation of seismic waves;
- transition of systems through resonant domains under a varying forcing frequency and amplitude;
- one-sided impacts provoked by backlashes with varying points of contact;
- oscillation of structures of varying mass and stiffness;
- action of moving loads;
- oscillation of structures with strongly nonlinear damping elements.

Analytical and numerical methods for non-stationary calculations related to discrete systems with concentrated mass and stiffness are developed in details in a number of papers (see, for example, Kobrinsky AE and Kobrinsky AA 1973). Unsteady processes in deformable systems with distributed mass and stiffness described by the wave equations have been investigated much less. The majority of solutions were until recently derived under greatly simplifying restrictions: valid within only the initial part of the process, by separating out the periodic solutions, at small nonlinearity, etc.(Mitropol'sky 1955; Babitsky 1998).

The successes of computer facilities and development of the finite element method (FEM) have greatly expanded opportunities of the numerical analysis of dynamic processes in deformable bodies and media, including unsteady loading conditions.

The traditional approach within dynamic finite-element analysis considered by Zienkiewicz and Cheung (1967); Rao (1995), and also in many other papers consists of the following.

The displacement $\mathbf{u}(\mathbf{r},t)$ of an arbitrary point $\mathbf{r}$ of the element is represented at the time moment t as the sum

$$\mathbf{u}(\mathbf{r},t) = \sum_{k=1}^{n_k} \mathbf{\Phi}_k(\overline{\mathbf{r}})\mathbf{u}_k(t),$$

where $k=1,2,...,n_k$ is an index of the node, $\mathbf{u}_k(t)$ are the nodal displacements at the given time, and $\mathbf{\Phi}_k(\overline{\mathbf{r}})$ are components of an interpolation matrix. These components, as well as those for the static analysis, depend only on the element configuration and local coordinates $\overline{\mathbf{r}}$ of the points, but do not depend on time. The velocity $\dot{\mathbf{u}}(\mathbf{r},t)$ and acceleration $\ddot{\mathbf{u}}(\mathbf{r},t)$ of the element point are connected to the velocities $\dot{\mathbf{u}}_k(t)$ and accelerations $\ddot{\mathbf{u}}_k(t)$ of the element nodes by the same matrix. The accelerations are assumed to be finite that allows integrating them with respect to time numerically using any finite-difference procedure.

The specified approach leads to good results for numerical investigation of problems, in which wave effects are not important. Such problems were named by Belytschko (1976) 'inertial'. First of all, this refers to the stationary dynamic characteristics, including computation of the natural frequencies and response analysis of the forced vibrations. Procedures called 'transient analysis' of unsteady processes and developed on the basis of the same approach also give in a number of cases approximately valid results. However, the traditional FEM does not take into account the possibility of strong discontinuities in stress, strain, and velocity fronts and wave propagation over the elements with a finite speed. These phenomena are of particular importance for 'wave' problems characterized by the fact that a time scale and the time that waves take to propagate over a structure may be of the same order.

Including time in the interpolation matrix as the fourth coordinate, as discussed by Argyris and Scharpf (1969); Oden (1969); Hughes and Hulbert (1988), and some other authors, does not entirely eliminate the aforementioned disadvantages. To describe the above phenomena, an interpolation matrix should be arranged to be discontinuous, varying in time relevant to the wave equations for each element separately. Some attempts in this direction for special loading cases were undertaken by Oden et al.(1976), but their realization, as a general numerical procedure, is hardly possible.

In investigations of Li and Wiberg (1996, 1999) and also Li and Yao (2002), the discontinuities of the velocity vector at discrete time levels is realized using a time-discontinuous Galerkin finite element method. In recent years, some 'meshless' methods have been proposed for numerical solving different problems in solid mechanics (Belytschko at al. 1996; De and Bathe 2001, and others). The perspective and restrictions of these methods for simulating of discontinuous wave propagation require further study.

An alternative approach was proposed by Shorr (1976a,b) in application to 1-D wave processes and was generalized to multi-dimensional wave problems by Shorr (1997, 1999). The essence of this approach implies on the following assumptions.

The stress-strain state of a finite element system is considered at discrete time moments t_{i-1}, t_i, t_{i+1} separated by varying intervals Δt_i, Δt_{i+1}, where i is an index of the time step. In analyzing a discontinuous wave process, it is necessary to distinguish at the moment t_{i-1} infinitesimally close time instants t_{i-1}^- and t_{i-1}^+. In doing so, the use of the static interpolation matrix for representing element displacements by displacements of its nodes is valid only for the moment t_{i-1}^-, when each element is assumed to be in a quasi-static state. For this time, the element velocities and node displacements are known from the preceding calculation steps or initial conditions and all mechanical characteristics of the element, including strains and stresses, can be determined. In contrast to the transient FEM, the function $\mathbf{u}(\mathbf{r},t)$ exploited for discrete instants is not differentiated with respect to time.

At t_{i-1}^- the displacements in a common node of neighboring elements are continuous, while in the general case their velocities are distinct and the node is not in equilibrium. As a result, strong discontinuities of the velocities and forces arise between elements. Such discontinuities at any point of the solid must immediately (i.e., at the instant t_{i-1}^+) decay to new node velocities and forces. External forces and boundary conditions that are assumed referring to the nodes can also change arbitrarily, remaining constant during the following time step.

In reality, the strong discontinuities (disturbances) of velocities and forces propagate into elements from their nodes in all directions, interacting with each other in a highly complicated manner. To make numerical simulation realizable, this process is averaged, assuming the disturbances entirely cover all the elements within the same time interval Δt_i. The transient velocity and force propagation over the element is calculated on the base of the laws of mass and momentum conservation, providing the element boundaries in the nodes remain nonseparable. The value of current interval Δt_i is determined from the equation of mechanical energy balance of the whole system. At the time $t_i^- = t_{i-1}^+ + \Delta t_i$, the mechanical state of the element again arrives at a quasi-static state, analogous to the previous one, velocity and nodes displacements in which take new values. This allows us to formulate a recurrence procedure for the numerical simulation of the problem.

As the method represents propagation of strong discontinuities in velocities, stresses, and strains with finite wave speed, this approach may be called, as distinct from ordinary (non-wave) finite element method, 'the method of wave finite element modeling' or *'wave finite element method'* (WFEM).

The above procedure describes transient wave propagation without formulating differential equations of motion and does not require their approximate finite-difference solution. Similar setting is sometimes referred to as 'direct numerical analysis' (Mechta and Davids 1966). By analogy, the term 'direct mathematical modeling' (DMM) has been used by Shorr and Mel'nikova (1988) and in some other author's papers for numerical analysis of 1-D wave propagation in solids. The method DMM was successfully applied to various transient problems in mechanics and engineering. In Shorr (1999) the method DMM was shown to be a specific case of the general WFEM applied to 1-D problems when time intervals Δt_i are constant. On the other hand, the method DMM can be assumed as a convenient numerical realization of the classical method of 'characteristics'. In the limit, by increasing the number of elements and relevant decreasing time steps, the method leads for 1-D problems to exact wave solutions in solids.

At finite speed of wave propagation, disturbances from the given node propagate for a time interval Δt_i only within those elements, which directly adjoin to the node and do not reach the other elements. The task of step-by-step computation of the mechanical structure of n degrees of freedom in nodes is broken down into n simple algebraic systems of equations, with a small number of unknowns for each node. Therefore, in the wave approach, the necessity to treat the structure stiffness and mass matrices calculation as a whole and finding at each step the solution of the very high order equations system is excluded. The values of Δt_i can be easily calculated using successive approximations.

In the book, the wave finite element method is systematically described for the first time.

The book consists of two parts: the seven chapters of the first part contain theoretical background defined to various problems; in the second, also including seven chapters, a number of mechanics and engineering applications are demonstrated.

In Chapter 1, foundations of WFEM, beginning from its simplest 1-D modification – method DMM, with some illustrative examples are described in details. Chapter 2 is concerned with problems of the DMM simulation of longitudinal and torsional elastic waves in rods and transverse waves in stretched strings and cables. A single wave speed of a known value and direction is inherent in all these problems; this leads to an identical numerical calculation procedure. Propagation of 1-D longitudinal waves in a rod of inelastic material with viscoelastic, elastic-plastic, and elastic-viscoplastic properties is studied in Chapter 3. To this goal, a special DMM algorithm based on the concept of a discrete-continual model of an inelastic body presented by Shorr (1984) and developed in Shorr (1995, 1998) is used.

Chapter 4 discusses the problem of coupled longitudinal-torsional waves in a pre-twisted rod, which is a typical 1-D mechanical structure. In this case, two kinds of waves propagate simultaneously, interacting with each other; this requires making use the general WFEM approach. Two computation models of bending wave propagation in a Timoshenko beam are described in Chapter 5: a special structural bending/shear model for DMM and a more general approach based on WFEM. The problems of stepped force and moment suddenly affecting a beam are considered. Numerical simulation of 1-D plane, spherical, and cylindrical waves arising in plates, elastic continua, and some other structures is studied in Chapter 6.

The topic of the Chapter 7 is a description of the general approach to multi-dimensional wave simulation based on WFEM. A specific code referred to 2-D wave propagation in a rectangular plane region with application to problems of longitudinal loading and in-plane bending of a plate, and other examples, are presented. Some results are compared with other transient numerical solutions. The Chapter includes additional remarks of the WFEM approach that may be of theoretical interest.

Chapter 8 contains a number of mechanics and engineering examples connected with the problem of impact loading of elastic and inelastic solids. The concept of 'floating boundary condition' suggested by Shorr (1995) is used to simulate the repeated impact/rebound interaction between colliding bodies. The impact interaction of a pre-twisted rod with a rigid body is considered for the first time, and an analysis of the DMM accuracy in application to impact problems is carried out. The wave approach to experience the forced vibration of solids, including resonant response under fluctuated frequency and phase, bending vibration of a turbine blade damped by dry friction inserts, and some other nonlinear problems are presented in Chapter 9. Unsteady vibro-impact loading of deformable structures, with multiple collisions in fixed or distributed varying points is considered in Chapter 10.

Chapter 11 describes 1-D and 2-D numerical simulation of dynamic processes in strips, beams, and plates setting up by loads moving with sub/supersonic velocity. Chapter 12 contains the numerical analysis of a classical problem of applied mechanics – dynamic loading of a plane edge of a solid. The results of 2-D numerical solution relevant to constant and also impulse load suddenly applied to an elastic thin plate and half-space (the generalized Lamb's problem) are compared with some known analytical solutions. The solution is extended to the case of a bounded domain in view of wave reflections from its boundaries. In Chapter 13, two special dynamic problems of solid mechanics are simulated. The first refers to slipping of a chain from a platform under action of its own weight (the Kaly's problem). A paradox of this problem connected with loss of a part of mechanical energy discussed by Panovko (1985) is elucidated, as soon as the elastic waves are taken into account. In the second, wave propagation in a structure interacting with 'active' media is considered. In this case, energy input into the system and self-exciting oscillation arise. Waves in a stretched string supported on an 'anti-elastic' or 'anti-viscous' foundation and self-exciting transverse oscillations of a string in a nonlinear viscous medium are calculated.

Chapter 14 contains examples of the DMM application to some unsteady engineering problems. This approach was effectively used by Kaplunova (1990a,b) in the investigation of 'longitudinal dynamics' of a train. As examples, train oscillation under starting and braking and in the case of carriage collision are studied.

Although the WFEM and DMM were developed with reference to problems in mechanics, these methods, due to a known mathematical analogy of various physical processes, can be successfully applied to numerical modeling of other continua. Chapter 14 also demonstrates application of the DMM method to some electrical engineering and hydraulics problems.

The book contains a significant number of the numerical solutions referred to not trivial problems of unsteady dynamics of solids. One would have great difficulty in obtaining similar solutions using other methods, even where other methods are possible. At the same time, as an illustration of possibilities and accuracy of the method proposed, the solutions of a number of simple problems are compared with known analytical or graph-analytical solutions.

All computations were carried out using PC Pentium with the FORTRAN programs. A part of the 1-D examples from Shorr and Mel'nikova (1988), which were carried out earlier using universal computers of the previous generation, have been renewed for the PC.

Some results of computations by the WFEM and DMM methods were compared to the data obtained by the traditional FEM transient approach. To this end, the author used accessible to him 'in home' programs, which were supervised by transient analysis options of widely known software packages NASTRAN, ANSYS, ABAQUS and others. It is well to bear in mind that the references in the book to FEM calculations relate not to any concrete software packages, but to typical algorithms of the non-wave FEM.

For simplification of practical use of the wave method, some FORTRAN programs with the necessary comments are given in the Appendix. Since the method DMM approximates certain kinds of problems with increase of elements number to exact results (of course, for the accepted design model), some of examples can be used for testing algorithms of the transient analysis of FEM software packages.

The solutions by the DMM method give very clear representation of the wave processes in solids, allowing the method to be exploited in elementary texts illustrating the general principles of solid dynamics.

Theory

1 Foundation of the Wave Finite Element Method

1.1 Direct Mathematical Modeling of Wave Propagation in an Elastic Rod

1.1.1 Background Equations

1.1.1.1. **A.** As a simple mechanical model, we consider a rectilinear homogeneous elastic rod of length L and constant cross-sectional area A. The rod moves along its x-axis with velocity v_0 and is loaded by forces F_0^+ and $F_0^- = -F_0^+$ applied to its ends (Fig.1.1a). The positive index refers to the right end, the negative index to the left end. The positive direction of the forces is taken to coincide with that of the x-axis; therefore, a positive (tensile) stress in the rod is determined as $\sigma_0 = F_0^+ / A = -F_0^- / A$ (Fig.1.1b).

The strain $\varepsilon_0 = \sigma_0 / E$, where E is Young's modulus, is assumed to be small. The stressed-inertial state of the deformed moving rod may be regarded a quasi-static.

Let the boundary forces suddenly change at a time t to arbitrary constant quantities F^+ and F^-, so that values of relevant boundary stresses become $\sigma^+ = F^+ / A$ and $\sigma^- = -F^- / A$, respectively, while the stress-strain state over the rod, excluding its boundaries, remains as yet unchanged.

The differences $F^\pm - F_0$ and $\sigma^\pm - \sigma_0$ constitute 'strong' discontinuities of force and stress arising between the disturbed boundary domains and the inner undisturbed part of the rod. Such discontinuities in any part of the solid exist only instantaneously and must immediately decay. As equilibrium of infinitesimal parts of the rod near the boundaries is broken, unbalanced domains begin expanding and propagating into the rod as waves with some speed c, their behavior governed by the laws of solid mechanics.

Additional strains in the disturbed domain, due to Hooke's law, are given by

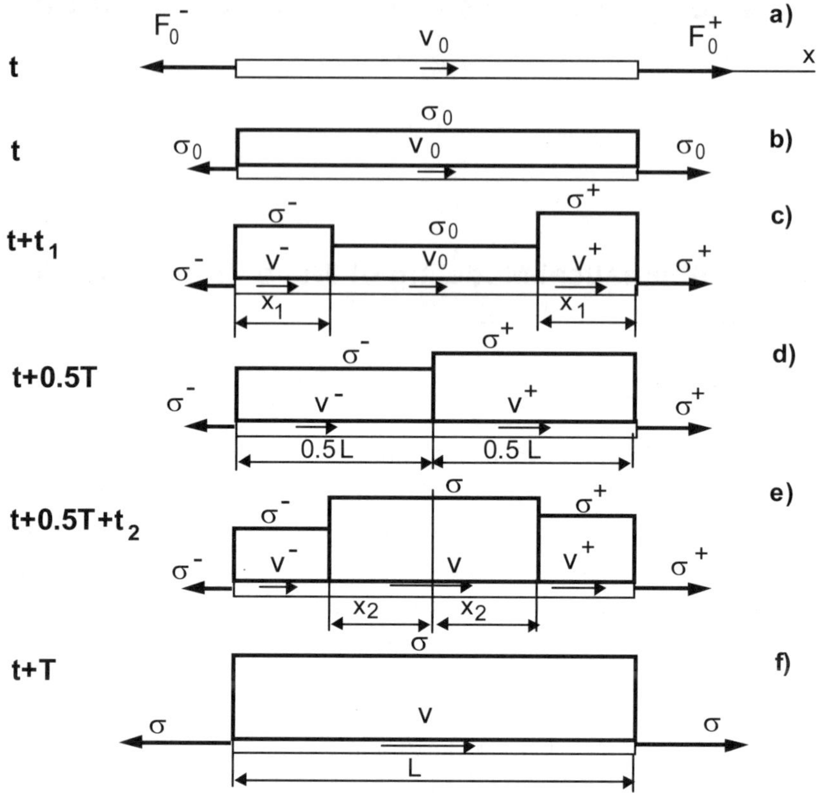

Fig. 1. 1. Propagation of stress and velocity counter waves in a rod

$$\varepsilon^{+}-\varepsilon_{0}=(\sigma^{+}-\sigma_{0})/E,\quad \varepsilon^{-}-\varepsilon_{0}=(\sigma^{-}-\sigma_{0})/E \tag{1.1a}$$

or in a more compact notation

$$\varepsilon^{\pm}-\varepsilon_{0}=(\sigma^{\pm}-\sigma_{0})/E. \tag{1.1b}$$

Assuming the speed c be constant, consider a state of the rod at an instant t_1, when the length of disturbed domains becomes $x_1 = c/t_1$ (Fig. 1.1c). The ratio v/c of the body particles velocity v to wave speed c is assumed to be small in comparison with unity.

The law of momentum conservation for the disturbed domains leads to

$$\rho A x_1 (v^{\pm}-v_0)=(F^{\pm}-F_0)t_1$$

or

$$\rho c(v^{\pm} - v_0) = \pm(\sigma^{\pm} - \sigma_0) \tag{1.2}$$

where ρ is density of the rod material and $v^{\pm}$ are the velocities of these domains propagating from corresponding rod boundaries. The difference $v^{\pm} - v_0$ also may constitute a strong discontinuity.

The displacement difference $(v^{\pm} - v_0)t_1$ of the disturbed domain boundaries brings its elongation $(\varepsilon^{\pm} - \varepsilon_0)x_1$. The equality

$$(v^{\pm} - v_0)t_1 = \pm(\varepsilon^{\pm} - \varepsilon_0)x_1$$

then yielding

$$(\varepsilon^{\pm} - \varepsilon_0)c = \pm(v^{\pm} - v_0). \tag{1.3}$$

It follows from Eqs.(1.1)-(1.3) that

$$(\rho c^2 - E)(\sigma^{\pm} - \sigma_0) = 0.$$

As in the general case, $\sigma^{\pm} \neq \sigma_0$, the wave speed is in fact constant and equal to

$$c = \sqrt{E / \rho} \tag{1.4}$$

corresponding to the well-known formula of longitudinal wave speed in a rod.

The time t_1 and distance $x_1 = ct_1$ are not represented explicitly in Eqs.(1.1)-(1.3); these equations are, therefore, valid for any time instant and cross section position until the waves from opposite boundaries meet at the rod mid-point, i.e. for $t_1 \leq 0.5T$, where $T = L/c$ is the time of wave propagation along the whole length of the rod. At this instant, strong discontinuities of forces, stresses, strains, and velocities appear at this point (Fig.1.1d). A new disturbed domain with stress σ and velocity v arises at the rod center, propagating to both ends of the rod. The state of the rod at the instant $t + 0.5T + t_2$, at which the length of the new disturbed domain becomes $x_2 = ct_2$ (Fig.1.1e), is described by equations analogous to Eqs.(1.1)-(1.3) yielding

$$\rho c(v - v^{\pm}) = \pm(\sigma^{\pm} - \sigma). \tag{1.5}$$

Eliminating the stresses σ^{+} and σ^{-} from Eqs.(1.2) and (1.5), we find

$$\rho c(2v^{\pm} - v_0 - v) = \pm(\sigma - \sigma_0),$$

from which the new velocity of the rod expressed in terms of boundary velocities may be obtained, thus

$$v = v^+ + v^- - v_0 . \tag{1.6}$$

Repeating the same procedure for the velocities v^+ and v^-, we obtain the new stress in the rod

$$\sigma = \sigma^+ + \sigma^- - \sigma_0 \tag{1.7}$$

also expressed in terms of boundary values.

At the instant $t+T$ a new quasi-static state with stress σ, strain $\varepsilon = \sigma / E$, and velocity v is established over the whole rod (Fig.1.1f). If boundary forces again suddenly change at this instant, the calculation procedure can be prolonged the same way.

B. Equations (1.6)-(1.7) can be represented in the form

$$\left.\begin{aligned} v - v_0 &= (v^+ - v_0) + (v^- - v_0), \\ \sigma - \sigma_0 &= (\sigma^+ - \sigma_0) + (\sigma^- - \sigma_0) \end{aligned}\right\}, \tag{1.8}$$

which shows that the total change of the stressed-inertial state of the rod during time T is the result of summation of disturbances traveling from both ends of the rod.

Equations (1.8) can also be obtained using the principle of superposition of linear elastic waves.

Substituting the velocities $v^{\pm}$ and the stresses $\sigma^{\pm}$ from Eqs.(1.2) into Eq.(1.6) and Eq.(1.7), respectively, we obtain

$$v - v_0 = (\sigma^+ - \sigma^-) / \rho c \tag{1.9}$$

and

$$\sigma - \sigma_0 = \rho c (v^+ - v^-). \tag{1.10}$$

Equations (1.9) and (1.10) have distinct mechanical meanings. The first one directly follows from the law of momentum conservation for the whole rod during the time T. As to the second, we may establish it using Hooke's law for the whole rod

$$\sigma - \sigma_0 = E(\varepsilon - \varepsilon_0)$$

and noting the condition of rod continuity

$$\varepsilon - \varepsilon_0 = [(u^+ - u_0^+) - (u^- - u_0^-)] / L,$$

where $u_0^\pm$ and $u^\pm$ are the longitudinal displacements of the rod ends at the instants t and $t + T$, respectively, and finally the kinematical equation

$$u^\pm - u_0^\pm = (v^\pm - v_0)L / c.$$

C. Let us show that deduced equations satisfy the law of mechanical energy conservation for the entire duration of wave propagation in the rod.

The change of kinetic energy of the right domain x_1 in Fig.1.1c for the time t_1 is

$$\Delta K^+ = 0.5\rho x_1 A[(v^+)^2 - v_0^2] = 0.5(v^+ + v_0)(\sigma^+ - \sigma_0)t_1, \qquad (1.11)$$

where use has been made of Eq.(1.2).

The change of potential strain energy for the same conditions is

$$\Delta P^+ = 0.5x_1 A[(\sigma^+)^2 - \sigma_0^2] / E = 0.5(\sigma^+ + \sigma_0)(v^+ - v_0)t_1. \qquad (1.12)$$

Adding expressions (1.11) and (1.12) yields

$$\Delta K^+ + \Delta P^+ = A(\sigma^+ v^+ - \sigma_0 v_0)t_1 = \Delta W^+, \qquad (1.13)$$

where ΔW^+ is the total work supplied to this domain x_1 in a time t_1.

An analogous equality is valid for the left domain x_1 in Fig.1.1c and for the rod as a whole.

Thus, the laws of momentum and energy conservation, just as the condition of continuity and Hooke's law, are satisfied throughout. Therefore, the presented form of solution to the problem of longitudinal wave propagation in an elastic rod is exact for this one-dimensional approach, provided the boundary forces $F^\pm$ do not change within the time interval $\Delta t = T = L / c$.

1.1.1.2. **A**. Let a rod, at rest at $t = 0$, be affected by time-varying boundary forces $F_b^\pm(t)$ and longitudinal load $q(x,t)$ distributed along its length. Divide the length L into n elements of an equal magnitude $\Delta x = L / n$ and label them as $j = 1,2,...,n$. The numeration of elements boundaries, i.e., of the nodes between elements, is $j = 1,2,...,n+1$. Quantities referred to nodes will be noted with an upper or lower asterisk.

For a homogeneous rod with constant values of Young's modulus E and density ρ, the wave speed c determined by the Eq.(1.4) is the same for all the elements; therefore, the time $\Delta t = \Delta x / c$ of wave propagation along each element is identical.

Replace the distributed loads $q(x_{j-1},t)$ and $q(x_j,t)$ acting on the halves of neighboring elements $j-1$ and j by the point force $F_j^*(t) = 0.5\Delta x[q(x_{j-1},t) + q(x_j,t)]$ applied to the node j For the boundary elements the forces are $F_1^*(t) = 0.5\Delta x q(x_1 t)$ and $F_{n+1}^*(t) = 0.5\Delta x q(x_n t)$. We represent the given time functions $F_j^*(t)$, $F_1^-(t) = F_b^-(t) + F_1^*(t)$, and $F_{n+1}^+(t) = F_b^+(t) + F_{n+1}^*(t)$ approximately by step-wise values, constant over the time intervals Δt. All the external loads will then vary simultaneously at the discrete time instants $t_{i-1} = (i-1)\Delta t,\ i = 1,2,...,n_t$, where i is an index of time steps and n_t is the total step number under consideration.

In doing so, Eqs.(1.1)-(1.13), which referred to the whole rod, are now valid for elements, using their boundary parameters, and for each time step i. In particular, for the adjacent elements j-1 and j (see Fig.1.2, where the elements are conditionally shown as moved apart) one must take Eqs.(1.2) in the form

$$\left.\begin{aligned} \rho c(v_{j-1}^+ - v_{j-1,0}) &= \sigma_{j-1}^+ - \sigma_{j-1,0}, \\ \rho c(v_j^- - v_{j,0}) &= -(\sigma_j^- - \sigma_{j,0}) \end{aligned}\right\}, \tag{1.14}$$

where $\sigma_{j-1,0}$, $\sigma_{j,0}$ and $v_{j-1,0}$, $v_{j,0}$ are the element stresses and velocities, respectively, at the beginning of the given time step.

The boundary stresses $\sigma_{j-1}^+, \sigma_j^-$ and velocities v_{j-1}^+, v_j^- appear as a result of the decay of strong stress $\sigma_{j-1,0} - \sigma_{j,0}$ and velocity $v_{j-1,0} - v_{j,0}$ discontinuities, which form between the neighboring elements at the termination of each preceding step. Sudden application of an external force F_j^* also leads to a strong stress discontinuity.

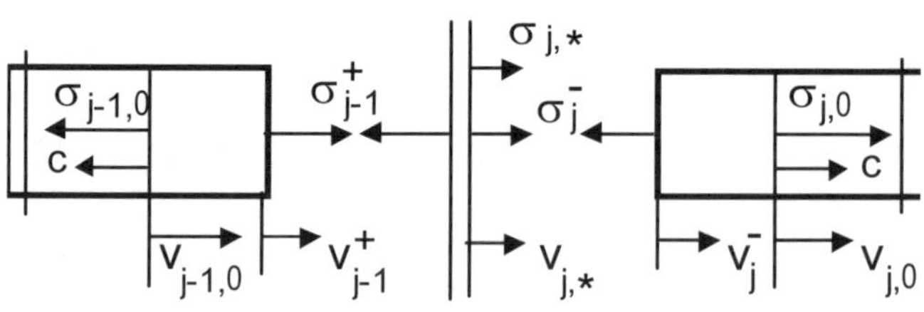

Fig. 1.2. Wave propagation over the elements *j-1* and *j* due to their interaction

B. During each step Δt, fixed conditions of inner boundary equilibrium

$$\sigma_j^* + \sigma_j^- - \sigma_{j-1}^+ = 0, \tag{1.15a}$$

where $\sigma_j^* = F_j^* / A$, and continuity

$$v_j^- = v_j^+, \tag{1.15b}$$

must be satisfied.

Substituting Eqs.(1.14) in Eqs.(1.15a,b), we arrive for inner nodes $j = 2,3,\ldots,n$ at

$$\left.\begin{array}{l} \sigma_{j-1}^+ = 0.5[\sigma_{j,0} + \sigma_{j-1,0} + \sigma_j^* + \rho c(v_{j,0} - v_{j-1,0})], \\ \text{with } v_{j-1}^+ = v_{j,0} + (\sigma_{j-1}^+ - \sigma_{j,0})/\rho c \end{array}\right\}, \tag{1.16a}$$

or

$$\left.\begin{array}{l} v_{j-1}^+ = 0.5[v_{j,0} + v_{j-1,0} + (\sigma_{j,0} - \sigma_{j-1,0} + \sigma_j^*)/\rho c], \\ \text{with } \sigma_{j-1}^+ = \sigma_{j,0} + \rho c(v_{j-1}^+ - v_{j,0}) \end{array}\right\}. \tag{1.16b}$$

Determining all boundary parameters of the element j, we can find its new stressed-inertial state, subject to Eqs.(1.6)-(1.7), by

$$\left.\begin{array}{l} \sigma_j = \sigma_j^- + \sigma_j^+ - \sigma_{j,0}, \\ v_j = v_j^- + v_j^+ - v_{j,0} \end{array}\right\}. \tag{1.17}$$

The initial conditions for a rod at rest are

$$\left.\begin{array}{l} u_{j,in} = 0, \quad j = 1,2,\ldots,n+1, \\ v_{j,in} = 0, \quad j = 1,2,\ldots,n \end{array}\right\}. \tag{1.18}$$

The initial stress $\sigma_{j,in}$ may be then determined in terms of nodal displacements as

$$\sigma_{j,in} = E(u_{j+1,in} - u_{j,in})/\Delta x. \tag{1.19}$$

However, it is convenient to present its initial values corresponding to Eq.(1.19) explicitly because the governing equations contain the stresses. Henceforth, we shall often do thus. In the given case, we have $\sigma_{j,in} = 0,\ j = 1,2,\ldots,n$.

C. The boundary conditions referred to the end elements $j = 1$ and $j = n$ are determined from Eqs.(1.14). This leads for the given boundary stresses $\sigma_1^- = F_b^- / A$ and $\sigma_n^+ = F_b^+ / A$ to

$$\left.\begin{aligned} v_1^- &= v_{1,0} - (\sigma_1^- - \sigma_{1,0})/\rho c, \\ v_n^+ &= v_{n,0} + (\sigma_n^+ - \sigma_{n,0})/\rho c \end{aligned}\right\}. \tag{1.20}$$

The other boundary conditions due to specific problem formulations will be considered later. Eqs.(1.15) can also be generalized for special distributed or point boundary conditions.

1.1.1.3. Equations (1.16)-(1.20) form a set of very simple algebraic recurrence relations, the number being equal to the number of the nodes. Solving these relations step-by-step for all the elements of the rod, an arbitrary wave process can be simulated. Obviously, the new mechanical state of the element j at the instant $t+\Delta t$ depends only on the states of the neighboring elements $j-1$ and $j+1$ at the preceding time instant t and also on the external loads acting at its boundaries during the time interval Δt. The states of all other elements, as the other external loads, play no part since the wave traveling from these do not reach the jth element within the reference time interval.

Using a numerical procedure, the elements may be tabulated in any order but the computational algorithm is simplified by sequential transition from element $j-1$ to element j.

The wave solutions based on the equations presented are exact for the one-dimensional approach with the above-assumed step-wise time and space approximations of the external distributed loads and boundary conditions. This results in unconditional stability of the computations.

Decreasing the size of the elements and consequently the appropriate time interval, we can obtain a solution for arbitrary varying loads and other factors with any desired accuracy. Of great importance is the fact that increasing the number of elements does not affect the stability of the computations.

To note an interesting property, it follows from Eqs.(1.16)-(1.17) that

$$\left.\begin{aligned} \sigma_j &= 0.5[\sigma_{j+1,0} + \sigma_{j-1,0} + \sigma_{j+1}^* - \sigma_j^* + \rho c(v_{j+1,0} - v_{j-1,0})], \\ v_j &= 0.5[v_{j+1,0} + v_{j-1,0} + (\sigma_{j+1,0} - \sigma_{j-1,0} + \sigma_{j+1}^* + \sigma_j^*)/\rho c] \end{aligned}\right\}. \tag{1.21}$$

Equations (1.21) show that the mechanical state of the inner element j at the previous instant t does not affect its state at the following instant $t+\Delta t$ as its energy and momentum transfer into adjacent elements. However, this does not apply to the boundary elements.

Computationally, it is convenient to exploit directly Eqs.(1.16)-(1.17), because they enable us to obtain all the determined quantities at the nodes, in particular, its displacements.

1.1.1.4. **A.** Considering two infinitesimally close rod cross sections, one can deduce, instead of Eqs.(1.2)-(1.3), the analogous partial differential equations

$$\rho\frac{\partial v}{\partial t}=\frac{\partial \sigma}{\partial x};\quad \frac{\partial \varepsilon}{\partial t}=\frac{\partial v}{\partial x}, \tag{1.22a}$$

or

$$\rho\frac{\partial^2 \varepsilon}{\partial t^2}=\frac{\partial^2 \sigma}{\partial x^2}, \tag{1.22b}$$

which are valid for a rod with arbitrary homogeneous mechanical properties.

Adding Hooke's law $\sigma = E\varepsilon$ to Eq.(1.22b), we get the well-known wave equation for an elastic rod in term of stresses

$$c^2\frac{\partial^2 \sigma}{\partial x^2}=\frac{\partial^2 \sigma}{\partial t^2},\quad c^2 = E/\rho. \tag{1.22c}$$

It has the same form in terms of velocity, strain, and displacement.

B. Let us integrate Eq.(1.22c) by the method of characteristics for initial conditions corresponding to the problem of stress and velocity discontinuities decaying under the interaction of elements $j-1$ and j (see Fig.1.2 with $\sigma_j^* = 0$):

$$v(x,0)=\begin{cases} v_{j-1,0} & \text{with } x<0,\\ v_{j,0} & \text{with } x>0,\end{cases}\qquad \sigma(x,0)=\begin{cases} \sigma_{j-1,0} & \text{with } x<0,\\ \sigma_{j,0} & \text{with } x>0,\end{cases}$$

with the coordinate x-origin at the elements boundary. Then we obtain the solution

$$v(x,t)=0.5[v_{j,0}+v_{j-1,0}+(\sigma_{j,0}-\sigma_{j-1,0})/\rho c],$$

which is valid for $-ct < x < ct$, i.e. within the perturbed domains.

This expression coincides with the first Eq.(1.16b), as it should do for the exact solution. Thus, the approach described may in some sense be assumed as a convenient numerical realization of the method of characteristics.

Dealing with more complex problems, approximate numerical solutions to the differential wave equation (1.22) with appropriate boundary and other conditions are required. The proposed method, in contrast, allows us to describe wave propagation without composing a set of differential equations of motion and, hence, without their approximate numerical solution. For this reason, the approach was named by Shorr (1976a,b) as the method of direct mathematical modeling (DMM) of wave propagation in solids (by analogy with the term used by Mechta and Davids 1966) for numerical analysis of plastic waves). Its connection with the more general wave finite element modeling (WFEM) and the ordinary finite element method (FEM) will be considered in the subsequent sections of the book.

1.1.2 Numerical Examples

The simple examples presented below illustrate the DMM numerical procedure and the accuracy of its results in comparison with analytical solutions. Some examples are also compared with FEM results.

The geometry and loading of the rods considered in the examples are shown in Fig.1.3. Hereafter, we use in conjunction with dimensional parameters f, dimensionless ones denoted as $\bar{f} = f / f^o$. Scale factors f^o are chosen to simplify the calculation formulae in their most intuitive mechanical presentation. In some cases, we use the same letters to denote the dimensional and scaled quantities.

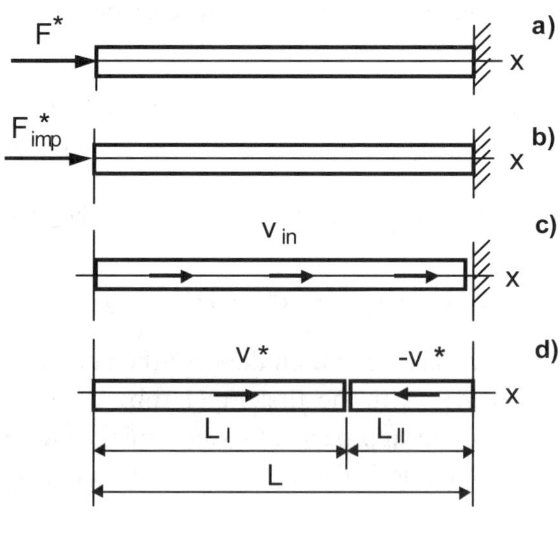

Fig. 1.3. Sketches of the rods considered

1.1.2.1. **Problem 1.1. Constant force suddenly applied to the free boundary of a one-end clamped rod (Fig.1.3a). A.** In accordance with this figure, where F^* is 'stepped', i.e. a suddenly applied constant compressive force, the following dimensionless quantities are introduced:

$$\bar{x} = \frac{x}{L},\ \bar{t} = \frac{tc}{L},\ \bar{\sigma} = \frac{\sigma A}{F^*},\ \bar{v} = \frac{v\rho c A}{F^*},\ \bar{u} = \frac{uEA}{F^* L}. \tag{1.23a}$$

In this case

$$\Delta\bar{x} = \Delta\bar{t} = 1/n, \tag{1.23b}$$

where n is a number of elements.

Thus, Eqs.(1.14) for any element $j = 1,2,...,n$ are

$$\left.\begin{aligned} \bar{v}_j^+ &= \bar{v}_{j,0} + \bar{\sigma}_j^+ - \bar{\sigma}_{j,0}, \\ \bar{v}_j^- &= \bar{v}_{j,0} - \bar{\sigma}_j^- + \bar{\sigma}_{j,0} \end{aligned}\right\}. \tag{1.24a}$$

The governing Eqs.(1.16) with $\sigma_j^* = 0$, valid for the inner nodes $j = 2,3,...,n$, are

$$\left.\begin{aligned} \bar{\sigma}_{j-1}^+ &= 0.5(\bar{\sigma}_{j,0} + \bar{\sigma}_{j-1.0} + \bar{v}_{j,0} - \bar{v}_{j-1,0}), \\ \bar{v}_{j-1}^+ &= 0.5(\bar{v}_{j,0} + \bar{v}_{j-1,0} + \bar{\sigma}_{j,0} - \bar{\sigma}_{j-1,0}) \end{aligned}\right\}. \tag{1.24b}$$

The initial conditions are $\bar{\sigma}_{j,in} = 0,\ \bar{v}_{j,in} = 0,\ j = 1,2,...,n$, and $\bar{u}_{j,in} = 0,\ j = 1,2,...,n+1$, with the permanent boundary conditions $\bar{\sigma}_1^- = -1,\ \bar{v}_n^+ = 0$, and $\bar{\sigma}_j^* = 0$. Obviously, the condition $\bar{v}_n^+ = 0$ with $\bar{u}_{n+1}(0) = 0$ provides the permanent fixing of the right end of the rod.

Using Eqs.(1.20) in nondimensional terms with given boundary conditions, we obtain for the element $j = 1$ and $j = n$, respectively

$$\bar{v}_1^- = \bar{v}_{1,0} + 1 + \bar{\sigma}_{1,0},\quad \bar{\sigma}_n^+ = \bar{\sigma}_{n,0} - \bar{v}_{n,0}. \tag{1.25}$$

B. At the first step ($i = 1$), we obtain from Eqs.(1.25) the boundary parameters $\bar{v}_1^- = 1,\ \bar{\sigma}_n^+ = 0,$ with all the other quantities of velocities and stresses remaining zero. It follows from Eqs.(1.17) that the first element parameters at the end of this step become $\bar{\sigma}_1 = -1,\ \bar{v}_1 = 1$.

At the second step (i = 2), one takes these quantities as the new values $\bar{\sigma}_{1,0} = -1,\ \bar{v}_{1,0} = 1$, with the border velocity $\bar{v}_1^-$ of the first element seen from Eqs.(1.25) unchanged. Using Eqs.(1.24b) for the node $j = 2$, we then obtain $\bar{\sigma}_1^+ = \bar{\sigma}_2^- = -1$ and $\bar{v}_1^+ = \bar{v}_2^- = 1$. Hence, the stress and the velocity of the first element at the time $t = 2\Delta t$ remain unchanged, i.e.

$\bar{\sigma}_1 = -1$, $\bar{v}_1 = 1$, and the stress and the velocity of the second element obtain the same quantities $\bar{\sigma}_2 = -1$, $\bar{v}_2 = 1$; the process thereafter is continuing in a similar manner.

The stress and velocity of the last element $j = n$ are given the values $\bar{\sigma}_n = -1$, $\bar{v}_n = 1$ at the step $i = n$. At the next step $i = n+1$ the boundary stress $\bar{\sigma}_n^+$, in view of the second Eq.(1.25), is seen to be duplicated, $\bar{\sigma}_n^+ = -2$, with the reflected stress and velocity of the last element $\bar{\sigma}_n = -2$, $\bar{v}_{n,} = 0$.

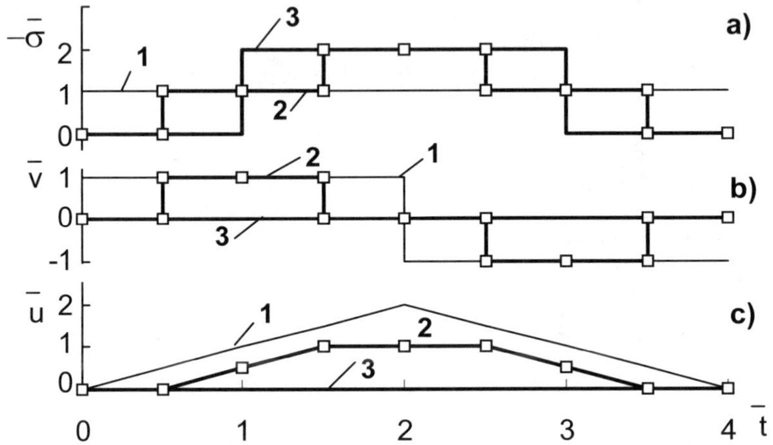

Fig. 1.4. Time variation of stresses –a), velocities –b), and displacements –c) in a free-fixed rod affected by a suddenly applied force; 1) parameters at the node *j*=1 (thin lines), 2) – at the node *j*=2 (marker lines), 3) –at the node *j*=3 (bold lines)

The time variations of the compressive stresses $\bar{\sigma}_1^-$, $\bar{\sigma}_1^+ = \bar{\sigma}_2^-$, $\bar{\sigma}_2^+$, velocities $\bar{v}_1^-$, $\bar{v}_1^+ = \bar{v}_2^-$, $\bar{v}_2^+$, and displacements $\bar{u}_1$, $\bar{u}_2$, $\bar{u}_3$ at the nodes of the rod consisting of two elements are shown in Fig.1.4. After the four transitions of waves along the rod, the process is completely repeated.

A simple FORTRAN program illustrating the algorithm described is presented in the Appendix.

The numerical results entirely coincide with the well-known analytical solution considered by many authors (see, e.g., Babitsky 1998).

***1.1.2.2.* Problem 1.2. Impulse-induced wave in a free-fixed rod (Fig.1.3b). A.** A square impulse induced by a constant compressive force F^*_{imp} during the time t_{imp} is equal to $F^*_{imp} i_{imp} \Delta t$, where i_{imp} is a number of the impulse steps. To describe a very short impulse, it is necessary to take $i_{imp} = 1$ ($\bar{t}_{imp} = 1/n$) and use a sufficiently large number of elements *n*.

Initial and boundary conditions at the right end of the rod remain the same as the former case; the boundary conditions at the left end for $\bar{\sigma} = \sigma A / F^{\bullet}_{imp}$ become

$$\bar{\sigma}_1^- = \begin{cases} -1 & \text{with } 1 \le i \le i_{imp}, \\ 0 & \text{with } i > i_{imp}. \end{cases} \tag{1.26}$$

The numerical procedure also remains exactly the same.

In Fig.1.5a,b space-time wave patterns of the impulse-induced stress $\bar{\sigma}(\bar{x},\bar{t})$ and the velocity $\bar{v}(\bar{x},\bar{t})$ for $\bar{t}_{imp} = 0.05$ and *n*=20 are displayed, respectively.

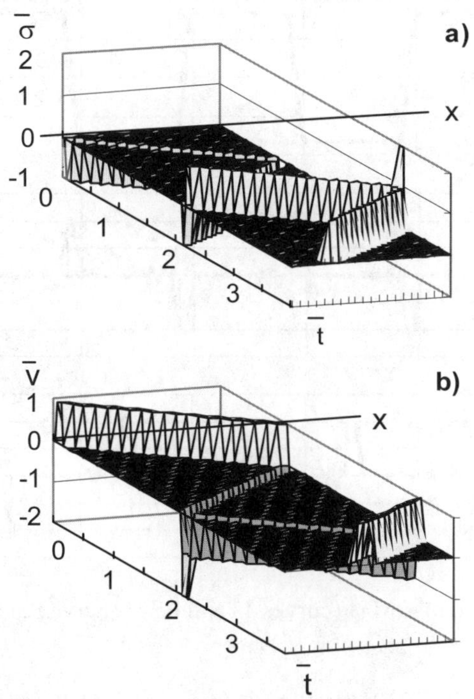

Fig. 1.5. Traveling wave diagrams of stresses – a) and velocities –b) induced by a short time impulse in a free-fixed rod

The perturbed domain restricted by the strong discontinuities of compressive stress $\bar{\sigma}_j = -1$ and velocity $\bar{v}_j = 1$ propagates along the rod with the wave speed $\bar{c} = \Delta\bar{x} / \Delta\bar{t} = 1$ from $\bar{t} = 0$ up to $\bar{t} = 1$ without distortion. Upon reflection from the fixed end at $\bar{t} = 1$, the stress wave does not change, while the velocity wave alters to $\bar{v}_j = -1$. The perturbed domain remains in contact with the support over the short impulse time $\bar{t}_{imp}$, during which the reaction stress is $\bar{\sigma}_n^+ = -2$, i.e. is doubled. After returning to the free end and reflecting from it at $\bar{t} = 2$, the stress wave changes to $\bar{\sigma}_j = 1$, while the velocity wave does not change. The boundary velocity becomes $\bar{v}_1^- = -2$ and retains this value over the impulse time $\bar{t}_{imp}$ until the perturbed domain remains adjacent to the free end of the rod. At the instants $\bar{t} = 3$ and $\bar{t} = 4$ the reflections are repeated, but with contrast direction of sign change. Further, the wave process continues in a similar manner.

B. It would be of interest to compare the computational results using the

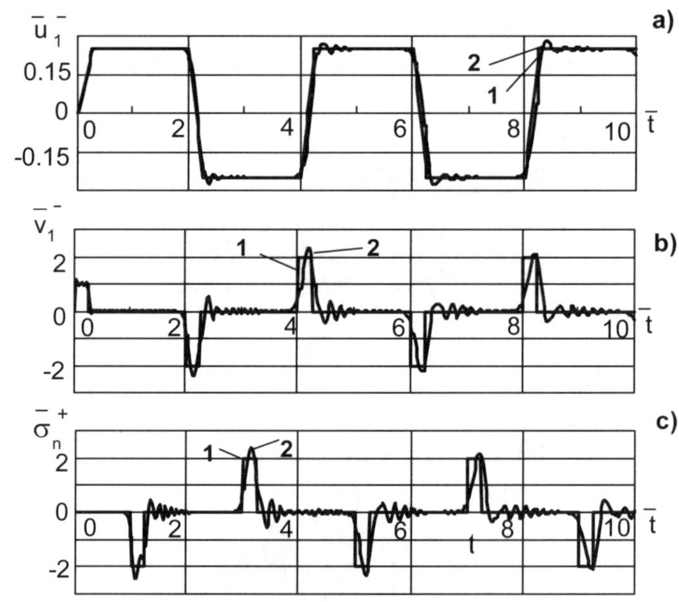

Fig. 1.6. Comparison of DMM (curves 1) and FEM (curves 2) solutions for Problem 1.2

methods DMM and FEM for the elementary 1-D problems, especially in view of the fact that the exact solutions are known.

Such comparison of the DMM and FEM results referring to the displacement $\bar{u}_1$ and velocity $\bar{v}_1^-$ at the free end, and the stress $\bar{\sigma}_n^+$ at clamped end for Problem 1.2 is shown in Fig.1.6a, b, c respectively. The curves 1 that coincide with the analytical solution are obtained by the DMM, the curves 2 - by traditional FEM. The calculations are carried out for the identical conditions: number of elements $n=40$, impulse time $\bar{t}_{imp}=0.25$ ($i_{imp}=10$) and the same time step $\Delta\bar{t}=0.025$.

The given value of time step satisfies the Courant-Friedrichs-Lewy criterion (1928) $\Delta t \le \Delta x / c$ needed to ensure stability of the finite difference solution used in transient analysis of FEM. The standard quantities of Newmark's integration parameters $\alpha=0.25$ and $\beta=0.5$ providing the unconditional stability of the FEM solution are also taken.

Figure 1.6 demonstrates that for the problem considered the continuous displacement curves of DMM and FEM almost agree; however, additional oscillations and distortion of maximum quantities accompany stress and velocity jumps simulating by FEM.

***1.1.2.3.* Problem 1.3. Interaction of different counter-waves in a free-free rod (Fig.1.7a).** Two tensile forces $-F_1^-$ and F_n^+ of the opposite directions, applied to the free ends of the rod, act during an impulse time t_{imp}. The forces generate longitudinal impulses that are the same in magnitude $F^*_{imp}t_{imp}$ but different in the form: the right impulse is rectangular, the left triangular. Then,

$$\sigma_1^- = \begin{cases} 4\bar{t}/\bar{t}_{imp} & \text{with} \quad 0 \le \bar{t}/\bar{t}_{imp} \le 0.5, \\ 4(1-\bar{t}/\bar{t}_{imp}) & \text{with} \quad 0.5 \le \bar{t}/\bar{t}_{imp} \le 1, \\ 0 \quad \text{with} \quad \bar{t}/\bar{t}_{imp} > 1; \end{cases}$$

$$\bar{\sigma}_n^+ = \begin{cases} 1 \quad \text{with} \quad 0 \le \bar{t}/\bar{t}_{imp} \le 1, \\ 0 \quad \text{with} \quad \bar{t}/\bar{t}_{imp} \ge 1 \end{cases}$$

where $\bar{\sigma}=\sigma A/F^*_{imp}$, $\bar{t}=tc/L$.

The number of elements is taken n=240 with the time step $\Delta\bar{t}=1/240$, the impulse duration is $\bar{t}_{imp}=0.25$. Any damping is neglected.

A transformation of the stress waves induced by these impulses at certain time instants is shown in Fig.1.7b and 1.7c. Strong stress discontinuities caused by the rectangular impulse are seen in Fig.1.7b, relevant to the DMM solution. The wave configuration does not change after the waves superpose during their meeting and then sequentially reflect from the free ends of the rod. Such pattern of elastic wave propagation exactly coincides with theoretical prediction.

The solution based on the ordinary FEM with the same number of elements is presented in Fig.1.7c. The results are qualitatively identical,

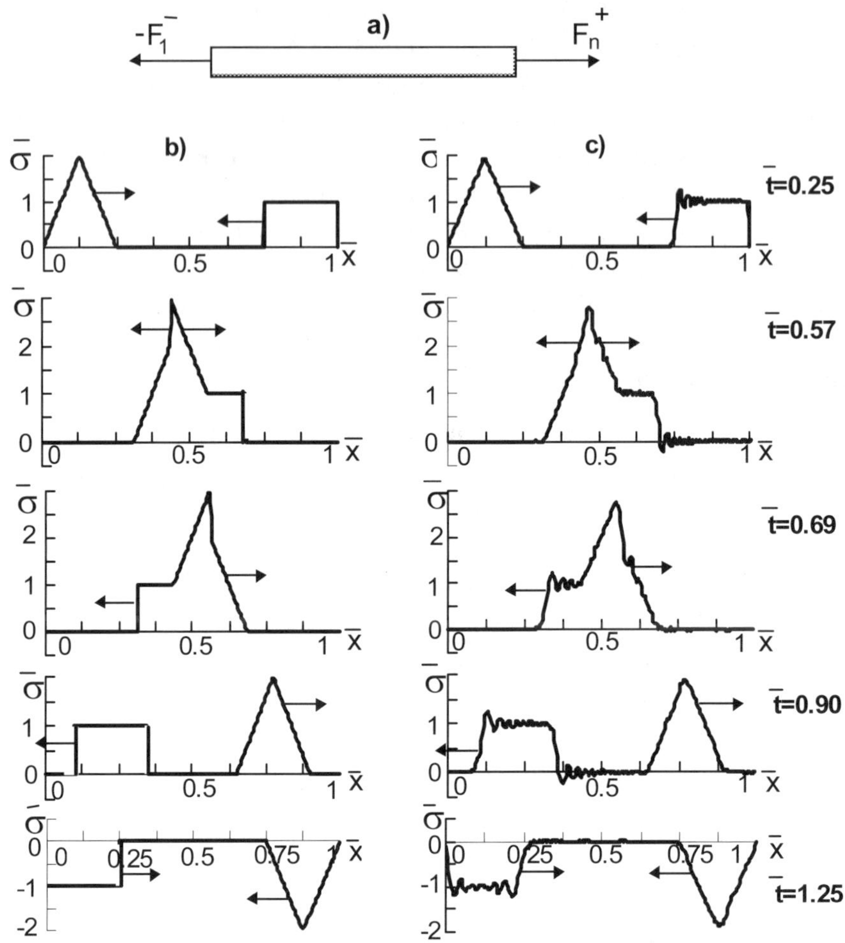

Fig. 1.7. Superposition of different counter-waves in a free-free rod; a) sketch of the system, b) DMM solution, c) FEM solution

and distortion of the triangular wave that increases and decreases gradually is insignificant. However, the borders of the rectangular wave are eroded and oscillations accompanying this wave are intensified with time.

1.1.2.4. **Problem 1.4. Impact of a moving rod against a rigid surface (Fig.1.3b).** Let a rod moving with initial velocity v_{in} suddenly impact a rigid surface. Instead of relationships (1.23a), we now take

$$\bar{v} = \frac{v}{v_{in}}, \quad \bar{\sigma} = \frac{\sigma}{\rho c v_{in}}, \quad \bar{u} = \frac{uc}{v_{in} L}, \tag{1.27}$$

with the initial conditions given by

$$\bar{\sigma}_{j,0} = 0, \; \bar{v}_{j,0} = 1, \; j = 1,2,...,n; \quad \bar{u}_{j,0} = 0, \; j = 1,2,...,n+1,$$

and boundary conditions $\bar{\sigma}_1^- = 0, \; \bar{v}_n^+ = 0$. The numerical procedure is unchanged.

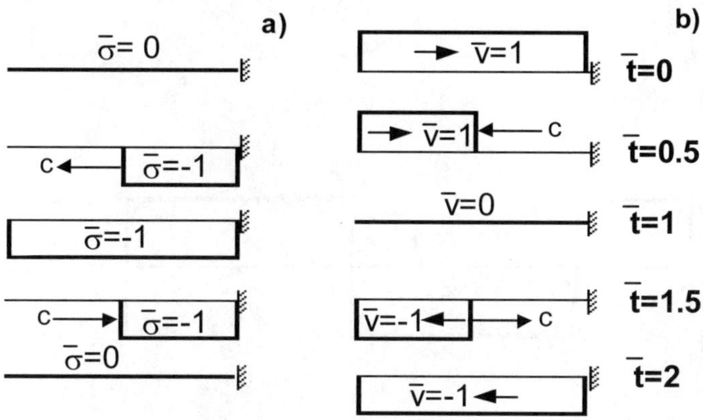

Fig.1.8. Distribution of stresses –a) and velocities –b) along the moving rod for time instants $\bar{t}$ after sudden stopping

Distributions of the stress $\bar{\sigma}_j$ and velocity $\bar{v}_j$ along the rod for some time instants $0 \le \bar{t} \le 2$ are shown in Fig.1.8a,b. After stopping the end $\bar{x} = 1$ at the initial moment $\bar{t} = 0$, the compressive stress wave front travels to the free end $\bar{x} = 0$. The whole rod stops at $\bar{t} = 1$, being entirely in compression. The rod rebounds at $\bar{t} = 2$ when it restores the initial velocity, but in inverse direction, and is entirely unloaded. The contact stress is $\bar{\sigma}_n^+ = -1$ or

$$\sigma_{cont} = -\rho c v_{in} \tag{1.28}$$

and is independent of the rod length.

The contact duration is $\bar{t}_{cont} = 2$ or

$$t_{cont} = 2L/c \tag{1.29}$$

and is independent of the impact velocity. The number of elements does not affect the DMM results.

Comparison of the DMM (curves 1) and the FEM results (curves 2) referring to displacement $\bar{u}_1$, velocity $\bar{v}_1^-$, and stress $\bar{\sigma}_n^+$ for n=40 and the same time step $\Delta\bar{t} = 0.025$ are displayed in Fig.1.9. No rebounding is

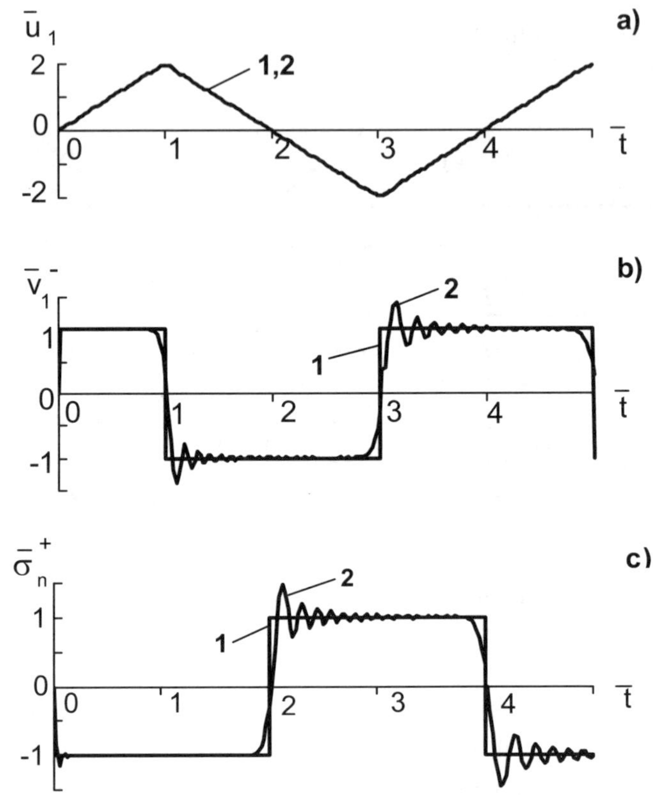

Fig.1.9. Comparison of DMM (curves 1) and FEM (curves 2) solutions for an initially moving rod after sudden stopping

taken into account here (a shock is assumed as 'adhered'). As in the previous cases, the correlation of displacements is satisfactory, while the FEM pattern of velocity and stress with time is not in good agreement with analytical and the DMM results.

***1.1.2.5.* Problem 1.5. Collision of rods of a different length (Fig.1.3d).** Consider the longitudinal elastic collision of two rods with initial velocities v_{in} and $-v_{in}$. Their lengths L_I and L_{II} are assumed to be related by the integers $L_I / L_{II} = n_I / n_{II}$. Then, the element length of the rods can be taken as identical $\Delta x = L_I / n_I = L_{II} / n_{II}$. The rods during contact can be considered as a single rod with total length $L = L_I + L_{II}$ and total number of elements $n = n_I + n_{II}$.

Using the same relationships (1.27), with $\bar{u} = uc / v_{in} L_{II}$, to denote the dimensionless quantities, the initial conditions are

$$\bar{v}_{j,0} = \begin{cases} 1 \text{ with } 1 \le j \le n_I, \\ -1 \text{ with } n_I < j \le n, \end{cases}; \quad \bar{\sigma}_{j,0} = 0 \text{ with } 1 \le j \le n, \tag{1.30}$$

and boundary conditions are $\bar{\sigma}_1^- = 0$, $\bar{\sigma}_n^+ = 0$. The moment of rebound is determined by the change in sign of the stress at the point $j = n_I + 1$, when this calculated stress becomes positive. In this case, it is necessary to take $\bar{\sigma}_{n_I}^+ = 0$, $\bar{\sigma}_{n_I+1}^- = 0$, considering each rod separately.

Patterns of the rod motion and deformation during and after the collision, and the displacement $\bar{u}_n^+$ for the colliding rods with elements number $n_I = 2$ and $n_{II} = 1$ are shown in Fig.1.10. The dimensionless displacement $\bar{u}_j$ is related to the length L_{II} of the shorter rod. The rods are deformed jointly during the first four time intervals. Then, the shorter rod *II* rebounds and moves in the reverse direction as if a rigid body with the same velocity as before the collision. From the instant $\bar{t} = 1$, the mass center of the longer rod *I* becomes immovable and the rod begins to oscillate as a free elastic body. Its initial kinetic energy of translational movement is completely transformed into energy for the elastic oscillations.

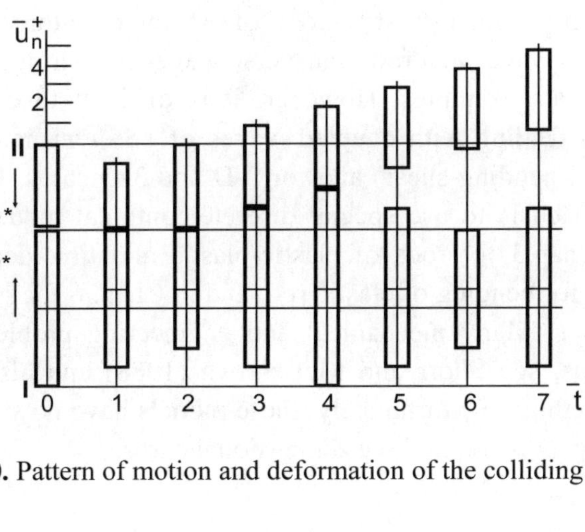

Fig. 1.10. Pattern of motion and deformation of the colliding rods

If the rod collision was an impact of two rigid bodies of masses $m_I = \rho A L_I$ and $m_{II} = \rho A L_{II}$, then using the laws of balances for momentum

$$m_I v_I + m_{II} v_{II} = (m_I - m_{II}) v_{in}$$

and kinetic energy

$$m_I v_I^2 + m_{II} v_{II}^2 = (m_I + m_{II}) v_{in}^2$$

we should obtain with $m_I / m_{II} = 2$ the quite different rebound velocities of the rods, namely, $\bar{v}_I = -1/3$ and $\bar{v}_{II} = 5/3$. Hence, the wave approach essentially corrects the rod collision phenomenon.

Analysis of the presented examples verifies that all the DMM numerical results exactly coincide with the equivalent analytical solutions. In spite of the different problem formulations, the simple numerical procedure remains the same and only the initial and boundary conditions have to be stated.

1.2 Wave Approach to Finite Element Modeling

1.2.1 Background Equations of the Wave Finite Element Method (WFEM)

1.2.1.1. The method of direct mathematical modeling of wave propagation (DMM) in the form set forth in Sect.1.1. is very effective for solving one-dimensional problems, which treat waves of a single nature (elastic longitudinal or torsion waves in a rod, transverse waves in a string), as it is seen from the previous examples. However, it is difficult to extend it directly to problems dealing with coupled waves of different nature and speed (elastic-plastic, bending-shear) and for 2-D and 3-D cases. For 1-D problems, one approach is to use special discrete-continual models as it will be shown in Chap.3 for rods of elastic-plastic and time-dependent materials, in Chap.5 for bending of elastic rod, and in Chap. 6 for spherical and cylindrical waves. Many mechanical and engineering problems are solved by this means, see Shorr and Mel'nikova (1988) and also other references on this method. Unfortunately, these models have no sufficient generality, especially, in two-and three-dimensional cases.

An alternative approach – the 'wave finite element method' (WFEM), which was proposed by Shorr (1997) and has been developed in Shorr (1999), is also based on direct mathematical modeling but uses more general assumptions, allowing widespread application to arbitrary complex problems. In detail, this approach will be outlined in Chap.7. In this section, WFEM is formulated in conformity to 1-D problems, where its connection with the DMM method is shown.

1.2.1.2. **A.** Consider again the problem of wave propagation in a rod with the loading conditions described in Subsect.1.1.1, but the time interval Δt_i at the calculation step i and corresponding wave speed $c_j = \Delta x_j / \Delta t_i$ for the element j are thus far undetermined. In analyzing wave propagation, the infinitesimally close time instants t_{i-1}^- and t_{i-1}^+ must be distinguished. Assume that at the instant t_{i-1}^- each element j is in a quasi-static state with known velocity $v_{j,0}$ and boundary (nodal) displacements $u_{j,0}^{\pm}$. Then, all the mechanical characteristics of the element at this instant can be determined, namely:

- the strain

$$\varepsilon_{j,0} = (u_{j,0}^+ - u_{j,0}^-) / \Delta x_j, \tag{1.31}$$

- the momentum

$$M_{j,0} = \rho A \Delta x_j v_{j,0}, \tag{1.32}$$

- the kinetic energy

$$K_{j,0} = 0.5 \rho A \Delta x_j v_{j,0}^2, \tag{1.33}$$

- the potential energy of deformation

$$P_{j,0} = 0.5 EA (u_{j,0}^+ - u_{j,0}^-)^2 / \Delta x_j, \tag{1.34}$$

- the forces affecting the element in its nodes

$$F_{j,0}^{\pm} = \frac{\partial P_{j,0}}{\partial u_{j,0}^{\pm}} = \pm EA (u_{j,0}^+ - u_{j,0}^-) / \Delta x_j, \tag{1.35}$$

- the stress

$$\sigma_{j,0} = F_{j,0} / A = E (u_{j,0}^+ - u_{j,0}^-) / \Delta x_j, \tag{1.36a}$$

where the inner force

$$F_{j,0} = F_{j,0}^+ = -F_{j,0}^-. \tag{1.36b}$$

Certainly, the stress may also be determined in the given case as $\sigma_{j,0} = E\varepsilon_{j,0}$.

In the general case, the velocities $v_{j-1,0}$ and $v_{j,0}$ of the neighboring elements $j-1$ and j are distinct and their common node j is not in equilibrium. Therefore, strong discontinuities of the velocities and forces (stresses) arise between these elements at the instant t_{i-1}^-. Such discontinuities immediately (i.e. at the instant t_{i-1}^+) decay to new boundary velocities v_{j-1}^+, v_j^- and stresses $\sigma_{j-1}^+, \sigma_j^-$. The external force applied to the node j can also change arbitrarily. All these quantities remain constant during the interval Δt_i and must therefore satisfy the interelement boundary conditions (1.15).

B. To analyze propagation of the force and velocity waves over the element, we shall use the law of momentum conservation, applying it sequentially to the two phases of the process, which have been considered in Subsect.1.1.1. Replacing in Eqs.(1.2) the wave speed $c = (E/\rho)^{0.5}$ by as yet the undetermined quantities $c_{j-1} = \Delta x_{j-1}/\Delta t_i$ and $c_j = \Delta x_j/\Delta t_i$, we obtain for the *first half* of the interval Δt_i, i.e., until the waves arrive at the central points of the elements,

$$\left.\begin{aligned} v_{j-1}^+ &= v_{j-1,0} + (\sigma_{j-1}^+ - \sigma_{j-1,0})\Delta t_i / \rho\Delta x_{j-1}, \\ v_j^- &= v_{j,0} - (\sigma_j^- - \sigma_{j,0})\Delta t_i / \rho\Delta x_j \end{aligned}\right\}. \tag{1.37}$$

Inserting Eqs.(1.37) into (1.15) we obtain, with $\Delta x = \Delta x_{j-1} = \Delta x_j$, the new boundary velocity

$$v_{j-1}^+ = v_j^- = 0.5[v_{j,0} + v_{j-1,0} + (\sigma_{j,0} - \sigma_{j-1,0} + \sigma_j^*)\Delta t_i / \rho\Delta x]. \tag{1.38}$$

Hence, the boundary stresses are

$$\left.\begin{aligned} \sigma_{j-1}^+ &= 0.5[\sigma_{j,0} + \sigma_{j-1,0} + \sigma_j^* + \rho\Delta x(v_{j,0} - v_{j-1,0})/\Delta t_i], \\ \sigma_j^- &= \sigma_{j-1}^+ - \sigma_j^* \end{aligned}\right\}. \tag{1.39}$$

The boundary quantities between the elements j and $j+1$ are determined with the analogous equations.

During the *second half* of the interval Δt_i, the waves reflected from the central point of the element j arrive at the opposite element ends, while the boundary quantities $\sigma_j^\pm$ and $v_j^\pm$ stay constant. Applying the law of momentum conservation to the whole element j during the entire interval Δt_i, we obtain the new value of the element velocity

$$v_j = v_{j,0} + (\sigma_j^+ - \sigma_j^-)\Delta t_i / \rho\Delta x. \qquad (1.40a)$$

Taking into account Eqs.(1.37), we come again to the second expression (1.17)

$$v_j = v_j^- + v_j^+ - v_{j,0} \qquad (1.40b)$$

with new nodal displacements

$$u_j^\pm = u_{j,0}^\pm + v_j^\pm \Delta t_i. \qquad (1.41)$$

As it has been shown in Subsect.1.1.1, the mechanical states of all the elements at the instant $t_i^- = t_{i-1}^+ + \Delta t_i$ are again quasi-static.

Thanks to the new velocity v_j and the new node displacements $u_j^\pm$, all the mechanical characteristics of the element at instant t_i^- can be expressed in terms of the interval Δt_i using equations analogous to Eqs.(1.31)-(1.36).

***1.2.1.3.* A.** To conclude the governing equation system, it is necessary to determine the time interval Δt_i for each calculation step by applying the law of energy calculation to the whole rod. This law can be taken here in two equivalent forms:

$$\Delta P_{i\Sigma} + \Delta K_{i\Sigma} = \Delta W_{i\Sigma}^* \qquad (1.42a)$$

or

$$P_{i\Sigma} + K_{i\Sigma} = W_{i\Sigma}^*, \qquad (1.42b)$$

were

$$\Delta P_{i\Sigma} = \sum\nolimits_{j=1}^{n} \Delta P_{ij}$$

and

$$\Delta K_{i\Sigma} = \sum\nolimits_{j=1}^{n} \Delta K_{ij}$$

are the changes of potential and kinetic energy of the rod, respectively, during the time interval Δt_i and

$$\Delta W_{i\Sigma}^\bullet = \sum\nolimits_{i=1}^{n+1} \Delta W_{ij}^\bullet$$

is the work of all outer forces applied in nodes during this time. The quantities $P_{i\Sigma}$ and $K_{i\Sigma}$ are the corresponding energy components at the time instant t_i^-, and $W_{i\Sigma}^*$ is the total work introduced into the system during the whole process.

According to Eqs.(1.34) and (1.40)-(1.41), the change of kinetic energy of the element j is

$$\Delta K_{ij} = 0.5\rho A\Delta x(v_j^2 - v_{j,0}^2) = 0.5\rho A\Delta x(v_j + v_{j,0})(v_j - v_{j,0}) = \\ = 0.5A(\sigma_j^+ - \sigma_j^-)(v_j^+ + v_j^-)\Delta t_i. \tag{1.43}$$

Analogously, taking into account Eqs.(1.34) with (1.31) and (1.36), the change of the potential energy of the element is

$$\Delta P_{ij} = 0.5EA[(u_j^+ - u_j^-)^2 - (u_{j,0}^+ - u_{j,0}^-)^2]/\Delta x = \\ = 0.5A(\sigma_j + \sigma_{j,0})(v_j^+ - v_j^-)\Delta t_i. \tag{1.44}$$

The work introduced into the element in a time Δt_i is

$$\Delta W_{ij} = A(\sigma_j^+ v_j^+ - \sigma_j^- v_j^-)\Delta t_i. \tag{1.45}$$

B. Inserting Eqs.(1.43)-(1.45) in Eq.(1.42a), we arrive with $A \neq 0$ and $\Delta t_i \neq 0$ at the equation

$$\sum_{j=1}^{n}(\sigma_j + \sigma_{j,0} - \sigma_j^- - \sigma_j^+)(v_j^+ - v_j^-) = 0. \tag{1.46}$$

In view of Eqs.(1.37) referred to the same element j, we find

$$\sigma_j^- + \sigma_j^+ = (v_j^+ - v_j^-)\rho\Delta x/\Delta t_i + 2\sigma_{j,0}$$

and

$$\sigma_j = \sigma_{j,0} + E\Delta\varepsilon_j = \sigma_{j,0} + E(v_j^+ - v_j^-)\Delta t_i/\Delta x.$$

Therefore, Eq.(1.46) takes the form

$$\sum_{j=1}^{n}\left(\frac{E\Delta t_i}{\Delta x} - \frac{\rho\Delta x}{\Delta t_i}\right)(v_j^+ - v_j^-)^2 = 0. \tag{1.47}$$

It is obvious that Eq.(1.47) is satisfied in the case considered with the constant time interval

$$\Delta t_i = \Delta t = \Delta x\sqrt{\rho/E}, \tag{1.48a}$$

or with the wave speed

$$c = \Delta x/\Delta t = \sqrt{E/\rho} \tag{1.48b}$$

independently of velocities $v_j^{\pm}$ values.

This is in full agreement with the wave theory.

Applying the condition of energy balance to the single element in the form $\Delta P_j + \Delta K_j = \Delta W_j$, each term of Eq.(1.47) must be zero, from where the same expressions (1.48a) and (1.48b) are obtained. In other words, determination of the interval Δt_i based on the law of the energy balance for the whole system provides the energy balance of each element. This is typical for all 1-D problems with waves of a single nature, which will be studied in Chap.2.

1.2.1.4. **A.** In the above, we have dealt with a homogeneous rod of a constant element length Δx. However, the previous result is also true under certain conditions for other models.

Consider the propagation of one-dimensional longitudinal waves in a nonhomogeneous rod of variable cross-section. Assume that the rod is divided into n elements of different length Δx_j; cross-sectional area A_j, Young's modulus E_j, and density ρ_j are averaged over the length Δx_j.

The governing Eqs.(1.37) reduce to

$$\left.\begin{aligned} v^+_{j-1} &= v_{j-1,0} + (F^+_{j-1} - F_{j-1,0})\Delta t_i / \rho_{j-1}A_{j-1}\Delta x_{j-1}, \\ v^-_j &= v_{j,0} + (F^-_j + F_{j,0})\Delta t_i / \rho_j A_j \Delta x_j \end{aligned}\right\}. \quad (1.49a)$$

with inverse

$$\left.\begin{aligned} F^+_{j-1} &= F_{j-1,0} + (v^+_{j-1} - v_{j-1,0})\rho_{j-1}A_{j-1}\Delta x_{j-1} / \Delta t_i, \\ F^-_j &= -F_{j,0} + (v^-_j - v_{j,0})\rho_j A_j \Delta x_j / \Delta t_i \end{aligned}\right\}. \quad (1.49b)$$

Taking into account an external visco-linear friction with constant coefficient of viscosity η_v, we replace friction forces distributed along the halves of $(j-1)$th and jth elements by a point force at the jth node $F^*_{v,j} = -0.5\eta_v(\Delta x_j + \Delta x_{j-1})v_j$, adding it to the given external force F^*_j. Then, the compatibility conditions at the elements' common boundary are

$$\left.\begin{aligned} &v_j = v^+_{j-1} = v^-_j, \\ &F^*_j - 0.5\eta_v(\Delta x_j + \Delta x_{j-1})v_j - F^-_j - F^+_{j-1} = 0 \end{aligned}\right\} \quad (1.50)$$

and Eq.(1.38) reduces to

$$v_j = \frac{\rho_j A_j \Delta x_j v_{j0} + \rho_{j-1}A_{j-1}\Delta x_{j-1}v_{j-1,0} + (F^*_j + F_{j0} - F_{j-1,0})\Delta t_i}{\rho_j A_j \Delta x_j + \rho_{j-1}A_{j-1}\Delta x_{j-1} + 0.5\eta_v(\Delta x_j + \Delta x_{j-1})\Delta t_i}. \quad (1.51)$$

The expressions for the kinetic energy K_j and potential energy P_j are

$$\left.\begin{aligned} K_j &= 0.5\rho_j A_j \Delta x_j v_j^2, \\ P_j &= 0.5E_j A_j (u_j^+ - u_j^-)^2 / \Delta x_j \end{aligned}\right\}. \tag{1.52}$$

By repeating the deduction of Subsect. 1.2.1.3, we are able to find that

$$\sum_{j=1}^{n} A_j \Delta x_j \left(\frac{E_j \Delta t_i}{\Delta x_j} - \frac{\rho_j \Delta x_j}{\Delta t_i} \right) (v_j^+ - v_j^-)^2 = 0. \tag{1.53}$$

If the length Δx_j of the element j is established so that the expression

$$\rho_j \Delta x_j^2 / E_j = \Delta t_i^2 \tag{1.54}$$

becomes constant, Eq.(1.53) is satisfied at $\Delta t_i = \Delta t = \text{const}$ for any values of $v_j^\pm$, and consequently, for all types of loading and boundary conditions. In this case, the wave speed $c_j = \Delta x_j / \Delta t = (E_j / \rho_j)^{0.5}$ is different for each element but the time interval $\Delta t = \Delta x_j / c_j$ is the same. The proposed numerical simulation of wave propagation then leads to an exact description of the problem presented.

If the equality (1.54) is not satisfied, it is necessary to determine the interval Δt_i for the whole system as a minimal positive root of Eq.(1.53), taking into account that the velocities $v_j^\pm$ also depend on this interval.

B. In the general case, the value of Δt_i can be calculated using the following procedure. Let us first evaluate the minimum quantity of the time interval Δt_{min} correlated to the elements dimension of the model under question. For example, this interval for a nonhomogeneous rod is

$$\Delta t_{min} = (\Delta x_j \sqrt{\rho_j / E_j})_{min}.$$

Write the left part of Eq.(1.53) as a function $\Phi(\Delta t)$ and calculate sequentially values of this function $\Phi(\Delta t^{(k)})$ with $\Delta t^{(k)} = \Delta t^{(k-1)} + \alpha \Delta t^{(0)}$, where $\Delta t^{(0)} = \beta \Delta t_{min}$ is a starting value of the argument, $k = 1,2,...$ and $\alpha < 1$, $\beta < 1$. Their recommended quantities are $\alpha \approx 0.4 - 0.5$ and $\beta \approx 0.2 - 0.5$. After the function $\Phi(\Delta t^{(k)})$ changes sign, its first root can be easily determined using an ordinary iteration procedure. It is desirable that the ratio ν of the modulus of the residual energy misbalance $|\Phi(\Delta t_i)|$ to the maximum full energy $[P_{i\Sigma} + K_{i\Sigma}]_{max}$ of the system, which has been calculated at any preceding moment, is small $(\nu \approx 10^{-4} - 10^{-6})$.

1.2.1.5. **A.** In traditional finite-element transient dynamic analysis, the 1-D displacements $u(\xi,t)$ of element points ξ, where $0 \le \xi \le \Delta x$, are expressed in terms of time-varying nodal displacements $u_1(t),\ u_2(t)$ by an interpolation matrix, which does not depend on time. In our case,

$$u(\xi,t)=(1-\xi/\Delta x)u_1(t)+(\xi/\Delta x)u_2(t). \tag{1.55}$$

The point velocity $v(\xi,t)=\partial u(\xi,t)/\partial t$ and acceleration $a(\xi,t)=\partial^2 u(\xi,t)/\partial t^2$ are expressed in terms of nodal velocities and accelerations by the same matrix. The strains are

$$\varepsilon(\xi,t)=\partial u(\xi,t)/\partial\xi=[u_2(t)-u_1(t)]/\Delta x \tag{1.56a}$$

and the stresses for an elastic material

$$\sigma(\xi,t)=E\varepsilon(\xi,t). \tag{1.56b}$$

Making use of Eqs.(1.55)-(1.56), the vectorial correlation of the type (1.35) between the boundary displacements $\mathbf{u}_l(t)$ and forces $\mathbf{F}_k(t)$ affecting the element at its nodes can be written as

$$\mathbf{F}_k(t)=\mathbf{B}_{kl}\mathbf{u}_l(t), \tag{1.57}$$

where $\mathbf{B}_{kl}$ is the stiffness matrix of the element. In our case, $k=1,2$ and the components b_{kl} are

$$b_{11}=b_{22}=EA/\Delta x,\ b_{12}=b_{21}=-EA/\Delta x. \tag{1.58}$$

At any time, all the nodes are assumed to be in equilibrium, allowing the stiffness matrix of the whole mechanical system to be determined (see, e.g., Zienkiewicz 1987).

The given expressions mean that all the above dynamic quantities vary along the element length without jumps, the changes of each nodal parameter immediately propagating over the element with speed of $c=\infty$, and these changes have an instant bearing on the whole mechanical system.

B. In contrast to the transient FEM, the method proposed exploits the correlation (1.55) only for discrete time instants t_{i-1}^- in the form

$$u(\xi,t_{i-1}^-)=(1-\xi/\Delta x)u_1(t_{i-1}^-)+(\xi/\Delta x)u_2(t_{i-1}^-), \tag{1.59}$$

which is not differentiated with respect to time. The same is related to Eq.(1.57). Moreover, the stiffness matrix $\mathbf{B}_{kl}$ is calculated and used separately for each element but not for the whole system because the nodes are not in equilibrium at these moments.

As transient wave propagation is directly calculated on the basis of the conservation laws for mass and momentum, this approach describes strong discontinuities of velocities, strains, forces, and stresses and their propagation with finite wave speed $c = \Delta x / \Delta t$. From this reasoning, the approach may be called 'wave finite element modeling' or '*wave finite element method' (WFEM)*. The method of direct mathematical modeling (DMM) of wave propagation is its particular case for some 1-D problems. Using the procedure to compute time intervals Δt_i from the law of energy conservation, we shall call it the WFEM algorithm. We shall also use the term DMM algorithm for 1-D problems, where the constant time interval Δt can be determined beforehand.

Representation of dynamic processes in the WFEM approach as consecutive change of quasi-static states and transitive dynamic steps is, to some extent, similar to the 'moving pictures principle': object movement, fixed and then viewed at frequent but discrete time instants, is perceived by the observer as a continuous process.

On the other hand, the intermittent transition from one shot to another allows discontinuous patterns of motion to simulate shock waves.

1.2.2 Numerical Examples

1.2.2.1. As it was revealed above, the results of the simulation of one-dimensional wave propagation in nonhomogeneous rods using the WFEM algorithm with the condition (1.54) must coincide exactly with those of the DMM algorithm and analytical solutions.

To confirm this numerically, consider a nonhomogeneous rod of a constant cross section A divided now into n elements of *different* length Δx_j, so that

$$\sum_{j=1}^{n} \Delta x_j = L ,$$

with different material properties E_j, ρ_j.

Equations (1.49), (1.50), and (1.52) with $A_j = A = \text{const}$ and $F_j^* = -0.5\eta_v(\Delta x_{j-1} + \Delta x_j)v_j$ written in dimensionless form yield

$$\bar{v}_j^{\pm} = \bar{v}_{j,0} \pm (\bar{\sigma}_j^{\pm} - \bar{\sigma}_{j,0})\Delta\bar{t}_i / \mu_j \Delta\bar{x}_m, \tag{1.60}$$

$$\bar{v}_j = \bar{v}_{j-1}^{+} = \bar{v}_j^{-} = \frac{\mu_j \bar{v}_{j,0} + \mu_{j-1}\bar{v}_{j-1,0} + (\bar{\sigma}_{j,0} - \bar{\sigma}_{j-1,0})\Delta\bar{t}_i / \Delta\bar{x}_m}{\mu_j + \mu_{j-1} + 0.5\bar{\eta}_v(\bar{l}_j + \bar{l}_{j-1})\Delta\bar{t}_i}, \tag{1.61}$$

and

$$\left.\begin{aligned}\overline{K}_j &= 0.5\mu_j\overline{v}_j^2\Delta\overline{x}_m,\\ \overline{P}_j &= 0.5\overline{E}_j(\overline{u}_j^+ - \overline{u}_j^-)^2/\overline{l}_j\Delta\overline{x}_m\end{aligned}\right\},\tag{1.62}$$

where

$$\begin{aligned}&\mu_j = \overline{\rho}_j\overline{l}_j,\ \overline{\rho}_j = \rho_j/\rho_m,\ \overline{l}_j = \Delta x_j/\Delta x_m,\ \overline{E}_j = E_j/E_m,\\ &\Delta\overline{x}_m = \Delta x_m/L,\ \Delta\overline{t}_i = \Delta t_i/T,\ \Delta x_m = L/n,\ T = L/c_m,\\ &\overline{\eta}_v = \eta_v T/A\rho_m.\end{aligned}\tag{1.63}$$

The quantity T corresponds to the time of wave propagation along the rod with the speed c_m. Since

$$L = \Delta t_i \sum_{j=1}^{n} c_j = c_m T\ ,$$

where $c_j = (E_j/\rho_j)^{0.5}$, then the mean wave speed of the rod is

$$c_m = (\sum_{j=1}^{n} c_j)/n\ .$$

Obviously, $\overline{c}_j = (\overline{E}_j/\overline{\rho}_j)^{0.5}$ and the sum $\sum_{j=1}^{n}\overline{l}_j = n$.

Equation (1.42b) reduces to

$$\sum_{j=1}^{n}(\overline{K}_j + \overline{P}_j) = \sum_{i=1}^{i}\sum_{j=1}^{n}(\overline{\sigma}_j^+\overline{v}_j^+ - \overline{\sigma}_J\overline{v}_j^-)\Delta\overline{t}_i\ .\tag{1.64}$$

Using Eqs.(1.60)-(1.64) with necessary initial and boundary conditions, we can numerically simulate wave propagation in a rod with different contribution of element length $\overline{l}_j$, density $\overline{\rho}_j$, and Young's modulus $\overline{E}_j$.

Under the condition (1.54), the constant time interval is $\Delta t = T/n$ and $\Delta\overline{t} = \Delta\overline{x}_m$, Eq.(1.54) then requiring that

$$\frac{\overline{l}_j^2}{\overline{c}_j^2} = \frac{\overline{\rho}_j\overline{l}_j^2}{\overline{E}_j} = 1.\tag{1.65}$$

Equation (1.65) can be satisfied with different relationship between $\overline{\rho}_j$, $\overline{E}_j$, and $\overline{l}_j$.

***1.2.2.2.* Problem 1.5. A nonhomogeneous free-fixed rod loaded by a suddenly applied constant force (Fig.1.3a).**

When friction forces are absent ($\overline{\eta}_v = 0$), the nondimensional boundary conditions are

$$\left.\begin{array}{l}\bar{\sigma}_1^- = -1,\ \bar{v}_1^- = \bar{v}_{1,0} + (1+\bar{\sigma}_{1,0})\Delta\bar{t}_i / \mu_1\Delta\bar{x}_m, \\ \bar{v}_n^+ = 0,\ \bar{\sigma}_n^+ = \bar{\sigma}_{n,0} - \bar{v}_{n,0}\mu_n\Delta\bar{x}_m / \Delta\bar{t}_i\end{array}\right\}. \quad (1.66)$$

A relative element length $\bar{l}_j$ is chosen from a series of random quantities ξ_j that are adjusted for the two following conditions:

i) A ratio $k = \xi_{max} / \xi_{min}$, where ξ_{max} and ξ_{min} are the maximal and minimal values of quantities ξ_j, can vary in a range $1 \le k \le 2$, indicating that $\xi_{max} - \xi_{min} = 2/3$;

ii) A mean value of ξ_j is

$$k = \frac{1}{n}\sum_{j=1}^{n}\xi_j = 1.$$

The accepted sequence $\xi_j = f(j)$ for n=10 is presented in Table 1.1.

Table 1.1. Series of random quantities accepted for calculations

j	1	2	3	4	5	6	7	8	9	10
ξ_j	0.667	0.888	1.335	1.060	0.920	0.798	1.166	1.050	1.182	0.935

Below, some variants of nonhomogeneity are considered.

a) With $\bar{l}_j = 1,\ \bar{\rho}_j = 1$, and $\bar{E}_j = 1$ we return to a homogeneous rod, and the calculation using the WFEM algorithm gives exactly the same pattern, as shown in Fig.1.4.

b) Let the relative mass $\mu_j = \bar{\rho}_j\bar{l}_j$ of the elements be constant, e.g. $\mu_j = 1$. Then, $\bar{\rho}_j = 1/\bar{l}_j$ and Eq.(1.65) is satisfied by $\bar{E}_j = \bar{l}_j$. This means, for an element to be longer, its density $\bar{\rho}_j$ and elastic compliance $1/\bar{E}_j$ must be lower. In this case, the nonhomogeneity does not influence numerical results, since all parameters of Eqs.(1.60) - (1.66) characterizing this effect take the value 1. Evolution of the stress $\bar{\sigma}_n^+$ versus time $\bar{t}_i$ within three time intervals, taking the length nonuniformity $\bar{l}_j = \xi_j$ according to Table 1.1, is shown in Fig.1.11a. The stress pattern is stable and exactly the same as in Fig.1.4.

c) In more general cases, Eq.(1.63) may be satisfied taking

$$\bar{c}_j = \sqrt{\bar{E}_j / \bar{\rho}_j} = \bar{l}_j,$$

where the individual characteristics of $\bar{E}_j, \bar{\rho}_j$ influence the process of wave propagation. Making use of the same presentation as above the numerical results for $\bar{l}_j = \xi_j, \bar{E}_j = 1, \bar{\rho}_j = 1/\bar{l}_j^2$ are shown in Fig.1.11b and for $\bar{l}_j = \xi_j, \bar{E}_j = \bar{l}_j^2, \bar{\rho}_j = 1$ in Fig.1.11c. The calculations are carried out using both DMM and WFEM algorithms. The stress pattern is very complicated; nevertheless, both algorithms yield the same results.

The stress experiences a few changes from one wave transition along the rod to another. This is due to multiple reflections from inner boundaries between different elements.

As far as the presented solutions for nonhomogeneous rods with step-wise altering parameters satisfy all the laws of elastic solid not only for the whole rod but for each of its element, the results in Fig.1.11 are exact up to calculation errors. Using the double-precision procedure, the latter are not significant. It is noted that the stresses $\bar{\sigma}_n^+$, due to the nature of the algorithm, remain constant during the step $\Delta\bar{t}$, but the curves in Fig.1.11 are smoothed. This is not visible in the graphs for the scale used.

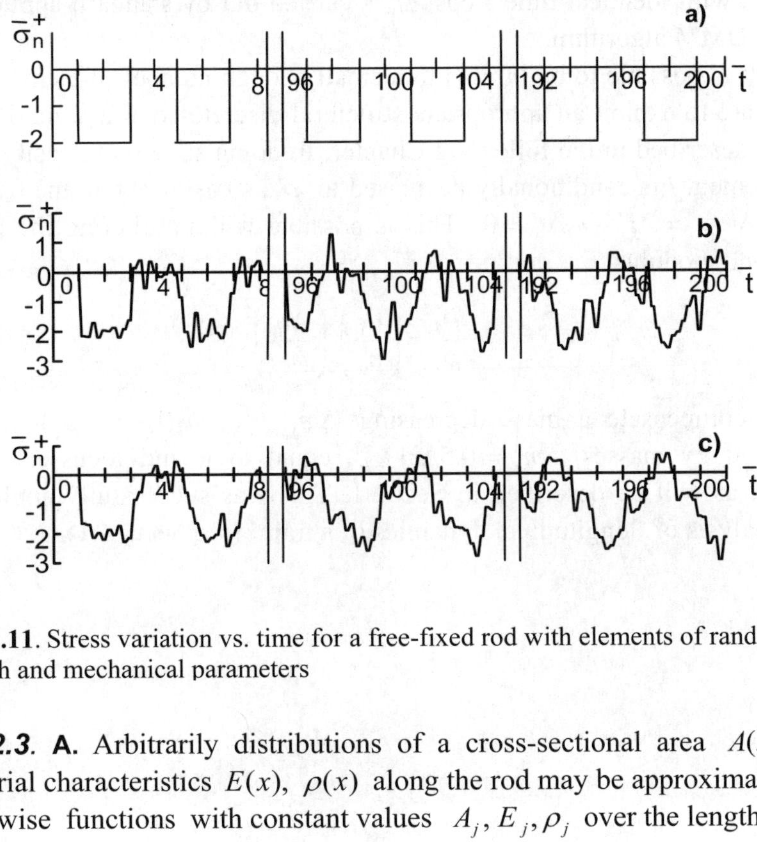

Fig.1.11. Stress variation vs. time for a free-fixed rod with elements of random length and mechanical parameters

***1.2.2.3*. A.** Arbitrarily distributions of a cross-sectional area $A(x)$ and material characteristics $E(x)$, $\rho(x)$ along the rod may be approximated by step-wise functions with constant values A_j, E_j, ρ_j over the length Δx_j.

The time interval $\Delta t_j = \Delta x_j(\rho_j / E)^{0.5}$ needed for an elastic wave to propagate along the length Δx_j may vary from element to element. In this case, it is possible to proceed as follows.

Let us allocate an element Δx_0 with the minimal value of time $\Delta t_0 = \Delta t_{\min}$ and discretize it into sub-elements n_0 of length $\Delta x_0' = \Delta x_0 / n_0$, so that the time of wave passage through each of them decreases up to $\Delta t_0' = \Delta t_0 / n_0$. Divide the time Δt_j of wave transition through other elements by the quantity $\Delta t_0'$ and find for them the increased number n_j of sub-elements that must be taken as an integer of the ratio $\Delta t_j / \Delta t_0'$. The rest of the time is

$$\Delta t_{j,rest} = \Delta t_j - n_j \Delta t_0'. \tag{1.67}$$

Increasing the referent number n_0, the residual times for all the elements can be reduced to acceptable small values. The computation of a system with identical time steps $\Delta t_0'$ is carried out by standard application of the DMM algorithm.

B. It is possible to be limited to a small enough number of elements n_0 if we are to exploit an appropriate structural discrete-continual model of a body, described in the following Chapter. In doing so, a real density ρ_j of the element j is conditionally decreased to ρ_j', so as to obtain the residual time $\Delta t_{j,rest} = \Delta t_j - n_j \Delta t_0' = 0$. This is possible without altering the length Δx_j and modulus E_j, putting

$$\frac{\rho_j'}{\rho_j} = \left(\frac{n_j}{n_0}\right)^2 \left(\frac{\Delta t_0}{\Delta t_j}\right)^2. \tag{1.68}$$

To compensate a mass decreasing $\Delta m_{j,rest} = \Delta m_j(1 - \rho_j' / \rho_j)$, this is replaced by masses $\Delta m_j^{\pm} = 0.5 \Delta m_{j,rest}$, equal to it and focussed in the nodes, as will be described in Sect.2.1. This was successfully applied in the analysis of 'longitudinal dynamics of a train' (see Sect.14.1).

2 Simulation of Simple One-Dimensional Wave Processes

The propagation of elastic waves associated with longitudinal and torsional oscillation of rod-like bodies and transverse oscillation of thin stretched strips, strings, and cables is described mathematically by identical equation system - both in the differential form and by a finite element wave approach. The characteristic parameters are the unique internal force factor and one component of particle velocity. The time-independent speed of wave propagation has a known constant direction, though it may vary on specific elements. The specified generality of given problems allows them to be united in common group of simple one-dimensional wave processes.

2.1 Longitudinal Waves in a Rod

2.1.1 Collision of Rods of Different Sizes and Mechanical Parameters

2.1.1.1. The governing Eqs.(1.49)-(1.51) taken in dimensionless form for a nonhomogeneous rod of a variable cross section with $\Delta t_j = \Delta t = \text{const.}$ are

$$\overline{v}_j^{\pm} = \overline{v}_{j,0} + (\overline{F}_j^{\pm} \mp \overline{F}_{j,0}) / \mu_j \tag{2.1a}$$

with inverse

$$\overline{F}_j^{\pm} = \pm \overline{F}_{j,0} + (\overline{v}_j^{\pm} - \overline{v}_{j,0}) \mu_j . \tag{2.1b}$$

Inserting Eqs.(2.1) into conditions of the node continuity, $\overline{v}_{j-1}^{+} = \overline{v}_j^{-}$, and equilibrium, $\overline{F}_j^{*} - \overline{F}_{j-1}^{+} - \overline{F}_j^{-} - 0.5\overline{\eta}_v(\Delta\overline{x}_{j-1} + \Delta\overline{x}_j)\overline{v}_j^{-} = 0$, implies that the new element velocity and inner force are given by

$$\overline{v}_{j-1}^{+} = \overline{v}_j^{-} = \frac{\mu_j \overline{v}_{j,0} + \mu_{j-1}\overline{v}_{j-1,0} + \overline{F}_j^{*} + \overline{F}_{j,0} - \overline{F}_{j-1,0}}{\mu_j + \mu_{j-1} + 0.5\overline{\eta}_v(\Delta\overline{x}_{j-1} + \Delta\overline{x}_j)} \tag{2.2}$$

$$\bar{v}_j = \bar{v}_j^+ + \bar{v}_j^- - \bar{v}_{j,0}; \ \bar{F}_j = \bar{F}_j^+ - \bar{F}_j^- - \bar{F}_{j,0}, \tag{2.3}$$

with the new node displacements defined by

$$\bar{u}_j = \bar{u}_{j,0} + \bar{v}_j^- \Delta\bar{t}\ , \tag{2.4}$$

where

$$\mu_j = \bar{A}_j \bar{\rho}_j \bar{c}_j = \bar{A}_j \sqrt{\bar{E}_j \bar{\rho}_j}\,, \tag{2.5a}$$

and

$$\begin{gathered} \bar{v} = v/v^o,\ \bar{F} = F/v^o A^o \rho^o c^o,\ \bar{A} = A/A^o,\ \bar{\rho} = \rho/\rho^o,\ \bar{E} = E/E^o, \\ \bar{c} = c/c^o,\ \Delta\bar{x} = \Delta x/x^o,\ \Delta\bar{t} = \Delta t/t^o,\ \bar{u} = u/v^o t^o, \\ \bar{\eta}_v = \eta_v x^o / A^o \rho^o c^o,\ c^o = \sqrt{E^o/\rho^o},\ x^o = c^o t^o. \end{gathered} \tag{2.5b}$$

The reference parameters f^o and necessary boundary conditions must be taken with regard to the concrete problem peculiarity.

The total numerical procedure described in Sect.1.1 does not change.

***2.1.1.2.* Problem 2.1. Collision of two rods (Fig.2.1a).** Let the first colliding rod have length L_j, cross-sectional area A_I, Young's modulus E_I, mass density ρ_I, and velocity v_I, with the corresponding parameters of the second being L_{II}, A_{II}, E_{II}, ρ_{II}, v_{II}, respectively, where $v_{I,0} = v_0$ and $v_{II,0} = -v_0$ The rods are separated into n_I and n_{II} elements, selecting their numbers so that ratio $\bar{n}_{I,II} = n_I / n_{II}$ is sufficiently close to ratio

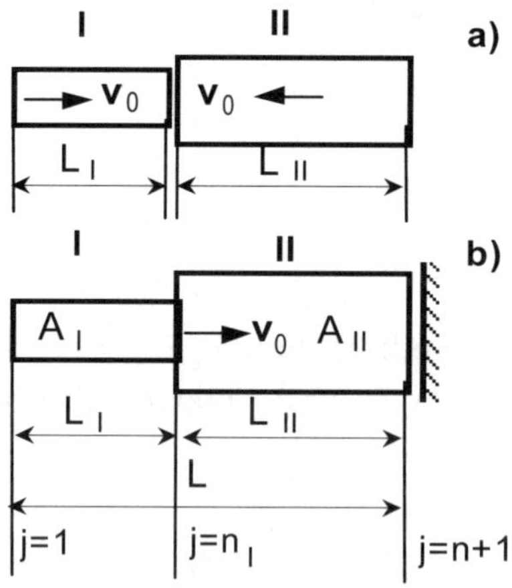

Fig.2.1. Schemes of colliding rods – a) and a suddenly stopped rod –b)

$$\overline{n}_{I,II} = \frac{L_I c_{II}}{L_{II} c_I} = \frac{L_I}{L_{II}}\sqrt{\frac{E_I \rho_{II}}{E_{II}\rho_I}}$$

with

$$\Delta t_I = L_I / c_I n_I = \Delta t_{II} = L_{II} / c_{II} n_{II}.$$

After the collision at the instant $t = 0$ and until the rebound, the both rods may be regarded as a single nonhomogeneous rod with $n = n_I + n_{II}$ elements and $n+1$ element boundaries.

Scaling the dimensionless quantities with the velocity v_0 and with the corresponding parameters of the second rod, the initial conditions of motion for such a united rod are

$$\overline{v}_{j,in} = \begin{cases} 1 & \text{with } 1 \le j \le n_I \\ -1 & \text{with } n_I + 1 \le j \le n; \end{cases}$$

$$\overline{F}_{j,in} = 0 \quad \text{with } 1 \le j \le n; \quad , \tag{2.6a}$$

$$\overline{u}_{j,in} = 0 \quad \text{with } 1 \le j \le n+1$$

with the boundary conditions given by

$$\overline{F}_1^- = 0,\ \overline{F}_n^+ = 0. \tag{2.6b}$$

External forces and damping are absent ($\overline{F}_j^* = 0,\ \overline{\eta}_v = 0$).

The rebound is determined as the instant, at which the sign of the contact force $\overline{F}_{n_I}^+$ becomes positive. The stress in the rod I is $\overline{\sigma}_{j,I} = \overline{F}_j / \overline{A}_I$, with the stress in the rod II $\overline{\sigma}_{j,II} = \overline{F}_J$, and the parameter μ_j

$$\mu_j = \begin{cases} \overline{\rho}_I \overline{A}_I \overline{c}_I & \text{with } 1 \le j \le n_I, \\ 1 & \text{with } n_I + 1 \le j \le n. \end{cases} \tag{2.7}$$

Calculation results referred to some parameter combinations of the colliding rods are presented in Table 2.1.

Here, $\overline{v}_I$, $\overline{v}_{II}$ are the average rebound velocities of the first and the second rod, respectively, and $\overline{\sigma}_{max}$ is the maximal contact stress during the collision. We also denote the ratio of the rod masses as $\overline{m} = \overline{A}_I \overline{\rho}_I \overline{L}_I$ and partial conversion in the rod oscillation energy, as

$$\Delta\overline{K} = 1 - (\overline{m}\overline{v}_I^2 + \overline{v}_{II}^2)/(\overline{m}+1).$$

Table 2.1. Calculation cases for collision of two different rods

No.	Ratio of rod parameters							
	L_i/L_{II}	A_I/A_{II}	ρ_I/ρ_{II}	E_I/E_{II}	c_I/c_{II}	m_I/m_{II}	T_I/T_{II}	n_I/n_{II}
1	1	1	1	1	1	1	1	1/1
2	1	2	1	1	1	2	1	1/1
3	2	1	1	4	2	2	1	1/1
4	$\sqrt[3]{3}\approx$ 1.442	$\sqrt[3]{3}\approx$ 1.442	$\sqrt[3]{3}\approx$ 1.442	3	$\sqrt[3]{3}\approx$ 1.442	3	1	1/1
5	1	1	2	1	$1/\sqrt{2}\approx$ 0.707	2	$\sqrt{2}\approx$ 1.414	17/12
6	$\sqrt{2}\approx$ 1.414	1	$\sqrt{2}\approx$ 1.414	$\sqrt{2}\approx$ 1.414	1	2	$\sqrt{2}\approx$ 1.414	17/12
7	2	1	1	1	1	2	2	2/1
8	$\sqrt{2}\approx$ 1.414	1	$\sqrt{2}\approx$ 1.414	$1/\sqrt{2}\approx$ 0.707	$1/\sqrt{2}\approx$ 0.707	2	2	2/1
9	2	1	2	2	1	4	2	2/1
10	1	1	1	0.25	0.5	1	2	2/1
11	1	1	1.31	131	10	1.31	0.1	1/10
12	20	1	1	1	1	20	20	20/1
13	20	20	1	1	1	400	20	20/1

An elementary non-wave solution for the collision of two rigid bodies having the same velocity values gives

$$\bar{v}_I = (\bar{m} - 3)/(m + 1),$$

$$\bar{v}_{II} = (3\bar{m} - 1)/(m + 1),$$

and corresponds to $\Delta\bar{K} = 0$.

The ratio of the times

$$\bar{T}_I = T_I / T_{II} = L_I c_{II} / L_{II} c_I$$

needed for waves transition through the rods is equal to their oscillation period ratio for the first natural longitudinal mode.

To simulate the ratio quantity $\bar{T}_I = \sqrt{2} \approx 1.414$ with the ratio of integers, we have taken $n_I = 17,\ n_{II} = 12,$ yielding $n_I / n_{II} \approx 1.417$.

Table 2.1. (Cont).

No.	Collision characteristics				Non-wave solution	
	$\overline{v}_I$	$\overline{v}_{II}$	$\overline{\sigma}_{max}$	$\Delta\overline{K}\%$	$\overline{v}_I$	$\overline{v}_{II}$
1	-1	1	1	0	-1	1
2	-0.333	1.667	1.333	0	$-1/3\approx$ -0.333	$5/3\approx$ 1.667
3	-0.333	1.667	1.333	0	$-1/3$	$5/3$
4	0	2	1.500	0	0	2
5	-0.170	1.343	1.172	38	$-1/3\approx$ -0.333	$5/3\approx$ 1.667
6	-0.170	1.343	1.172	38	-1/3	5/3
7	0	1	1	67	-1/3	5/3
8	0	1	1	67	-1/3	5/3
9	-0.333	1.667	1.333	36	1/5=0.2	11/5=2.2
10	-0.778	0.778	0.667	40	-1	1
11	-0.567	1.052	1.858	34	-0.732	1.268
12	0.900	1.000	1.000	18	0.810	2.81
13	0.990	2.810	1.905	0.17	0.990	2.99

Observing the results presented in Table 2.1, one can see that the colliding process depends not only on the mass ratio $\overline{m} = m_I / m_{II}$, but also on the relationship between all others parameters. According to Eq.(2.7), the coefficient μ_j can be represented as

$$\mu_j = \begin{cases} \left(\dfrac{m_I}{m_{II}}\right)\left(\dfrac{T_I}{T_{II}}\right) & \text{with } 1 \le j \le n_I, \\ 1 & \text{with } n_I + 1 \le j \le n. \end{cases} \tag{2.8}$$

Therefore, the time ratio $\overline{T}_I = T_I / T_{II}$ is of decisive importance.

For T_I / T_{II} =1, the kinetic energy does not decrease $(\Delta\overline{K} = 0)$ and the calculation results for the rebound velocities using the DMM algorithm and elementary non-wave solution are the same for different mass ratio m_I / m_{II} (see variants 1-4 of Table 2.1). However, the wave solution enables to obtain the contact stress that remains undetermined using non-wave approach.

For $T_I / T_{II} \neq 1$, results depend both on the ratio m_I / m_{II} and T_I / T_{II} and significantly differ from elementary solutions; moreover, this difference can be fundamental (variants 9 and 12). If the two ratios m_I / m_{II} and T_I / T_{II} are equal, the results are also identical (see variants 5-6, 7-8). The rebound velocities of rods with the same masses, $m_I / m_{II} = 1$, but different time ratio, $T_I / T_{II} \neq 1$, are also identical, however, the velocity is less than that predicted by the elementary solution (variant 10). If the difference of the colliding rod masses becomes very great, the results of wave analysis again approximate the elementary solution (variant 13).

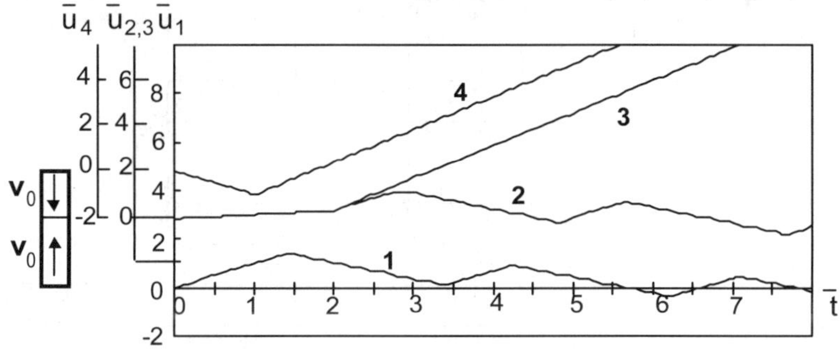

Fig. 2.2. Boundary displacements of colliding rods vs. time

The maximal impact stress $\bar{\sigma}_{max}$ can exceed the stress $\bar{\sigma} = 1$ corresponding to complete stopping of the rod with smaller cross-sectional area, especially, if the difference of rod stiffness (variants 11) or mass (variant 13) is large.

The displacements $\bar{u}_j$ of the rods boundaries against time $\bar{t}$ for variant 6 are shown in Fig.2.2., where indexes $j = 1,2$ relate to the first rod and $j = 3,4$ to the second. The length of the rods is depicted in conditional scale. The post-rebound oscillations of the first rod, whose oscillation period $\bar{T}_{I,0} = 2\bar{T}_I \approx 2.283$ is greater, than oscillation time of the second rod, are clearly seen.

2.1.2 Sudden Stopping of a Rod of a Variable Cross Section

2.1.2.1. **Problem 2.2. Sudden stopping of a rod of two sections.** Consider a problem of sudden stopping of a rod, initially moving in the longitudinal direction with velocity v_0, in application to the rod of two sections (see Fig.2.1b). The material of the rod is assumed to be homogeneous with $\overline{\rho}_I = 1$, $\overline{E}_I = 1$, the section length ratio is taken $L_I / L_{II} = 1$ and cross-sectional area ratio $\overline{A}_I = 0.5$. Under these assumptions, the number of sections elements may be taken as $n_I = n_{II}$, including $n_I = 1$, $n_{II} = 1$, i.e. $n = 2$. The associated initial conditions are

$$\left.\begin{aligned} \overline{v}_{j,in} &= 1 \\ \overline{F}_{j,in} &= 0 \end{aligned}\right\} \text{ with } 1 \le j \le n, \qquad , \qquad \overline{u}_{j,in} = 0 \quad \text{with } 1 \le j \le n+1 \tag{2.9a}$$

with boundary conditions

$$\overline{F}_1^- = 0, \ \overline{v}_n^+ = 0. \tag{2.9b}$$

The variation of the free end displacement $\overline{u}_1 = u_1 c / v_0 L,$ the stress $\overline{\sigma}_{n_I}^+ = F_{n_I}^+ / \overline{A}_I \rho c v_0$ at the right end of the first rod section, and the stress $\overline{\sigma}_n^+ = F_n^+ / \rho c v_0$ at the contact face, with time $\overline{t} = tc / L$, are shown in Fig.2.3 a,b,c, respectively. The dimensionless displacement, time, and

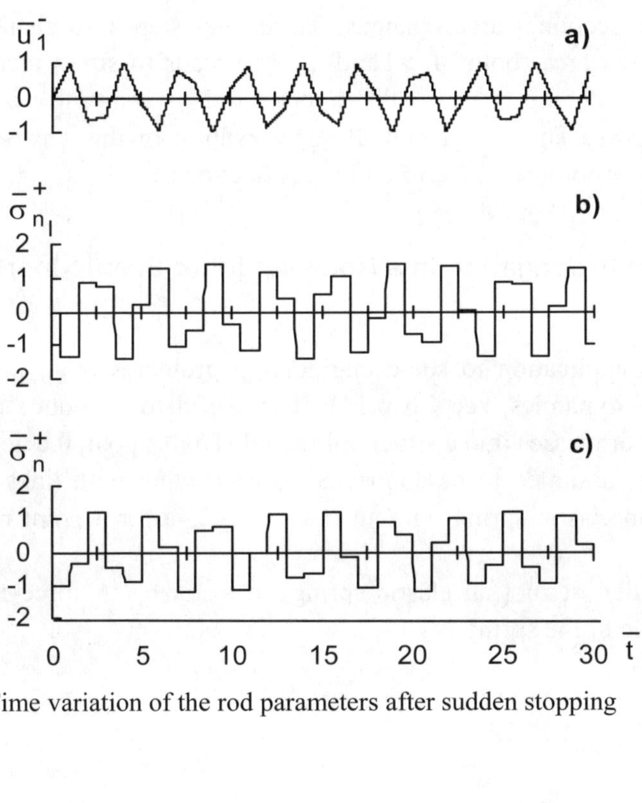

Fig. 2.3. Time variation of the rod parameters after sudden stopping

length $\overline{L}_I = L_I / L$ of the first rod are scaled with the common length of the rod L. To verify the code, calculations are made with $n = 2$ and $n = 50$.

For both numbers of elements the results are the same.

2.1.2.2. A pattern of parameter evolution with mainly oscillation period $\overline{T} \approx 3.25 - 3.30$ is rather complicated. Dimensionless eigenfrequencies $\bar{f} = fL / c$ for a two-step rod with boundary conditions (2.9b) can be determined analytically from the characteristic equation

$$\cos(2\pi\bar{f}) + (1 - \overline{A}_I)\sin(2\pi\bar{f}\overline{L}_I)\sin[2\pi\bar{f}(1 - \overline{L}_I)] = 0,$$

giving the first eigenfrequency of $\bar{f}_1 \approx 0.304$ and oscillation period of $\overline{T}_1 = 1/\bar{f}_1 \approx 3.28$. The pattern then repeats, starting from the time instant $\bar{t} = 23$, although not strongly accurate. The integer 23 is the minimal integer that may be divided to the period $\overline{T}_1$ with minimum remainder.

The calculations for different combinations of the rod sections length $\overline{L}_I$ and area $\overline{A}_I$ allow us to make the following deductions.

First, the maximum stress in a rod with ratio $\overline{A}_I > 1$ always arises at the contact face. Second, the most stressed cross section of a rod with ratio $\overline{A}_I < 1$ may be both the contact face and the weakest section at the point where cross-sectional area changes. Third, any step-wise change of the cross-sectional area (both $\overline{A}_I > 1$ and $\overline{A}_I < 1$) leads to stress increasing in comparison with the stress in the stopped rod of constant cross section where $\overline{\sigma}_{max} = 1$. This is a result of superposition of the waves reflected from the inner boundaries between the rod sections.

2.1.3 Wave Propagation in a Rod with Inner Elastic-Inertial Links

2.1.3.1. In application to some engineering problems (e.g., in the train longitudinal dynamics, see Chap.14), it is useful to introduce additional springs and/or masses into a structural model. To this goal, the neighboring elements are assumed to be connected to each other with links that may constitute an elastic spring without mass (Fig.2.4a) or a point rigid mass (Fig.2.4b).

A. Consider, at first an elastic spring at a node j. A force-elongation characteristic of the spring is

$$\delta_{js} = a_j F_{js}, \tag{2.10}$$

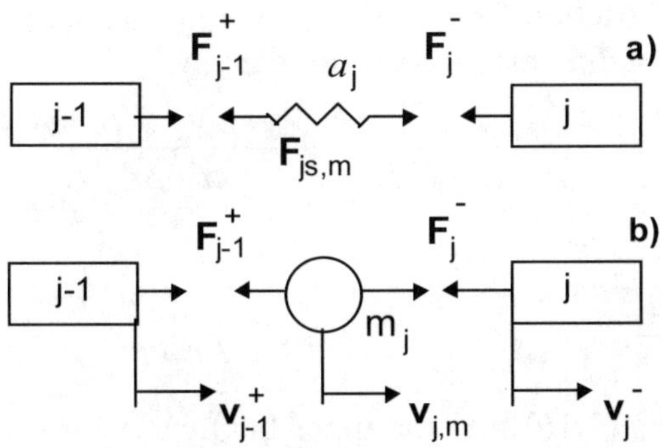

Fig. 2.4. Connection of elements through a spring –a) or rigid mass – b)

where a_j is a spring compliance coefficient.

Let $\delta_{js,0}$ be a spring elongation at the beginning of the current time step, $\Delta\delta_{js}$ its small change within the interval Δt, and $\delta_{js,m}$ the mean value of elongation

$$\delta_{js,m} \approx \delta_{js,0} + 0.5\Delta\delta_{js}. \tag{2.11}$$

The condition of displacement continuity of the elements $j-1$ and j boundary is

$$\Delta\delta_{js} = (v_j^- - v_{j-1}^+)\Delta t. \tag{2.12}$$

The mean elongation determines the mean force

$$F_{js,m} = \delta_{ls,m} / a_s, \tag{2.13}$$

which is transmitted by the spring within the interval Δt.

As the spring force F_{js} is a continuous function in time, while the boundary forces F_{j-1}^+ and F_j^- are discontinuous, the condition of equilibrium for the node j during time interval Δt can be satisfied only in average terms, namely (see Fig.2.4a),

$$F_{j-1}^+ = -F_j^- = F_{js,m}. \tag{2.14}$$

This averaging is of no importance as the number of elements increases. An impulse $F_{j-1}^+\Delta t = -F_j^-\Delta t$ is transmitted through the spring without alteration. It then follows from Eqs.(2.11)-(2.14) that

$$F_{j-1}^+ = -F_j^- = [\delta_{js,0} + 0.5(v_j^- - v_{j-1}^+)\Delta t] / a_j. \tag{2.15}$$

In the absence of friction forces, Eq.(2.15) together with (2.1a) yield a governing equation in dimensionless form, namely

$$\overline{F}_{j-1}^{+} = \frac{\mu_{j-1}\mu_j\overline{\delta}_{js,0} + 0.5[\,\mu_{j-1}\mu_j(\overline{v}_{j.0} - \overline{v}_{j-1,0}) + \mu_{j-1}\overline{F}_{j,0} + \mu_j\overline{F}_{j-1,0}\,]\Delta\overline{t}}{\mu_{j-1}\mu_j\overline{a}_j + 0.5(\mu_{j-1} + \mu_j)\Delta\overline{t}}, \tag{2.16}$$

where

$$\overline{a} = aE^o A^o / x^o, \;\; \overline{\delta} = \delta E^o A^o / x^o F^o. \tag{2.17}$$

It follows from Eq.(2.16) that the inner boundary force $\overline{F}_{j-1}^{+}$ decreases when the spring compliance $\overline{a}_j$ grows. In limit, with $\overline{a}_j \to \infty$, the force $\overline{F}_{j-1}^{+} \to 0$ and the rod 'breaks' into pieces.

B. The effect of a point (concentrated, lumped) mass m_j (Fig.2.4b) may be described using the law of mass momentum conservation during the time interval Δt

$$\Delta v_{jm} = -(F_{j-1}^{+} + F_j^{-})\Delta t / m_j, \tag{2.18}$$

where Δv_{jm} is a change of mass velocity. The small mean velocity Δv_{jm} is given by

$$v_{jm,m} \approx v_{jm,0} + 0.5\Delta v_{jm}, \tag{2.19}$$

where $v_{jm,0}$ is a mass velocity at the beginning of the given step.

As the mass velocity is a continuous function in time, while the element boundary velocities v_{j-1}^{+} and v_j^{-} are discontinuous, the condition of continuity for the node j during time Δt can only be satisfied in the average form

$$v_{j-1}^{+} = v_j^{-} = v_{jm,m}. \tag{2.20}$$

It follows from Eqs.(2.18)-(2.20) that

$$v_{j-1}^{+} = v_j^{-} = v_{jm,0} - 0.5(F_{j-1}^{+} + F_j^{-})\Delta t / m_j. \tag{2.21}$$

Equation (2.21) taken in dimensionless form leads to

$$\overline{v}_{j-1}^{+} = \overline{v}_j^{-} = \frac{\overline{v}_{jm,m} + 0.5(\mu_{j-1}\overline{v}_{j-1,0} + \mu_j\overline{v}_{j,0} + \overline{F}_{j,0} - \overline{F}_{j-1,0})\Delta\overline{t} / \overline{m}_j}{+0.5(\mu_{j-1} + \mu_j)\Delta\overline{t} / \overline{m}_j}, \tag{2.22a}$$

where use has been made of Eq.(2.1b) and

$$\overline{m}_j = m_j / \rho^o A^o x^o. \tag{2.22b}$$

If the mass is absent ($\overline{m}_j = 0$), Eq.(2.22a) coincides with Eq.(2.2) for $\overline{\eta}_v = 0$. When $\overline{m}_j \to \infty$, the element boundary j moves with constant velocity $\overline{v}_{jm,0}$.

C. Equations (2.11), (2.13), and (2.14) yield the change of spring elongation

$$\Delta\overline{\delta}_{js} = 2(\overline{a}_j \overline{F}^+_{j-1} - \overline{\delta}_{js,0}). \tag{2.23}$$

Analogously, Eqs.(2.19) and (2.20) yield the change of mass velocity

$$\Delta\overline{v}_{jm} = 2(\overline{v}^+_{j-1} - \overline{v}_{jm,0}). \tag{2.24}$$

Now, all the other element parameters can be calculated for the current step. New initial values of $\overline{\delta}_{js,0}$ or $\overline{v}_{jm,0}$ for the next step are

$$\left.\begin{aligned} \overline{\delta}_{js,0}(\overline{t} + \Delta\overline{t}) &= \overline{\delta}_{js,0}(\overline{t}) + \Delta\overline{\delta}_{js}, \\ \overline{v}_{jm,0}(\overline{t} + \Delta\overline{t}) &= \overline{v}_{jm,0}(\overline{t}) + \Delta\overline{v}_{jm} \end{aligned}\right\}. \tag{2.25}$$

Because of equalities (2.11) and (2.19), only mean values of the spring force $F_{js,m}$ and mass velocity $v_{jm,m}$ may be considered valid. Choosing the time interval $\Delta\overline{t}$ sufficiently small, a smooth character of spring deformation or mass motion can be described with any desired accuracy. The interval $\Delta\overline{t}$ can be diminished, dividing the elements to sub-elements without changing the number of springs or masses.

Should the need arise, the springs and masses can be connected in a parallel or sequential way.

D. We shall now demonstrate that the condition of energy balance is satisfied in the presence of inner links. For example, a complete energy alteration of the link consisting of a sequential spring/mass connection, within an interval Δt, is given by

$$\Delta E = 0.5m(v_m^2 - v_{m,0}^2) + 0.5a_s(F_s^2 - F_{s,0}^2). \tag{2.26a}$$

Taking into account Eqs.(2.11) to (2.14) and Eqs.(2.19) to (2.21), we obtain from Eq.(2.26a) that

$$\Delta E = -[(F_j^- - F_{s,m})v_j^- - (v_{s,m} - v_{j-1}^+)F_{j-1}^+]\Delta t, \tag{2.26b}$$

where $F_{s,m} = F_{j-1}^+$ and $v_{s,m} = v_j^-$ are the force and velocity at the link point between the spring and the mass.

As $F_{s,m}v_j^- - v_{s,m}F_{j-1}^+ = 0$, the value of energy change ΔE is equal to the work

$$\Delta W = -(F_j^- v_j^- + F_{j-1}^+ v_{j-1}^+)\Delta t$$

induced to the link from adjacent elements.

The energy balance of the links is independent of the magnitude of time interval Δt; therefore, the condition (1.54) for correlation of the calculation parameters is valid for a rod with inner elastic-inertial links, as before.

***2.1.3.2*. Problem 2.3. Wave propagation in a rod with interelement springs.** A rod consists of n elements connected with n-1 springs. A force F_0 is suddenly applied to the first element; the other end of the rod remains free (Fig.2.5a).

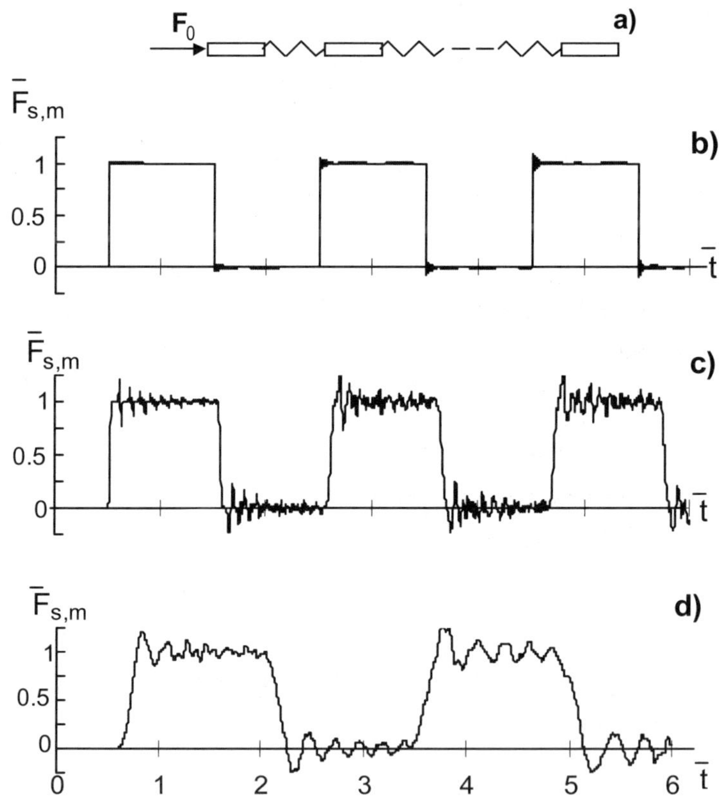

Fig. 2.5. A rod with interelement springs; sketch of the problem –a); force in the middle point of the rod vs. time: b) $\alpha = 10^{-4}$, c) $\alpha = 1$, d) $\alpha = 10^4$

Using $\overline{F} = F / F_0$, Eq.(2.16) yields

$$\overline{F}^{+}_{j-1} = -\overline{F}^{-}_{j} = \frac{\overline{\delta}_{js,0} + 0.5(\overline{v}_{j,0} - \overline{v}_{j-1,0} + \overline{F}_{j,0} + \overline{F}_{j-1,0})\Delta\overline{t}}{\overline{a} + \Delta\overline{t}} \tag{2.27}$$

with $\Delta\overline{t} = 1/n$.

The initial conditions are

$$\left.\begin{array}{ll} \overline{F}_{j.in} = 0, \ \overline{v}_{j,in} = 0, & 1 \le j \le n; \\ \overline{u}_{j,in} = 0, & 1 \le j \le n+1; \\ \overline{\delta}_{js,in} = 0, & 1 \le j \le n-1 \end{array}\right\} \tag{2.28}$$

with the boundary conditions given by

$$\overline{F}^{-}_{1} = -1, \ \overline{F}^{+}_{n} = 0. \tag{2.29}$$

To elucidate the spring influence upon the wave propagation in a rod, calculations are made for different relationships between elements and springs longitudinal compliance, while the compliance of the whole system has not been varied. The summary compliance of all the elements over the length $L = n\Delta x$ is

$$a_{e\Sigma} = L / EA, \tag{2.30a}$$

the summary compliance of all the springs is

$$a_{s\Sigma} = (n-1)a_s, \tag{2.30b}$$

and the total system compliance is $a_\Sigma = a_{e\Sigma} + a_{s\Sigma}$.

To ensure the quantity a_Σ remains constant for varying a_s, the Young's modulus E must be altered. To this end, the modulus E is scaled to the value of E^o for a rod without springs setting $\overline{E} = E / E^o$. Using Eq.(2.17) with $x^o = L$ and putting $\overline{a}_\Sigma = 1$, we obtain $\overline{a}_\Sigma = 1/\overline{E} + (n-1)\overline{a}_s = 1$, and so

$$\overline{E} = 1/[1-(n-1)\overline{a}_s] \tag{2.31}$$

The 'springs-elements' compliance ratio is

$$\alpha == \frac{a_{s\Sigma}}{a_{e\Sigma}} = (n-1)\overline{E}\overline{a}_s = \frac{(n-1)\overline{a}_s}{1-(n-1)\overline{a}_s} \tag{2.32a}$$

The value of $\overline{a}_s$ needed for calculation may be found as a function of α

$$\overline{a}_s = \frac{\alpha}{(1+\alpha)(n-1)}. \tag{2.32b}$$

It is seen, $\overline{a}_s = 0$ with $\alpha = 0$ and $\overline{a}_s = 1/(n-1)$ with $\alpha \to \infty$.

The number of the elements for the following example is $n = 20$, each with 10 sub-elements where springs are absent. Damping is neglected.

The results of calculation as a function of force $\overline{F}_{s,m}$ in the 11th (middle) spring situated at the rod mid-point, with respect to the time $\bar{t}$, for $\alpha = 10^{-4}$, $\alpha = 10^{-1}$, and $\alpha = 10^{4}$ are shown in Fig. 2.5b,c,d. With $\alpha = 10^{-4}$ (Fig.2.5b), the wave front of the force passes the rod mid-point practically without distortion, as for a compact elastic rod in the absence of strings. The wave pattern with $\alpha = 10^{4}$ (Fig.2.5d) is very close to the analytical solution for a system of rigid bodies connected with elastic springs, $\alpha \to \infty$, a problem considered by Zhukovsky in 1905 (published in 1937). In this case, the maximal oscillation period increases from $\overline{T} = 2$ for a free-free continuous rod, to $\overline{T} \approx 3$. This approximates $\overline{T} = \pi$, as it might be for oscillating rigid body with mass $\overline{m} = 0{,}5$ and string compliance $\overline{a} = 0.5$. The minimal visible period $\overline{T}_{min} \approx 0.24$ is also sufficiently close to the oscillation period of the single element of the mass $\overline{m}_e = 1/n$ connected with neighboring immobile elements through two springs of compliance $\overline{a} = 0.5/(n-1)$. This gives for $n = 20$ the value $\overline{T} = 2\pi[2n(n-1)]^{-0.5} \approx 0.23$.

Figure.2.5c illustrates the intermediate situation that is rather difficult for analytical analysis. The DMM algorithm provides a very simple way to solve this problem, previously exploited by Kapluniva (1990) to investigate the train longitudinal dynamics.

2.2 Torsional Waves in a Rod

2.2.1 Sudden Stopping of a Rotating Shaft

2.2.1.1. It is known that one-dimensional longitudinal and torsional deformations of an elastic rod of circular cross section are described by a similar set of equations (see, e.g. Steidel 1971). This allows us to extend the algorithms obtained for analysis of longitudinal wave propagation upon the torsional waves. Correlation between the corresponding parameters applied to our notation is presented in Table 2.2. (Explanation of the string parameters will be given in Sect. 2.3.).

In particular, Eq.(2.5a) takes the form

$$\mu_j = \bar{J}_{pj}\bar{\rho}_j\bar{c}_j = \bar{J}_{pj}\sqrt{\bar{G}_j\bar{\rho}_j}, \tag{2.33}$$

where J_{pj} is a polar second moment of cross section area, G_j is the shear modulus, and c_j is the torsional wave speed

Table 2.2 Analogous parameters of simple 1-D wave processes

Wave type		Longitudinal in a rod	Torsional in a rod	Lateral in a string
Parameters	Load	Outer force F^*	Outer torque M^*	Outer force Q^*
		Inner force F_j	Inner moment M_j	Inner force Q_j
	Deformation	Strain ε_j	Relative angle θ_j	Slope angle φ_j
	Displacement	Linear u_j	Angular φ_j	Transversal y_j
	Velocity	Linear v_j	Angular ω_j	Transversal v_j
	Geometry	Area A_j	Polar moment of area J_{pj}	Area A_j
	Stiffness	Young's modulus E_j	Shear modulus G_j	Tension force N

$$c_j = \sqrt{G_j / \rho_j} \tag{2.34}$$

The same approach can be approximately employed to analyze torsion wave propagation in a rod of non-circular cross section. In this case, the torsional wave speed is determined as

$$c_j = \sqrt{\frac{G_j I_j}{\rho_j J_{pj}}}, \tag{2.35}$$

where I_j is a geometrical stiffness of the cross section in torsion.

***2.2.1.2.* Problem 2.4. Sudden stopping of a rotating shaft of two sections.** Let a shaft consisting of two step-wise changed sections be loaded by a torque M_0 and rotate with angular velocity ω_0 (Fig. 2.6a); the sections are separated into n_I and n_{II} elements. The right end of the shaft is suddenly brought to a halt at the instant $t = 0$.

The initial conditions are

$$M_{j,0} = M_0,\ \omega_{j,0} = \omega_0,\ 1 \le j \le n, \tag{2.36}$$

where $n = n_I + n_{II}$.

Taking the initial angular displacement at the left end $\varphi_{1,0}=0$, we get

$$\varphi_{j,0}=\begin{cases}\dfrac{M_0(j-1)\Delta x}{GJ_{pI}}, & 1\le j\le n_I+1,\\[2ex] \dfrac{M_0}{G}\left[\dfrac{n_j}{J_{jI}}+\dfrac{(j-n_I-1)}{J_{pII}}\right]\Delta x, & n_I+1\le j\le n+1\end{cases}. \tag{2.37}$$

The initial tangential stress at the shaft surface is $\tau_{j,in}=0.5M_0d_j/J_{pj}$, where d_j is the shaft diameter of the corresponding section.

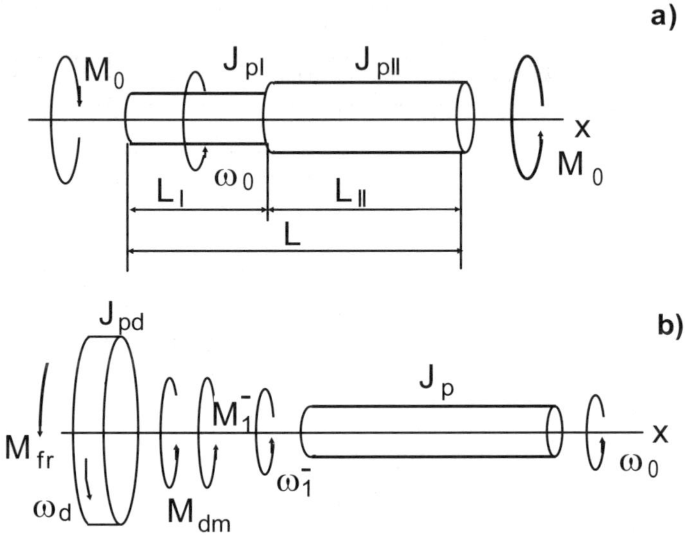

Fig. 2.6. Sketches of rotating shafts: a) two sections; b) disk/shaft connection

The boundary conditions are

$$M_1^-=-M_0,\ \omega_n^+=0. \tag{2.38}$$

If one makes the inversion $A_I\to J_{pI}$, $A_{II}\to J_{pII}$, $E\to G$, and takes moment M instead of force F, the problem, in the case $M_0=0$, entirely coincides with the analogous problem described at Subsect.2.1.2. However, the stresses $\overline{\sigma}_{nI}^+$ indicated in Fig.2.3 must be changed to $\overline{\tau}_{nI}^+=(\overline{\sigma}_{nI}^+)^{3/4}$.

In the case $M_0\ne 0$, the shock stresses due to the shaft stopping are algebraically summarized with the initial stresses.

If the direction of the initial moment and rotation velocity are contrast ($M_0 < 0$), the maximum stress at the front of the leading wave increases. With $M_0 > 0$, the static and dynamic stresses are at first subtracted but later, due to inner reflections of the waves, the maximum stress neglecting damping becomes greater than the static.

2.2.2 Setting a Disk in Motion by Sudden Connection with Rotating Shaft

2.2.2.1. **Problem 2.5. Impact setting a disk in motion.** Let a disk, initially at rest, start to rotate at $t = 0$ as the result of sudden contact with a rotating shaft of angular velocity ω_0 (Fig. 2.6b).

The initial conditions for the disk and the shaft are, respectively,

$$\omega_d = 0, \quad M_{j,0} = 0, \ \omega_{j,0} = \omega_0, \quad 1 \le j \le n. \tag{2.39}$$

The boundary conditions of the left end of the shaft can be established from the appropriate set of equations from Subsect.2.1.3.1.B, modified for torsion. In doing so, we obtain:

a) From the law of angular momentum (moment of momentum) conservation for the disk within an interval Δt:

$$J_{pd}\Delta\omega_d = (M_{dm} - \eta_{\omega d}\omega_{dm})\Delta t\,; \tag{2.40a}$$

b) From the conditions of kinematical and dynamic 'disk-shaft' connection at the point $j = 1$:

$$\left.\begin{aligned} &\omega_{dm} \approx \omega_{d0} + 0.5\Delta\omega_d = \omega_1^-, \\ &M_{dm} = -M_1^- \end{aligned}\right\}; \tag{2.40b}$$

c) From the law of angular momentum conservation for the first shaft element

$$M_1^- = -M_{1,0} + \rho J_p c(\omega_1^- - \omega_{1,0})\,. \tag{2.40c}$$

In the above, J_{pd} is the moment of disk inertia related to rotation axis, $\eta_{\omega d}$ is the coefficient of outer linear viscous friction of the disk, ω_{d0} is the value of the disk angular velocity at the beginning of current time step, and ω_{dm} and M_{dm} are the mean quantities of disk velocity and torque affected the disk by the shaft, respectively.

Equations (2.40) yield in dimensionless terms

$$\left.\begin{aligned} \Delta\overline{\omega}_d &= \frac{\overline{M}_{1,0}+\overline{\omega}_{1,0}-(1+\overline{\eta}_{\omega d})\overline{\omega}_{d0}}{\overline{J}_{pd}+0.5(1+\overline{\eta}_{\omega d})\Delta\bar{t}}\Delta\bar{t}, \\ \overline{\omega}_1^- &= \overline{\omega}_{d0}+0.5\Delta\overline{\omega}_d, \\ \overline{M}_1^- &= -\overline{M}_{1,0}+\overline{\omega}_1^- -\overline{\omega}_{1,0}, \\ \overline{\omega}_d &= \overline{\omega}_{d0}+\Delta\overline{\omega}_d \end{aligned}\right\}, \tag{2.41}$$

where

$$\overline{\omega}=\frac{\omega}{\omega_0},\ \overline{M}=\frac{M}{\rho J_p c\omega_0},\ \overline{J}_{pd}=\frac{J_{pd}}{\rho J_p L},\ \overline{\eta}_{\omega d}=\frac{\eta_{\omega d}}{\rho J_p c},\ \Delta\bar{t}=\frac{\Delta tc}{L}=\frac{1}{n}. \tag{2.42}$$

We remark that the disk remains immobile if $\overline{J}_{pd}\to\infty$ or $\overline{\eta}_{\omega d}\to\infty$, and the system has free end conditions with $\overline{J}_{pd}=0$ and $\overline{\eta}_{\omega d}=0$.

Simulation of smooth change of the disk velocity is provided using $\Delta\overline{\omega}_d \ll 1$, which requires the number of elements be

$$n \gg 1/2\overline{J}_{pd}. \tag{2.43}$$

The angular velocity at the right end of the shaft is assumed constant, so the appropriate boundary condition is given by

$$\overline{\omega}_n^+ = 1. \tag{2.44}$$

2.2.2.2. The disk angular velocity $\overline{\omega}_d$ and the torque $\overline{M}_d \approx \overline{M}_{dm}$, implied to the disk from the shaft, are represented in Fig.2.7 against the dimensionless time $\bar{t}=tc/L$.

Diagrams of Fig.2.7a,b are calculated in the absence of damping, diagrams of Fig.2.7c,d are referred to the friction factor of $\overline{\eta}_{\omega d}=2$. For the number of elements $n=50$, the disk/shaft moment inertia ratio is taken $\overline{J}_{pd}=2$ that satisfies Eq.(2.43).

Superposition of two processes is clearly seen

The long oscillation period of the curves in Fig. 2.7a,b is close to the theoretical value of the first torsion eigenmode period $\overline{T}_0$ of a rod with rigid disk at one end and clamped at the other. This period is determined as the minimal root of the characteristic equation $\nu\tan\nu=1/\overline{J}_{pd}$, with where $\nu=0.653$ and $\overline{T}_0=2\pi/\nu\approx 9.62$. The spike peaks are repeated over the interval $\Delta\overline{T}=2$ needed for a wave to pass along the shaft and back.

With moderate external friction of the disk, its velocity approximates that of the shaft (Fig.2.7c) and the mean value of the torque becomes equal to the friction moment $\overline{M}_d \approx \overline{\eta}_{\omega d}\overline{\omega}_d$; in our case, $\overline{M}_d \approx 2$ (Fig.2.7d). How-

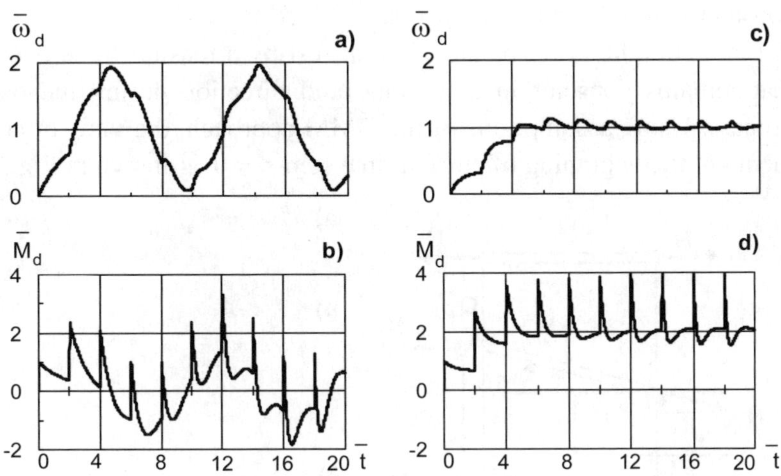

Fig.2.7. Angular velocity –a), c) and torque –b), d) of a disk set in motion by a rotating shaft; a) and b) $\overline{\eta}_{\omega.d} = 0$; c) and d) $\overline{\eta}_{\omega.d} = 2$

ever, the spike peaks remain visible, as before, because the inner friction in the shaft is not taken here into account.

The strong external friction does not allow the disk to rotate, and the shaft deformations and stresses, with the second condition (2.39b), must increase with no limit.

2.3 Transverse Waves in Strings and Cables

2.3.1 Waves in a String Stretched by a Constant Force

2.3.1.1. The background equations of the vibration for thin taut strings (cables, strips, lines etc.) are usually based on the following concepts:

a) The flexural stiffness of a string weakly influences transverse oscillations and may by neglected. Then, the bending moment from all the loads must be put to zero at any point of the string, i.e., the resulting force must be always directed along the tangent to its deformed axis.

b) The change of the string length associated with elastic elongation a few affects transversal oscillations and may be also neglected.

c) Transverse displacements are assumed to be small and the tension force N determined from static equilibrium conditions may be taken as constant within a dynamic process.

Let a straight string be stretched at rest by a tension force N (Fig.2.8a) that remains constant in magnitude and direction during the oscillation process. Using assumptions of the DMM approach, the view of string element j at the beginning of current time step $t_1 = 0$ is shown in Fig.2.8b.

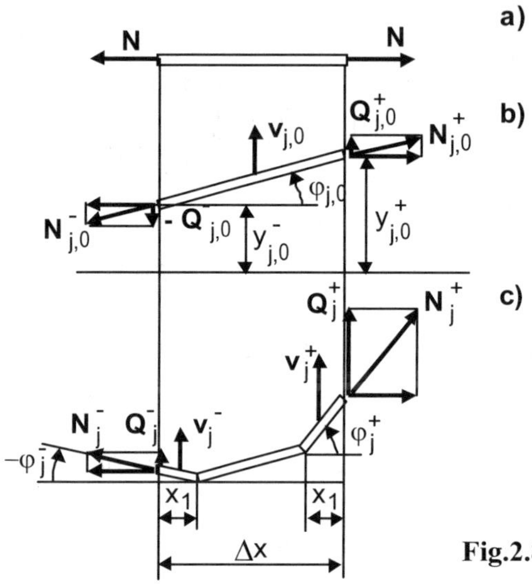

Fig.2.8. The DMM model of a taut string

Here, $y^{\pm}_{j,0}$ are the transverse deflections of element boundaries,

$$\varphi_{j,0} = \frac{y^{+}_{j,0} - y^{-}_{j,0}}{\Delta x} \tag{2.45}$$

is the slope of the string deformed axis, $Q^{\pm}_{j,0}$ are the inner transverse forces affecting the element, $v_{j,0}$ is the transverse element velocity, and $N_{j,0}$ is the resulting tension of the element. (In Fig.2.8 real correlation of forces $Q^{\pm}_{j}$ and N is significantly disturbed).

The equilibrium conditions, with a small slope of the element axis, yield

$$N_{j,0} \approx N = \text{const}, \quad Q^{+}_{j,0} = -Q^{-}_{j,0} = Q_{j,0} \approx N\varphi_{j,0} \tag{2.46}$$

i.e., the tension force N plays the role of element stiffness in transverse deformation.

The pattern of element deformation at any instant $0 < t_1 \le \Delta t$ under transverse wave propagation is demonstrated in Fig.2.8c. Assuming the wave speed c be constant, the length of the perturbed zones is $x_1 = ct_1$.

The following equations must be satisfied within time interval Δt :

i) The law of transverse momentum conservation

$$Q_j^{\pm} \mp Q_{j,0} = \rho c A(v_j^{\pm} - v_{j,0}), \tag{2.47}$$

where ρ is the mass density and A is cross-sectional area.

ii) The condition of string continuity

$$v_j^{\pm} - v_{j,0} = \pm c(\varphi_j^{\pm} - \varphi_{j,0}) . \tag{2.48}$$

iii) The condition of string moment equilibrium in the deformed state $Q_j^{\pm} = \pm N \varphi_j^{\pm}$, or taking into account Eq.(2.46),

$$Q_j^{\pm} \mp Q_{j,0} = \pm N(\varphi_j^{\pm} - \varphi_{j,0}). \tag{2.49}$$

According to Eqs.(2.47)-(2.49), transverse disturbances propagate along the stretched string with the speed

$$c = \sqrt{N / \rho A}. \tag{2.50}$$

Conditions of $(j-1)$th and jth elements connection are

$$\left. \begin{aligned} Q_{j-1}^{+} + Q_j^{-} &= F_j^{*}, \\ v_{j-1}^{+} &= v_j^{-} \end{aligned} \right\}, \tag{2.51}$$

where F_j^{*} is an external lateral force implied to the string at the node j

Equations (2.45)-(2.51) are entirely identical to background equations of longitudinal and torsional wave dynamics of a rod, for which all the previous algorithms of this Chapter for solving the analogous string problems may be used. Correlation of the corresponding parameters was presented above in Table 2.2.

***2.3.1.2.* Problem 2.6. Oscillation of a string under impulse loading.** Consider a two-side fixed in the lateral direction string loaded at time instant $t = 0$ by distributed impulse forces so that it obtains the initial uniform velocity v_{in} (Fig.2.9a). Then, the initial conditions in nondimensional

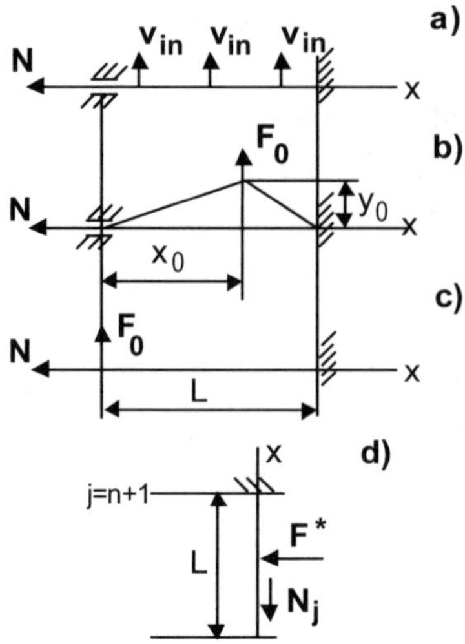

Fig.2.9. Schemes of string systems under consideration

form are

$$\left.\begin{aligned}\overline{v}_{j,in} &= 1,\\ \overline{Q}_{j,in} &= 0\end{aligned}\right\}, \quad 1 \le j \le n,$$
$$\overline{y}_{j,in} = 0, \qquad 1 \le j \le n+1, \tag{2.52a}$$

with the boundary conditions taking the form

$$v_1^- = 0, \; \overline{v}_n^+ = 0, \tag{2.52b}$$

where $\overline{v} = v / v_{in}$, $\overline{Q} = Q / \rho c A v_{in}$, and $\overline{y} = yc / L v_{in}$.

Damping is neglected.

The variations of the deflection $\overline{y}$ and transverse force $\overline{Q}$ along the axial location $\overline{x} = x / L$ for some selected values of time $\overline{t} = tc / L$ are plotted in Fig.2.10a,b.

Thanks to the wave departure from the fixed ends, the deflection curve takes a trapezoidal form with stopped ramp sides. The deflection line becomes triangular when the waves meet at the string mid-point at $\overline{t} = 0.5$. Thereafter, the deflections begin decreasing. At the time $\overline{t} = 1$ the string is entirely unloaded but its velocity is $\overline{v} = -1$ that initiates string deformation in the opposite direction, and so forth.

The trapezoidal-triangular form of oscillating string deflection was studied analytically (Krupenin 1985) and was observed experimentally (Krupenin and Veprick 1985).

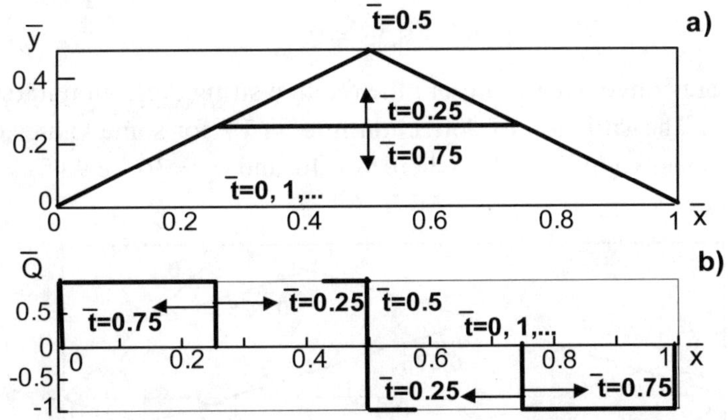

Fig.2.10. String deflections – a) and transverse forces – b) affected by evenly distributed initial velocity

2.3.1.3. **Problem 2.7. A suddenly released deformed string.** A static point force F_0 loads a string (fixed as in above) at any node j_0+1 corresponding to the point $x_0 = j_0 L/n$ (see Fig.2.9b). One can readily check that the reactions of supports, equal to lateral boundary forces at the string ends, are

$$Q_1^- = -F_0(L-x_0)/L, \quad Q_n^+ = -F_0 x_0/L \tag{2.53a}$$

and the maximum static deflection is

$$y_0 = F_0 x_0 (L-x_0)/NL. \tag{2.53b}$$

Accordingly, the initial static conditions in nondimensional form are

$$\begin{aligned} &\overline{v}_{j,in} = 0, \qquad 1 \le j \le n; \\ &\overline{Q}_{j,in} = \begin{cases} 1-\overline{x}_0, & 1 \le j \le j_0 \\ -\overline{x}_0, & j_0+1 \le j \le n; \end{cases} \\ &\overline{y}_{j,in} = \begin{cases} (1-\overline{x}_0)(j-1)/n, & 1 \le j \le j_0+1, \\ \overline{x}_0(n-j+1)/n, & j_0+1 \le j \le n+1, \end{cases} \end{aligned} \tag{2.54}$$

where

$$\overline{Q} = Q/F_0, \ \overline{v} = v\rho c A/F_0, \ \overline{y} = yN/F_0 L, \ \overline{x} = x/L, \ \overline{x}_0 = j_0/n,$$

and $\overline{y}_0 = \overline{x}_0(1-\overline{x}_0)$.

At the time $t=0$, the force F_0 is suddenly removed and the released string begins to freely oscillate under boundary conditions

$$\overline{v}_1^- = 0, \overline{v}_n^+ = 0. \tag{2.55}$$

It is more convenient to present the relative string deflection in the form $\widetilde{y} = y / y_0$. The variation of deflection line $\widetilde{y}(\overline{x})$ for some values of time $\overline{t} = tc / L$ is shown in Fig.2.11, where $n = 40$ and $j_0 = 30$, e.g. $\overline{x}_0 = 0.75$.

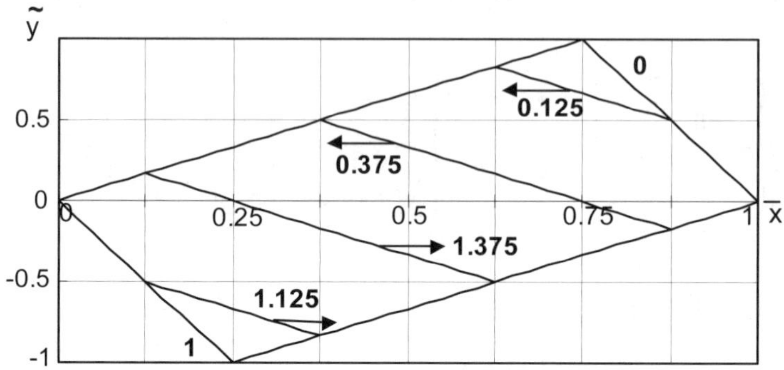

Fig.2.11. String deflections after release of the static force for instants $\overline{t}$ denoted by indexes

With $\overline{x}_0 > 0.5$ and $0 < \overline{t} < 1$, the deflection wave travels towards the point $\overline{x} = 0$, changing the sign of maximal deflection. Then, the wave returns to its initial position, etc. Smirnov (1934) proposed an original graphical acceptance to build the deformed deflection line.

2.3.1.4. **Problem 2.8. Impulse loading of a one-side fixed string.** A short-time sinusoidal impulse is applied to the free end of a one-side fixed string (Fig.2.9c) starting at the time $t = 0$. The initial conditions are now

$$\left.\begin{array}{ll} v_{j,in} = 0, \quad Q_{j,in} = 0, & 1 \le j \le n; \\ y_{j,in} = 0, & 1 \le j \le n+1 \end{array}\right\} \tag{2.56}$$

with the boundary conditions given by

$$Q_1^- = \begin{cases} F_0 \sin 2\pi \dfrac{(i-0.5)}{(i_* + 0.5)}, & i = 1,2,\ldots,i_* + 1 \\ 0, & i > i_* + 1 \end{cases} \quad . \tag{2.57}$$

$$v_n^+ = 0$$

Here, i is a step index and i_* is a number of steps of the sinusoidal impulse duration assumed to be significantly less than the number of elem-

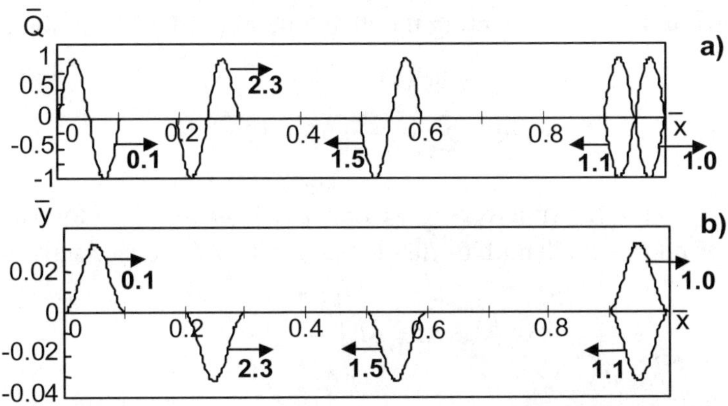

Fig. 2.12. Wave disposition of the transverse forces – a) and deflections – b) for instants depicted next to the curves

ents, $i_* << n$. Disposition of the inner force $\overline{Q}(\overline{x},\overline{t}\,)$ and the deflection $\overline{y}(\overline{x},\overline{t}\,)$ waves for some time instants $\overline{t} = tc / L$ with $n = 500$ and $i_* = 50$ is depicted in Fig.2.12a,b, where $\overline{Q} = Q / F_0$ and $\overline{y} = yN / LF_0$.

The single sinusoidal force and deflection waves travel along the string with the same constant speed c without distortion (in the absence of damping). The force wave reflects from the fixed end without altering, whereas the deflection wave changes in sign. The waves behavior reverses under reflection from the free end as it can be seen from the curves corresponding to the time $\overline{t} = 2.3$.

In the course of wave contact with the right fixed end, the maximum reaction force $\overline{Q}_n^+$ is, as usual, double that of the amplitude of the applied force $\overline{F}_0 = 1$.

2.3.2 Waves in a Cable Stretched by its Own Weight

2.3.2.1. In some cases, the tension force N may vary along the cable length, in particular, when the cable is hung vertically (Fig.2.9d).

Regarding the cable weight as the external distributed force, the weight $N_{jw}^{\pm}$ of each half of the element can be referred to its corresponding boundary (Fig.2.13), namely,

$$N_{jw}^{\pm} = 0.5 \rho g A \Delta x_j \,, \tag{2.58}$$

where g is acceleration due to gravity.

The tension force N_j affecting the *j*th element, indexed from the bottom, is

$$N_j = \rho g A(\sum_{k=1}^{j-1} \Delta x_k + 0.5\Delta x_j). \tag{2.59}$$

As the variable transverse wave speed according to (2.50) is $c_j = (N_j / \rho A)^{0.5}$, the length of *j*th element, with Δt =const, is given by

$$\Delta x_j = c_j \Delta t = \Delta t \sqrt{\frac{N_j}{\rho A}}. \tag{2.60}$$

Evidently, the sum $\sum_{j=1}^{n} \Delta x_j = L.$

The above set of equations in nondimensional terms is

$$\overline{N}_j = 0.5\Delta\overline{x}_j + \overline{x}_j,\ \Delta\overline{x}_j = \Delta\overline{t}\sqrt{\overline{N}_j},\ \overline{x}_j = \sum_{k=1}^{j-1}\Delta\overline{x}_k,\ \sum_{j=1}^{n}\Delta\overline{x}_j = 1, \tag{2.61a}$$

where

$$\overline{x}_j = x_j / L,\ \overline{t} = tc_0 / L,\ \overline{N}_j = N_j / \rho g A L,\ c_0 = \sqrt{gL}. \tag{2.61b}$$

Equations (2.61a) yield a quadratic equation in $\Delta\overline{x}_j$

$$\Delta\overline{x}_j^2 - 0.5\Delta\overline{t}^2\Delta\overline{x}_j - \Delta\overline{t}^2\overline{x}_j = 0. \tag{2.62}$$

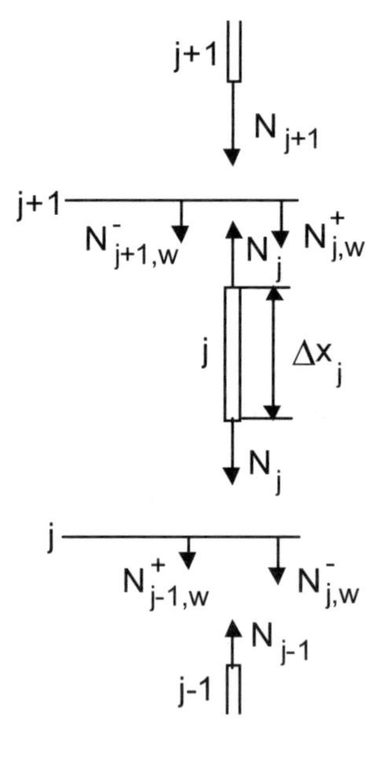

Fig.2.13. Calculated model of a cable stretched by its own weight

Writing Eq.(2.62) for indexes j and $j+1$ and subtracting one from another, we get, after some simple algebraic transformations,

$$\Delta\bar{x}_{j+1} - \Delta\bar{x}_j = 0.5\ \Delta\bar{t}^2,$$

implying that

$$\Delta\bar{x}_j = 0.5\Delta\bar{t}^2 j. \tag{2.63}$$

The whole cable dimensionless length is

$$\bar{L} = \sum_{j=1}^{n} \Delta\bar{x}_j = 0.25n(n+1)\Delta\bar{t}^2 = 1, \tag{2.64}$$

where

$$\Delta\bar{t}^2 = 4/n(n+1) \tag{2.65}$$

and

$$\Delta\bar{x}_j = 2j/n(n+1). \tag{2.66}$$

The variable tension force in the jth element may be found as

$$\bar{N}_j = \frac{\Delta\bar{x}_j^2}{\Delta\bar{t}^2} = \frac{j^2}{n(n+1)}, \tag{2.67}$$

and the position of the $(j+1)$th node between the elements j and $j+1$ is

$$\bar{x}_{j+1} = \sum_{k=1}^{j} \Delta\bar{x}_k = \frac{j(j+1)}{n(n+1)}. \tag{2.68}$$

As the elements length Δx_j and transverse wave speed

$$\bar{c}_j = j/\sqrt{n(n+1)} \tag{2.69}$$

are variable, the equations of Subsect.2.1.1.1 for a nonhomogeneous rod, represented in the string dynamics terms (see Table 2.2), may be exploited. According to Eq.(2.5a), $\mu_j = \bar{c}_j$.

The tension force at the free bottom end of the cable is

$$\bar{N}_{1w}^{-} = 0.5\Delta\bar{x}_1 = [n(n+1)]^{-1}.$$

With $n >> 1$ we note that $\bar{N}_{1w}^{-} << 1$; heretofore, the condition of free end is simulated quite well.

***2.3.2.2.* Problem 2.9. A freely hung cable affected by a short-time force.** A lateral short-time point force F^*, applied to the cable mid-point (see Fig.2.9d) affects a cable described above. We denote its value scaled by the cable weight as $\overline{F}^* = F^* / \rho g A L$. The initial conditions for the elements inner force $\overline{Q}_{j,in}$, velocity $\overline{v}_{j,in}$, and nodes deflection $\overline{y}_{j,in}$ are zero. To represent the condition for action of the force $\overline{F}^*$, we need to find the index j_* of the element approximated the cable mid-point $\overline{x}_{j+1} \approx 0.5$. Substituting $\overline{x}_{j_*+1} = 0.5$ in Eq.(2.68), we come to the quadratic equation in j_*

$$j_*^2 + j_* - 0.5n(n+1) = 0, \tag{2.70a}$$

from where

$$j_* = 0.5[\sqrt{1+2n(n+1)} - 1]. \tag{2.70b}$$

The closest integer to j_* locates the required node element and its upper node $j_* + 1$, where the force $\overline{F}^*$ is applied.

If the shortest duration of the force $\overline{F}^*$ is assumed to be equal to the single time step $\Delta\overline{t}$, the boundary conditions become

$$\overline{Q}_1^- = 0, \qquad \overline{v}_n^+ = 0,$$
$$\overline{Q}_{j_*+1}^* = \begin{cases} \overline{F}^* & \text{with } i = 1 \text{ and } j = j_* \\ 0 & \text{with } i \neq 1 \text{ or } j \neq j_*. \end{cases} \tag{2.71}$$

The impulse force is assumed to be $\overline{F}* = 0.1$. Taking the number n of elements as $n = 50$, the value of free end tension is $\overline{N}_{1w}^- \approx 0.0004$. In accordance with Eq.(2.7a), the index $j_* = 35$ corresponds to the cable mid-point near the node $j_* + 1 = 36$.

Variation of dimensionless free end deflection $\overline{y}_1 = y_1 / L$ with relative time $\tilde{t} = \overline{t} / \overline{T}$, where $\overline{T}$ is the time of wave passing along the cable, is

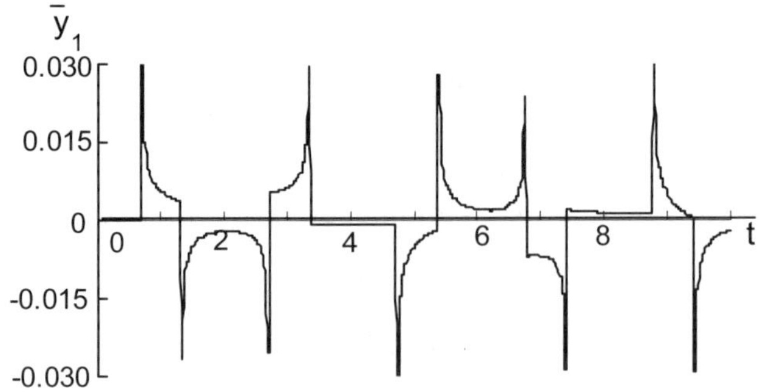

Fig.2.14. Deflections at the free end of a cable under an impulse force applied to the mid-point

shown in Fig.2.14. With $\Delta\bar{t}$ =const, the time $\overline{T}$ is equal to $\overline{T} = n\Delta\bar{t} = 2n/\sqrt{n(n+1)}$, or in our case, $\overline{T}$ =1.98, whereas $\overline{T} \to 2$ with $n \to \infty$.

Pair of transverse waves starts from the cable mid-point at $\bar{t} = 0$. The waves travel with different and varying current speeds; however, the mean speed value over the time $\overline{T}$ is constant and equal to $\bar{c}_m = 1/\overline{T} \approx 0.5$. The first peak in Fig.2.14 corresponds to the first arrival of the backward wave at the free end, the second one to the forward wave, which arrives at the same point with inverse sign due to reflection from the fixed end. The following wave interaction is rather complicated.

The detailed distribution of the node deflections at some instants $\tilde{t}$ in a

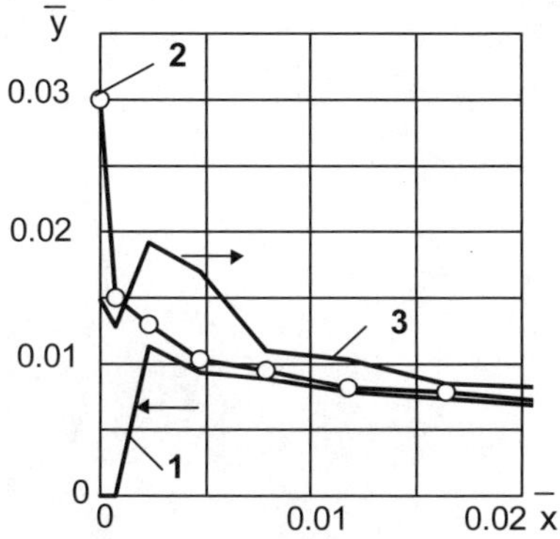

Fig.2.15. Deflections of the cable nodes near the free end for some instants:
1) $\bar{t}$ = 0.66; 2) $\bar{t}$ = 0.70; 3) $\bar{t}$ = 0.76

small domain closely approximating the free end is plotted in Fig.2.15, arrows showing the direction of wave motion. Disposition of the nodes is depicted by white dots on curve 2 corresponding to the time step $i = i_* + 1 = 36$ of the wave first arrival at the free end.

It should be once more emphasized that the energy balances for each element, so that the whole system's energy balance, are satisfied during the all process.

Standing waves of a hung cable were studied by Morse (1948) and strong oscillations of the hung cable with free end were observed by Pierce (1974).

3 Wave Propagation in an Inelastic Rod

3.1 Longitudinal Waves in an Inelastic Rod

3.1.1 Discrete-Continual Model of an Inelastic Rod

3.1.1.1. To extend the approach of direct mathematical modeling (DMM), described in Chaps. 1 and 2 in application to an elastic rod, to an inelastic rod, we assume that each finite element is conditionally divided into two parts: an internal continual elastic-inertial part (A) of realistic length Δx_j and inelastic non-inertial border links (B) (see Fig. 3.1, where adjacent halves of the elements $j-1$ and j are shown). A space separation of the mechanical properties like this is of no importance when using a large number of small elements. Moreover, this assumption, first proposed by Shorr (1984), allows us to describe the well-known experimental effect that the leading waves in a rod of any material always propagate with the elastic speed $c = \sqrt{E/\rho}$. Plastic or viscous deformations develop signifi-

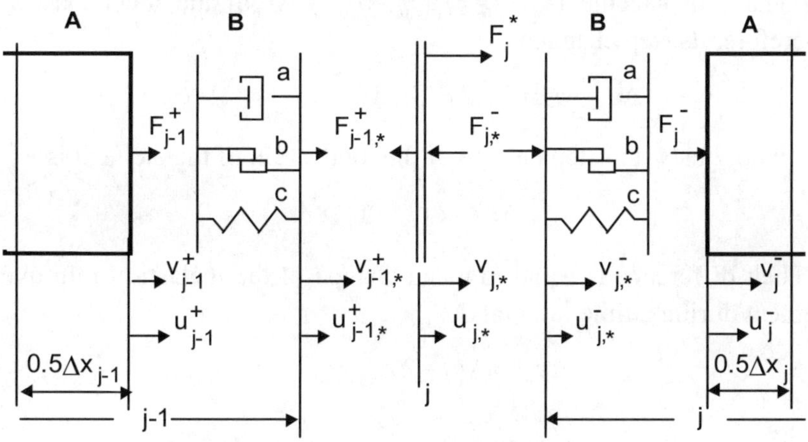

Fig. 3.1. 'Discrete-continual' model of adjacent inelastic elements

cantly slower and their behavior can be adequately described by constitutive equations, which do not take inertia into account.

The boundaries between the elastic inertial part of an element and its inelastic links will be called the 'inner' borders and those between adjacent elements - the 'outer' borders. The latter coincide with the nodes. The node parameters will be, as previously used, with an 'asterisk' in the superscript, with the outer borders parameters having an 'asterisk' in the subscript. The external loads F_j^* and local boundary conditions are assumed to be constant over the time steps Δt_i and referred to nodes.

Wave propagation in internal parts is entirely described by the equations of previous chapters. In particular, Eqs.(1.49b) connecting the inner border forces $F_j^\pm$ with velocities $v_j^\pm$ hold, thus

$$F_j^\pm = \pm F_{j,0} + \rho_j c_j A_j (v_j^\pm - v_{j,0}) \tag{3.1}$$

As the inelastic links are assumed to be non-inertial, the longitudinal forces applied to them must be equal over the time step, implying that

$$F_{j,*}^\pm = F_j^\pm , \tag{3.2a}$$

where, as previously,

$$F_j^\pm = \pm \sigma_j^\pm A_j . \tag{3.2b}$$

The elastic strain $\varepsilon_{je,0}$ is determined, as usual, by the difference of the boundary displacements $\varepsilon_{je,0} = (u_{j,0}^+ - u_{j,0}^-) / \Delta x_j$ of the inner elastic part. Therefore, its step change is

$$\Delta\varepsilon_{je} = (\Delta u_j^+ - \Delta u_j^-) / \Delta x_j = (v_j^+ - v_j^-) / c_j . \tag{3.3}$$

Analogously, the step change of the total strain of the element is

$$\Delta\varepsilon_j = (v_{j,*}^+ - v_{j,*}^-) / c_j . \tag{3.4}$$

Their difference is equal to mean change of the inelastic strain over the element during a time interval Δt

$$\Delta\varepsilon_{jp} = \Delta\varepsilon_j - \Delta\varepsilon_{je} = (v_{jp}^+ - v_{jp}^-) / c_j , \tag{3.5a}$$

where

$$v_{jp}^\pm = v_{j,*}^\pm - v_j^\pm \tag{3.5b}$$

is an additional links velocity arising from the influence of the inelastic strain change $\Delta\varepsilon_{jp}^{\pm}$ in the adjoining halves of the element.

Expressing the additional inelastic displacements $\Delta u_{jp}^{\pm} = v_{jp}^{\pm}\Delta t$ of the element borders through the inelastic strain change of the half element length

$$\Delta u_{jp}^{\pm} = \pm 0.5\Delta\varepsilon_{jp}^{\pm}\Delta x\,, \tag{3.6}$$

we find

$$v_{jp}^{\pm} = \pm 0.5c\Delta\varepsilon_{jp}^{\pm}\,, \tag{3.7}$$

and substituting Eqs.(3.7) into Eq.(3.5a), we obtain

$$\Delta\varepsilon_{jp} = 0.5(\Delta\varepsilon_{jp}^{-} + \Delta\varepsilon_{jp}^{+})\,. \tag{3.8}$$

3.1.1.2. The sum of work $\Delta W_j^{\pm}$ done by the forces $F_j^{\pm}$ over the inner displacements $v_j^{\pm}\Delta t$ is, as previously, equal to the change of the total mechanical energy of the inner element part $\Delta W_j^{-} + \Delta W_j^{+} = \Delta E_j$. The work $\Delta W_{j,*}^{\pm}$ of the same forces $F_{j,*}^{\pm} = F_j^{\pm}$ over the outer displacements $v_{j,*}^{\pm}\Delta t$ is

$$\Delta W_{j,*}^{\pm} = F_{j,*}^{\pm}v_{j,*}^{\pm}\Delta t = F_j^{\pm}(v_j^{\pm} + v_{jp}^{\pm})\Delta t = \Delta W_j^{\pm} \pm 0.5F_j^{\pm}\Delta\varepsilon_{jp}^{\pm}\Delta x_j\,. \tag{3.9}$$

On the other hand, the energy dissipated in each half of the element due to inelastic deformation can be determined as

$$\Delta E_{jp}^{\pm} = 0.5\sigma_{jpm}^{\pm}\Delta\varepsilon_{jp}^{\pm}A_j\Delta x_j\,, \tag{3.10}$$

where $\sigma_{jpm}^{\pm}$ is a middle stress in the corresponding link over the time step.

Taking into account that

$$\sigma_{jpm}^{\pm} = \sigma_j^{\pm}\,, \tag{3.11}$$

we ensure, due to Eq.(3.2b),

$$\Delta E_j + \Delta E_{jp} = \Delta W_{j,*}\,, \tag{3.12}$$

where $\Delta E_{jp} = \Delta E_{jp}^{-} + \Delta E_{jp}^{+}$ and $\Delta W_{j,*} = \Delta W_{j,*}^{-} + \Delta W_{j,*}^{+}$.

Therefore, the law of the energy conservation, including the inelastic dissipation of energy, is precisely satisfied for each element over each time step. If the signs of $\Delta\varepsilon_{jp}^{\pm}$ and $\sigma_{jpm}^{\pm}$ coincide, the dissipated energy $\Delta E_{jp} > 0$, i.e. always increases. In particular, the waves induced by initial impulse must decay.

3.1.1.3. A change of the inelastic strain $\Delta\varepsilon^{\pm}_{jp}$, in general, depends on the deformation history, which is determined by the previously acting stresses in the corresponding halves of the element, and on the stress $\sigma^{\pm}_{j}$ acting over the current step. This allows $\Delta\varepsilon^{\pm}_{jp}$ to be represented in the form

$$\Delta\varepsilon^{\pm}_{jp} = 2\left(\frac{\sigma^{\pm}_{j}}{E_j}\varphi^{\pm}_{j} + \psi^{\pm}_{j}\right) \tag{3.13a}$$

and, according to Eqs.(3.7) and (3.2b),

$$v^{\pm}_{jp} = \left(\frac{F^{\pm}_{j}}{A_j E_j}\varphi^{\pm}_{j} \pm \psi^{\pm}_{j}\right)c_j. \tag{3.13b}$$

The non-dimensional coefficients $\varphi^{\pm}_{j}$ and $\psi^{\pm}_{j}$ are determined from the constitutive equations of the material, as it will be demonstrated below. They are assumed to be constant over the separate time step, but may vary from step to step due to the material behavior under varying stresses. If the coefficient $\varphi^{\pm}_{j}$ depends on the stress $\sigma^{\pm}_{j}$, it is to be determined by successive approximations.

3.1.2 Governing Equations

3.1.2.1. The conditions of interelement equilibrium and continuity referred to outer boundaries of the elements $j-1$ and j (see Fig.3.1) are, respectively,

$$\left.\begin{aligned} F^{+}_{j-1,*} + F^{-}_{j,*} &= F^{*}_{j}, \\ v^{+}_{j-1,*} = v^{-}_{j,*} &= v^{*}_{j} \end{aligned}\right\}. \tag{3.14}$$

Taking account of Eq.(3.2a), (3.14) and excluding the velocities v^{+}_{j-1} and v^{-}_{j} from Eqs.(3.1), (3.8), and (3.13b), we find for a nonhomogeneous rod

$$\left.\begin{aligned} F^{+}_{j-1} &= \frac{F_{j-1,0} + \rho_{j-1}c_{j-1}A_{j-1}(v^{*}_{j} - v_{j-1,0}) - E_{j-1}A_{j-1}\psi^{+}_{j-1}}{1+\varphi^{+}_{j-1}}, \\ F^{-}_{j} &= \frac{-F_{j,0} + \rho_j c_j A_j (v^{*}_{j} - v_{j,0}) + E_j A_j \psi^{-}_{j}}{1+\varphi^{-}_{j}} \end{aligned}\right\}. \tag{3.15}$$

By considering the force of external viscous friction $F^{*}_{jv} = -\eta_{jv}v^{*}_{j}$ applied to the node j, where $\eta_{jv} = 0.5\eta_v(\Delta x_{j-1} + \Delta x_j)$, and inserting

Eqs.(3.15) into (3.14), we obtain a governing equation to calculate the node velocity between the outer borders of the elements $j-1$ and j, thus

$$v_j^* = (D_1 + D_2 + D_3)/D_4, \tag{3.16a}$$

where

$$\left.\begin{aligned} D_1 &= [A_{j-1}(\rho_{j-1}c_{j-1}v_{j-1,0} + E_{j-1}\psi_{j-1}^+) - F_{j-1,0}](1+\varphi_j^-),\\ D_2 &= [A_j(\rho_j c_j v_{j,0} - E_j\psi_j^-) + F_{j,0}](1+\varphi_{j-1}^+),\\ D_3 &= F_j^*(1+\varphi_{j-1}^+)(1+\varphi_j^-),\\ D_4 &= \rho_{j-1}c_{j-1}A_{j-1}(1+\varphi_j^-) + \rho_j c_j A_j(1+\varphi_{1-1}^+) + \eta_{jv}(1+\varphi_{j-1}^+)(1+\varphi_j^-) \end{aligned}\right\}. \tag{3.16b}$$

Thereafter, the forces F_{j-1}^+, F_j^- and the velocities v_{j-1}^+, v_j^- can be found using Eqs.(3.15) and (3.1). Repeating the same procedure for the node $j+1$, we obtain the velocity v_{j+1}^*, etc. New values of the inner force and velocity in the jth element at the instant $t+\Delta t$ are determined as

$$\left.\begin{aligned} F_j &= F_j^+ - F_j^- - F_{j,0},\\ v_j &= v_j^+ + v_j^- - v_{j,0} \end{aligned}\right\}, \tag{3.17a}$$

with the new value of node displacement given by

$$u_j = u_{j,0} + v_j^*\Delta t. \tag{3.17b}$$

The changes of inelastic strains in the links due to Eqs.(3.13a) and (3.2b) are

$$\Delta\varepsilon_{jp}^{\pm} = 2\left(\pm\frac{F_j^{\pm}}{A_j E_j}\varphi_j^{\pm} + \psi_j^{\pm}\right), \tag{3.18a}$$

and their new values

$$\varepsilon_{jp}^{\pm}(t+\Delta t) = \varepsilon_{jp}^{\pm}(t) + \Delta\varepsilon_{jp}^{\pm}. \tag{3.18b}$$

3.1.2.2. **A.** Some interesting results follow from the equations given above:

i) The difference of displacements of inner borders in adjoining elements over a time Δt is equal to the sum of the inelastic deformation of their corresponding halves

$$(v_j^- - v_{j-1}^+)\Delta t = 0.5(\Delta\varepsilon_{j-1,p}^+\Delta x_{j-1} + \Delta\varepsilon_{jp}^-\Delta x_j).$$

ii) The mean mass velocity v_{jm} of the adjoining halves of the elements at the instant $0.5\Delta t$

$$v_{jm} = \frac{\rho_{j-1}c_{j-1}A_{j-1}v_{j-1}^{+} + \rho_j c_j A_j v_j^{-}}{\rho_{j-1}c_{j-1}A_{j-1} + \rho_j c_j A_j}$$

does not depend on inelastic mechanical properties in the absence of external friction, since in this case

$$v_{jm} = \frac{\rho_{j-1}c_{j-1}A_{j-1}v_{j-1,0} + \rho_j c_j A_j v_{j,0} - F_{j-1,0} + F_{j,0} + F_j^{*}}{\rho_{j-1}c_{j-1}A_{j-1} + \rho_j c_j A_j}.$$

iii) In the general case, the node velocity is

$$v_j^{*} = 0.5(v_{j-1}^{+} + v_j^{-}) + 0.25(c_{j-1}\Delta\varepsilon_{j-1,p}^{+} - c_j\Delta\varepsilon_{jp}^{+}).$$

iv) In specific cases, calculation formulae may in fact become simpler. In connection with a homogeneous rod of constant cross section

$$v_{jm} = 0.5(v_{j-1}^{+} + v_j^{-})$$

and

$$v_j^{*} = v_{jm} + 0.25c(\Delta\varepsilon_{j-1,p}^{+} - \Delta\varepsilon_{jp}^{-}).$$

Without external forces, when $\sigma_{j-1}^{+} = \sigma_j^{-}$ and $\Delta\varepsilon_{j-1,p}^{+} = \Delta\varepsilon_{j,p}^{-}$, the node velocity

$$v_j^{*} = v_{jm} = 0.5[v_{j,0} + v_{j-1,0} + (F_{j,0} - F_{j-1,0})/\rho cA] \qquad (3.19)$$

does not also depend on inelastic material properties. However, the border forces, calculated from Eqs.(3.15) after excluding the velocity v_j^{*} as

$$F_{j-1}^{+} = -F_j^{-} = \frac{F_{j,0} + F_{j-1,0} + (v_{j,0} - v_{j-1,0})\rho cA - 2EA\psi_j}{2(1+\varphi)}, \qquad (3.20)$$

are affected by coefficients $\psi_j = \psi_{j-1}^{+} = \psi_j^{-}$ and $\varphi = \text{const}$.

The same is true in regard of velocities v_{j-1}^{+} and v_j^{-}, and the boundary velocities $v_{1,*}^{-}$ and $v_{n,*}^{+}$ at the ends of the rod. Some of these simplifications will be exploited in the subsequent sections of the present Chapter.

B. Equation (3.16a) taken in dimensionless terms yields

$$\overline{v}_j^{*} = (\overline{D}_1 + \overline{D}_2 + \overline{D}_3)/\overline{D}_4, \qquad (3.21a)$$

where

$$\left.\begin{aligned}
\overline{D}_1 &= [\mu_{j-1}(\overline{v}_{j-1,0} + \overline{c}_{j-1}\overline{\psi}^{+}_{j-1}) - \overline{F}_{j-1,0}](1+\varphi^{-}_{J}),\\
\overline{D}_2 &= [\mu_j(\overline{v}_{j,0} - \overline{c}_j\overline{\psi}^{-}_{j}) + \overline{F}_{j,0}](1+\varphi^{+}_{j-1}),\\
\overline{D}_3 &= \overline{F}^{*}_{j}(1+\varphi^{+}_{j-1})(1+\varphi^{-}_{j}),\\
\overline{D}_4 &= \mu_{j-1}(1+\varphi^{-}_{j}) + \mu_j(1+\varphi^{+}_{j-1}) + \overline{\eta}_{jv}(1+\varphi^{+}_{j-1})(1+\varphi^{-}_{j})
\end{aligned}\right\}. \qquad (3.21b)$$

Here, in addition to relations (2.5), we also have

$$\overline{\psi} = \frac{\psi c^{o}}{v^{o}}, \; \overline{\eta}_{jv} = \frac{\eta_{jv}}{\rho^{o} c^{o} A^{o}} = 0.5\overline{\eta}_{v}(\Delta\overline{x}_{j-1} + \Delta\overline{x}_{j}), \; \overline{\eta}_{v} = \frac{\eta_{v} L}{\rho^{o} c^{o} A^{o}}.$$

No governing equations, which have been previously deduced, are dependent on concrete inelastic material properties. However, any constitutive equation of a material must describe its behavior under arbitrary loading trajectories, including the alternating-sign. The wide range of inelastic material models is schematically presented in Fig.3.1 in the form of parallel units of the link: a) viscoelastic, b) hysteretic (in particular, plastic), and c) additional reversible (in particular, high-elastic). Using the DMM algorithm, the inner elastic-inertial part plays the role of the principal elastic unit. Excluding some of these units or adding some others in parallel-sequential way, one can describe inelastic behavior of different materials as it was used by Shorr (1984, 1995, and 1998).

Graphical interpretation of the inelastic units is, of course, not necessary.

Linear and nonlinear viscoelastic, elastic-plastic, and elastic-viscoplastic material models are considered in the next two sections. A model taking into account internal hysteretic material friction in the form, suitable for wave analysis, was proposed by Shorr and Mel'nikova (1988) and has been exploited by Shorr (1990) for studying the impulse-induced stress fading

3.2 Waves in a Viscoelastic Rod

3.2.1 Background Equations

3.2.1.1. A unit of viscous material is usually displayed graphically as a dash-pot. A sequential connection of such dash-pot with an elastic spring corresponds to the Maxwell model; an analogous combination of parallel connection forms the Voigt model. Their sequential combination is sometimes called as the Bürger's model, which is considered below. The notations of the stress and strain in these units are presented in Fig.3.2a. Here, η_c and η_v are Newtonian viscosity coefficients and E_v is a high-elastic modulus, which is usually significantly less than Young's modulus E. All these parameters for linear viscoelastic models are constant in time but may vary along the rod.

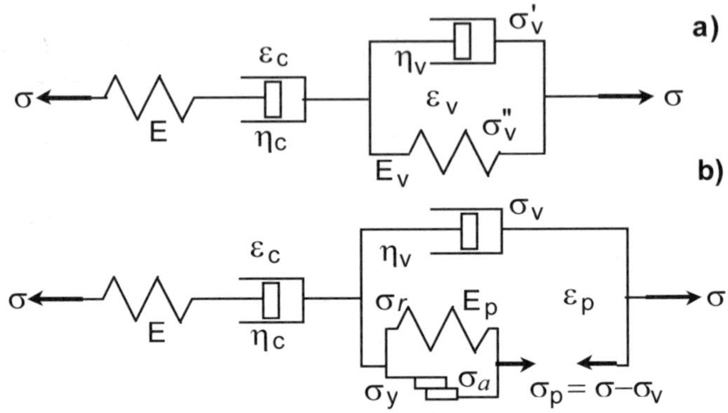

Fig. 3.2. Models considered: a) viscoelastic, b) elastic-viscoplastic

A. The constitutive equation of the Maxwell's unit is

$$\dot{\varepsilon} = \dot{\varepsilon}_e + \dot{\varepsilon}_c = \frac{1}{E}\dot{\sigma} + \frac{\sigma}{\eta_c} \tag{3.22}$$

where $\dot{f} = \partial f / \partial t$.

The change in the elastic strain is represented by deformation of the inner part of an element. For the links of the element j we must take $\sigma = \sigma_j^\pm$. Hence, the change in the viscous strain at the relevant element halves over the time Δt is

$$\Delta\varepsilon_{jc}^\pm = \frac{\sigma^\pm \Delta t}{\eta_c} = \frac{2\sigma_j^\pm}{E}\xi_c, \tag{3.23a}$$

where

$$\xi_c = \Delta t / 2\tau_c . \tag{3.23b}$$

Here, $\tau_c = \eta_c / E$ is the relaxation time of the material. To describe smooth time change of the strain, it is necessary to take a time interval so that $\xi_c << 1$.

B. The constitutive equation of the Voigt's unit

$$\dot{\varepsilon}_v = (\sigma - E_v \varepsilon_v)/\eta_v$$

leads to the linear differential equation

$$\dot{\varepsilon}_v + \frac{1}{\tau_v}\varepsilon_v = \frac{1}{E_v \tau_v}\sigma, \tag{3.24}$$

where $\tau_v = \eta_v / E_v$ is the retardation time of the material.

Integrating Eq.(3.24) over the limits from t to $t + \Delta t$ with $\sigma = \text{const}$, we obtain the change of strain in the Voigt's unit during the step Δt

$$\Delta\varepsilon_v = (\sigma / E_v - \varepsilon_{v,0})[1 - \exp(-2\xi_v)], \tag{3.25a}$$

where $\varepsilon_{v,0}$ is the value of strain in this unit at the beginning of the current step and

$$\xi_v = \Delta t / 2\tau_v. \tag{3.25b}$$

Expanding Eq.(3.25a) in the small parameter ξ_v with an accuracy of the second order, i.e.,

$$\xi_v^2 << 1, \tag{3.25c}$$

we get

$$\Delta\varepsilon_v \approx 2\left(\frac{\sigma}{E_v} - \varepsilon_{v,0}\right)\xi_v(1 - \xi_v). \tag{3.26}$$

On the other hand, using the general procedure of the DMM for the element j, it is appropriate to take into account the fact that the momentum balance for the links during the time step is carried out exactly if the sum of the mean stresses in the viscous and high-elastic branches are equal to the full stress $\sigma = \sigma_j^{\pm}$, i.e.,

$$(\sigma'_v)_{jm}^{\pm} + (\sigma''_v)_{jm}^{\pm} = \sigma_j^{\pm}, \tag{3.27a}$$

where

$$\left.\begin{aligned} (\sigma'_v)_{jm}^{\pm} &= \eta_v \Delta\varepsilon_{jv}^{\pm} / \Delta t, \\ (\sigma''_v)_{jm}^{\pm} &= E_v \varepsilon_{jvm}^{\pm} = E_v(\varepsilon_{jv,0}^{\pm} + 0.5\Delta\varepsilon_{jv}^{\pm}) \end{aligned}\right\}. \tag{3.27b}$$

Equations (3.27) may be shown to yield

$$\Delta\varepsilon_{jv}^{\pm} = 2\left(\frac{\sigma_j^{\pm}}{E_v} - \varepsilon_{jv,0}^{\pm}\right)\frac{\xi_v}{1 + \xi_v}. \tag{3.28}$$

Equations (3.26) and (3.28) are identical due to the condition (3.25c); however, the form (3.28) is more preferable because it is limited by the condition $\xi_v < 1$ that is less severe than the restriction (3.25c). This allows Shorr (1998) to generate complex inelastic models with multiple parallel Maxwell's units of different relaxation time. The formula (3.25a) is useful for very small retardation time, when ensuring condition (3.25c) is too difficult.

By comparing the sum of strains in the inelastic links $\Delta\varepsilon_{jp}^{\pm} = \Delta\varepsilon_{jc}^{\pm} + \Delta\varepsilon_{jv}^{\pm}$ from Eqs.(3.23a) and (3.28) with general expression (3.13a), we see that for the viscoelastic model under consideration

$$\left.\begin{aligned} \varphi_j^{\pm} &= \varphi = \xi_c + \frac{E}{E_v}\frac{\xi_v}{1+\xi_v}, \\ \psi_j^{\pm} &= -\varepsilon_{jv,0}^{\pm}\frac{\xi_v}{1+\xi_v} \end{aligned}\right\}. \tag{3.29}$$

The new value of inelastic strain in Voigt's unit is $\varepsilon_{jv}^{\pm} = \varepsilon_{jv,0}^{\pm} + \Delta\varepsilon_{jv}^{\pm}$.

3.2.1.3. **A.** The viscosity coefficients η of some materials are not constant but depend on the stress, accumulated strain, the rate of strain, and other factors. In numerical calculation, it is convenient to represent an experimental relation $f(\sigma,\varepsilon,\dot{\varepsilon}) = 0$, in applying to Maxwell's model, in the form

$$\dot{\varepsilon}_c = \mu(\sigma,\varepsilon_c)\sigma,$$

where $\mu = \eta^{-1}$ is the reciprocal of the traditional viscosity coefficient.

We take the relaxation time related to the ($\pm$) link in the time interval Δt as

$$\tau_{jc}^{\pm} = [E_j \mu_{jc}^{\pm}(\sigma_{jm}^{\pm},\varepsilon_{jm}^{\pm})]^{-1},$$

where $\sigma_{jm}^{\pm} = \sigma_j^{\pm} =$ const. and also the mean value of viscous strain $\varepsilon_{\mathrm{jm}}^{\pm} =$ const.

As the given relaxation time depends on the stress and the viscous strain in the link, the calculations must be carried out using successive approximations. Some examples of numerical simulation of wave propagation in a rod of nonlinear material viscosity are demonstrated in Shorr (1998).

B. Taking into account the external viscous friction with coefficient η_v and adding the constitutive equation of Maxwell's material (3.22) to Eqs.(1.22a), we obtain

$$\rho\frac{\partial v}{\partial t} = \frac{\partial \sigma}{\partial x} - \eta_v v; \quad \frac{\partial v}{\partial x} = \frac{\partial \varepsilon}{\partial t}; \quad \frac{\partial \varepsilon}{\partial t} = \frac{1}{E}\frac{\partial \sigma}{\partial t} + \frac{\sigma}{\eta_C}, \tag{3.30a}$$

and excluding the stress from Eqs.(3.30a), we obtain

$$\frac{\partial^2 v}{\partial x^2} - \frac{\rho}{E}\frac{\partial^2 v}{\partial t^2} - \left(\frac{\rho}{\eta_c} + \frac{\eta_v}{E}\right)\frac{\partial v}{\partial t} - \frac{\eta_v}{\eta_c} v = 0. \tag{3.30b}$$

The analogous equation (so-called 'telegraph' equation) is widely exploited in electrical engineering for studying transient processes in electrical cables. Equations (3.21a,b) with $\mu = 1$, $\psi = 0$, and $\varphi = \xi_c = 0.5E\Delta t / \eta_c$ accurately corresponds to the solution of Eq.(3.30b), using DMM approach. Therefore, the DMM algorithm can be readily applied to some problems of electrical engineering (see Chap. 14).

3.2.2 Numerical Examples

3.2.2.1. **Problem 3.1. A semi-infinite viscoelastic rod of Maxwellian material affected by the impact on the free end.** To illustrate the accuracy of the method, consider a semi-infinite rod of viscoelastc material with $\xi_v = 0, \psi = 0$. The striking body applied to the face $j = 1$ is assumed to be of significant mass and stiffness and hence the boundary velocity $v_{1,*}^- = v_0$ (or $\bar{v}_{1,*}^- = 1$) may be accounted as constant.

Equation (3.20) in dimensionless form yields

$$\bar{\sigma}_{j-1}^+ = (\bar{\sigma}_{j,0} + \bar{\sigma}_{j-1,0} + \bar{v}_{j,0} - \bar{v}_{j-1,0})/(2 + \Delta\bar{t}), \tag{3.31}$$

where realistic time is scaled with relaxation time $\bar{t} = t / \tau_c$, so that $\Delta\bar{t} = \Delta t / \tau_c = 2\xi_c = 2\varphi$.

The initial conditions are

$$\bar{\sigma}_{j,in} = 0, \ \bar{v}_{j,in} = 0, \ j = 1,2,... \tag{3.32a}$$

The boundary condition $\bar{v}_{1,*}^+ = 1$ at the left end $j = 1$, after using the second Eq.(3.15), leads to

$$\bar{\sigma}_1^- = (\bar{\sigma}_{1.0} - 1 + \bar{v}_{1,0})/(1 + 0.5\Delta\bar{t}). \tag{3.32b}$$

As the disturbed zone spreads with each step on one element, it is sufficient to limit the calculated number of elements by $n = i$. This quantity and the node index $j = i + 1$ for the right border of the last element increase as the leading wave advances, but the silent boundary conditions

$$\sigma_{n=i}^+ = 0, \ v_{n=i}^+ = 0 \tag{3.32c}$$

for this altering border remain invariable.

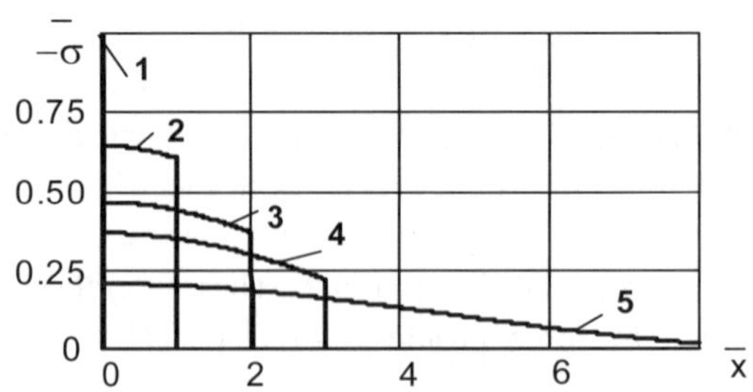

Fig. 3.3. Distribution of stresses over the length of the rod of Maxwell's material under constant velocity at the free end; 1) $\bar{t}=0.02$, 2) $\bar{t}=1$, 3) $\bar{t}=2$, 4) $\bar{t}=3$, 5) $\bar{t}=8$

Fig.3.3 shows the distribution of the compressive stress $\bar{\sigma}$ over the length $\bar{x}$, where $\bar{x}=x/c\tau_c$, for some points of time $\bar{t}$. Numerical results with short time intervals $\Delta\bar{t}\le 0.02$ are very close to the analytic solution obtained by Lee and Kanter (1953).

For the problem considered, the analytic time dependence of the stress $\bar{\sigma}_i^-$ in the leading wave calculated by the DMM algorithm can be directly established. For the element transmitting the leading wave, whose index j coincides with step index i, we have $\bar{\sigma}_{j,0}=\bar{\sigma}_{j+1,0}=0$ and $\bar{v}_{j,0}=\bar{v}_{j+1,0}=0$, so that

$$\bar{\sigma}_j^+=0,\ \ \bar{v}_j^+=0,\ \ \bar{\sigma}_j=\bar{\sigma}_j^-=(\bar{\sigma}_{j-1,0}-\bar{v}_{j-1,0})/(2+\Delta\bar{t}),$$

and $v_j=\bar{v}_j^-=-\bar{\sigma}_j$.

Applying this to the first element, we obtain $\bar{\sigma}_1=-(1+0.5\Delta\bar{t})^{-1}$, $\bar{v}_1=-\bar{\sigma}$, etc. With the element $j=i$, we have $\bar{\sigma}_i=-(1+0.5\bar{t}/i)^{-i}$, since $\Delta t=\bar{t}/i$. Decreasing the element dimension and the time step, we pass to the limit

$$\bar{\sigma}(\bar{t})=\lim_{i\to\infty}[-(1+0.5\bar{t}/i)^{-i}]=-\exp(-0.5\bar{t})$$

that coincides exactly with the analytical solution.

3.2.2.2. **Problem 3.2. . A free-fixed viscoelastic rod of Maxwellian material affected by the sinusoidal impulse.** Let a one-clamped rod of length L of the same material as above be loaded at the free end by a short-time sinusoidal impulse during the steps i_* The initial and boundary conditions are the same as in Subsect.2.3.1.4., where the analogous problem applied to an elastic string was considered, see Eqs.(2.56)-(2.57). In dimensionless form referred to the longitudinal waves these conditions are, respectively,

$$\bar{v}_{j,in} = 0,\ \bar{\sigma}_{j,in} = 0,\ \bar{u}_{j,in} = 0, \tag{3.33a}$$

and

$$\left.\begin{aligned} \bar{\sigma}_1^- &= \begin{cases} \sin 2\pi \dfrac{(i-0.5)}{(i_*+0.5)}, & i = 1,2,\ldots,i_*+1 \\ 0, & i > i_*+1 \end{cases}, \\ \bar{v}_{n,*}^+ &= 0 \end{aligned}\right\}. \tag{3.33b}$$

Unlike the previous Subsection, the time $\bar{t}$ is scaled here to $T = L/c$. Therefore, $\Delta\bar{t} = \Delta\bar{x} = 1/n$ where n is a number of elements, the nondimensional relaxation time is $\bar{\tau}_c = \tau_c c/L$, and $\xi_c = \varphi = 0.5/\bar{\tau}_c n$.

The second boundary condition (3.33b) for the clamped end leads to

$$\bar{\sigma}_n^+ = (\bar{\sigma}_{n,0} - \bar{v}_{n,0})/(1+\varphi).$$

The stress wave distributions along the length of the rod for n=250, $i_* = 25$, and $\xi_c = 0.004$ referred to various instants before and after reflection from the fixed end are shown in Fig.3.4a,b, respectively

The viscoelastic wave propagates with the same constant speed as the elastic wave. Its sinusoidal form is conserved both for direct and reflected waves, however, the magnitude progressively fades.

-

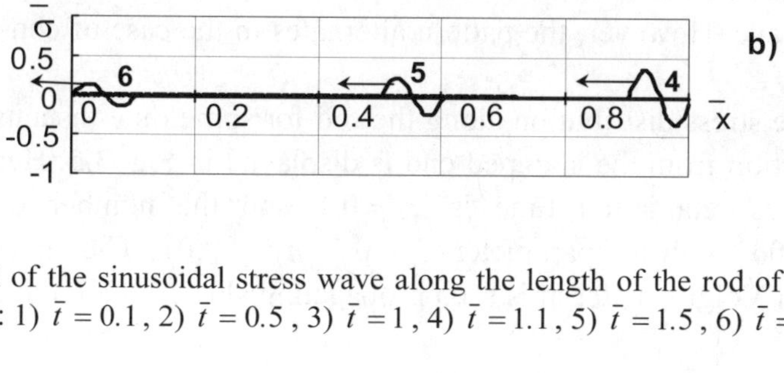

Fig.3.4. Travel of the sinusoidal stress wave along the length of the rod of Maxwell's material: 1) $\bar{t} = 0.1$, 2) $\bar{t} = 0.5$, 3) $\bar{t} = 1$, 4) $\bar{t} = 1.1$, 5) $\bar{t} = 1.5$, 6) $\bar{t} = 2$

***3.2.2.3.* Problem 3.3. A free-fixed viscoelastic rod of Voigt's material affected by a suddenly applied force.** The third example is referred to a viscoelastic rod with $\xi_c = 0, \varphi = 0$ subjected to a constant force suddenly applied to the free end. The relatively high-elastic modulus is taken as $\overline{E}_v = 0.2$.

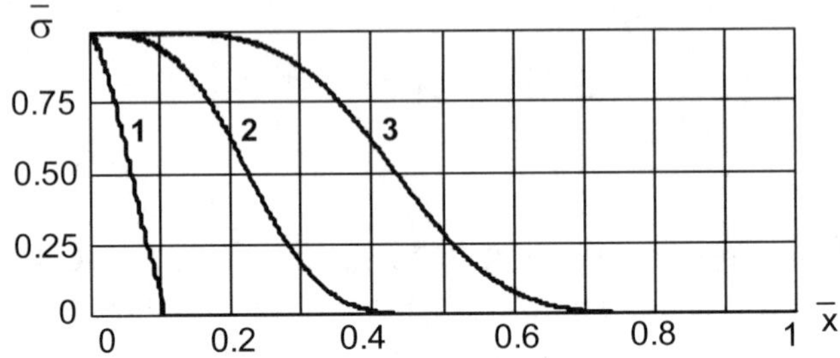

Fig. 3.5. Distribution of stresses over the length of the rod of Voigt's material under constant force at the free end; 1) $\bar{t} = 0.1$, 2) $\bar{t} = 0.5$, 3) $\bar{t} = 1$

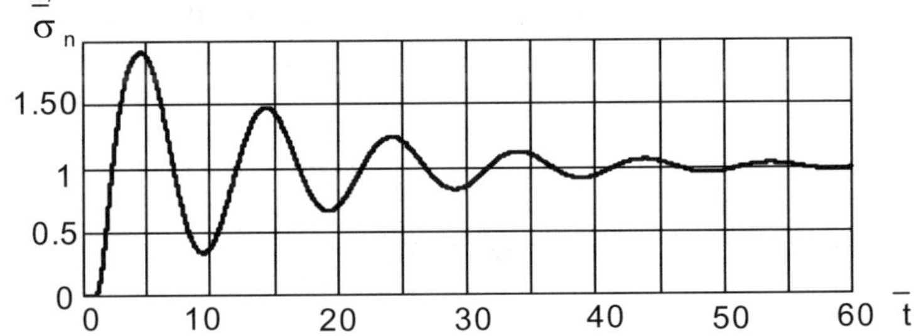

Fig. 3.6. Stress at the clamped end of the rod of Voigt's material vs. time under the constant force at the free end

Calculations show that the stress wave induced by a short-time impulse load propagates, as for Maxwell's material, with the same speed as the associated elastic one, since such impulse follows immediately after the leading wave. However, the pattern alternates in the case of constant force action.

The stress distribution along the rod for some time instants before wave reflection from the clamped end is displayed in Fig. 3.5. Here, the dimensionless retardation time is $\bar{\tau}_v = 0.1$ and the number of elements is $n = 500$, with the parameter $\xi_v = 0.5/n\bar{\tau}_v = 0.01$. The stress wave in the rod of Voigt's material is seen propagating slower than the elastic leading wave. In our case, its visible averaged speed is about $\overline{c}_v = c_v / c \approx 0.40 \div 0.42$.

To illustrate the time-dependent variation of the fading stress $\overline{\sigma}_n$ at the clamped end, Fig. 3.6 is presented using less elements $n = 50$ but a significant number of reflections, which is taken up to 60. The retardation time is $\overline{\tau}_v = 0.4$ or $\xi_v = 0.025$. The visible period of oscillation is $\overline{T}_f \approx 9.8$ instead of $\overline{T}_f = 4$ for the elastic rod. This determines the propagation time $\overline{T}_v = 0.25\overline{T}_f \approx 2.45$ and the relative wave speed $\overline{c}_v = 1/\overline{T}_v \approx 0.41$.The calculated quantities correlate with the growth of the compliance from $1/E$ for an elastic rod to the sum $1/E + 1/E_v$ for a rod with high-elastic unit. The ratio of these quantities for $\overline{E}_v = 0.2$ is $k = (1+\overline{E}_v)/\overline{E}_v = 6$ and the relative propagation time is just $\overline{T}_v = \sqrt{k} = 2.45$.

3.3 Waves in an Elastic-Viscoplastic Rod

3.3.1 Elastic-Plastic Models

3.3.1.1. To describe wave propagation in a rod of elastic-plastic material using the DMM algorithm, we can employ any theory of plasticity that takes into account the material behavior under alternating-sign stresses, including the known Bauschinger effect, e.g., the models of Jwan (1967), Shorr (1984), Lippmann and Winter (1987), and others. In this Section, the simplest Ishlinsky‘s (1954) model described by the theory of linear (kinematical) hardening is employed. Its stress-plastic strain diagram $\sigma = f(\varepsilon_p)$, where $\varepsilon_p = \varepsilon - \sigma / E$, is shown in Fig.3.7a. Plastic deformation is assumed to be small.

Initial yield points of material for tension $\sigma_{yt} > 0$ and compression $\sigma_{yc} < 0$, in the absence of previous plastic strain ($\varepsilon_p = 0$), are assumed to be of the same magnitude $\sigma_{yt} = |\sigma_{yc}| = \sigma_{yi}$. The width of the elastic domain, equal to $2\sigma_y$ with $\sigma_y = \sigma_{yi}$, remains constant under the subsequent deformation, while this domain itself, as a whole, is displaced in the direction of the stress action, simultaneously with growth of the plastic strain.

A current position of the middle point of the elastic domain is determined as

$$\sigma_r = E_p \varepsilon_p, \tag{3.34}$$

where E_p is the modulus of linear plastic hardening connected with the or-

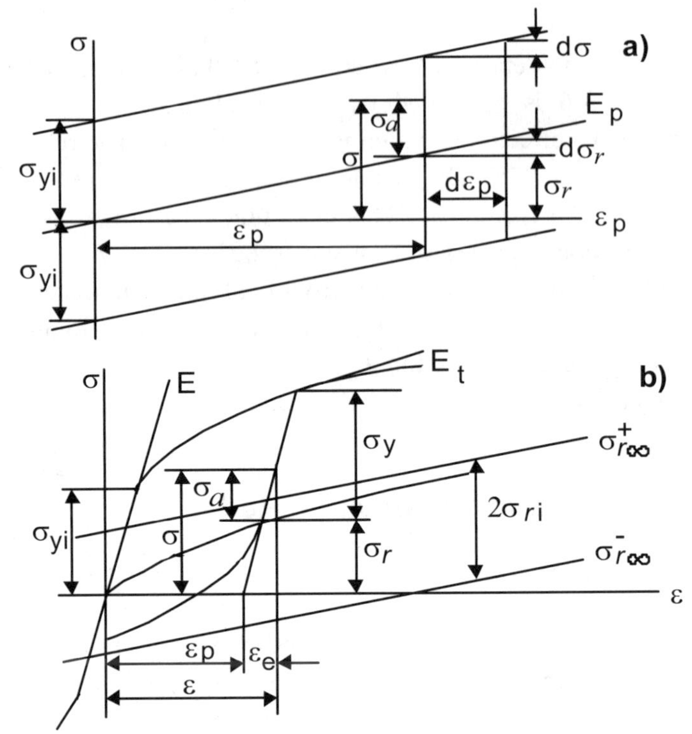

Fig. 3.7. Stress-strain diagrams for elastic-plastic models:
a) $E_p = \text{const}, \sigma_y = \sigma_{yi} = \text{const}$, b) $E_p = f(\sigma_r, \varepsilon_p, \text{sign}\sigma_a), \sigma_y = f(\varepsilon_{ps})$

dinary tangential modulus $E_t = d\sigma / d\varepsilon$ by the expression $E_p = E_t / (1 - E_t)$.

Kadashevich and Novozhilov (1958) suggested presenting the total stress σ under plastic deformation ε_p as the sum of 'residual' σ_r and 'active' σ_a components

$$\sigma = \sigma_r + \sigma_a. \tag{3.35}$$

The strain alternates elastically as long as the active stress remains within the elastic domain $-\sigma_y \le \sigma_a \le \sigma_y$. In this case, $d\varepsilon_p = 0$, $d\sigma_r = 0$, and $d\sigma = d\sigma_a$. When the active stress arrives at one of the borders of the elastic domain, i.e.

$$|\sigma_a| = \sigma_y, \tag{3.36a}$$

and the total stress σ continues increasing in magnitude, so that

$$\sigma_a d\sigma > 0, \tag{3.36b}$$

the plastic strain also restores increasing in the direction of the active stress action according to the stress-plastic strain diagram; then,

$$d\varepsilon_p = \frac{d\sigma_r}{E_p} = \frac{d\sigma}{E_p}, \quad d\sigma_a = 0. \tag{3.37}$$

When unloading (with $\sigma_a d\sigma < 0$), the active stress returns into the elastic domain and plastic flow stops. If the sign of active stress alters, the process is developed in the opposite direction and the values of the plastic strain and residual stress decrease; moreover, they may alternate the sign. In other words, the kinematical hardening under alternating-sign loading is reversible.

The conditions for plastic flow can be written as

$$d\varepsilon_p = \begin{cases} 0 \text{ with} |\sigma_a| < \sigma_y, \text{ or } |\sigma_a| = \sigma_y \text{ and } \sigma_a d\sigma \le 0, \\ \dfrac{d\sigma}{E_p} \text{ with} |\sigma_a| = \sigma_y \text{ and } \sigma_a d\sigma \ge 0 \end{cases}. \tag{3.38}$$

3.3.1.2. Using the DMM algorithm, the value of the plastic strain $\varepsilon^{\pm}_{jp,0}$ and the relevant residual stress $\sigma^{\pm}_{jr,0} = E_p \varepsilon^{\pm}_{jp,0}$ in the links at the beginning of current time step are known from the previous step calculations. We assume first an elastic deformation, calculating the elastic border stresses $\sigma^{\pm}_j$. If the plastic strain does not change, the total stress in the link is constant over the time step and coincides with outer border stress. Then, the active stress is

$$\sigma^{\pm}_{ja} = \sigma^{\pm}_j - \sigma^{\pm}_{jr.0}. \tag{3.39}$$

If $|\sigma^{\pm}_j - \sigma^{\pm}_{jr,0}| \le \sigma_y$, then due to the first condition (3.38), the assumption of elastic deformation is true.

Otherwise, with $|\sigma^{\pm}_j - \sigma^{\pm}_{jr,0}| > \sigma_y$, the plastic strain begins to increase again. Its change $\Delta\varepsilon^{\pm}_{jp}$ corresponding to the stress-plastic strain diagram is accompanied by the growth of total stress from current yield point

$$\sigma^{\pm}_{jy} = \sigma^{\pm}_{jr,0} + \text{sign}\,\sigma^{\pm}_{ja}\sigma_y \tag{3.40}$$

to $\sigma^{\pm}_{jy} + \Delta\sigma^{\pm}_{jr}$, where $\Delta\sigma^{\pm}_{jr} = E_p \Delta\varepsilon^{\pm}_{jp}$. Its mean value over the time step is

$$\sigma_{jm}^{\pm} = \sigma_{jy}^{\pm} + 0.5 E_p \Delta\varepsilon_{jp}^{\pm} \tag{3.41}$$

and must, as before, be equal to the border stress $\sigma_j^{\pm}$ which, of course, can differ from the value of the stress obtained in the elastic calculation. Due to Eq.(3.21),

$$\sigma_j^{\pm} = \frac{\sigma_{j,0} + \sigma_{j-1,0} + (v_{j,0} - v_{j-1,0})\rho c - 2E\psi_j^{\pm}}{2(1+\varphi_j^{\pm})}, \tag{3.42}$$

and it is therefore deduced that

$$\Delta\varepsilon_{jp}^{\pm} = 2(\sigma_j^{\pm} - \sigma_{jy}^{\pm}) / E_p. \tag{3.43a}$$

Inserting Eq.(3.40) into (3.43a) and taking in account that $\mathrm{sign}\sigma_{ja}^{\pm} = \mathrm{sign}(\sigma_j^{\pm} - \sigma_{jr,0}^{\pm})$, we obtain

$$\Delta\varepsilon_{jp}^{\pm} = 2\{\sigma_j^{\pm} - [\sigma_{jr,0}^{\pm} + \mathrm{sign}(\sigma_j^{\pm} - \sigma_{jr,0}^{\pm})\sigma_y]\} / E_p. \tag{3.43b}$$

Comparing all these results with expression (3.13a) and using a nondimensional form of the DMM algorithm with coefficients $\varphi_j^{\pm}$, $\psi_j^{\pm}$, we get for the conditions of the elastic-plastic deformation applying to the element j (Shorr 1995)

$$\varphi_j^{\pm} = 0,\ \overline{\psi}_j^{\pm} = 0 \quad \text{with } \left|\overline{\sigma}_j^{\pm} - \overline{\sigma}_{jr,0}^{\pm}\right| \le \overline{\sigma}_y,$$

$$\left.\begin{aligned} \varphi_j^{\pm} &= \frac{1}{\overline{E}_p}, \\ \overline{\psi}_j^{\pm} &= -\varphi_j^{\pm}[\overline{\sigma}_{jr,0}^{\pm} + \mathrm{sign}(\overline{\sigma}_j^{\pm} - \overline{\sigma}_{jr,0}^{\pm})\overline{\sigma}_y] \end{aligned}\right\} \text{ with } \left|\overline{\sigma}_j^{\pm} - \overline{\sigma}_{jr,0}^{\pm}\right| > \sigma_y. \tag{3.44}$$

where $\overline{E}_p = E_p / E$. In this Section, the stress is scaled by the initial yield point $\overline{\sigma} = \sigma / \sigma_{yi}$ and the related strain and velocity are, correspondingly, $\overline{\varepsilon} = \varepsilon E / \sigma_{yi}$ and $\overline{v} = v\rho c / \sigma_{yi}$.

***3.3.1.3.* A. Problem 3.4. An elastic-plastic rod affected by a linearly increasing force.** To illustrate elastic-plastic wave propagation, we consider again a one-clamped rod with a stress $\overline{\sigma}_1^-$ applied to the free end and linearly increasing from $\overline{\sigma}_1^- = 0$ to $\overline{\sigma}_1^- = 1.25$ during i_* steps. So, the maximal applied stress is somewhat greater than the yield point. Let the relative plastic modulus be $\overline{E}_p = 0.04$. The boundary condition at the clamped end $\overline{v}_{n,*}^{+} = 0$ leads to the boundary stress

$$\overline{\sigma}_n^+ = (\overline{\sigma}_{n,0} - \overline{v}_{n,0} - \overline{\psi}_n^+)/(1+\varphi). \tag{3.45}$$

As the stresses σ_j and total strains ε_j are referred to elements, we exploit below the mean value of plastic strain over the element

$$\overline{\varepsilon}_{jp,m} = 0.5(\overline{\varepsilon}_{jp}^- + \overline{\varepsilon}_{jp}^+).$$

The distribution of stresses $\overline{\sigma}$, plastic $\overline{\varepsilon}_p$, and full $\overline{\varepsilon}$ strains along the rod for the time instant $\overline{t} = 1$, i.e. before wave reflection from the clamped end, is shown in Fig.3.8 calculated for 500 elements and load increasing during $\overline{t}_* = 0.05$ ($i_* = 25$). The stress-strain diagram for above parameters is indicated in the same Figure.

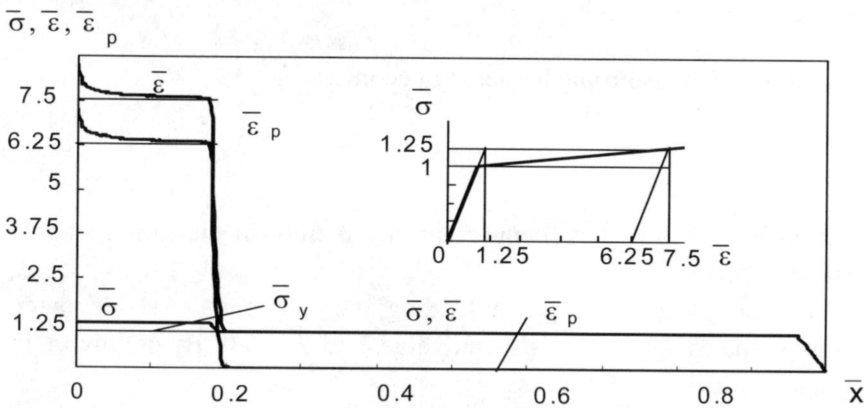

Fig. 3.8. Stresses and also plastic and full strains in an elastic-plastic rod under linearly increasing force at the free end

Retardation of the plastic wave from the elastic one is clearly seen. The relative plastic wave speed is about $\overline{c}_p \approx 0.2$, closely coinciding with theoretical value $\overline{c}_p = (\overline{E}_t)^{0.5}$ obtained from the deformation theory of plasticity. As $\overline{E}_t = \overline{E}_p/(1+\overline{E}_p)$, the theoretical speed for $\overline{E}_p = 0.04$ is $\overline{c}_p = 0.196$. If the force at the free end applied suddenly (with $i_* = 1$), both the leading elastic wave front and the plastic front become steeper, with the calculated steepness growing as number of elements increases.

The stable plastic strain of the level $\overline{\varepsilon}_p \approx 6.25$ is established after advancement of the plastic wave front. This level is determined by the anisotropic linear hardening with the plastic modulus $\overline{E}_p = 0.04$ (see the elastic-plastic diagram in Fig.3.8).

B. Some local increasing of the plastic strain over the value $\bar{\varepsilon}_p = 6.25$ immediately near the free end is seen in Fig.3.8. This is caused by small stress oscillations of period $2\Delta\bar{t}$ due to discrete character of plastic links in the model considered. With $\bar{E}_p << 1$, small stress oscillations about 1-2% noticeably increase plastic strain. Although this local calculated effect is of no practical meaning, it can be eliminated by smoothing the stress over the period $2\Delta\bar{t}$, as shown in Chap.1.

3.3.1.4. **A.** Isotropic hardening, which enlarges the width of the elastic domain as a plastic strain grows, is readily included in calculation procedure. By setting the yield point σ_y in active stresses as a function of 'accumulated' plastic deformation $\sigma_y(\varepsilon_{ps})$, where

$$\varepsilon_{ps} = \int_0^{\varepsilon_p} |d\varepsilon_p|, \tag{3.46}$$

the modulus of the isotropic hardening becomes

$$E_y = \frac{d\sigma_y}{d\varepsilon_{ps}} = E_y(\varepsilon_{ps}). \tag{3.47}$$

The influence of this hardening appears mainly in the initial stage of plastic deformation.

Under multiple alternating-sign loading, the yield point of stable materials approximates, usually, a constant value, and $E_y \to 0$. By definition, the isotropic hardening is not reversible.

When the active stress arrives at the current yield point $|\sigma_a| = \sigma_y(\varepsilon_{ps})$, the increase of total stress $\sigma = \sigma_r + \sigma_a$ is (see Fig.3.7b)

$$d\sigma = d\sigma_r + \mathrm{sign}\sigma_a d\sigma_y, \tag{3.48}$$

and, in accordance with Eqs.(3.34) and (3.47),

$$d\varepsilon_p = \frac{d\sigma}{E_p + E_y(\varepsilon_{ps})}. \tag{3.49}$$

The module E_p and E_y are connected with tangential modulus $E_t = d\sigma/d\varepsilon$ and Young's modulus E by the relation

$$\frac{1}{E_y + E_p} = \frac{1}{E_t} - \frac{1}{E}.$$

Using the DMM algorithm, both the value of accumulated plastic strain $\varepsilon^{\pm}_{jps,0}$ (and, hence, the values of yield point $\sigma^{\pm}_{jy,0}$) and modulus $E^{\pm}_{jy}$ at the beginning of current step are assumed known. Repeating the deduction of the previous subsections, we come to the similar equations for the conditions of elastic-plastic deformation

$$\varphi_j^{\pm}=0,\ \overline{\psi}_j^{\pm}=0 \quad \text{with } \left|\overline{\sigma}_j^{\pm}-\overline{\sigma}_{jr,0}^{\pm}\right|\leq\overline{\sigma}_{jy,0}^{\pm},$$

$$\left.\begin{aligned}\varphi_j^{\pm}&=\frac{1}{\overline{E}_p+\overline{E}_{jy}^{\pm}},\\ \overline{\psi}_j^{\pm}&=-\varphi_j^{\pm}[\overline{\sigma}_{jr,0}^{\pm}+\text{sign}(\overline{\sigma}_j^{\pm}-\overline{\sigma}_{jr,0}^{\pm})\overline{\sigma}_{jy,0}^{\pm}]\end{aligned}\right\} \text{with } \left|\overline{\sigma}_j^{\pm}-\overline{\sigma}_{jr,0}^{\pm}\right|>\sigma_{jy}^{\pm}. \tag{3.50}$$

The value of $\overline{E}_{jy}^{\pm}=E_{jy}^{\pm}/E$ is assumed to be constant over the small strain change $\Delta\overline{\varepsilon}_{jps}^{\pm}$.

B. To describe nonlinear anisotripic hardening under alternating-sign loading, a model of restricted area of residual stresses was proposed by Shorr (1975) - see also Birger et al. (1975) - and given a more detailed exposition in Shorr (1979).

It was assumed that a nonlinear function $\sigma_r=f(\varepsilon_p)$ under monotone increase of plastic deformation in any direction approaches some limit straight lines $\sigma_{r\infty}=\text{sign}\sigma_a\sigma_{ri}+E_{pi}\varepsilon_p$ (Fig.3.7b), where σ_{ri} and E_{pi} are experimental characteristics of the material. The residual plastic stresses σ_r under any arbitrary loading trajectories alter only within the area of $2\sigma_{ri}$.

These assumptions lead to the equation

$$E_p=\frac{d\sigma_r}{d\varepsilon_p}=E_{pi}+\beta[\sigma_{ri}-\text{sign}\sigma_a(\sigma_r-E_{pi}\varepsilon_p)], \tag{3.51}$$

where β is also an experimental constant of material.

The value of E_p depends on ε_p,σ_r and loading direction.

Integrating (3.51) over the current step with $\text{sign}\sigma_a$=const., we obtain

$$\Delta\sigma_r=E_{pi}\Delta\varepsilon_p+\text{sign}\sigma_a(E_{p,0}-E_{pi})[1-\exp(-\beta|\Delta\varepsilon_p|)]/\beta$$

or, with $\beta|\Delta\varepsilon_p|<<1$,

$$\Delta\sigma_r\approx E_{p,0}\Delta\varepsilon_p. \tag{3.52}$$

Here, $E_{p,0}$ is determined from Eq.(3.51) using the values of $\varepsilon_{p,0}$, $\sigma_{r,0}$, and $\sigma_{a,0}$ at the beginning of current step. The further calculation order remains the same as above.

3.3.2 An Elastic-Viscoplastic Model

3.3.2.1. Under dynamic loading, the inelastic deformations may have viscoplastic behavior. Due to the model in Fig.3.2b, where all the material characteristics ($E_p, \sigma_y, \eta_c, \eta_v$) are assumed to be constant, the following equations are valid:

$$\left.\begin{aligned} &\sigma - \sigma_{vm} = \sigma_{rm} + \sigma_{am}, \Delta\varepsilon_{p\Sigma} = \Delta\varepsilon_c + \Delta\varepsilon_p, \\ &\sigma_{rm} = E_p \varepsilon_{pm} \approx E_p(\varepsilon_{p,0} + 0.5\Delta\varepsilon_p), \\ &\sigma_{vm} = \eta_v \dot{\varepsilon}_p \approx \eta_v \Delta\varepsilon_p / \Delta t, \sigma = \eta_c \dot{\varepsilon}_c \approx \eta_c \Delta\varepsilon_c / \Delta t \end{aligned}\right\}, \tag{3.53}$$

where σ_{rm}, σ_{vm}, and σ_{am} are the mean values of these stresses over the step Δt.

Under plastic flow,

$$\left.\begin{aligned} &\sigma_a = \sigma_{am} = \text{sign}\sigma_{r,0}\sigma_y = \text{const}, \\ &\text{sign}\sigma_{r,0}\Delta\varepsilon_p > 0 \end{aligned}\right\}. \tag{3.54}$$

Otherwise, $\Delta\varepsilon_p = 0$, the viscoplastic branch of the link is ‘locked’, and the change in inelastic strain is purely viscous

$$\Delta\varepsilon_{p\Sigma} = \Delta\varepsilon_c = 2\sigma\xi_c / E, \tag{3.55}$$

where

$$\xi_c = 0.5\Delta t / \tau_c, \tau_c = \eta_c / E.$$

If conditions (3.54) are satisfied, we find from Eqs.(3.53)

$$\sigma = \text{sign}\sigma_{r,0}\sigma_y + E_p(\varepsilon_{p,0} + 0.5\Delta\varepsilon_p) + \eta_v \frac{\Delta\varepsilon_p}{\Delta t},$$

from where, taking into account that $\text{sign}\sigma_{r,0} = \text{sign}(\sigma - \sigma_{r,0})$,

$$\Delta\varepsilon_p = \frac{2\xi_v}{E_p(1+\xi_v)}[\sigma - \sigma_{r,0} - \text{sign}(\sigma - \sigma_{r,0})\sigma_y], \tag{3.56}$$

where

$$\xi_v = 0.5\Delta t / \tau_v, \tau_v = \eta_v / E_p.$$

Comparing Eq.(3.55) and (3.56) with expression (3.13a), we obtain for the element j in nondimensional form

$$\varphi_j^{\pm} = \xi_c,\ \overline{\psi}_j^{\pm} = 0 \quad \text{with } \left|\overline{\sigma}_j^{\pm} - \overline{\sigma}_{jr,0}^{\pm}\right| \le \overline{\sigma}_y,$$

$$\left.\begin{aligned} \varphi_j^{\pm} &= \xi_c + \frac{1}{\overline{E}_p}\frac{\xi_v}{1+\xi_v}, \\ \overline{\psi}_j^{\pm} &= -\frac{1}{\overline{E}_p}\frac{\xi_v}{1+\xi_v}[\overline{\sigma}_{jr,0}^{\pm} + \text{sign}(\overline{\sigma}_j^{\pm} - \overline{\sigma}_{jr,0}^{\pm})\overline{\sigma}_y] \end{aligned}\right\} \text{with } \left|\overline{\sigma}_j^{\pm} - \overline{\sigma}_{jr,0}^{\pm}\right| > \sigma_y. \tag{3.57}$$

3.3.2.2. **Problem 3.5. A semi-infinite elastic-viscoplastic rod subjected to a suddenly applied force.** Just as in Subsect.3.2.2.1, we assume a constant velocity of the free end but with negative relative value of $\overline{v}_{1,*}^- = -5$. Time is scaled with the retardation time $\overline{t} = t/\tau_v$ and, correspondingly, $\overline{x} = xc/\tau_v$. It is assumed that $\overline{E}_p = 0.25$, $\xi_c = 0\,(\tau_c \to \infty)$, and $\xi_v = 0.05\ (\Delta\overline{t} = 2\xi_v = 0.1)$. The calculations are carried out until $\overline{t} = \overline{x} = 100$ with the maximal number of elements $n = 1000$.

Figure 3.9 shows the distributions of the stress $\overline{\sigma}$ and the total strain $\overline{\varepsilon}$ over the length of the rod at a number of instants $\overline{t}$. Fig.3.10 demonstrates the dynamic time-dependent stress-strain diagram in some points $\overline{x}$.

Directly after the impact, the stress at the free end ($\overline{x} = 0$) increases elastically until $\overline{\sigma} = -\overline{v}_{1,*}^- = 5$ and essentially exceeds the initial static yield

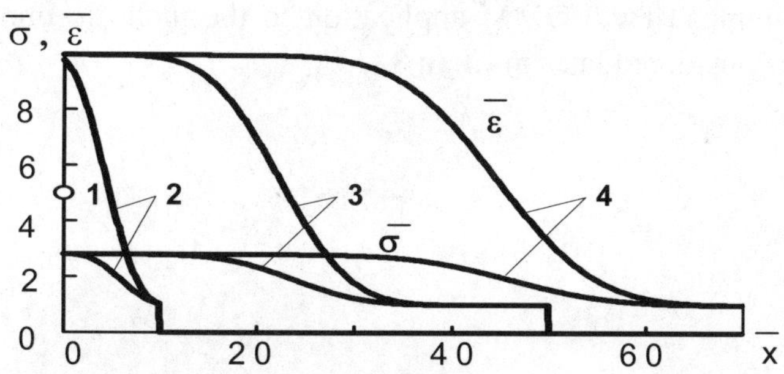

Fig. 3.9. Stresses and total strains in a semi-infinite elastic-viscoplastic rod under a suddenly applied force; 1) $\overline{t} = 0$, 2) $\overline{t} = 10$, 3) $\overline{t} = 50$, 4) $\overline{t} = 100$

the point of impact the cross section is situated, the faster the stress arrives at the static curve.

The viscoplastic waves, characterized by visible appearing of the plastic strain $\overline{\varepsilon}_p = \overline{\varepsilon} - \overline{\sigma}$ and increasing of the stress over the initial yield point, propagate slower than the elastic wave. The viscoplastic wave speed varies depending on the strain level, with the mean quantity that is near the theoretical value of plastic wave speed $\bar{c}_p = [\bar{E}_p/(1+\bar{E}_p)]^{0.5}$, in our case

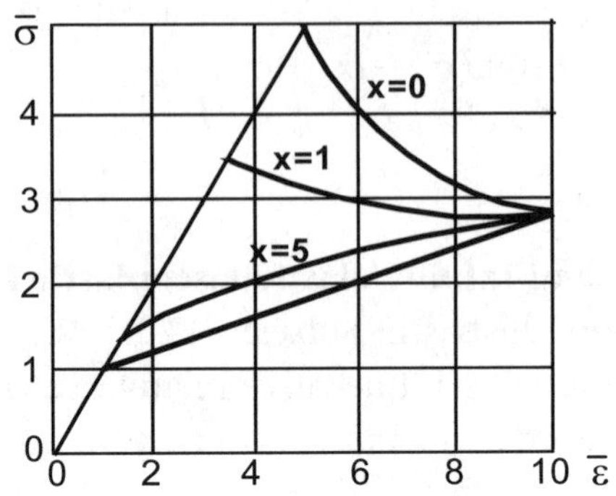

Fig. 3.10. Dynamic stress-strain diagram for an elastic-viscoplastic rod

$\bar{c}_p \approx 0.45$. After the viscoelastic wave front goes through any point, stable 'plateaus' of constant stresses and strains form.

All the numerical results presented agree well with known experimental data and analogous results obtained in Stepanov (1978) by numerical integration of the differential wave equation using the method of characteristics.

Some examples of the DMM application to the inelastic impact problems will be considered later in Chap.8.

4 Coupled Longitudinal-Torsional Waves in a Pre-Twisted Rod

A pre-twisted rod is a typical 1-D mechanical system, in which two kinds of waves arise and propagate simultaneously, interacting with each other. This requires exploiting the general WFEM approach.

4.1 Basic Equations

4.1.1 Governing Equations for a Pre-Twisted Rod

An elastic homogeneous rod of two-symmetrical cross sections is considered. The rod is pre-twisted (or 'naturally' twisted), that is the local principal axes of the cross section η, ζ rotate relative to the rod x-axis with a rate $\theta_{in}(x) = d\varphi_{in} / dx$, see Fig. 4.1a.

The theory of pre-twisted rods was studied by many authors, beginning from Kirchhoff (1859) and Clebsch (1862). The last century, the theory has obtained significant development in connection with design of air-

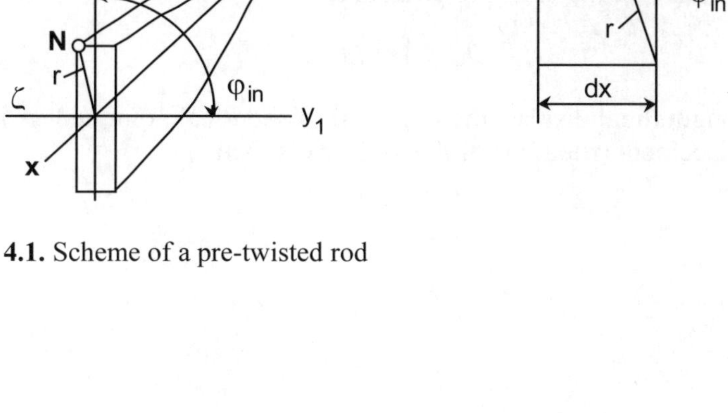

Fig. 4.1. Scheme of a pre-twisted rod

screws and axial compressor and turbine blades (see, by example, Shorr 1954, 1959, and 1968; the review in Vorob'ev and Shorr 1983; and also in Srinivasan 1997). In the case of two-symmetrical cross sections, a set of governing equations of a pre-twisted rod decays in two independent sets for bending and longitudinal-torsional deformations. The latter is

$$\left.\begin{aligned} F &= \beta_{11}\varepsilon + \beta_{12}\theta \\ M &= \beta_{21}\varepsilon + \beta_{22}\theta \end{aligned}\right\}, \tag{4.1}$$

where F is a longitudinal force, M is a torsional moment, ε is an elastic longitudinal strain, θ is a relative angle of elastic twisting, and β_{ij} are components of a stiffness matrix.

Respective points of different cross sections of the pre-twisted rod having the same local coordinates lie at the spiral fiber NN. We see that, according to Fig.4.1b, a value of increment ds can be determined as $ds = \gamma_{in}(r)dx = rd\varphi_{in}$, hence $\gamma_{in}(r) = \theta_{in}(x)r$. Let $\gamma_{in,m} = \theta_{in}r_m$ be a maximal angle between the spiral fiber far removed from the x-axis and this axis. Assuming moderate pre-twist when

$$\gamma_{in.m}^2 << 1, \tag{4.2}$$

the components β_{ij}, as shown by Shorr (1954) and also by Knowles and Reissner (1960), are

$$\beta_{11} = EA,\ \beta_{12} = \beta_{21} = \theta_{in}EJ_p,\ \beta_{22} = GJ_{t0}(1+\beta^2), \tag{4.3a}$$

where A is an area and J_{t0} is a geometrical stiffness of the cross section of the corresponding untwisted (prismatic) rod in torsion; $J_p = \int_A r^2 dA$ is a cross-sectional polar second moment (moment of inertia). Here

$$\beta = \theta_{in}\sqrt{\frac{EJ_r}{GJ_{t0}}} \tag{4.3b}$$

is a characteristic parameter of pre-twist and

$$J_r = \int_A r^4 dA.$$

If u is a longitudinal displacement of a cross-sectional point and φ is an angular displacement (rotation) of the η, ζ - axes then

$$\varepsilon = \frac{\partial u}{\partial x},\quad \theta = \frac{\partial \varphi}{\partial x}. \tag{4.4}$$

4.1.2 Wave Model of a Pre-Twisted Rod

4.1.2.1. Using wave finite element modeling, we assume that the rod is divided into n equal elements of dimension Δx and the elements are in a quasi-static state at a time instant t_{i-1}^{-}. The longitudinal $v_{j,0}$ and the angular $\omega_{j,0}$ velocities, as well as the boundary (nodal) displacements $u_{j,0}^{\pm}$ and $\varphi_{j,0}^{\pm}$ of each element $j=1,2,...,n$ are assumed to be known.

The mean values of element deformations $\varepsilon_{j,0}$ and $\theta_{j,0}$ are, respectively,

$$\varepsilon_{j,0} = \frac{u_{j,0}^{+} - u_{j,0}^{-}}{\Delta x}, \quad \theta_{j,0} = \frac{\varphi_{j,0}^{+} - \varphi_{j,0}^{-}}{\Delta x}. \tag{4.5}$$

Making use of Eqs.(4.1) and (4.5), we can find all the mechanical characteristics of the element j at the instant t_{i-1}^{-}:

The potential energy is given by

$$\begin{aligned} P_{j,0} = 0.5[\, & \beta_{11}(u_{j,0}^{+} - u_{j,0}^{-})^2 + 2\beta_{12}(u_{j,0}^{+} - u_{j,0}^{-})(\varphi_{j,0}^{+} - \varphi_{j,0}^{-}) + \\ & + \beta_{22}(\varphi_{j,0}^{+} - \varphi_{j,0}^{-})^2\,] / \Delta x \end{aligned} \tag{4.6}$$

with the kinetic energy

$$K_{j,0} = 0.5\rho(Av_{j,0}^2 + J_p\omega_{j,0}^2)/\Delta x\ . \tag{4.7}$$

The forces $F_{j,0}^{\pm}$ and the moments $M_{j,0}^{\pm}$ applied to the element in its nodes are

$$\left.\begin{aligned} F_{j,0}^{+} &= \frac{\partial P_{j,0}}{\partial u_{j,0}^{+}} = [\,\beta_{11}(u_{j,0}^{+} - u_{j,0}^{-}) + \beta_{12}(\varphi_{j,0}^{+} - \varphi_{j,0}^{-})] / \Delta x \\ M_{j,0}^{+} &= \frac{\partial P_{j,0}}{\partial \varphi_{j,0}^{+}} = [\,\beta_{21}(u_{j,0}^{+} - u_{j,0}^{-}) + \beta_{22}(\varphi_{j,0}^{+} - \varphi_{j,0}^{-})] / \Delta x \end{aligned}\right\} \tag{4.8a}$$

and also

$$F_{j,0}^{-} = -F_{j,0}^{+},\ M_{j,0}^{-} = -M_{j,0}^{+}. \tag{4.8b}$$

The inner force $F_{j,0}$ and the inner moment $M_{j,0}$ in any cross section of the element j are

$$F_{j,0} = F_{j,0}^{+},\ M_{j,0} = M_{j,0}^{+}. \tag{4.9}$$

A normal stress $\sigma(\eta,\zeta)$ and components $\tau_{x\eta}(\eta,\zeta)$ and $\tau_{x\zeta}(\eta,\zeta)$ of a tangential stress can be determined using formulae (Shorr 1960)

$$\sigma(\eta,\zeta) = E(\varepsilon_{j,0} + \theta_{in}\theta_{j,0} r^2), \; r^2 = \eta^2 + \zeta^2 \tag{4.10a}$$

and

$$\tau_{x\eta}(\eta,\zeta) = G\left(\frac{\partial \psi}{\partial \eta} + \zeta\right)\theta_{j,0}, \; \tau_{x\zeta}(\eta,\zeta) = G\left(\frac{\partial \psi}{\partial \zeta} - \eta\right)\theta_{j,0} \tag{4.10b}$$

where $\psi(\eta,\zeta)$ is an ordinary torsion function of a cross section.

4.1.2.2. Denote the forces and the moments affecting the element j in its nodes during time interval Δt_i by $F_j^{\pm}$ and $M_j^{\pm}$, and the corresponding boundary longitudinal and angular velocities by $v_j^{\pm}$ and $\omega_j^{\pm}$, respectively. It follows from the laws of momentum and angular momentum balance of each half of the element j during the half-interval $0.5\Delta t$ that

$$\left.\begin{aligned} F_j^{\pm} &= \pm F_{j,0} + \rho A(v_j^{\pm} - v_{j,0})\Delta x / \Delta t \\ M_j^{\pm} &= \pm M_{j,0} + \rho J_p(\omega_j^{\pm} - \omega_{j,0})\Delta x / \Delta t \end{aligned}\right\}. \tag{4.11}$$

Analogously, these laws when applied to the whole element j during the interval Δt_i lead to

$$\left.\begin{aligned} v_j &= v_{j,0} + (F_j^+ + F_j^-)\Delta t_i / \rho A \Delta x, \\ \omega_j &= \omega_{j,0} + (M_j^+ + M_j^-)\Delta t_i / \rho J_p \Delta x \end{aligned}\right\}, \tag{4.12}$$

where v_j and ω_j are new longitudinal and angular element velocities at the instant $t_i^- = t_{i-1}^- + \Delta t_i$.

Combining Eqs.(4.11) and (4.12), we obtain

$$v_j = v_j^+ + v_j^- - v_{j,0}, \quad \omega_j = \omega_j^+ + \omega_j^- - \omega_{j,0}. \tag{4.13}$$

The new values of nodal displacements are

$$\left.\begin{aligned} u_j^{\pm} &= u_{j,0}^{\pm} + v_j^{\pm}\Delta t_i, \\ \varphi_j^{\pm} &= \varphi_{j,0}^{\pm} + \omega_j^{\pm}\Delta t_i \end{aligned}\right\}. \tag{4.14}$$

Moreover, the work of boundary forces and moments applied to the element in its nodes during the interval Δt_i is

$$\Delta W_j = (F_j^+ v_j^+ + F_j^- v_j^- + M_j^+ \omega_j^+ + M_j^- \omega_j^-)\Delta t_i. \tag{4.15}$$

To determine the boundary parameters of the adjoining elements j-1 and j at their common node, we use the conditions of continuity

$$v^+_{j-1} = v^-_j,\ \omega^+_{j-1} = \omega^-_j \tag{4.16a}$$

and equilibrium

$$\left.\begin{aligned} F^+_{j-1} + F^-_j - F^*_j - F^*_{v,j} = 0, \\ M^+_{j-1} + M^-_j - M^*_j - M^*_{\omega,j} = 0 \end{aligned}\right\}. \tag{4.16b}$$

Here, F^*_j and M^*_j are the external force and moment applied to the node j at the instant t^+_{i-1}, and

$$F^*_{v,j} = -\eta_v v^-_j,\quad M^*_{\omega,j} = -\eta_\omega \omega^-_j \tag{4.17}$$

are external visco-linear friction force and moment with viscous coefficients η_v, η_ω respectively.

Inserting Eqs.(4.11) into Eqs.(4.16), we obtain

$$v^-_j = \frac{v_{j,0} + v_{j-1,0} + (F_{j,0} + F^*_j - F_{j-1,0})\Delta t_i / \rho A \Delta x}{2 + \eta_v \Delta t_i / \rho A \Delta x} \tag{4.18a}$$

and

$$\omega^-_j = \frac{\omega_{j,0} + \omega_{j-1,0} + (M_{j,0} + M^*_j - M_{j-1,0})\Delta t_i / \rho J_p \Delta x}{2 + \eta_\omega \Delta t_i / \rho J_p \Delta x}, \tag{4.18b}$$

that allows expressing all the parameters at the instant t^-_i in terms of the time interval Δt_i.

To determine the potential energy P_j and kinetic energy K_j at the instant t^-_i, parameters $u^\pm_{j,0}, \varphi^\pm_{j,0}, v_{j,0}, \omega_{j,0}$ in Eqs.(4.6) and (4.7) have to be replaced by parameters $u^\pm_j, \varphi^\pm_j, v_j, \omega_j$, respectively.

The law of energy balance for the whole rod requires

$$\sum_{j=1}^{n} (\Delta K_j + \Delta P_j - \Delta W_j) = 0, \tag{4.19a}$$

where $\Delta K_j = K_j - K_{j,0}$ and $\Delta P_j = P_j - P_{j,0}$, or

$$\sum_{j=1}^{n} (K_j + P_j) - \sum_{i=1}^{n_t} \sum_{j=1}^{n} W_{ji} = 0. \tag{4.19b}$$

The last expression is more preferable in any calculation procedure.

With reference to general WFEM, the time interval Δt_i has to be determined from Eq.(4.19b) for each step.

4.1.2.3. To reduce the calculation algorithm to the simplest form, the following dimensionless quantities are introduced:

$$\bar{x}=\frac{x}{r_p},\ \bar{t}=\frac{tc_v}{r_p},\ \bar{F}=\frac{F}{F^o},\ \bar{M}=\frac{M}{F^o r_p},\ \bar{v}=\frac{v\rho Ac_v}{F^o},\ \bar{\omega}=\frac{\omega\rho Ar_p c_v}{F^o},$$

$$\bar{u}=\frac{uEA}{F^o r_p},\ \bar{\varphi}=\frac{\varphi EA}{F^o},\ \bar{\varepsilon}=\frac{\varepsilon EA}{F^o},\ \bar{\theta}=\frac{\theta EAr_p}{F^o},\ \bar{\theta}_{in}=\frac{\theta_{in}EAr_p}{F^o},$$

$$\bar{W}=\frac{WEA}{(F^o)^2 r_p},\ \bar{K}=\frac{\bar{K}EA}{(F^o)^2 r_p},\ \bar{P}=\frac{\bar{P}EA}{(F^o)^2 r_p},\ \bar{\eta}_v=\frac{\eta_v}{\rho Ac_v},\ \bar{\eta}_\omega=\frac{\eta_\omega}{\rho J_p c_v},$$

$$\bar{\beta}_{11}=\frac{\beta_{11}}{E}=1,\ \bar{\beta}_{12}=\frac{\beta_{12}}{EAr_p}=\theta_{in}r_p,\ \bar{\beta}_{22}=\frac{\beta_{22}}{EJ_p}=\frac{GJ_{t0}}{EJ_p}(1+\beta^2). \tag{4.20}$$

Here, F^o is an arbitrary reference force, $c_v=(E/\rho)^{0.5}$ is a longitudinal wave speed in an untwisted rod, and $r_p=(J_p/A)^{0.5}$ is a radius of inertia for cross section in torsion.

If n is a number of elements and L is a length of a rod, then $\Delta x=L/n$ and $\Delta\bar{x}=\lambda_p/n$, where $\lambda_p=L/r_p$ represents a torsional 'slenderness' of the rod. On the other hand,

$$\Delta\bar{x}=\frac{c\Delta t}{r_p}=\bar{c}\Delta\bar{t},\ \bar{c}=\frac{c}{c_v}, \tag{4.21a}$$

where $c=\Delta x/\Delta t$ is a real wave speed in the pre-twisted rod. Therefore,

$$\Delta\bar{t}=\frac{\lambda_p}{n\bar{c}}. \tag{4.21b}$$

Equation (4.21b) shows that both the relative time step $\Delta\bar{t}$ and relative wave speed $\bar{c}$ can be taken as unknown step parameters for a homogeneous rod.

As the speed of a torsional wave in an untwisted rod is $c_{\omega 0}=(GJ_{t0}/\rho J_p)^{0.5}$, then

$$\bar{c}_{\omega 0}=\frac{c_\omega}{c_v}=\sqrt{\frac{GJ_{t0}}{EJ_p}}. \tag{4.22}$$

The magnitude of the ratio $\bar{c}_\omega$ may be significantly less than unity for a rod of an elongated cross section.

Disposition of any cross section scaled by the rod length is described by

$$\widetilde{x} = x / L = \overline{x} / \lambda_p. \quad (4.23a)$$

A relative process time is characterized by

$$\widetilde{t} = t / T_v = \overline{t} / \lambda_p, \quad (4.23b)$$

where $T_v = L / c_v$ is the time that the longitudinal wave takes to propagate along the length L in the untwisted rod.

Three problems of wave propagation in a pre-twisted rod are considered below. The first two are relatively simple; however, some of their results may be compared with analytical solutions and experimental data. The third one, presented in Chap.8 - an impact of a rigid body against a pre-twisted rod - is studied, as far as we know, for the first time.

4.2 Wave Propagation Induced by a Force and Torque

4.2.1 Waves Induced by a Constant Load

4.2.1.1. **Problem 4.1. A pre-twisted rod subjected to a longitudinal force and torque. A.** Consider a one-clamped uniformly pre-twisted rod of an elongated rectangular cross section of width h and height b, with $\overline{h} = h / b << 1$ and length L (Fig. 4.2).

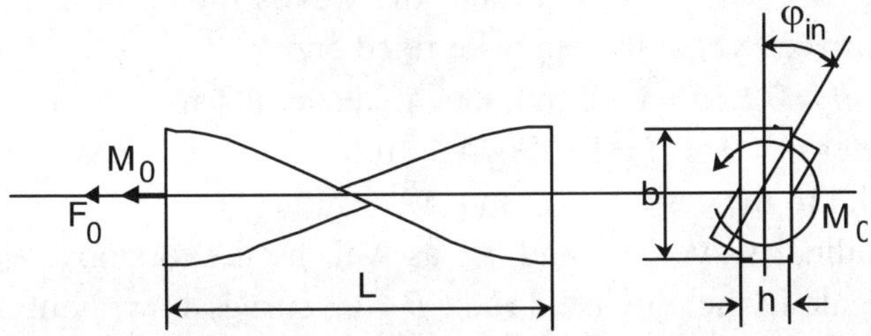

Fig. 4.2. Sketch to loading of a pre-twisted one-clamped rod

The total pre-twist angle is φ_{in} and the relative angle is $\theta_{in}=\varphi_{in}/L$. A longitudinal force F_0 applied to the free end of the rod varies step-wise with time steps i=1,2...n_F according to

$$F_0 = \begin{cases} i/n_F \text{ with } 1 \le i \le n_F \\ 1 \quad \text{with } i \ge n_F \end{cases}, \quad (4.24)$$

i.e., the force increases during n_F steps and then becomes constant. A similar equation relates to the torque M_0. The loads are suddenly applied with n_F=1.

The initial conditions in dimensionless notation are

$$\overline{v}_{j,in} = 0,\ \overline{\omega}_{j,in} = 0,\ \overline{u}^{\pm}_{j,in} = 0,\ \overline{\varphi}^{\pm}_{j,in} = 0.\ j = 1,2,...,n \tag{4.25}$$

The boundary conditions with the reference force $F^o = F_0$ are

$$\overline{F}_1^- = -\overline{F}_0,\ \overline{M}_1^- = -\overline{M}_0,\ \overline{v}_n^+ = 0,\ \overline{\omega}_n^+ = 0. \tag{4.26}$$

The geometrical characteristics from Eqs.(4.3a), (4.3b), and (4.20) for a rod of the elongated rectangular cross section are

$$A = bh,\ J_p = b^3h/12,\ r_p = b/\sqrt{12},\ J_{t0} = bh^3/3,$$

$$\lambda_p = \sqrt{12}L/b,\ \beta = \theta_{in}\frac{b^2}{h}\sqrt{\frac{1+\mu}{30}},\ \overline{c}_{\omega 0} = \overline{h}\sqrt{\frac{2}{1+\mu}}, \tag{4.27}$$

$$\overline{\beta}_{11} = 1,\ \overline{\beta}_{12} = \beta\overline{h}\sqrt{\frac{5}{2(1+\mu)}},\ \overline{\beta}_{22} = \frac{2(1+\beta^2)\overline{h}^2}{1+\mu}.$$

B. At first, the system is assumed to be undamped ($\eta_v = \eta_\omega = 0$). Distributions of the inner force $\overline{F}$, inner moment $\overline{M}$, longitudinal strain $\overline{\varepsilon}$, and relative rotation angle $\overline{\theta}$ along the rod at the time instant $\tilde{t} = 0.8$ are shown in Figs.4.3-4.4. At this instant, the waves traveling from the free end have not arrived yet at the opposite fixed end.

It is taken $\overline{h} = 0.1$, $\mu = 1/3$, number of elements n=100, and the pre-twist parameter $\beta = 0$ or $\beta = 1$. Fig.4.3 refers to the case $\overline{F}_0 = 1$ and $\overline{M}_0 = 0$, Fig.4.4 to the case $\overline{F}_0 = 0$ and $\overline{M}_0 = 1$.

The longitudinal waves $\overline{F}$ and $\overline{\varepsilon}$, as well as the torsional waves $\overline{M}$ and $\overline{\theta}$, propagate in the untwisted rod ($\beta = 0$, curves 1) without distortion and independently of one another with wave speeds $\overline{c}_v = 1$ and $\overline{c}_{\omega 0} = 0.1225$, respectively. This entirely correlates with the exact analytical solution.

In the pre-twisted rod ($\beta = 1$, curves 2) all the waves propagate in conjunction with one other. Two domains can be clearly seen in Figs.4.3-4.4. The domain I propagates from the free end of the rod, to which the external loads have been applied, with 'low' speed $\overline{c}_{min} \approx \overline{c}_\omega = 0.1732$, where $\overline{c}_\omega = \overline{c}_{\omega 0}(1+\beta^2)^{0.5}$ is a partial torsion speed accounting the pre-twist. The deformation-load relationships in this domain are determined by Eqs.(4.1) of the pre-twisted rods for the corresponding boundary conditions at the free end.

Equations (4.1) in nondimensional notation lead to

$$\left.\begin{aligned}\bar{\varepsilon} = \bar{\alpha}_{11}\bar{F},\ \bar{\theta} = \bar{\alpha}_{12}\bar{F} \quad \text{with}\ \bar{F}_0 = 1,\ \bar{M}_0 = 0,\\ \bar{\varepsilon} = \bar{\alpha}_{21}\bar{M},\ \bar{\theta} = \bar{\alpha}_{22}\bar{M} \quad \text{with}\ \bar{F}_0 = 0,\ \bar{M}_0 = 1,\end{aligned}\right\}, \tag{4.28a}$$

where

$$\bar{\alpha}_{11} = \frac{\bar{\beta}_{22}}{\bar{\Delta}},\ \bar{\alpha}_{12} = \bar{\alpha}_{21} = -\frac{\bar{\beta}_{12}}{\bar{\Delta}},\ \bar{\alpha}_{22} = \frac{\bar{\beta}_{11}}{\bar{\Delta}},\ \bar{\Delta} = \bar{\beta}_{11}\bar{\beta}_{22} - \bar{\beta}_{11}^{\ 2}. \tag{4.28b}$$

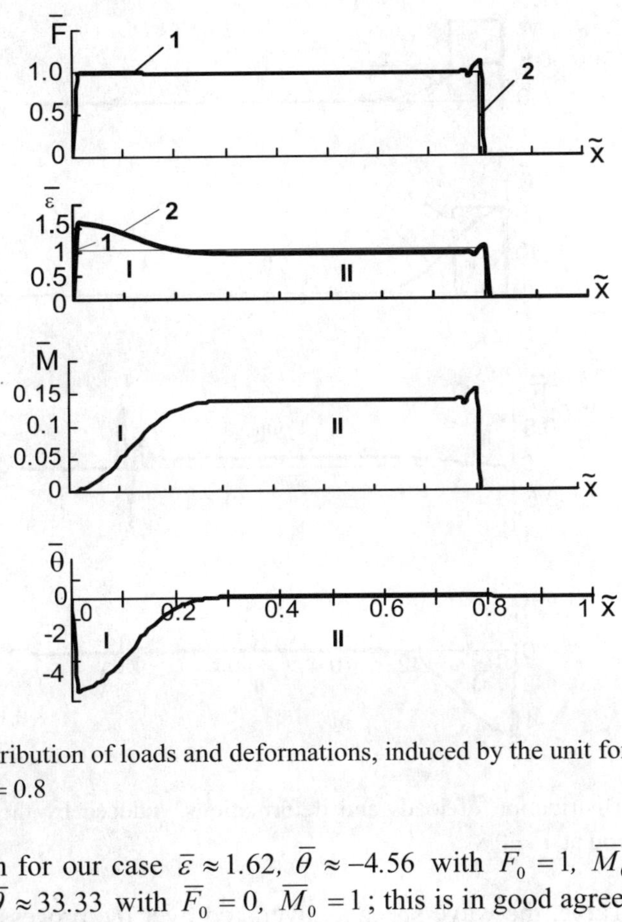

Fig. 4.3. Distribution of loads and deformations, induced by the unit force, along the rod at $\tilde{t} = 0.8$

We obtain for our case $\bar{\varepsilon} \approx 1.62,\ \bar{\theta} \approx -4.56$ with $\bar{F}_0 = 1,\ \bar{M}_0 = 0,$ and $\bar{\varepsilon} \approx -4.56,\ \bar{\theta} \approx 33.33$ with $\bar{F}_0 = 0,\ \bar{M}_0 = 1$; this is in good agreement with the pattern in Figs.4.3-4.4.

The deformation-load relationships in the domain II following the leading wave with 'high' speed $\bar{c}_{max} \approx \bar{c}_v = 1$ is more complex. We see that in this domain $\bar{\varepsilon} \approx \bar{F}$ and $\bar{\theta} \approx \bar{M}$; this being associated with the unified speed of the leading coupled longitudinal-torsional wave. The outstripping propagation of the longitudinal strain $\bar{\varepsilon} \approx 1$, with $\bar{F}_0 = 1$, $\bar{M}_0 = 0$, induces the moment $\bar{M} \approx \bar{\beta}_{12}\bar{\varepsilon} \approx 0.137$ (Fig.4.3). On the other hand, by $\bar{F}_0 = 0$ when $\bar{M}_0 = 1$, the longitudinal strain is only $\bar{\varepsilon} \approx \bar{F} \approx \bar{\beta}_{12}\bar{\theta} \approx 0.137$, so the succeeding values of torsional parameters become $\bar{M} \approx \bar{\theta} \approx \bar{\beta}_{12}^{\,2} \approx 0.02$ (Fig.4.4).

The leading wave affected by the constant torque $\bar{M}_0$ reaches the value of the speed $\bar{c} \approx 1$ not immediately but progressively (see Table 4.1).

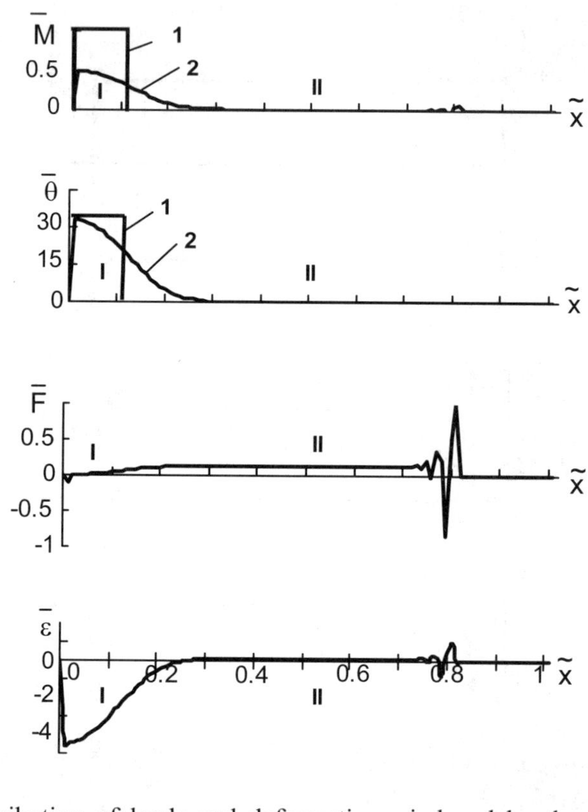

Fig. 4.4. Distribution of loads and deformations, induced by the unit torque, along the rod at $\tilde{t} = 0.8$

In this Table, the wave speed $\bar{c}_m$ averaged over the process time is presented in dependence of the pre-twist parameter β and the calculated step index i. The greater the pre-twist is, the sooner the speed increases.

Table 4.1. A wave speed $\bar{c}_m$ vs. step index i and pre-twist parameter β

$\beta \setminus i$	1	2	5	10	100
0.	0.122	0.122	0.122	0.122	0.122
0.5	0.153	0.256	0.458	0.625	0.942
1.0	0.221	0.350	0.568	0.722	0.967
1.5	0.302	0.446	0.663	0.797	0.990
2.0	0.387	0.537	0.741	0.857	1.014

4.2.1.3. Let the force $\bar{F}_0$ vary as indicated in Eq.(4.24) with $n_F = 5$. Taking into account external damping, the deformations after multiple reflections from the rod ends approximate the state of static equilibrium. Fig.4.5 shows the alteration of relative angle decreasing (detwist angle) at the free end $\bar{\theta}(0)$ and at clamped end $\bar{\theta}(1)$ against time $\tilde{t}$.

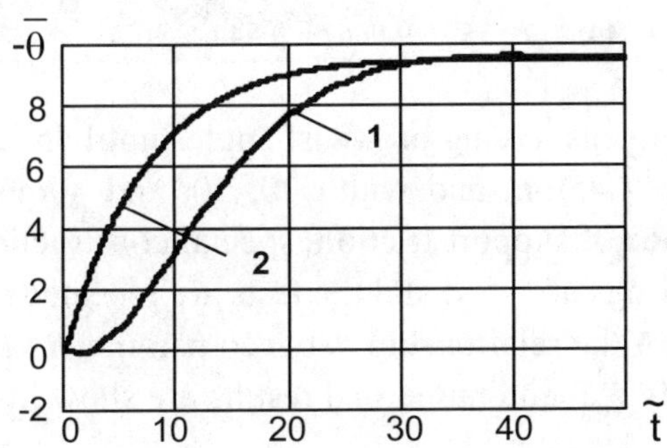

Fig.4.5. Relaxation of relative detwisting angles to steady-state condition

Here, the number of elements is $n = 10$, the step number is increased to $n_t = 5000$ corresponding to 500 reflections, the pre-twist parameter is $\beta = 1$, the ratio of cross-sectional thickness to width is $\bar{h} = 0.04833$, and damping coefficients are $\bar{\eta}_v = \bar{\eta}_\omega = 0.01$. In Fig.4.5 the reflection number is shown only to 50, as the pattern does not noticeably alter in what follows. In steady-state condition, the difference between $\bar{\theta}(0)$ and $\bar{\theta}(1)$ approaches zero.

The stationary magnitudes are determined numerically with high accuracy, as can be seen from Table 4.2 where the calculated values of angles $\bar{\theta}_{st}(0) \approx \bar{\theta}_{st}(1)$ are compared with theoretical ones $\bar{\theta}_{th}$ for different values of parameter β . Here, as shown by Shorr (1960)

$$\theta_{th} = -\frac{F_0 J_p \theta_{in}}{G J_{t0} A (1+\beta^2)} \tag{4.29a}$$

or

$$\overline{\theta}_{th} = -\frac{\beta}{1+\beta^2} \frac{1}{\overline{h}} \sqrt{\frac{5(1+\mu)}{8}}. \tag{4.29b}$$

Experimental data for detwisting of pre-twisted duralumin rods of elongated rectangular cross section under expanding force are presented in Shorr (1959).

Table 4.2. Stationary numerical $\overline{\theta}_{st}$ and theoretical $\overline{\theta}_{th}$ detwist angles for different values of β

$\theta \setminus \beta$	0	0.25	0.50	0.75	1.00	1.25	1.50	1.75	2.00
$-\overline{\theta}_{st}$	0	4.435	7.554	9.066	9.444	9.214	8.718	8.137	7.557
$-\overline{\theta}_{th}$	0	4.444	7.555	9.066	9.444	9.214	8.718	8.136	7.555

About 40 specimens having pre-twist angles until 75° at the base 100mm with thickness h=1.45mm and width 20, 30, and 40mm were tested. To avoid the influence of support friction, special construction with two freely rotating ball-bearings are used and the tests are repeated several times. Test data in the form of the relationship between parameters θ^* and β in comparison with analytical and numerical results are show in Fig.4.6. Here,

$$\theta^* = \beta \frac{|\theta|}{\theta_{in}}. \tag{4.30}$$

The experimental values of θ^*_{exp} are obtained using Eq.(4.30) with measured angles θ_{exp} of detwisting. The analytical values of θ^* are determined from Eqs.(4.29a) and (4.30) as

$$\theta^*_{th} = \frac{\nu\beta}{1+\beta^2}, \tag{4.31a}$$

where

$$\nu = \frac{J_p F_0}{G L_{t0} A} \left(= \frac{(1+\mu) F_0 b}{2 E h^3} \right) \tag{4.31b}$$

is a loading factor.

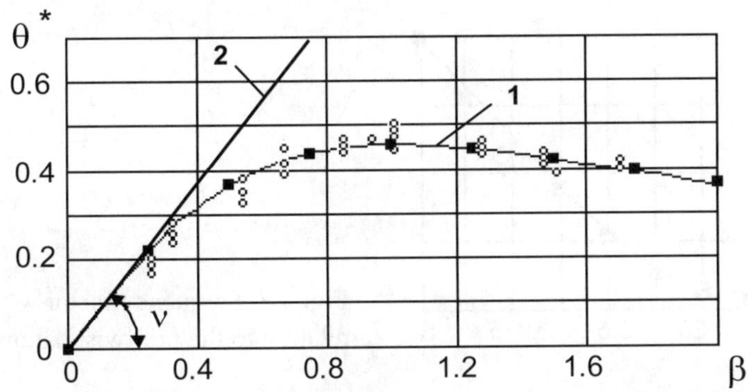

Fig. 4.6. Generalized detwist angle θ^{*} as a function of pre-twist parameter β

Calculated values of θ^{*} using wave modeling are

$$\theta^{*}_{wm} = \left|\overline{\theta}\right| \frac{\beta F_0}{EAr_p\theta_{in}} \left(= \left|\overline{\theta}\right| \nu\overline{h} \sqrt{\frac{8}{5(1+\mu)}} \right). \tag{4.31c}$$

The expressions in parentheses refer to the elongated rectangular cross section.

All the data in Fig.4.6 are obtained with the identical loading factor $\nu = 0.0911$. The correlation between numerical (black dots), analytical (solid curve), and experimental (white dots) results are close.

Existence of the maximum at the curve $\theta^{*} = f(\beta)$ is affected by growth of the rod stiffness in torsion while the pre-twist angle increasing. Do not taking into account this phenomenon, the function $\theta^{*} = f(\beta)$ is linear that is correct only for $\beta^2 << 1$ (curve 2 in Fig.4.6).

4.2.2 Impulse-Induced Waves

4.2.2.1. **A**. The experimental frequencies f_{min} of the first coupled longitudinal-torsion mode for pre-twisted cantilever rods of rectangular cross section are studied by Vorob'ev and Shorr (1983).

The relative thickness of specimens is $\overline{h} = 1/12 = 0.0833$. The results are expressed using a frequency factor $\kappa = f / f_{\theta,0}$, where $f_{\theta,0}$ is the first theoretical eigenfrequency of torsional vibration for the corresponding untwisted rod.

The experimental quantity of $\kappa_{min} = f_{min} / f_{\theta,0}$ as a function of the pre-twist parameter β is displayed by white dots in Fig.4.7.

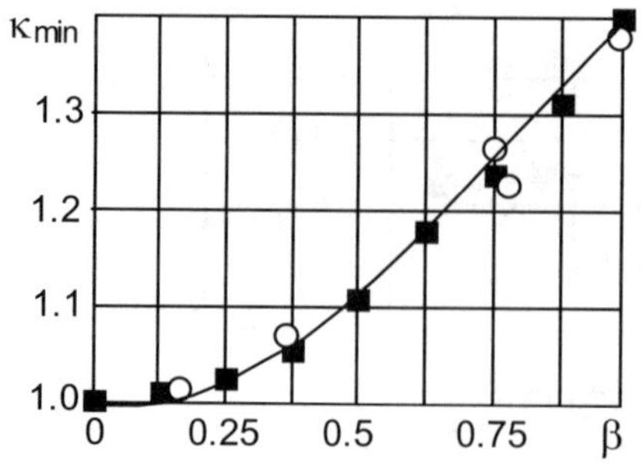

Fig. 4.7. Frequency factor κ_{min} in relation to the pre-twist parameter β

The theoretical values of the frequency factor $\kappa_{1,2} = f_{1,2} / f_{\theta,0}$ for two lowest oscillation modes 1,2 of a pre-twist rod are (Shorr 1960),

$$(\kappa_{1,2})^2 = 0.5[\kappa_\varepsilon^2 + \kappa_\theta^2 \mp \sqrt{(\kappa_\varepsilon^2 - \kappa_\theta^2)^2 + 4\theta_{in}^2 r_p^2 \kappa_\varepsilon^4}\,], \tag{4.32a}$$

where $\kappa_\varepsilon = f_\varepsilon / f_{\theta,0}$, $\kappa_\theta = f_\theta / f_{\theta,0}$, and $f_{\theta,0} = \sqrt{GJ_{t0} / \rho J_p} / 4L$.

For the first family of coupled longitudinal-torsion modes (with single node at the clamped end),

$$\kappa_\theta = \sqrt{1+\beta^2}, \quad \kappa_\varepsilon = \sqrt{\frac{EJ_p}{GJ_{t0}}}. \tag{4.32b}$$

In respect of an elongated rectangular cross section, the frequency factors are given by

$$\kappa_\varepsilon = \frac{1}{h}\sqrt{\frac{1+\mu}{2}} >> 1, \quad \kappa_1 \approx \kappa_\theta, \quad \kappa_2 \approx \kappa_\varepsilon . \tag{4.32c}$$

The minimum theoretical value of $\kappa_{min} = \kappa_1$ is shown in Fig.4.7 by solid curve.

B. Problem 4.2. Coupled oscillation of a pre-twisted rod induced by a torque. Using wave modeling, the eigenfrequencies can be approximately obtained as the resonance frequencies under harmonical excitation or as frequencies of impulse-induced oscillations. Replacing Eq.(4.24) by

$$M_0 = \begin{cases} i/n_F & \text{with} 1 \le i \le n_F, \\ 0 & \text{with} i \ge n_F \end{cases} . \tag{4.33}$$

and putting $n_F = 1$, we get a one-step torque impulse.

The time dependence of angular displacement $\overline{\varphi}$ and longitudinal displacement $\overline{u}$ at the free end of a cantilever rod subjected to the torque $\overline{M}_0 = -1$ is shown in Fig.4.8. The rod is assumed to be undamped.

Steady step-wise oscillation of the angle $\overline{\varphi}$ arises in the untwisted rod (Fig.4.8a) where $\beta = 0$ and $\kappa_{\theta,0} = 1$. Its visible relative period is $\widetilde{\tau}_0 \approx 40$, with analytical value of $\widetilde{\tau}_0 = \tau_0 c_v / L = 4/\overline{c}_{\omega 0} \approx 39.39$. This corresponds to a wave speed of $\overline{c}_{\omega 0} \approx 0.1021$ and a relative torsional frequency of $\widetilde{f}_{\theta,0} = 1/\widetilde{\tau}_0 \approx 0.0255$. The analytical minimal longitudinal eigenfrequency is $\widetilde{f}_{\varepsilon,0} = 0.25$ with the frequency factor of $\kappa_{\varepsilon,0} = \widetilde{f}_{\varepsilon,0.} / \widetilde{f}_{\theta,0} \approx 9.80$. The longitudinal displacements $\overline{u}$ are absent.

In the case of a pre-twisted rod, both oscillations of angle $\overline{\varphi}$ (Fig.4.8b) and displacement $\overline{u}$ (Fig.4.8c) arise. The period of the angle oscillations $\widetilde{\tau}$ decreases and the frequency increases (for $\beta = 1$ we have $\widetilde{\tau} \approx 28.15$ and $\kappa_{min} \approx 1.4$). The angle amplitudes gradually decrease, since a part of the Initial torque impulse energy is transferred to the energy of longitudinal waves. In the curve of $\overline{u}(\widetilde{t}\,)$ we see slow waves with the same period and phase as for the angle oscillation and fast step-wise waves, which fre-

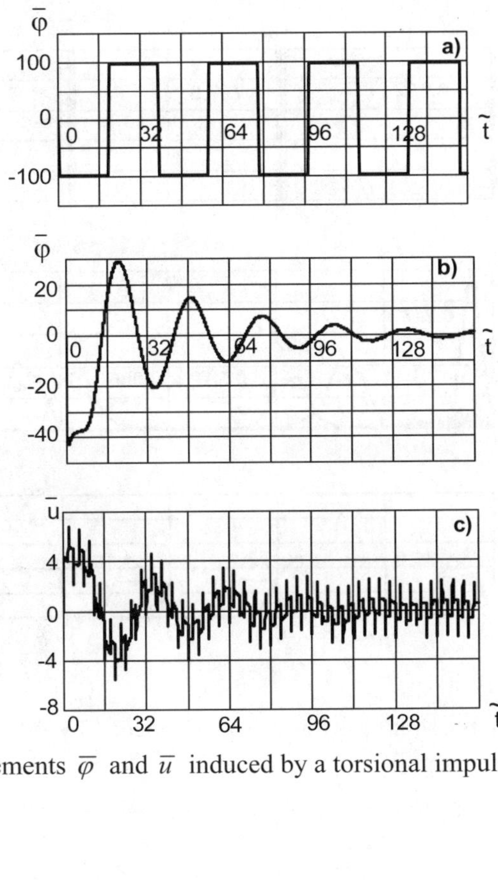

Fig. 4.8. Displacements $\overline{\varphi}$ and $\overline{u}$ induced by a torsional impulse vs. time $\widetilde{t}$

quency factor hardly exceeds the value $\kappa_{\varepsilon,0} \approx 9.80$ of the untwisted rod. This quantity follows also from Eq. (4.32a) as κ_2 by taking sign (+). Besides, the traces of initial impulse reflections from the fixed end appear in the form of undamped spike peaks during all the process.

A comparison of numerical κ_{nm} and theoretical κ_{th} frequency factors for some values of β is presented in Table 4.3; the factor κ_{nm} is also plotted in Fig.4.7 by black dots. Correlation between numerical, theoretical, and experimental frequencies is very good.

Table 4.3. Numerical κ_{nm} and theoretical κ_{th} frequency factors for different values of β

β	0	0.25	0.50	0.75	1.00
κ_{nm}	1.000	1.019	1.107	1.238	1.399
κ_{th}	1.000	1.031	1.116	1.247	1.401

C. Distribution of relative full energy $\widetilde{E} = (P+K)/W_{in}$ along the rod

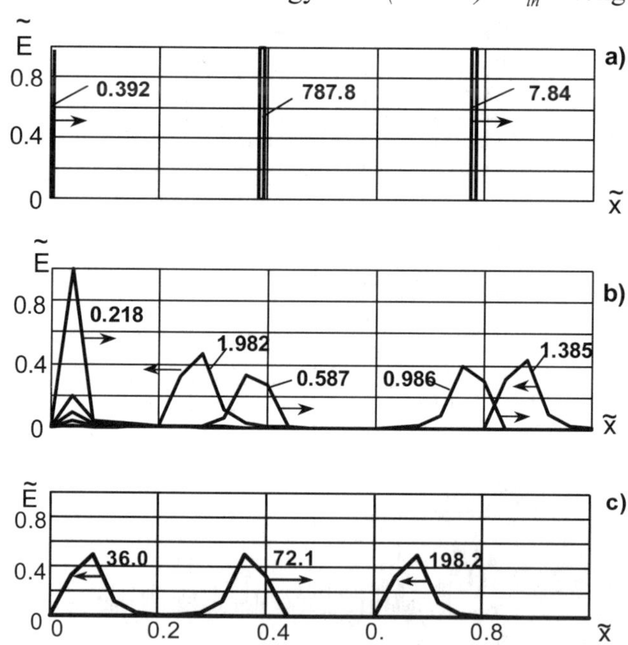

Fig. 4.9. Distribution of relative full energy $\widetilde{E}$ induced by the unit torque along the rod at the different time

length (with $n = 25$) at some instants $\tilde{t}$ is shown in Fig.4.9a with $\beta = 0$ and in Fig.4.9b,c with $\beta = 1$.

Here, W_{in} is the energy of the initial torque impulse, which is different for the cases under consideration but remains constant during the whole process. Numerical labels indicate time instants. The values of energy $\tilde{E}$ in Fig.4.9b and 4.9c are conditionally referred to the coordinate $\tilde{x}$ at the corresponding elements end and connected with the polygonal line.

With $\beta = 0$ the energy wave travels along the rod with constant speed $\overline{c}_{\omega} \approx 0.1021$ as a concentrated disturbance. With $\beta \neq 0$ the energy wave is eroded at the beginning, moreover, its speed is close to $\overline{c} \approx 1$. Then, its configuration becomes also permanent, as it can be clearly seen from comparison the waves at $\tilde{t}_1 = 1.982$ (Fig.4.9b) and at $\tilde{t}_2 = 100\tilde{t}_1 = 198.2$ (Fig. 4.9c). The energy values between peak domains are nonzero but too small to be visible in the graphical representation.

5 Bending Waves in a Beam

5.1 Basic Equations

5.1.1 Wave Model of the Timoshenko Beam

5.1.1.1. Studying the wave propagation in a beam, we take the following usual assumptions:

i) The beam possesses the symmetry plane xy, with x the axis of the beam, and transverse deflections $y(x,t)$ within this plane;

ii) The material of the beam is elastic and homogeneous with density ρ, Young's E and shear G module;

iii) The longitudinal ε_x and shear $\varepsilon_{xy} = \varepsilon_{xy}$ strains are small compared with unity;

iv) The square of the deformed axis slope $\psi = \partial y / \partial x$ is small compared with unity, then $\sin\psi \approx \psi$, $\cos\psi \approx 1$. At first, the cross-sectional area A and the moment of inertia of the beam cross section J are assumed constant.

Applying the numerical method, additional assumptions are made, namely:

i) The external forces, given or determined from the local boundary conditions, are applied to the nodes and remain constant during time steps Δt_i;

ii) The condition, which the element length Δx must obey, is

$$\alpha^2 << 1, \tag{5.1}$$

where $\alpha = 0.5\Delta x / r$ and $r = \sqrt{J / A}$ is a radius of inertia of the beam cross section.

As $\Delta x = L / n$, where L is a length of the beam and n is a number of elements, the condition of Eq.(5.1) can always be satisfied, as n increases.

To correctly describe wave propagation, it is necessary to exploit a Timoshenko type theory of beam transversal vibration, which takes into account shear and section rotation effects.

The well-known equations of elastic beam deformation are

$$M_z = EJ\chi, \quad F_y = GA\gamma / k_s, \tag{5.2}$$

and

$$\gamma = \psi - \varphi, \tag{5.3}$$

where M_z is a bending moment, F_y is a shear force, k_s is a shear coefficient dependent on the section form, φ is a rotation angle of cross section due to beam curving, $\psi = \partial y / \partial x$ is a slope of the beam deformed axis, γ is a shear angle, and the rate of the rotation angle is $\chi = \partial\varphi / \partial x$.

Ignoring the shear influence (as is usual in Bernoulli-Euler type theory), $\gamma = 0$ and $\varphi = \psi = \partial y / \partial x$; then, the rate of rotation angle coincides with the curvature χ of the deformed axis and is given by $\chi = \partial^2 y / \partial x^2$. In general case it is remarked that $\chi \neq \partial^2 y / \partial x^2$.

5.1.1.2. Assume, according to the previously described wave approach, that each beam element j is in a quasi-static state at the time instant t_{i-1}^-, i.e., its transverse linear velocity in the y direction is $v_{j,0}$, the rotation velocity about z-axis is $\omega_{j,0}$, the lateral (transverse) deflections of its nodes are $y_{j,0}^{\pm}$, and the rotation angles of the boundary sections are $\varphi_{j,0}^{\pm}$. All these quantities are known from previous calculation steps or initial boundary conditions. The velocities $v_{j,0}$ and $\omega_{j,0}$ allow us to determine the following:

the element momentum in the transverse direction

$$M_{vj,0} = \rho A \Delta x v_{j,0}, \tag{5.4}$$

the element angular momentum about the z- axis

$$M_{\omega j,0} = \rho I \Delta x \omega_{j,0}, \tag{5.5}$$

the full kinetic energy of the element

$$K_{j,0} = 0.5\rho\Delta x(A v_{j,0}^2 + I\omega_{j,0}^2). \tag{5.6}$$

In view of the condition of Eq.(5.1), $I \approx J$.

A knowledge of the displacements $y_{j,0}^{\pm}$ and $\varphi_{j,0}^{\pm}$ enables determination of the following parameters:

The mean slope of the beam deformed axis over the element j

$$\psi_{jm,0} = \frac{y_{j,0}^{+} - y_{j,0}^{-}}{\Delta x}, \tag{5.7}$$

the mean rate of rotation angle

$$\chi_{jm,0} = \frac{\varphi^{+}_{j,0} - \varphi^{-}_{j,0}}{\Delta x}, \tag{5.8}$$

the mean deflection

$$y_{jm,0} = 0.5(y^{+}_{j,0} + y^{-}_{j,0}), \tag{5.9}$$

the mean rotation angle

$$\varphi_{jm,0} = 0.5(\varphi^{+}_{j,0} + \varphi^{-}_{j,0}), \tag{5.10}$$

the mean shear angle

$$\gamma_{jm,0} = \psi_{jm,0} - \varphi_{jm,0}, \tag{5.11}$$

and Eqs.(5.7)-(5.10) yield

$$y^{\pm}_{j,0} = y_{jm,0} \pm 0.5\psi_{jm}\Delta x; \; \varphi^{\pm}_{j,0} = \varphi_{jm,0} \pm 0.5\chi_{jm}\Delta x. \tag{5.12}$$

The full potential energy $P_{j,0}$ of the element is given by

$$P_{j,0} = 0.5(EJ\chi^{2}_{jm,0} + GA\gamma^{2}_{jm,0} / k_s)\Delta x, \tag{5.13a}$$

or taking into account Eqs.(5.8)-(5.11),

$$\begin{aligned} P_{j,0} = 0.5\{ & EJ(\varphi^{+}_{j,0} - \varphi^{-}_{j,0})^2 + \\ & + GA[(y^{+}_{j,0} - 0.5\varphi^{+}_{j,0}\Delta x) - (y^{-}_{j,0} + 0.5\varphi^{-}_{j,0}\Delta x)]^2 / k_s \} / \Delta x \end{aligned} \tag{5.13b}$$

The forces $F^{\pm}_{j,0}$ and the moments $M^{\pm}_{j,0}$ affecting the element j in its nodes can be determined as

$$F^{\pm}_{j,0} = \frac{\partial P_{j,0}}{\partial y^{\pm}_{j,0}}, \; M^{\pm}_{j,0} = \frac{\partial P_{j,0}}{\partial \varphi^{\pm}_{j,0}}, \tag{5.14}$$

hence

$$\left.\begin{aligned} F^{\pm}_{j,0} &= \pm GA[y^{+}_{j,0} - y^{-}_{j,0} - 0.5(\varphi^{+}_{j,0} + \varphi^{-}_{j,0})\Delta x] / k_s\Delta x, \\ M^{\pm}_{j,0} &= \pm EJ(\varphi^{+}_{j,0} - \varphi^{-}_{j,0}) / \Delta x \mp 0.5F^{\pm}_{j,0}\Delta x \end{aligned}\right\}. \tag{5.15a}$$

Using Eqs.(5.13b) and treating the partial derivatives (5.14), we obtain

$$F^{\pm}_{j,0} = \pm F_{jm,0}, \quad M^{\pm}_{j,0} = \pm M_{jm,0} - 0.5F_{jm,0}\Delta x, \tag{5.15b}$$

where the mean values of inner force $F_{jm,0}$ and moment $M_{jm,0}$ are

$$F_{jm,0} = GA\gamma_{jm,0} / k_s, \quad M_{jm,0} = EJ\chi_{jm,0}, \tag{5.16}$$

corresponding to Eqs.(5.2).

Evidently, in the state of equilibrium,

$$F_{j,0}^{+} + F_{j,0}^{-} = 0, \quad M_{j,0}^{+} + M_{j,0}^{-} + F_{j,0}^{+}\Delta x = 0.$$

It is readily confirmed that Eq.(5.13b) can be represented as the work $W_{j,0}$, which the loads statically applied to the element in its nodes perform over the actual nodes displacements at the time instant t_{i-1}^{-}

$$P_{j,0} = W_{j,0} = 0.5(F_{j,0}^{+}y_{j,0}^{+} + F_{j,0}^{-}y_{j,0}^{-} + M_{j,0}^{+}\varphi_{j,0}^{+} + M_{j,0}^{-}\varphi_{j,0}^{-}). \tag{5.17}$$

5.1.1.3. **A.** At the infinitesimally close instant t_{i-1}^{+}, forces, bending moments, and velocities at the element borders can suddenly vary by finite quantities. Corresponding to the wave approach, these parameters denoted by $F_{j,*}^{\pm}, M_{j,*}^{\pm}, v_{j,*}^{\pm}, \omega_{j,*}^{\pm}$ are assumed to remain constant during the time step Δt_i. The principal peculiarity of bending waves implies that only the force and angular velocity can propagate over the element without alteration, whereas the moment and the transverse velocity alter with time. Therefore, they must be averaged over the step. We denote the averaged values by $F_j^{\pm}, M_j^{\pm}, v_j^{\pm}, \omega_j^{\pm}$, where

$$F_j^{\pm} = F_{j,*}^{\pm}, \omega_j^{\pm} = \omega_{j,*}^{\pm}. \tag{5.18}$$

All the equations considered below in this Section are valid within a time interval Δt_i; however, the value of Δt_i remains so far undetermined.

As the fronts of the forces $F_{j,*}^{\pm}$ travel from one element end to the other, additional bending moments arise and increase from zero to $\pm F_{j,*}^{\pm}\Delta x$; their average values in a time Δt_i are $\pm 0.5F_{j,*}^{\pm}\Delta x$. Adding these moments to the external ones, we obtain

$$M_j^{\pm} = M_{j,*}^{\pm} \pm 0.5F_{j,*}^{\pm}\Delta x. \tag{5.19}$$

Likewise, as the fronts of the angular velocities $\omega_{j,*}^{\pm}$ travel along the element length, the additional transverse velocities of the corresponding element ends due to rotation increase from zero to $\pm\omega_{j,*}^{\pm}\Delta x$ with the average values of $\pm 0.5\omega_{j,*}^{\pm}\Delta x$. Therefore, the full transverse border velocities are

$$v_{j,*}^{\pm} = v_j^{\pm} \pm 0.5\omega_{j,*}^{\pm}\Delta x. \tag{5.20}$$

We emphasize that the additional moments affect the element, whereas the additional velocities only refer to the element borders, i.e. to its corresponding nodes.

Taking into account Eqs.(5.18)-(5.20), we find from the law of momentum conservation in the transverse direction

$$v_{j,*}^{\pm} = v_{j,0} \pm 0.5\omega_{j,*}^{\pm}\Delta x + \frac{(F_{j,*}^{\pm} \mp F_{j,0})\Delta t_i}{\rho A \Delta x}, \tag{5.21}$$

and from the law of angular momentum conservation we obtain

$$\omega_{j,*}^{\pm} = \omega_{j,0} + \frac{(M_{j,*}^{\pm} \pm 0.5F_{j,*}^{\pm}\Delta x \mp M_{j,0})\Delta t_i}{\rho I \Delta x}. \tag{5.22}$$

Henceforth, the subscript m in $F_{jm,0}$ and $M_{jm,0}$ is omitted.

The same equations in the terms of averaged parameters are given by

$$v_j^{\pm} = v_{j,0} + \frac{(F_j^{\pm} \mp F_{j,0})\Delta t_i}{\rho A \Delta x}, \tag{5.23}$$

and

$$\omega_j^{\pm} = \omega_{j,0} + \frac{(M_j^{\pm} \mp M_{j,0})\Delta t_i}{\rho I \Delta x}. \tag{5.24}$$

The correlations, inverse to (5.21)-(5.22), are

$$F_{j,*}^{\pm} = \pm F_{j,0} + \frac{(v_{j,*}^{\pm} - v_{j,0} \mp 0.5\omega_{j,*}^{\pm}\Delta x)\rho A \Delta x}{\Delta t_i}, \tag{5.25}$$

$$M_{j,*}^{\pm} = \pm M_{j,0} \mp 0.5F_{j,*}^{\pm}\Delta x + \frac{(\omega_{j,*}^{\pm} - \omega_{j,0})\rho I \Delta x}{\Delta t_i}. \tag{5.26}$$

Eliminating $\omega_{j,*}^{\pm}$ from Eqs.(5.21), and $F_{j,*}^{\pm}$ from Eq.(5.26), we get the formulae for $v_{j,*}^{\pm}$ and $M_{j,*}^{\pm}$ in equivalent forms

$$v_{j,*}^{\pm} = v_{j,0} \pm 0.5\omega_{j,0}\Delta x + [F_{j,*}^{\pm}(1+\alpha^2) \mp F_{j,0} \pm (M_{j,*}^{\pm} \mp M_{j,0})\alpha / r]\Delta t_i / \rho A \Delta x, \tag{5.27}$$

and

$$M_{j,*}^{\pm} = \pm M_{j,0} - 0.5F_{j,0}\Delta x + [\omega_{j,*}^{\pm}(1+\alpha^2) - \omega_{j,0} \mp (v_{j,*}^{\pm} - v_{j,0})\alpha / r]\rho I \Delta x / \Delta t_i. \tag{5.28}$$

It is necessary to note that the terms of order α^2 which due to Eq.(5.1) are relatively small, ensure the correct satisfaction of energy balance and must not be truncated in calculations.

Equations (5.21)-(5.28) connect the element border parameters in a time interval Δt_i with each other and with inner parameters of the element at the beginning of the step.

B. Using the law of momentum conservation in a time Δt_i in application to the element as a whole, we obtain

$$v_j = v_{j,0} + \frac{(F^+_{j,*} + F^-_{j,*})\Delta t_i}{\rho A \Delta x}, \qquad (5.29)$$

and doing so using the law of angular momentum conservation,

$$\omega_j = \omega_{j,0} + \frac{[M^+_{j,*} + M^-_{j,*} + 0.5(F^+_{j,*} - F^-_{j,*})\Delta x]\Delta t_i}{\rho I \Delta x} \qquad (5.30a)$$

or, from Eq.(5.19),

$$\omega_j = \omega_{j,0} + \frac{(M^+_j + M^-_j)\Delta t_i}{\rho I \Delta x}. \qquad (5.30b)$$

Substituting the expression for the forces $F^\pm_j$ from Eqs.(5.23) into (5.29), and for the moments $M^\pm_j$ from Eqs.(5.24) into (5.30b), we arrive at the new values of element velocities v_j and ω_j at the instant $t^-_i = t^+_{i-1} + \Delta t_i$, thus

$$\left.\begin{aligned} v_j &= v^+_j + v^-_j - v_{j,0} \\ \omega_j &= \omega^+_j + \omega^-_j - \omega_{j,0} \end{aligned}\right\}. \qquad (5.31)$$

The new nodal deflections $y^\pm_j$ and rotation angles $\varphi^\pm_j$ are

$$y^\pm_j = y^\pm_{j,0} + v^\pm_{j,*}\Delta t_i, \varphi^\pm_j = \varphi^\pm_{j,0} + \omega^\pm_{j,*}\Delta t_i. \qquad (5.32)$$

Thus, the same situation as at the beginning of the current step is repeated but with changed values of the element velocities and nodes displacements.

5.1.1.4. **A.** The second term of Eq.(5.19) can be justified also by another way.

In the time $0.5\Delta t_i$ the bending moment induced by the force $F^\pm_{j,*}$ increases from zero to $\pm 0.5 F^\pm_{j,*} \Delta x$; its mean value during this half-interval is only $\pm 0.25 F^\pm_{j,*} \Delta x$. However, in the following half-interval the moment increases from $\pm 0.5 F^\pm_{j,*} \Delta x$ to $\pm F^\pm_{j,*}\Delta x$ with a mean value of $\pm 0.75 F^\pm_{j,*}\Delta x$.

In accordance with the DMM assumptions, both these moments, being external, have to be referred to the element ends and their average value in the time Δt_i will be $\pm 0.5\, F^{\pm}_{j,*}\, \Delta x$

B. Equations (5.15a) can be presented in the form of the matrix expression $\mathbf{F}_0 = \mathbf{B}\mathbf{y}_0$, where $\mathbf{F}_0^{\mathrm{T}} = \{F_0^-, F_0^+, M_0^-, M_0^+\}$, $\mathbf{y}_0^{\mathrm{T}} = \{y_0^-, y_0^+, \varphi_0^-, \varphi_0^+\}$, and

$$b_{11} = b_{22} = -b_{12} = -b_{21} = GA / k_s \Delta x,$$
$$b_{33} = b_{44} = EJ / \Delta x + 0.25\, GA\Delta x / k_s,\ b_{34} = b_{43} = -EJ / \Delta x + 0.25\, GA \Delta x / k_s,$$
$$b_{13} = b_{14} = b_{31} = b_{41} = -b_{23} = -b_{24} = -b_{32} = -b_{42} = 0.5 GA / k_s.$$

C. The relations of the Subsect.5.1.1 for the quasi-static state of a beam element can be obtained also by other way closer to the traditional finite-element approach. From the theory of the bending for Timoshenko beam it follows that the functions $\varphi_0(\xi)$ and $y_0(\xi)$ for any element point $\xi = x / \Delta x$ $(0 \le \xi \le 1)$ should look like

$$\varphi_0(\xi) = \varphi_0^- + \frac{\Delta x}{EJ} M_{m,0}\xi + \frac{\Delta x^2}{2EJ} F_{m,0}\xi(1-\xi),$$

$$y_0(\xi) = y_0^- + \Delta x \int_0^{\xi} \varphi_0(\xi_1) d\xi_1 + \frac{k_s \Delta x}{GA} F_{m,0}\xi.$$

This allows us to express $\varphi_0(\xi)$ and $y_0(\xi)$ through border displacements $\varphi_0^{\pm}$ and $y_0^{\pm}$. All the results of the Section considered, under condition (5.1), remain in force.

5.1.2 Finite Element Simulation of Bending Waves

5.1.2.1. **A.** The equilibrium conditions of the node j in a time Δt_i are

$$\left.\begin{aligned} F^+_{j-1,*} + F^-_{j,*} - F^*_j + \eta_v v_{j,*}\Delta x = 0, \\ M^+_{j-1,*} + M^-_{j,*} - M^*_j + \eta_\omega \omega_{j,*}\Delta x = 0 \end{aligned}\right\}, \tag{5.33}$$

where F_j^* and M_j^* are the external loads applied to the node; the outer linear viscous friction is taken into account.

The conditions of the beam continuity in a time Δt_i are

$$v_{j,*} = v^+_{j-1,*} = v^-_{j,*},\ \omega_{j,*} = \omega^+_{j-1,*} = \omega^-_{j,*}. \tag{5.34}$$

Equations (5.25) and (5.28) referred to the corresponding borders of elements $(j-1)$ and j, together with Eqs.(5.33)-(5.34), connect the unknowns $F^+_{j-1,*}$, $M^+_{j-1,*}$, $v^+_{j-1,*}$, $\omega^+_{j-1,*}$, $F^-_{j,*}$, $M^-_{j,*}$, $v^-_{j,*}$, $\omega^-_{j,*}$ with each other.

This system of linear algebraic equations enables us to determine all the parameters relevant to the node j. The nodal velocities are

$$v_{j,*} = \frac{v_{j,0} + v_{j-1,0} + (F_j^* + F_{j,0} - F_{j-1,0})\Delta t_i / \rho A \Delta x}{2(1 + 0.5\eta_v \Delta t_i / \rho A)}, \tag{5.35}$$

and

$$\omega_{j,*} = \frac{\omega_{j,0} + \omega_{j-1,0} + \Delta\omega}{2(1 + 0.5\eta_\omega \Delta t_i / \rho I + \alpha^2)}, \tag{5.36a}$$

where

$$\Delta\omega = [M_j^* + M_{j,0} - M_{j-1,0} + 0.5(F_{j,0} + F_{j-1,0})\Delta x]\Delta t_i / \rho I \Delta x + (v_{j,0} - v_{j-1,0})\alpha / r. \tag{5.36b}$$

If required, the border shear forces and bending moments can be determined using Eqs.(5.25) and (5.28).

Later, the nodes are indexed from $j = 1$ to $j = n + 1$, so the deflections of the ($j - 1$)th element borders can be denoted $y_{j-1}^- = y_{j-1}$, $y_j^+ = y_j$, and the same is true for $\varphi_{j-1}^\pm$.

B. Below, formulae for the basic boundary beam conditions using some combinations of Eqs.(5.21) to (5.28) are deduced.

The conditions referred to the right end of the element $j - 1$ are:

Free end: $F_{j-1,*}^+ = 0$, $M_{j-1,*}^+ = 0$.

Velocities of this end are

$$\left.\begin{aligned} v_{j-1,*}^+ &= v_{j-1,0} + 0.5\omega_{j-1,0}\Delta x - (F_{j-1,0} + M_{j-1,0}\alpha / r)\Delta t_i / \rho A \Delta x, \\ \omega_{j-1,*}^+ &= \omega_{j-1,0} - M_{j-1,0}\Delta t_i / \rho I \Delta x \end{aligned}\right\}. \tag{5.37}$$

Fixed node: $v_{j-1,*}^+ = 0$, $\omega_{j-1,*}^+ = 0$.

Reaction shear force and bending moment are

$$\left.\begin{aligned} F_{j-1,*}^+ &= F_{j-1,0} - v_{j-1,0}\rho A \Delta x / \Delta t_i, \\ M_{j-1,*}^+ &= M_{j-1,0} - 0.5F_{j-1,0}\Delta x - (\omega_{j-1,0} - v_{j-1,0}\alpha / r)\rho I \Delta x / \Delta t_i \end{aligned}\right\}. \tag{5.38}$$

Pinned support: $v_{j-1,*}^+ = 0$, $M_{j-1,*}^+ = 0$.

Reaction force and angular velocity are

$$\left.\begin{aligned} F_{j-1,*}^{+} &= [F_{j-1,0} + M_{j-1,0}\alpha / r - (v_{j-1,0} + 0.5\omega_{j-1,0}\Delta x)\rho A\Delta x / \Delta t_i]/(1+\alpha^2), \\ \omega_{j-1,*}^{+} &= \omega_{j-1,0} - (M_{j-1,0} - 0.5F_{j-1,*}^{+}\Delta x)\Delta t_i / \rho I\Delta x \end{aligned}\right\} \tag{5.39}$$

Treating an *intermediate pinned support at the node j* with condition $v_{j,*} = 0$ and regarding the reaction force, which is a sum of border forces for adjacent elements, as the external force F_j^*, we can obtain from the first Eq.(5.33) and Eqs.(5.25) related to these borders that

$$F_j^* = F_{j-1,*}^{+} + F_{j,*}^{-} = F_{j-1,0} - F_{j,0} - (v_{j-1,0} + v_{j,0})\rho A\Delta x / \Delta t_i. \tag{5.40}$$

The same value of the reaction force F_j^* is obtained from Eq.(5.35) with $v_{j,*} = 0$.

Assuming external moments are absent, $M_j^* = 0,\ \eta_\omega = 0$, the second Eq.(5.33) leads to $M_{j-1,*}^{+} + M_{j,*}^{-} = 0$, and Eqs.(5.26) yield

$$M_{j-1,*}^{+} = -M_{j,*}^{-} = 0.5[M_{j-1,0} + M_{j,0} - 0.5F_j^*\Delta x + (\omega_{j,0} - \omega_{j-1,0})\rho I\Delta x / \Delta t_i]. \tag{5.41}$$

Using Eqs.(5.28) we can obtain $\omega_{j-1,*}^{+}$, $\omega_{j,*}^{-}$ and, by means of Eqs.(5.25), determine the values of forces $F_{j-1,*}^{+}$ and $F_{j,*}^{-}$ separately.

A way of building equations for more complex boundary conditions, which can vary from one time step to other, is analogous.

5.1.2.2. A. The work $\Delta W_{j,*}$ brought to the element in a time Δt_i in its nodes is

$$\Delta W_{j,*} = (F_{j,*}^{+}v_{j,*}^{+} + F_{j,*}^{-}v_{j,*}^{-} + M_{j,*}^{+}\omega_{j,*}^{+} + M_{j,*}^{-}\omega_{j,*}^{-})\Delta t_i. \tag{5.42}$$

The work ΔW_j of the averaged border parameters in the same time is

$$\Delta W_j = (F_j^{+}v_j^{+} + F_j^{-}v_j^{-} + M_j^{+}\omega_j^{+} + M_j^{-}\omega_j^{-})\Delta t_i. \tag{5.43}$$

It is readily confirmed that, due to Eqs.(5.18)-(5.20), the work difference is zeroing, i.e. $\Delta W_{j,*} - \Delta W_j \equiv 0$.

Therefore, the energy balance of the element is

$$\Delta W_j = \Delta K_j + \Delta P_j, \tag{5.44}$$

where ΔK_j and ΔP_j are the increments of the element kinetic and potential energy in a step, respectively.

Taking into account Eqs.(5.20) to (5.24), the expression

$$\Delta K_j = 0.5\rho\Delta x[A(v_j^2 - v_{j,0}^2) + I(\omega_j^2 - \omega_{j,0}^2)]$$

may be reduced after some simple algebraic transformations to

$$\Delta K_j = 0.5[(F_j^+ + F_j^-)(v_j^+ + v_j^-) + (M_j^+ + M_j^-)(\omega_j^+ + \omega_j^-)]\Delta t_i. \quad (5.45)$$

Then, the increment of potential energy $\Delta P_j = \Delta W_j - \Delta K_j$ must be equal to

$$\Delta P_j = \Delta P_j^{(1)} = 0.5[(F_j^+ - F_j^-)(v_j^+ - v_j^-) + (M_j^+ - M_j^-)(\omega_j^+ - \omega_j^-)]\Delta t_i. \quad (5.46)$$

On the other hand, this increment is given by

$$\Delta P_j = \Delta P_j^{(2)} = P_j - P_{j,0}, \quad (5.47)$$

where the energy P_j can be determined just as the energy $P_{j,0}$, changing in Eq.(5.13b) the quantities $y_{j,0}^{\pm}$ and $\varphi_{j,0}^{\pm}$ to $y_j^{\pm}$ and $\varphi_j^{\pm}$, respectively.

The new values of the inner force F_j and moment M_j at the instant $t_i^- = t_{i-1}^+ + \Delta t_i$ are expressed in terms of new nodal displacements as

$$F_j = GA[y_j^+ - y_j^- - 0.5(\varphi_j^+ - \varphi_j^-)\Delta x]/k_s\Delta x, \quad (5.48)$$

and

$$M_j = EJ(\varphi_j^+ - \varphi_j^-)/\Delta x. \quad (5.49)$$

Using Eqs.(5.20), (5.32), and (5.47) - (5.49), we come to expression

$$\Delta P_j^{(2)} = 0.5[(F_{j,0} + F_j)(v_j^+ - v_j^-) + (M_{j,0} + M_j)(\omega_j^+ - \omega_j^-)]\Delta t_i. \quad (5.50)$$

Due to Eqs.(5.23), (5.32), and (5.48), we have

$$F_j^+ - F_j^- - (F_{j,0} + F_j) = A(v_j^+ - v_j^-)\left(\frac{\rho\Delta x}{\Delta t_i} - \frac{G\Delta t_i}{k_s\Delta x}\right) \quad (5.51)$$

and, due to Eqs.(5.24), (5.32), and (5.49),

$$M_j^+ - M_j^- - (M_{j,0} + M_j) = J(\omega_j^+ - \omega_j^-)\left(\frac{\rho\Delta x}{\Delta t_i} - \frac{E\Delta t_i}{\Delta x}\right), \quad (5.52)$$

Finally, setting $\Delta P_j^{(1)}$ to $\Delta P_j^{(2)}$ in view of Eqs.(5.51) and (5.52), the equation of element energy balance takes the form

$$\left[(v_j^+ - v_j^-)^2 A\left(\frac{\rho\Delta x}{\Delta t_i} - \frac{G\Delta t_i}{k_s\Delta x}\right) + (\omega_j^+ - \omega_j^-)^2 J\left(\frac{\rho\Delta x}{\Delta t_i} - \frac{E\Delta t_i}{\Delta x}\right)\right]\Delta t_i = 0. \quad (5.53)$$

In the general case when $\Delta t_i \neq 0$ and, simultaneously, $v_j^+ \neq v_j^-$ and $\omega_j^+ \neq \omega_j^-$, Eq.(5.53) is satisfied only by such value of the time interval $\Delta t_i = \Delta x / c_{ij}$ that corresponds to the wave speed

$$c_{ij} = \sqrt{\frac{(v_j^+ - v_j^-)^2 A c_v^2 + (\omega_j^+ - \omega_j^-)^2 I c_\omega^2}{(v_j^+ - v_j^-)^2 A + (\omega_j^+ - \omega_j^-)^2 I}}, \quad (5.54)$$

where $c_v = \sqrt{G/\rho k_s}$ and $c_\omega = \sqrt{E/\rho}$.

The speed c_v describes the propagation of the shear strain wave; the speed c_ω corresponding to 'pure' bending is affected by section rotation connected with elongation of longitudinal fibers.

If the value of c_v were equal to c_ω, Eq.(5.53) would be satisfied with a constant quantity of time step $\Delta t = \Delta x / c_v = \Delta x / c_\omega$ just as in the problems of longitudinal or torsional wave propagation. However, in reality, both these waves arise and propagate simultaneously with different speeds $c_v \neq c_\omega$, interacting with each other. In this case, due to Eq.(5.54) with $\Delta x = \text{const}$, the wave speed c_{ij} based on the energy balance and, consequently, time step Δt_i might alter not only in time, but also from one element to other. Letting the current time interval Δt_i be constant over all the elements, the dimensions Δx_j might be different and also changing in time.

In either case, to build an exact numerical finite element procedure is not possible. However, the problem can be approximately solved using the methods described in Chap.1.

B. Referring to the general approach of the WFEM, the current time interval Δt_i has to be determined using the mechanical energy balance of the whole beam. The balance equation is more convenient taken in the form (1.42b)

$$K_{i\Sigma} + P_{i\Sigma} = W_{i\Sigma}^*. \quad (5.55)$$

Here, $K_{i\Sigma}$ and $P_{i\Sigma}$ are the whole beam kinetic and potential energy, respectively, and $W_{i\Sigma}^*$ is the total work introduced into the beam during the whole process. All these quantities are readily calculated for each step. The solution procedure is carried out starting from any value of Δt_i; the real time interval Δt_i is determined using the successive approximations described in Sect.1.2. The use of this numerical method is illustrated below in Subsect.5.3.3.

There is no principal difficulty in extending this approach to a curved beam and to the problems of longitudinal-transversal or coupled bending-torsion deformation of beams and frames.

5.2 Direct Mathematical Modeling of Bending Waves Propagation

5.2.1 Structural Bending/Shear Model of a Beam

5.2.1.1. Along with the general WFEM, it is possible to obtain perfectly good results using the DMM approach with the special structural model of a beam proposed by Shorr (1985) and developed in Shorr and Mel'nikova (1988).

The ratio of the shear wave speed to the 'pure' bending wave speed is $\bar{c}_v = c_v / c_\omega = 1/\sqrt{\beta}$, where

$$\beta = \frac{Ek_s}{G}. \tag{5.56}$$

As strictly $k_s > 1$ and $E/G \approx 2.6 - 2.7$, the realistic value of $\bar{c}_v$ is less than 0.6, i.e. the shear waves, like high-elastic or plastic waves, lag behind the leading bending waves. This allows us to take advantage of the composed structural model with additional borders 'springs' (see Subsect. 2.1.3 and Chap 3).

We represent the full shear transverse deflection $y_s = \alpha_s F_y \Delta x$ of an element induced by the force F_y as a sum $y_s = y_{s0} + 2\tilde{y}_s$ where the real shear compliance is $a_s = \gamma / F_y = k_s / GA$. Let $y_{s0} = \alpha_{s0} F_y \Delta x$ and $\tilde{y}_s = 0.5\tilde{\alpha}_s F_y \Delta x$, where the basis compliance $\alpha_{s0} = 1/EA$ refers to the whole continual part of the bending element, while the quantity $\tilde{\alpha}_s$ describes the additional compliance of the each shear border spring (Fig.5.1). Hence, we are able to deduce that

$$\tilde{a}_s = \frac{k_s}{GA} - \frac{1}{EA} = \frac{\beta - 1}{EA}. \tag{5.57}$$

Replacing the value GA/k_s by EA in the first term of Eq.(5.53), the element energy balance is exactly satisfied by a constant time interval

$$\Delta t_i = \Delta t = \Delta x \sqrt{\frac{\rho}{E}} = \frac{\Delta x}{c_\omega}. \qquad (5.58)$$

Denote shear spring forces at the beginning and end of the current step as $\widetilde{F}^{\pm}_{j,0}$ and $\widetilde{F}^{\pm}_{j}$, respectively. Their mean values in a step

$$\widetilde{F}^{\pm}_{jm} = 0.5(\widetilde{F}^{\pm}_{j,0} + \widetilde{F}^{\pm}_{j})$$

must be equal to boundary forces $\widetilde{F}^{\pm}_{jm} = F^{\pm}_{j} = F^{\pm}_{j,*}$.

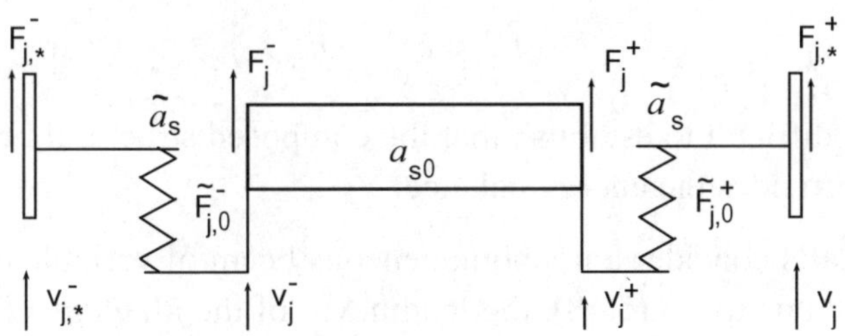

Fig. 5.1. Structural bending/shear model of a beam

The spring transverse deformation over the step is

$$\Delta\widetilde{y}^{\pm}_{j} = 0.5\widetilde{a}_s(\widetilde{F}^{\pm}_{j} - \widetilde{F}^{\pm}_{j,0})\Delta x = \widetilde{a}_s(F^{\pm}_{j} - \widetilde{F}^{\pm}_{j,0})\Delta x, \qquad (5.59)$$

with the additional transverse border velocity accounting Eq.(5.57) given by

$$\widetilde{v}^{\pm}_{j} = \frac{\Delta\widetilde{y}^{\pm}_{j}}{\Delta t} = (\beta - 1)\frac{F^{\pm}_{j} - \widetilde{F}^{\pm}_{j,0}}{\rho A c_\omega}. \qquad (5.60)$$

Equation (5.20) now is changed to

$$v^{\pm}_{j,*} = v^{\pm}_{j} \pm 0.5\omega^{\pm}_{j,*}\Delta x + \widetilde{v}^{\pm}_{j} \qquad (5.61)$$

that allows reducing Eq.(5.21) to

$$v^{\pm}_{j,*} = v_{j,0} \pm 0.5\omega^{\pm}_{j,*}\Delta x + \frac{\beta F^{\pm}_{j,*} \mp F_{j,0} - (\beta - 1)\widetilde{F}^{\pm}_{j,0}}{\rho A c_\omega}, \qquad (5.62)$$

from where

$$F^{\pm}_{j,*} = [\pm F_{j,0} + (\beta - 1)\widetilde{F}^{\pm}_{j,0} + (v^{\pm}_{j,*} - v_{j,0} \mp 0.5\omega^{\pm}_{j,*}\Delta x)\rho A c_\omega] / \beta. \qquad (5.63)$$

The right parts of Eqs.(5.51) and (5.52) after replacing GA/k_s by EA with condition (5.58) become zero, hence

$$F_j = F_j^+ - F_j^- - F_{j,0}, \tag{5.64}$$

and

$$M_j = M_j^+ - M_j^- - M_{j,0}. \tag{5.65}$$

A new value of the shear spring force at the beginning of the next step is

$$\widetilde{F}_j^{\pm} = 2F_j^{\pm} - \widetilde{F}_{j,0}^{\pm}. \tag{5.66}$$

It is not difficult to establish that the composed structural bending model correctly provides the energy balance.

5.2.1.2. Let's consider a nonhomogeneous beam of variable cross section. In this case due to Eq.(5.58), the length Δx_j of the jth element with density ρ_j and Young's modulus E_j must be chosen so that time interval

$$\Delta t_j = \Delta x_j / c_j \tag{5.67}$$

with $c_j = \sqrt{E_j / \rho_j}$ becomes constant, $\Delta t_j = \Delta t$.

Moreover, the square of element parameters ratio $(\Delta x_j / r_j)^2$ with $r_j = \sqrt{J_j / A_j}$ must satisfy the condition (5.1).

Keeping this in mind, we introduce nondimensional quantities scaled by basis values of velocity v^o and other corresponding parameters, as in Subsect.2.1.1.1:

$$\left.\begin{aligned}
&\overline{v} = v / v^o, \overline{\omega} = \omega r^o / v^o, \overline{F} = F / v^o A^o \rho^o c^o, \overline{M} = M r^o / v^o J^o \rho^o c^o, \\
&\overline{x} = x / r^o, \overline{t} = t c^o / r^o, \overline{y} = y c^o / v^o r^o, \overline{\varphi} = \varphi c^o / v^o, \overline{c} = c / c^o, \\
&\mu = A\rho c / A^o \rho^o c^o, \lambda = J\rho c / J^o \rho^o c^o, \\
&\overline{\eta}_v = \eta_v r^o / A^o \rho^o c^o, \overline{\eta}_\omega = \eta_\omega r^o / J^o \rho^o c^o
\end{aligned}\right\}, \tag{5.68}$$

where

$$r^o = \sqrt{J^o / A^o}, \; c^o = \sqrt{E^o / \rho^o}.$$

In addition, we denote

$$\alpha = 0.5\Delta x / r^o = 0.5\Delta\overline{x}, \; \Delta x^o = c^o \Delta t = L / n, \; \alpha^o = 0.5\Delta x^o / r^o = 0.5\Delta\overline{x}^o \tag{5.69}$$

and take into account that

$$\alpha=\alpha^{o}\bar{c},\ \Delta\bar{x}=\bar{c}\Delta\bar{t},\ \Delta\bar{t}=\Delta t c^{o}/r^{o}=\Delta\bar{x}^{o}=2\alpha^{o}=\text{const}, \tag{5.70}$$

where, as above, $\alpha^{2}<<1$.

The basic system of jth element equations in nondimensional terms, where over-bars here and later in this Chapter are omitted, is

$$\left.\begin{aligned} &M_{j,*}^{\pm}=M_{j}^{\pm}\mp\alpha_{j}F_{j}^{\pm},\quad F_{j,*}^{\pm}=F_{j}^{\pm},\\ &v_{j,*}^{\pm}=v_{j}^{\pm}\pm\alpha_{j}\omega_{j}^{\pm}+(\beta_{j}-1)(F_{j}^{\pm}-\widetilde{F}_{j,0}^{\pm})/\mu_{j},\quad \omega_{j,*}^{\pm}=\omega_{j}^{\pm},\\ &F_{j}^{\pm}=\pm F_{j,0}+(v_{j}^{\pm}-v_{j,0})\mu_{j},\quad M_{j}^{\pm}=\pm M_{j,0}+(\omega_{j}^{\pm}-\omega_{j,0})\lambda_{j},\\ &y_{j}^{\pm}=y_{j,0}^{\pm}+2\alpha^{o}v_{j,*}^{\pm},\quad \varphi_{j}^{\pm}=\varphi_{j,0}^{\pm}+2\alpha^{o}\omega_{j,*}^{\pm} \end{aligned}\right\}. \tag{5.71}$$

Equations (5.31) and (5.64)-(5.66) in nondimensional terms remain unchanged.

5.2.2 Solution Procedure

5.2.2.1. Using Eqs.(5.71) for the adjacent boundaries of the elements $j-1$ and j, we may express the boundary forces $F_{j-1,*}^{+}$ and $F_{j,*}^{-}$, and moments $M_{j-1,*}^{+}$ and $M_{j,*}^{-}$ by nodal velocities $v_{j,*}=v_{j-1,*}^{+}=v_{j,*}^{-}$ and $\omega_{j,*}=\omega_{j-1,*}^{+}=\omega_{j,*}^{-}$ as

$$\left.\begin{aligned} &F_{j-1,*}^{+}=[F_{j-1,0}+(\beta_{j-1}-1)\widetilde{F}_{j-1,0}^{+}+\mu_{j-1}(v_{j,*}-v_{j-1,0}-\alpha_{j-1}\omega_{j,*})]/\beta_{j-1}\\ &F_{j,*}^{-}=[-F_{j,0}+(\beta_{j}-1)\widetilde{F}_{j,0}^{-}+\mu_{j}(v_{j,*}-v_{j,0}+\alpha_{j}\omega_{j,*})]/\beta_{j} \end{aligned}\right\}, \tag{5.72}$$

and

$$\left.\begin{aligned} &M_{j-1,*}^{+}=M_{j-1,0}+\omega_{j,*}(\lambda_{j-1}+\mu_{j-1}\alpha_{j-1}^{2}/\beta_{j-1})-\lambda_{j-1}\omega_{j-1,0}\\ &-\alpha_{j-1}[\mu_{j-1}(v_{j,*}-v_{j-1,0})+F_{j-1,0}+(\beta_{j-1}-1)\widetilde{F}_{j-1,0}^{+}]/\beta_{j-1},\\ &M_{j,*}^{-}=-M_{j,0}+\omega_{j,*}(\lambda_{j}+\mu_{j}\alpha_{j}^{2}/\beta_{j})-\lambda_{j}\omega_{j,0}\\ &+\alpha_{j}[\mu_{j}(v_{j,*}-v_{j,0})-F_{j,0}+(\beta_{j}-1)\widetilde{F}_{j,0}^{-}]/\beta_{j} \end{aligned}\right\}. \tag{5.73}$$

Equations (5.33) in dimensionless form are

$$\begin{aligned} &F_{j-1,*}^{+}+F_{j,*}^{-}-F_{j}^{*}+(\alpha_{j-1}+\alpha_{j})\eta_{v}v_{j,*}=0,\\ &M_{j-1,*}^{+}+M_{j,*}^{-}-M_{j}^{*}+(\alpha_{j-1}+\alpha_{j})\eta_{\omega}\omega_{j,*}=0 \end{aligned}.$$

Inserting Eqs.(5.72) and (5.73) into these equations, we obtain the system of two linear algebraic equations

$$\left.\begin{aligned} a_{11}v_{j,*}+a_{12}\omega_{j,*}=b_1 \\ a_{21}v_{j,*}+a_{22}\omega_{j,*}=b_2 \end{aligned}\right\}, \tag{5.74}$$

where

$$\left.\begin{aligned} &a_{11}=\mu_{j-1}/\beta_{j-1}+\mu_j/\beta_j+(\alpha_{j-1}+\alpha_j)\eta_v, \\ &a_{12}=a_{21}=\alpha_j\mu_j/\beta_j-\alpha_{j-1}\mu_{j-1}/\beta_{j-1}, \\ &a_{22}=\lambda_{j-1}+\lambda_j+(\alpha_{j-1}+\alpha_j)\eta_\omega+\mu_{j-1}\alpha_{j-1}^2/\beta_{j-1}+\mu_j\alpha_j^2/\beta_j, \\ &b_1=[F_{j,0}-(\beta_j-1)\widetilde{F}_{j,0}^-+\mu_j v_{j,0}]/\beta_j- \\ &\quad -[F_{j-1,0}+(\beta_{j-1}-1)\widetilde{F}_{j-1,0}^+-\mu_{j-1}v_{j-1,0}]/\beta_{j-1}+F_j^*, \\ &b_2=M_{j,0}+\lambda_j\omega_{j,0}+\alpha_j[F_{j,0}-(\beta_j-1)\widetilde{F}_{j,0}^-+\mu_j v_{j,0}]/\beta_j-M_{j-1,0}+ \\ &+\lambda_{j-1}\omega_{j-1,0}+\alpha_{j-1}[F_{j-1,0}+(\beta_{j-1}-1)\widetilde{F}_{j-1,0}^+-\mu_{j-1}v_{j-1,0}]/\beta_{j-1}+M_j^* \end{aligned}\right\}. \tag{5.75}$$

The determinant of the system (5.74) can be recast in the form

$$\Delta=\left(\frac{\mu_{j-1}}{\beta_{j-1}}+\frac{\mu_j}{\beta_j}\right)(\lambda_{j-1}+\lambda_j)+\frac{\mu_{j-1}\mu_j}{\beta_{j-1}\beta_j}(\alpha_{j-1}+\alpha_j)^2+\Delta_\eta,$$

where the damping term $\Delta_\eta=f(\eta_v,\eta_\omega)\geq 0$; thus Δ is observed to be always positive.

5.2.2.2. Applying the above method to a homogeneous beam or to the node connecting similar elements, the coefficients $a_{12}=a_{21}=0$ and the system (5.74) reveals that

$$v_{j,*}=b_1/a_{11},\ \omega_{j,*}=b_2/a_{22}. \tag{5.76}$$

In the last case, taking $\alpha_{j-1}=\alpha_j=\alpha$ etc, we further deduce that

$$v_{j,*}=\frac{\mu(v_{j,0}+v_{j-1,0})+F_{j,0}-F_{j-1,0}+\beta F_j^*-(\beta-1)(\widetilde{F}_{j,0}^-+\widetilde{F}_{j-1,0}^+)}{2(\mu+\alpha\eta_v\beta)} \tag{5.77a}$$

and

$$\omega_{j,*}=\frac{\omega_M+\omega_F}{2[(\lambda+\alpha\eta_\omega)\beta+\alpha^2\mu]}, \tag{5.77b}$$

where

$$\omega_M = \beta[\lambda(\omega_{j,0} + \omega_{j-1,0}) + M_{j,0} - M_{j-1,0} + M_j^*],$$

$$\omega_F = \alpha[F_{j,0} + F_{j-1,0} + \mu(v_{j,0} - v_{j-1,0}) - (\beta - 1)(\widetilde{F}_{j,0}^- - \widetilde{F}_{j-1,0}^+)]$$

After finding the velocities $v_{j-1,*}^+ = v_{j,*}^- = v_{j,*}$ and $\omega_{j-1,*}^+ = \omega_{j,*}^- = \omega_{j,*}$, one can easily determine all the other parameters associated with $(j-1)$th element and then proceed to consider the next element j, employing sequentially Eqs.(5.72),(5.73),(5.71),(5.64),(5.65), and (5.31).

5.3 Numerical Examples

5.3.1 A Stepped Force Affecting a Beam

In this Subsection we shall exploit the DMM approach described above.

***5.3.1.1.* Problem 5.1. A homogeneous beam affected by a stepped force applied to any point, Fig. 5.2a. Initial phase**. All the beam elements are at rest at $t = 0$. We place the origin $x = 0$ at the point where a force $F^* = 1$ is suddenly applied at the time $t = 0$ and scale all parameters by this force, Eq.(5.68) having additionally the relation $v^o = F^* / A\rho c$.

Here we focus attention on the initial phase of the process before reflections from ends of the beam. Within this phase, the waves propagate in both directions in the same manner independently from ends fixing. Due to this symmetry, only the positive half $x \geq 0$ of the beam affected by the force $F_1^* = 0.5$ is considered.

The boundary conditions at the origin x=0 (the node $j = 1$) are

$$\left.\begin{aligned} F_{1,*}^- &= F_1^* = 0.5, \\ \omega_{1,*}^- &= 0, \end{aligned}\right\} \qquad (5.78)$$

where symmetry of the problem has also been taken into account.

Inserting the conditions (5.78) into Eqs.(5.72) and (5.73), we obtain with $\lambda = \mu = 1$

$$\left.\begin{aligned} v_{1,*}^- &= v_{1,0} + F_{1,0} + 0.5\beta - (\beta - 1)\widetilde{F}_{1,0}^-, \\ M_{1,*}^- &= -M_{1,0} - \omega_{1,0} + 0.5\alpha \end{aligned}\right\}. \qquad (5.79)$$

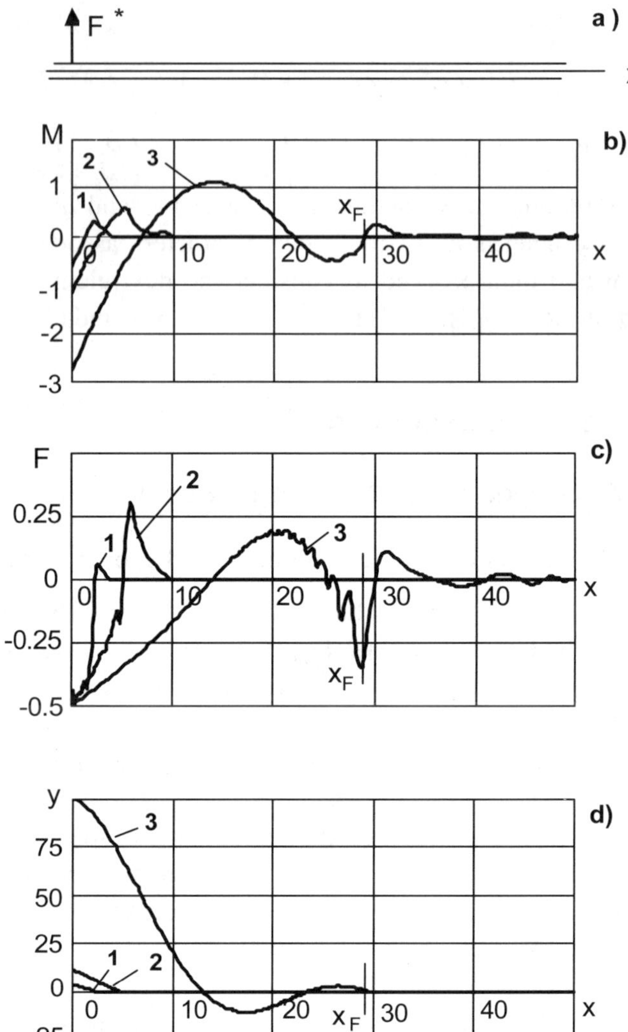

Fig.5.2. Propagation of bending waves affected by a suddenly applied force F^*: a) loading sketch; b),c),d) distribution of moment M, force F, and deflection y, respectively, at the time instants t: 1) $t = 4$, 2) $t = 10$, 3) $t = 50$

The calculations are carried out for a beam of a rectangular cross section with $k_s = 1.2$ and the ratio $E/G = 2(1+\mu) = 2.6$, implying $\beta = 3.12$. Damping is at this stage neglected.

Distributions of the dimensionless bending moment M, shear force F, and deflection y over the length x of the beam relating to some time instants t are presented in Fig.5.2b, c, d, respectively. The element dimension factor is $\alpha = 0.1$ and the time steps n_t are considered up to $n_t = 250$ corresponding to $t = 2\alpha n_t = 50$. The number of elements effected by the propagating wave is also $n=n_t$.

The more detail patterns of moment and force distribution calculated with α =0.01 and $\beta = 3.078$ for the short instant $t = 4$ are shown in Fig.5.3a,b, respectively. The white dots correspond to the results of a very complicated graph-analytic solution carried out previously for this problem using the same values of t and β by Makushin (1952).

Two distinct zones can be recognized in the perturbed domain. The first begins directly after the leading wave and propagates with dimensionless speed $c = c_\omega = 1$. Its current positions are determined by the coordinate $x = t$. Throughout this zone, the bending moments and shear forces are already distinguished from zero; however, deflections remain insignificant.

The leading border of the second zone runs with the speed $c \approx c_v = 1/\sqrt{\beta}$, i.e. $c = 0.566$ for $\beta = 3.12$ and $c = 0.570$ for $\beta = 3.078$. Its positions $x_F = ct$ are shown in Fig.5.2 (for $t = 50$) and Fig.5.3 with vertical bars. The deflections within the second zone quickly increase. A particularly noteworthy point is that the wave direction along part of the beam is opposite to the applied force.

For a small value of time ($t < 10$), the shear force changes jump-like, while the bending moment curve has a sharp inflection at the shear front $x = x_F$. If the value of time becomes large ($t >> 10$), the leading wave takes on the appearance of a week forerunner and the first zone remains practically at rest, while the second one, the growing deformation, propagates with the speed nearly c_v.

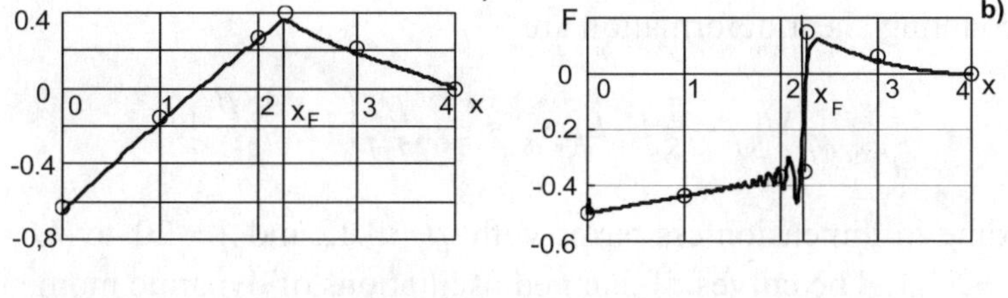

Fig.5.3. The same loading as in Fig. 5.2: a) bending moment M, b) shear force F at the instant $t = 4$

Using the DMM algorithm, the effects caused by the difference between the speeds c_ω and c_v are clearly noticeable, although the speed c_v is not explicitly present in the structural model. With $\alpha << 1$, numerical results do not depend on the element dimension.

***5.3.1.2.* Problem 5.2. Sudden loading of a fixed-fixed beam.** We elaborate the previous problem assuming the beam of the length L is fixed at its ends and a force $F^* = 1$ is now suddenly applied to its mid-point (Fig.5.4a). As previously, only the right half of the beam is considered. Then, the problem initial conditions and boundary conditions at the point $j=1$ remain the same; the boundary conditions at the right fixed end $j=n+1$, where n is a number of elements within the half length of the beam, are

$$v^+_{n,*} = 0; \ \ \omega^+_{n,*} = 0. \tag{5.80}$$

Support reactions due to Eqs.(5.80) and (5.72)-(5.73) are given by

$$\left.\begin{aligned} F^+_{n,*} &= [F_{n,0} - v_{n,0} + (\beta - 1)\widetilde{F}^+_{n,0}] / \beta, \\ M^+_{n,*} &= M_{n,0} - \omega_{n,0} - \alpha F^+_{n,*} \end{aligned}\right\} \tag{5.81}$$

The beam slenderness ratio $\lambda = L/r$ is assumed to be relatively small ($\lambda = 20$) to detect the shear influence; then the number of elements with $\alpha = 0.1$ must be taken as $n = 0.5L/\Delta x = \lambda/4\alpha = 50$. Damping is now accounted.

The bending moment M_1^- and deflection y_1 at the beam mid-point versus relative time *t,* for various friction coefficients $\eta_v = \eta_\omega$, are shown in Fig.5.4b,c. In accordance with our accepted sign rule, a boundary moment M_1^- is positive when counter-clockwise, while an internal moment $M_{1,0}$ of the adjacent first element section, when clockwise. To allow comparison with Fig.5.2 and 5.3, a quantity $(-M_1^-)$ is displayed in Fig.5.4a.

If the force F^* applied statically, the theoretical values of M_1^- and y_1 accounting shear deformation are

$$M_{st} = \frac{1}{8} F^* L, \ \ y_{st} \approx \frac{F^* L^3}{192 EJ}\left(1 + \frac{48\beta}{\lambda^2}\right), \tag{5.82}$$

leading in dimensionless terms with $\beta = 3.12$ and $\lambda = 20$ to $M_{st} = 2.5$ and $y_{st} = 57.3$. The curves of damped oscillations of dynamic moment M_1^- and deflection y_1 approach these quantities very well.

In the absence of external friction, free non-fading oscillations due to reflections from ends of the beam arise. They differ from harmonic osciltions in view of the influence of initial conditions. The moment and de-

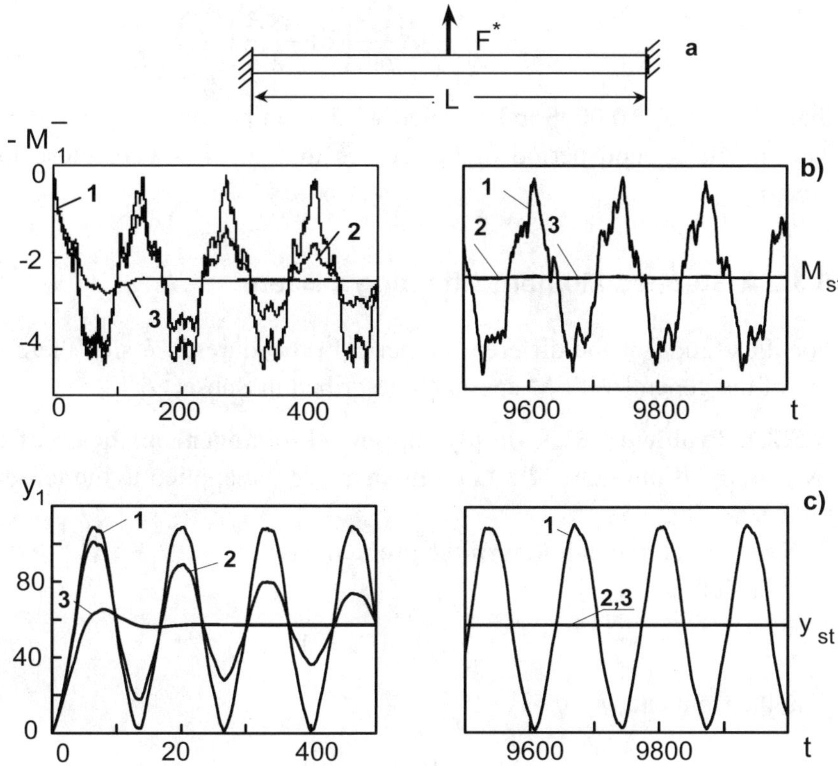

Fig.5.4. Sudden loading of a fixed-fixed beam; a) loading sketch, b) moment -*M*), c) deflection *y* vs. time for external friction coefficients
$\eta_v = \eta_\omega = \eta$: 1) $\eta = 0$, 2) $\eta = 0.005$, 3) $\eta = 0.05$

flection oscillation swings are slightly less than the duplicated static values, since wave motion over the beam does not come to an end for the instant.

The DMM algorithm provides the computation stability without any fading for practically unlimited number of steps n_t and reflections $n_r = n_t / n$. The latter are equal to the number of wave transitions along half of the beam in a time t. This has been confirmed by calculations up to $n_t = 50000$ ($t = 2\alpha n_t = 10000$) and $n_r = 1000$ (see Fig.5.4).

The theoretical nondimensional value of the first eigenfrequency for the beam with given boundary conditions can be approximately determined accounting the shear effect as

$$\bar{f} = \frac{fr}{c_\omega} \approx \frac{11.2}{\pi\lambda^2}\left(1 + \frac{48\beta}{\lambda^2}\right)^{-0.5},$$

that leads to $\bar{f} = 0.0076$ and a scaled oscillation period of $\bar{\tau}_f = 1/\bar{f} \approx 132$. The visible ground period of the curves in Fig.5.4 is very close to this quantity.

5.3.2 A Stepped Moment Affecting a Beam

For illustration of the different numerical procedures, we shall here make use of the general WFEM approach described in Subsect.5.1.2.

5.3.2.1. **Problem 5.3. A simply supported homogeneous beam affected by a stepped moment *M**.** Let a moment M^* be applied to the left end of the beam, Fig. 5.5a.

The boundary conditions of the problem are:
at the left end, $j = 1$,

$$v_{1,*}^- = 0, \;\; M_{1,*}^- = M^*, \tag{5.83a}$$

at the right end, $j = n+1$,

$$v_{n,*}^+ = 0, \;\; M_{n,*}^+ = 0. \tag{5.83b}$$

Due to Eqs.(5.39), these lead in nondimensional terms, respectively, to

$$\left.\begin{aligned} F_{1,*}^- &= \frac{-F_{1,0} + \alpha(M_{1,0} + M^*) - (v_{1,0} - \alpha\omega_{1,0})/\tau}{1+\alpha^2}, \\ \omega_{1,*}^- &= \omega_{1,0} + (M_{1,0} + M^* - \alpha F_{1,*}^-) \end{aligned}\right\}, \tag{5.84}$$

and

$$\left.\begin{aligned} F_{n,*}^+ &= \frac{F_{n,0} + \alpha M_{n,0} - (v_{n,0} + \alpha\omega_{n,0})/\tau}{1+\alpha^2}, \\ \omega_{n,*}^+ &= \omega_{n,0} - (M_{n,0} - \alpha F_{n,*}^+) \end{aligned}\right\}, \tag{5.85}$$

where the ratio $\tau = \Delta t / \Delta x$ must be determined at each step from energy balance of the system, exploiting successive approximations.

All the quantities are scaled by the moment $M^o = -M^*$, replacing in Eqs.(5.68) the basis velocity v^o by $M^o / rA\rho c$, i.e., putting $\overline{M} = M / M^o$,

$\overline{F} = Fr / M^o$, $\overline{v} = vrA\rho c / M^o$ etc. As above, the overbars will be omitted.

5.3.2.2. **A**. Some numerical results for the similar problem in reference to a 'beam/slab' model were obtained by Nigul (1965). The Timoshenko type bending theory was used, but the calculated model differs from a beam in that the plane strain state in the lateral direction z was assumed. Hence, the modulus E must be replaced by $E_r = E/(1-\mu^2)$.

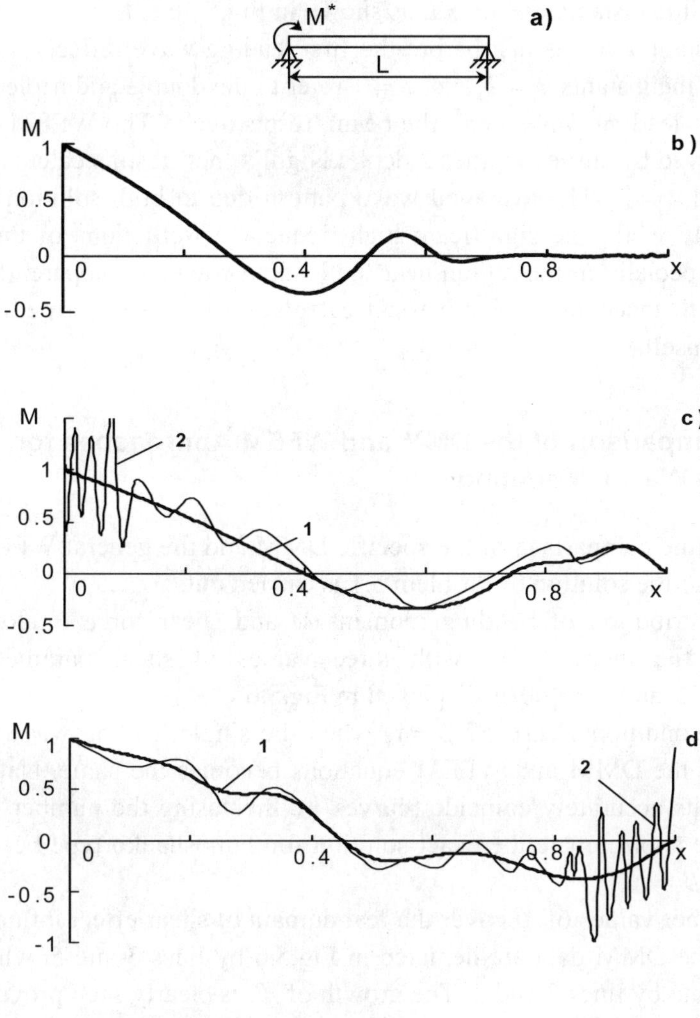

Fig.5.5. A beam affected by a bending moment; a) sketch of the problem; b), c), d) distributions of moment M along the beam at $\widetilde{t}$: b) $\widetilde{t} = 1$, c) $\widetilde{t} = 2$, d) $\widetilde{t} = 3$. Numerical results: 1) WFEM, 2) 'net' method

The numerical solution was carried out by the ‘net’ method. To compare the WFEM and ‘net’ results, we take

$$L/H = 15,\ \lambda = L/r \approx 52,\ n = 208,\ \alpha = 0.5\lambda/n = 0.125, \text{ and } \mu = 0.3$$

where H is a height of the beam cross section.

The reciprocal of the shear coefficient is $1/k_s = 0.86$, hence $\beta = E_r k_s / G = 2k_s/(1-\mu) = 3.322$.

B. The distribution of bending moment M along the length of the beam for three time instants $\tilde{t} = tc_\omega / L$ is shown in Fig.5.5b,c,d.

The instant $\tilde{t} = 1$ is just before the first leading wave reflects from the right end, the instants $\tilde{t} = 2$ and $\tilde{t} = 3$ refer to the double and triple transition of the leading wave along the beam, respectively. The WFEM results are displayed by curves 1; lines 2 depict Nigul’s ‘net’ results calculated for $\tilde{t} = 2$ and $\tilde{t} = 3$. The averaged wave pattern due to both solutions coincides fairly well. The significant high-frequency oscillations of the ‘net’ results, especially in the region near the leading wave, are apparently connected with inaccuracy of numerical calculation that was warned by the author himself.

5.3.3 Comparison of the DMM and WFEM Approaches for Bending Waves Modeling

Below, some comparison of the specific DMM and the general WFEM approaches to the solution of Problem 5.1 is carried out.

The distribution of bending moment M and shear force F along the beam at the instant t=10 with three values of shear parameter β for $\alpha = 0.02$ and $n = 300$ is displayed in Fig.5.6.

In the conditional case of $\beta = 1$, when the single leading wave arises, the set of the DMM and WFEM equations becomes the same. Naturally, their results accurately coincide (curves 1). Increasing the number of elements, we approximate the exact solution for Timoshenko type beam theory with $\beta = 1$.

Two other values of β cover the real domain of shear effect influence in beams. The DMM data are depicted in Fig.5.6 by lines 3 and 5, while the WFEM data by lines 2 and 4. The growth of β is clearly seen provocating the retardation of the strong shear wave from the weak leading wave. Some high-frequency oscillations appear near these fronts. The averaged DMM and WFEM results differ insignificantly, while the computation

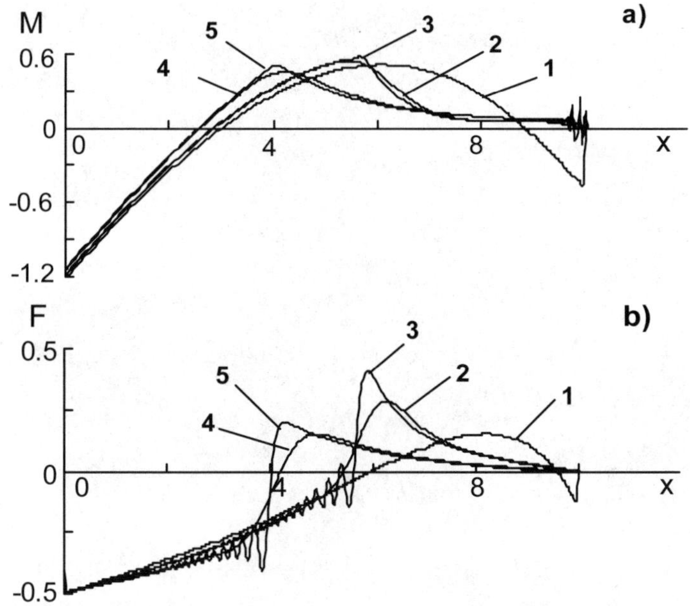

Fig.5.6. To comparison of the DMM and WFEM results for Problem 5.1; a) bending moment, b) shear force for some values of β 1) $\beta = 1$; 2,3) $\beta = 3$; 4,5) $\beta = 6$; DMM - curves 1,3,5, WFEM – curves 1.2.4

time of the first procedure is noticeably less. Therefore, to exploit the general WFEM approach is only useful for more complicated problems, for example, beam/frame bending, coupled bending/torsional oscillations of turbine blades etc.

6 One-Dimensional Waves in Elastic Continua and Structures

6.1 Plane Waves

1-D waves can arise not only in rods, strings, and beams, as we have seen in earlier chapters, but also in plates, solid continua, and in more complicated structures.

6.1.1 Longitudinal Waves

6.1.1.1. All time-dependent quantities associated with 1-D wave processes in solids are, by definition, functions of a single space coordinate. Relative to a Cartesian coordinate system, we take as the governing (longitudinal) direction the *x*-axis.

If all the solid particles move in any common direction, a wave of plane deformation propagates along this axis. However, the particle displacements can be, in general, not coincident with the direction of wave propagation.

Assume, initially, that the directions x, y, z are principal and the normal stress σ_x is nonzero with the tangential stresses $\sigma_{xy} = \sigma_{yz} = \sigma_{zx} = 0$.

Then, from the general equations of elasticity

$$\varepsilon_x = \frac{\sigma_x - \mu(\sigma_y + \sigma_z)}{E}, \quad \varepsilon_y = \frac{\sigma_y - \mu(\sigma_z + \sigma_x)}{E}, \quad \varepsilon_z = \frac{\sigma_z - \mu(\sigma_x + \sigma_y)}{E} \tag{6.1}$$

the 'lateral' normal stresses σ_y and σ_z can be presented in the form

$$\sigma_y = k_y \sigma_x, \sigma_z = k_z \sigma_x, \tag{6.2}$$

where

$$\left.\begin{aligned} k_y &= \frac{\mu(1+\mu-\alpha_z)}{(1-\alpha_y)(1+\mu-\alpha_z)-\mu(1+\mu-\alpha_y)}, \\ k_z &= \frac{\mu(1+\mu-\alpha_y)}{(1-\alpha_z)(1+\mu-\alpha_y)-\mu(1+\mu-\alpha_z)} \end{aligned}\right\}. \tag{6.3}$$

The constants α_y, α_z connect the stresses σ_y, σ_z with the 'lateral' strains $\varepsilon_y, \varepsilon_z$, namely,

$$\alpha_y = E\varepsilon_y / \sigma_y, \quad \alpha_z = E\varepsilon_z / \sigma_z. \tag{6.4}$$

The governing equation for plane longitudinal waves yields

$$\varepsilon_x = \sigma_x / E_r, \tag{6.5}$$

where E_r is the reduced elastic modulus

$$E_r = \frac{E}{1-\mu(k_y+k_z)}. \tag{6.6}$$

Its values for the particular cases (see Fig. 6.1) are the following:

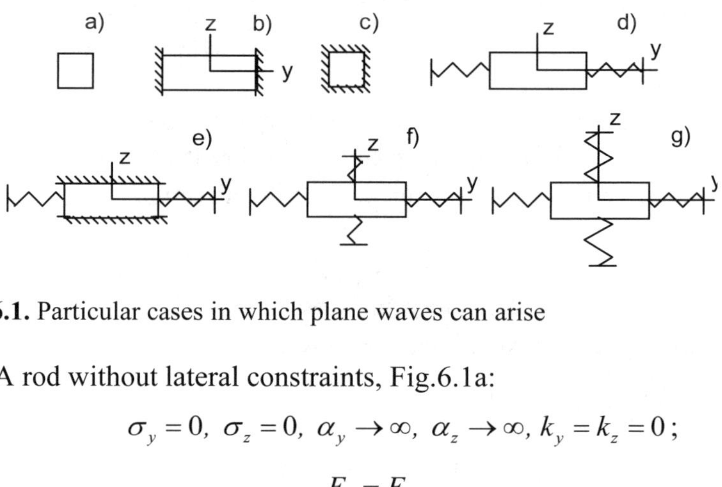

Fig.6.1. Particular cases in which plane waves can arise

- A rod without lateral constraints, Fig.6.1a:

$$\sigma_y = 0, \ \sigma_z = 0, \ \alpha_y \to \infty, \ \alpha_z \to \infty, \ k_y = k_z = 0;$$

$$E_r = E. \tag{6.7a}$$

- A wide plate without any constraint in the out-of-plate direction z and with full constraint in the other lateral direction y, Fig.6.1b:

$$\sigma_z = 0, \ \varepsilon_y = 0, \ \alpha_y = 0, \ \alpha_z \to \infty, \quad k_y = \mu, \ k_z = 0;$$

$$E_r = E/(1-\mu^2). \tag{6.7b}$$

- An elastic body with full constraints in the both lateral directions, Fig.6.1c:

$$\varepsilon_y = \varepsilon_z = 0,\ \alpha_y = \alpha_z = 0,\ k_y = k_z = \mu/(1-\mu),$$

$$E_r = \frac{(1-\mu)E}{(1+\mu)(1-2\mu)}. \tag{6.7c}$$

Neglecting the inertial effects in the lateral directions and exploiting Eq.(6.5), the DMM algorithm described in the previous chapters can be used, where the wave speed is given by

$$c = \sqrt{E_r/\rho}. \tag{6.8}$$

All the nondimensional expressions remain unchanged.

6.1.1.2. Using Eqs.(6.2)-(6.6), the wave processes in complicated structures induced by lateral interaction of an elastic rod (or fiber) with ambient elastic medium can be readily elucidated.

We assume that the medium deformations ε'_y, ε'_z are connected with the stresses σ'_y, σ'_z by relations

$$\varepsilon'_y = \alpha'_y \sigma'_y / E,\ \varepsilon'_z = \alpha'_z \sigma'_z / E, \tag{6.9a}$$

where the conditions of the rod/medium interaction yield

$$\sigma'_y = \sigma_y,\ \sigma'_z = \sigma_z,\ \varepsilon'_y = -\varepsilon_y,\ \varepsilon'_z = -\varepsilon_z, \tag{6.9b}$$

i.e. $\alpha_y = -\alpha'_y,\ \alpha_z = -\alpha'_z$.

Allowing the coefficients α_y, α_z to vary in the range from 0 to ∞, the several additional cases shown in Fig.6.1 can also be studied:

- A wide plate without constraint in the out-of-plate direction z elastically interacting with the medium in the direction y, Fig.6.1d, implying

$$\sigma_z = 0,\ \alpha_z \to \infty,\ \alpha_y = -\alpha'_y,\ k_z = 0,\ k_y = \mu(1+\alpha'_y),$$

$$E_r = \frac{1+\alpha'_y}{1+\alpha'_y - \mu^2} E. \tag{6.10a}$$

- A plane elastic layer constrained in the direction z and elastically interacting with medium in the direction y, Fig.6.1e, implying

$$\varepsilon_z = 0,\ \alpha_z = 0,\ \alpha_y = -\alpha'_y,$$

$$k_y = \mu(1+\mu)/(1+\alpha'_y - \mu^2),\ k_z = \mu(1+\mu+\alpha'_y)/(1+\alpha'_y - \mu^2),$$

$$E_r = \frac{1+\alpha'_y - \mu^2}{(1+\mu)[(1+\mu)(1-2\mu^2)+(1-\mu)\alpha'_y)]}E. \tag{6.10b}$$

- A rod (fiber) interacting elastically with homogeneous medium in both lateral directions, Fig.6.1f, implying

$$\alpha_y = \alpha_z = -\alpha',\ k_y = k_z = \mu/(1+\alpha' - \mu),$$

$$E_r = \frac{(1+\alpha' - \mu)}{(1+\mu)(1-2\mu)+\alpha'}E. \tag{6.10c}$$

- A rod (fiber) interacting elastically with nonhomogeneous medium, Fig.6.1g. The reduced modulus E_r is to be determined by the general Eqs.(6.3)-(6.4) with $\alpha_y = -\alpha'_y,\ \alpha_z = -\alpha'_z$.

6.1.2 Transverse and Coupled Waves

6.1.2.1. Unlike the previous Subsection, consider all the solid particles moving in the common direction (say, y), normal to the x-axis of wave propagation. Such wave movement is referred to transverse. In this case, the single elasticity equation

$$\varepsilon_{xy} = \sigma_{xy}/G \tag{6.11}$$

is valid, with $\varepsilon_{yx} = \varepsilon_{xy},\ \sigma_{yx} = \sigma_{xy}$, and all other stress and strain components are zero.

The standard set of the DMM equations for the longitudinal fiber element is

$$\left.\begin{aligned} \sigma^{\pm}_{xy} &= \sigma_{xy,0} \pm \rho c_g(v^{\pm}_y - v_{y,0}), \\ v^{\pm}_y - v_{y,0} &= \pm c_g(\varepsilon^{\pm}_{xy} - \varepsilon_{xy,0}), \\ \sigma^{\pm}_{xy} - \sigma_{xy,0} &= G(\varepsilon^{\pm}_{xy} - \varepsilon_{xy,0}) \end{aligned}\right\}, \tag{6.12}$$

from which the transverse wave speed is given by

$$c_g = \frac{\Delta x}{\Delta t} = \sqrt{\frac{G}{\rho}}. \tag{6.13}$$

This speed provides the element energy balance

$$\Delta W = \Delta E ,$$

where

$$\Delta W = (\sigma_{xy}^{+} v_y^{+} - \sigma_{xy}^{-} v_y^{-})\Delta t,$$

$$\Delta E = 0.5\left[\rho(v_y^2 - v_{y,0}^2) + \frac{\sigma_{xy}^2 - \sigma_{xy,0}^2}{G}\right]\Delta x,$$

and also $v_y = v_y^{+} + v_y^{-} - v_{y,0}$ and $\sigma_{xy} = \sigma_{xy}^{+} + \sigma_{xy}^{-} - \sigma_{xy,0}$.

The calculation procedure of DMM does not require any change.

***6.1.2.2.* A.** In a linear elastic system, longitudinal and transverse waves propagate with their own speeds independently of each other. However, for any nonlinear problem, in particular, in the case of the compressed multi-layered plates interacting with dry frictional slip, these waves become coupled and require on-line consideration.

To demonstrate such possibilities and the accuracy of the general WFEM approach applied to coupled plane waves analysis, we consider a simpler linear situation where both wave types arise and propagate simultaneously.

B. Problem 6.1. Elastic half-space affected at the free surface by uniformly distributed 'pendulum' load. Let us assume that the slope angle ϕ of a load traction p to the y-axis linearly varies in time from $\phi = 0$ to $\phi = \pi$ and back again (Fig. 6.2a), so that

$$\phi(\bar{t}) = \begin{cases} 2\pi(\bar{t} - \bar{t}_n) & \text{with } 0 \le \bar{t} - \bar{t}_n \le 0.5, \\ 2\pi[1 - (\bar{t} - \bar{t}_n)] & \text{with } 0.5 \le \bar{t} - \bar{t}_n \le 1 \end{cases},$$

where $\bar{t} = t/T$, with the period T of the angle $\phi(\bar{t})$ variation, and a relative time $\bar{t}_n = n_t - 1$ is referred to the initial moment of the nth period $(n_t = 1,2,...)$.

The load p projections to x,y-axes

$$p_x = p\sin\phi, \; p_y = -p\cos\phi$$

provoke a plane longitudinal wave with normal stress σ_x and a plane transverse wave with tangential stress σ_{xy}, respectively.

The boundary conditions at the node $j = 1$ referred to the free surface are

$$\bar{\sigma}_{1x}^{-} = -\sin\phi,\ \bar{\sigma}_{1xy}^{-} = \cos\phi,$$

where $\bar{\sigma} = \sigma / p$.

The boundary conditions at the varying opposite node $j = i + 1$, which overtakes the leading wave front $\bar{x} = i\Delta\bar{x}$ by one element length, do not influence the results. Here, i is an index of time steps, $\bar{x} = x/L,\ \Delta\bar{x} = 1/n,$ n is an accepted number of elements within the length $L = Tc,$ and c is a longitudinal wave speed in solid determined by Eq.(6.8).

The kinetic and potential energy of the element in nondimensional terms are, respectively,

$$\bar{K} = 0.5(\bar{v}_{jx}^2 + \bar{v}_{jy}^2)\Delta\bar{x},\ \bar{P}_j = 0.5[(\bar{u}_{jx}^{+} - \bar{u}_{jx}^{-})^2 + \bar{c}_g(\bar{u}_{jy}^{+} - \bar{u}_{jy}^{-})^2]/\Delta\bar{x},$$

where

$$\bar{v} = v\rho c/p,\ \bar{u} = u\rho c/pT,\ \bar{K} = K\rho c/p^2,\ \bar{P} = P\rho c/p^2,\ \bar{W} = W\rho c/p^2,$$

and

$$\bar{c}_g = \sqrt{\frac{G}{E_r}} = \sqrt{\frac{1-2\mu}{2(1-\mu)}}.$$

The work brought to the element over a varying time interval Δt_i is

$$\Delta\bar{W}_{ji} = (\bar{\sigma}_{jx}^{+}\bar{v}_{jx}^{+} - \bar{\sigma}_{jx}^{-}\bar{v}_{jx}^{-} + \bar{\sigma}_{jxy}^{+}\bar{v}_{jxy}^{+} - \bar{\sigma}_{jxy}^{-}\bar{v}_{jxy}^{-})\Delta\bar{t}_i.$$

Calculation of the intervals $\Delta\bar{t}_i$ is carried out by the standard WFEM algorithm described previously.

C. The normal $\bar{\sigma}_x$ and tangential $\bar{\sigma}_{xy}$ stresses at the point $\bar{x}_* = 0.5$ against time $\bar{t}$ are shown in Fig.6.2b,c, respectively, for $n = 400$ and $\bar{c}_g = 0.5345$ (with $\mu = 0.3$). To avoid small oscillations with period of $2\Delta\bar{t}$, the procedure of final result smoothing is exploited. The identical phases of stress curves and load position are marked by indexes I, II, III.

The lag of the shear wave $\bar{\sigma}_{xy}$ from the longitudinal one $\bar{\sigma}_x$ is clearly seen. The last wave arrives at the point $\bar{x}_* = 0.5$ exactly at the time $\bar{t} = 0.5$, while a visible strong increase of the shear stress begins after the time $\bar{t} \approx 0.88$, reaching the middle value 0.5 at $\bar{t} \approx 0.94$; whereas the theoretical value of this time displayed in Fig.6.2c by vertical line is $\bar{t} = 0.5\bar{c}_g^{-0.5} = 0.9355$.

As the treated problem is linear, the propagation of waves of each kind can be calculated separately in an identical way. Doing so, we obtain num-

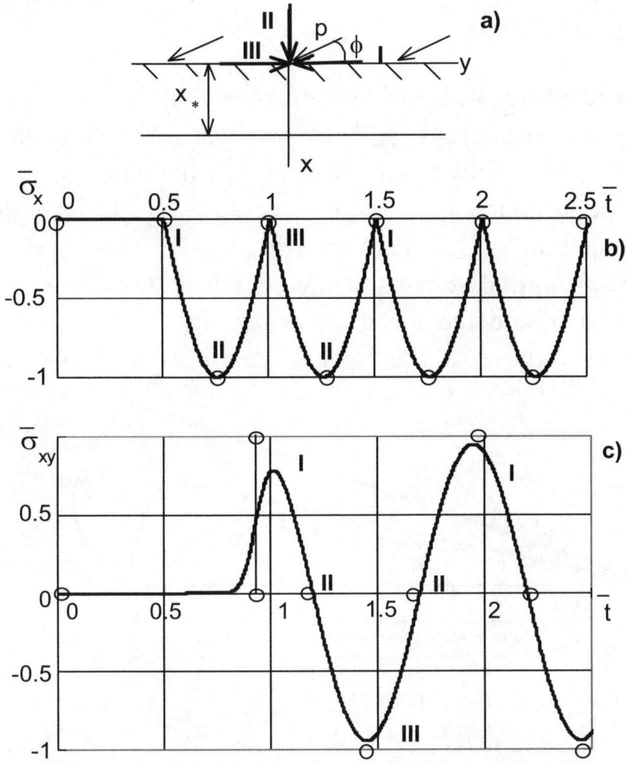

Fig.6.2. Elastic half-space affected by 'pendulum' load; a) sketch of the problem, b) normal and c) tangential stresses at the point $\bar{x}_* = 0.5$ vs. time

erical results depicted in Fig.6.2b,c by white dots, for which the time positions coincide with analytical predictions. Sufficient accuracy of the WFEM approach when applied to coupled wave analysis is seen, excluding the bounded initial region where the more slowly traveling shear stresses vary not so sharply as the analytical results.

6.2 Spherical and Cylindrical Waves

For both these types of 1-D waves, the governing direction of wave propagation is radial. As the problem of spherical waves is of great interest in seismology and some other applications, (see Hopkins 1960 and also Mechta and Devids 1966), it is considered in more details using the DMM approach.

6.2.1 Spherical Waves

***6.2.1.1. Static state*. A**. Consider a small spatial finite element cut from a centrally symmetrical elastic body by two near spherical surfaces of radii r^- and $r^+ = r^- + \Delta r$ and two pairs of close meridian planes, as it is shown in Fig.6.3. The arbitrary small angles $\Delta\varphi$ and $\Delta\psi$ do not influence the following deduction

Denote radial normal stresses at the spherical surfaces $r^\pm$ of the area $(r^\pm)^2\Delta\varphi\Delta\psi$ as $\sigma_r^\pm$ and the mean circumferential normal stresses at the meridian planes of the areas $r\Delta r\Delta\varphi$ and $r\Delta r\Delta\psi$ as σ_φ and σ_ψ, respectiv-

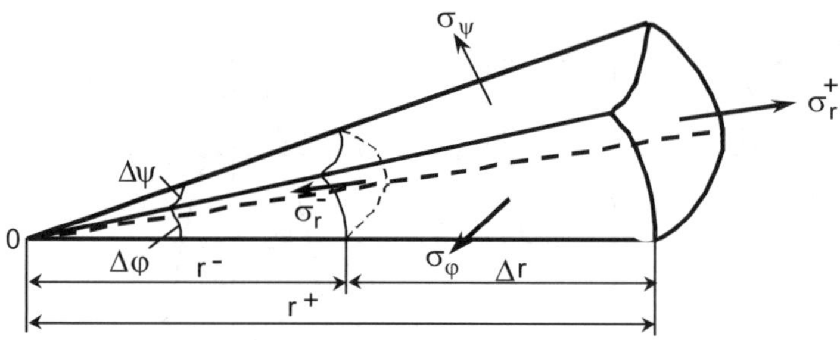

Fig.6.3. Scheme of a spherical element

ely, with $r = 0.5(r^- + r^+)$ and $\sigma_\psi = \sigma_\varphi$. The tangential stresses are absent because of the system central symmetry. The static subscript 0 is so far omitted.

The radial equilibrium equation of the element being at rest at an instant t_{i-1}^- for any angles $\Delta\varphi, \Delta\psi$ with $(\Delta r / r)^2 << 1$ yields

$$(\sigma_r^+ - \sigma_r^-)r + 2(\sigma_r - \sigma_\varphi)\Delta r = 0\,. \tag{6.14}$$

Decreasing Δr, we come to the known differential equation of the spherical body

$$\frac{d\sigma_r}{dr} + 2\frac{\sigma_r - \sigma_\varphi}{r} = 0.$$

The principal distinction between the radii r^+ and r^- is valid only for the central element with $r^- = 0$. In this case, $\Delta r = r^+$, $r = 0.5r^+$, and Eq.(6.14a) yields $\sigma_r^+ = \sigma_\varphi$. For other elements we assume $(\Delta r / r)^2 << 1$, hence

$$\frac{\Delta r}{r^\pm} \approx \frac{\Delta r}{r}(1 \mp \frac{\Delta r}{r}) \approx \frac{\Delta r}{r}.$$

Omitting the angles $\Delta\varphi, \Delta\psi$, we conditionally call the quantities r^2 or $r\Delta r$ as 'areas' and $F_r = \sigma_r r^2$ or $F_\varphi = \sigma_\varphi r\Delta r$ as 'forces'.

The general elasticity equations reduce for the centrally symmetrical case with $\varepsilon_\varphi = \varepsilon_\psi$ to

$$\varepsilon_r = \frac{\sigma_r - 2\mu\sigma_\varphi}{E}, \ \varepsilon_\varphi = \frac{(1-\mu)\sigma_\varphi - \mu\sigma_r}{E}, \tag{6.15a}$$

and vice versa

$$\sigma_r = E_r\left(\varepsilon_r + \frac{2\mu}{1-\mu}\varepsilon_\varphi\right), \ \sigma_\varphi = \frac{E_r}{1-\mu}(\varepsilon_\varphi + \mu\varepsilon_r), \tag{6.15b}$$

where the reduced elastic modulus E_r is expressed by the previous formula (6.7c).

The radial ε_r and circumferential ε_φ strains are functions of the radial displacement u given by

$$\varepsilon_r = \frac{\partial u}{\partial r}, \ \varepsilon_\varphi = \frac{u}{r}, \tag{6.16}$$

and their mean values over the element length can be expressed by the element boundary displacements $u^\pm = u(r^\pm)$ as

$$\varepsilon_r = \frac{u^+ - u^-}{\Delta r}, \ \varepsilon_\varphi \approx \frac{u^+ + u^-}{2r}. \tag{6.17}$$

It is convenient for the subsequent analysis to express the strain ε_r and the stress σ_φ by means of Eq.(6.15) in the terms of stress σ_r and strain ε_φ, thus

$$\varepsilon_r = \frac{\sigma_r}{E_r} - \frac{2\mu}{1-\mu}\varepsilon_\varphi, \ \sigma_\varphi = \frac{\mu}{1-\mu}\sigma_r + \frac{E}{1-\mu}\varepsilon_\varphi. \tag{6.18}$$

B. The first terms of Eqs.(6.18) containing the stress σ_r are directly caused by the radial force action, including the inertial loads, whereas the second ones are connected only with volumetric deformational behavior of the material. Due to the DMM principles, we incorporate the 1-D structural model of the finite spherical element as a composition of three parts: a basis continual-inertial part I of the length Δr and two non-inertial parts II, each of the length $0.5\Delta r$. A radial strain of the part I is $\varepsilon_r = \sigma_r / E_r$ with absence of strain ε_φ; additional radial strains $\tilde{\varepsilon}_r^\pm = -2\mu\varepsilon_\varphi^\pm/(1-\mu)$ of the parts II are induced by the transition of the element boundaries to other radii. The full radial strain is given by

$$\varepsilon_{r,*} = \varepsilon_r + 0.5(\widetilde{\varepsilon}_r^{+} + \widetilde{\varepsilon}_r^{-}). \tag{6.19}$$

Denoting the displacements of the whole element boundaries by $u_*^{\pm} = u^{\pm} + \widetilde{u}^{\pm}$ and the radial displacements for borders of the parts I and II by $u^{\pm}$ and $\widetilde{u}^{\pm}$, we have

$$\varepsilon_{r*} = \frac{u_*^{+} - u_*^{-}}{\Delta r}. \quad \varepsilon_{\varphi}^{\pm} \approx \frac{u_*^{\pm}}{r^{\pm}}, \quad \widetilde{\varepsilon}_r^{\pm} \approx -\frac{2\mu}{1-\mu}\frac{u_*^{\pm}}{r^{\pm}}, \tag{6.20}$$

Then we obtain for $(\Delta r / r)^2 << 1$ that

$$u^{\pm} = u_*^{\pm}\left(1 \pm \frac{\mu}{1-\mu}\frac{\Delta r}{r}\right). \tag{6.21}$$

The circumferential stresses for the parts I and II, in compliance with Eqs.(6.18) and (6.20), are

$$\sigma_{\varphi} = \frac{\mu}{1-\mu}\sigma_r = \frac{E_r \mu}{1-\mu}\left(\frac{u^{+} - u^{-}}{\Delta r}\right), \quad \widetilde{\sigma}_{\varphi}^{\pm} = \frac{E}{1-\mu}\varepsilon_{\varphi}^{\pm} = \frac{E}{1-\mu}\left(\frac{u_*^{\pm}}{r^{\pm}}\right). \tag{6.22}$$

C. The potential energy of a spherical element

$$P = 0.5(\sigma_r \varepsilon_r + 2\sigma_{\varphi}\varepsilon_{\varphi})r^2 \Delta r$$

expressed in the terms σ_r and $\varepsilon_{\varphi}^{\pm}$ can be separated to three parts $P = P_I + P_{II}^{+} + P_{II}^{-}$, where

$$P_I = \frac{\sigma_r^2 r^2 \Delta r}{2E_r}, \quad P_{II}^{\pm} = \frac{E}{1-\mu}(\varepsilon_{\varphi}^{\pm})^2 \frac{r^2 \Delta r}{2}. \tag{6.23}$$

The radial boundary forces statically applied to the element in its nodes can be determined in the terms of boundary displacements as

$$F_{r*}^{\pm} = \frac{\partial P}{\partial u_*^{\pm}} = \pm \frac{E_r r^2}{\Delta r}\left(1 \pm \frac{\mu}{1-\mu}\frac{\Delta r}{r}\right)\left[u_*^{+}\left(1 + \frac{\mu}{1-\mu}\frac{\Delta r}{r}\right) - u_*^{-}\left(1 - \frac{\mu}{1-\mu}\frac{\Delta r}{r}\right)\right] +$$
$$+ \frac{E r \Delta r}{1-\mu}\left(\frac{u_*^{\pm}}{r^{\pm}}\right) \tag{6.24}$$

For element boundary equilibrium conditions (see Fig.6.4), Eq.(6.24) corresponds to

$$F_{r*}^{\pm} = F_r^{\pm} - F_{r\varphi}^{\pm}, \tag{6.25}$$

where

$$F_r^{\pm} = \pm\sigma_r r^2, \quad F_{r\varphi}^{\pm} = -(\sigma_\varphi + \tilde{\sigma}_\varphi^{\pm}) r\Delta r. \tag{6.26}$$

The condition of static equilibrium for the element as a whole

$$F_{r*}^{+} + F_{r*}^{-} + F_{r\varphi}^{+} + F_{r\varphi}^{-} = 0 \tag{6.27}$$

is a consequence of Eqs.(6.25) and (6.26).

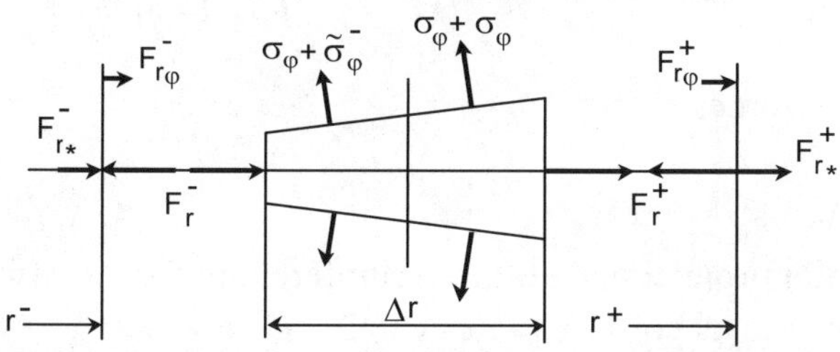

Fig.6.4. To radial equilibrium conditions of a spherical element

It is readily checked that a total work $W = 0.5(F_{r*}^{+}u_*^{+} + F_{r*}^{-}u_*^{-})$ statically introduced to the proposed element structural model is exactly equal to the element potential energy P.

6.2.1.2. Spherical wave propagation. **A**. Using the DMM algorithm we assume, as usual, that the element radial velocity $v_{j,0}$ and the radial displacements $u_{j,0}^{\pm}$ of the inertial part I at the instant t_{i-1}^{-} are known.

Henceforth, the subscript r referred to radial quantities is omitted and the element length is $\Delta r = \text{const}$. By analogy with the longitudinal waves in a rod, we assume the border velocities $v_j^{\pm}$ of the part I during time step $\Delta t = t_i^{-} - t_{i-1}^{+}$ remain constant; then the border stresses of this part are $\sigma_j^{\pm} = \sigma_{j,0} \pm \rho c(v_j^{\pm} - v_{j,0})$ and the wave speed satisfying the energy balance is $c = \Delta r / \Delta t = (E_r / \rho)^{0.5}$. This quantity coincides with the analytical speed for elastic spherical waves (see Kolsky 1953).

The new border displacements of the part I are

$$u_j^{\pm} = u_{j,0}^{\pm} + v_j^{\pm}\Delta t. \tag{6.28}$$

If the full displacements change from $u_{j,0*}^{\pm}$ to $u_{j,*}^{\pm}$ with the mean velocity $v_{j,*}^{\pm} = (u_{j,*}^{\pm} - u_{j,0*}^{\pm}) / \Delta t$, the full mean displacements are

$$u^{\pm}_{j,m*} = u^{\pm}_{j,0*} + 0.5v^{\pm}_{j,*}\Delta t. \tag{6.29}$$

The velocities $v^{\pm}_{j}$ and $v^{\pm}_{j,*}$ are connected by the same expression (6.21) as the corresponding displacements, namely,

$$v^{\pm}_{j} = v^{\pm}_{j,*}\left(1 \pm \frac{\mu}{1-\mu}\frac{\Delta r}{r_j}\right). \tag{6.30}$$

Then, the boundary stresses for part I are

$$\sigma^{\pm}_{j} = \sigma_{j,0} \mp \rho c v_{j,0} \pm \rho c v^{\pm}_{j,*}\left(1 \pm \frac{\mu}{1-\mu}\frac{\Delta r}{r_j}\right) \tag{6.31}$$

and the boundary forces

$$F^{\pm}_{j} = \pm\sigma^{\pm}_{j} r^{\pm 2}_{j}. \tag{6.32}$$

The mean radial projections of the circumferential forces affecting the element in a time Δt, according to Eqs.(6.22), are

$$F^{\pm}_{j,r\varphi} = -\left[\frac{\mu}{1-\mu}\sigma^{\pm}_{j} + \frac{E}{1-\mu}\left(\frac{u^{\pm}_{j,m*}}{r^{\pm}_{j}}\right)\right] r_j \Delta r. \tag{6.33}$$

With reference to Eqs.(6.25) and (6.32)-(6.33), the conditions of the element boundaries equilibrium during the interval Δt yield

$$F^{\pm}_{j,*} = F^{\pm}_{j,0*} + \beta^{\pm}_{j} v^{\pm}_{j,*}, \tag{6.34}$$

where

$$\left.\begin{aligned} F^{\pm}_{j,0*} &= \pm(\sigma_{j,0} \mp \rho c v_{j,0})\left(1 \pm \frac{\mu}{1-\mu}\frac{\Delta r}{r}\right) r^{2}_{j} + \frac{E}{1-\mu} u^{\pm}_{j,0*}\Delta r, \\ \beta^{\pm}_{j} &= \rho c\left(1 \pm \frac{\mu}{1-\mu}\frac{\Delta r}{r}\right)^{2} r^{2}_{j} + \frac{E}{2(1-\mu)}\Delta r \Delta t \end{aligned}\right\}. \tag{6.35}$$

B. Taking into account the equilibrium condition $F^{+}_{j-1,*} + F^{-}_{j,*} = 0$ of the node j between elements $j-1$ and j, and equating their velocities $v^{+}_{j-1,*} = v^{-}_{j,*} = v_{j,*}$, we obtain the governing equation

$$v_{j,*} = -\frac{F^{+}_{j-1,0*} + F^{-}_{j,0*}}{\beta^{+}_{j-1} + \beta^{-}_{j}}. \tag{6.36}$$

Once the velocity $v_{j,*}$ (as previously $v_{j-1,*}$) is determined, all the other quantities for the element $j-1$ can be sequentially calculated that admits in turn to progress to the next node.

For nonhomogeneous media with density ρ_j and elastic modulus $E_{j,r}$ depending on radius (i.e. on the element index j) the element length Δr_j must satisfy the requirement for constant time interval

$$\Delta t = \Delta r_j / c_j = \Delta r_j \sqrt{\rho_j / E_{j,r}} = \text{const}. \tag{6.37}$$

Equations (6.34)-(6.36) remain valid with $\Delta r = \Delta r_j$, $\rho = \rho_j$, $E = E_j$, and $c = c_j$. The boundary conditions at the given spherical surface $r_j \neq 0$ are established in the ordinary way. For example, for a free surface at the node $j=1$ when $F_{1,*}^- = 0$ we get from Eq.(6.34) $v_{1,*}^- = -F_{1,0*}^- / \beta_1^-$.

C. To describe the conditions at the center of the compact spherical domain, the central element bounded by a small radius $r_0 = \Delta r$ has to be singled out. In this case, $\sigma_0 = \sigma_{0,\varphi}$, $\varepsilon_0 = \varepsilon_{0,\varphi} = (1-2\mu)\sigma_0 / E$, and $u_0 = r_0 \varepsilon_{0,\varphi} = \alpha_0 F_0^+$, where $F_0^+ = \sigma_0 r_0^2$ and $\alpha_0 = (1-2\mu)/Er_0$.

Thus, the central element can be regarded as an elastic fixation of the left boundary of the next (first) element. The sum of the boundary forces $F_{1,*}^- = F_{1,0*}^- + \beta_1^- v_{1,*}$ for the first element and $F_{0,*}^+ = (u_0 + v_{1,*} 0.5\Delta t)/\alpha_0$ for the central one must satisfy the equation $F_{0,*}^+ + F_{1,*}^- = 0$ from which

$$v_{1,*} = -\frac{F_{1,0*}^- \alpha_0 + u_0}{\beta_1^- \alpha_0 + 0.5\Delta t}. \tag{6.38}$$

6.2.2 Explosion in a Spherical Cavity of an Elastic Medium

6.2.2.1. **Problem 6.2. Homogeneous elastic medium with a spherical cavity subjected to suddenly applied pressure.** Denote the cavity radius by r_0 and arbitrarily changing pressure in the cavity by $p(t)$. A function $p(t)$ will be represented step-wise with constant values p_i over each time step Δt.

Introducing the dimensionless quantities

$$\bar{r} = \frac{r}{r_0},\ \bar{t} = \frac{ct}{r_0},\ \bar{p} = \frac{p}{p_0},\ \bar{\sigma} = \frac{\sigma}{p_0},\ \bar{F} = \frac{F}{p_0 r_0^2},\ \bar{v} = \frac{\rho c v}{p_0},\ \bar{u} = \frac{E_r u}{p_0 r_0},\ \bar{\beta} = \frac{\beta}{\rho c r_0^2},$$

and also $\bar{E} = E / E_r$, where $p_0 = p(0)$ is a magnitude of pressure in the cavity at the initial moment $t = 0$, and assuming the elements length $\Delta\bar{r}^2 = (\Delta r / r_0)^2 << 1$, the boundary condition $\bar{\sigma}_1^- = -\bar{p}_i$ at the cavity face leads to $\overline{F}_{1,*}^{-} = \overline{F}_{1,0*}^{-} + \overline{\beta}_1^{-}\overline{v}_{1,*}^{-} = -\overline{\sigma}_1^{-}$, where from $\overline{v}_{1,*}^{-} = -(\overline{\sigma}_1^{-} + \overline{F}_{1,0*}^{-})/\overline{\beta}_1^{-}$.

6.2.2.2. Numerical results for the particular case of constant pressure $\overline{p}=1$, i.e. $\overline{\sigma}_1^{-} = -1$, with $\Delta\overline{r} = 0.01$ and $\mu = 0.3$ are shown in Fig.6.5-6.6.

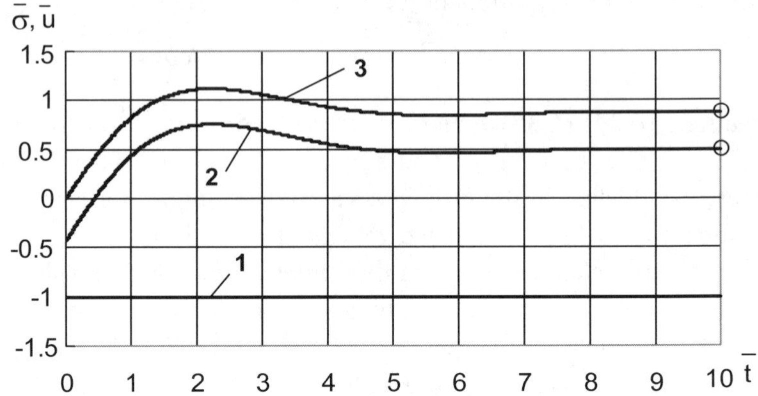

Fig.6.5. Time evolution of stresses and displacements at the cavity surface under constant pressure: 1)- $\overline{\sigma}_1$, 2) - $\overline{\sigma}_{1,\varphi}$, 3) $-\overline{u}_1$

Evolution of the radial $\overline{\sigma}_1$ and the circumferential $\overline{\sigma}_{1,\varphi}$ stress related to the cavity surface and the displacement $\overline{u}_1$ of this face versus time are presented in Fig.6.5. The distribution of stresses $\overline{\sigma}, \overline{\sigma}_\varphi$, and displacement $\overline{u}$ along the radius $\overline{r}$ for some times $\overline{t}$ are illustrated in Fig.6.6 a,b,c, respectively.

In spite of the fact that the system is free from damping forces, the dynamic process fades due to energy spreading under wave propagation over the increasing deformed material volume. Within the leading wave region, where radial displacements have not yet had sufficient time to develop, material is practically subjected to the not uniform three-sided compression with constant stress ratio of $\sigma_\varphi/\sigma = \mu/(1-\mu) \approx 0.429$. In particular, this refers to the cavity surface at the explosion moment. As the radial displacements increase, the circumferential stresses change their sign to positive. With relative time $\overline{t} >> 1$, distribution of the stress and radial displacement closely arrives at the analytical solution for the static loading, which yields (see Timoshenko and Googier 1970)

$$\overline{\sigma} = -\overline{r}^{-3},\ \overline{\sigma}_\varphi = 0.5\overline{r}^{-3},\ \overline{u} = 0.5(1-\mu)\overline{r}^{-2}/(1-2\mu).$$

These quantities are also doted in Fig. 6.5 - 6.6.

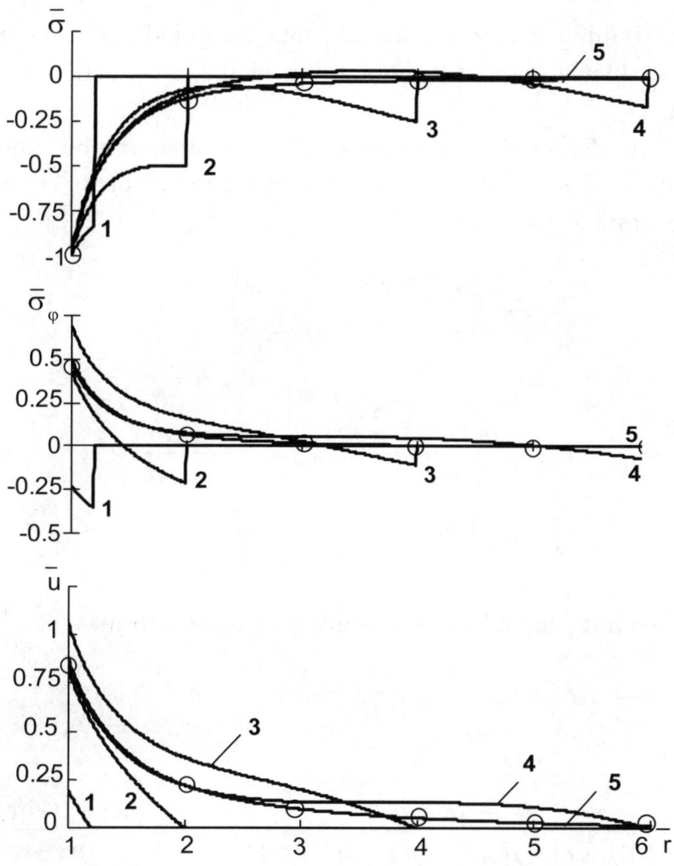

Fig.6.6. Distribution of stresses and displacements along the radius of a sphere for time instants $\bar{t}$: 1) $\bar{t}=0.2$, 2) $\bar{t}=2$, 3) $\bar{t}=3$, 4) $\bar{t}=5$, 5) $\bar{t}=10$

6.2.3 Cylindrical Waves

6.2.3.1. Dilatation radial waves. **A.** We shall next consider a circular body referred to the cylindrical co-ordinates r,φ,z. The strain ε_z in the axial z direction may be connected with the corresponding stress σ_z by the expression

$$\varepsilon_z = \alpha \frac{\sigma_z}{E}. \tag{6.39}$$

The case of $\alpha \to \infty$ $(\sigma_z = 0)$ relates to a thin plate with free lateral faces, the value $\alpha = 0$ $(\varepsilon_z = 0)$ describes a massive solid in cylindrical coordinates. Putting $0 < \alpha < \infty$, one can analyze cylindrical wave ordinates. Putting $0<\alpha<\infty$, one can analyze cylindrical wave propagation in circular plates elastically interfacing in the z direction with ambient medium.

The circumferential σ_φ and the axial σ_z stresses can be expressed from the equation of elasticity (6.1) in terms of the radial stress σ_r and circumferential strain ε_φ as

$$\left.\begin{aligned}\sigma_\varphi &= k_{\sigma\varphi}\sigma_z + E\beta_\varphi\varepsilon_\varphi,\\ \sigma_z &= k_{\sigma z}\sigma_z + E\beta_z\varepsilon_\varphi\end{aligned}\right\}, \tag{6.40}$$

where

$$\left.\begin{aligned}k_{\sigma\varphi} &= \frac{\mu(1+\mu-\alpha)}{1-\mu^2-\alpha}, \quad k_{\sigma z} = \frac{\mu(1+\mu)}{1-\mu^2-\alpha},\\ \beta_\varphi &= \frac{1-\alpha}{1-\mu^2-\alpha}, \quad \beta_z = \frac{\mu}{1-\mu^2-\alpha}\end{aligned}\right\}. \tag{6.41}$$

The governing equation for radial waves takes a form

$$\varepsilon_r = \frac{\sigma_r}{E_r} - k_{\varepsilon r}\varepsilon_\varphi, \tag{6.42}$$

where

$$E_r = \frac{E(1-\mu^2-\alpha)}{(1+\mu)[(1+\mu)(1-2\mu)-\alpha(1-\mu)]}, \quad k_{\varepsilon r} = \frac{\mu(1+\mu-\alpha)}{1-\mu^2-\alpha}. \tag{6.43}$$

For a plate with free lateral faces we note that $E_r = E/(1-\mu^2)$ and $k_{\varepsilon r} = \mu$. The value of E_r for a large solid coincides with that of Eq.(6.7c), while $k_{\varepsilon r} = \mu/(1-\mu)$. As it has been shown above, the radial wave speed under the DMM approach is $c = \sqrt{E_r/\rho}$.

B. The consequent deduction would repeat that of the spherical waves with some insignificant changes:

The static radial equilibrium equation

$$\sigma_r^+ r^+ - \sigma_r^- r^- - \sigma_{\varphi m}\Delta r = 0$$

approximates, with $(\sigma_r^+ - \sigma_r^-)/\Delta r \to \partial\sigma_r/\partial r$, the differential equation

$$\frac{\partial\sigma_r}{\partial r} + \frac{\sigma_r - \sigma_\varphi}{r} = 0.$$

Additional radial strains $\tilde{\varepsilon}_r^\pm = -k_{\varepsilon r}\varepsilon_\varphi^\pm$ with $\varepsilon_\varphi^\pm = u_*^\pm / r^\pm$ lead to

$$u^{\pm} = u_*^{\pm}\left(1 \pm 0.5k_{\varepsilon r}\frac{\Delta r}{r}\right), \quad v^{\pm} = v_*^{\pm}\left(1 \pm 0.5k_{\varepsilon r}\frac{\Delta r}{r}\right).$$

Conditional areas of spherical r_j^2 and circumferential $r_j\Delta r$ element faces have to be overall changed by $r_j h$ and $h\Delta r$, respectively, where h is a plate width.

The mean radial projection of the circumferential forces is

$$F_{j,r\varphi}^{\pm} = -0.5h\Delta r\left(k_{\sigma\varphi}\sigma_j^{\pm} + E\beta_{\varphi}\frac{u_{j,*}^{\pm}}{r^{\pm}}\right). \tag{6.44}$$

The terms of Eq.(6.34) become

$$\left.\begin{aligned} F_{j,0*}^{\pm} &= \pm hr_j(\sigma_{j,0} \mp \rho c v_{j,0})\left(1 \pm 0.5k_{\sigma\varphi}\frac{\Delta r}{r_j}\right) + 0.5hE\beta_{\varphi}\frac{\Delta r}{r_j}u_{j,0*}^{\pm}, \\ \beta_j^{\pm} &= \rho c h r_j\left(1 \pm 0.5k_{\sigma\varphi}\frac{\Delta r}{r_j}\right)\left(1 \pm 0.5k_{\varepsilon r}\frac{\Delta r}{r_j}\right)0.25hE\beta_{\varphi}\frac{\Delta r\Delta t}{r_j} \end{aligned}\right\} \tag{6.45}$$

The governing Eq.(6.36) remains valid.

6.2.3.2. Shear tangential waves. Along with the plane waves, the radial 1-D waves in circular plates can be provoked by particles moving in the circumference direction φ. For this case, the equation of static circumference equilibrium

$$\sigma_{r\varphi}^{+}r^{+} - \sigma_{r\varphi}^{-}r^{-} + \sigma_{\varphi rm}\Delta r = 0,$$

where $\sigma_{r\varphi}^{\pm}$ are the tangential stresses on the element cylindrical surfaces and $\sigma_{\varphi rm}$ is the mean tangential stress on the radial planes, approximates with $(\sigma_{r\varphi}^{+} - \sigma_{r\varphi}^{-})/\Delta r \to \partial\sigma_{r\varphi}/\partial r$ the differential equation

$$\frac{\partial\sigma_{r\varphi}}{\partial r} + 2\frac{\sigma_{r\varphi}}{r} = 0.$$

It follows from the element moment equilibrium that $\sigma_{\varphi rm} = \sigma_{r\varphi m}$ where $\sigma_{r\varphi m} = 0.5(\sigma_{r\varphi}^{+} + \sigma_{r\varphi}^{-})$. Usual elasticity and kinematics relations between shear strain $\varepsilon_{r\varphi}$, tangential stress $\sigma_{r\varphi}$, and circumference displacement u_{φ} yield

$$\varepsilon_{r\varphi} = \frac{\sigma_{r\varphi}}{G}, \quad \varepsilon_{r\varphi} = \frac{\partial u_{\varphi}}{\partial r} - \frac{u_{\varphi}}{r}.$$

We obtain for static state, using the DMM approach of parameter separation $\sigma_{r\varphi*} = \sigma_{r\varphi} + \tilde{\sigma}_{r\varphi}$, that

$$\sigma_{r\varphi,0} = G\frac{u^{+}_{\varphi,0} - u^{-}_{\varphi,0}}{\Delta r},\ \tilde{\sigma}^{\pm}_{r\varphi,0} = -G\frac{u^{\pm}_{\varphi,0}}{r^{\pm}}. \tag{6.46}$$

The displacements $u^{\pm}_{\varphi,0}$ and $\tilde{u}^{\pm}_{\varphi,0}$ relate to the borders of the elastic-inertial part I and the non-inertial part II, respectively. The terms of Eq.(6.36) are

$$\left.\begin{aligned} F^{\pm}_{j,0*} &= \pm hr_j(\sigma_{j\varphi,0} \mp \rho c_g v_{\varphi,0})\left(1 \pm 0.5\frac{\Delta r}{r_j}\right) \pm 0.5hG\frac{\Delta r}{r_j}u^{\pm}_{\varphi,0*}, \\ \beta^{\pm}_j &= \rho c_g hr_j\left(1 \pm 0.5\frac{\Delta r}{r_j}\right)^2 \pm 0.25hG\frac{\Delta r\Delta t}{r_j} \end{aligned}\right\}, \tag{6.47}$$

where $c_g = \sqrt{G/\rho}$.

The given expressions allow us to examine numerically all the particular cases of the tangential wave arising. There are some problems when both types of cylindrical waves become coupled.

7 Numerical Simulation of Multi-Dimensional Wave Processes

7.1 Foundation of the General WFEM Approach

7.1.1 Governing Equations

7.1.1.1. **A**. The general WFEM approach proposed by Shorr (1997, 1999) and described below is suitable for analysis of any multi-dimensional wave processes. For the sake of simplicity and clearness, the methodology is presented in application to 2-D waves and a Cartesian x, y-coordinate system. Strain is assumed to be elastic and small; element rotation is also believed to be small.

The basic notations are taken according to Fig.7.1, where the diagrams in column I relate to an element, those in the column II to one of its node. Here, j is an element index, $1 \le j \le n$, where n is a number of the elements; k is a node index, $1 \le k \le n_1$, where n_1 is a number of the all nodes of a system; k_j are indexes of the nodes referred to the element j, their number being n_j; j_k are indexes of the elements adjoining the node k, their number being n_k. Components of the velocity vector $\mathbf{v}_j$ of the jth element are $v_{j,x}, v_{j,y}$, an angular velocity is ω_j, and the displacement vector $\mathbf{u}_k$ of the kth node has components $u_{k,x}, u_{k,y}$. The force vector applied to the node k from the element j and denoted by $\mathbf{F}_{j_k}$ has components $F_{j_k,x}, F_{j_k,y}$ where $j_k = 1,2,...,n_k$; the force vector affecting the element j in its node k is $\mathbf{F}_{k_j}$ with components $F_{k_j,x}, F_{k_j,y}$, $k_j = 1,2,...,n_j$; the associated inner force is $\mathbf{F}'_{k_j} = -\mathbf{F}_{k_j}$.

We assume that the state of the finite element system at discrete time instants t_i, $i = 0,1,2,...$, is quasi-static (this definition will be made more precise below). The index $i = 0$ refers here to the initial moment of a wave process. The 'element-node' states under wave transition from any instant t_{i-1} to t_i during a finite time interval Δt_i are a subject of our analysis.

B. By investigating wave propagation in a solid, it is necessary to distin-

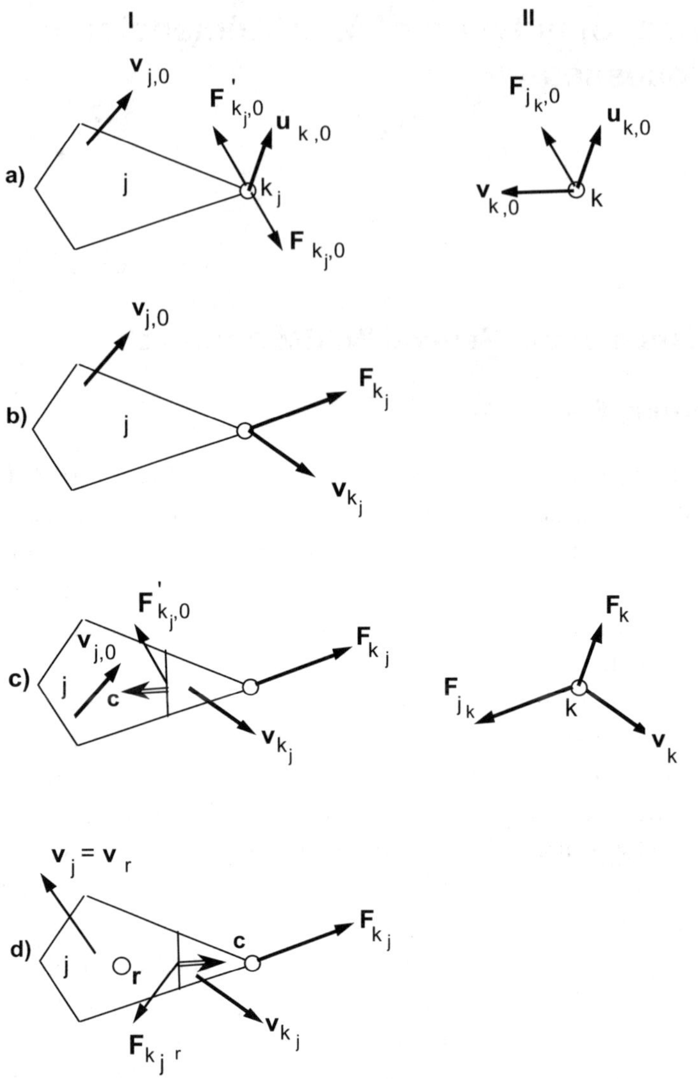

Fig.7.1. States of the element j and its node k_j during any time interval Δt_i

guish between infinitesimally close time instants t_{i-1}^- and t_{i-1}^+. In doing so and adding to the quantities for the instant t_{i-1}^- subscript 0, we assume at this time (Fig.7.1a):

i) The linear $\mathbf{v}_{j,0}$ and angular $\omega_{j,0}$ velocities of the element j and the displacement vectors $\mathbf{u}_{k_j,0}$ of all its nodes n_j are known;

ii) The vectorial sum of the forces $\mathbf{F}_{k_j,0}$ applied to the element in its nodes is zero

$$\sum_{k_j=1}^{n_j} \mathbf{F}_{k_j,0} = 0; \tag{7.1}$$

iii) The forces $\mathbf{F}_{k_j,0}$ are connected with node displacements $\mathbf{u}_{k_j,0}$ by means of a static stiffness matrix $\mathbf{B}_j$ using in the traditional finite element analysis

$$\mathbf{F}_{j,0} = \mathbf{B}_j \mathbf{u}_{j,0}, \tag{7.2}$$

where $\mathbf{F}_{j,0} = \{\mathbf{F}_{k_j,0}\}^{\mathrm{T}}$ and $\mathbf{u}_{j,0} = \{\mathbf{u}_{k_j,0}\}^{\mathrm{T}}$ are the vectors of all the nodal forces $\mathbf{F}_{k_j,0}$ and displacements $\mathbf{u}_{k_j,0}$ of the element *j*; vector $\mathbf{f}^{\mathrm{T}}$ is a transpose to vector **f**;

iv) The displacements in common nodes of neighboring elements are continuous, thus $\mathbf{u}_{k_j,0} = \mathbf{u}_{k,0}$, while the vectorial sum of forces applied to a node may be non-zero and the velocities of the elements adjoining the node may differ, i.e.

$$\sum_{j_k=1}^{n_k} F_{j_k,0} \neq 0, \tag{7.3a}$$

and

$$\mathbf{v}_{k_j,0} \neq \mathbf{v}_{k,0}\ . \tag{7.3b}$$

The listed conditions always hold at the initial time $t = 0$ if all the elements of non-deformed (or statically deformed) body move rectilinearly with the same initial velocity or a body rotates with initial angular velocity.

Using the assumptions i) to iii), all the necessary mechanical parameters of an element at t_{i-1}^{-} can be determined, namely:

The momentum vector

$$\mathbf{M}_{j,v0} = m_j \mathbf{v}_{j,0}; \tag{7.4}$$

The angular momentum

$$M_{j,\omega 0} = I_j \omega_{j,0}; \tag{7.5}$$

The kinetic energy

$$K_{j,0} = 0.5[m_j(v_{j,x0}^2 + v_{j,y0}^2) + I_j \omega_{j,0}^2]; \tag{7.6}$$

The potential energy of elastic deformation

$$P_{j,0} = 0.5\mathbf{u}_{j,0}^{\mathrm{T}}\mathbf{B}_j\mathbf{u}_{j,0}. \tag{7.7}$$

The vector of element boundary forces determined by Eq.(7.2) satisfies the equation

$$\mathbf{F}_{j,0} = \frac{\partial P_{j,0}}{\partial \mathbf{u}_{j,0}}. \tag{7.8}$$

Here, m_j is an element mass and I_j is a mass moment of inertia.

The strains and stresses can be determined from nodal displacements using ordinary static FEM algorithm.

Rotary inertia of element can be neglected when the number of elements is great; however, it may be accounted in necessary cases (see Chaps.4 and 5).

***7.1.1.2*. A**. At the instant t_{i-1}^-, strong discontinuities in velocities and forces arise at nodes as a result of the above condition iv). As the discontinuities in any point of a solid immediately decay, the velocity of the element j in its node k_j at a time instant t_{i-1}^+ becomes $\mathbf{v}_{k_j} = \mathbf{v}_k \neq \mathbf{v}_{j,0}$, where $\mathbf{v}_k$ is a new value of the nodal velocity, and the forces applied to the element j in its nodes become $\mathbf{F}_{k_j} \neq \mathbf{F}_{k_j0}$ (Fig.7.1b).

The equilibrium condition for the node k that is applicable to the n_k neighboring elements becomes

$$\sum_{j_k=1}^{n_k} \mathbf{F}_{j_k} + \mathbf{F}_k = 0, \tag{7.9}$$

where $\mathbf{F}_{j_k} = -\mathbf{F}_{k_j}$, $j_k = 1,\dots,n_k$, and $\mathbf{F}_k = \mathbf{F}_k^* - \eta_k \mathbf{v}_k$.

Here, $\mathbf{F}_k^*$ is a vector of the node surface or volume external forces that can change step-wise at the instant t_{i-1}^+. External linear viscous friction with a viscous coefficient η_k is also taken into account. The nodal velocity and forces are assumed to be constant in the current time step.

In reality, the strong discontinuities (disturbances) of the velocities $\mathbf{v}_{k_j} - \mathbf{v}_{j,0}$ and the forces $\mathbf{F}_{k_j} - \mathbf{F}_{k_j,0}$ generated at this instant should propagate into element j from its nodes in all directions, interacting with each other in a complicated manner. To make numerical simulation realizable, the following additional assumptions are introduced in the proposed approach:

i) Disturbances entirely cover all the elements within the consequent time interval $\Delta t_i = t_i^- - t_{i-1}^+$;

ii) Disturbances from a given node arrive at the other nodes simultaneously to the end of the current step at t_i^-;

iii) External forces and boundary conditions refer only to nodes and do not vary during the time interval Δt_i;

iv) Waves traveling from each node k_j are taken up by equal parts m_j/n_j of the element mass m_j.

We remark that values of Δt_i vary over time steps and have to be determined through calculation.

B. We could conditionally imagine two phases of the wave process.

During the *first half* of the interval Δt_i, within $t_{i-1}^+ \le t \le t_{i-1}^+ + 0.5\Delta t_i$, we do not assume interaction between the disturbances propagating from different nodes. Wave fronts spread from nodes into the unperturbed element domain, in which the inner forces $\mathbf{F}'_{k_j,0} = -\mathbf{F}_{k_j,0}$ remain unchanged.

The law of momentum balance of the mass part m_j/n_j related to the node k_j (see Fig.7.1c)

$$m_j(\mathbf{v}_{k_j} - \mathbf{v}_{j,0})/n_j = 0.5(\mathbf{F}_{k_j} + \mathbf{F}'_{k_j,0})\Delta t_i$$

effects the velocities $\mathbf{v}_{k_j}$ as a function of forces $\mathbf{F}_{k_j}$

$$\mathbf{v}_{k_j} = \mathbf{v}_{j,0} + 0.5 n_j \Delta t_i (\mathbf{F}_{k_j} + \mathbf{F}'_{k_j,0})/m_j, \tag{7.10a}$$

and vice versa

$$\mathbf{F}_{k_j} = -\mathbf{F}'_{k_j,0} + 2m_j(\mathbf{v}_{k_j} - \mathbf{v}_{j,0})/n_j\Delta t_i. \tag{7.10b}$$

Replacing the notations $\mathbf{v}_{j,0}$, $\mathbf{v}_{k_j}$, $\mathbf{F}'_{k_j,0}$, $\mathbf{F}_{k_j}$ related to the element point k_j by $\mathbf{v}_{j_k,0}$, $\mathbf{v}_{j_k}$, $\mathbf{F}'_{j_k,0}$, $\mathbf{F}_{j_k}$ related to the node k, while $\mathbf{F}_{j_k} = -\mathbf{F}_{k_j}$, and inserting Eq.(7.10b) into Eq.(7.9) for all the elements surrounding this node, the new value of the node velocity can be calculated as

$$\mathbf{v}_k = \frac{\sum_{j_k=1}^{n_k} \mathbf{v}_{j_k,0} m_{j_k}/n_{j_k} + 0.5\Delta t_i(\mathbf{F}_k^* + \sum_{j_k=1}^{n_k} F'_{j_k,0})}{\sum_{j_k=1}^{n_k} m_{j_k}/n_{j_k} + 0.5\eta_k \Delta t_i}. \tag{7.11}$$

The same formula is obtainable directly from the law of momentum conservation in a time $0.5\Delta t_i$ applied to the set of corresponding parts of the all elements adjoining the node k

$$\sum_{j_k=1}^{n_k} m_{jk}(\mathbf{v}_k - \mathbf{v}_{j_k,0}) / n_{jk} = 0.5(\mathbf{F}_k^* - \eta_k \mathbf{v}_k + \sum_{j_k=1}^{n_k} \mathbf{F}'_{j_k,0})\Delta t_i .$$

In this way, we define new nodal velocity $v_{k_j} = v_k$ for each element n_k and, using Eq.(7.10b), new forces $\mathbf{F}_{k_j}$ of their parts disturbed.

C. At the instant $t_{i-1}^+ + 0.5\Delta t_i$, all the disturbances converge to a conditional 'point of contact' that may be regarded as an inner element node, in which $\mathbf{F}_k^* = 0$, $\eta_k = 0$. Quantities referred to this point are marked by the subscript *r*.

The new velocity at this point becomes $\mathbf{v}_r$; new forces $\mathbf{F}_{k_j r}$, being reflected from the 'inner node', affect outwards the element parts k_j. The fronts of reflected waves propagate into previously disturbed domains characterized by the parameters $\mathbf{v}_{k_j}$ and $\mathbf{F}_{k_j}$.

New disturbances reach the outer (real) nodes during the *second half* of the interval Δt_i, which lasts within $t_{i-1}^+ + 0.5\Delta t_i \le t \le t_{i-1}^+ + \Delta t_i = t_i^-$ (see Fig.7.1d). The velocity $\mathbf{v}_r$ covers the whole element to the termination of this interval, hence, the new element velocity becomes $\mathbf{v}_j = \mathbf{v}_r$. Repeating the above procedure, we must insert quantities $\mathbf{v}_j, \mathbf{v}_{k_j}, \mathbf{F}_{k_j r}, \mathbf{F}_{k_j}$ instead of $\mathbf{v}_{k_j}, \mathbf{v}_{j_k,0}, \mathbf{F}_{k_j}, \mathbf{F}'_{k_j,0}$, respectively, into Eqs.(7.10b) and (7.11), and as well put $m_{j_k} / n_{j_k} = m_j / n_i$.

Then,

$$\mathbf{F}_{k_j r} = -\mathbf{F}_{k_j} + 2m_j(\mathbf{v}_j - \mathbf{v}_{k_j}) / n_j \Delta t_i \tag{7.12}$$

and

$$\mathbf{v}_j = \left(\frac{m_j}{n_j} \sum_{k_j=1}^{n_j} \mathbf{v}_{k_j} + 0.5\Delta t_i \sum_{k_j=1}^{n_j} \mathbf{F}_{k_j} \right) / m_j . \tag{7.13}$$

Inserting $\mathbf{F}_{k_j}$ from Eq.(7.10b) into (7.13), we obtain

$$\mathbf{v}_j = \frac{2}{n_j} \sum_{k_j=1}^{n_j} \mathbf{v}_{k_j} - \mathbf{v}_{j,0}, \tag{7.14}$$

where Eq.(7.1) has been taken into account.

The vectorial sum of forces $\mathbf{F}_{k_j r}$ is readily shown to be zero. Furthermore, using Eqs.(7.1), (7.10b), and (7.14) for each element j_k enclosing the node *k,* one can check that the law of momentum conservation in the whole time interval Δt_i is satisfied for the set of these elements.

Note that both the impulses of the nodal forces $\mathbf{F}_{k_j}$ affecting the element j and the element momentum alteration during each half-interval $0.5\,\Delta t_i$ are the same, while the velocity alteration of the perturbed parts of the element in these half-intervals are different.

Since the node velocity $\mathbf{v}_k$ is assumed to be constant in the interval Δt_i, the new value of node displacement is

$$\mathbf{u}_{k_j} = \mathbf{u}_{k_j,0} + \mathbf{v}_{k_j} \Delta t_i \,. \tag{7.15}$$

Thus, at the time instant $t_i^- = t_{i-1}^- + \Delta t_i$ we arrive again at the quasi-static mechanical state of the element, analogous to the previous one, velocity and nodes displacements in which are of new values. This allows, as in the 1-D case, formulation of a recurrent procedure for the numerical simulation of the problem.

7.1.1.3. The above expressions, taken alone, do not allow us to determine the magnitude of the current time interval Δt_i. To this goal, as it has been discussed in Chap.1, it is necessary to start from the equation of mechanical energy balance for the whole system written for the current step or for the total wave process.

In the latter case

$$W_{i\Sigma} = K_{i\Sigma} + P_{i\Sigma}, \tag{7.16a}$$

where

$$W_{i\Sigma} = \sum_{i=1}^{i} \sum_{j=1}^{n} \Delta W_{ji}, \quad K_{i\Sigma} = \sum_{j=1}^{n} K_{ij}, \quad P_{i\Sigma} = \sum_{j=1}^{n} P_{ij} \,. \tag{7.16b}$$

Here, ΔW_{ji} is a work of inner forces introduced to the jth element in the step i

$$\Delta W_{ji} = \sum_{k_j=1}^{n_j} (F_{k_j,x} v_{k_j,x} + F_{k_j,y} v_{k_j,y}) \Delta t_i \,. \tag{7.17}$$

The kinetic energy K_{ij} of the jth element at the instant t_i^-, neglecting rotation, is

$$K_{ij} = 0.5 m_j (v_{j,x}^2 + v_{j,y}^2) \,. \tag{7.18}$$

The potential energy P_{ij} of the jth element at t_i^- is conveniently determined, exploiting an equation of the type (7.7), thus

$$P_{ij} = 0.5\mathbf{u}_j^{\mathrm{T}}\mathbf{B}_j\mathbf{u}_j. \quad (7.19)$$

Determination of the interval Δt_i using successive approximations creates in principle no problems.

7.1.2 Waves in a Plane Region. Code WPRD

7.1.2.1. A stiffness matrix for static stress-strain state of a solid. A theory of the static finite element method including a stiffness matrix calculation has been well-studied (see, e.g., Zienkievicz and Cheung 1967). Some deductions related to a 2-D plane square (quadrilateral) element and needed for our goal are briefly described below.

A. Consider a plane square element of dimension $\Delta x = \Delta y$. Enumerating its nodes by $k = 1 \div 4$ and using local nondimensional coordinates $\xi = x_1/\Delta x$, $\eta = y_1/\Delta y$ with $0 \le \xi, \eta \le 1$ (Fig.7.2), the displacement vector $\mathbf{u}\{u_x, u_y\}^{\mathrm{T}}$ is approximated by a function

$$\mathbf{u}(\xi,\eta) = (1-\xi-\eta+\xi\eta)\mathbf{u}_1 + \xi(1-\eta)\mathbf{u}_2 + \eta(1-\xi)\mathbf{u}_3 + \xi\eta\mathbf{u}_4, \quad (7.20)$$

where $\mathbf{u}_k\{u_{kx}, u_{ky}\}^{\mathrm{T}}$ is the displacement vector of the nodes, which coordinates are $\xi = 0, \eta = 0$; $\xi = 1, \eta = 0$; $\xi = 0, \eta = 1$; $\xi = 1, \eta = 1$.

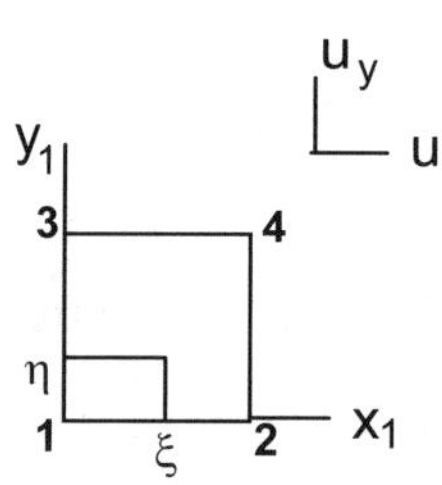

Fig.7.2. A plane square element

The strain components expressed by the nodes displacements are

$$\left.\begin{aligned} \varepsilon_\xi &= \frac{\partial u_x}{\partial x_1} = -[(1-\eta)(u_{1x}-u_{2x}) + \eta(u_{3x}-u_{4x})]/\Delta x, \\ \varepsilon_\eta &= \frac{\partial u_y}{\partial y_1} = -[(1-\xi)(u_{1y}-u_{3y}) + \xi(u_{2y}-u_{4y})]/\Delta x, \end{aligned}\right\}. \quad (7.21a)$$

and

$$\varepsilon_{\xi\eta} = \frac{\partial u_x}{\partial y_1} + \frac{\partial u_y}{\partial x_1} = -[(1-\xi)(u_{1x} - u_{3x}) + \xi(u_{2x} - u_{4x}) + (1-\eta)(u_{1y} - u_{2y}) + \eta(u_{3y} - u_{4y})] / \Delta x \tag{7.21b}$$

Putting the condition of plane stress state (PSsS), $\sigma_\zeta = 0$, or plane strain state (PSnS), $\varepsilon_\zeta = 0$, into the equations of elasticity associated with 2-D problems

$$\left.\begin{aligned} \varepsilon_\xi &= \frac{\sigma_\xi - \mu(\sigma_\eta + \sigma_\zeta)}{E},\ \varepsilon_\eta = \frac{\sigma_\eta - \mu(\sigma_\zeta + \sigma_\xi)}{E},\ \varepsilon_\zeta = \frac{\sigma_\zeta - \mu(\sigma_\xi + \sigma_\eta)}{E}, \\ \varepsilon_{\xi\eta} &= \frac{2(1+\mu)}{E}\sigma_{\xi\eta},\ \varepsilon_{\eta\zeta} = 0,\ \varepsilon_{\zeta\xi} = 0 \end{aligned}\right\}, \tag{7.22}$$

we obtain the reversal of Eqs.(7.22) in generalized form

$$\sigma_\xi = E_r(\varepsilon_\xi + \mu_r \varepsilon_\eta),\quad \sigma_\eta = E_r(\varepsilon_\eta + \mu_r \varepsilon_\xi),\quad \sigma_{\xi\eta} = E_r g_r \varepsilon_{\xi\eta}, \tag{7.23}$$

where: for the PSsS

$$E_r = \frac{E}{1-\mu^2},\quad \mu_r = \mu,\quad g_r = \frac{1-\mu}{2}; \tag{7.24a}$$

for the PSnS

$$E_r = \frac{(1-\mu)E}{(1+\mu)(1-2\mu)},\quad \mu_r = \frac{\mu}{1-\mu},\quad g_r = \frac{1-2\mu}{2(1-\mu)}. \tag{7.24b}$$

The notations $\sigma_{\xi\eta}$ and $\varepsilon_{\xi\eta}$ are referred here to tangential stress and strain, respectively.

B. The potential energy P of the element, with dimension h in z direction, given by

$$P = 0.5h\Delta x^2 \int_0^1\int_0^1 (\sigma_\xi \varepsilon_\xi + \sigma_\eta \varepsilon_\eta + \sigma_{\xi\eta}\varepsilon_{\xi\eta})\, d\xi d\eta$$

yields, with use of Eqs.(7.23),

$$P = 0.5h\Delta x^2 E_r \int_0^1\int_0^1 (\varepsilon_\xi^2 + \varepsilon_\eta^2 + 2\mu_r \varepsilon_\xi \varepsilon_\eta + g_r \varepsilon_{\xi\eta}^2)\, d\xi d\eta. \tag{7.25}$$

The vector of the forces affecting the element in its node k can be calculated as

$$\mathbf{F}_k = \frac{\partial P}{\partial \mathbf{u}_k} = \frac{\partial P}{\partial \varepsilon_\xi}\frac{d\varepsilon_\xi}{d\mathbf{u}_k} + \frac{\partial P}{\partial \varepsilon_\eta}\frac{d\varepsilon_\eta}{d\mathbf{u}_k} + \frac{\partial P}{\partial \varepsilon_{\xi\eta}}\frac{d\varepsilon_{\xi\eta}}{d\mathbf{u}_k}, \tag{7.26}$$

where derivative $\partial P / \partial \varepsilon_\xi$ and the others are determined from Eq.(7.25), and derivative $d\varepsilon_\xi / d\mathbf{u}_k$ and others - from Eqs.(7.21).

Treating the required derivatives and integrals over the element area and passing on to the general force vector

$$\mathbf{F} = \{F_{1x}, F_{2x}, F_{3x}, F_{4x}, F_{1y}, F_{2y}, F_{3y}, F_{4y}\}^{\mathrm{T}} \tag{7.27a}$$

and to the general displacement vector

$$\mathbf{u} = \{u_{1x}, u_{2x}, u_{3x}, u_{4x}, u_{1y}, u_{2y}, u_{3y}, u_{4y}\}^{\mathrm{T}}, \tag{7.27b}$$

which include all the element nodes, we obtain the equation

$$\mathbf{F} = E_r h \mathbf{B}\mathbf{u}, \tag{7.28}$$

where **B** is a nondimensional symmetrical stiffness matrix of order 8x8.

An analysis shows only 6 among 64 components of this matrix are distinct (see, e.g., Strang and Fix 1973), or with sign accounting, 8 components. These are

$$\left.\begin{array}{l} b_1 = (1+g_r)/3,\ b_2 = -(2-g_r)/6_r,\ b_3 = (1-2g_r)/6,\ b_4 = -(1+g_r)/6, \\ b_5 = (\mu_r + g_r)/4,\ b_6 = (\mu_r - g_r)/4,\ b_7 = -b_6, b_8 = -b_5 \end{array}\right\}. \tag{7.29}$$

Components $b_{lm} = b_{ml}$ of the matrix **B** are expressed by the quantities $b_1 \div b_8$. An expanded form of this matrix corresponding to the node numeration in Fig.7.2. is

$$\mathbf{B} = \begin{bmatrix} b_1 & b_2 & b_3 & b_4 & b_5 & b_6 & b_7 & b_8 \\ b_2 & b_1 & b_4 & b_3 & b_7 & b_8 & b_5 & b_6 \\ b_3 & b_4 & b_1 & b_2 & b_6 & b_5 & b_8 & b_7 \\ b_4 & b_3 & b_2 & b_1 & b_8 & b_7 & b_6 & b_5 \\ b_5 & b_7 & b_6 & b_8 & b_1 & b_3 & b_2 & b_4 \\ b_6 & b_8 & b_5 & b_7 & b_3 & b_1 & b_4 & b_2 \\ b_7 & b_5 & b_8 & b_6 & b_2 & b_4 & b_1 & b_3 \\ b_8 & b_6 & b_7 & b_5 & b_4 & b_2 & b_3 & b_1 \end{bmatrix}. \tag{7.30}$$

C. The stresses averaged over the element volume and expressed by the nodal displacements due to Eqs.(7.21) and (7.23) are

$$\left.\begin{aligned}\sigma_{\xi m} &= 0.5E_r[u_{2x}-u_{1x}+u_{4x}-u_{3x}+\mu_r(u_{3y}-u_{1y}+u_{4y}-u_{2y})]/\Delta x\\ \sigma_{\eta m} &= 0.5E_r[u_{3y}-u_{1y}+u_{4y}-u_{2y}+\mu_r(u_{2x}-u_{1x}+u_{4x}-u_{3x})]/\Delta x\\ \sigma_{\xi\mu m} &= 0.5E_r g_r(u_{3x}-u_{1x}+u_{4x}-u_{2x}+u_{2y}-u_{1y}+u_{4y}-u_{3y})/\Delta x\end{aligned}\right\}. \quad (7.31)$$

Sometimes, stress intensity

$$\sigma_{\text{int}} = \tfrac{1}{\sqrt{2}}\sqrt{(\sigma_\xi-\sigma_\eta)^2+(\sigma_\eta-\sigma_\zeta)^2+(\sigma_\zeta-\sigma_\xi)^2+6\left(\sigma_{\xi\eta}^2+\sigma_{\eta\zeta}^2+\sigma_{\zeta\xi}^2\right)} \quad (7.32a)$$

may be of use within the analysis. In our case, the mean value of σ_{int} yields

$$\sigma_{imt} = \sqrt{\mu_{r1}(\sigma_{\xi m}^2+\sigma_{\xi m}^2)-\mu_{r2}\sigma_\xi\sigma_\eta+3\sigma_{\xi\eta m}^2}\,, \quad (7.32b)$$

where:

for the PSsS

$$\mu_{r1}=1,\quad \mu_{r2}=1; \quad (7.33a)$$

for the PSnS

$$\mu_{r1}=1-\mu+\mu^2,\quad \mu_{r2}=1+2\mu-2\mu^2. \quad (7.33b)$$

Note that we call the stress σ_{int} determined by Eq.(7.32a) 'stress intensity' according to Kolsky (1953) and other authors. However, in some papers on FEM the same expression is named 'equivalent stress' or 'Von Mises stress'. On the other hand, in those papers the term 'stress intensity' is referred to duplicated value of maximum tangential stress.

D. Along with the 'element' stresses averaged over the element volume, some other means of averaging are possible. By example, the 'node' stres-

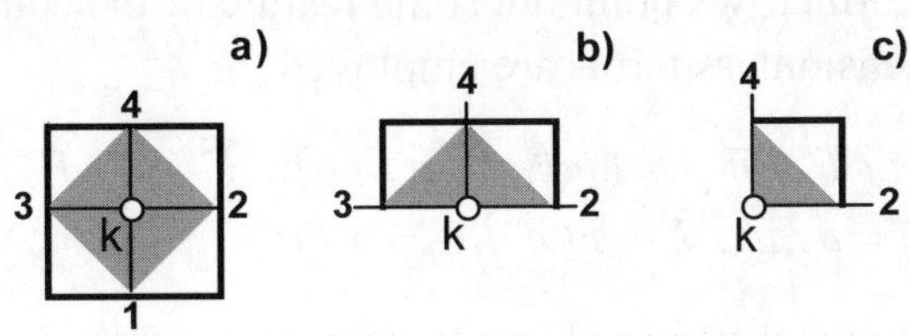

Fig.7.3. To calculation of 'node' stresses

ses averaged over some parts of elements adjoining the node can be calculated. These parts are displayed in Fig.7.3 as shaded.

For an inner node k using the notations in Fig.7.3a we obtain

$$\left.\begin{aligned} \sigma_{\xi k} &= 0.5E_r[u_{2x} - u_{3x} + \mu_r(u_{4y} - u_{1y})]/\Delta x \\ \sigma_{\eta k} &= 0.5E_r[u_{4y} - u_{1y} + \mu_r(u_{2x} - u_{3x})]/\Delta x \\ \sigma_{\xi\mu k} &= 0.5E_r g_r(u_{4x} - u_{1x} + u_{2y} - u_{3y})/\Delta x \end{aligned}\right\}; \tag{7.34a}$$

for a node k at the bottom side (Fig.7.3b)

$$\left.\begin{aligned} \sigma_{\xi k} &= 0.5E_r[u_{2x} - u_{3x} + 2\mu_r(u_{4y} - u_{ky})]/\Delta x \\ \sigma_{\eta k} &= 0.5E_r[2(u_{4y} - u_{ky}) + \mu_r(u_{2x} - u_{3x})]/\Delta x \\ \sigma_{\xi\mu k} &= 0.5E_r g_r[u_{2y} - u_{3y} + 2(u_{4x} - u_{kx})]/\Delta x \end{aligned}\right\}; \tag{7.34b}$$

for a corner node k (Fig.7.3c)

$$\left.\begin{aligned} \sigma_{\xi k} &= E_r[u_{2x} - u_{kx} + \mu_r(u_{4y} - u_{ky})]/\Delta x \\ \sigma_{\eta k} &= E_r[u_{4y} - u_{ky} + \mu_r(u_{2x} - u_{kx})]/\Delta x \\ \sigma_{\xi\eta k} &= E_r g_r(u_{4x} - u_{kx} + u_{2y} - u_{ky})/\Delta x \end{aligned}\right\}, \tag{7.34c}$$

and so on. The element local rotation ω_z can be also determined as

$$\omega_z = 0.5(u_{2y} - u_{1y} + u_{4y} - u_{3y} + u_{1x} - u_{3x} + u_{2x} - u_{4x})/\Delta x\,.$$

7.1.2.2. A rectangular domain. Code WPRD. A square element allows treating, in principle, the plane wave problems for rather complicated domains by means of approximating arbitrary boundary contours by step-like ones. However, such element is, of course, the most effective to analyze wave propagation in a rectangular domain. For this goal, a special numerical code WPRD (Waves in a Plane Rectangular Domain) has been elaborated. All the numerical solutions of 2-D problems presented in this book are examined using this code.

Before we go any further, we point out some feature of the code.

The following dimensionless terms are employed:

$$\begin{aligned} &\bar{x} = x/L,\ \bar{t} = t/T,\ \bar{m} = m/m^o,\ \bar{E}_r = E_r/E,\ \bar{F} = F/F^o, \\ &\bar{v} = v/v^o,\ \bar{u} = u/u^o,\ \bar{\varepsilon} = \varepsilon/\varepsilon^o,\ \bar{\sigma} = \sigma/\sigma^o, \end{aligned}\quad, \tag{7.35a}$$

where L is a length set equal to one of the domain lateral sides L_x or L_y, and in some cases, to element length Δx or other linear parameters. The other quantities are $T=L/c_r$, $c_r=\sqrt{E_r/\rho}$, and also

$$m^o=\rho hL^2,\ F^o=\rho hc_rLv^o,\ u^o=Tv^o=F^o/E_rh,\ \varepsilon^o=u^o/L,\ \sigma^o=E_r\varepsilon^o \tag{7.35b}$$

The scaled element mass is determined by $\overline{m}_j=\rho h\Delta x^2/m^o=\Delta\overline{x}^2$; the node number of all the elements is identical and equal to n_j=4. Hence, Eqs.(7.10b) and (7.14) yield, respectively,

$$\overline{\mathbf{F}}_{k_j}=-\overline{\mathbf{F}}'_{k_j,0}+\frac{\Delta\overline{x}^2}{2\Delta\overline{t}_i}(\overline{\mathbf{v}}_{k_j}-\overline{\mathbf{v}}_{j,0}), \tag{7.36}$$

$$\overline{v}_j=\tfrac{1}{2}\sum_{k_j=1}^{4}\overline{v}_{k_j}-\overline{v}_{j,0}. \tag{7.37}$$

The number n_k of the elements adjoining the node k depends on the node disposition: within the domain n_k=4, along a lateral side n_k=2, and at a corner node n_k=1. Eq.(7.11) yields

$$\overline{v}_k=\frac{0.5\Delta\overline{x}^2\sum_{j_k=1}^{n_k}\overline{v}_{j_k,0}+\Delta\overline{t}_i(\overline{F}_k^*+\sum_{j_k=1}^{n_k}\overline{F}_{j_k,0})}{0.5n_k\Delta\overline{x}^2+\overline{\eta}_k\Delta\overline{t}_i}, \tag{7.38}$$

where $\overline{\eta}_k=\eta_kT/m^o$.

The boundary conditions at the nodes referred to the lateral sides must be considered separately for each of the coordinate directions. If one of the sides related to a corner node is free, while the other in the same direction is fixed, this direction is assumed to be inhibited. Notice, although the tangential stresses in mutually normal sections are equal $\sigma_{\xi\eta}=\sigma_{\eta\xi}$, their mean values over finite element sides may be different.

The usual smoothing procedure of oscillations with period $2\Delta\overline{t}_i$, or over the length $2\Delta\overline{x}$, can be used for finish results presentation

7.2 Numerical Examples

7.2.1 Sudden Longitudinal Loading of a One-Side Fixed Plate

7.2.1.1. **Problem 7.1. A thin rectangular one-side fixed plate subjected to pressure p_0 suddenly applied in its plane (Fig.7.4).** Two boundary conditions at the fastened face $x=0$ are under consideration: a) a tide ('welded') contact in both directions, $v_x(0,y,t)=0, v_y(0,y,t)=0$, Fig.7.4a;

b) a free sliding without friction in direction y along the contact face, $v_x(0,y,t)=0$ and $F_y(0,y,t)=0$, Fig.7.4b. Nodal coordinates $\bar{x}=x/L$ and $\bar{y}=y/L$ are scaled by the length $L=L_x$, and time $\bar{t}=t/T$ by $T=L_x/c_r$. A quantity $\bar{t}=1$ corresponds to the time required for a wave to travel the plate length L_x with the speed $c_r=\sqrt{E/\rho(1-\mu^2)}$. A side ratio is taken as $L_x/L_y=2$ and calculated mesh as $n_x=24, n_y=12$ for Fig.7.4-7.5 and $n_x=60, n_y=30$ for Fig.7.6. Due to the plate and loading symmetry about x-axis, only the upper half of the plate $y\geq 0$ needs to be considered.

Deformed patterns of an initially quadratic mesh at two times for the contact conditions a) and b) are displayed in Fig.7.4c,e and 7.4d,f, respectively. In Fig.7.5, the 2-D distributions of relative stress intensity

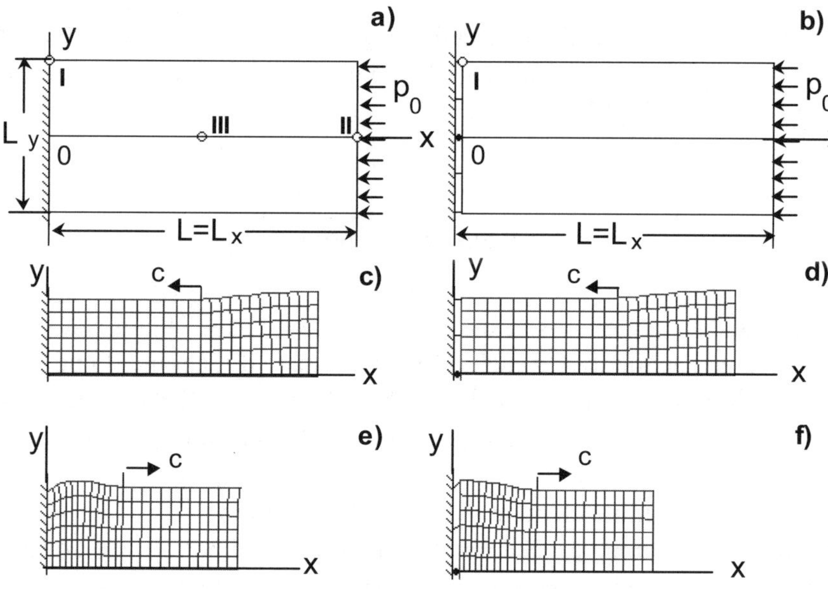

Fig.7.4. Pressure p_0 suddenly applied to a free-fixed plate; a, b) different boundary conditions, c), d) deformed pattern at time $\bar{t}=0.5$; e), f) the same at $\bar{t}=1.5$

$\bar{\sigma}_{\text{int}}=\sigma_{\text{int}}/p_0$ over the plate for the same times are shown, where Fig.7.5b relates to the fixation case a) and Fig.7.5c to the case b).

For the given problem, the real calculated process time $\bar{t}_i=\sum_{i=1}^{n_i}\Delta\bar{t}_i$ differs very slightly from the quantity $\bar{s}_i=i\Delta\bar{x}=i/n_x$ of the relative path traveled by the leading wave in a time of i steps. So, for i=12 the calculated time is $\bar{t}_i=0.506$ against $\bar{s}_i=0.5$; for i=36 these times are $\bar{t}_i=1.522$ and 1.523 against $\bar{s}_i=1.5$ in the cases a) and b), respectively.

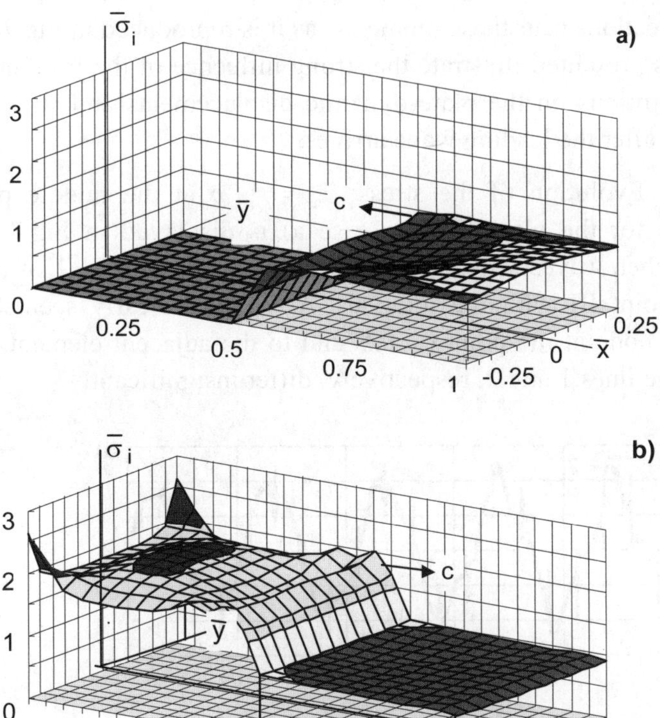

Fig.7.5. Maps of the stress intensity $\overline{\sigma}_{int}$ related to the Problem 7.1 for time instants $\bar{t}$: a) $\bar{t} = 0.5$, b),c) $\bar{t} = 1.5$

The leading wave meets the plate mid-point $\bar{x} = 0.5$ in direct and opposite directions near these moments, as it is reproduced in Fig.7.4 -7.5.

The maps presented illustrate the strong influence of the fastening faces friction conditions on the plate dynamic displacements and stresses near the corner I after the leading wave arrives.

***7.2.1.2.* A.** Evolution of the stress $\bar{\sigma}_x = \sigma_x / p_0$ at the middle point III versus time for the plate fixation case a) is displayed in Fig.7.6a. The moments, when waves reflected from borders $\bar{x} = 0$ and $\bar{x} = 1$ of the plate reach the point III with the intervals $\Delta\bar{t} = 1$, are clearly seen. Stresses related to a node at the point $\bar{x} = 0.5$ and to the adjacent element that are shown by the lines 1 and 2, respectively, differ insignificantly.

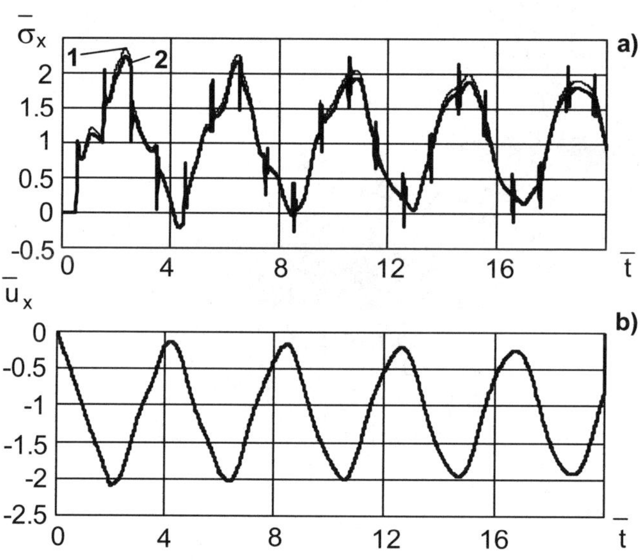

Fig.7.6. Evolution of stresses at the point III –a) and horizontal displacements at the point II –b) (see Fig.7.4a) vs. time

B. Putting in Eqs.(7.35) $F^o = p_0 L_x$, we determine a scaled displacement

$$\bar{u} = u / u^o = uE / p_0 L_x (1 - \mu^2). \tag{7.39}$$

Time evolution of the displacement $\bar{u}_x$ at the central point II on the free surface is plotted in Fig.7.6b. The oscillations are seen occurring around a middle value $\bar{u}_m \approx -1.09$ that is close to the static displacement $\bar{u}_{st} = -1/(1 - \mu^2) \approx 1.10$ of the point II for a narrow plate approximating a rod. The mean visible oscillation period for stress and displacement is

$\bar{\tau} \approx 4.17$, which is close to the time $\bar{\tau} = 4\sqrt{1-\mu^2} \approx 4.19$ for the first vibration mode of a rod. An expected period for a very wide plate is $\bar{\tau} = 4.00$. Calculations of the plate harmonic oscillations using ordinary FEM code with the same mesh has led to $\bar{\tau} \approx 4.10$.

In the fixation case b) the mean visible period is a few greater, $\bar{\tau} \approx 4.23$.

A cause of slight amplitude decrease in Fig.7.6 in the absence of damping will be discussed below in Subsect.7.2.5.

7.2.2 Sudden in-Plane Bending of a Deep Plate

Problem 7.2. Unsteady bending of a thin rectangular plate fixed at both opposite ends. A plate is subjected to constant pressure p_0 suddenly

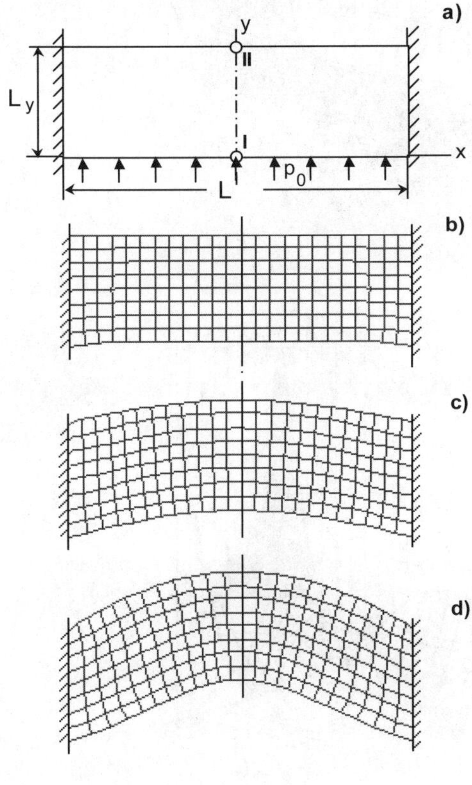

Fig.7.7. Pressure p_0 suddenly applied to the bottom side of a plate; a) sketch of the Problem, b) deformed mesh pattern at time $\bar{t} = 0.344$, c) at $\bar{t} = 1.029$, d) at $\bar{t} = 2.328$

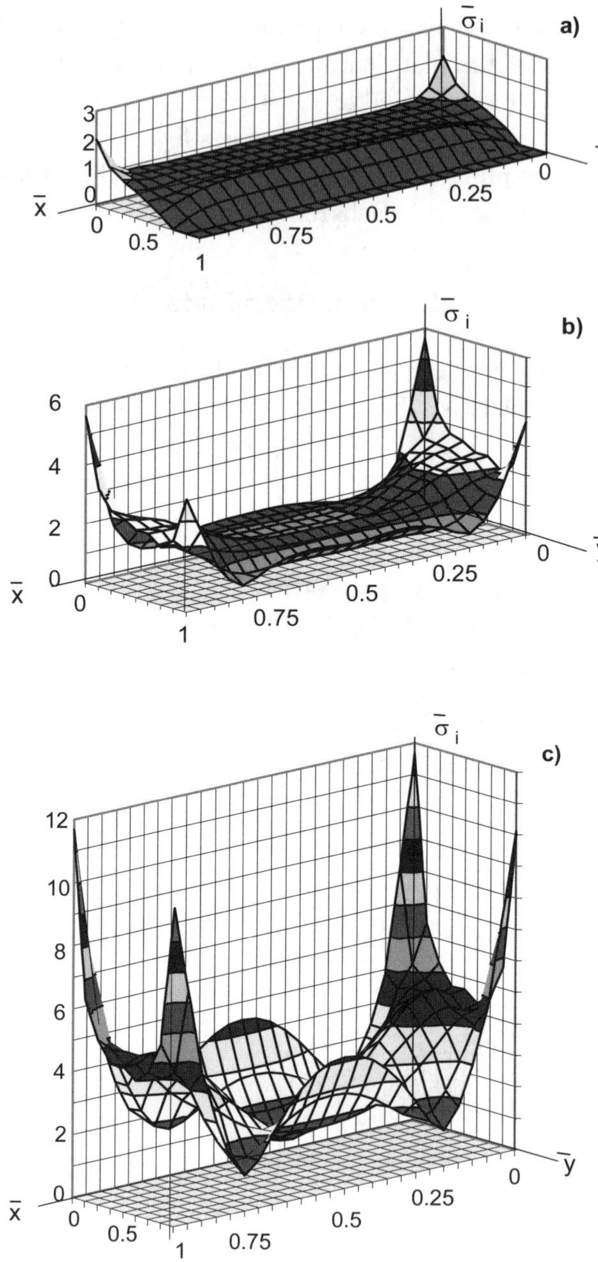

Fig.7.8. Maps of the stress intensity $\overline{\sigma}_{int}$ related to the Problem 7.2 for instants $\bar{t}$: a) $\bar{t} = 0.258$, b) $\bar{t} = 0.945$, c) $\bar{t} = 2.245$

applied in its plane to bottom surface y=0 (Fig.7.7a). The scaled quantities $\bar{x}, \bar{y}, \bar{t}$, and $\bar{\sigma}$ remain the same as for Problem 7.1. Due to symmetry to y-axis, only a right half $x \geq 0$ of the plate is simulated. The side ratio is taken as $L_x / L_y = 3$ and a calculated mesh for Figs.7.7-7.8 as $n_x = 24, n_y = 8$.

Deformed mesh patterns for the three times $\bar{t}$ are displayed in Fig.7.7b,c,d, respectively. The first time relates to a moment when the leading wave arrives at the opposite upper surface; the last corresponds to the maximum dynamic deformation of the plate.

In Fig.7.8a,b,c, the distribution of stress intensity $\bar{\sigma}_{\text{int}}$ over the plate for the times $\bar{t}$, those are a few less than in Fig.7.7, are shown. One can see from these figures, how the initially plane wave front traveling in y direction (Fig.7.7b and Fig.7.8a) is eroded after multiple reflections from free and fixed sides and gradually modified into pattern of combined bending/shear plate oscillation (Fig.7.7c,d and Fig.7.8b,c). A significant stress concentration in the corner points is observed. Due to FEM code with the same mesh, the static stress intensity in these points is about $\bar{\sigma}_{\text{int},st} \approx 5.2 \div 5.4$; its duplicated (dynamic) value is close to the ones displayed in Fig.7.8c. Of course, the real corner stress depends on a support stiffness and fillet radius.

Additional remarks to numerical simulation of Problem 7.2 are given in Subsect.7.2.5.

7.2.3 A Plate Longitudinally Impacted by a Heavy Body

Problem 7.3. An elongated one-side fixed plate lengthwise impacted in its plane by a heavy body, Fig. 7.9a. The ratio of the striking body mass M to the plate mass $M_{\text{pl}} = \rho L_x L_y h$ is assumed to be significantly greater than unity. This allows us to consider a body velocity v_M in the x direction approximately constant over an initial phase of contact duration. Similarly to the case b) of Problem 7.1, free sliding in lateral direction y is assumed for both ends of the plate, with boundary conditions

$$\left.\begin{aligned} v_x(0,y,t) = v_M,\ \ v_x(L_x,y,t) = 0, \\ F_y(0,y,t) = 0,\ \ \ F_y(L_x,y,t) = 0 \end{aligned}\right\}. \tag{7.40}$$

The plate side ratio is taken as $\bar{L} = L_x / L_y = 10$

Compressive stresses $-\bar{\sigma}_x(0,0,\bar{t})$ and $-\bar{\sigma}_x(L_x,0,\bar{t})$ at the middle point

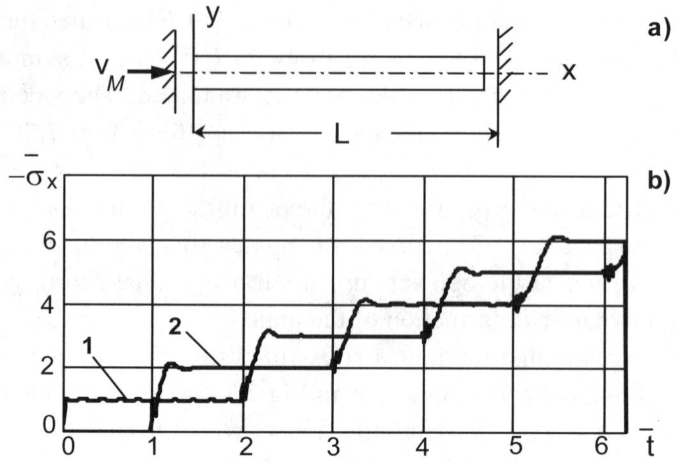

Fig.7.9. A plate impacted by a heavy body; a) sketch of the Problem, b) compressive stresses: 1) at the contact face, 2) at the clamped end.

of the plate end faces versus time $\bar{t}$ are shown in Fig.7.9 where curve I relates to the impacted face and curve II to the fixed one.

The relative time in this figure is $\bar{t} = tc_r / L_x$, whereas the stress $\bar{\sigma}_x$ for convenience of comparison with results of 1-D rod impact calculation (see below Chap.8) is scaled by a rod wave speed $c = c_r(1-\mu^2)^{0.5}$, i.e., $\bar{\sigma}_x = \sigma_x / \rho c v_M$. The time evolution of the stresses $\bar{\sigma}_x$ relevant to the boundary conditions (7.40) differs little from the solution of the same problem simulated by the 1-D rod approach.

7.2.4 A Wide Plate Subjected to a Bending Moment

7.2.4.1. **Problem 7.4. A wide plate (slab) subjected on one side to longitudinal stresses that are linearly distributed along the plate height (Fig.7.10a).** The solution of a similar task was obtained by Nigul (1965) using numerical integration of 3-D equations of the dynamic theory of elasticity by a method of characteristics (Nigul called this approach as the method of three-dimensional 'networks'). The problem was solved in the following setting: A slab of the thickness H=2h freely lies on two extended along the z-axis supports, which are connected with the slab at its middle plane. The distance between supports along the x-axis (slab length) is L. The study also assumed a plane strain.

At the moment $t = 0$, normal stresses are suddenly applied to the left face of the slab. The stresses are assumed to be linearly distributed along the slab thickness, so that the permanent boundary condition at x=0 is

$$\sigma_x(0, y, t) = \sigma_{\max} y / h. \tag{7.41a}$$

The stresses create a moment distributed along the z-axis,

$$M_z = \int_{-h}^{h} \sigma_x(y) y dy = 1.5 \sigma_{\max} h^2, \tag{7.41b}$$

which bends the slab in the plane xy.

The solution is limited to an initial stage of process, until the forward front propagating with the speed c_r of a dilatation wave reaches an opposite end of the slab, i.e. within the time limits $0 \le t < L / c_r$. Because of anti-symmetry of a task in reference to the middle plane y=0, the calculations are carried out for the top half $y \ge 0$ of the slab.

It is accepted that the vertical displacement $u_y(0, y, t)$, and consequently, also the vertical velocity v_y in section x=0 are absent, thus

$$v_y(0, y, t) = 0. \tag{7.42}$$

The lateral surfaces of the slab $y = \pm h$ are free from stresses. As a grid dimension, the quantity $\Delta x = \Delta y = h / 19$ for numerical integration was used.

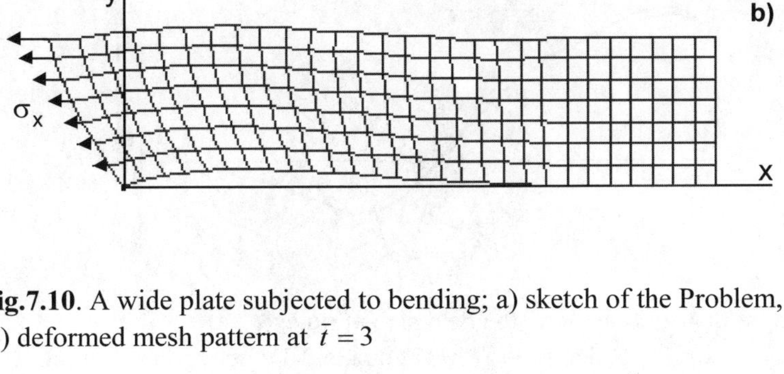

Fig.7.10. A wide plate subjected to bending; a) sketch of the Problem, b) deformed mesh pattern at $\bar{t} = 3$

***7.2.4.2.* A.** In use of WFEM, the top half of the plate is broken in a plane xy by a mesh $\Delta x = \Delta y$ into $n_x \times n_y$ elements and a half of the slab thickness h is taken as a characteristic linear size $L = h$. Then

$$\bar{x} = x / h, \ \bar{y} = y / h, \ \Delta\bar{x} = \Delta\bar{y} = 1 / n_y, \ \bar{t} = tc_r / h.$$

The value $\bar{t} = 1$ corresponds to the time, within which the leading wave passes a distance $x = h$ with the speed c_r.

Figure 7.10b demonstrates a picture of slab deformation at $\bar{t} = 3$, when a perturbed domain propagates over the length of 21 elements, with the

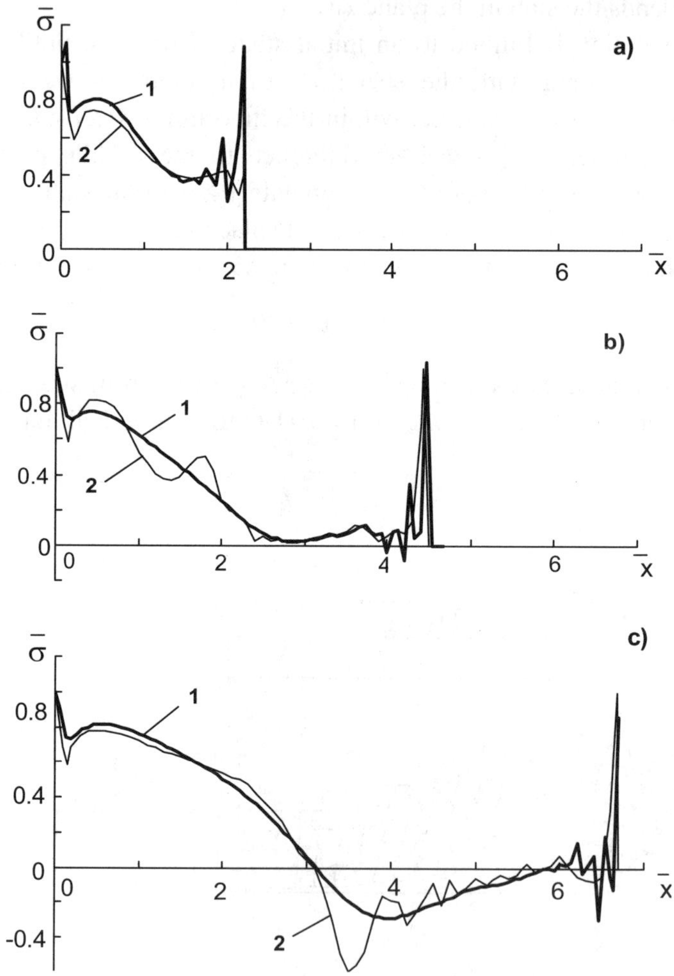

Fig.7.11. Stress distribution along the bent slab at times $\bar{t}$: a) $\bar{t} = 2.2$, b) $\bar{t} = 4.4$, c) $\bar{t} = 6.67$; 1) due to WFEM, 2) due to 3-D 'networks' method.

mesh of $n_x = 28$, $n_y = 7$. The deformation pattern completely coincides with the diagram presented in Nigul (1965).

B. In the cited paper, the diagrams of distribution of a dimensionless normal stress $\tilde{\sigma}_x(\bar{x},1,\bar{t})$ at the slab top surface $\bar{y}=1$ along its length $\bar{x}$ for three moments of time $\bar{t}=42/19,\ 84/19,$ and $126/19$ were given; here we denote relative stress by $\tilde{\sigma}=\sigma/\sigma_{\max}$. For comparison with the WFEM calculations, where the number of elements was limited by $n_x=100$ and $n_y=15$, the close moments of time $\bar{t}=33/15,\ 66/15,$ and $100/15$ were taken (Fig.7.11a,b,c).

The network's calculations were carried out for the maximal value of stress $\sigma_{\max}=1/(1-\mu)\approx 1.4286$. Dimensionless stress in the WFEM calculations is scaled by the given value, i.e., the maximum stress is accepted as $\tilde{\sigma}_{\max}=1$ that is reflected in the curves of Fig.7.11. The lines 1 show there the results of the WFEM calculations and the lines 2 of the method of 3-D networks. It is visible that the WFEM approach gives very close concurrence with averaged values of curves designed by the networks but prevents them from poorly reliable oscillations.

Under Nigul's numerical integration, the stresses at the leading wave front $\tilde{\sigma}_x(\bar{x}=\bar{t},\bar{y},\bar{t})$, based on the preliminary theoretical analysis, were beforehand accepted equal to the stresses $\tilde{\sigma}_x(0,\bar{y},\bar{t})$ at the face $\bar{x}=0$; in our notations, their maximal value is $\tilde{\sigma}_{\max}=1$. From Fig.7.11 it is visible that the stress values at the leading wave front obtained by WFEM are very close to this magnitude, although they are directly resulted by numerical calculation

7.2.5 Additional Remarks

7.2.5.1. **A**. In application of the WFEM to 1-D problems, 'local' time intervals Δt_{ij} evaluated from the energy balance of the elements coincide with the 'global' values Δt_i obtained from the energy balance of the whole system. This leads for a given finite element structure to the exact wave solution (see Chaps.1 and 2). As this takes place, the forces $\mathbf{F}_{k_j r}$ determined by Eq.(7.12) for a wave process at discrete time instants t_i^- coincide with the forces $\mathbf{F}_{k_j B}$ calculated at the same instants on the base of the static stiffness matrix $\mathbf{B}_j$ using Eq.(7.2).

In the case of general multi-dimensional problems, both force sets also provide the condition of the element static equilibrium at the instants t_i^-. Determining the local values of Δt_{ij}, we would come to the energetically exact solution for each element separately, even though the complete equality of the force sets $\mathbf{F}_{k_j r}$ and $\mathbf{F}_{k_j B}$

is not observed. However, the local intervals Δt_{ij} in the general case are different, and to build any numerical step-by-step algorithm with different values of steps Δt_{ij} is impossible. To align the steps by means of a re-meshing techniques is a complicated procedure and, as a rule, is accompanied by violation of the laws of conservation. The opportunity of meshless methods (see, e.g., Belytschko at al. 1996) for simulating wave processes in solids seems while problematical.

B. In use of a global magnitude of the step Δt_i, as in all the numerical methods, the solution becomes inevitably approximated. However, the quantity Δt_i calculated due to the WFEM approach is shown as a 'weight-mean' (with respect to potential energy) value of the local intervals Δt_{ij}. In this sense, the calculated interval Δt_i can be considered as the most optimal characteristic for steps averaging over the system and its use in numerical step-by-step procedure is well warranted.

As for distinction of the statically balanced force sets $\mathbf{F}_{k_j r}$ and $\mathbf{F}_{k_j B}$, the following remark is assumed useful. Due to St.Venant's principle, two statically equivalent force systems placed over a small bounded domain identically affect a stress-strain state in regions, distant from that domain. The force sets $\mathbf{F}_{k_j r}$ and $\mathbf{F}_{k_j B}$ are precisely these and their distinction could not significantly influence the total wave pattern of the whole system. The reference to St.Venant's principle in our situation is, of course, not quite correct; however, the available calculation results described above and below confirm the optimistic expectations.

C. Although ordinary dynamic FEM codes exploit non-waves elements, they have 'transient' options that can be used for approximate wave problem descriptions. Some solutions referred to transient multi-dimensional problems have been numerically obtained on the base of the characteristic's method. As far as possible, we try to compare the WFEM results and other transient numerical solutions in application to some 2-D wave problems (see Subsect.7.2.4 and, below, Chap.12). Some results of similar comparison are also discussed in Shorr and Mel'nikova (2002).

7.2.5.2. **A**. After repeated reflections from borders, the propagation of counter waves results in occurrence of oscillations, which behavior depends on the loading affecting a system. The oscillations induced by permanent loads must not fade in a bounded undamped system. However, simulations of 2-D wave processes show that magnitude of calculated amplitudes in some cases slightly decreases (see, for example, Fig.7.6). A practical meaning of this effect is not significant, as neglecting damping is feasible only for the first few periods after the loading. But its theoretical aspect is interesting to consider in more detail. We shall do this by reference to Problem 7.2. For the analysis, all subsequent diagrams are presented with unsmoothed curves.

B. Nondimensional deflections $\bar{u}_y$ of a plate are given by Eq.(7.39). The time

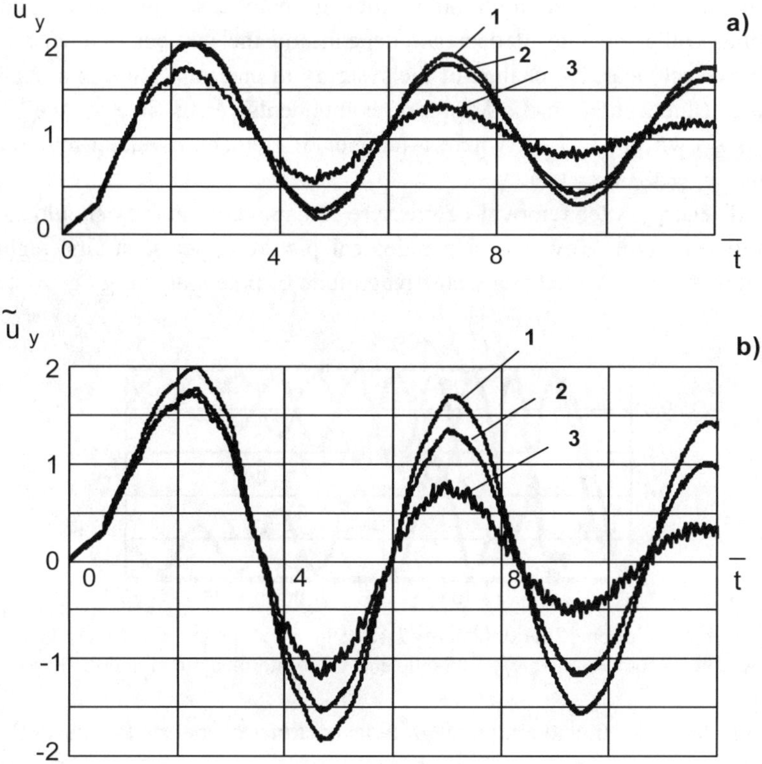

Fig.7.12 Time evolution of the deflection at the point I (see Fig.7.7a):
a) with constant pressure, b) with pressure removed at $\bar{t} \approx 2.38$; number of elements: 1) $n_x = 90,\ n_y = 30$; 2) $n_x = 60,\ n_y = 20$; 3) $n_x = 18,\ n_y = 6$

change of a deflection $\tilde{u}_y = \bar{u}_y / \bar{u}_{y,st}$ at the middle point I of the bottom side of a plate (see Fig.7.7a) under action of constant pressure p_0 (the loading case I) is shown in Fig.7.12a. The deflections are related to the maximum static deflection $\bar{u}_{y,st}$ and calculated for various numbers of elements. For the plate side ratio $L_x / L_y = 3$, the analytical value $\bar{u}_{y,st}$ is about 2.1 (Timoshenko and Goodier 1970).

The deflection achieves the first maximum $\bar{u}_{1,max} \approx 4.2$ correlated with $\tilde{u}_{1,max} \approx 2$ at the moment $\bar{t} \approx 2.38$, after which the oscillations with the visible period of $\bar{\tau} \approx 4.7 \div 4.8$ begin. Calculations due to the FEM programs give the same values

In Fig.7.12b, the deflection curves for the same point are displayed provided the moment of time, when the deflection has achieved the first maximum, the pressure was removed and the plate began to oscillate freely because of the received impulse (the loading case II).

C. The calculated oscillation amplitudes in both cases are seen gradually decreasing, while the rate of decrease depends on the number of elements. To make this effect clear, the change of the system full energy E (line 1) and also its potential P (line 2) and kinetic K (line 3) components versus time for the loading case II is shown in Fig.7.13, where a number of elements is taken intentionally moderate ($n_x = 48,\ n_y = 16$).

The full energy after removal of pressure remains constant, as should be in a conservative system. However, a paradoxical picture appears, at first sight, for energy components: while the average magnitude of potential energy grows, com-

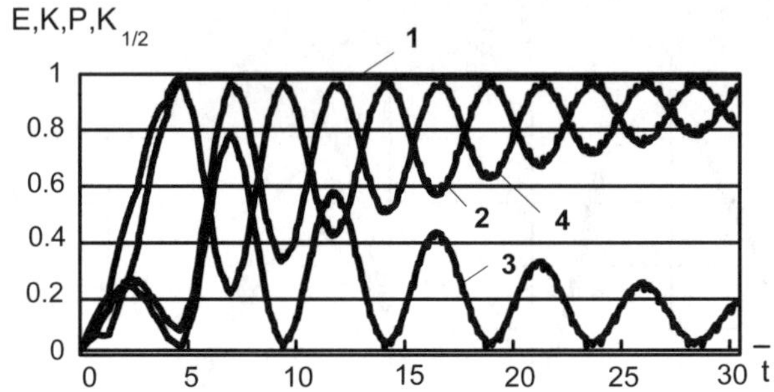

Fig.7.13. Time evolution of the full energy E (line 1) and its potential P (line 2) and kinetic K (line 3) components; $K_{1/2}$ - kinetic energy at intermediate moments (line 4).

ing nearer to total, the average magnitude of kinetic energy (so as deflection amplitudes) decreases.

D. The picture clarifies if we keep in mind that, according to the WFEM approach, the above mentioned diagrams map not a continuous dynamic process, but only values of considered parameters at the discrete time moments t_i separated by intervals Δt_i. However, this approach allows finding values of some parameters at the intermediate moments of time $t_{i,1/2} = t_i + 0.5\Delta t_i$. At those moments the disturbances from the node k are assumed distributing over the parts $0.25 n_k \Delta x$ of adjoining elements, where the number of elements n_k depends on a node arrangement (see Subsect.7.1.2.2.). The kinetic energy of a system at those moments can be determined as

$$K_{1/2} = 0.5\rho h(0.25 n_k \Delta x)^2 \sum_{k=1}^{n_1} v_k^2 , \tag{7.43}$$

and node displacements as

$$u_{k,1/2} = u_{k,0} + 0.5 v_k \Delta t_i . \tag{7.44}$$

The change of the system kinetic energy $K_{1/2}$ versus time is put in Fig.7.13 by the line 4.

It follows from calculations and given diagrams that the change of kinetic energy $K_{1/2}$ at the moments $t_{i,1/2}$ coincides with change of potential energy P at the moments t_i, 'downloading' of energy components takes place; so, the unfading oscillations in conservative system are kept. But the approximate modeling of wave process in separate elements results in arising of contra-phase fluctuations of neighboring nodes displacements, which lead to strain and stress fluctuations with digitization period of $2\Delta t_i$.

In consequence, an original dispersion redistribution of energy between elements appears: ordered 'macro-vibrations' of the conservative system gradually weaken, passing in 'micro-fluctuations' of elements with the digitization period.

E. The considered phenomenon has common features with the known 'hourglass' effect in transient option of FEM (see, for example, Flanagan and Belytschko 1981), but is distinguished by the following:

i) Before occurrence of the reflected waves, the effect of energy dispersion is shown poorly;

ii) Dispersion does not affect the general stability of computing process, since the total mechanical energy of the conservative system remains strictly constant;

iii) With an increase in the number of elements and reduction in a time step, the dispersion effect weakens, as is seen from Fig.7.12.

Thus by increase of element number, the use of the WFEM approach ensures the sufficient accuracy of solutions within the limits of desirable time or a number of the oscillation periods. The examples of Chap.12 and other our calculations substantiate this conclusion. With the presence of damping forces, the considered dispersion effect becomes insignificant, as is superseded by energy dissipation.

Applications

8 Impact Loading of a Deformable Body

8.1 Principle of Floating Boundary Conditions (FBC)

8.1.1 Application of the FBC Principle to WFEM

8.1.1.1. Many engineering systems, especially impact and vibro-impact mechanisms, consist of a number of units contacted each other upon some surfaces, or between which small gaps arise from time to time. Numerical methods for wave simulation in complex deformable structures must take into account that repeated contacts and short-time rebounds can appear at arbitrary points of bodies and at different time instants.

Influence of local contact deformation on impact response will be considered below, in Sect.8.4. Here, we attack the problem of making compatible the WFEM approach requirements with gaps appearing and vanishing.

One of the fundamental assumptions of the WFEM for ensuring the momentum and energy conservation is that both the external boundary conditions of a body and the internal conditions of finite elements interaction remain constant during each time step. However, in the general case the transition from a gap to a contact and vice versa can happen at any arbitrary moment of a time step. This comes into conflict with the WFEM assumption. Avoiding this, we use the principle of 'floating' boundary conditions (FBC principle) proposed by Shorr (1995).

The essence of this implies that the precise satisfaction of the configuration of the colliding body boundaries corresponding to the problem setting is assumed to be of secondary importance for calculation results. Thus the 'real' boundary can temporarily be changed at a local contact point for somewhat differing one so as to satisfy the WFEM requirements. As far as the mass, momentum, and the energy of the bodies remain without alteration, this temporary change does not affect the wave process as a whole, whereas local boundary disturbances become negligible for short time intervals. A lot of numerical calculations confirm the validity of the FBC principle.

Although the boundary configuration change is purely a calculating procedure, some conditional mechanical interpretation is called on below for its clarification.

The approach can be treated both to external links and to boundaries between some elements.

8.1.1.2. For simplicity, consider a boundary between the last element $j = n$ of an elastic rod and a rigid wall (Fig.8.1). Denote a value of the rod-wall gap at the beginning of a step by δ_0 and at the final step moment by δ. Four situations referred to these gap quantities during a current time step may occur:

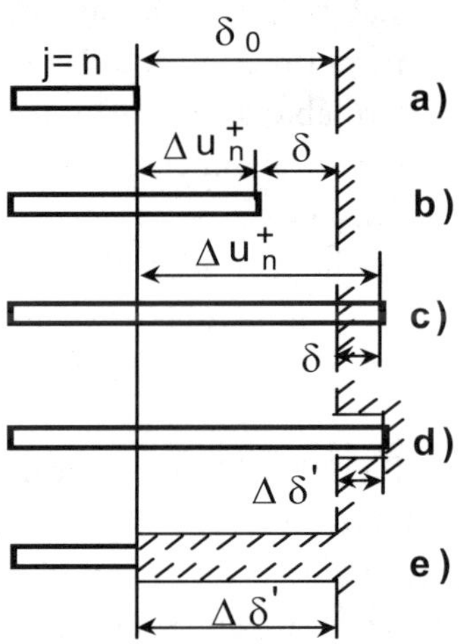

Fig.8.1. To formulation of floating boundary conditions (FBC)

A. A constant or varying gap, $\delta_0 > 0, \delta \geq 0$;
B. A change of the initial gap, $\delta_0 > 0$, into the contact, $\delta = 0$;
C. A permanent contact, $\delta_0 = 0, \delta = 0$;
D. A change of the initial contact, $\delta_0 = 0$, into a final gap, $\delta \geq 0$.

Cases A or B. Let there be no contact at the step beginning, $\delta_0 > 0$ (Fig.8.1a). Calculating the boundary velocity v_n^+ of the element $j = n$ from the free boundary condition $F_n^+ = 0$, where F_n^+ is the wall reaction force, we get (see Sect.1.2)

$$v_n^+ = v_{n,0} + \frac{F_{n,0}\Delta t_i}{\rho_n A_n \Delta x_n}. \tag{8.1}$$

The calculated gap δ at the step end is given by

$$\delta = \delta_0 + \Delta\delta , \tag{8.2}$$

where $\Delta\delta = -\Delta u_n^+ = -v_n^+ \Delta t_i$ and both $\delta \geq 0$ and $\delta < 0$ are possible.

If $\delta \geq 0$ (the case **A**, Fig.8.1b) the assigned condition $F_n^+ = 0$ is true and the calculation procedure can be continued. The calculated value $\delta < 0$ points to the contact occurring within the time interval $t_i < t < t_i + \Delta t_i$ (the case **B**, Fig.8.1c).

To bring a moment of boundary condition change to the end or to the beginning of the step, we assume an initial or final gap temporarily taken as $\delta_0' = \delta_0 + \Delta\delta'$ or $\delta' = \delta_0 + \Delta\delta'$, respectively, by means of a corresponding local change of the wall configuration. A minimal quantity of $|\Delta\delta'|$ can be determined by comparison of the magnitude of $|\delta|$ with δ_0. If $|\delta| \leq \delta_0$ we consider the boundary moving back for $|\delta|$, i.e. put $\Delta\delta' = |\delta|$, and the contact occurs at the end of the step, Fig.8.1d. If $|\delta| > \delta_0$ we consider the boundary moving forward for δ_0, i.e. put $\Delta\delta' = -\delta_0$, and the contact occurs immediately at the beginning of the step, Fig.8.1e. So, the starting gap δ' for the next step or the gap δ_0' for the current one become zero. In the last case, the step must be recalculated with boundary condition $v_n^+ = 0$. This recalculation concerns only the relevant node.

Committing in memory the introduced value of $\Delta\delta'$, the real position of the boundary can be restored in calculation when a gap appears again.

Cases C or D. Now let there be a contact at the beginning of the current step, i.e. the gap $\delta_0 = 0$. Assuming that the contact remains over the step, we determine from the boundary condition $v_n^+ = 0$ the reaction force

$$F_n^+ = -F_{n,0} - \frac{\rho_n A_n v_{n,0} \Delta x_n}{\Delta t_i}, \tag{8.3}$$

where both $F_n^+ \leq 0$ and $F_n^+ > 0$ are possible.

If $F_n^+ \leq 0$ the condition $v_n^+ = 0$ is true and calculations can be continued (the case **C**). By contrast, we put $F_n^+ = 0$ and recalculate this step under the free boundary, as above (the case **D**).

A final gap for $\delta_0 = 0$ and $\Delta\delta' = 0$ is $\delta = -\Delta u_n^+$. The reduced value with $\Delta\delta' \neq 0$ yields

$$\delta_r = \delta - \Delta\delta'. \tag{8.4}$$

With $\Delta\delta' < 0$ the reduced gap δ_r will always be positive and $\delta_r > \delta$. However, with $\Delta\delta' > 0$ the quantity δ_r may become negative. In this case, it is necessary to put $\delta_r = 0$ and find a reduced value of $\Delta\delta'_r = \delta$. As $\Delta\delta'_r < \Delta\delta'$, the real boundary position will be entirely restored through the subsequent steps. The maximum temporary difference between the floating and real boundary positions can attain the magnitude of $\Delta\delta'_{\max} = 0.5 v_n^+ \Delta t_i$, and its ratio to a finite element length is

$$\frac{\Delta\delta'_{\max}}{\Delta x} = 0.5 \frac{v_n^+}{c}.$$

We remark that due to WFEM setting the ratio $v/c << 1$, therefore the ratio $\Delta\delta'_{\max} / \Delta x << 1$.

The recalculations are not necessary if the contact occurrence is always related to the end of the step, however the maximum temporary boundary distortion may be doubled in this case.

8.1.2 Special Cases of Bodies Impact Interaction

The basic FBC approach described above can be readily extended to some special cases of deformed-rigid and deformed-deformed bodies impact interaction.

8.1.2.1. An elastic rod impacts a rigid wall that moves lengthwise with arbitrary velocity $v_w(t)$. For the cases **A** and **B**, Eq.(8.1) is unchanged and a calculated gap at the step end is determined by the rod-wall coming together as

$$\delta = \delta_0 + (v_{w,m} - v_n^+)\Delta t_i, \tag{8.5}$$

where $v_{w,m}$ is the mean wall velocity for a time step.

For the cases **C** and **D**, as far as the contact between the rod and the wall be not violated,

$$v_n^+ = v_{w,m} \tag{8.6}$$

and the reaction force is

$$F_n^+ = -F_{n,0} + \frac{\rho A_n (v_{w,m} - v_{n,0})\Delta x_n}{\Delta t_i}. \tag{8.7}$$

Otherwise, the numerical procedure remains valid. A wall boundary velocity may be given or may have to be determined from the conditions of rod-wall interaction.

8.1.2.2. Neighboring rod elements j-1 and j have a one-side contact that can from time to time change to a gap (Fig.8.2). For the case **A** (Fig.8.2a), the boundary velocities v_{j-1}^{+} and v_j^{-} of the elements are determined with $F_{j-1}^{+}=0$ and $F_j^{-}=0$ independently and a new value of the calculated gap is $\delta=\delta_0+\Delta\delta$ where $\Delta\delta=(v_j^{-}-v_{j-1}^{+})\Delta t_i$. In the case **B**, when the starting positive gap δ_0 changes to negative calculated gap $\delta<0$, it is necessary to increase temporarily the initial gap to $\delta_0'=\delta_0+\Delta\delta'$ where $\Delta\delta'=|\delta|$, see Fig.8.2b. One can conditionally imagine this procedure by means of the element's local shape altering as shown in Fig.8.2c; then the final gap becomes $\delta'=0$ (Fig.8.2d). As it has been mentioned above, these local border alterations in no way influence the integral element dynamical characteristics.

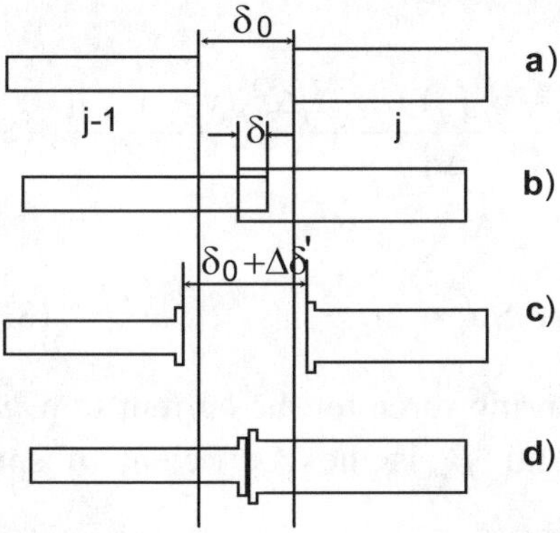

Fig.8.2. FBC in application to an inner boundary of rod elements

For the case **C**, while the element boundaries move together, we take $v_{j-1}^{+}=v_j^{-}$, and the calculation is carried out as for a solid rod. In the case **D**, the real elements boundary configurations are restored by the numerical procedure described above.

8.1.2.3. **A.** The FBC may cover not only boundary configuration but also some other characteristics of colliding bodies referred to their impact interaction. The next type of impact interaction relates to a contact between a rod and an elastic spring that is one-side connected with the inner node j (Fig.8.3a).

Under the spring-rod contact ($\delta=\delta_0=0$), the node velocity v_j and the mean compressive force $F_{sp,m}=-F_j$ determined from Chap.2 are

$$v_j=\frac{\rho_{j-1}A_{j-1}\Delta x_{j-1}v_{j-1,0}+\rho_jA_j\Delta x_jv_{j,0}+(F_{j,0}-F_{j-1,0}+F_{sp,0})\Delta t_i}{\rho_{j-1}A_{j-1}\Delta x_{j-1}+\rho_jA_j\Delta x_j+0.5\beta_{sp}\Delta t_i^2},\qquad(8.8)$$

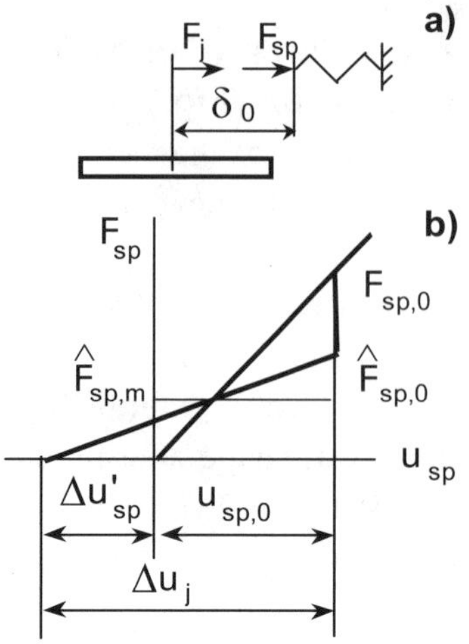

Fig.8.3. FBC in application to a rod/spring one-side connection; a) connection sketch, b) temporary change of a spring characteristic

and

$$F_{sp,m} = F_{j,0} - F_{j-1,0} - \frac{[\rho_{j-1} A_{j-1} \Delta x_{j-1}(v_j - v_{j-1,0}) + \rho_j A_j \Delta x_j (v_j - v_{j,0})]}{\Delta t_i}, \quad (8.9)$$

where

$$F_{sp,m} = F_{sp,0} + 0.5\beta_{sp} v_j \Delta t_i \,. \quad (8.10)$$

Here, $F_{sp,0} = \beta_{sp} u_{sp,0}$ is the starting spring force for the current step, $u_{sp,0}$ is the relevant spring deformation, and β_{sp} is the coefficient of spring stiffness.

With $\delta_0 > 0$ the spring is free, its deformation $u_{sp,0} = 0$, just as the force $F_{sp,0} = 0$. A calculated step change for the gap is $\Delta\delta = -v_j \Delta t_i$. With $v_j > 0$ and $\delta = \delta_0 + \Delta\delta < 0$, we always assume a contact is translated to the finish of the step, so as $\delta' = \delta_0 + \Delta\delta' = 0$ where $\Delta\delta' = |\delta|$, while the final force F_{sp} and spring deformation u_{sp} stay zero.

If the spring is in contact with the rod at the step beginning $(\delta_0 = 0,\ F_{sp,0} > 0)$, a final calculated spring force is

$$F_{sp} = 2F_{sp,m} - F_{sp,0}\,, \quad (8.11)$$

with permissible values such that $F_{sp} \geq 0$.

In the case $v_j < 0$ when the calculated node displacement $\Delta u_j = v_j \Delta t_i$ becomes negative, so that $|\Delta u_j| > u_{sp,0}$ and $F_{sp} < 0$, the contact changes from $\delta_0 = 0$ into a gap $\delta > 0$ within the current interval. Then we also assume a gap be appeared only at the final moment of the step, for which we put $\delta' = 0$.

B. To save in this situation a real spring/rod energetic characteristics, we conditionally may present an initial portion of the function $F_{sp}(u_{sp})$ in the form of polygonal line, as shown in Fig.8.3b.

In doing so,

i) the initial force $F_{sp,0}$ is assumed to step-wise decrease to a value $F_{sp,0}$;

ii) the contact force F_{sp} at the end of the time interval becomes zero with mean value $F_{sp,m} = 0.5F_{sp,0}$;

iii) the work $W_j = F_j\Delta u_j = -F_{sp,m}v_j\Delta t_i$ introduced to the rod from the spring during the time Δt_i is equal to the real potential energy $P_{sp,0} = 0.5F_{sp,0}^2 / \beta_{sp}$ of the spring at the step beginning.

Substituting, with $v_j \neq 0$, the values of the forces

$$F_j = P_{sp,0} / v_j\Delta t_i,$$
$$F_{j-1}^+ = F_{l-1,0} + (v_j - v_{j-1,0})\rho_{j-1}A_{j-1}\Delta x_{j-1} / \Delta t_i,,$$
$$F_j^+ = -F_{j,0} + (v_j - v_{j,0})\rho_j A_j \Delta x_j / \Delta t_i$$

into the node equilibrium equation

$$F_{j-1}^+ + F_j^- - F_j = 0,$$

we obtain a quadratic equation in v_j

$$av_j^2 + bv_j + c = 0, \tag{8.12a}$$

where

$$\begin{aligned} a &= \rho_{j-1}A_{j-1}\Delta x_{j-1} + \rho_j A_j \Delta x_j, \\ b &= (F_{j-1,0} - F_{j,0})\Delta t_i - (\rho_{j-1}A_{j-1}\Delta x_{j-1}v_{j-1,0} + \rho_j A_j \Delta x_j v_{j,0}), \\ c &= -0.5F_{sp,0}^2 / \beta_{sp}. \end{aligned} \tag{8.12b}$$

Since $a > 0$ and $c < 0$, then $\sqrt{b^2 - 4ac}$ is real, and a minimal root of Eq.(8.12a) providing the energy balance for the transient step

$$v_j = -\frac{\sqrt{b^2 - 4ac} + b}{2a}. \tag{8.13}$$

An additional spring elongation $\Delta u'_{sp} = |\Delta u_j| - u_{sp,0}$ (Fig.8.3b) is removed in the next step transmitting into a new initial gap $\delta_0 = \Delta u'_{sp}$.

Note that the FBC may be arbitrarily referred to one or another (or to both) contact faces. Therefore, to turn to the described relatively complicated procedure is recommended only when necessary (for example, see below Problem 10.2).

8.2 An Elastic Rod Impacted by a Rigid Body

As a prototype problem for a number of impact and vibro-impact machines and mechanisms (pneumatic hammer, devices for material dynamic tests, etc), a calculated model in the form of a rod impacted by a rigid body may be used.

8.2.1 A Rod of a Constant Cross Section

***8.2.1.1.* A**. The problem of an impact of a rigid body against the free end of an elastic one-side clamped rod was analytically considered for the first time by Navier (1823), Saint-Venant (1883), Boussinesq (1883) and was later described by a number of authors, by example, Timoshenko and Goodier (1970). This problem may be treated as an excellent to verify numerical methods intended for simulation of wave propagation in solids.

Using DMM, no difficulties arise by including the equations of a body-rod impact interaction in the boundary conditions of a rod.

Problem 8.1. A free-fixed elastic rod impacted by a rigid body. We assume that a rigid body of the mass M moving lengthwise with an initial velocity $v_{\mathrm{M},in}$ impacts the left end of the rod element $j=1$ at $t=0$ (Fig.8.4a).

In the case of mass-rod contact, the boundary conditions at the node $j=1$ are

$$\mathrm{M}\Delta v_{\mathrm{M}} = -F_1^- \Delta t, \tag{8.14a}$$

and

$$v_{\mathrm{M},m} = v_{\mathrm{M},0} + 0.5\Delta v_{\mathrm{M}} = v_1^-, \tag{8.14b}$$

where $v_{\mathrm{M},0}$ is the mass velocity at the beginning of the current time step, $v_{\mathrm{M},m}$ is its mean velocity over the step, and

$$\Delta v_{\mathrm{M}} = 2(v_{\mathrm{M},m} - v_{\mathrm{M},0}) \tag{8.15}$$

is the change of velocity in it. The body velocity is approximated by the linear alteration for a short time step.

Employing Eq.(1.49), $v_1^- = v_{1,0} + (F_1^- + F_{1,0})/\rho c A$, we find in dimensionless terms that $\overline{v} = v/v_{\mathrm{M},in}$ and $\overline{F} = F/\rho c A v_{\mathrm{M},in}$ are, respectively,

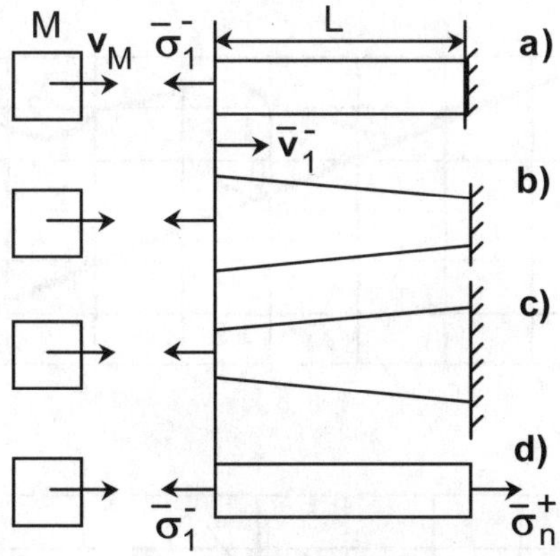

Fig.8.4. Rods of different configuration impacted by a rigid body

$$\bar{v}_1^- = \frac{\bar{v}_{\mathrm{M},0} + 0.5\gamma(\bar{v}_{1,0} + \bar{F}_{1,0})}{1 + 0.5\gamma}, \tag{8.16a}$$

and

$$\bar{F}_1^- = -\frac{\bar{F}_{1,0} + \bar{v}_{1,0} - \bar{v}_{\mathrm{M},0}}{1 + 0.5\gamma}, \tag{8.16b}$$

where

$$\gamma = \frac{\rho c A \Delta}{\mathrm{M}} = (\overline{\mathrm{M}} n)^{-1}. \tag{8.17}$$

Here, $\overline{\mathrm{M}} = \mathrm{M}/\rho AL$ is the ratio of striking body mass to rod one and n is a number of elements. It follows from Eqs.(8.15) to (8.17) that

$$\Delta\bar{v}_{\mathrm{M}} = -\gamma \bar{F}_1^-. \tag{8.18}$$

To describe a smooth time variation of the mass velocity, it is sufficient to take $\gamma \ll 1$. Conditions of the mass-rod transmission from contact to gap and vice versa are determined by FBC procedure (see Sect.8.1). Neither external nor internal damping are taken into account.

B. Figure 8.5 illustrates the change in the mass/rod dynamic parameters versus time $\bar{t} = tc/L$ after an impact for $\overline{\mathrm{M}} = 1$ (n=50). The displacement $\bar{u}_{\mathrm{M}}$ of the mass (curve 1) and $\bar{u}_1$ of the free end of the rod (curve 2), velocity $\bar{v}_{\mathrm{M}}$ of the mass (curve 1) and $\bar{v}_1^-$ of the rod (curve 2), and stress

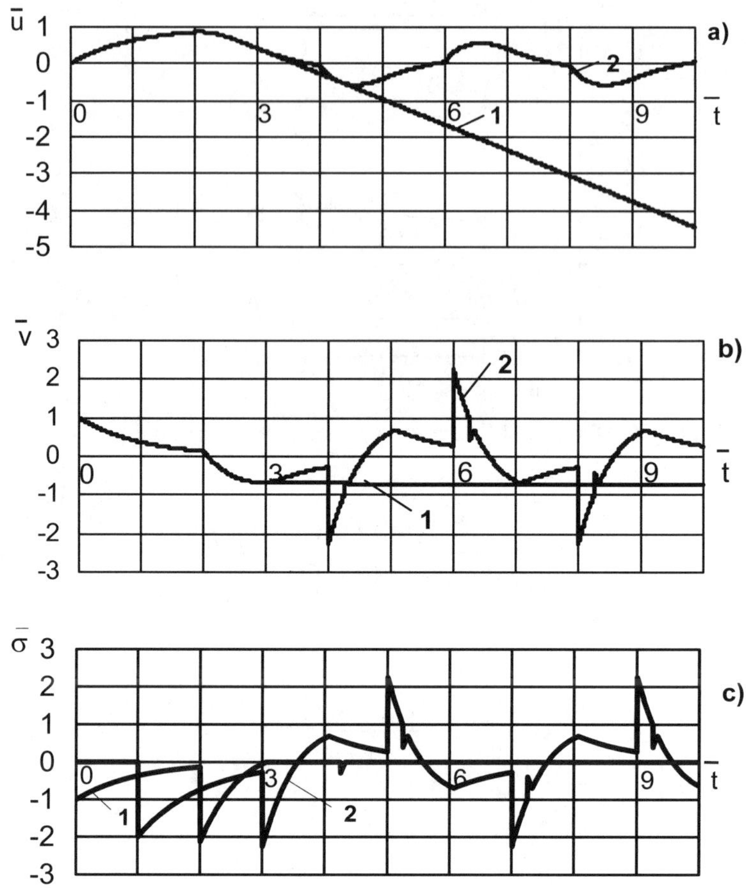

Fig.8.5. Change of the mass/rod dynamic parameters vs. time after an impact by a rigid body

$\overline{\sigma}_1^- = -\overline{F}_1^-$ at the rod free face (curve 1) and $\overline{\sigma}_n^+ = \overline{F}_n^+$ at the clamped end (curve 2) are displayed in Fig.8a,b,c, respectively.

All the details of wave process induced by the impact are clearly shown in these figures. A wave from the initial impact arrives at the clamped end for the first time at $\overline{t} = 1$, for the second at $\overline{t} = 3$, and then returns regularly again with oscillation period $\overline{T} = 4$. Between the moments $\overline{t} \approx 3.069$ and $\overline{t} \approx 4.251$ the mass is separated from the rod. The stress at the free end becomes zero, and the velocities $\overline{v}_M$ and $\overline{v}_1^-$ diverge when a gap appears. During a short time, the free rod face overtakes the striking body, the impact is repeated, and the velocities $\bar{v}_M$ and $\bar{v}_1^-$ coincide; then a compressive stress emerges again. The final rebound takes place at the moment $\bar{t} = 4.326$. After that, undamped oscillations of complex but regular character, with mentioned period, are established; the narrow spikes of stress and velocity are connected with the superposition of waves induced by the two impacts and reflections from both ends of the rod.

The wave pattern before the first rebound and the effect of the repeated impact are in entire agreement with the analytical analysis carried out by Veklich and Malyshev (1972) and in other investigations.

***8.2.1.2.* A. Problem 8.2. Impact of an 'adhering' mass against a rod.** Contrary to the previous problem, the striking mass is assumed to be 'adhered' to the rod after the impact, i.e. the body accompanies the rod without rebound. In this case, the rod and the mass mean velocities, and the displacements of their common face must be, respectively, the same: $\bar{v}_1^- = \bar{v}_{\mathrm{M},m}$ and $\bar{u}_1 = \bar{u}_\mathrm{M}$. All other conditions of the Problem 8.1 remain valid. The stresses $\bar{\sigma}_1^-$ and $\bar{\sigma}_n^+$ for $\overline{\mathrm{M}} = 1$ (n=50) are shown in Fig.8.6. The oscillation pattern is noticeably changed in comparison with Fig.8.5c.

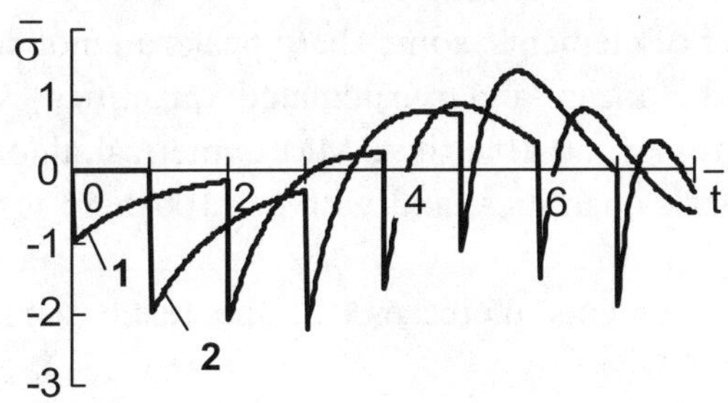

Fig.8.6. Stresses in a rod impacted by 'adhering' body; 1) $\bar{\sigma}_1^-$, 2) $\bar{\sigma}_n^+$

B. In parallel with the model of separate striking rigid body, another possible formulation of impact modeling was proposed by Pupyrjev and Pavlovskaya (1996). Doing so, the mass of striking body is added to the mass of the first rod element that is assumed moving with the initial velocity $v_{\mathrm{M},in}$, whereas the stiffness of this element is correspondingly increased because the time step Δt remains identical for all the elements. If the number of elements is increased by one and the additional element has the same length $\Delta x = L/n$, its density is taken as $\rho_1 = \rho\overline{\mathrm{M}}n$.

Clearly, this approach is valid only for an adhering mass, since it cannot describe repeated impacts.

8.2.2 The DMM Accuracy in Application to Impact Problems

To verify the accuracy of the DMM/FBC approach to simulation of impact problems, some numerical and analytical results transformed in nondimensional form are compared below.

8.2.2.1. For the case $\overline{\mathrm{M}} = 1.31$, the quantities of stress $\bar{\sigma}_n^+$ for typical time moments $\bar{t}^{\mp}$, and final rebound velocity $\bar{v}_r$ are determined with different number n of the elements.

The results are presented in Table 8.1, where two different stress values relate to infinitesimally close time moments $\bar{t}^-$ and $\bar{t}^+$ before and after the stress jumps. The stresses obtained by analytical solution are given in the last row of Table 8.1.

Due to DMM, the element boundary stress $\sigma_j^{\pm}$ relates to the mean value within a time interval Δt . Therefore, to provide a more correct numerical-analytical comparison, peak stresses σ_i shown in the upper row of the table cells are recalculated for the corresponding step beginning values $\sigma_{i,0}$ using the linear time extrapolation $\sigma_{i,0} = 0.5(3\sigma_i - \sigma_{i+1})$. They are presented in the bottom row of the cells.

With a small number of elements, some sharp peaks are not detected and divergence between the mean and recalculated quantities is sensitive. However, beginning from n=50-100, the DMM numerical algorithm gives very accurate stress peak quantities, and with $n \geq 100$ there is no need of their recalculation.

As the number of elements increases, all the results monotonically approach a limit.

Some kind of analytical or other numerical solutions, which could describe such details of wave interaction under repeated impacts and after a mass rebound, are not known by the author.

8.2.2.2. Analytical impact characteristics for mass ratio $\overline{\mathrm{M}} = 1,2,4,6$ obtained by Saint-Venant and Flamant (1883) and described in Timoshenko and Goodier (1970) are tabulated in the first columns of Table 8.2. In it $\bar{t}_{imp}$ is the impact duration before the first rebound, $\bar{\sigma}_1(2)$ and $\bar{\sigma}_1(4)$ are stresses at the contact face at the moments $\bar{t} = 2$ and $\bar{t} = 4$ after the first and the second rebounds, respectively, and $\bar{\sigma}_{n,\max}$ is a maximum stress at the clamped end.

The DMM numerical results shown in the second columns of Table 8.2 are in full agreement with the theoretical ones.

Table 8.1. Numerical and analytical stresses $\bar{\sigma}_n^+$ and rebound velocity $\bar{v}_r$ for different element number n

Number of elements n		10	50	100	400	Analytic
Quantities $\bar{\sigma}_n^+$ at $\bar{t}^{\mp}$		-1.9265 -1.9974	-1.9849 -1.9999	-1.9962 -2.0000	-1.9981 -2.0000	-2.0000
		-0.4514 -0.4335	-0.4378 -0.4344	-0.4362 -0.4345	-0.4349 -0.4345	-0.4345
		-2.2030 -2.4204	-2.3860 -2.4340	-2.4101 -2.4344	-2.4284 -2.4346	-2.4345
	~4.46	0.6593	0.6589	0.6587	0.6595	0.6600
	5^-	0.4514 0.4335	0.4378 0.4344	0.4362 0.4346	0.4349 0.4345	0.4345
	5^+	-	2.3860 2.4340	2.4101 2.4344	2.4284 2.4346	2.4345
	~5.05	1^+	-0.8533 -0.9213	-0.8877 -0.9225	-0.9139 -0.9227	
	~5.42	3^-	0.8521	0.8504	0.8559	
$\bar{v}_r$		-0.8984	3^+	-0.8586	-0.8586	

Table 8.2. . Numerical and analytical stresses for different mass ratio $\overline{\text{M}}$

$\overline{\text{M}}$	$\bar{t}_{imp}$		$\bar{\sigma}_1(2)$		$\bar{\sigma}_1(4)$		$\bar{\sigma}_{n,max}$	
	Theor.	DMM	Theor.	DMM	Theor.	DMM	Theor.	DMM
1	3.069	3.069	2.1353	2.1354	0	0	2.270	2.271
2	4.708	4.709	2.3679	2.3680	2.135	2.1354	2.736	2.736
4	5.900	5.901	2.6065	2.6066	2.974	2.9744	3.212	3.213
6	7.419*	7.409	2.7165	2.7165	-	3.4687	3.504	3.504

*) This quantity, probably, contains a misprint.

8.2.2.3. Figure 8.7 shows results of DMM calculation of a rod impacted by a heavy body of the mass ratio $\overline{\text{M}} = 8.77$. The shock wave travels along the rod more than nine times until the rebound takes place at $\bar{t}_{imp} = 9.165$. The value of the maximum stress at the clamped end reaches $\bar{\sigma}^+_{n,\max} = 4.134$ at $\bar{t} = 5$. Residual oscillations are of the same kind as for the mass $\overline{\text{M}} = 1$ (cp. Fig.8.7 and 8.5).

In Makushin (1952), the mass-rod impact with the given parameters was calculated graphically up to the moment of the mass rebound, using the characteristic's method. The time dependencies $\bar{\sigma}_1^-(\bar{t})$ and $\bar{\sigma}_n^+(\bar{t})$ obtained by that way within indicated bounds were close to those shown in Fig.8.7, and the graphical results were $\bar{t}_{imp} \approx 9.1$ and $\bar{\sigma}^+_{n,\max} \approx 4.16$ at $\bar{t} = 5$.

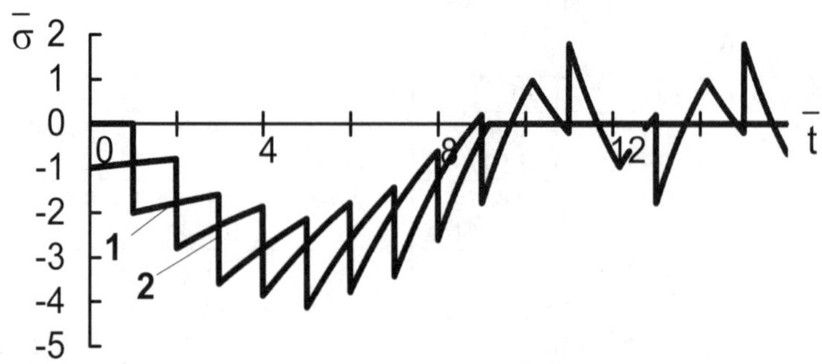

Fig.8.7. Stresses in a rod impacted by a heavy body; 1) $\bar{\sigma}_1^-$, 2) $\bar{\sigma}_n^+$

8.2.2.4. The next two examples refer to comparison of the impact pattern calculated by the ordinary FEM code and the DMM results which, as it has been shown just above, coincide with the analytical ones.

A. An entirely free rod impacted by a rigid body of the same mass $\overline{M} = 1$, which is assumed, as in Subsect.8.2.1.2, to be 'adhered' to the rod, is experienced. In Fig.8.8a the boundary velocities $\bar{v}_1^-$ and $\bar{v}_n^+$, and in Fig.8.8b the boundary displacements $\bar{u}_1$ and $\bar{u}_{n+1}$ calculated by FEM and DMM codes are displayed.

The time step is taken in both algorithms as $\Delta\bar{t} = 0.0065$, whereas a connection between step value and number of elements is governed by the corresponding code orders.

The most interesting velocity peak values referred to $\bar{t}$ = 0, 1, 3, and 5 are presented in Table 8.3.

B. The boundary stresses referred to a free-clamped rod with account of the mass rebound are shown in Fig.8.9 and in Table 8.4.

Comparison of the FEM and DMM results in Figs.8.8 and 8.9 and in corresponding tables shows:

i) The displacement and uninterrupted velocity curves (until the contact remains) are close;

ii) The other velocity and stress curves are qualitatively similar, however, FEM gives the accurate stress $\bar{\sigma}_1^-(0) \approx -1$ and $\bar{\sigma}_n^+(1) \approx -2$, and velocity $\bar{v}_1^-(0) = 1$ only for their first peaks;

iii) Thereupon, both stress and velocity reflected waves begin eroding and their peaks calculated by FEM progressively decrease, while the DMM results remain stable, as it is especially well seen from Table 8.4;

iv) Due to FEM, the stress at the free surface does not vanish after the

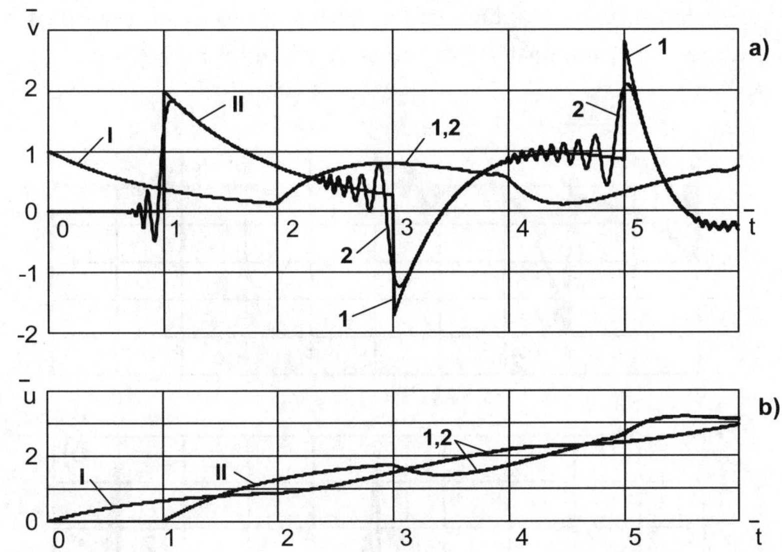

Fig.8.8. Comparison of DMM (lines 1) and FEM (lines 2) solutions for a free-free rod impacted by an 'adhering' rigid body; a) velocity, b) displacement; I – impacted face, II – opposite free face

Table 8.3. Boundary velocities calculated by the DMM and FEM codes

Method	$n, \Delta \bar{t}$	Quantities of $\bar{v}_{max}(\bar{t})$ or $\bar{v}_{min}(\bar{t})$			
		$\bar{v}_1^-(0)$	$\bar{v}_n^+(1)$	$\bar{v}_n^+(3)$	$\bar{v}_n^+(5)$
DMM	154, 0.0065	1.000	1.994	1.710	2.816
FEM	50, 0.0065	1.000	1.823	1.250	2.102

final rebound but oscillates within some small limits, and the wave pattern is distorted by some spurious (parasitic) oscillation.

Note that an investigation of ordinary FEM assurance in conformity to wave process simulation is not the subject of this book. Therefore, it is not improbable that the FEM results for the problem considered may provide more reasonable approximation to the analytical ones without loss of stability by matching number of elements, time steps, artificial damping coefficients, and gap parameters. However, when an analytical solution is unknown the choice of optimal calculation parameters becomes problematical.

For this reason, the advantage of the DMM approach in regard of a 1-D impact numerical simulation is, by the author's opinion, obvious.

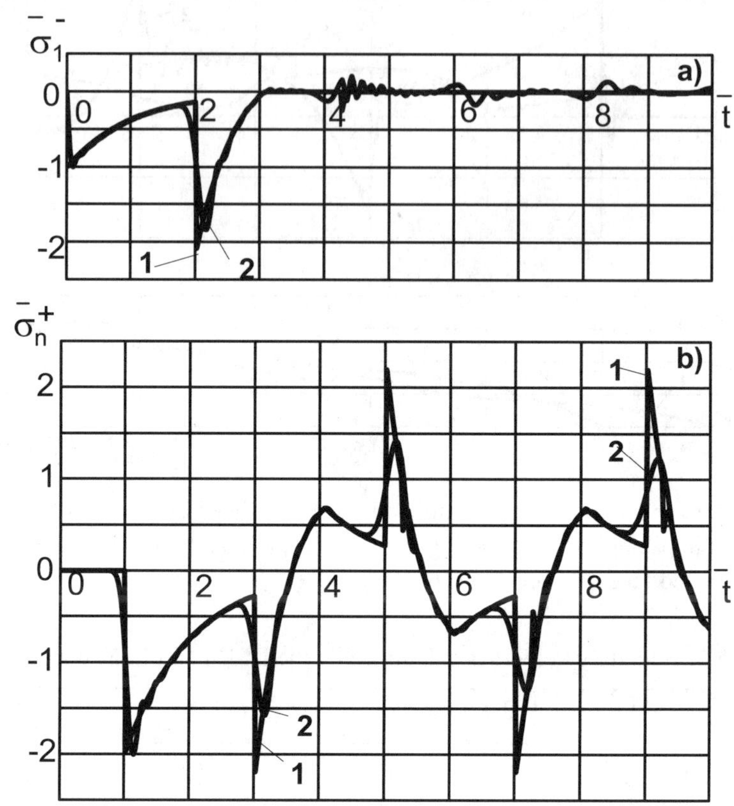

Fig.8.9. Comparison of DMM (1) and FEM (2) solutions for a cantilever rod impacted by a rebounding body; a) impacted face, b) clamped end

8.2.3 A Rod of a Variable Cross Section

***8.2.3.1* A.** As usual in DMM, an arbitrary function of cross-sectional area A of a distance x from the free end is approximated by step-wise function, for example,

$$\overline{A}_j = 1 + (\overline{A}_n - 1)\left(\frac{j-1}{n-1}\right)^{\nu},$$

where $\overline{A}_j = A_j / A_1$, $\overline{A}_n = A_n / A_1$, and ν is a constant

Table 8.4. Boundary stresses calculated by the DMM and FEM codes

Method	n, $\Delta\bar{t}$	Quantities of $\bar{\sigma}_{max}(\bar{t})$ or $\bar{\sigma}_{min}(\bar{t})$						
		$\bar{\sigma}_1^-(0)$	$\bar{\sigma}_1^-(2)$	$\bar{\sigma}_n^+(1)$	$\bar{\sigma}_n^+(3)$	$\bar{\sigma}_n^+(5)$	$\bar{\sigma}_n^+(7)$	$\bar{\sigma}_n^+(9)$
DMM	20, 0.05	0.999	2.133	1.999	2.265	2.265	2.265	2.265
	40, 0.025	1.000	2.135	1.999	2.270	2.270	2.270	2.270
	100, 0.01	1.000	2.136	2.000	2.271	2.271	2.271	2.271
FEM	20, 0.025	1.001	1.840	2.006	1.571	1.422	1.301	1.227
	50, 0.01	1.013	1.811	1.934	1.650	1.517	1.419	1.344

A body-rod mass ratio is determined now as $\overline{\text{M}} = \text{M} / \rho c A_m$, where A_m is a mean value of cross-sectional area, and the coefficient γ, according to Eq.(8.17), is

$$\gamma = \frac{A_1}{\overline{\text{M}} n A_m}. \tag{8.19}$$

For linear area change with $\nu = 1$ this leads to $\gamma = 2/(1+\overline{A}_n)\overline{\text{M}}n$.

The reduced force and stress are $\overline{F}_j = F_j / \rho c A_1 v_{\text{M},in}$ and $\bar{\sigma}_j = \overline{F}_j / \overline{A}_j$, respectively. A ratio of a rod cross-section size change to its length is assumed to be small.

B. Some examples of DMM numerical solution related to impact of a rigid body against a one-side clamped rod with linear change of cross-sectional area were studied by Mel'nikova (1985).

Problem 8.3. A free-fixed rod of linearly changing cross-sectional area impacted by a rigid body. The next two diagrams illustrate the dependence of the stresses $\bar{\sigma}_1^-$ and $\bar{\sigma}_n^+$ on time $\bar{t}$, with the body-rod mass ratio $\overline{\text{M}} = 1$ and $\overline{\text{M}} = 10$, for a rod whose cross-sectional area linearly decreases from the free end to the clamped one (Fig.8.4b, with $\overline{A} = 0.1$), and for a rod whose area increases (Fig.8.4c, with $\overline{A} = 10$).

In the case of a narrowing rod (Fig.8.10), the clamped end is more stressed. Very sharp spikes and deep slits in the curve $\bar{\sigma}_n^+(\bar{t})$ induced by the number of alternating rebounds and impacts arise. Residual rod oscillations are rather intensive because the significant part of the mass initial kinetic energy transmitted into the rod remains in it.

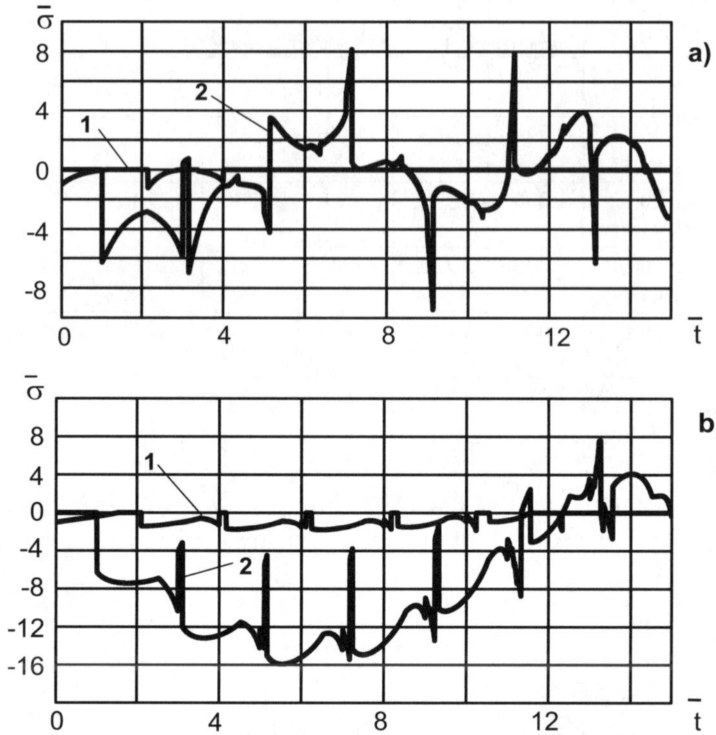

Fig.8.10. Stresses in a narrowing rod impacted by a rigid body; *a*) $\overline{\mathrm{M}}=1$, *b*) $\overline{\mathrm{M}}=10$; 1) $\overline{\sigma}_1^-$, 2) $\overline{\sigma}_n^+$

Moreover, some unexpected effect occurs. After the last rebound, the heavy left part of the narrowing rod, being free from the striking mass, generates the stresses in the weak clamped section which can exceed the maximum stress within the contact time.

In the case of a rod of widening cross-sectional area (Fig.8.11), the maximum compressive stress occurs direct at the contact face. Residual rod oscillations become less, especially, for an impact of a heavy mass when almost the whole initial kinetic energy returns to the mass after its rebound (e.g., the rebound velocity for $\overline{\mathrm{M}} = 10$ is $\overline{v}_r = -0.997$)

8.2.3.2. Impact loading of a rod is exploited for experimental study of material dynamic characteristics, see, e.g., Kolsky (1953). For this purpose, investigators have attacked different devices inducing impulsive tensile stresses.

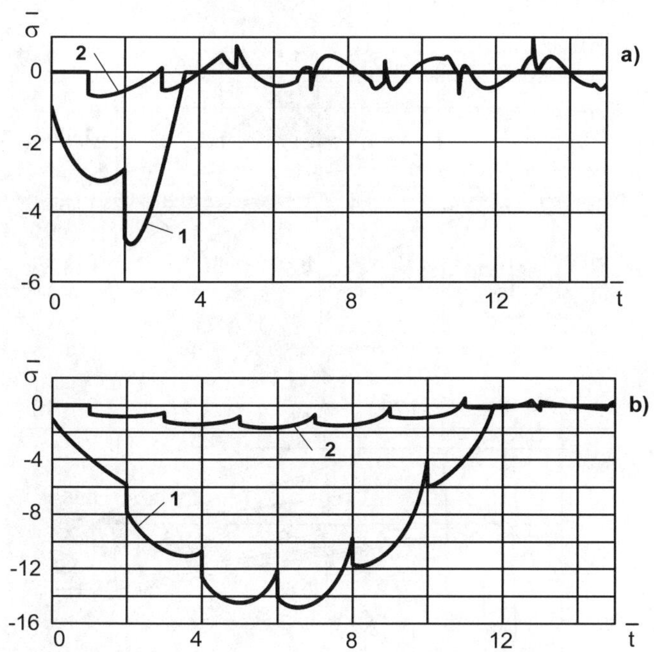

Fig.8.11. Stresses in a widening rod impacted by a rigid body; *a)* $\overline{\mathrm{M}}=1$, *b)* $\overline{\mathrm{M}}=10$; 1) $\overline{\sigma}_1^-$, 2) $\overline{\sigma}_n^+$

A. A study of tensioning impact of a wire was begun by J.Hopkinson (1872) and continued by B.Hopkinson (1905). The dynamic stresses in a wire modeled by a free-fixed rod are readily calculated by DMM, changing a sign of the mass initial velocity $v_{\mathrm{M},in}$ to positive. Moreover, Taylor (1946) showed that the wire rupture in B.Hopkinson's tests caused by maximal tension stress had occurred after the third reflection.

B. Problem 8.4. A free-free rod impacted by a rigid body. As it has been shown previously in Chap.1, a compression wave reflecting from a free end converts to a tension wave.

Let the both ends of an impacted rod from the Problem 8.1 be free (see Fig.8.4d). Replacing the clamped boundary condition $\overline{v}_n^+=0$ by the condition of the free end $\overline{F}_n^+=0$, a solution of wave propagation can be obtained.

Figure 8.12 shows the stress distribution along the rod axis for some time $\overline{t}$ depicted near the curves. Fig.8.12a is relevant to a rod of constant cross-section, $\overline{A}_n=1$, Fig.8.12b to a widening rod with $\overline{A}_n=3$. In the both

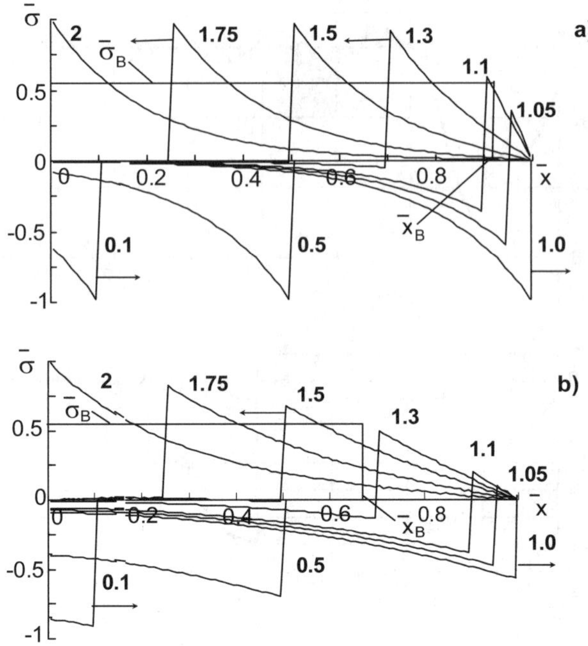

Fig.8.12. Direct and reflected stress waves in a free-free rod impacted by a small rigid body

cases the rod is impacted by a rigid body of the small mass ratio $\overline{\mathrm{M}} = 0.2$.

For the rod with constant area both the direct compressive and reflected tensile stress waves travel without distortion. A zone near the free end $\bar{x} = 1$ where the build-up of generated tensile stresses occurs until they reach maximum values is relatively short (from $\bar{x} = 1$ to $\bar{x} \approx 0.7$). In contrast to that, a compressive stress wave in the widening rod becomes weaker as it approaches the free end, while the reflected tensile stress wave that moves away from the end becoming stronger. As a result, the build-up zone in the latter case expands, covering the entire rod length.

As soon as a tensile stress at any point $\bar{x}_B$ reaches the material rupture stress, a part of the rod $1 - \bar{x}_B$ will separate from the remaining part $\bar{x}_B$. Having established a point $\bar{x}_B$ disposition from the test and exploiting calculated diagrams as in Fig.8.12, one can evaluate the magnitude of the rupture stress $\sigma_B = \bar{\sigma}_B \rho c\, v_{\mathrm{M},in}$. The wider is the build-up zone, the more accurate the rupture stress value could be determined from the position $\bar{x}_B$ Varying the mass ratio $\overline{\mathrm{M}}$, initial mass velocity $v_{\mathrm{M},in}$, and a rod configuration $\bar{A}_n$, a broad spectrum of materials can be investigated.

C. The effect of wave reflection was exploited by B Hopkinson (1914) who suggested a use of a 'metering rod' for experimental study of wave propagation in materials. To this goal, a rod is beforehand slitted at any point $\bar{x}_*$ into two parts so that a free part $1-\bar{x}_*$ flies off when a tensile stress occurs at this point. Measuring the momentum of the both separated parts for different $\bar{x}_*$, a magnitude and duration of the impulse applied can be calculated. Similar and other devices are used for the experimental study of dynamical characteristic of brittle materials, see, e.g., Goldsmith (1960).

D. Taking for a contacting body and a rod with free end inverted initial conditions $v_{\mathrm{M},in}=0,\ v_{j,0}=-v_{in}$, we come to the problem of impact of an elastic rod, moving with initial velocity $-v_{in}$, against a rigid body being at rest.

8.3 An Inelastic Rod Impacted by a Rigid Body

For the first time, the DMM numerical simulation of the problem of an elastic-viscoplastic rod impacted by a rigid body was employed in Shorr (1984). A number of calculation results related to this topic in application to different material rheological properties were presented in Shorr (1995, 1998).

8.3.1 A Rod of Viscoelastic Material

8.3.1.1. **Problem 8.5. A viscoelastic one-side fixed rod impacted by a rigid body.** Exploiting the setting of Chap.3, inelastic deformation is included in the DMM algorithm by additional element boundary velocities $v_{j,c}^{\pm}=\pm(\sigma_j^{\pm}\varphi_j^{\pm}/E_j+\psi_j^{\pm})c_j$, where the coefficients $\varphi_j^{\pm},\psi_j^{\pm}$ depend on the material properties. In doing so, the condition (8.14b) is replaced by

$$v_{\mathrm{M},m}=v_{1,*}^{-}=v_1^{-}+v_{1,c}^{-}, \tag{8.20}$$

and the governing Eqs.(8.16)-(8.17) of the rigid body/inelastic rod interaction take the form

$$\bar{v}_{1,*}^{-}=\frac{0.5\gamma(\bar{v}_{1,0}+\bar{F}_{1,0}+\psi_1^{-})+\bar{v}_{\mathrm{M},0}(1+\varphi_1^{-})}{1+0.5\gamma+\varphi_1^{-}}, \tag{8.21a}$$

$$\bar{F}_1^{-}=-\frac{\bar{F}_{1,0}+\bar{v}_{1,0}-\bar{v}_{\mathrm{M},0}-\psi_1^{-}}{1+0.5\gamma+\varphi_1^{-}}. \tag{8.21b}$$

Equation (8.18) is not changed. The boundary velocity v_1^- in the FBC procedure has to be substituted to $v_{1,*}^-$.

8.3.1.2. Figure 8.13 shows how the relative retardation time $\bar{\tau}_v = \tau_v c / L$ affects the stress $\bar{\sigma}_n^+$ at the clamped end of a homogeneous viscoelastic rod of Voigt material that is described by the coefficients

$$\varphi = \frac{E}{E_v} \frac{\xi_v}{1+\xi_v}, \quad \psi = -\varepsilon_{v,0} \frac{\xi_v}{1+\xi_v}, \tag{8.22}$$

where E_v is a high-elastic modulus, $\xi_v = 0.5\Delta t / \tau_v$ with $\tau_v = \eta_v / E_v$, and η_v is Newtonian viscosity (see Fig.3.2a).

The rod is assumed to be of variable cross-sectional area linearly shrinking from the free end to the clamped one with $\bar{A}_n = 0.8$. The mass ratio is $\bar{\mathrm{M}} = 1$, the number of elements is n=100, and the ratio of moduli $\bar{E}_v = E_v / E = 0.2$.

At the values $\bar{\tau}_v >> 1$, the stress curves are close to the elastic ones but with slight damping. As the relative retardation time $\bar{\tau}_v$ decreases, the damping at first increases (Fig.8.13a) and the most intensive damping relates to $\bar{\tau}_v$ of the order about unity (Fig.8.13b). Then, with time $\bar{\tau}_v < 1$, the wave process is changed in principle (Fig.8.13c,d). The propagation time of the mechanical perturbation along the rod alternates from $\bar{t} = 1$ to $\bar{t} \approx 2.45$, with the oscillation period becomes about $\bar{T} \approx 9.8$ instead of $\bar{T} = 4$.

This correlates with the growth of the material compliance by the ratio $\sqrt{(1+\bar{E}_v)/\bar{E}_v}$ which is equal to 2.45 for $\bar{E}_v = 0.2$. The damping of the oscillations decreases again, as the material acquires high-elastic properties, and becomes small with $\bar{\tau}_v << 1$ (Fig.8.13d)

8.3.1.3. The viscosity coefficient η of many materials is not usually constant but varies over time, in particular, by physical aging, or depends on the stress, accumulated strain, and on the rate of strain. In these cases, the DMM calculations are completed using succesive approximations, an example of which has been given in Shorr (1998).

8.3.2 A Rod of Elastic-Plastic Material

8.3.2.1. **Problem 8.6. An elastic-plastic one-side fixed rod of a constant area impacted by a rigid body.** We assume the material of the rod to have the kinematic hardening, with relative tangential modulus $\bar{E}_t = E_t / E$

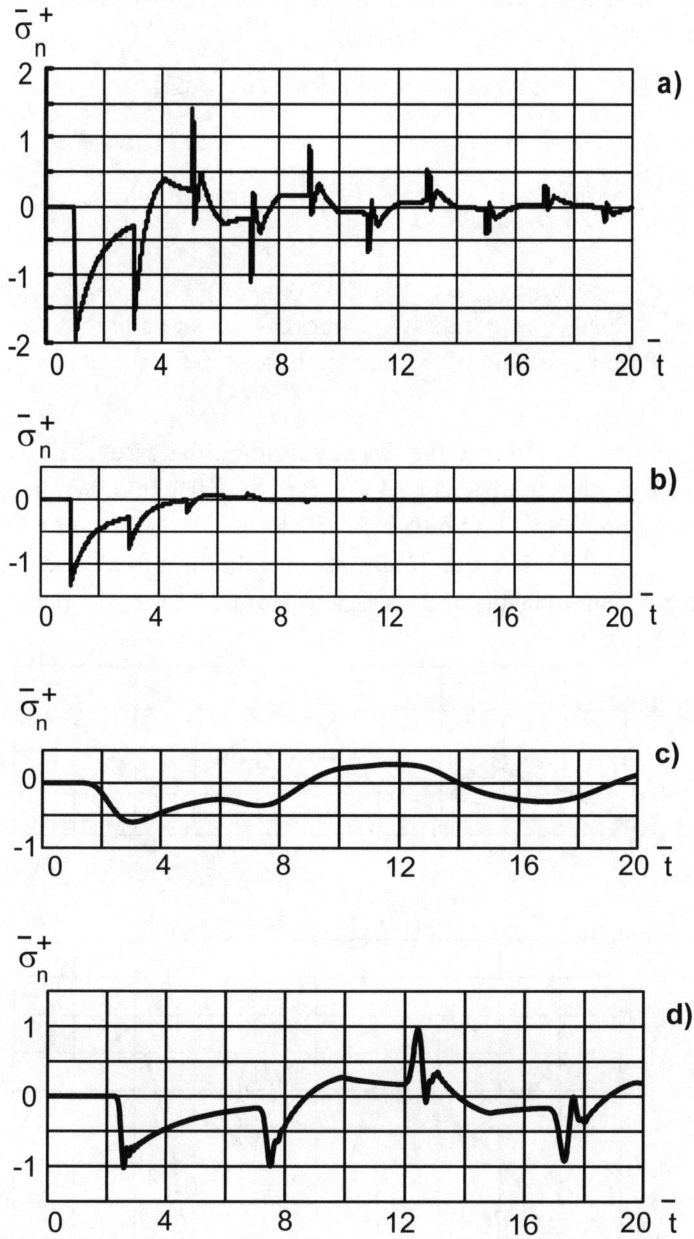

Fig.8.13. A rod of a Voigt's material impacted by a rigid body; relative retardation time: $a)\ \bar{\tau}_v = 20,\ b)\ \bar{\tau}_v = 5,\ c)\ \bar{\tau}_v = 0.1,\ d)\ \bar{\tau}_v = 0.0005$

The Bauschinger's effect is taken into account. In this case (see Eqs.(3.44) of Chap.3),

$$\varphi_j^{\pm} = \psi_j^{\pm} = 0 \text{ with } \left|\overline{\sigma}_j^{\pm} - \overline{\sigma}_{jr,0}^{\pm}\right| \le \overline{\sigma}_y, \tag{8.23}$$

$$\left.\begin{aligned} &\varphi_j^{\pm} = (1-\overline{E}_t)/\overline{E}_t, \\ &\psi_j^{\pm} = -\varphi_j^{\pm}[\overline{\sigma}_{jr,0}^{\pm} + \overline{\sigma}_y \operatorname{sign}(\overline{\sigma}_j^{\pm} - \overline{\sigma}_{jr,0}^{\pm})] \end{aligned}\right\} \text{ with } \left|\overline{\sigma}_j^{\pm} - \overline{\sigma}_{jr,0}^{\pm}\right| > \overline{\sigma}_y \tag{8.24}$$

where $\overline{\sigma}_y = \sigma_y / \rho c v_{\mathrm{M},in}$ is a relative initial yield point and $\overline{\sigma}_{jr,0}^{\pm} = \sigma_{jr,0}^{\pm} / \rho c v_{\mathrm{M},in}$ is a relative value of the so-called 'residual micro-stresses' at the beginning of the current time step for the plastic links of the element j.

8.3.2.2. Figure 8.14 shows the time evolution of stresses $\overline{\sigma}_1^-$ and $\overline{\sigma}_n^+$ under the impact by the solid mass $\overline{\mathrm{M}} = 1$ for $\overline{E}_t = 0.1$ and two values of the initial yield point $\overline{\sigma}_y = 0.5$ and 1.5. If the initial yield point $\overline{\sigma}_y > \overline{\sigma}_{e,\max}$, where $\overline{\sigma}_{e.\max} = 2.31$ is a maximum stress value in the identical elastic rod (see Fig.8.5), only elastic strain arises in a rod.

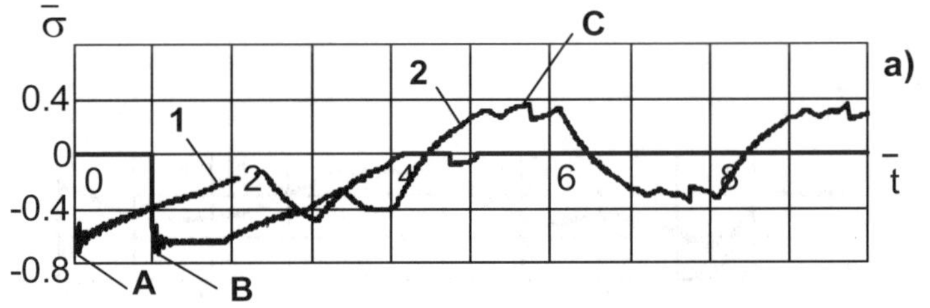

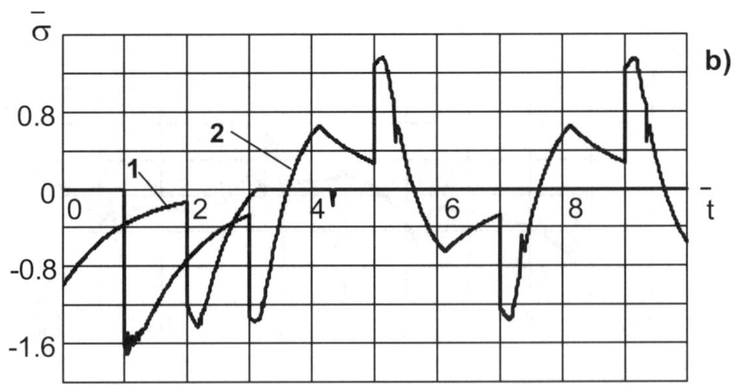

Fig.8.14. A rod of an elastic-plastic material impacted by a rigid body; relative yield point $\overline{\sigma}_y$: *a)* $\overline{\sigma}_y = 0.5$, *b)* $\overline{\sigma}_y = 1.5$; 1) $\overline{\sigma}_1^-$, 2) $\overline{\sigma}_n^+$

With $\overline{\sigma}_y < 1$ the level of stress decreases considerably. With $1 < \overline{\sigma}_y < \overline{\sigma}_{e.\max}$ initial shock stresses do not change, however, the peak quantities are truncated. From Fig.8.14 and also from Shorr (1995), in which a detail pattern of the stress wave propagation in an elastic-plastic rod was studied, it follows that the leading elastic wave has the magnitude of the undeformed material yield point. The waves connected with plastic hardenning and subsequent unloading caused by the decreasing of the striking body velocity travel with lower speeds.

Three zones of plastic strain (see Fig.8.14a) can be extracted: A - at the free end directly after the initial shock, B - at the clamped end during the first reflection of the compression wave, C - at the same place during the reflection of the tensile wave. In spite of the fact that the absolute value of stresses are significantly less up to this time, they are higher than the current value of yield point which decreases with stress sign alternation because of the Bauschinger's effect.

8.4 Influence of Contact Deformation on Impact Response

Experimental impact investigations show that the real stress in an elastic rod increases not so sharply as indicated in previous presented diagrams. The most probable cause is a local compliance enhancement of contact surfaces of the colliding bodies. This effect can be approximately taken into account including the additional local compliance in boundary conditions, as was proposed by Sears (1908).

8.4.1 Basic Equations

***8.4.1.1.* A.** The experimental relationship $u_c = f(F_c)$ of an elastic contact deformation u_c with a force F_c is nonlinear, and can be described by Hertz' formula. Linearizing it within some range of the force, one put

$$\Delta u_c = \alpha_c \Delta F_c \,, \qquad (8.25)$$

where the contact compliance coefficient α_c is assumed to be constant.

In doing so, α_c is equivalent to the compliance of an elastic spring of stiffness $\beta_c = 1/\alpha_c$. Exploiting DMM, the value of α_c can change for each calculation step; so, there are no difficulties in using any arbitrary nonlinear function $u_c = f(F_c)$. Below, only the first linear section of this function is taken into account. Due to the definition of a one-side contact, a compression force must be $F_c \geq 0$.

B. Problem 8.7. A one-side clamped rod impacted by a rigid body accounting contact compliance. In this case, due to contact compliance, a striking rigid body and the left end $j = 1$ of an elastic rod will additionally come together at

$$\Delta u_c = (v_{M,m} - v_1^-)\Delta t\,, \tag{8.26}$$

where the condition of contact during a time Δt is assumed to be true. As this takes place, the contact force changes from $F_{c,0}$ at the step beginning to F_c at its finish. The mean force value is $F_{c,m} = F_{c,0} + 0.5\Delta F_c$, where $\Delta F_c = F_c - F_{c,0}$, and must be equal to the rod boundary force $F_{c,m} = F_1^-$.

Adding these conditions to the equations of Subsect.8.1.1, we may determine the mean contact force

$$F_{c,m} = \frac{\rho c A(v_{M,0} - v_{1,0}) - F_{1,0} + F_{c,0}\gamma_c}{1 + 0.5\gamma + \gamma_c}, \tag{8.27}$$

where $\gamma_c = 2n\overline{\alpha}_c$.

Here, $\overline{\alpha}_c = \alpha_c EA/L$ is the relative contact compliance. With growth of the element number, $\gamma_c \to \infty$ and the force $F_{c,m} \to F_{c,0}$, i.e., the rate of this force is as small as to approximate continuous change. The new value of contact force is $F_c = F_{c,0} + \Delta F_c$. Repeated impacts after body rebounds may be analyzed by the same procedure FBC as we have described above.

8.4.1.2. Using a graph-analytical procedure, Biderman and Maljukova (1964) solved the problem of an elastic rod impacted by a rigid body accounting contact compliance. They took the striking body-rod mass ratio $\overline{\mathrm{M}} = 0.886$ and very large relative compliance $\overline{\alpha}_c = \alpha_c EA/L = 1.352$.

Figure 8.15 demonstrates results of the DMM calculation of the contact stress $\overline{\sigma}_1^-$ and clamped end stress $\overline{\sigma}_n^+$ versus time $\bar{t} = tc/L$ for $\alpha_c = 0$, for the given compliance, and more moderate value of $\overline{\alpha}_c = 0.1352$.

Softening of the impact due to contact deformation eliminates stress peaks and decreases maximum stress values. The striking mass rebounds at the moment $\bar{t}_* = 4.72$ with the velocity $\bar{v}_r = -0.998$; i.e., the energy expenditure for the remainder rod oscillations, with the given elastic contact case, is very small.

The rebound ignoring the contact deformation might have occurred

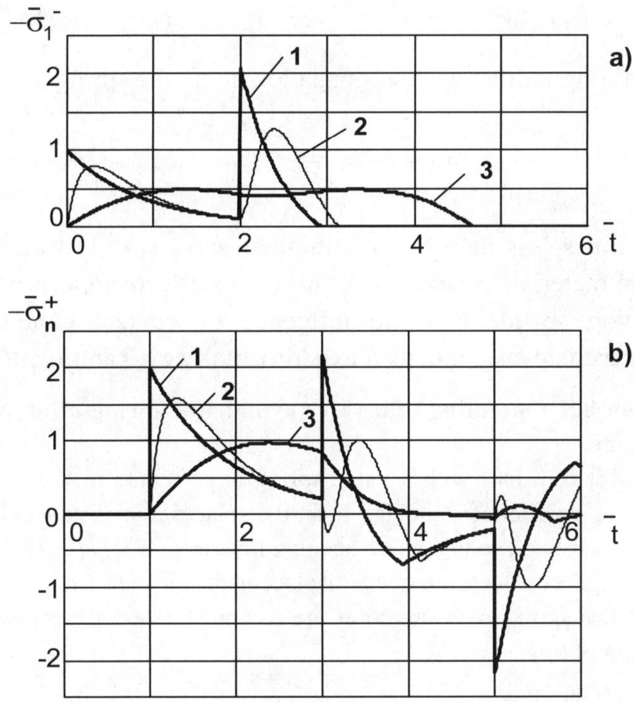

Fig.8.15. Influence of the contact compliance on the stresses in an impacted rod for compliances: 1) $\overline{\alpha}_c = 0$, 2) $\overline{\alpha}_c = 0.1352$, 3) $\overline{\alpha}_c = 1.352$; *a)* $\overline{\sigma}_1^-$; *b)* $\overline{\sigma}_n^+$

earlier at $\bar{t}_* = 2.96$ and the velocity would be of $\overline{v}_r = -0.698$.

The DMM evaluation of the contact stress $\overline{\sigma}_1^-$ closely coincides with the above-cited results but gives a more reliable pattern of stress $\overline{\sigma}_n^+$ evolution than the more complex graph-analytical solution.

8.4.2 Impact Loading of a Valve Cylindrical Spring

8.4.2.1. The DMM approach may be applied to the approximate calculation of a cylindrical spring dynamics, replacing the spring by an equivalent prismatic rod of the same length, mass, and stiffness, see Biderman (1952). Let D be the mean spring diameter, d the wire diameter, i the number of operating coils, and s the coil step. The spring mass is $M_{sp} = \pi\rho D i A_{sp}$ and its axis compliance is $\alpha_{sp} = \pi D^3 i / 4GJ_{sp}$, where A_{sp} and J_{sp} are the wire cross-sectional area and polar moment of inertia, respectively. Then, the equivalent rod parameters are

$$L_{eq} = si,\ \ A_{eq} = \pi D^2 / 4,\ \ \rho_{eq} = 4\rho A_{sp} / Ds,\ \ E_{eq} = 16GJ_{sp}s / \pi^2 D^5. \quad (8.28)$$

The speed of longitudinal wave propagation along the spring

$$c_{eq} = \sqrt{\frac{E_{eq}}{\rho_{eq}}} = \frac{sd}{\pi D^2}\sqrt{\frac{G}{2\rho}} \quad (8.29)$$

is about 1000 times less than the longitudinal wave speed in a prismatic rod of the same material. Hence, the spring wave effects appear even with moderate loading speeds and the influence of contact conditions is therewith weaker that was confirmed experimentally by Ramsauer (1909).

8.4.2.2. Problem 8.8. Operating of a valve cylindrical spring of an internal-combustion engine.

A. A sketch of a camshaft with a valve spring is presented in Fig.8.16a. The cam has parabolic profile of a height h and displaces the distance l with a circumference velocity v_{cr}, so that valve opening time is $t_{cr} = v_{cr} / l$.

The cam-spring contact relative displacement $\tilde{u}_x = u_x / h$ and velocity $\tilde{v}_x = v_x / v_{x,\max}$ in the spring axis direction are assumed to be described by the following function of time $\tilde{t} = t / t_{cr}$

$$\tilde{v}_x(\tilde{t}) = \begin{cases} \tilde{t} / \tilde{t}_1 \ \text{ with } \ 0 \le \tilde{t} \le \tilde{t}_1, \\ (1 - 2\tilde{t})/(1 - 2\tilde{t}_1) \ \text{ with } \ \tilde{t}_1 \le \tilde{t} \le 1 - \tilde{t}_1, \\ -(1 - \tilde{t}) / \tilde{t}_1 \ \text{ with } \ 1 - \tilde{t}_1 \le \tilde{t} \le 1 \end{cases} \quad (8.30)$$

where t_1 is an arrival time of maximum valve velocity $v_{x,\max}$.

As the velocity v_x changes gradually, the impact is relatively soft. Neglecting the influence of previous impacts, the spring is assumed to be initially at rest.

Taking into account the spring preloading F_{pr}, the initial conditions become

$$v_{j,in}(x,0) = 0,\ \ F_{j,in}(x,0) = F_{pr},\ \ u_{j,in} = 0. \quad (8.31)$$

The varying boundary conditions at the cam-spring contact face over time step *i,* taking into account a local contact compliance α_c are

$$v_{x,m} = v_1^- + \frac{\Delta u_c}{\Delta t},\ \ F_{x,m} = F_1^-, \quad (8.32)$$

where $v_{x,m}$ is the mean value of valve velocity, $F_{x,m}$ is the mean contact force during the current time interval Δt, and $\Delta u_c = 2\alpha_c(F_{x,m} - F_{x,0})$ is the additional contact displacement. The opposite spring end is assumed to be fixed. To calculate the contact force $F_{x,m}$, it is sufficient to put $\gamma = 0$ and change $v_{\mathrm{M},0}$ to $v_{x,0}$ in Eq.(8.27).

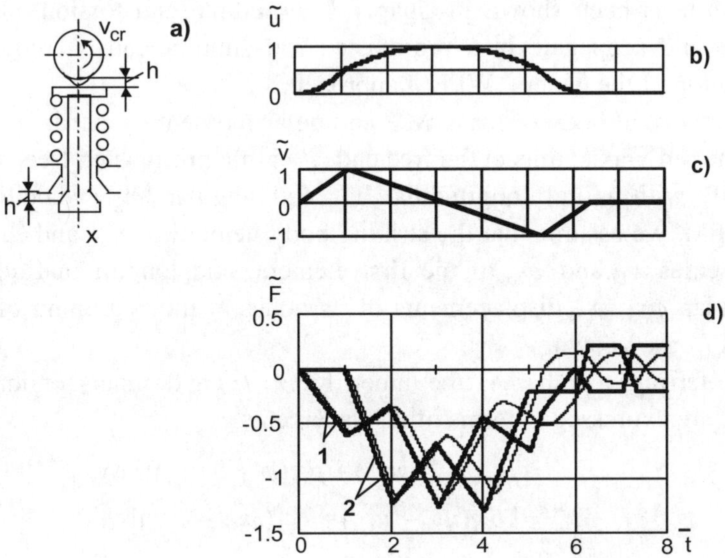

Fig.8.16. A sketch of a cam/spring interaction –a), and dynamic parameters of a valve spring vs. time $\bar{t}$: b) displacement $\tilde{u}$, *c*) velocity $\tilde{v}$, *d*) forces $\tilde{F}$; 1) $\tilde{F}_1^-$, 2) $\tilde{F}_n^+$

B. For numerical example, the valve/spring quantities are taken according to Makushin (1952). A change of the contact cam-spring face displacement $\tilde{u}$ and velocity $\tilde{v}$ versus time $\bar{t}$ are displayed in Fig.8.16b,c, respectively. Fig.8.16d shows the time evolution of the forces $\tilde{F}_1^-$ and $\tilde{F}_n^+$ at the spring ends without contact compliance and pre-loading (bold curves), where $\tilde{F} = F / F_{st}$ and $\bar{t} = t / T$. The thin lines correspond to the moderate contact compliance of $\bar{\alpha}_c = 0.1$. After the cam departure at $\bar{t} = 6.39$, a few residual oscillations of the spring are seen. To avoid a valve opening without pressure from the cam, the pre-load must not be less than $\tilde{F}_{pr} = 0.23$. These results are in good agreement with the more laborious graphic solution of Makushin (1952).

8.5 A Pre-Twisted Rod Impacted by a Rigid Body

8.5.1 Impact Interaction of a Rigid Body with a Pre-Twisted Rod

8.5.1.1. A rigid body is assumed to impact a uniformly pre-twisted rod of constant two-symmetrical cross section.

As it as been shown in Chap.4, longitudinal and torsion elastic wave arise and propagate in a pre-twisted rod simultaneously, requiring exploitation of the general WFEM approach.

Let a rigid body of mass M_B and polar moment of inertia I_{pB}, referred to the rod x-axis, impact the free end $j=1$ of a pre-twisted free-fixed rod at $t=0$, with initial longitudinal $v_{B,in}$ and angular $\omega_{B,in}$ velocities. Using WFEM, we assume that the striking body velocities $v_{B,0}$ and $\omega_{B,0}$, just as velocities $v_{1,0}$ and $\omega_{1,0}$ of the first element, and longitudinal $u_{1,0}$, $u_{2,0}$ and angular $\varphi_{1,0}$, $\varphi_{2,0}$ displacements of its nodes at the beginning of a current step t_i, are known.

Referring to Chap.4, the inner force $F_{1,0}$ and inner torsion moment $M_{1,0}$ are expressed in terms of displacements as

$$\left.\begin{aligned} F_{1,0} &= [\beta_{11}(u_{2,0}-u_{1,0})+\beta_{12}(\varphi_{2,0}-\varphi_{1,0})]/\Delta x, \\ M_{1,0} &= [\beta_{21}(u_{2,0}-u_{1,0})+\beta_{22}(\varphi_{2,0}-\varphi_{1,0})]/\Delta x \end{aligned}\right\}. \tag{8.33}$$

The coefficients β_{ij} are clarified in Chap.4. The boundary force F_1^- and torsion moment M_1^- are connected to relevant quantities by usual equations

$$\left.\begin{aligned} F_1^- &= -F_{1,0} + \rho A(v_1^- - v_{1,0})\Delta x/\Delta t_i, \\ M_1^- &= -M_{1,0} + \rho J_p(\omega_1^- - \omega_{1,0})\Delta x/\Delta t_i \end{aligned}\right\}. \tag{8.34}$$

The mean force $F_{B,m}$ and the mean moment $M_{B,m}$ applied to the striking body during the time interval Δt_i, under body to rod interaction, must be taken as

$$F_{B,m} = -F_1^-, \quad M_{B,m} = -M_1^-, \tag{8.35}$$

and the mean body velocities $v_{B,m}$ and $\omega_{B,m}$ are

$$v_{B,m} = v_1^-, \ \omega_{B,m} = \omega_1^-. \tag{8.36}$$

The laws of striking body momentum and angular momentum conservation in a short time Δt_i yield

$$\mathrm{M}_B \Delta v_B = F_{B,m}\Delta t_i, \quad \mathrm{I}_{pB}\Delta\omega_B = M_{B,m}\Delta t_i, \tag{8.37}$$

where

$$\Delta v_B = 2(v_{B,m} - v_{B,0}), \quad \Delta\omega_B = 2(\omega_{B,m} - \omega_{B,0}) \tag{8.38}$$

are changes in the relevant velocities in a time Δt_i.

Substituting Eqs.(8.35)-(8.38) into Eqs.(8.34), we obtain

$$v_1^- = \frac{\rho A\Delta x v_{1,0} + F_{1,0}\Delta t_i + 2\mathrm{M}_B v_{B,0}}{\rho \mathrm{A}\Delta \mathrm{x} + 2\mathrm{M}_\mathrm{b}}, \tag{8.39}$$

and

$$\omega_1^- = \frac{\rho J_p \Delta x \omega_{1,0} + M_{1,0}\Delta t_i + 2\mathrm{I}_{pB}\omega_{B,0}}{\rho J_p \Delta x + 2\mathrm{I}_{pB}}. \tag{8.40}$$

Determining the work

$$\Delta W_1 = (F_1^- v_1^- + M_1^- \omega_1^-)\Delta t_i \tag{8.41}$$

introduced to the rod from the striker, we can calculate the value of the current time interval Δt_i exploiting the standard WFEM procedure.

8.5.1.2. Further, the usual dimensionless quantities

$$\bar{v} = v / v^o, \ \bar{\omega} = \omega / \omega^o, \ \bar{F} = F / F^o, \ \bar{M} = M / M^o$$

are used where, with reference to Eq.(4.20),

$$\left.\begin{aligned} v^o = \omega^o r_p, \ F^o = \rho A c_v v^o, \ M^o = \rho J_p c_v \omega^o, \\ r_p = \sqrt{J_p / A}, \ c_v = \sqrt{E/\rho}, \ \bar{x} = x / r_p, \ \bar{t} = t c_v / r_p \end{aligned}\right\}. \tag{8.42}$$

Exploiting these expressions, Eqs.(8.39)-(8.40) are transformed to

$$\bar{v}_1^- = \frac{\bar{v}_{B,0} + 0.5\gamma_\mathrm{M}(\bar{v}_{1,0} + \bar{F}_{1,0}\Delta\bar{t}_i / \Delta\bar{x})}{1 + 0.5\gamma_\mathrm{M}}, \tag{8.43}$$

and

$$\bar{\omega}_1^- = \frac{\bar{\omega}_{B,0} + 0.5\gamma_\mathrm{I}(\bar{\omega}_{1,0} + \bar{M}_{1,0}\Delta\bar{t}_i / \Delta\bar{x})}{1 + 0.5\gamma_\mathrm{I}}, \tag{8.44}$$

where

$$\gamma_\mathrm{M} = (\bar{\mathrm{M}}_B n)^{-1}, \ \gamma_\mathrm{I} = (\bar{\mathrm{I}}_{pB} n)^{-1}, \ \bar{\mathrm{M}}_B = \mathrm{M}_B / \rho A L, \ \mathrm{I}_{pB} = \mathrm{I}_{pB} / \rho J_p L. \tag{8.45}$$

Now, substituting Eqs.(8.43)-(8.44) into Eqs.(8.34) written in nondimensional terms, we find the contact force and moment in the forms

$$\bar{F}_1^- = \frac{(\bar{v}_{B,0} - \bar{v}_{1,0})\Delta\bar{x} / \Delta\bar{t}_i - \bar{F}_{1,0}}{1 + 0.5\gamma_\mathrm{M}}, \tag{8.46}$$

and

$$\overline{M}_1^- = \frac{(\overline{\omega}_{B,0} - \overline{\omega}_{1,0})\Delta\overline{x} / \Delta\overline{t}_i - \overline{M}_{1,0}}{1 + 0.5\gamma_{\mathrm{I}}} . \tag{8.47}$$

To ensure a smooth character of the body velocity change, the number of elements n must be chosen so that the parameters γ_{M} and γ_{I} satisfy the conditions

$$\gamma_{\mathrm{M}} << 1, \ \gamma_{\mathrm{I}} << 1 \tag{8.48}$$

To complete the posing of the impact problem, conditions of the striking body to the rod contact behavior must be formulated. The simplest assumption implies that both the longitudinal and torsion contacts are tight as it has been taken above in Eqs.(8.36).

Two impact types are considered below: i) an impact in the lengthwise direction and ii) a turning impact about the rod axis.

Internal and external damping are neglected.

8.5.2 Lengthwise and Turning Impacts

***8.5.2.1.* Problem 8.9. A free-fixed pre-twisted rod of an elongated rectangular cross section impacted lenghtwise by a rigid body.**

The initial conditions are assumed to be

$$\overline{v}_{B,in} = 1, \ \overline{\omega}_{B,in} = 0 . \tag{8.49}$$

Equations (8.43) – (8.47) are valid as far as the contact force remains compressive, i.e., accounting the sign rule,

$$\overline{F}_1^- > 0 . \tag{8.50}$$

If a calculated value of $\overline{F}_1^-$ at any time step becomes negative, we put simultaneously $\overline{F}_1^- = 0$ and $\overline{M}_1^- = 0$ and determine the velocities from Eqs.(8.36) as

$$\left.\begin{aligned} \overline{v}_1^- &= \overline{v}_{1,0} + \overline{F}_{1,0}\Delta\overline{t}_i / \Delta\overline{x}, \\ \overline{\omega}_1^- &= \overline{\omega}_{1,0} + \overline{M}_{1,0}\Delta\overline{t}_i / \Delta\overline{x} \end{aligned}\right\}, \tag{8.51}$$

while the striker velocities $\overline{v}_B$ and $\overline{\omega}_B$ remain constant during this step.

Possible repeated impacts are described using the FBC procedure (see

Sect.8.1) applied to the analysis of the gap change in the longitudinal direction. The behavior of torsion moment and deformation depends on the ratio of the striker/body moment of inertia $\bar{I}_{pB}$. We shall confine ourselves to its limit cases of $\bar{I}_{pB}$<<1 and $\bar{I}_{pB}$>>1.

The influence of the pre-twist is dictated by the characteristic parameter β (see Sect.4.1) that is determined for a rod of a length L with rectangular cross section of sides $h \times b$ by the expression

$$\beta = \varphi_{in} \frac{b^2}{Lh} \sqrt{\frac{1+\mu}{30}}, \tag{8.52}$$

where φ_{in} is a full pre-twisting angle along the rod length L.

Stress in the pre-twisted rod is distributed over the cross-sectional area nonuniformly. The maximum normal stress $\sigma_{\max}$ under tension or compression occurs at the cross section center and can be calculated from the mean value σ_m as $\sigma_{\max} = K_0 \sigma_m$, where for a rectangular cross section

$$K_0 = 1 + 1.25\beta^2 /(1+\beta^2). \tag{8.53}$$

Equations (8.52)-(8.53) will be treated later. The other stress components can be also calculated using expressions for pre-twisted rods, see Vorob'ev and Shorr (1983).

***8.5.2.2.* A.** Let the rotational inertia of a striking body be negligibly small in comparison with the rod inertia, $\bar{I}_{pB}$<<1, or in the limit $\gamma_{\mathrm{I}} \to \infty$.

We see from Eqs.(8.37),(8.38),(8.46), and (8.49) for this case

$$\bar{\omega}_{B,m} = \bar{\omega}_1^- = \bar{\omega}_{1,0} + \overline{M}_{1,0} \Delta\bar{t}_i / \Delta\bar{x}, \quad \overline{M}_{B,m} = \overline{M}_1^- = 0, \tag{8.54}$$

i.e., the contact face of the pre-twisted rod is free in rotation. However, the coupling of longitudinal and torsion deformations caused by pre-twist is conserved, and the striker rotates following the left end of the rod.

The relative maximum compressive stress $-\bar{\sigma}_1^-$, at the contact face, and $-\bar{\sigma}_n^+$, at the fixed end, versus relative time $\tilde{t} = tc_v / L$ (scaled by the rod length L) are displayed in Fig.8.17a,b, respectively. In this Figure we assume that $\overline{\mathrm{M}}_B = 1$, $\gamma_{\mathrm{M}} = 0.01$, $\lambda_p = L / r_p = 10$, and the side ratio of rectangular cross section is $\bar{h} = 0.1$.

Only the stresses induced by the longitudinal force and determined by Eq.(8.53) are shown.

The curves in Fig.8.17 correspond to the three values of the pre-twist parameter β. As a whole, the normal stress evolution in time for pre-

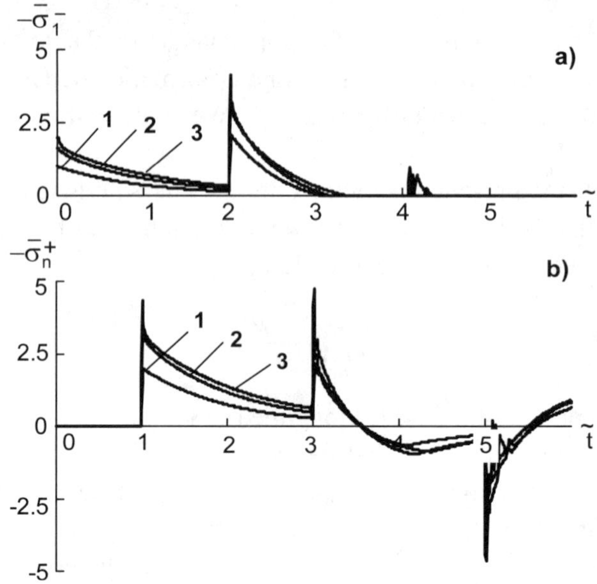

Fig.8.17. Compressive stresses $\overline{\sigma}_1^-$ and $\overline{\sigma}_n^+$ in a pre-twisted rod impacted lengthwise by a rigid body for different β : 1) $\beta = 0$, 2) $\beta = 1$, 3) $\beta = 2$

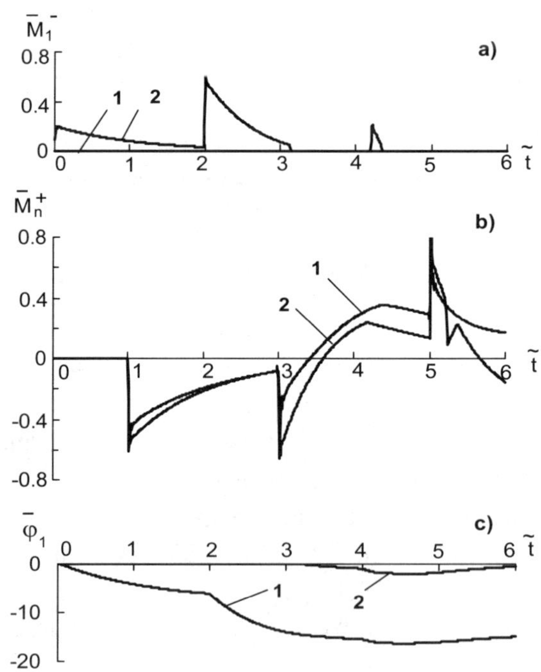

Fig.8.18. Torsion moments $\overline{M}_1^-$, $\overline{M}_n^+$, and angular displacement $\overline{\varphi}_1$ in a pre-twisted rod impacted lengthwise by a rigid body; 1) $\overline{I}_{pB} << 1$, 2) $\overline{I}_{pB} >> 1$

twisted rod including the repeated impact is similar to the untwisted one; however, the maximum magnitude of the impact stress is significantly greater.

B. Now, the rotational inertia of a striking body is far greater than the rod inertia, $\bar{\mathrm{I}}_{pB}$>>1, or in the limit $\gamma_{\mathrm{I}} \to 0$.

The left boundary of the rod, along with the striking body, does not rotate, $\overline{\omega}_B = \overline{\omega}_1^- = 0$; and the boundary moment, due to Eq.(8.47), is

$$\overline{M}_1^- = -(\overline{M}_{1,0} + \overline{\omega}_{1,0}\Delta\bar{x} / \Delta\bar{t}_i)\,. \tag{8.55}$$

The torsion moments and angular displacements behave differently depending on striker/rod inertia ratio $\bar{\mathrm{I}}_{pB}$. Time dependence of the contact moment $\overline{M}_1^-$, the moment $\overline{M}_n^+$ at the fixed end, and the angular displacement $\overline{\varphi}_1$ versus time are shown in Fig.8.18a,b,c, respectively, with the pre-twist parameter $\beta = 2$ and two limit quantities of $\gamma_{\mathrm{I}} \to 0$ and $\gamma_{\mathrm{I}} \to \infty$.

With small rotating inertia of the striking body ($\gamma_{\mathrm{I}} \to \infty$, curves 1), the contact moment is absent and the angle $\overline{\varphi}_1$ quickly increases.

With large striker rotating inertia ($\gamma_{\mathrm{I}} \to 0$, curves 2), the contact moment increases at once, while the angular displacement appears only after the body rebound.

The shock wave of the torsion moment propagates with the same speed as the longitudinal force.

***8.5.2.3.* Problem 8.10. A free-fixed pre-twisted rod subjected to a turning impact by a rotating rigid body.** Without concretely defining a mechanical model of a given problem, see Babitsky (1998), we assume that the striker/rod contact at the rod boundary (*j*=1) is provided by the turning movement of a rigid body with its initial conditions of

$$\bar{v}_{B,in} = 0,\ \overline{\omega}_{B,in} = 1\,. \tag{8.56}$$

In this case, the computation WFEM procedure remains the former, but interchanging the expressions of the longitudinal and torsion parameters.

The next example is carried out with $\bar{\mathrm{I}}_{pB} = 1$, $\overline{\mathrm{M}}_B << 1$ (in the limit, $\gamma_B \to \infty$), $\beta = 1$, *n*=50, $\bar{h} = 0.1$ .The calculation results referred to torsion moments $\overline{M}_1^-$, $\overline{M}_n^+$ and angular velocities $\overline{\omega}_B$, $\overline{\omega}_1^-$ are presented in Fig.8.19a,b, respectively.

In Fig.8.19a the curve 1 relates to the moment at the impacted end $\overline{M}_1^-$ and the curve 2 to the moment $\overline{M}_n^+$ at the fixed end.

In Fig.8.19b the curve 1 relates to the striker and the curve 2 to the impacted end of the rod.

A torsion wave is clearly seen propagating with a slow speed, passing the length of the rod in the time $\tilde{t} \approx 5.5$. This is close to ratio of $1/\bar{c}_\omega = 5.77$ referred to given parameters $\bar{h}$ and β. The impact duration before the striker rebound increases as much as the passing time; this is well illustrated by Fig.8.19b.

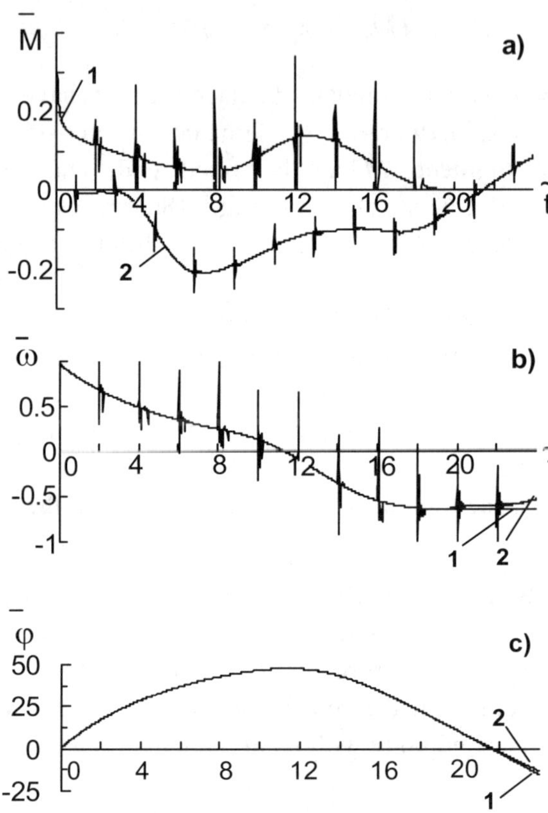

Fig.8.19. Torsional moments $\overline{M}_1^-$, $\overline{M}_n^+$ and angular velocities $\overline{\omega}_B$, $\overline{\omega}_1^-$ in a pre-twisted rod subjected to turning impact

Reflections of the fast longitudinal wave from the rod boundaries appear in the form of regularly repeated sharp spikes of moments and velocities.

9 Unsteady Forced Vibration of Solids

9.1 Wave Approach to Study of Forced Vibration

Using the wave approach, a diversity of unsteady (non-stationary, transient) dynamic processes in elastic and inelastic solids can be numerically simulated, including nonlinear problems.

9.1.1 Response of an Elastic Rod to Harmonic Excitation

9.1.1.1. **A**. Exploiting a dynamic model of a constant cross-sectional rod with free end at $x=0$ and fixed at $x=L$, its longitudinal natural frequencies (eigenfrequencies) are

$$f_k = \frac{kc}{4L}, \quad c = \sqrt{\frac{E}{\rho}}, \quad k = 1,3,... \tag{9.1a}$$

and the associated modes represented by displacements (eigenmodes) are

$$u_k(x) = u_k(0)\cos\frac{k\pi x}{2L}, \tag{9.1b}$$

where $u_k(0)$ is an arbitrary displacement at the free end.

The mode shapes represented by stresses relevant to Eq.(9.1b) are

$$\sigma_k(x) = E\frac{du_k(x)}{dx} = \sigma_k(L)\sin\frac{k\pi x}{2L}, \tag{9.2a}$$

where the stress $\sigma_k(L)$ at the fixed end is connected with the displacement $u_k(0)$ by expression

$$\sigma_k(L) = -\frac{\pi Ek}{2L}\sin\frac{\pi k}{2}u_k(0). \tag{9.2b}$$

When an undamped rod is subjected to a longitudinal forcing harmonic load

$$q_k(x,t) = q_k(x)\sin 2\pi ft, \tag{9.3}$$

with the distribution $q_k(x)$ analogous to the eigenmode function $u_k(x)$

$$q_k(x) = q_k(0)\cos\frac{k\pi x}{2L} \ , \tag{9.4}$$

the analytical solution of forced rod vibration takes the same form as for a one-degree-of-freedom system.

In the case of resonance excitation by the frequency $f = f_k$, amplitudes increase linearly in time with the increment of π for each oscillation period $T_k = 1/f_k$.

B. For resonance simulation by DMM, we use nodal external forces $F_{i,j}$ that approximate the forcing load by time/space step-wise function. For Eqs.(9.3)-(9.4) we take the nodal forces in a nondimensional form $\overline{F}_{i,j} = F_{i,j} / F_{st,k}$, where the reference static compressive load $F_{st,k}$ is

$$F_{st,k} = q_k(0)\int_0^L \cos\frac{k\pi x}{2L}dx = q_k(0)L\upsilon_k \ , \tag{9.5a}$$

where

$$\upsilon_k = \begin{cases} 1 & \text{with } k = 0, \\ 2/k\pi & \text{with } k = 1,5\ldots \\ -2/k\pi & \text{with } k = 3,7\ldots \end{cases} . \tag{9.5b}$$

Thus,

$$\overline{F}_{i,j} = \frac{1}{n\upsilon}\cos\frac{\pi k(j-1)\Delta\bar{x}}{2}\sin\frac{\pi\bar{f}(i-0.5)\Delta\bar{t}}{2} \ , \tag{9.6}$$

where $j = 2,3,\ldots,n$ is an index of the node, $i = 1,2,\ldots$ is an index of the time step, $\Delta\bar{x} = \Delta\bar{t} = 1/n$, and $\bar{f} = f/f_1$. Here, $f_1 = 0.25c/L$ is the first natural frequency of a cantilever rod. For the nodes $j = 1$ and $j = n+1$, half of the force value from Eq.(9.6) has to be taken.

The DMM solution is obtained by substitution of the nodal external forces from Eq.(9.6) into the governing equations of the method. Below, the initial conditions are assumed zero, $\bar{u}(\bar{x},0) = 0$, $\bar{v}(\bar{x},0) = 0$, and $\bar{\sigma}(\bar{x},0) = 0$, where $\bar{\sigma} = \sigma/\sigma_{st,k}$ with $\sigma_{st,k} = -F_{st,k}/A$.

9.1.1.2. **Problem 9.1. An initial phase of resonance stress development in a rod. A.** The four types of a rod harmonic loading taken below in numerical analysis are presented in Fig.9.1. Here, a) a load distribution associated with the first natural mode obtained from Eq.(9.1b) by k=1;

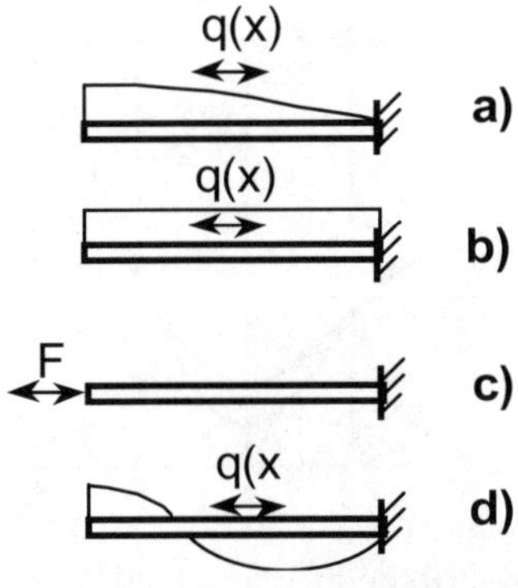

Fig.9.1. Sketches of harmonic loading applied to a rod

b) an evenly distributed load for which the index k in Eq.(9.4) must be put zero; c) a point force effected the free end; and d) a load distribution associated with the second natural mode obtained from Eq.(9.1b) by k=3. Damping is until neglected.

B. Time development of the resonance stress $\overline{\sigma}_n^+$ at the clamped end relevant to the first mode load distribution (Fig.9.1a) with exciting frequency $\overline{f} = 1$ is shown in Fig.9.2a. Fig.9.3 demonstrates a more detailed pattern for the initial phase, where stress distributions along the rod (Fig.9.3a) indicated for some time instants from $\overline{t} = 1$ to $\overline{t} = 6$ are associated in Fig.9.3b with stress change at the clamped end $\overline{x} = 1$ (line 1) and at the midpoint $\overline{x} = 0.5$ (line 2).

From these diagrams we can see that just from the rise the stress wave takes a form of a 'standing' wave, which is very close to the theoretical eigenmode described by Eq.(9.4) with k=1. As to the rate of the wave am-

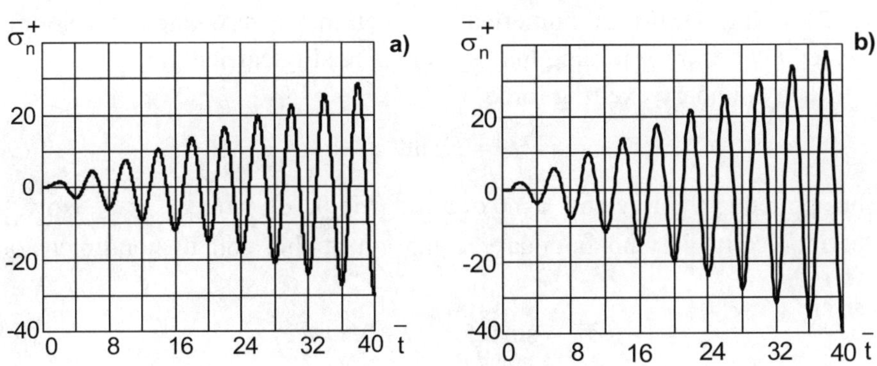

Fig.9.2. Development of resonance stresses in an undamped rod under harmonic · excitation; a) distributed forcing load, b) boundary forcing load

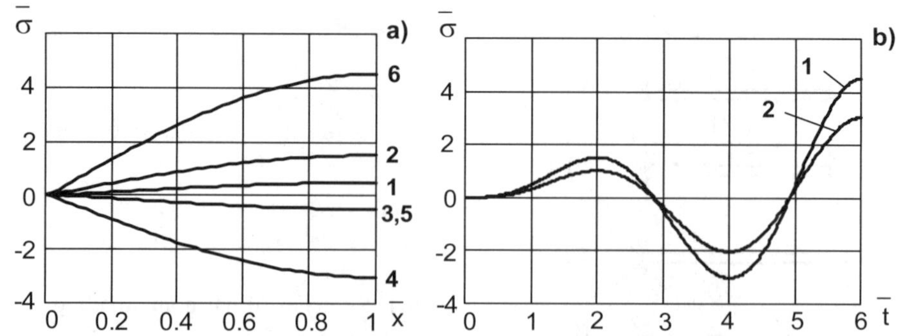

Fig.9.3. An initial phase of resonant process under distributed forcing load

plitude increase, $\Delta\bar{\sigma}_n^+ = \bar{\sigma}_n^+(\bar{t}+\bar{T}) - \bar{\sigma}_n^+(\bar{t})$ where the oscillation period is $\bar{T}=4$, it depends on the accuracy of the harmonic function step-wise approximation, i.e. on the number of elements. This trend is confirmed by data of the row a) of Table 9.1, where the increment $\Delta\bar{\sigma}_n^+$ given for some values of n approaches π.

Table 9.1. Stress amplitude increment $\Delta\bar{\sigma}_n^+$ depending on element number

Loading type from Fig.9.1	Number of elements n					
	10	25	50	100	200	400
a)	2.506	2.889	3.015	3.079	3.110	3.126
b)	3.270	3.746	3.873	3.937	3.968	3.984
c)	4.000					

C. Using DMM, a numerical simulation of resonance development under any arbitrary forcing load system is readily carried out.

Let a boundary exciting force

$$F_0(t) = F_0 \sin 2\pi f t \tag{9.7}$$

be applied to the free end $x=0$ of a rod (Fig.9.1c), while $F_0 < 0$. Now, the harmonically varying boundary condition at this end in nondimensional form is

$$\bar{\sigma}_1^- = \sin 0.5\pi \bar{f}(i-0.5)\Delta\bar{t}\,. \tag{9.8}$$

Time development of the resonance stress $\bar{\sigma}_n^+$ relevant to the frequency $\bar{f}=1$ is shown in Fig.9.2b. Stress and velocity distributions along the rod at certain times for the initial phase are presented in Fig.9.4a,c and as function of time in Fig.9.4b,d. The stresses refer to the clamped end (line 1) and mid-point (line 2), and the velocities - to the free end (line 1) and mid-point (line 2).

The stress and velocity waves induced by the boundary harmonic force are clearly seen to be traveling and are radically different from the previous ones. Therefore, it is of some interest to trace the course of the resonant amplification in the context of wave propagation.

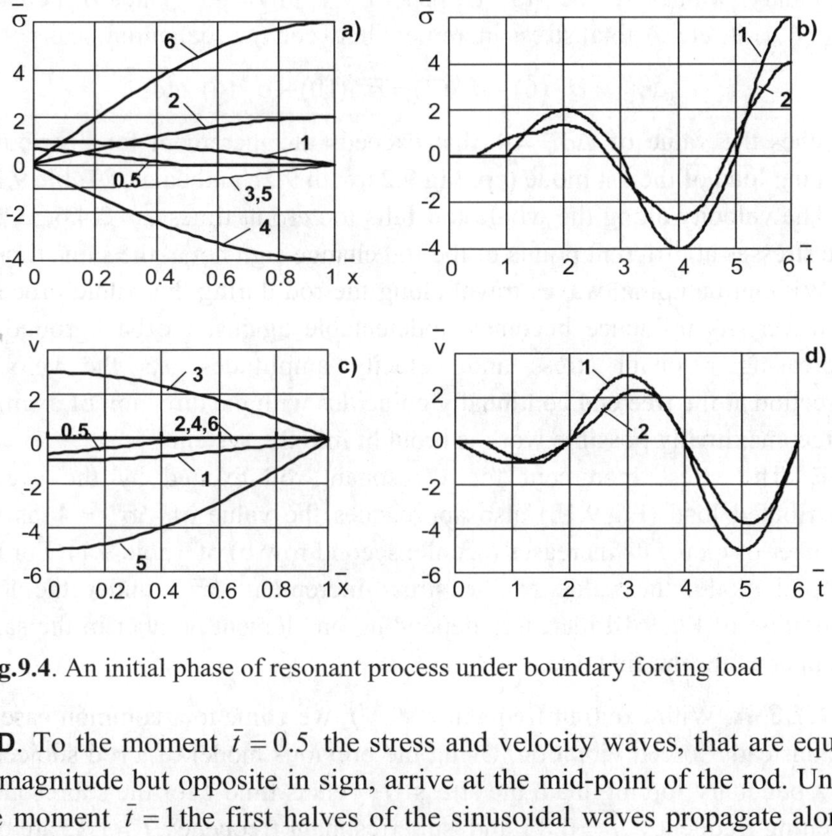

Fig.9.4. An initial phase of resonant process under boundary forcing load

D. To the moment $\bar{t} = 0.5$ the stress and velocity waves, that are equal in magnitude but opposite in sign, arrive at the mid-point of the rod. Until the moment $\bar{t} = 1$ the first halves of the sinusoidal waves propagate along the whole rod, the boundary values at the free end become $\bar{\sigma}_1^- = 1$, $\bar{v}_1^- = -1$, and beginning from this moment the waves are reflected from the clamped end. Within the interval $1 < \bar{t} < 2$, the leading fronts of the second halves of the direct waves also reach the clamped end; after their reflection from it, the stress at the fixed boundary increases to $\bar{\sigma}_n^+(2) = 2$ while the velocity drops to $\bar{v}_n^+(2) = 0$. If an external force at the free end were absent, the rod would be to the moment $\bar{t} = 3$ entirely unloaded while the velocity at the free border would become $\bar{v}_1^-(3) = 2$.

However, due to negative half of the forcing sinusoidal load action within the interval $2<\bar{t}<3$, the stress at the free end takes the value $\bar{\sigma}_1^-(3)=-1$, and the velocity increases to $\bar{v}_1^-(3)=3$.

The waves arrive a second time at the clamped boundary within the interval $3<\bar{t}<4$; Then, being reflected from it, the stress becomes $\bar{\sigma}_n^+(4)=-4$ and the velocity again drops to $\bar{v}_n^+(4)=0$. After repeating this process within the next two intervals $4<\bar{t}<5$ and $5<\bar{t}<6$, the boundary values come to $\bar{\sigma}_1^-(5)=1,$ $\bar{v}_1^-(5)=-5$ and $\bar{\sigma}_n^+(6)=6,$ $\bar{v}_n^+(6)=0$, etc. A total stress increment between the sequential peaks

$$\Delta\bar{\sigma}_n^+ = \bar{\sigma}_n^+(6)-\bar{\sigma}_n^+(2)=\bar{\sigma}_n^+(10)-\bar{\sigma}_n^+(6) \text{ etc,}$$

reaches the value of $\Delta\bar{\sigma}_n^+ = 4$ that exceeds the increment for distributed forcing load of the 1st mode (cp. Fig.9.2a with 9.2b and data of Table 9.1).

The velocity along the whole rod falls to zero at times $\bar{t}=2,4,6,...$, but the stresses at different points of the rod change sign not at the same time.

Without damping, waves travel along the rod during the whole process; however, its influence becomes undetectable against the background of increasing resonant stress and velocity amplitudes. As the velocity direction at the free end continually coincides with the direction of exciting force, maximally possible work is brought into the system.

E. The stress increment for a resonant rod excited by the evenly distributed load (Fig.9.1b) also approaches the value of $\Delta\bar{\sigma}_n^+ = 4$ as the number of elements increases (see the second row b) of Table 9.1). For the second mode, the value of the stress increment $\Delta\bar{\sigma}_n^+$ under the load condition of Fig.9.1d increases depending on element number in the same manner as for the first one.

9.1.1.3. **A**. With exciting frequency $\bar{f} \neq f_k$ we come to a common case of an unsteady forced vibration. Using the previous model of a rod subjected to a boundary forcing load, the stress $\bar{\sigma}_n^+$ versus time $\bar{t}$ for the subresonant exciting frequency $\bar{f}=0.85$ and superresonant frequency $\bar{f}=1.15$ are displayed in Fig.9.5a,b, respectively. The stress growth is bounded and the typical beating phenomenon is seen.

B. In many cases there is no necessity to display each time a full oscillogram. An amplitude curve, i.e. an envelope that unites the absolute values of extreme points of functions or their maxima, fairly completely describes a non-stationary process. Below, the envelope of any oscillation function will be noted by the same letter.

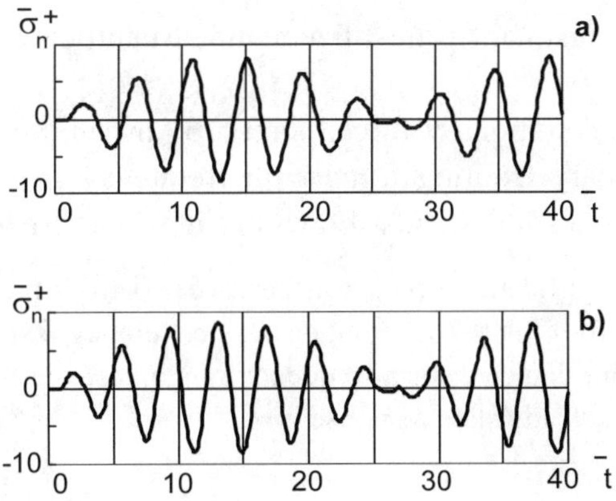

Fig.9.5. Development of stress forced oscillation in an undamped rod; a) $\bar{f} = 0.85$, b) $\bar{f} = 1.15$

To include the external viscous friction into a computational model, a term $\overline{F}_j = -\overline{\eta}\Delta\overline{x}\overline{v}_j$ must be added in Eq.(2.2) as that has been done in Chap.2. Here, $\overline{\eta} = \eta L / \rho c A$ is the nondimensional viscous coefficient per unit length of a rod.

In the case of constant forcing load amplitude, the value of the nondimensional stress determined as $\overline{\sigma} = \sigma / \sigma_{st}$ coincides for $\bar{t} \to \infty$ with the standard stress amplification factor $\xi_\sigma = \sigma / \sigma_{st}$, which, in turn, is connected with a logarithmic decrement δ by expression

$$\xi_\sigma = \pi / \delta \,. \tag{9.9}$$

In the most interesting engineering applications of damping, the influence of external linear viscous friction on resonance frequencies can be ne-

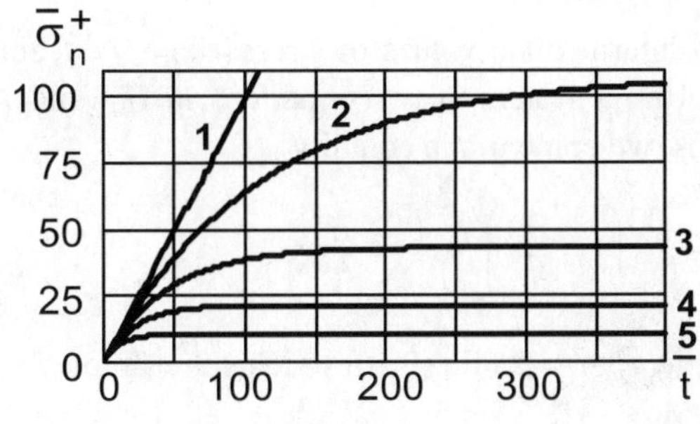

Fig.9.6. Establishment of steady-state vibration under boundary forcing load with external viscous friction; 1) $\overline{\eta} = 0$, 2) $\overline{\eta} = 0.02$, 3) $\overline{\eta} = 0.05$, 4) $\overline{\eta} = 0.1$, 5) $\overline{\eta} = 0.2$

glected and the first resonant time of a damped cantilever rod remains $\bar{t} \approx 4$.

Establishment of the stationary forced stress $\bar{\sigma}_n^+$ over time $\bar{t}$ calculated in respect of a boundary exciting force with frequency $\bar{f} = 1$ for various values of the viscous coefficient $\bar{\eta}$ is shown in Fig.9.6 where $\delta < 0.3$.

C. The resonance amplification effect can be revealed from the outset of the excitation as it is seen from Fig.9.7 where the stress envelopes $\bar{\sigma}_n^+(\bar{t})$, referred to marked time instants, are depicted for a frequency range near the first resonance. A white dot refers to the steady state response.

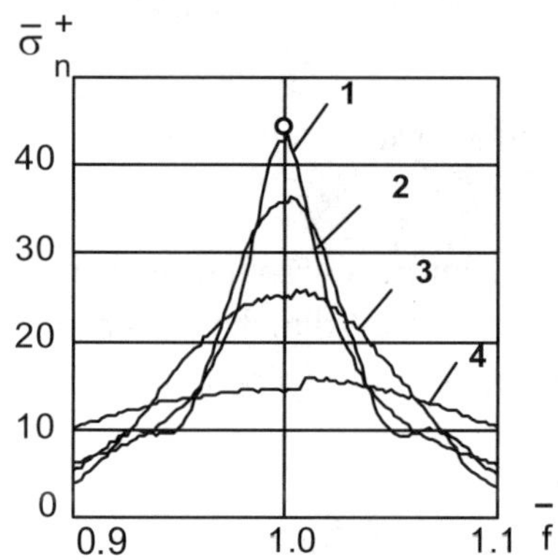

Fig.9.7. Unsteady stress response referred to time instants $\bar{t}$:

The intermediate envelopes allow us to find the preliminary resonance domains in a particular frequency range without solving an eigenvalue problem. Moreover, the established resonance stress magnitude $\bar{\sigma}_\infty$ can also be approximately evaluated taking into account that the curve trend in Fig.9.6 is close to exponential and may be approximated by the function

$$\bar{\sigma}(\bar{t}) = \bar{\sigma}_\infty[1 - \exp(-\kappa\bar{t})]. \tag{9.10a}$$

Calculating the two intermediate values of stress $\bar{\sigma}_1 = f(\bar{t}_1)$ and $\bar{\sigma}_2 = f(\bar{t}_2)$, we obtain from Eq.(9.10a) a system of two equations in $\bar{\sigma}_\infty$ and κ. Eliminating κ from these equations, we come to the equality

$$\left(1 - \frac{\bar{\sigma}_1}{\bar{\sigma}_\infty}\right)^{t_2} = \left(1 - \frac{\bar{\sigma}_2}{\bar{\sigma}_\infty}\right)^{t_1}. \tag{9.10b}$$

For the particular ratio $\bar{t}_2 / \bar{t}_1 = 2$, Eq.(9.10b) yields the simple formula

$$\bar{\sigma}_\infty = \frac{\bar{\sigma}_1^2}{2\bar{\sigma}_1 - \bar{\sigma}_2}. \tag{9.10c}$$

For example, taking from Fig.9.7 the two points $\overline{\sigma}_1(20)=15.9$ and $\overline{\sigma}_2(40)=25.9$ corresponding, respectively, to $\overline{t}=20$ and $\overline{t}=40$ we obtain $\overline{\sigma}_\infty=42.6$ while the limit stress value calculated on the base of more than 100 periods (at $\overline{t}=300$) is about $\overline{\sigma}_\infty=43.9$ (see white dot in Fig.9.7).

Notice, that a visible jump in the curves in Fig.9.7 at the frequency range of $\overline{f}=1.002-1.009$ is provoked by a change of peak quantity to unity within the time $\overline{t}$ chosen.

9.1.2 Response of a Rod of Inelastic Material

9.1.2.1. Using the algorithms of Chap.3, resonance response to harmonic excitation of structures with various inelastic material properties can be readily simulated.

Problem 9.2. An initial phase of resonance stress and strain development in a structure of inelastic material. The previous model of a fixed-free rod subjected to a boundary forcing load is considered to illustrate peculiarities of the wave approach to this problem.

Equation (9.8) describes a harmonic varying boundary load at the free end independently from material behavior. The boundary condition at the clamped end $\overline{v}^+_{n,*}=0$ leads to the boundary stress

$$\overline{\sigma}^+_n=(\overline{\sigma}_{n,0}-\overline{v}_{n,0}-\psi)/(1+\varphi), \tag{9.11a}$$

where inelastic coefficients φ and ψ have been determined in Chap.3.

The change in the inelastic strain $\Delta\overline{\varepsilon}_{n,c}$ of the border element $j=n$ due to Eq.(3.13a) is

$$\Delta\overline{\varepsilon}_{n,c}=2(\overline{\sigma}^+_n\varphi+\psi). \tag{9.11b}$$

As in nondimensional terms we have $\overline{\sigma}=\overline{\varepsilon}$, a full deformation change is $\Delta\overline{\varepsilon}_n=\Delta\overline{\sigma}+\Delta\overline{\varepsilon}_{n,c}$. The sequential results are presented in the form of the stress-time evolution graphs and stress-strain diagrams for some initial periods of forced vibration under the first resonance frequency $\overline{f}=1$.

***9.1.2.2.* A. A rod of a Maxwell viscoelastic material.** In this case, due to Eqs.(3.29) and (3.23b),

$$\varphi=\frac{\Delta t}{2\tau_c},\ \psi=0,$$

where $\tau_c=\eta_c/E$ is the relaxation time.

Time development of the resonance stress at the clamped end is shown in Fig.9.8a, while a stress-strain diagram for the last element is built in Fig.9.8b. It is assumed that $\overline{\tau}_c = \tau_c c / L = 5$ and the number of elements $n = 25$. The thin lines are referred to the strong elastic material. The stress-strain loops are very close to an ellipse.

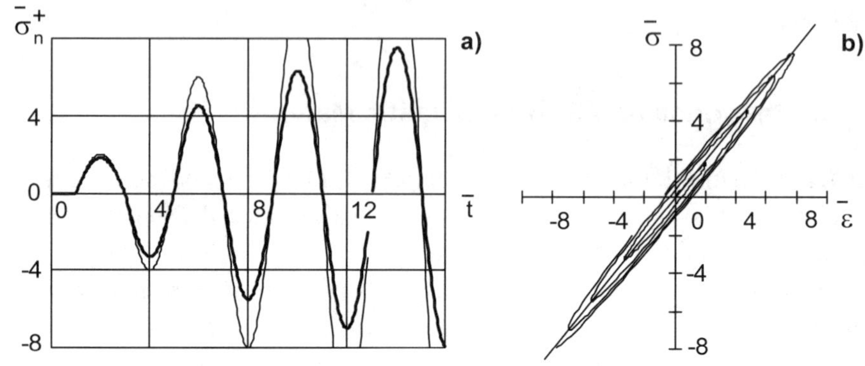

Fig.9.8. Development of resonance stress in a rod of viscoelastic material

B. A rod of elastic-plastic material with kinematic hardening. Its behavior is described by both the inelastic coefficients φ and ψ depending, due to Eqs.(3.44), on an initial yield point $\overline{\sigma}_y = \sigma / \sigma_0$ and the relative modulus $\overline{E}_a = E_a / E$ of plastic kinematic hardening.

Calculation results of resonance stress development at the same points as previous for $\overline{\sigma}_y = 5$ and $\overline{E}_a = 0.1$ are presented in Fig.9.9. Some analogous points in Fig.9.9a and 9.9b are depicted with the same numerical indexes. The process remains elastic before the maximum stress reaches the value of the yield limit $\overline{\sigma}_y$ (point 4). Then, peaks of stress oscillogram are 'cut off' and oscillation becomes rapidly steady-state.

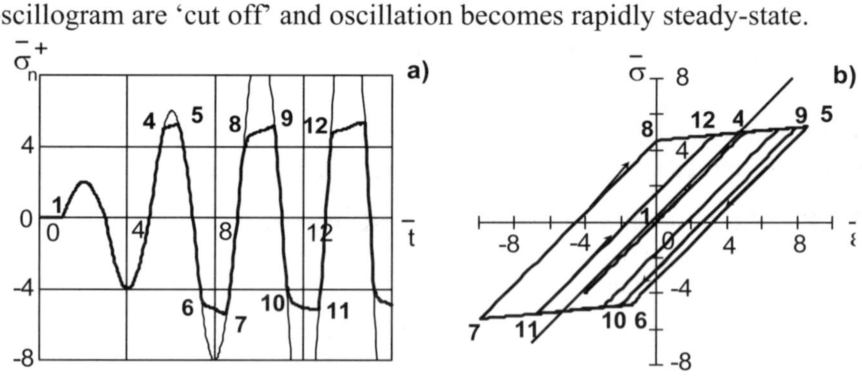

Fig.9.9. Development of resonance stress in a rod of elastic-plastic material

C. A rod of a material with hysteretic damping. A phenomenological theory, making it possible to describe an arbitrary unsteady dynamic process in a hysteretic material, has been proposed by Shorr (1989). This approach is based on the assumption that an experimental curve of stress-inelastic strain beginning from the each point of loading reverse has a constant character for a given hysteretic material. This dependence is approximated by the nonlinear function $\bar{\varepsilon}_c = \bar{B}\bar{\sigma}^m$ where $m \geq 2$.

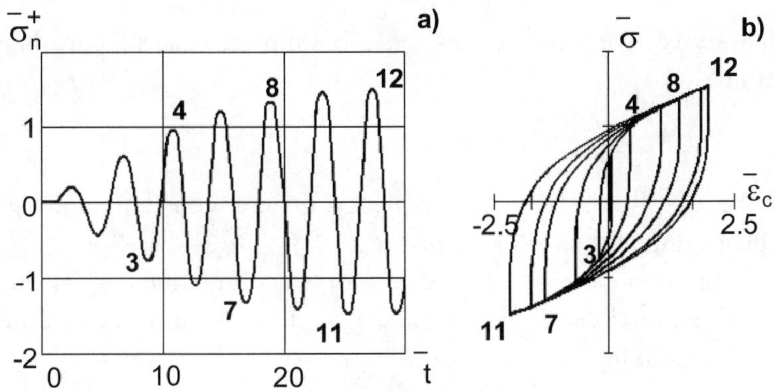

Fig.9.10. Development of resonance stress in a rod of hysteretic material

Calculations are carried out, as usual for nonlinear processes, by successive approximation.

The result of the DMM application to the problem considered is shown in Fig.9.10, where $\bar{B} = 0.0114$ and $m = 3.5$; unlike the previous diagrams, only an inelastic strain $\bar{\varepsilon}_c$ is plotted to the x-coordinate in Fig.9.10b. In the given case, vibration becomes steady-state and the loops are closed to the 6th -7th cycles, as damping parameters are severe. Inner hysteretic nonlinear damping reproduces the real dynamic material behavior more adequately than a model of linear viscous friction usually exploited in calculations; however, hysteretic simulation is significantly more laborious.

9.1.3 Transition through Resonance Domains under Quasi-Harmonic Excitation

Transition of an elastic body through a resonance domain treated in a number of publications is usually applied to discrete systems. Transient processes within distributed systems are experienced significantly less.

9.1.3.1. Let the forcing load be quasi-periodical

$$F_0(t) = F_a(t)\sin\phi(t)\,, \tag{9.12}$$

where $F_a(t)$ is a slowly altering amplitude and $\phi(t)$ is a rapidly changing phase angle. The current circular frequency is determined as

$$\omega(t) = 2\pi f(t) = \frac{d\phi}{dt}\,. \tag{9.13}$$

In the above, we have considered the simplest case of pure harmonic excitation

$$F_0(t) = F_a \sin(\omega t + \phi_{in})\,, \tag{9.14}$$

where the amplitude F_a and frequency ω are constant, and ϕ_{in} is an initial phase angle; thus $\phi(t) = 2\pi f t + \phi_{in}$.

In the common case, approximating arbitrary functions $F_a(t)$ and $\phi(t)$ by step-wise functions $F_{a,m}(t_{im})$ and $\phi_m(t_{im})$ relevant to the middle point of a step *i*, i.e. taking

$$\int_{t_i}^{t_i+\Delta t} F_a(t_i)dt \approx F_{a,m}(i-0.5)\Delta t \quad \text{and} \quad \int_{t_i}^{t_i+\Delta t} \phi(t_i)dt \approx \phi_m(i-0.5)\Delta t\,,$$

where $t_{im} = (i-0.5)\Delta t$, we can numerically attack by DMM any unsteady behavior of a system.

In particular, for a constant force amplitude F_a and linearly altering frequency

$$\left.\begin{aligned} f(t) &= f_{in} + vt \\ \phi(t) &= 2\pi(f_{in} + 0.5vt)t + \phi_{in} \end{aligned}\right\}. \tag{9.15}$$

Nondimensional frequency $\bar{f}(\bar{t})$ and force $\bar{F}_{i,j}$ applied in a time step *i* to a node *j* are expressed for $\phi_{in} = 0$ as

$$\bar{f} = \bar{f}_m + 0.25vt \tag{9.16a}$$

and

$$\bar{F}_{i,j} = \bar{F}_j \sin\{0.5\pi[\bar{f}_{in} + 0.125\bar{v}(i-0.5)\Delta\bar{t}](i-0.5)\Delta\bar{t}\}\,, \tag{9.16b}$$

where the relative frequency rate is $\bar{v} = v/f_1^2 = 16v(L/c)^2$.

***9.1.3.2.* Problem 9.3. A fixed-free rod excited by a transient quasi-harmonic load.** A load is assumed to be distributed along the rod in accordance with sketches of Fig.9.1a,b and d. Vibration is damped by inner viscous friction.

A. Let the forcing frequency increase from $\bar{f}_{in} = 0.9$ to $\bar{f}_{fin} = 3.4$ in relative time $\bar{t} = 160$ that corresponds to the frequency rate of $\bar{\nu} = 0.015625$. The number of elements is taken as n=25 and the relaxation time $\bar{\tau}_c = 10$.

In Fig.9.11 curve 1 relates to the even load distribution which excites all the natural oscillation modes, curve 2 corresponds to the first natural mode

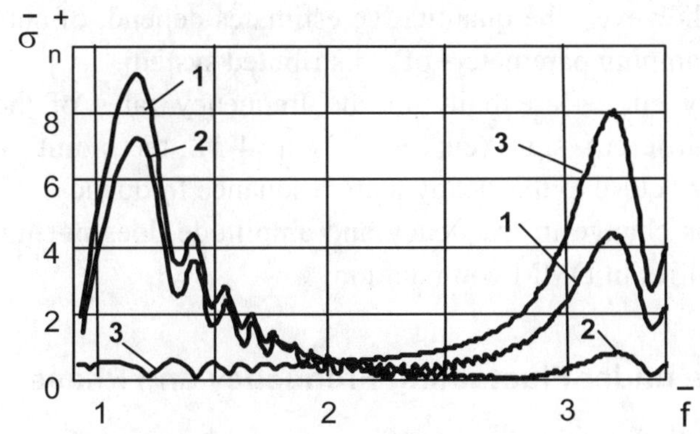

Fig.9.11. Stress response of a rod excited by the differently distributed quasi-harmonic loads with the frequency rate of $\bar{\nu} \approx 0.016$

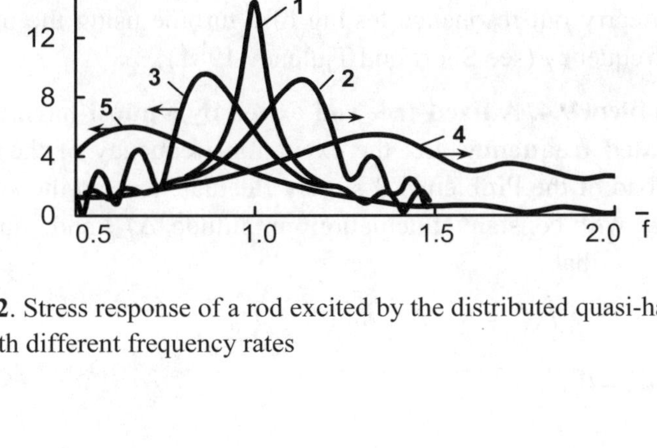

Fig.9.12. Stress response of a rod excited by the distributed quasi-harmonic load with different frequency rates

($\bar{f}_1 = 1$) and curve 3 to the second mode ($\bar{f}_2 = 3$). These two last forcing load distributions excite only their 'own' modes, as may be clearly seen from the diagram and is implied by the theory of vibration.

B. Consider now unsteady stress response to quasi-harmonic excitation with different frequency rates. The rate direction can be positive ($\bar{\nu} > 0$) or negative ($\bar{\nu} < 0$). The load distribution is taken to be similar to the first mode (see Fig.9.1a).

In Fig.9.12 curve 1 relates to the constant resonance frequency $\bar{f} = 1$ ($\bar{\nu} = 0$), curves 2 and 3 to the moderate frequency rate $\bar{\nu} = \pm 0.01$, and curves 4 and 5 to the higher frequency rate $\bar{\nu} = \pm 0.05$.

Qualitatively, the transient response pattern is like the ordinary one for a discrete system, however, the quantitative estimates depend, of course, on the forcing and damping parameters of a distributed system.

If the unsteady curves are built for the frequency rates of the same magnitude but different sign (curves 2-3 or 4-5), the point of their intersection is very close to the steady-state resonance frequency.

A simultaneous change in frequency and amplitude does not introduce additional difficulties in DMM computation.

9.1.4 Response under Fluctuating Frequency and Phase

In engineering, frequency and phase of forcing loads are in number of situations not stable but slowly fluctuating within some borders around the bases resonance parameters.

As an example, fluctuation of rotation speed of an engine at an operating regime can be named. Because individual machine units (e.g., turbine blades) sometimes have a significant scatter of natural frequencies, it is advisable to carry out resonance testing of a turbine using the method of 'swinging' frequency (see Shorr and Tjulenev 1981)

9.1.4.1. **Problem 9.4. A fixed-free rod exited by a quasi-harmonic load with fluctuated frequency.** Let the excitation frequency of the unsteady distributed load of the Problem 9.3 slowly fluctuate around the *k*th natural frequency f_k with constant 'fluctuation' amplitude Δf_{fl} and 'fluctuation' frequency f_{fl} so that

$$f(t) = f_1 + \Delta f_{fl} \sin(2\pi f_{fl} t)\,. \tag{9.17}$$

Then for $\phi_{in} = 0$

$$F(t) = F_a \sin\left\{2\pi\left[f_k t - \frac{\Delta f_{fl}}{2\pi f_{fl}}\cos(2\pi f_{fl} t)\right]\right\} \tag{9.18a}$$

and in nondimensional terms

$$\bar{F}_{i,j} = \bar{F}_j \sin[0.5\pi \bar{f}_k \bar{t} - B_{fl}\cos(0.5\pi \bar{f}_{fl}\bar{t})], \tag{9.18b}$$

where $\bar{f}_{fl} = f_{fl}/f_1$, $\Delta\bar{f} = \Delta f_{fl}/f_1$ and $B_{fl} = \Delta\bar{f}_{fl}/\bar{f}_{fl}$.

Below, it is taken $k = 1$, i.e. $\bar{f}_1 = 1$.

Changes in the stress envelop $\bar{\sigma}_n^+$ versus time $\bar{t}$ and versus the current forcing frequency $\bar{f} = 1 + \Delta\bar{f}_{fl}\sin(0.5\pi\bar{f}_{fl}\bar{t})$ for two fluctuation variants $\Delta\bar{f}_{fl} = 0.05$, $\bar{f}_{fl} = 0.04$ (curves 2) and $\Delta\bar{f}_{fl} = 0.1$, $\bar{f}_{fl} = 0.06$ (curves 3) are displayed in Fig.9.13a and 9.13b, respectively. The forcing frequencies $\bar{f}(\bar{t})$ for these variants are also depicted in Fig.9.13a. Curves 1 show stress response for constant exciting frequency $\bar{f} = 1$ with the same inner viscous friction of $\bar{\tau}_c = 10$.

After some fluctuation periods, steady state loop-wise cycles of stress are established. Their configuration does not depend on the way, in which the loop has been arrived at. The wider a fluctuation range $\Delta\bar{f}_{fl}$ and the greater a ratio $\bar{f}_{fl}$ are, the smaller is the maximum loop stress in comparison with the stable resonance peak.

Numerical experience of a ramp frequency fluctuation described by Shorr and Mel'nikova (1988) has shown an analogous result.

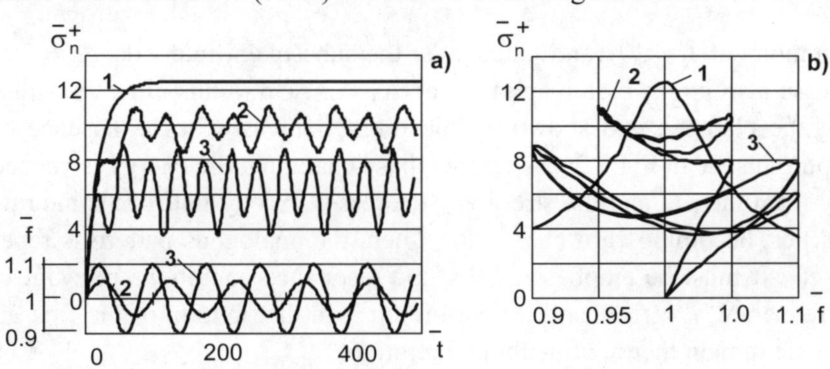

Fig.9.13. Stress response of a rod excited by the load with frequency fluctuated around the first eigenfrequency

9.1.4.2. Energy delivery to a system under resonance conditions is provided by coincidence of the phases of forcing loads and body velocities at the points the forces are applied. The solution of the next problem demonstrates what occurs if this coincidence is temporarily violated.

Problem 9.5. A fixed-free rod excited by a quasi-harmonic load with suddenly changed phase. At any instant $\bar{t} = \bar{t}_*$, the phase $\phi(\bar{t}) = 0.5\pi\bar{f}\bar{t}$ of the distributed harmonic forcing load $q(\bar{x},\bar{t}) = q(\bar{x})\sin 0.5\pi\bar{f}\bar{t}$ is assumed to suddenly jump by a magnitude of $\Delta\phi = \pi$. This leads to sudden sign change of the forcing load that becomes $q(\bar{x},\bar{t}) = -q(\bar{x})\sin 0.5\pi\bar{f}\bar{t}$, with $\bar{t} \geq \bar{t}_*$.

In Fig.9.14 the line 1 depicts the stress in the first element of the rod that changes in a similar manner as the external distributed forcing load. At the

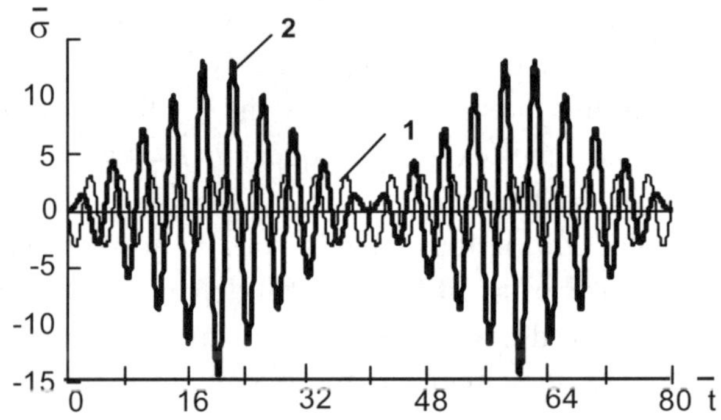

Fig.9.14. Decrease of resonance stress in an undamped rod at $\bar{f} = 1$ caused by phase alternation

given moment $\bar{t}_* = 20$ (and latter, over the subsequent intervals $\Delta\bar{t}_* = 20$) its phase also jumps by a magnitude of $\Delta\phi = \pi$. Up to this time, the stress $\bar{\sigma}_n^+$ at the clamped end shown by the line 2 increases in the absence of damping just as in Fig.9.2a. After the phase changing, the energy is carried away from the rod and the stress $\bar{\sigma}_n^+$ decreases exactly with the same rate as earlier, becoming zero at $\bar{t} = 40$. Then, the analogous pattern is repeated etc. It must be emphasized that the resonance conditions relevant to the frequency $\bar{f} = \bar{f}_1 = 1$ and to the forcing load distribution of the first eigenmode remain therewith without alteration.

Figure 9.15 brings out this phenomenon in a damped rod with the relaxation time of $\bar{\tau}_c = 10$. Here, an envelope of the curve 1 relates to exciting with an uninterrupted phase, while the envelope of the curve 2 to the suddenly alternating phase with intervals of $\Delta\bar{t}_* = 16$. In the latter case, the ascending/descending branches of the 'resonance' curve 2 are not identical and the energy loss because of damping is compensated by the work input into the system.

An exciting phase violation is exploited in some axial compressors to weaken rotating blades vibration provoked by air wakes from stator vanes. To this goal, the vanes are arranged with different circumferential steps (Tjulenev VN 1981)). The expected efficiency of this setting is usually evaluated by steady-state spectrum analysis of the exciting force distribution. If the vane step alters twice per rotor round, so that each phase lag is equal to π, the steady-state exciting harmonic, due to vane number, drops to zero. However, the nonstationary analysis presented above intimates that some resonance stresses can be progressing within each of exciting half-cycles.

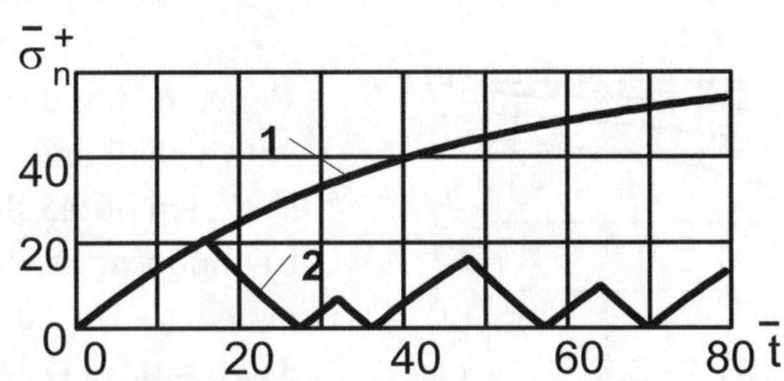

Fig.9.15. Stress response of a damped rod at $\bar{f} = 1$ called by phase alternation

9.2 Unsteady Forced Vibration of Nonlinear Systems

9.2.1 Torsional Vibration of a Shaft with a Nonlinear Clutch

For decreasing unsteady dynamic loads transmitting by shafts from drivers to executive units, nonlinear elastic clutches of different types are widely exploited. The response analysis of these systems is usually carried out making use of their schematization by discrete models of one/two degree-of-freedom, see Mitropol'sky (1955) and also Goloskokov and Philippov (1977).

Below, interesting peculiarities of unsteady dynamics of trans-mission with distributed mass and stiffness, in application to a shaft-nonlinear clutch system, are studied using the DMM approach.

***9.2.1.1.* A. Problem 9.6. A transmission section including a shaft with a nonlinear elastic clutch.** A transmission section consists of a shaft connected at the right end with a nonlinear elastic clutch (Fig.9.16a). The shaft is loaded at the left end by a quasi-harmonically varying torque

$$M(t) = M_0 \sin \phi(t) \tag{9.19}$$

and is damped by distributed torsion moment of viscous friction

$$m_c(x,t) = -\eta_c \omega(x,t), \tag{9.20}$$

where ω is a dynamic angular velocity of the shaft at a point x. Only the

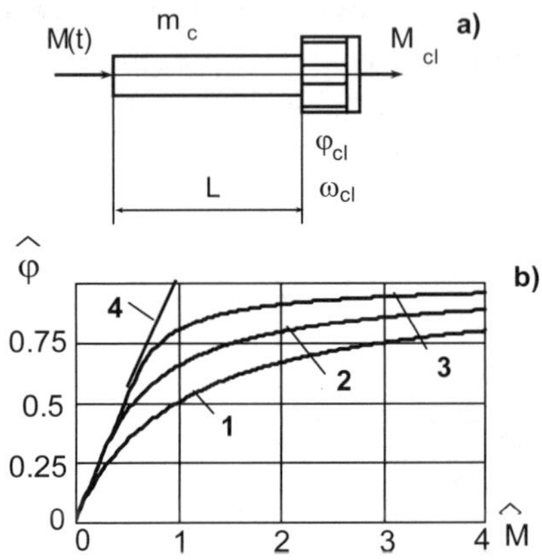

Fig.9.16. A transmission section with a shaft and elastic clutch; a) sketch of the shaft, b) nonlinear characteristic of the clutch; 1) $\hat{M}_l = 0$, 2) $\hat{M}_l = 0.2$, 3) $\hat{M}_l = 0.5$, 4) $\hat{M}_l = 1$

dynamic components of shaft moving and deformation will be considered in the following analysis.

Inertia of other transmission parts is assumed to be as much great that the varying velocity component ω_{cl}^{+} as far as dynamic rotation angle φ_{cl}^{+} at the external clutch face can be taken zero. Then, the elastic angular displacement of the clutch interacting parts is $\varphi_{cl} = \varphi_{cl}^{+} - \varphi_{cl}^{-} = -\varphi_{cl}^{-}$, where φ_{cl}^{-} is the clutch rotation angle at its face connected to the right end of the shaft.

Let a forcing frequency $f(t)$ linearly alter in a time t_* from an initial value f_{in} to any given magnitude f_* and later remain constant. In this case

$$f(t) = \begin{cases} f_{in} + \nu t & \text{with} \quad t \le t_*, \\ f_* & \text{with} \quad t \ge t_* \end{cases}. \tag{9.21}$$

Then

$$\phi(t) = \begin{cases} 2\pi(f_{in} + 0.5\nu t)t & \text{with} \quad t \le t_*, \\ \phi_* + 2\pi f_*(t - t_*) & \text{with} \quad t \ge t_* \end{cases}, \tag{9.22}$$

where $\phi_* = \phi(t_*)$ and $\nu = (f_* - f_{in})/t_*$.

In the general case, the clutch angular displacement φ_{cl} nonlinearly depends on the clutch moment $\varphi_{cl}(M_{cl})$. An additional friction moment $M_{cl,c} = -\eta_{cl}\omega_{cl}$ simulating the clutch damping effect is assumed to be applied to the right end of the shaft.

B. The governing DMM equations of torsional wave propagation taken in corresponding terms remain the same as for the longitudinal waves. The specific clutch-to-shaft boundary conditions at the right node of the element $j = n$, due to Fig.9.16a, are

$$\omega_n^+ = \omega_{cl,m}^-, \quad M_n^+ = M_{cl,m} + M_{c\Sigma} \,, \tag{9.23}$$

where $M_{cl,m}$ and $\omega_{cl,m}^-$ are mean values of the clutch moment and velocity with respect to time step Δt; and $M_{c\Sigma} = -(0.5\eta_c\Delta x + \eta_{cl})\omega_n^+$ is a total friction moment. The DMM usual assumption ($\omega_n^+ =$ const. over each calculation step) yields $\Delta\varphi_n^+ = \omega_n^+\Delta t$ with $\Delta\varphi_n^+ = \Delta\varphi_{cl}^- = -\Delta\varphi_{cl}$.

Taking into account the governing equations of Chap.2 and scaling all the quantities by the amplitude of the forcing torque M_0, we come to a system of nonlinear algebraic equations

$$\left.\begin{aligned} \omega_n^+ &= (\omega_{n,0} - M_{n,0} + M_{cl,m})/(1+\eta_\Sigma), \\ \varphi_{cl} &= \varphi_{cl,0} - \omega_n^+\Delta t, \\ M_{cl,m} &= M_{cl,m}(\varphi_{cl,0}, \varphi_{cl}) \end{aligned}\right\}, \tag{9.24}$$

where $\varphi_{cl,0}$ and φ_{cl} are the angles at the beginning and termination of the current step, respectively, and $\eta_\Sigma = 0.5\eta_c\Delta x + \eta_{cl}$. For notational simplicity, bars over scaled quantities are henceforth omitted.

The system (9.24) has to be solved at each computational step.

Applying Eqs.(9.24) to an elastic clutch with linear characteristic, when $\varphi_{cl} = \alpha_0 M_{cl}$, $\alpha_0 = \text{const}$ we obtain

$$\omega_n^+ = \frac{\omega_{n,0} - M_{n,0} + M_{cl,0}}{1 + \eta_\Sigma + 0.5\beta_0\Delta}, \tag{9.25}$$

where $\beta_0 = 1/\alpha_0$ and $M_{cl,0} = \beta_0\varphi_{cl,0}$.

New clutch moment is

$$M_{cl} = 2[M_{n,0} - \omega_{n,0} + (1+\eta_\Sigma)\omega_n^+] - M_{cl,0}. \tag{9.26}$$

The clutch-to-shaft boundary conditions in the nonlinear characteristic case can be satisfied by sequential approximation, realized by some substeps starting from the known value $M_{cl,0}$.

9.2.1.2. **A.** To improve accuracy of the numerical analysis, a typical clutch nonlinear characteristic shown in Fig.9.16b was presented in Shorr and Mel'nikova (1988). by the analytical function

$$\hat{\varphi} = \begin{cases} \hat{M} \text{ with } 0 \le \hat{M} \le \hat{M}_l, \\ (\hat{M} - \hat{M}_l^2)/(1 - 2\hat{M}_l + \hat{M})^2 \text{ with } \hat{M}_l \le \hat{M} \le \infty \end{cases} . \tag{9.27}$$

Here, $\hat{\varphi} = |\varphi_{cl}| / \varphi_{cl,\lim}$ where $\varphi_{cl,\lim}$ is a limit magnitude of the clutch angular displacement and $\hat{M} = |M_{cl}| / M_{cl,\lim}$ where $M_{cl,\lim} = \beta_0 \varphi_{cl,\lim}$. The quantity $\hat{M}_l$ bounds a linear characteristic domain with compliance coefficient $\alpha_0 = 1/\beta_0$ if the limit domain takes place. The uninterrupted pass conditions from point $\varphi_{cl,0}$ to φ_{cl} guarantee an accurate satisfaction of conservation laws at every finite time step independently of its magnitude.

B. Consider at first the system behavior within the domain of linear clutch characteristic, $\hat{\varphi}_{cl} = \hat{M}_{cl} \le 1$. A value of the ratio $\bar{\alpha}_0 = \alpha_0 / \alpha_{st} = 3$. where $\alpha_{st} = L / GJ_p$ is the static shaft compliance in torsion, is taken for calculation. The eigenfrequencies of the shaft with adjoined clutch are governed by the characteristic equation $\bar{\alpha}_0 \lambda \tan \lambda = 1$ with $\lambda = 0.5\pi \bar{f}$. For $\bar{\alpha}_0 = 3$ this yields $\bar{f}_1 = 0.3483$ and $\bar{f}_2 = 2.066$. Thus, the elastic clutch of $\bar{\alpha}_0 = 3$ sets the operation range $0.4 < \bar{f} < 2$ free from elevated dynamic loads. The dynamic load in this region is affected by the frequency rate and system damping.

The moment $\bar{M}_{cl}$ at the clutch referred to the frequency rate $\bar{\nu} = 0.002$ for some friction coefficients $\bar{\eta}_{cl}$ is depicted in Fig.9.17. Within the domain of the shaft/clutch resonance $(\bar{f} \approx 0.4 \div 0.45)$, the moment $\bar{M}_{cl}$ steadily decreases with

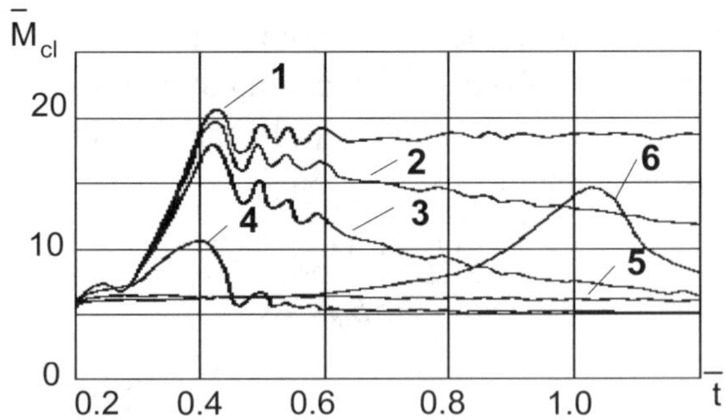

Fig.9.17. Unsteady response diagram of a linear clutch for the frequency rate $\bar{\nu} = 0.002$; damping coefficients: 1) $\bar{\eta}_{cl} = 0$, 2) $\bar{\eta}_{cl} = 10^{-3}$, 3) $\bar{\eta}_{cl} = 10^{-2}$, 4) $\bar{\eta}_{cl} = 10^{-1}$, 5) $\bar{\eta}_{cl} = 1$, 6) $\bar{\eta}_{cl} = 10$

damping growth to the static value that is given by $\overline{M}_{st} = 5$ (curves 1 to 5). However, as clutch damping becomes too great, the first resonance of the system shifts to the value of $\bar{f} \to 1$ and the moment $\overline{M}_{cl}$ begins significantly rising again (curve 6).

Note that the energy, being accumulated by the undamped or weakly damped system under resonance transition (curves 1 and 2), can support in what follows intensive oscillations over a wide frequency range.

C. For analysis of shaft with a nonlinear clutch behavior, the parameters $\overline{\alpha}_0 = 3$, $\overline{M}_{cl,\lim} = 100$, and $\widehat{M}_l = 0.05$ are taken below.

Figure 9.18 demonstrates response of the clutch moment $\overline{M}_{cl}$ to the forcing frequency $\bar{f}$ linearly increasing up to some value $\bar{f}_*$ and then remaining constant at this value. The frequency alters in both directions with the same rate magnitude of $\overline{\nu} = \pm 2 * 10^{-4}$ that are indicated by thin lines I and II, for which the frequency changes monotonously.

Computational results referred to given parameters show:

i) With stopping frequency $\bar{f}_* < \bar{f}_{1*}$, where $\bar{f}_{1*} \approx 0.37$ is the first 'critical' frequency, the steady oscillations are established upon a higher stable branch of the response curve (a line marked with round dots) independently of the direction of previous frequency altering, as it is depicted by arrows A and B.

ii) With stopping frequency $\bar{f}_* > \bar{f}_{2*}$, where $\bar{f}_{2*} \approx 0.39$ is the second 'critical' one, the steady oscillations are always established upon a bottom stable branch (a line with quadratic marks, the arrow C).

iii) Within the region $\bar{f}_{1*} < \bar{f}_* < \bar{f}_{2*}$, the level of steady oscillations depends on the direction of the frequency arrival at $\bar{f}_*$. If this comes from above, the oscillations are fixed upon the bottom branch, however, in the case of the frequen-

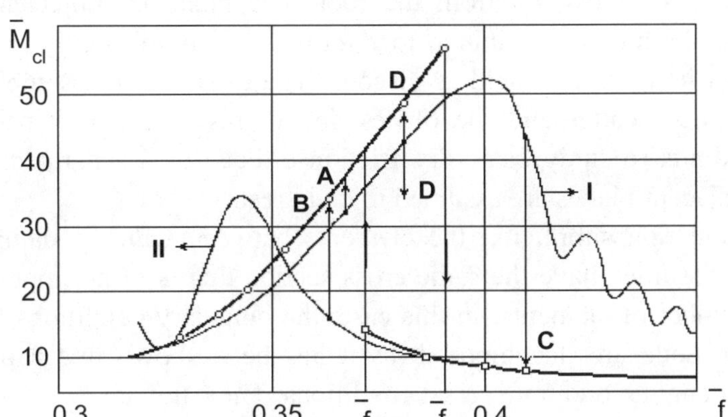

Fig.9.18. Response diagram of a nonlinear clutch: steady (bold lines) and unsteady with frequency rate $\overline{\nu} = \pm 0.0002$ (thin lines)

cy arriving from below, its further locus may by different, being effected first of all by the magnitude of the frequency rate.

For each value of stopping frequency $\bar{f}_*$, a 'critical' value of previous frequency rate $\bar{\nu}_*$ exists, such that at $\bar{\nu} < \bar{\nu}_*$ oscillations come nearer to the higher branch, while when $\bar{\nu} > \bar{\nu}_*$ they drop to the bottom one (arrows D). This magnitude $\bar{\nu}_*$ correlates with the intermediate unsteady branch of the nonlinear response curve. However, investigations of Shorr and Mel'nikova (1988, 1996) reveal that under some combinations of forcing torque phase and frequency rate very narrow domains of anomalous system behavior can exist when oscillations relax to the bottom branch jet in the case $\bar{\nu} < \bar{\nu}_*$.

9.2.2 Bending Vibration of a Turbine Blade Damped by a Dry Friction Device

9.2.2.1. To reduce resonance stresses in rotating turbine blades, dry friction damping devices of different types are placed between the platforms of adjacent blades of the bladed disk assembly. The dampers are pressed against the platforms by centrifugal forces. Due to relative motion of the vibrating blades and interblade inserts, dry friction between their contact faces provides energy dissipation and dynamic stresses decrease.

Problem 9.7. Forced vibration of a turbine blade damped by a dry friction device. A blade is schematized by a cantilever beam of variable cross section (Fig.9.19a). The blade has an elongated shank that allows special damping device to be inserted between the adjacent blade platforms at a distance L_d from the root. The blade is subjected to a forcing quasi-harmonic distributed load $q(x,t)$ and is inherently damped by external friction that is held as viscous. The usual blade assembly has some frequency scatter and the blades do not resonate simultaneously. This fact admits to study basic dry friction effects for a separated blade while the adjacent blades are assumed to be in rest.

For computation simplicity, the elements between which a damper is situated are assumed have the same cross section that is of no importance for great number of elements. In this case, the boundary conditions for an intermediate node are decomposed, as it has been shown in Chap.5, to independent angular and transversal conditions. The latter are

$$\left.\begin{aligned} &F_j^* + F_d(v_d) + F_{j,*}^- + F_{j-1,*}^+ = 0, \\ &v_{j,*}^- = v_{j-1,*}^+ = v_d \end{aligned}\right\}, \qquad (9.29)$$

where v_d is a support velocity coinciding under our assumptions with the relative velocity of the sliding damper units and $F_d(v_d)$ is a support reaction depending on the dry friction conditions.

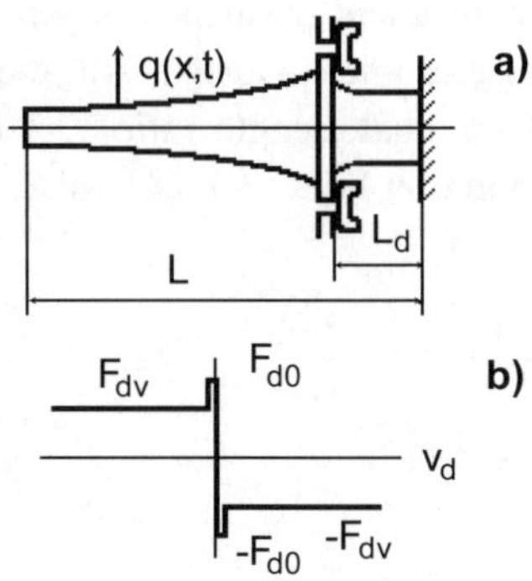

Fig.9.19. A turbine blade with damping device; a) sketch of the blade, b) dry friction diagram

Equations (9.29) together with Eqs.(5.53) and given function $F_d(v_d)$ form a nonlinear algebraic system, which is solved for a given time step using sequential approximation.

9.2.2.2. As an example, Fig 9.20 illustrates a calculated oscillogram of the damper velocity $\overline{v}_d$ and reaction force $\overline{F}_d$ obtained for a turbine blade model in Shorr and Mel'nikova (1988) with $L_{sh}/L = 0.1$. The friction force is scaled by the amplitude of quasi-harmonical forcing load taking $\overline{F}_d = \overline{F}_{d0} = \overline{F}_{dv} = 2$.

The instants of damper turning on/off are clearly seen from the diagram.

It is of interest to compare the maximal resonant bending moment $\overline{M}_{bl}$ in the blade airfoil with the moment $\overline{M}_{sh}$ in the blade shank. Fig.9.21 demonstrates these moments' dependence of the limit friction force $\overline{F}_d$.

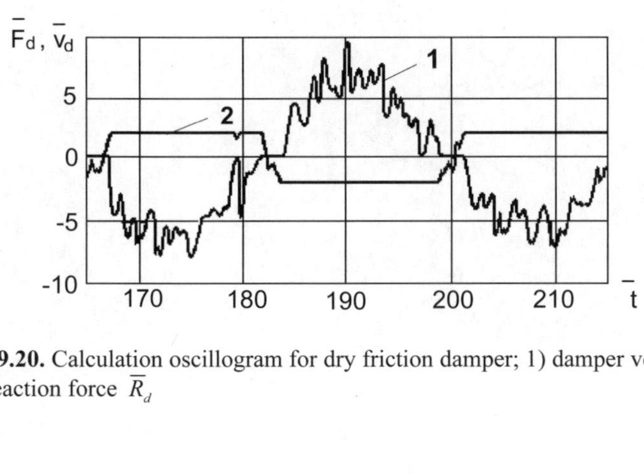

Fig.9.20. Calculation oscillogram for dry friction damper; 1) damper velocity $\overline{v}_d$, 2) reaction force $\overline{R}_d$

With $\overline{F}_d = 0$ just as with small friction, the shank moment $\overline{M}_{sh}$ exceeds the airfoil moment $\overline{M}_{bl}$. As the friction force grows and damping increases, both moments quickly fall, while with some value of $\overline{F}_d$ the moment $\overline{M}_{bl}$ may dominate. Under great value of friction force, the damper would begin to take the properties of a rigid support and damping decreases. Moreover, the resonant frequency is shifted to a greater value since the active blade length becomes shorter. All these phenomena are most conspicuous for advanced shank/blade length ratio $\overline{L}_{sh} / \overline{L}$, see Fig.9.21, where thick lines refer to $\overline{L}_{sh} / \overline{L}$ =0.1 and thin lines to $\overline{L}_{sh} / \overline{L}$ =0.3.

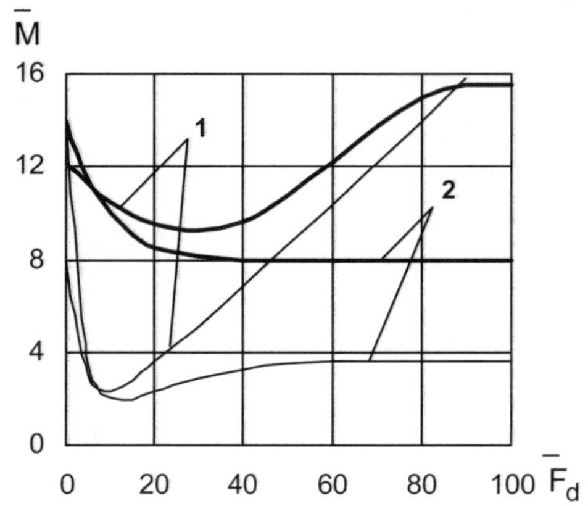

Fig.9.21. Maximum bending moments vs. dry friction force $\overline{F}_d$: 1) $\overline{M}_{bl}$, 2) $\overline{M}_{sh}$

Based on the given preliminary computations, optimal damper parameters, e.g., the mass of the damping inserts, can be chosen.

10 Unsteady Vibro-Impact Loading

Mechanisms operating under multiple numbers of collisions, for which the frequency is of the same order as their eigenfrequencies, are usually referred to vibro-impact systems. These systems include, as a rule, units with external or internal one-side contacts that lead to the arising and vanishing of gaps accompanied by repeated impacts. Analytical solutions of vibro-impact problems are developed chiefly for steady processes in discrete mechanical systems (see, e.g., Kobrinsky AE and Kobrinsky AA 1973), and to a lesser extent, in solids (see Babitsky 1978, 1998; and also Pal'mov (1998). The DMM setting allows detailed study of these problems in conformity to the latter, including unsteady regimes.

10.1 Multiple Collisions at Fixed Points of a Distributed System

10.1.1 Interaction of a Rod with a Viscoelastic Foundation

10.1.1.1. **Problem 10.1. Forced vibration of a rod interacting with a limiter.** Following Babitsky (1978), we consider as a prototype vibro-impact system a fixed-free rod of linear viscoelastic material subjected to the longitudinal harmonic force $F(t) = F_0 \cos\omega t$ that can be applied at any point of the rod. Under forced vibration, the free end of the rod interacts with a foundation limiter consisting of parallel viscoelastic units of a stiffness β_{fd} and viscosity η_{fd}. The foundation is initially placed in a gap (clearance) $\delta_{in} \geq 0$, Fig.10.1a. Resonance vibration of a similar viscoelastic rod in the absence of the limiter has been studied in Subsect.9.1.2 (see Fig.9.8).

Henceforth, the nondimensional variables are scaled by exciting force amplitude F_0 : $\overline{\sigma} = \sigma A / F_0$, $\overline{v} = v\rho c A / F_0$, etc. Also

$$\overline{\beta} = \beta L / EA, \;\; \overline{\eta} = \eta / \rho c A, \;\; \overline{u} = u / u_{st} \text{ and } \overline{\delta} = \delta / u_{st} \;\; (u_{st} = F_0 L / EA).$$

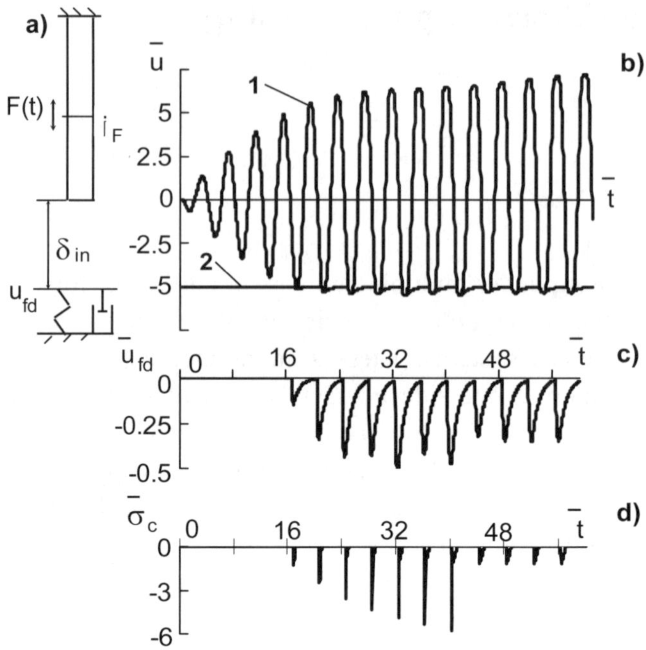

Fig10.1. Vibro-impact interaction of a rod with foundation; a) sketch of the problem, b), c), d) time development of deformations and stress

Varying boundary conditions for the rod/limiter interaction can be readily described using FBC procedure. In doing so, we assume at first that within a whole given step the gap remains for $\bar{\delta}_0 > 0$ and is absent for $\bar{\delta}_0 = 0$, where $\bar{\delta}_0$ is the starting gap of the step.

In the first case ($\bar{\delta}_0 > 0,$), the final step gap is calculated as

$$\bar{\delta} = \bar{\delta}_0 + (\bar{v}_{1,*}^- - \bar{v}_{fd,m})\Delta\bar{t}, \tag{10.1}$$

where the velocity $\bar{v}_{1,*}^-$ relates to the free rod end and $\bar{v}_{fd,m}$ is a mean velocity of the limiter during the interval $\Delta\bar{t}$.

In spite of the fact that the viscoelastic limiter is free, its mean velocity may be nonzero. For given foundation model we obtain that

$$\bar{v}_{fd,m} = \frac{\bar{F}_{fd,0}}{\bar{\eta}_{fd} + 0.5\bar{\beta}_{fd}\Delta\bar{t}}, \tag{10.2}$$

where $\bar{F}_{fd,0}$ is a compressive force of the elastic unit at the step beginning.

The calculated value of $\bar{\delta} \le 0$ shows arising of rod/limiter contact. Assuming due to the FBC approach that the contact is transmitted to the step end, a gap has to be conditionally increased to $\Delta\bar{\delta}' = |\bar{\delta}|$.

In the case $\bar{\delta}_0 = 0$, a common rod/limiter boundary velocity is

$$\bar{v}_{fd} = \bar{v}_{1,*}^{-} = \bar{v}_{1,0} + \bar{\sigma}_{1,0} - \bar{\sigma}_1^{-}(1+\varphi), \tag{10.3}$$

while the compressive rod/limiter contact force

$$\bar{F}_{cont} = -\bar{\sigma}_1^{-} = \frac{\bar{F}_{fd,0} - (\bar{\sigma}_{1,0} + \bar{v}_{1,0})(\bar{\eta}_{fd} + 0.5\bar{\beta}_{fd}\Delta\bar{t})}{1 + (1+\varphi)(\bar{\eta}_{fd} + 0.5\bar{\beta}_{fd}\Delta\bar{t})} \tag{10.4}$$

must be $\bar{F}_{cont} \ge 0$. If it is not, we put $\bar{F}_{cont} = 0$ and recalculate the given step under the free boundary condition, as above. A reduced final gap, taking into account the value of $\Delta\bar{\delta}'$, is determined as it has been described in Sect.8.1.

10.1.1.2. **A.** As an example, a rod excited by the force applied at the middle of its length is considered; the rod material is taken as Maxwell's with the relaxation time $\bar{\tau}_c$. The diagrams of Fig.10.1b to 10.1d demonstrate time development of the vibro-impact process under resonance frequency $\bar{f} = 1$ for a rod with $\bar{\tau}_c = 10$, the initial gap $\bar{\delta}_0 = 5$, and foundation elastic-viscous parameters being $\bar{\beta}_{fd} = 1$ and $\bar{\eta}_{ffd} = 1$. Until the contact moment $\bar{t} \approx 16$, the displacement amplitude of the free bottom end of the rod increases linearly, and after coming into contact, rapidly becomes stabilized (Fig.10.1b). Foundation displacement $\bar{u}_{fd}$ (Fig.10.1c) and contact stress $\bar{\sigma}_c = -\bar{\sigma}_1^{-}$ (Fig.10.1d) have expressed shock character; however, after some time their peaks also attain stable values.

B. In the next two figures, envelopes $\bar{u} = \bar{u}_{1,*}^{-}$ of the rod displacement amplitude versus time $\bar{t}$ are shown. Note that for an unsteady impact process the term 'amplitude' requires some precise definition. Here, amplitude is assumed to be the maximum semirange of the function over the first mode oscillation period of $\bar{T} = 4$. The other parameters are taken as $\bar{\tau}_c = 20$, $\bar{\delta}_0 = 5$, $\bar{\beta}_{fd} = 5$, and $\bar{\eta}_{fd} = 0$; the latter correspond to a strong elastic foundation.

Figure 10.2 illustrates establishment of the steady vibro-impact statement for different constant trans-resonance forcing frequencies $\bar{f}$ within the interval from 0.95 to 1.08. The unsteady responses for frequency changed from 0.95 to 1.15 with different rate $\bar{\nu}$, just as steady response

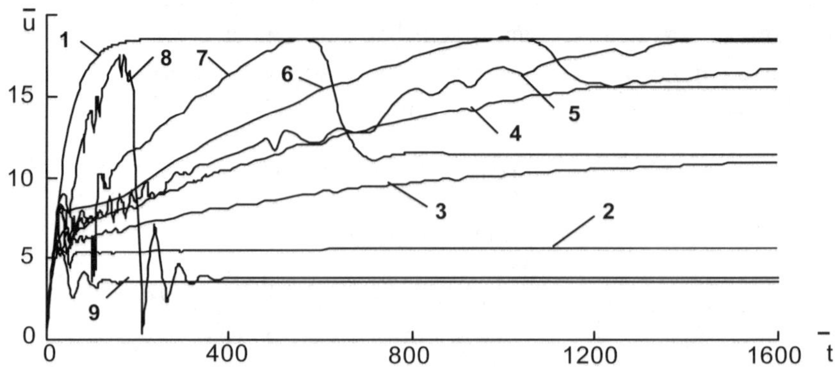

Fig.10.2. Establishment of steady vibro-impact state of a rod/foundation interaction; 1) vibration without limits, $\bar{f}$ =1; 2) to 9) vibration with the gap for some forcing frequencies $\bar{f}$: 2) $\bar{f}$ =0.950: 3) $\bar{f}$ =0.980; 4) $\bar{f}$ =1.000; 5) $\bar{f}$ =1.006; 6) $\bar{f}$ =1.010; 7) $\bar{f}$ =1.020; 8) $\bar{f}$ =1.075; 9) $\bar{f}$ =1.080

for $\bar{\nu} = 0$, are presented in Fig.10.3.

Outside of the region $\bar{f} \approx 0.94 - 1.06$ the gap is kept and the forced vibrations remain linear. For the sub-resonance frequencies $0.94 < \bar{f} \le 1$, the amplitudes progressively increase approximating the reference magnitude of the steady response curve. For the super-resonance frequencies $1 < \bar{f} < 1.06$, the amplitudes at first rapidly grow almost to the resonance value and then also collapse to the steady descending response curve.

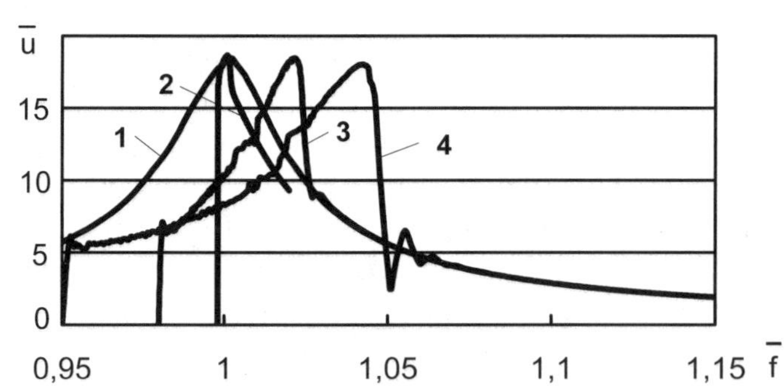

Fig.10.3. Unsteady response of a rod/foundation interaction with a gap for some forcing frequency rate $\bar{\nu}$; 1) steady state response, $\bar{\nu} = 0$; 2) $\bar{\nu}$ =3.67*10^{-7}; 3) $\bar{\nu}$ =1.67*10^{-6}; 4) $\bar{\nu}$ =3.33*10^{-6}

10.1.1.3. **A**. In the case when there is a pre-tightness (negative gap) of a value δ_{pt} between a rod and foundation, the initial conditions must be taken in the form

$$\bar{\sigma}_{j,0}(0) = -\bar{\sigma}_{pt},\ \bar{F}_{fd,0} = \bar{\sigma}_{pt}, \tag{10.5}$$

where the pre-stress is

$$\bar{\sigma}_{pt} = \frac{\beta_{fd}\delta_{pt}}{1+\beta_{fd}}. \tag{10.6}$$

In all other respects the calculation procedure remains unchanged.

B. In some cases, the time duration between the sequential impacts or their limited series is significantly greater than the time that elastic waves take to propagate along the system, so that oscillations associated with several previous impacts are able to almost die down due to damping. Then the vibro-impact behavior can be approximately studied on the basis of separate impact trains, as it has been considered in Subsect.8.4.2 for a valve spring. The next two problems are treated in this way.

10.1.2 Interaction of a Rod with a Hysteretic Foundation

10.1.2.1. **Problem 10.2. Soil processing by an impact mechanism.** A simplified mechanical part of a pneumatic hammer destined for soil pro-

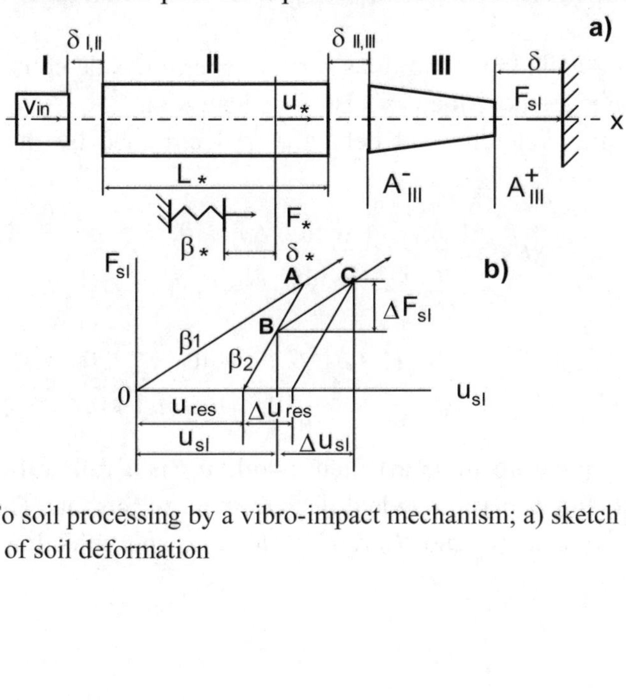

Fig.10.4. To soil processing by a vibro-impact mechanism; a) sketch of a system, b) diagram of soil deformation

cessing, that is a typical vibro-impact mechanism, is considered below.

The mechanism consists of three elastic rods (Fig.10.4a): a projectile I of cross-sectional area A_{I} and length L_{I}, a long intermediate rod II of area A_{II} and length L_{II}, and a striking rod III of a variable cross section and length L_{III}. The projectile longitudinally impacts the system with an initial velocity v_{in}; the intermediate rod is connected with a one-side clamped spring that compresses the top of the striking rod to soil. The soil is assumed having a linear hysteretic diagram of impression resistance and being partially recovered (Fig.10.4b).

The first loading runs along the line OA with a slope determined by a stiffness coefficient β_1 and the unloading is described by the line AB with a slope $\beta_2 \geq \beta_1$. The following loading, beginning from any point B, goes along the line BC in parallel to OA, etc.

Oscillations from previous impacts are assumed to have died down by the beginning of the current impact. Only dynamic change of loads and displacements are further under consideration. Then, at the first moment all units of the system are taken unloaded, the conditions of the rods II and III are zero, all the gaps: $\delta_{\mathrm{I,II}}$, $\delta_{\mathrm{II,III}}$ - between the rods, δ_* - between the rod II and the spring, and δ - between the tip of the rod III and the soil are absent.

The rods are divided into n_{I}, n_{II}, n_{III} finite elements of the same length $\Delta x = L_{\mathrm{II}} / n_{\mathrm{II}}$ in such a way that the length of the first element $L_{\mathrm{I}} = n_{\mathrm{I}} \Delta x$ and of the third one $L_{\mathrm{III}} = n_{\mathrm{III}} \Delta x$ be close enough to their given values.

The varying boundary conditions for the inner one-side contact faces of the system units are described by FBC (see Sect 8.1).

The dynamic hysteretic soil behavior is determined by the following equations:

$$\Delta F_{sl} = \begin{cases} \beta_1 \Delta u_{sl} & \text{with} \quad \Delta u_{sl} \geq 0, \\ \beta_2 \Delta u_{sl} & \text{with} \quad \Delta u_{sl} < 0; \end{cases} \tag{10.7}$$

$$\Delta u_{res} = \begin{cases} \Delta u_{sl} (1 - \beta_1 / \beta_2) & \text{with} \quad u_{sl} \geq 0, \\ 0 & \text{with} \quad u_{sl} < 0, \end{cases} \tag{10.8}$$

where F_{sl} is a pressure force affected a soil, u_{sl} is a full soil impression displacement, and u_{res} is a residual displacement of the soil. The different values of coefficients β_1 and β_2 refer to loading and unloading. The stiffness coefficient of the spring is denoted by β_*.

A variation of the cross-sectional area of the rod III (see notations in Fig.10.4.a) is described by the equation

$$A_j = A_{\mathrm{III}}^- + (A_{\mathrm{III}}^+ - A_{\mathrm{III}}^-)\left(\frac{j - n_{\mathrm{II}} + n_{\mathrm{III}}}{n_{\mathrm{III}}}\right)^{\nu}, \tag{10.9}$$

where $n = n_{\mathrm{I}} + n_{\mathrm{II}} + n_{\mathrm{III}}$, $\nu = \mathrm{const.}$

10.1.2.2. Numerical results are obtained for the following quantities:

$$L_{\mathrm{I}} / L_{\mathrm{II}} = 0.12,\ L_{\mathrm{III}} / L_{\mathrm{II}} = 0.4,\ A_{\mathrm{I}} / A_{\mathrm{II}} = 0.8,\ A_{\mathrm{III}}^- / A_{\mathrm{II}} = 1.2,\ A_{\mathrm{III}}^+ / A_{\mathrm{II}} = 0.4,$$
$$\nu = 3,\ \bar{\beta}_1 = 1,\ \bar{\beta}_2 = 2,\ \bar{\beta}_* = 10,\ L_* / L_{\mathrm{II}} = 0.68, \text{ where } \bar{\beta} = \beta L_{II} / EA_{II}.$$

The material of all the rods is the same. The numbers of the elements are chosen as $n_{\mathrm{I}} = 18, n_{\mathrm{II}} = 150$, and $n_{\mathrm{III}} = 60$ that provides the needed relationship between the rods length. The variation of the relative force $\bar{F}_{sl} = F_{sl} / \rho c A_{\mathrm{II}} v_{in}$ and displacements $\bar{u}_{sl} = u_{sl} c / L_{\mathrm{II}} v_{in}$, $\bar{u}_{res} = u_{res} c / L_{\mathrm{II}} v_{in}$ versus time $\bar{t} = tc / L_{\mathrm{II}}$ are shown in Fig.10.5a,b, respectively. The pressure force $\bar{F}_{sl}$ begins growing at the moment $\bar{t} = (n_{\mathrm{II}} + n_{\mathrm{III}}) / n_{\mathrm{II}} = 1.4$, when the leading wave arrives at the soil, and sharply falls in time $\Delta \bar{t} = 2n_{\mathrm{I}} / n_{\mathrm{II}} = 0.24$, which coincides with the rebound of the

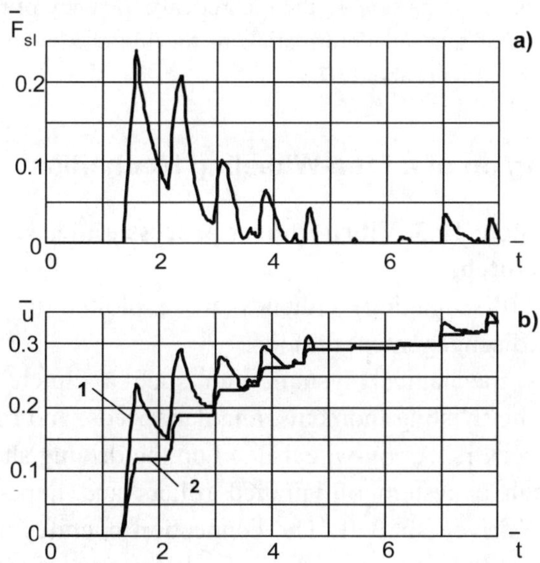

Fig.10.5. Time evolution of vibro-impact parameters: a) pressure force, b) soil impression displacements: 1) full, 2) residual

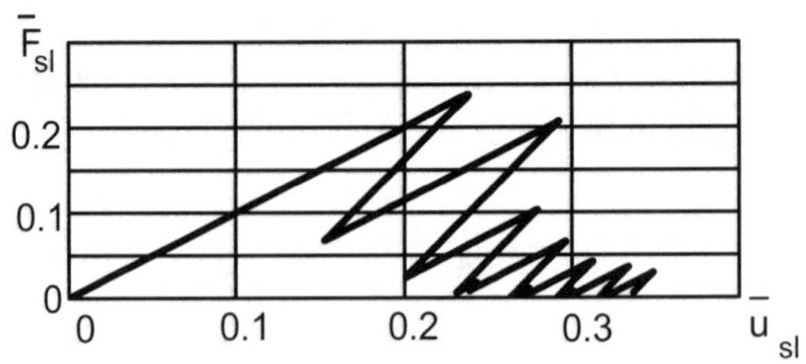

Fig.10.6. Diagram of soil deformation for loading/unloading pattern

rod I. The subsequent pressure force evolution is guided by the rods II and III oscillations and their repeated collisions with each other and the soil, as well as by superposition of reflected waves. A loading/unloading pattern is displayed in the diagram of soil deformation (Fig.10.6).

In the model, the position of the string that presses the rods to soil is assumed fixed. Therefore, the dynamic force $\overline{F}_{sl}$ decreases to zero and impression induced by the impact practically ceases to $\bar{t} \approx 4.8$. In reality, the spring moves together with the whole of system ensuring some static pressure at a contact face of the rod III to soil and additional small dynamic force appearing.

The energy balance during the whole dynamic process allows calculating its energetic characteristics, in particular, the theoretical efficiency of the mechanism (a ratio of the work of the soil deformation to the initial kinetic energy of the projectile). In our case, this is about 57%

10.1.3 Switching on of a Free-Wheeling Mechanism

10.1.3.1. A. Problem 10.3. Vibro-impact process under switching on of a free-wheeling clutch.

Free-wheeling (disengaging) clutches are exploited in a number of transmissions for disengagement of units.

An elementary mechanical system with such a clutch is shown in Fig. 10.7, where the twisting moments, angular speeds, and rotation angles are presented as vectors. A cog-wheel fixed on the driving shaft I transfers the torque through a system of jammed rollers and upper viscoelastic clutch ring to the driven shaft II. The connection operates only provided the torque is directed on jamming of rollers. If for any reason the rotation frequency of the driven shaft will exceed the rotation frequency of the driving one, the shafts become uncoupled and an angular gap δ occurs.

However, as movement of the driven shaft is delayed, the rollers will be

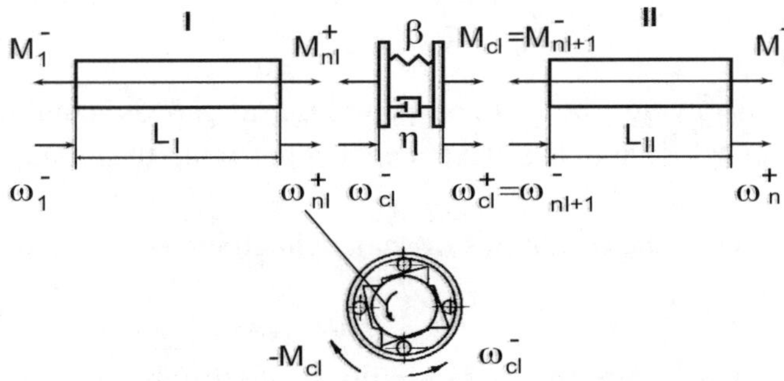

Fig.10.7. Sketch of a transmission part with a free-wheeling clutch

again jammed and coupling will be restored.

We denote the element number of the shafts by n_I and n_{II}, respectively, and by $n = n_I + n_{II}$ the common element number. Thus, $\omega^-_{nI+1} \equiv \omega^+_{cl}$ while $\omega^+_{nI} \le \omega^-_{cl}$.

Unlike in Sect.10.1, nondimensional velocities $\overline{\omega} = \omega / \omega_0$ are treated further with the constant angular velocity ω_0 referred to the left end of the driving shaft; the other variables are scaled by the expressions

$$\overline{M} = M / \rho c J_{pI} \omega_0, \; \overline{\beta} = \beta L_I / G J_{pI}, \; \overline{\eta} = \eta / \rho c J_{pI}, \; \overline{\varphi} = \varphi / \varphi^o, \; \overline{\delta} = \delta / \varphi^o$$

where $\varphi^o = \omega_0 L_I / c$ and $c = \sqrt{G/\rho}$.

B. Let's assume that at the beginning of a step an angular gap $\overline{\delta}_0 > 0$ exists between the rollers and the upper ring and the springs of the elastic unit of the clutch are compressed by a residual moment $\overline{M}_{cl,e0} \le 0$, while the full moment $\overline{M}_{cl}$ transmitted by the clutch is zero. Eq.(10.2) for a parallel viscoelastic non-inertial unit yields the relative angular velocity of the clutch parts

$$\overline{\omega}^+_{cl} - \overline{\omega}^-_{cl} = -\frac{\overline{M}_{cl,e0}}{\overline{\eta}_\Sigma}, \tag{10.10}$$

where $\overline{\omega}^\pm_{cl}$ are boundary velocities of these parts.

Here, $\overline{\eta}_\Sigma = \overline{\eta}_{cl} + 0.5\overline{\beta}_{cl}\Delta\overline{t}$ and $\overline{\beta}_{cl}$, $\overline{\eta}_{cl}$ are, as above, the stiffness and viscosity clutch coefficients. In this case, each shaft rotates independently, with boundary conditions

$$\overline{M}^+_{n_I} = 0, \; \overline{M}^-_{n_I+1} = \overline{M}_{cl} = 0, \tag{10.11}$$

and the step final gap is

$$\bar{\delta} = \bar{\delta}_0 + (\bar{\omega}_{cl}^- - \bar{\omega}_{nI}^+)\Delta\bar{t}\,. \tag{10.12}$$

With $\bar{\delta} \le 0$ showing the rollers jamming, a gap is conditionally increased to $\Delta\bar{\delta}' = |\bar{\delta}|$ and the next step begins with the contact condition $\bar{\delta}_0 = 0$.

C. Under a contact, the conditions of shafts/clutch interaction are

$$\bar{M}_{nI}^+ = \bar{M}_{cl,m} = \bar{M}_{nI+1}^-,\ \bar{\omega}_{nI}^+ = \bar{\omega}_{cl,m}^-,\ \bar{\omega}_{nI+1}^- = \bar{\omega}_{cl,m}^+\ , \tag{10.13}$$

where $\bar{M}_{cl,m}$ and $\bar{\omega}_{cl,m}^{\pm}$ are the mean values of clutch moments and angular borders velocities, respectively, and

$$\bar{\omega}_{cl,m}^+ - \bar{\omega}_{cl,m}^- = \frac{\bar{M}_{cl,m} - \bar{M}_{cl,e0}}{\bar{\eta}_\Sigma}\,. \tag{10.14}$$

Inserting equalities of Eq.(10.13), with basis DMM torsion equations

$$\bar{\omega}_j^{\pm} = \bar{\omega}_{j,0} \pm \bar{M}_j^{\pm} \mp \bar{M}_{j,0}\,,$$

into Eq.(10.14), we get

$$\bar{M}_{cl,m} = \frac{\bar{\eta}_\Sigma(\bar{M}_{nI+1,0} + \bar{M}_{nI,0} + \bar{\omega}_{n_I+1,0} - \bar{\omega}_{nI,0}) + \bar{M}_{cl,e0}}{1 + 2\bar{\eta}_\Sigma}\,. \tag{10.15}$$

The new moment value of clutch elastic unit is

$$\bar{M}_{cl,e} = 2\bar{M}_{cl,em} - \bar{M}_{cl,e0}\,, \tag{10.16}$$

where $\bar{M}_{cl,em} = \bar{\eta}\bar{M}_{cl,m} / \bar{\eta}_\Sigma$.

Equations (10.13)-(10.16) are valid with $\bar{M}_{cl,m} \le 0$. Otherwise, we put $\bar{M}_{cl,m} = 0$ and recalculate this step using Eqs.(10.10)-(10.12) and the FBC procedure described in Sect.(8.1).

10.1.3.2. **A.** To illustrate the effect of the clutch on/off engagement, the following initial conditions for the system shown in Fig.10.7 are taken:

$$\left.\begin{array}{l} \bar{M}_{j,in} = 0 \text{ with } 1 \le j \le n, \\ \bar{\omega}_{j,in} = \begin{cases} 1 \text{ with } 1 \le j \le n_I, \\ 0 \text{ with } n_{I+I} \le j \le n, \end{cases} \\ \bar{\delta}_{in} = 0 \end{array}\right\}. \tag{10.17}$$

The boundary angular velocity at the left end of the shaft I is assumed to remain equal to $\bar{\omega}_1^- = 1$ all the time and the drag moment at the right end of shaft II being

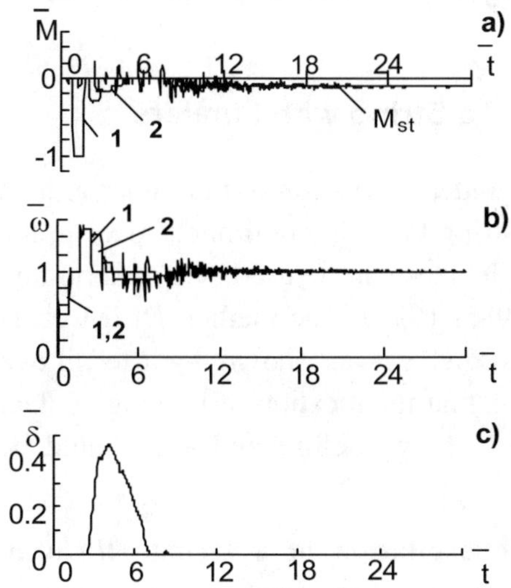

Fig.10.8. Calculated oscillograms of a free-wheeling clutch during engaging; a) moments 1) $\overline{M}_1^-$, 2) $\overline{M}_n^+$; b) angular velocities 1) $\overline{\omega}_{nI}^+$; 2) $\overline{\omega}_{nI+1}^- = \overline{\omega}_{cl}^+$, c) angular gap $\overline{\delta}$

correlated with its boundary velocity through use of the following equations:

$$\overline{M}_n^+ = \begin{cases} -\overline{M}_{st}\overline{\omega}_n^+\left|\overline{\omega}_n^+\right| \text{ with } \overline{\omega}_n^+ \geq 0, \\ 0 \quad \text{with } \overline{\omega}_n^+ < 0 \end{cases}. \tag{10.18}$$

Due to Eq.(10.18) the drag moment is never positive and coincides for the established regime $\overline{\omega}_n^+ = \overline{\omega}_1^- = 1$ with the given stationary torque $\overline{M}_{st} = M_{st} / \rho c J_{pl}\omega_0$.

Inserting the first expression from (10.18) into the boundary basis equation $\overline{M}_n^+ = \overline{M}_{n,0} + \overline{\omega}_n^+ - \overline{\omega}_{n,0}$, we come to nonlinear equation

$$\overline{\omega}_n^+(1+\overline{M}_{st}\left|\omega_n^+\right|) - (\overline{\omega}_{n,0} - \overline{M}_{n,0}) = 0, \tag{10.19}$$

that can readily be solved by sequential approximation, starting from the value of

$$\overline{\omega}_n^+ = \overline{\omega}_{n,0} - \overline{M}_{n,0}.$$

B. As a numerical example, the following quantities are taken: the number of elements $n_I = 20,\ n_{II} = 10$, the clutch coefficients $\overline{\beta}_{cl} = 25,\ \overline{\eta}_{cl} = 0.1$, and the stationary moment $\overline{M}_{st} = 0.1$. The moments $\overline{M}_1^-, \overline{M}_n^+$ transmitted by the shafts, the angular velocities $\overline{\omega}_{nI}^+, \overline{\omega}_{nI+1}^-$ at the shafts/clutch borders, and the gap $\overline{\delta}$ are plotted versus time in Fig.10.8a,b,c, respectively.

The significant impact torsion moment that exceeds the stationary moment $1/\overline{M}_{st}$ times is seen arising at the instant when the clutch is engaged. After the transient oscillation process, the system goes to a stationary state.

10.2 Multiple Collisions at Varying Points of a Distributed System

10.2.1 Vibro-Impact Interaction of a String with Limiters

For the study of resonant phenomena under oscillation of thin tubes in heat exchangers, the model of a stretched string vibrating in limited space in the presence of one or bilateral stopping devices can be used, see Amerio and Prouse (1975), and also Krupenin (1985, 1992). The method DMM gives ample opportunities for such analysis as it was shown by Mel'nikova (1987). The basic feature of this task is that the location of varying contact points of a string with limiters is not known beforehand and should be defined during computation.

***10.2.1.1*. Problem 10.4. Kinematic excitation of a string vibrating between two limiters.** Consider a taught string that is kinematically excited at both ends $j=1$ and $j=n+1$ with transverse deflection amplitude y_0 and forcing frequency f

$$y_1(t) = y_{n+1}(t) = y_0 \sin 2\pi f t\,. \tag{10.20}$$

Due to Eq.(10.20) and expressions of Sect.2.3, the varying boundary conditions for a time step i are

$$\left.\begin{aligned} v_{n,i}^{+} &= v_{1,i}^{-} = 2\pi f y_0 \cos 2\pi f (t_i - 0.5\Delta t), \\ Q_{1,i}^{-} &= Q_{1,0} - v_{1,i}^{-} + v_{1,0}, \\ Q_{n,i}^{+} &= Q_{n,0} + v_{n,i}^{+} - v_{n,0} \end{aligned}\right\}. \tag{10.21}$$

Two limiters elongated from the initial silent position of the string $y_j(0)=0$ to gaps (clearances) $\delta^- = \delta_{in}^-$ and $\delta^+ = \delta_{in}^+$ (Fig.10.9a) bound a movement of the string.

Henceforth, we use the nondimensional quantities

$$\bar{y} = \frac{y}{y_{IN}}, \quad \bar{\delta} = \frac{\delta}{y_{IN}}, \quad \bar{v} = \frac{vL}{y_{IN}c}, \quad \bar{Q} = \frac{QL}{y_{IN}T} \tag{10.22}$$

with $c = \sqrt{N/\rho A}$, omitting the function subscript y referred to the transversal direction.

Within the range $-\bar{\delta}_{in}^- < \bar{y}_{j,0} < \bar{\delta}_{in}^+$, no stress/limiters interaction at the node j exists at the step beginning and the node velocity is

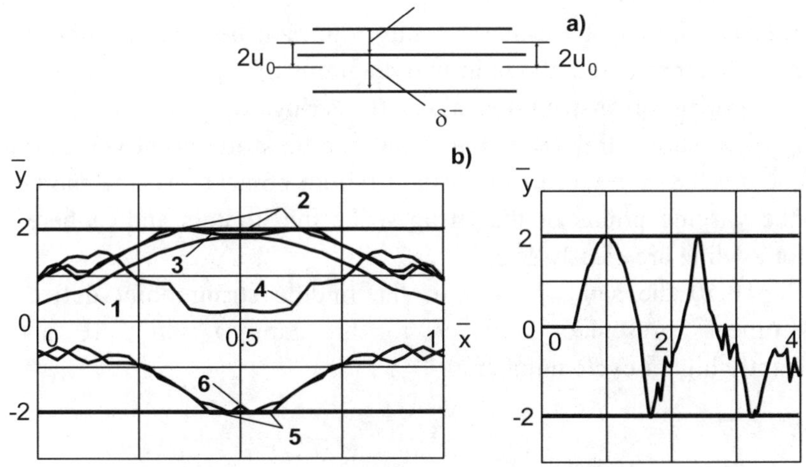

Fig.10.9. Kinematic excitation of a string between two limiters; a) sketch of the system; b) deflection along the string for time $\bar{t}$: 1) $\bar{t}$ =0.875, 2) $\bar{t}$ =2.375, 3) $\bar{t}$ =2.400, 4) $\bar{t}$ =2.650, 5) $\bar{t}$ =3.225, 6) $\bar{t}$ =3.250; c) string mid-point deflection vs. time

$$\bar{v}_j = \frac{\bar{v}_{j,0} + \bar{v}_{j-1,0} + \bar{Q}_{j,0} - \bar{Q}_{j-1,0}}{2(1+0.5\eta\Delta x)} . \tag{10.23a}$$

The deflection at the step end arrives at

$$\bar{y}_j = \bar{y}_{j,0} + \bar{v}_j \Delta\bar{t} . \tag{10.23b}$$

The condition of the string free motion during the whole step is

$$-\bar{\delta}_{in}^- < \bar{y}_j < \bar{\delta}_{in}^+ . \tag{10.24}$$

Under string/limiter contact the node starting velocity is $\bar{v}_j = 0$ and a reaction force of the limiter (see Sect.5.1.2.) is

$$\bar{R}_j = \bar{Q}_{j-1,0} - \bar{Q}_{j,0} - \bar{v}_{j-1,0} - \bar{v}_{j,0} . \tag{10.25}$$

The contact continuation conditions in the course of time $\Delta\bar{t}$ are:

$$\bar{R}_j < 0 \text{ at the upper limiter for which } \bar{y}_j = \bar{\delta}_{in}^+ , \tag{10.26a}$$

$$\bar{R}_j > 0 \text{ at the bottom limiter for which } \bar{y}_j = -\bar{\delta}_{in}^- . \tag{10.26b}$$

Transition from a gap to a contact and vice versa is described by the standard FBC procedure.

10.2.1.2. The initial phase of the string vibration between limiters with $\bar{\delta}^- = \delta^+ = 2$ is presented above in two diagrams of Fig.10.9. Figure 10.9b illustrates deflection distribution along the string for some time instants and Fig.10.9c shows the deflection at the middle string point versus time. The time $\bar{t} = 0.875$ refers to the instant before contact. All the moments when the varying points of the string strike the limiters and 'adhere' to them for a while are clearly seen.

In Fig.10.10 the same pattern of the middle string point deflection versus time is presented, however, for the gaps $\bar{\delta}_{in}^- = \bar{\delta}_{in}^+ = 10$ and a significantly higher cycle number.

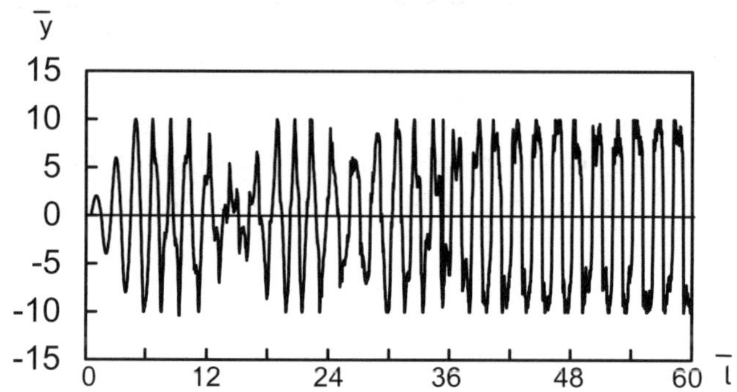

Fig.10.10. String mid-point deflection vs. time with double-side limiters, $\bar{\delta} = 10$

Without damping, the forced vibro-impact nonlinear oscillations induced by the frequency $\bar{f} = 1$ relevant to the free string first eigen-frequency are not steady due to presence of some beating.

Some other cases of string forced vibrations were considered by Mel'nikova (1987) and also by Krupenin and Mel'nikova (1991).

10.2.2 A System with Multiple Inner Gaps

10.2.2.1. **Problem 10.5. A rod with inner gaps expanded by suddenly applied longitudinal load.** In some mechanical systems consisting of significant number of units, transition parts with inner gaps separate elastic elements, as schematically shown in Fig.10.11a for a rod of constant cross section expanded by stress σ_0. These parts can translate both pressure and tensile loads due to alternating contact faces. Relevant links are also named as pressure or tension.

Denote a current value of the gap between pressure links of a node j by $\delta_j = u_j^- - u_{j-1}^+$ and its maximally possible value, which is equal to given total interelement clearance, by Δ_j. Evidently, $0 \le \delta_j \le \Delta_j$. The current gap between tension links is $\Delta_j - \delta_j$. The quantity Δ_j can vary along the rod. The calculation algorithm for this problem is similar to the previous one with the following peculiarities referred to the each step:

i) With contact at the pressure link, both the initial and the final gaps are $\delta_{j,0} = \delta_j = 0$ and the interaction stress between elements $j-1$ and j is

$$\sigma_{j-1}^+ = \sigma_j^- \le 0 .$$

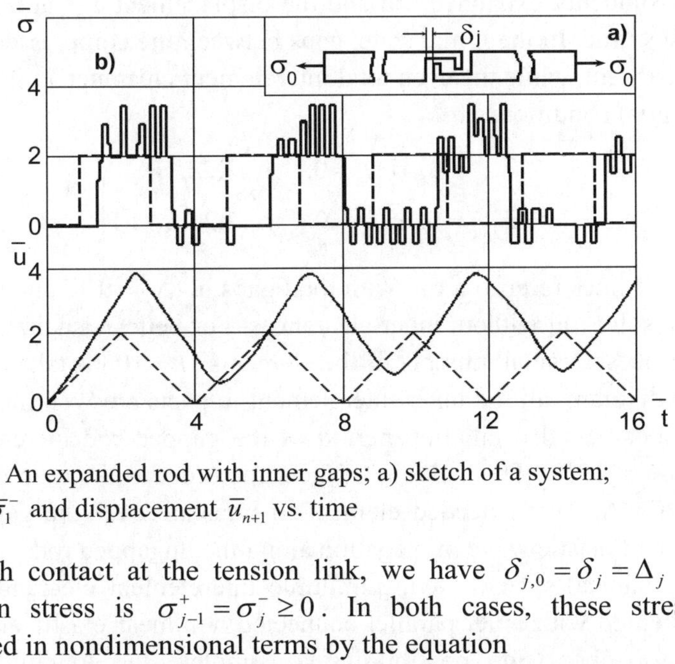

Fig.10.11. An expanded rod with inner gaps; a) sketch of a system; b) stress $\bar{\sigma}_1^-$ and displacement $\bar{u}_{n+1}$ vs. time

ii) With contact at the tension link, we have $\delta_{j,0} = \delta_j = \Delta_j$ and the interaction stress is $\sigma_{j-1}^+ = \sigma_j^- \ge 0$. In both cases, these stresses are determined in nondimensional terms by the equation

$$\bar{\sigma}_{j-1}^+ = 0.5(\bar{\sigma}_{j,0} + \bar{\sigma}_{j-1,0} + \bar{v}_{j,0} - \bar{v}_{j-1,0})$$

where, as usual, $\bar{\sigma} = \sigma / \sigma_0$, $\bar{v} = v\rho c / \sigma_0$ and the boundary velocities are equal; thus $\bar{v}_{j-1}^+ = \bar{v}_j^-$.

iii) Without any contact during the whole interval Δt when $\sigma_{j-1}^+ = \sigma_j^- = 0$, the boundary velocities of adjacent elements are calculated independently as

$$\bar{v}_{j-1}^+ = \bar{v}_{j-1,0} - \bar{\sigma}_{j-1,0}, \quad \bar{v}_j^- = \bar{v}_{j,0} + \bar{\sigma}_{j,0} ,$$

while the gap changes from $\bar{\delta}_{j,0}$ to

$$\bar{\delta}_j = \bar{\delta}_{j,0} + (\bar{v}_j^- - \bar{v}_{j-1}^+)\Delta\bar{t}\,. \tag{10.27}$$

The quantities u_j, δ_j and Δ_j are also scaled by the rod static elongation, e.g., $\bar{\delta}_j = \delta_j E/\sigma_0 L$, etc.

The FBC algorithm, which takes into account transitions from gaps to contacts and vice versa does not in principle differ from described in previous Subsection.

10.2.2.2. Figure 10.11b demonstrates the stress $\bar{\sigma}_1^-$ at the left immobile end of a suddenly expanded rod and the displacement $\bar{u}_{n+1}$ at the opposite end versus time. In the initial state, gaps between the compressed faces are assumed absent, while the even total interelement clearance is $\bar{\Delta}_j = 0.15$.

The initial conditions are

$$\left.\begin{array}{ll} \bar{v}_{j,in} = 0,\ \bar{\sigma}_{j,in} = 0, & j = 1,2,\ldots,n, \\ \bar{u}_{j,in} = 0,\ \bar{\delta}_{j,in} = 0, & j = 1,2,\ldots,n+1 \end{array}\right\}. \tag{10.28}$$

The bold lines refer to a rod with total gaps of $\bar{\Delta}_j = 0.15$ and the dashed lines to a solid rod without inner clearances. For better visualization of the impact process, a small number of the elements ($n = 10$) is taken.

In the diagram, all the inner interelement impacts are well mapped. The visual fundamental oscillation period of the gapped rod increases in the given case to 15% . This value is of the same order as the ratio of the time $\bar{t}_g = \bar{\Delta}\,/\bar{v} \approx \bar{\Delta} = 0.15$, needed element to translate over the gap, and the time $\bar{t} = 1$ of elastic wave propagation along the ungapped rod.

A mechanical system having multiple interelement clearances can be complemented with inner parallel-connected nonlinear elastic and viscous links that offers wide possibilities to simulate the longitudinal train oscillation (see Chap.14).

11 Oscillations of Mechanical Systems Affected by Moving Loads

Many mechanics problems result in consideration of the movement of one deformable body relative to another. As a specific case, the one-dimensional movement of a rigid body or given load relative to the deformable foundation may be cited. The analytical solutions have been obtained for some 1-D tasks by Philippov at al. (1974), Kaplunov and Muravsky (1986), and by other authors. Using the DMM approach, the dynamic analysis of mechanical systems under loads arbitrarily varying and moving with variable speed does not present major difficulties. The general WFEM can also be applied to the study of 2-D waves induced by moving loads.

11.1 General Approach to Simulation of Moving Loads

11.1.1 Equivalent Node Forces

11.1.1.1. Let a constant vertical force F_0 move over the surface of a deformable body with constant velocity v_0 in the horizontal positive direction of the x-axis. As examples of similar bodies, a tightened string or a beam on a viscoelastic foundation are considered below. As usual, these are divided into finite elements of length Δx.

The basic principle of numerical simulation of moving loads is to change their action by the action of equivalent varying but immobile forces F_j applied to relevant nodes.

The equivalent nodal forces are determined from the following conditions:

i) For each time step, 'active' nodes j which the moving load affects within a step Δt are separated. Let the indexes of these nodes vary from $j = j_1$ to $j = j_2$.

ii) A summary momentum

$$M_{\Sigma}=\sum_{j=j_1}^{j=j_2} F_j \Delta t$$

of the immobile nodal forces F_j in a time Δt is equal to the momentum $M_0 = F_0 \Delta t$ of the moving load F_0, from where

$$\sum_{j=j_1}^{j=j_2} F_j = F_0 \tag{11.1}$$

iii) The momentum M_0 is distributed over the active nodes proportionally to the times Δt_j, during which the force F_0 passes parts of the elements adjoining the corresponding node

$$M_j / M_0 = \kappa_j, \tag{11.2}$$

where $\kappa_j = \Delta t_j / \Delta t$.

The algorithm to the coefficient κ_j determination is described below.

iv) Taking into account that the nodal forces F_j creating the momentum M_j act during the whole step Δt, we find $F_j = M_j / \Delta t$, so as

$$F_j / F_0 = M_j / M_0 = \kappa_j. \tag{11.3}$$

Analogous assumptions are exploited for the analysis of moving bodies, distributed loads, in 2-D problems, and others.

***11.1.1.2.* A.** For the continuous horizontal movement of a rigid body of mass M along a deformable foundation, the change of the body momentum in the vertical direction during a step Δt is $M \Delta v_M$, where

$$\Delta v_M = 2(v_{M,m} - v_{M,0}).$$

Here, $v_{M,m}$ is the average and $v_{M,0}$ the starting speed of the body in the given step. The law of momentum conservation $M \Delta v_M = F_0 \Delta t$ yields

$$v_{M,m} = v_{M,0} + 0.5 F_0 \Delta t / M, \tag{11.4}$$

where F_0 is a vertical reaction force from the foundation.

The condition of Eq.(11.1) reducing the force F_0 to equivalent nodal forces F_j is kept, but in view of a sign of these forces,

$$F_j = -\kappa_j F_0. \tag{11.5}$$

The node velocities v_j are connected to forces F_j by the concrete equations of the foundation dynamic deformation. From the balance of work in-

introduced to the body and to active foundation nodes during a step

$$F_0 v_{M,m}\Delta t = -\sum_{j=j_1}^{j=j_2} F_j v_j \Delta t\,, \tag{11.6a}$$

we obtain

$$v_{M,m} = \sum_{j=j_1}^{j=j_2} \kappa_j v_j\,. \tag{11.6b}$$

B. Consider, as an example, motion of a mass along a tightened string. Due to the equations of Sect.2.3, a node velocity v_j can be treated as

$$v_j = \tilde{v}_j - 0.5F_j / \rho c A\,, \tag{11.7}$$

where

$$\tilde{v}_j = 0.5[v_{j,0} + v_{j-1,0} + (Q_{j,0} - Q_{j-1,0}) / \rho c A]\,.$$

Using Eq.(11.4) to (11.7) we come to the equality

$$v_{M,0} + \frac{F_0 \Delta t}{2M} = \sum_{j=j_1}^{j=j_2} \kappa_j \left(\tilde{v}_j - \kappa_j \frac{F_0}{2\rho c A} \right),$$

from which one finds the full reaction force

$$F_0 = \frac{2\rho c A \left(v_{M,0} - \sum\limits_{j=j_1}^{j=j_2} \kappa_j \tilde{v}_j \right)}{\rho c A \Delta t / M + \sum\limits_{j=j_1}^{j=j_2} \kappa_j^2}\,, \tag{11.8}$$

then nodal forces $F_j = -\kappa_j F_0$ and all other quantities needed for calculation.

To solve a problem referred to motion of a rigid body with rebounds, the FBC procedure can be exploited.

C. Although the approach for the equivalent nodal forces determination seems to be fairly simple, its practical realization requires detailed analysis of load varying disposition in relation to element boundaries. The algorithm must enable description of both the immobile loads and the loads moving with velocity exceeding the speed of wave propagation over a system ('supersonic' velocity).

Notice that account of the external load motion with supersonic velocity is not in contradiction with the basis WFEM assumption referred only to element velocity small in comparison with wave speed.

11.1.2 Equivalent Forces for Different Load/Wave Speeds Ratio

11.1.2.1. **A.** Consider again a load $F_0(t)$ moving with varying velocity $v_0(t)$ in the positive direction of the x-axis. The load is found at a point x_0 at the beginning of the given time step and takes a position $x = x_0 + v_0 \Delta t$ to the final step moment, while F_0 and v_0 are mean values of the relevant quantities in the time interval Δt (Fig.11.1a). The boundary coordinates of the element j_*, right x_* and left $x_* - \Delta x$, within which the final load position x may occur, are beforehand unknown but they can be readily determined by the evident conditions (for $v_0 \geq 0$)

$$x_* \geq x, \ x_* - \Delta x \leq x. \tag{11.9}$$

Elements length is assumed here to be constant $\Delta x_j = \Delta x$; however, this is of no consequence.

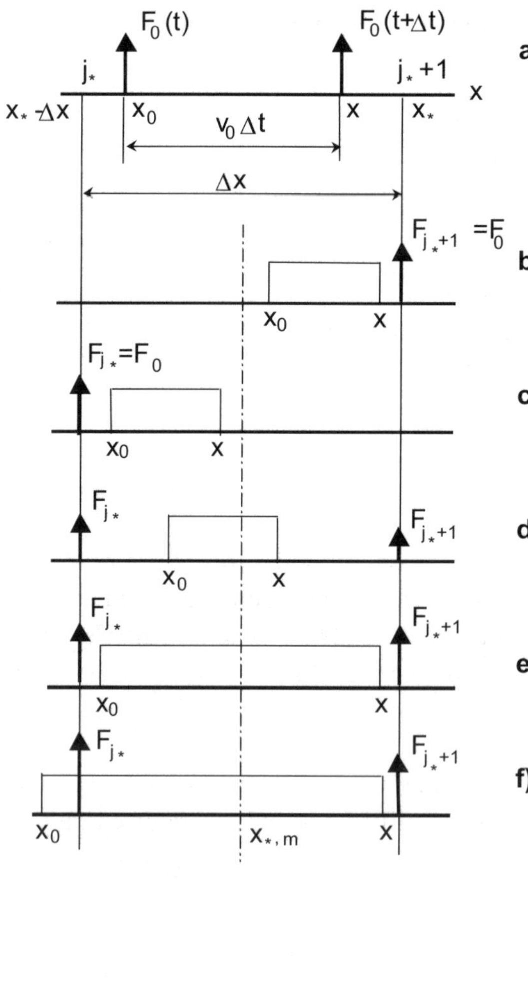

Fig.11.1. Different dispositions of a moving force accounted in Table 11.1

Using a sequential order of element tabulation, beginning from $j=1$, and taking into account that $x_* = j_* \Delta x$, the inequality $x_* \geq x$ becomes sufficient to calculate the integer index j_*.

During a time Δt for $v_0 \neq 0$, the momentum $M_0 = F_0 \Delta t$ of the force F_0 is assumed to be evenly distributed along the pass $x - x_0 = v_0 \Delta t$, while each of the infinitesimal momentum parts $dM = F_0 \Delta t dx/(x - x_0)$ relates to the length dx. Hence, the momentum M relevant to the time Δt_j is

$$M_j = M_0 \frac{\Delta x_j}{x - x_0}, \tag{11.10}$$

where $\Delta x_j = v_0 \Delta t_j$ is a length of the element portion, which the force F_0 passes in time Δt_j. Comparing Eq.(11.10) with (11.3), we see that a factor κ_j can be determined from the expression

$$\kappa_j = \frac{\Delta x_j}{x - x_0}, \tag{11.11}$$

as demonstrated below in Fig.11.1b to 11.1f for different correlation between the quantities $x_* - x$, $x_* - x_0$, and Δx.

If the quantity $x - x_0 \leq 0.5\Delta x$, and this interval is entirely situated within one half of the element j_*, the whole load F_0 must be referred to the corresponding element boundary. In this case, $\kappa_{j_*+1} = 1$ (Fig.11.1b) or $\kappa_{j_*} = 1$ (Fig.11.1c). If, as before, $x - x_0 \leq 0.5\Delta x$ but this interval is contained within both halves of the element j_*, then one part of the load $F_{j_*+1} = \kappa_{j_*+1} F_0$ with $\kappa_{j_*+1} = (x - x_{*,m})/(x - x_0)$ is assumed to be applied to the node $j_* + 1$ at the point x_*, while the remaining part $F_{j_*} = \kappa_{j_*} F_0$ with $\kappa_{j_*} = 1 - \kappa_{j_*+1}$, to the node j_* at the point $x_* - \Delta x$ (Fig.11.1d). Here, $x_{*,m} = x_* - 0.5\Delta x$.

The same approach is exploited to determine the components of the force F_0 in the cases $\Delta x \geq x - x_0 > 0.5\Delta x$ (Fig. 11.1e) or $x - x_0 > \Delta x$ (Fig. 11.1f). The last case can exist only for a 'supersonic' load velocity $v_0 > c$.

When the force F_0 stops at $v_0 = 0$ in a specific position $x = x_0 = x_{*,m}$, one takes $F_{j_*+1} = F_{j_*} = 0.5F_0$.

B. Instead of comparing the value $x - x_0$ with $0.5\Delta x$, Δx and so on, one can consider correlations between the differences $x_* - x$, $x_* - x_0$, and Δx to classify calculation cases. This approach is used for building Table 11.1, which contains the full set of formulae needed to determine the factor κ_j for components of the moving load referred to the positive velocity $v_0 \geq 0$, with arbitrary ratio of v_0 / c.

All the other nodes are free from loads within this time step. For the next step $x_0(t_{i+1}) = x(t_i)$.

Table 11.1. Determination of the factor κ_j

Correlation between $x_* - x$, $x_* - x_0$ and Δx		Formulae for force components factor κ_j	
		$0 \leq v_0 \leq c$	$v_0 > c$
$x_* - x \leq 0.5\Delta x$	$x_* - x_0 > 0.5\Delta x$	$\kappa_{j_*+1} = (x - x_* + 0.5\Delta x)/(x - x_0)$	
		$\kappa_{j_*} = 1 - \kappa_{j_*+1}$	If $\kappa_{j_*+1} \geq 1 - \Delta x/(x - x_0)$
	$x_* - x_0 < 0.5\Delta x$	$\kappa_{j_*+1} = 1$	then $\kappa_{j_*} = 1 - \kappa_{j_*+1}$,
	$x_* - x_0 = 0.5\Delta x$	$\kappa_{j_*+1} = 1$ with $v_0 > 0$	else $\kappa_{j_*} = \Delta x/(x - x_0)$; if $\kappa_{j_*+1} + \kappa_{j_*} \geq 1 - \Delta x/(x - x_0)$
		$\kappa_{j_*+1} = \kappa_{j_*} = 0.5$ with $v_0 = 0$	the $\kappa_{j_*-1} = 1 - (\kappa_{j_*+1} + \kappa_{j_*})$, else $\kappa_{j_*-1} = \kappa_{j_*}$ etc
$x_* - x > 0.5\Delta x$	$x_* - x_0 > 1.5\Delta x$	$\kappa_{j_*+1} = 0$; $\kappa_{j_*} = (x - x_* + 1.5\Delta x)/(x - x_0)$	
		$\kappa_{j_*-1} = 1 - \kappa_{j_*}$	If $\kappa_{j_*} \geq 1 - \Delta x/(x - x_0)$ then $\kappa_{j_*-1} = 1 - \kappa_{j_*}$,
	$x_* - x_0 \leq 1.5\Delta x$	$\kappa_{j_*+1} = 0$; $\kappa_{j_*} = 1$	else $\kappa_{j_*-1} = \Delta x/(x - x_0)$; if $\kappa_{j_*} + \kappa_{j_*-1} \geq 1 - \Delta x/(x - x_0)$ then $\kappa_{j_*-2} = 1 - (\kappa_{j_*} + \kappa_{j_*-1})$, else $\kappa_{j_*-2} = \kappa_{j_*-1}$; etc

11.1.2.2. **A.** The data of Table 11.1 can also be treated in some more complicated cases. If the load F_0 moves with velocity $v_0 < 0$ in the opposite direction to the x-axis, so that the final load position at the given step $x = x_0 + v_0 \Delta t$ is lesser than x_0, the following changes are needed in using Table 11.1:

i) To determine the right coordinate x_* of the element j_*, within which the starting load position x_0 is situated, we take

$$x_* = j_* \Delta x \geq x_0 \tag{11.12}$$

and calculate the integer index $j_* \geq x_0 / \Delta x$.

ii) All notations of the quantities x_0 must be changed to x and vice versa; for example, we put $\kappa_{j_*+1} = (x_0 - x_* + 0.5\Delta x)/(x_0 - x)$ for

$x_* - x_0 \le 0.5\Delta x$ and $x_* - x > 0.5\Delta x$, and so forth.

B. Let a moving distributed force of intensity $q(\xi)$ be bordered within the region $0 \le \xi \le l$, so that the full load is $F_0 = \int_0^l q(\xi)d\xi$ (Fig.11.2). The initial and final positions of the left border of this region are x_0' and $x' = x_0' + v_0\Delta t$, respectively.

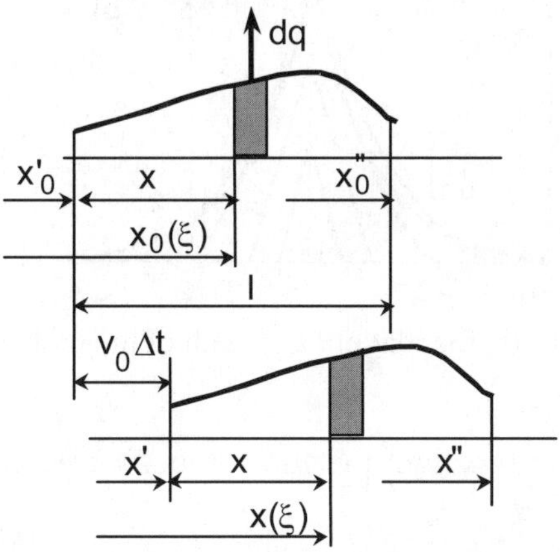

Fig.11.2. Sketch of a moving distributed load

Then, the initial and final positions of the infinitesimal load $dq = q(\xi)d\xi$ are $x_0(\xi) = x_0' + \xi$ and $x(\xi) = x' + \xi$. Applying the data of Table 11.1 to the given quantities $x_0(\xi)$ and $x(\xi)$, we obtain the factors $\kappa_j(\xi)$, from which the full nodal forces can be calculated as

$$F_j = \int_0^l q(\xi)\kappa_j(\xi)d\xi . \tag{11.13}$$

The algorithm just described was proposed by Shorr (1983) and has been generalized in Shorr and Mel'nikova (1988) to the cases of a load moving along a close trajectory, moving mass, rotary harmonic load, and reciprocally varying force.

11.2 Application of DMM to the Study of 1-D Waves Induced by Moving Loads

11.2.1 A Strip on a Viscoelastic Foundation

11.2.1.1. **Problem 11.1. An infinite strip on a viscoelastic foundation affected by a moving load.** A thin infinite strip with small flexible stiffness is modeled by an expanded string supported on a viscoelastic foundation. A transverse constant load F_0 moves with velocity $v_0(t)$, which may be constant or varying (Fig.11.3a).

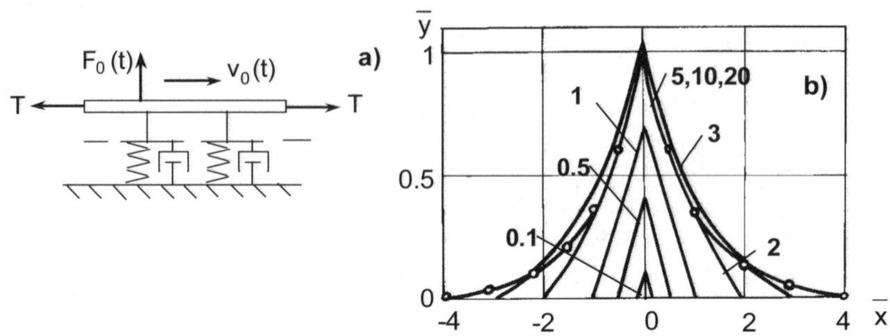

Fig.11.3. An infinite strip on a viscoelastic foundation; a) sketch of the problem, b) deflections from an immobile force

Taking account of the foundation reaction, the full force F_j affecting a node j in a time Δt is

$$F_j = F_{j,0} - k\Delta x y_{j,m} - \eta \Delta x v_j\,, \tag{11.14}$$

where $F_{j,0}$ is the varying external nodal force determined correspondingly Table 11.1, k is elastic and η viscous foundation factors referred to unit length, v_j is the node transverse velocity, and $y_{j,m}$ is the node deflection averaged over the time step.

For convenience of comparison with analytical results presented in Kaplunov and Muravsky (1986), the follow nondimensional quantities are introduced

$$\overline{F} = \frac{2F}{F_0},\ \overline{Q} = \frac{2Q}{F_0},\ \overline{v} = \frac{2v\rho c A}{F_0},\ \overline{y} = \frac{y}{y_{st}},\ \overline{x} = x\sqrt{\frac{k}{T}},\ \overline{t} = t\sqrt{\frac{k}{\rho A}},\ \overline{\eta} = \frac{\eta}{\sqrt{\rho A}}, \tag{11.15}$$

where $y_{st} = 0.5F_0/\sqrt{kT}$ is a maximum static strip deflection on the same elastic foundation under the immobile load F_0, $\overline{k} = 1$ and $\Delta\overline{x} = \Delta\overline{t}$; the wave speed is $c = \sqrt{T/\rho A}$.

Using common relationships of Sect.2.3 and expressions (11.15), the governing equation for the node velocity takes the form

$$\overline{v}_j = \frac{\overline{v}_{j,0} + \overline{v}_{j-1,0} + \overline{Q}_{j,0} - \overline{Q}_{j-1,0} + \overline{F}_{j,0} - \overline{y}_{j,0}\Delta\overline{x}}{2 + \Delta\overline{x}(\overline{\eta} + 0.5\overline{k}\Delta\overline{x})}, \tag{11.16}$$

where $\bar{y}_{j,0}$ is the starting nodal displacement at the given time step.

The condition $\Delta\bar{x}(\bar{\eta}+0.5\bar{k}\Delta\bar{x}) << 2$ provides a smooth change of the calculated parameters in time. The initial conditions are

$$\bar{y}_{j,in}=0,\ \bar{v}_{j,in}=0,\ \bar{Q}_{j,in}=0. \tag{11.17}$$

The load F_0 is assumed to be suddenly applied at the moment $t=0$ to the origin $x=0$ and then moving with velocity v_0 in positive x direction.

To describe wave propagation both forward and backwards from the origin, a calculated strip region is chosen so that the index of the origin node is $j_0=n/2+1$, where the total number of elements is $n=2\bar{t}_{\max}/\Delta\bar{t}$, with $\bar{t}_{\max}=5\div 20$ and $\Delta\bar{t}=0.01\div 0.05$.

The boundary conditions of the calculated region at $j=1$ and $j=n+1$ are of no meaning before $\bar{t}\le 0.5n\Delta\bar{x}$.

11.2.1.2. **A.** The strip deflections $\bar{y}$, after sudden application of an immobile force (with $\bar{v}_0=0$), for various time instants $\bar{t}$ are displayed in Fig. 11.3b. It is assumed that $\Delta\bar{t}=0.05$, $\bar{\eta}=1.2$, white dots referring to static analytical solution $\bar{y}(\bar{x})=\exp(-|\bar{x}|)$. The foundation viscosity (quantity of $\bar{\eta}$) is shown influencing only the rate of establishment of the limiting static state. The initial oscillations are damped even with $\bar{\eta}=0$ because of the increase of the strip region that accumulates the energy introduced.

B. Figure 11.4 illustrates the time/space development of the strip deflections under a force moving with different constant velocity $\tilde{v}_0=v_0/c$

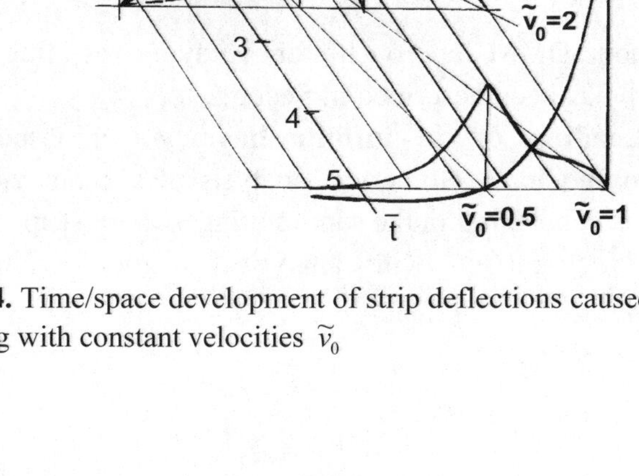

Fig.11.4. Time/space development of strip deflections caused by the load traveling with constant velocities $\tilde{v}_0$

that is scaled by the speed c: subsonic $\tilde{v}_0 = 0.5$, sonic $\tilde{v}_0 = 1$, and supersonic $\tilde{v}_0 = 2$ (dashed line); here, $\Delta\bar{t} = 0.05$, $\bar{\eta} = 0.4$.

In the first case, the perturbances propagate faster than the force travels; in the latest, the perturbances retard and are smoother. Force motion with sonic velocity leads to formation of a shock wave, whereas neglect of the flexible stiffness causes a jump of the deflection curve with the direct angle.

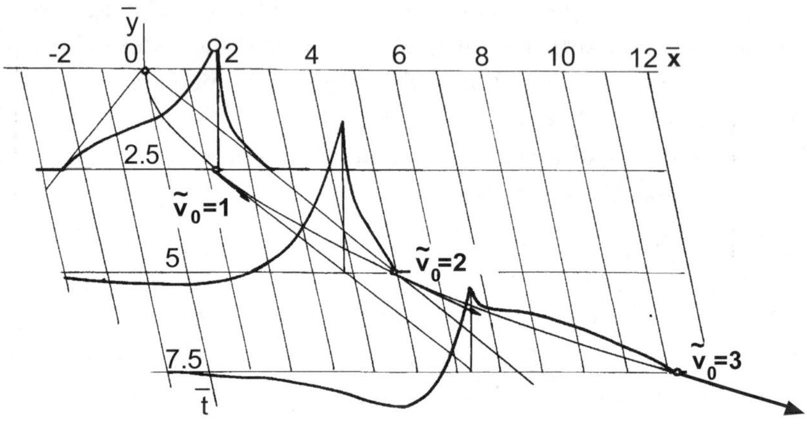

Fig.11.5. Time/space development of strip deflections caused by the load traveling with increasing velocity

C. Figure 11.5 shows the deflections under moving force, for which the velocity increases linearly from $\tilde{v}_0 = 0$ at $\bar{t} = 0$ to $\tilde{v}_0 = 3$ at $\bar{t} = 7.5$. The magnitude of the deflection at the point where $\tilde{v}_0 = 1$ (white dot) corresponds to the analytical solution (see Kaplunov and Muravsky 1986), from which the DMM result with $\Delta\bar{t} = 0.01$ is distinguished for 0.7%.

11.2.2 A Beam on a Viscoelastic Foundation

11.2.2.1. A common DMM approach for studying bending wave propagation in a beam has been described in Sect.5.2.

Problem 11.2. Loading of an infinite beam on a viscoelastic foundation by a moving load. Numerical analysis of a beam vibration under a moving load is considered in the same setting as for a strip.

For simplicity of comparison with analytical results obtained by Muravsky (1981), nondimensional quantities

$$\bar{k} = \frac{k\alpha r^2}{EA}, \bar{\eta} = \frac{\eta\alpha rc}{EA} \tag{11.18}$$

are introduced in addition to expression (5.49). Here, as above, the elastic k and viscous η foundation factors are referred to unit length.

As it has been shown in Shorr and Kaplunova (1986), the system of governing equations to the problem discussed yields

$$\bar{v}_{j,*} = \frac{\bar{v}_{j,0} + \bar{v}_{j-1,0} + \bar{F}_{j,0} - \bar{F}_{j-1,0} + \beta\bar{F}_j^* - (\beta - 1)(\tilde{F}_{j,0}^- + \tilde{F}_{j-1,0}^+) - \alpha\beta\bar{k}\bar{y}_{j,0}}{2[1 + \alpha\beta(\bar{\eta} + 0.5\alpha\bar{k})]} \tag{11.19a}$$

and

$$\bar{\omega}_{j,*} = \{ \beta(\bar{\omega}_{j,0} + \bar{\omega}_{j-1,0} + \bar{M}_{j,0} - \bar{M}_{j-1,0}) + \alpha[\bar{v}_{j,0} - \bar{v}_{j-1,0} + \bar{F}_{j,0} + \bar{F}_{j-1,0} - (\beta - 1)(\tilde{F}_{j,0}^- - \tilde{F}_{j-1,0}^+)]\} / 2\beta \tag{11.19b}$$

where $\bar{y}_{j,0}$ is the starting nodal deflection at the given step and

$$\bar{y} = \frac{yEA}{F_0 r}. \tag{11.20}$$

Regarding Eq.(11.19a) we remark that, in spite of condition (5.51) of $\alpha^2 << 1$, the term $\alpha^2\beta\bar{k}$ can be large and important for a stiff foundation with $\bar{k} >> 1$. In particular, for a rigid foundation with $\bar{k} \to \infty$ and $\bar{y}_{j,0} = 0$, Eq.(11.19a) leads to $\bar{v}_{j,*} \to -\bar{y}_{j,0} / \alpha \to 0$, as $\alpha \neq 0$.

A wave pattern for the most interesting calculated domain $\bar{x} \geq 0$ is shown in consequent figures.

11.2.2.2. **A**. Figure 11.6 shows distributions of scaled deflections $\tilde{y} = y / y_{st}$, bending moments $\tilde{M} = M / M_{st}$, and shear forces $\tilde{Q} = Q / Q_{st}$ at time instant $\bar{t} = tc / r = 40$ for different constant values of load velocity $\tilde{v}_0 = v_0 / c$ from zero to $\tilde{v}_0 = 2$. Here,

$$y_{st} = 0.5(4k^3 / \alpha^3)^{-0.25} F_0, \; M_{st} = 0.5(4k / \alpha)^{-0.25} F_0, \; Q_{st} = 0.5F_0 \tag{11.21}$$

are the magnitudes of corresponding parameters at the point $\bar{x} = 0$ under the static load F_0 applied to the beam on elastic foundation without taking account of shear strain.

Arrows mark the positions of the moving load at the given instant; the maximum static values for $\tilde{v}_0 = 0, \bar{x} = 0$ are shown by white dots. We put

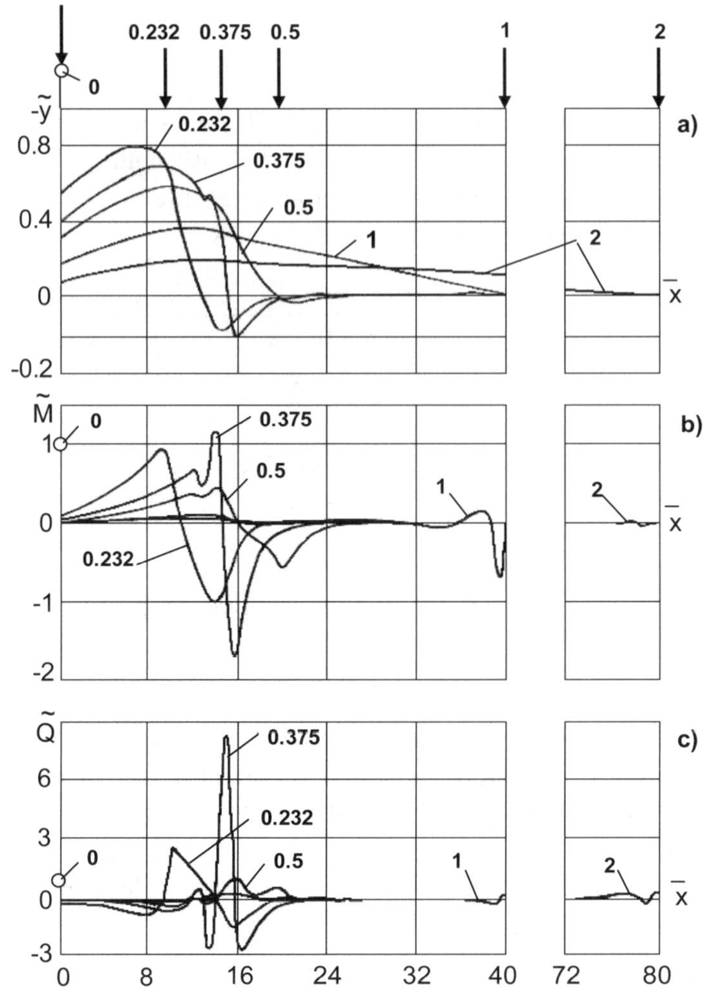

Fig.11.6. An infinite beam on a viscoelastic foundation under load traveling with constant velocity a) deflection, b) bending moment, c) shear force

$\alpha = 0.2$ and $\beta = 7.11$, $\bar{k} = 2*10^{-4}$, $\bar{\eta} = 2.6*10^{-3}$, as in Muravsky (1981).

Three 'critical' speeds of moving load are revealed by analytical solution: $\tilde{v}_{01} \approx 0.232$ is the speed of beam/foundation interaction, $\tilde{v}_{02} \approx 0.375$ is the speed of shear waves, and $\tilde{v}_{03} = 1$ is the speed of the longitudinal wave. The following effects predicted by theory appear in diagrams: i) a rapid sign change of deflection and bending moment at the current position of the moving load if it travels with critical speed $\tilde{v}_{01}$or $\tilde{v}_{02}$; ii) a local maximum of bending moment behind the leading wave for load velocity

$\widetilde{v}_{03} = 1$. For the supersonic velocity $\widetilde{v}_0 = 2$, the perturbances within the region $\bar{x} > 40$, i.e., ahead of leading longitudinal wave, are very small.

B. The time/space development of deflections $\widetilde{y}(\bar{x},\bar{t})$ and moments $\widetilde{M}(\bar{x},\bar{t})$ induced by the moving load, for which the velocity linearly increases from $\widetilde{v}_0 = 0$ to $\widetilde{v}_0 = 2$ at $\bar{t} = 40$, are shown in Fig.11.7. The load positions at various instants are displayed by white dots. The diagrams illustrate that the basic fronts of deflection and bending moment waves propagate with the speed of the shear strain $\widetilde{v}_{02}$; however, the speed of maximum deflection value is near $\widetilde{v}_{01}$.

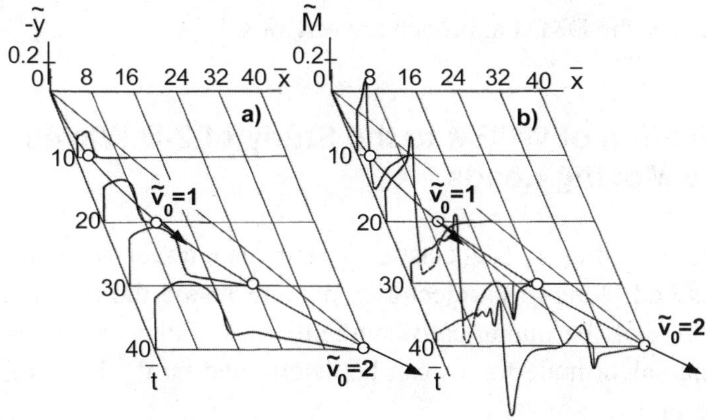

Fig.11.7. Time/space development of deflection - a) and bending moment - b) in a beam under the load traveling with increasing velocity

Furthermore, one can clearly observe the bending moment leading wave that arises under supersonic load traveling and has a speed of $\widetilde{v}_{03} = 1$.

***11.2.2.3*. Problem 11.3. Loading of a beam supported on a gapped foundation by a moving force**. The foundation from the Problem 11.2 is

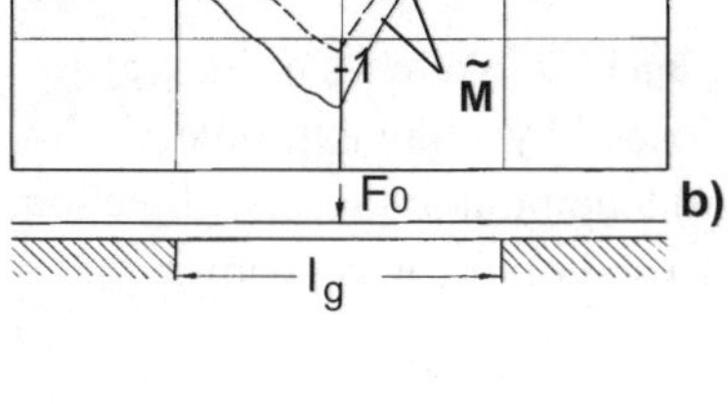

Fig.11.8. To load transition through the foundation gap; a) distribution of deflect-tions - $\widetilde{y}$ and bending moments $\widetilde{M}$ along the beam, b) scheme of the problem

now assumed to have a gap of relative length $\bar{l}_g = l_g / r$ (Fig.11.8b).

To take this peculiarity into account in DMM algorithm, it is sufficient to introduce that the foundation factors are $\bar{k} = 0$ and $\bar{\eta} = 0$ within interval $j_1 \leq j \leq j_2$, where j_1 and j_2 are node indexes referred to the gap boundaries. The pattern of deflection and bending moment distribution along the length of the gap and adjacent beam parts for an instant $\bar{t}_*$, when the load passes the gap mid-point, is shown in Fig.11.8a by the solid curves. The dashed lines relate to the unbroken foundation. The calculations are carried out with $\bar{l}_g = 12$, $\bar{t}_* = 60$, and $\tilde{v}_0 = 0.1$. The advantages of using the DMM approach are obvious.

11.3 Application of WFEM to the Study of 2-D Waves Induced by Moving Loads

Mobile loads affecting a 2-D elastic domain can travel both along its contour faces and along any trajectories passing inside the domain. Both these situations will be numerically studied below. For a rectilinear load trajectory, equivalent node forces can be determined on the basis of formulae of Table 11.1.

11.3.1 A Long Plate Loaded by a Transverse Moving Force

11.3.1.1. **Problem 11.4. A thin long plate with one free and other fixed long sides affected by transverse moving load (Fig.11.9a).** Consider a

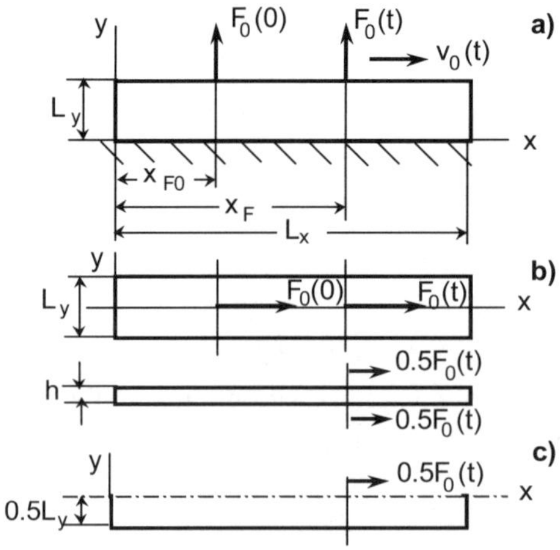

Fig.11.9. Sketches of long plates loaded by a moving force;
a) loading in transverse direction,
b) and c) longwise loading

thin long plate of width h and side ratio $L_x / L_y >> 1$, with one free and other fixed long sides. The plate is affected by a point force F_0, which is applied normal to the free long side and travels with varying velocity $v_0(t)$ along the positive direction of the longitudinal axis *x*. At the initial moment $t = 0$, the plate is at rest and the force suddenly affects a point $x = x_{F0}$, $y = L_y$.

The boundary conditions for the long sides are

$$u_x(x,0,t) = 0; u_y(x,0,t) = 0; F_x(x, L_y, t) = 0; F_y(x, L_y t) = F_0 \delta(x_F), \quad (11.22a)$$

where the delta-function is defined by

$$\delta(x_F) = \begin{cases} 0 \text{ with } x \neq x_F, \\ 1 \text{ with } x = x_F \end{cases} \quad (11.22b)$$

and $x_F = x_{F0} + \int_0 v_0(t_1) dt_1$ is a current position of the force F_0.

Using the 2-D code of WFEM (see Sect.7.2) and the algorithm for determination of equivalent node forces for moving load (Table 11.1), one can analyze in detail the varying stress-strain state and deformation of the given plate as functions of time. As in Sect.11.2, we chose the length L_x and the initial load position x_{F0}, so that the perturbances from the moving load do not reach the plate edges $x = 0$ and $x = L_x$ within the full time considered.

The formulation of Problem 11.4 in relation to the load motion along the plate is the same as above for a strip and a beam. The case of immobile load suddenly affected a thin plate will be specially discussed in Chap.12.

11.3.1.2. **A.** Here and later, nondimensional quantities are

$$\widetilde{x} = \frac{x}{L_y}, \widetilde{y} = \frac{y}{L_y}, \widetilde{t} = \frac{tc_r}{L_y}, \widetilde{v}_0 = \frac{v_0}{c_r}, \widetilde{u}_y = \frac{u_y}{u_{y,0}}, \widetilde{\sigma}_x = \frac{\sigma_x}{\sigma_{x,0}}, \quad (11.23)$$

where $c_r = \sqrt{E / \rho(1-\mu^2)}$ and $\sigma_{x,0} = F_0 / L_y h$.

It is assumed that $L_x / L_y = 15$, $n_x = 75$, and $\widetilde{x}_{F0} = 5$ (or $x_{F0} / L_x = 1/3$).

The variations of vertical displacement $\widetilde{u}_y(\widetilde{x},1)$ and normal stress $\widetilde{\sigma}_x(\widetilde{x},1)$ along the upper free long side of the plate at the time $\widetilde{t} \approx 5.4$ under the immovable load ($\widetilde{v}_0 = 0$) and the load moving with different constant velocities $\widetilde{v}_0$ are displayed in Fig. 11.10.

For the quantity $u_{y,0}$, the value of the first dynamic displacement maximum induced by the immovable load (at $\widetilde{t} \approx 2$) is taken.

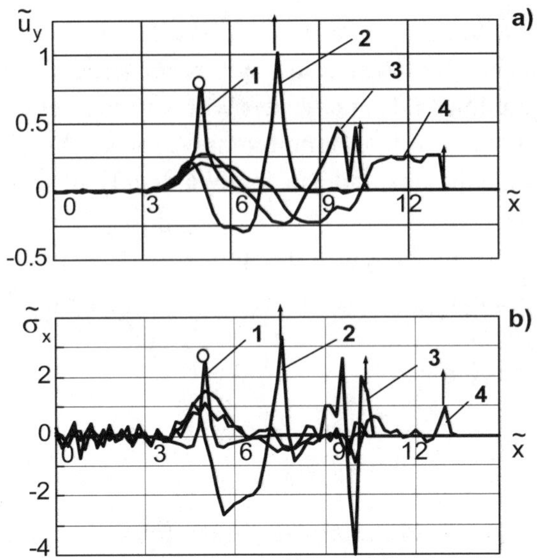

Fig.11.10. A plate affected by a transversal load moving with constant velocities $\tilde{v}_0$: 1) $\tilde{v}_0 = 0$, 2) $\tilde{v}_0 = 0.5$, 3) $\tilde{v}_0 = 1$, 4) $\tilde{v}_0 = 1.5$; a) transverse displacements, b) stresses

Disposition of the force F_0 at the initial time moment $\tilde{t} = 0$ is marked by the white dot, and at the time $\tilde{t} \approx 5.4$ by the arrows. This time has been chosen so that a backwards traveling elastic wave arrives at the plate‘s left side $x = 0$. Hence, the maximum curve values in Fig. 11.10 do not necessarily coincide with their real maximum. Notice that the time $\tilde{t} \approx 5.4$ is slightly later than $\tilde{t}_c = \tilde{x}_{F0}$=5, which would be needed to reach the point $x = 0$ with the speed c_r, because the average wave speed propagation c for the whole system, due to shear influence, is lesser then c_r. For the same reason, the load velocity $\tilde{v}_0 = 1$ is slightly greater than the real sonic

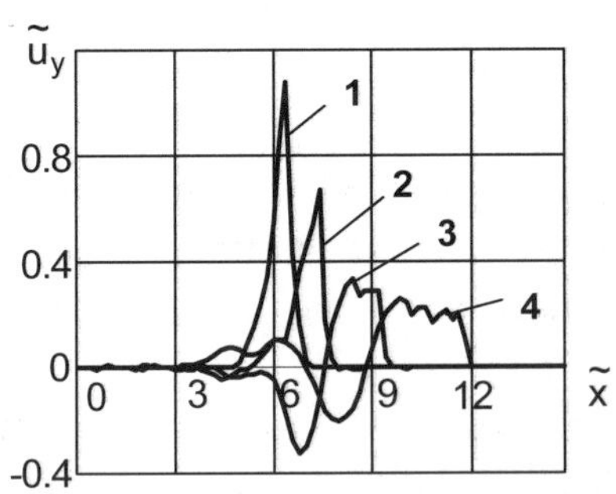

Fig.11.11. Displacements affected by a transversal load moving with increasing velocity; reference time $\tilde{t}$: 1) $\tilde{t} = 1.6$, 2) $\tilde{t} = 3.1$, 3) $\tilde{t} = 4.6$, 4) $\tilde{t} = 6$

speed $v_0 = c$, resulting in a double peak in the curves 3 in Fig.11.10. The calculations show that until the velocity $\tilde{v}_0 \approx 0.93$ only one peak of leading wave is present.

B. The pattern of displacement $\tilde{u}_y(\tilde{x},1)$ at certain time instants $\tilde{t}$ under a load moving with velocity, linearly increasing from $\tilde{v}_0 = 0$ at $\tilde{t} = 0$ to $\tilde{v}_0 = 2$ at $\tilde{t} = 6$, is shown in Fig. 11.11. Here, $L_x / L_y = 18$, $n_x = 90$, and $\tilde{x}_{F0} = 6$. The curves in Fig.11.11 relate to the scaled times $\tilde{t}$ when the increasing velocity of the moving load arrives at $\tilde{v}_0 = 0.5, 1, 1.5,$ and 2, respectively.

Some peculiarities of wave with sonic load speed $\tilde{v}_0 \approx 1$ and retardation of the displacement wave from the load position with supersonic load velocity are clearly seen.

11.3.2 A Long Plate Loaded by Longitudinal Moving Loads

11.3.2.1. **A. Problem 11.5. A long plate with free-free or fixed-fixed long sides affected by longitudinal moving loads.** A thin long plate is affected by two longitudinal forces, each of $0.5F_0$, applied to lateral surfaces of the plate at its middle line (see Fig. 11.9b). The forces synchronously move along the plate in the longitudinal direction x. Due to loading symmetry, only one half of the plate, $y \leq 0$, loaded on the face $y = 0$ by the force $0.5F_0$ (Fig.11.9c) is considered.

The boundary conditions along the axis of symmetry $y = 0$ are

$$u_y(x,0,t) = 0; F_x(x,0,t) = 0.5F_0\delta(x_F). \tag{11.24}$$

For the bottom long side, two variants of boundary conditions will be studied:

a) Fixed side,

$$u_x(x,-0.5L_y,t) = 0; u_y(x,-0.5L_y,t) = 0. \tag{11.25a}$$

b) Free side,

$$F_x(x,-0.5L_y,t) = 0; F_y(x,-0.5L_y,t) = 0. \tag{11.25b}$$

B. Numerical results for the plate with fixed sides, referred to some constant load velocities, are presented in Fig.11.12 and 11.13. The calculations are carried out with $L_x / L_y = 9$, $n_x = 90$, and $\tilde{x}_{F0} = 3$. The scaled longitudinal displacements are $\tilde{u}_x = u_x / u_{x,0}$ where $u_{x,0}$ is the value of the first displacement maximum induced by the immovable load in the point of its application.

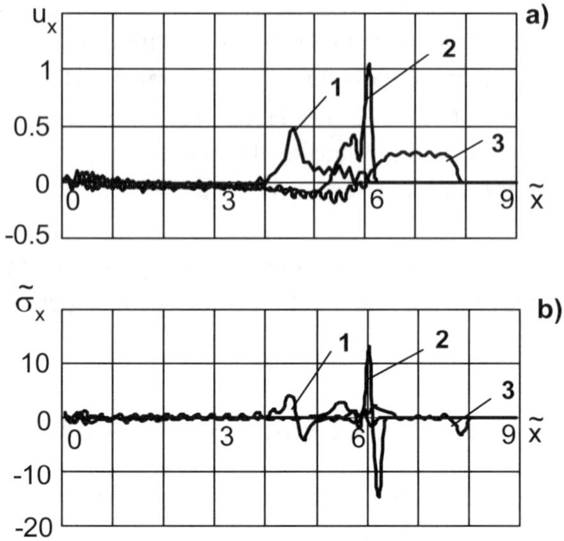

Fig.11.12. A plate affected by a longitudinal load moving with velocity $\tilde{v}_0 = \text{const.}$: 1) $\tilde{v}_0 = 0.5$, 2) $\tilde{v}_0 = 1$, 3) $\tilde{v}_0 = 1.5$; a) displacements, b) stresses

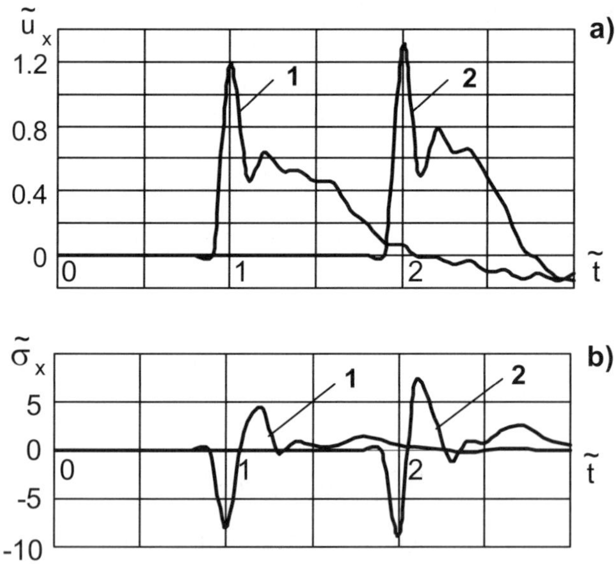

Fig.11.13. Time evolution of longitudinal displacements – a) and stresses –b) in the plate affected by a longitudinal load moving with velocity $\tilde{v}_0 = 1$ for points: 1) $\tilde{x} = 4$, 2) $\tilde{x} = 5$

In Fig.11.12, the distributions of displacement $\tilde{u}_x$ and stress $\tilde{\sigma}_x$ along the x-axis are displayed for $\tilde{t} = \tilde{t}_c \approx 3.2$, the time of which the backward wave reaches the short left end $x = 0$ of the plate. One can see that, as a whole, the wave patterns for transverse and longitudinal load direction, while traveling along the plate length, are similar. However, the disposition of the stress waves in the latter case is more apparent due to symmetrical reflections from both long sides.

Figure 11.13 illustrates the time evolution of displacements $\tilde{u}_x$ and stresses $\tilde{\sigma}_x$ at two points for the velocity $\tilde{v}_0 = 1$. Compression arising when the leading wave passes through these points rapidly changes to tension influenced by resistance of the disturbed part of the plate. For the same reason, positive displacement also alters the sign after a short time.

11.3.2.2. Some vibration peculiarities of the plate with free sides are illustrated in Fig.11.14. As above, these calculations are carried out with $L_x / L_y = 9$, $n_x = 90$, and $\tilde{x}_{F0} = 3$. In Fig.11.14a, allocations of longitudinal displacement $\tilde{u}_x$ along the $\tilde{x}$-axis for different load velocities at $\tilde{t} = 3$ are shown.

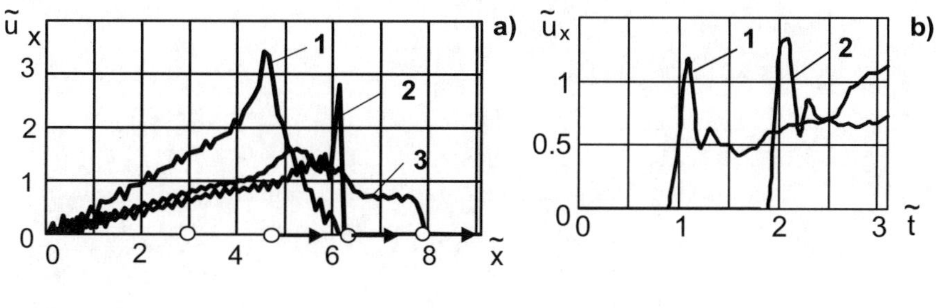

Fig.11.14. Longitudinal displacements along the plate with free sides;
a) $\tilde{u} = f(\tilde{x})$ for load velocity: 1) $\tilde{v} = 0.5$, 2) $\tilde{v} = 1$, and 3) $\tilde{v} = 1.5$;
b) $\tilde{u} = f(\tilde{t})$ for points: 1) $\tilde{x} = 4$ and 2) $\tilde{x} = 5$

Figure 11.14b demonstrates the manner in which a displacements $\tilde{u}_x$ at some points on the axis of the plate symmetry change with time for a load sonic velocity $\tilde{v}_0 = 1$. Before $\tilde{t}_* = \tilde{x}_* - \tilde{x}_{F0}$, the time of which the leading wave arrives at each of these points, the points stay in rest, at $\tilde{t}_*$ they experience a sharp splash, and then the displacements progressively increase because the disturbed part of the free plate continues its motion.

12 Dynamic Loading of a Free Plane Edge of a Solid

The problem of dynamic loading of a free plane edge of a 2-D domain is a classical task in solid mechanics. It is sometimes referred to 'the generalized Lamb's problem'. Either a thin plate, which is in a generalized plane stress, or a half-space in a plane strain are considered. Loads can be concentrating or distributed over some part of the free edge, pulsive, constant or varying by size and direction, periodic, etc. For a 2-D domain, infinite in x and y directions, a number of analytical solutions are available; however, an analysis of finite domains needs numerical solutions.

The software code WPRD (Waves in Plane Rectangular Domain) based on the wave approach, which was stated in Sect.7.1.2, allows effective simulation of the loading conditions mentioned above. Two examples were demonstrated in Sects.6.1.2 and 11.3.1. Further problems concerning the given area of the solid mechanics are considered below.

Dealing with a thin plate, we assume a specific load F [*N/m*] referred to the plate thickness h, dealing with a half-space, to the unit length of a loading line in z direction.

12.1 Constant Loads Suddenly Affecting a Thin Plate

12.1.1 A Point Force

12.1.1.1. **Problem 12.1. A plate affected by a point force (Fig.12.1).** Some domain of a thin rectangular plate $L_x \times L_y$ with a free upper edge $x = 0$ is considered. Three other sides of the plate can be fixed or free. The positive direction of the x-axis is taken, as usual in books on the theory of elasticity, downwards. A specific point force F_0 is applied to the free side at the origin $y = 0$.

Due to the symmetry, only the right half of the plate domain $y \geq 0$ affected by the force $0.5F_0$ is calculated.

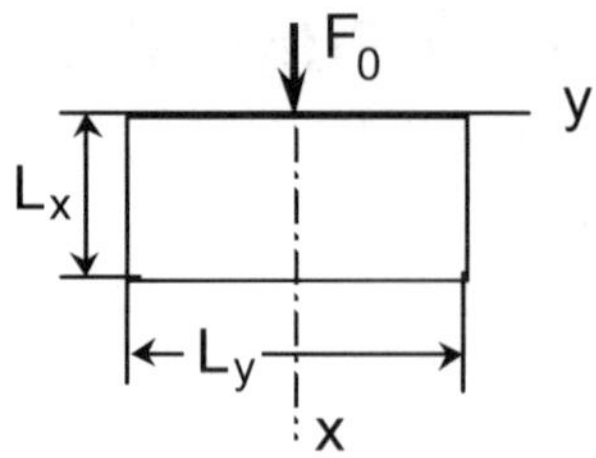

Fig.12.1. A plate affected by a point force

The boundary conditions at the axis of symmetry are

$$v_y(x,0,t)=0,\ \ F_x(x,0,t)=0\,. \tag{12.1}$$

The following nondimensional quantities are used:

$$\bar{x}=\frac{x}{L_x},\ \bar{y}=\frac{y}{L_x},\ \bar{t}=\frac{t}{t^o},\ \bar{u}=\frac{u}{u^o},\ \bar{\sigma}=\frac{\sigma}{\sigma^o}, \tag{12.2a}$$

where

$$t^o=L_x/c_r,\ u^o=F_0(1-\mu^2)/E,\ \sigma^o=F_0/\Delta y,\ c_r=\sqrt{E/\rho(1-\mu^2)}, \tag{12.2b}$$

and values of $\Delta y = \Delta x = L_x/n_x$ are determined by the chosen number n_x of elements along the length L_x.

For a finite plate, with a height H and width B, we take $L_x=H$ and $L_y=B$. For a semi-infinite plate, it is convenient to refer a length L_x to some given number n_{x0} of elements. As the distance x of wave propagation from the origin during time $t\approx x/c_r$ with calculated steps i is $x=i\Delta x$, the nondimensional time and space quantities become in this case $\bar{t}\approx\bar{x}=\bar{y}=i/n_{x0}$. Notice that calculation may be carried out with element number $n_x\neq n_{x0}$. Poisson‘s factor is taken as $\mu=0.3$.

12.1.1.2. **A.** The numerical WFEM solution for a finite plate with one free and three fixed edges was treated by Shorr (1999). In this Subsection, at first, a semi-infinite plate is modeled using solutions until the leading radial wave propagating from the origin reaches the borders of domain chosen. A 2-D distribution of vertical displacements $\bar{u}_x(\bar{x},\bar{y})$ at $\bar{t}=7/8$, with element number $n_x=n_{x0}=24$, is demonstrated in Fig.12.2.

B. An analytical solution for the static action of a point force on a semi-infinite plate, the so-called Flamant-Boussinesq‘s problem (1885, 1892), is well known. The horizontal displacements of the free edge points $x=0$ are $u_{y,st}(0,y)=-0.5(1-\mu)F_0/E$, and the normal vertical stress at any point x,y can be calculated by formula

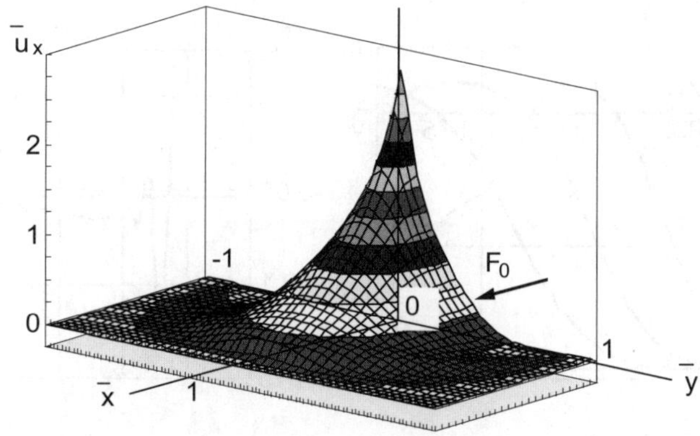

Fig.12.2. Distribution of vertical displacement $\bar{u}_x(\bar{x},\bar{y})$ under a constant point force F_0 at the time $\bar{t} = 7/8$

$$\sigma_{x,st}(x,y) = -\frac{2F_0}{\pi}\frac{x^3}{(x^2+y^2)^2}. \tag{12.3}$$

In our nondimensional terms these expressions are

$$\bar{u}_{y,st}(0,\bar{y}) = -\frac{1}{2(1+\mu)}, \quad \bar{\sigma}_{x,st}(\bar{x},\bar{y}) = -\frac{2}{\pi n_x}\frac{\bar{x}^3}{(\bar{x}^2+\bar{y}^2)^2}. \tag{12.4}$$

One can expect that an unsteady solution from a suddenly applied force would approximate these static quantities even without damping, as the energy introduced to the system spreads over the unlimited plate.

C. The distribution of horizontal displacement $\bar{u}_y(\bar{y})$ along the free edge for different times $\bar{t}$ is presented in Fig.12.3a (lines 1 to 4).

Hereafter, the basis number of elements is $n_{x0} = 36$ and the mesh is $n_x = n_y = 48$. A 'platform' of a constant value $\bar{u}_y \approx -0.385$ is seen to gradually form as the leading wave recedes from the point where the force has been imposed. The static theory predicts such phenomenon. The nondimensional analytical value of the horizontal static displacement for $\bar{u}_{y,st} = -0.3846$ (line 5) is very close to the numerical one.

The time variation of the normal stress $\bar{\sigma}_x(\bar{t})$ at $\bar{x} = 1/3$, on the axis of symmetry $\bar{y} = 0$, is shown in Fig.12.3b. The leading stress wave reaches this point at $\bar{t} = 1/3$, and then the stress gradually drops to the static value $\bar{\sigma}_{x,st}(1/3,0) = -2/\pi n_{x0}\bar{x} = -0.05305$.

In Fig.12.4a, the distributions of normal stress $\bar{\sigma}_x(\bar{y})$ along the horizontal line $\bar{x} = 1/3$ for different times are displayed (curves 1,2,3). The calculated stresses are averaged over elements due to Eqs.(7.31).

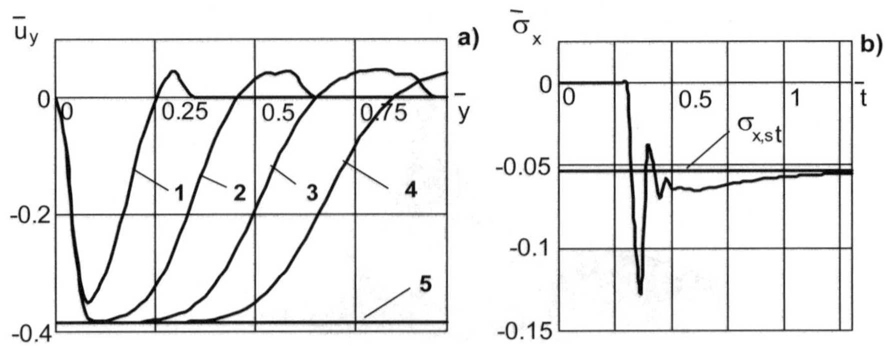

Fig.12.3. A constant point force; a) distribution of horizontal displacement $\bar{u}_y$ along the free face for instants $\bar{t}$: 1) $\bar{t}=1/3$, 2) $\bar{t}=2/3$, 3) $\bar{t}=1$, 4) $\bar{t}=1.25$; 5) analytical static value; b) variation of normal stress $\bar{\sigma}_x$ at the point $\bar{x}=1/3$, $\bar{y}=0$ vs. time

The stress in the node $\bar{x}=1/3, \bar{y}=0$ at the axis of symmetry at $\bar{t}=4/3$ is determined by Eq.(7.34b) separately and depicted by the white dot. This quantity lies very close to the analytical static curve shown by a line 4.

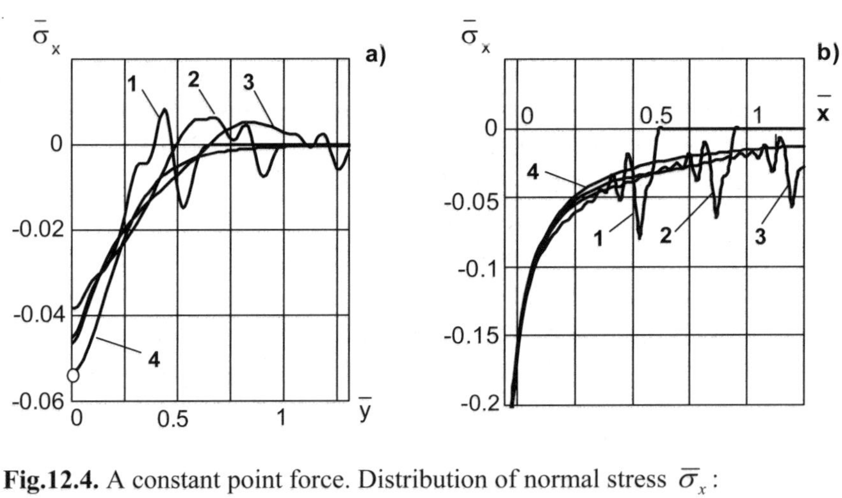

Fig.12.4. A constant point force. Distribution of normal stress $\bar{\sigma}_x$:
a) along the line $\bar{x}=1/3$; b) along the axis $\bar{y}=0$;
1) $\bar{t}=0.75$, 2) $\bar{t}=1$, 3) $\bar{t}=1.33$; 4) analytical static value

The distributions of stress $\bar{\sigma}_x(\bar{x})$ along the vertical axis of symmetry $\bar{y}=0$ for the same times are presented in Fig.12.4b (curves 1,2,3). When the distance between the leading front and the point under consideration increases, the unsteady stress approximates the static one (curve 4).

12.1.2 A Distributed Load

Problem 12.2. A plate affected by a vertical distributed load (Fig.12.5a). In contrast to the Problem 12.1, a finite plate of height H and width B is considered. The bottom side $x = H$ is fixed, the lateral sides $y = \pm 0.5B$ are assumed to be free, with the boundary conditions

$$v_x(H,y,t) = v_y(h,y,t) = 0\,, \tag{12.5a}$$

$$F_x(x,\pm 0.5B,t) = F_y(x,\pm 0.5B,t) = 0\,. \tag{12.5b}$$

The normal permanent traction $q[N/m^2]$ referred to the plate thickness is suddenly applied to the section $2y_q$ of the face $x = 0$, so that the distributed load qy_q affects a right half of the plate. A mesh $n_x = n_y = 24$ and a magnitude $\bar{y}_q = 5/6$ are taken.

The time evolution of stresses $\bar{\sigma}_x$, $\bar{\sigma}_y$, $|\bar{\sigma}_{xy}|$ at the point A adjoining the free face is demonstrated in Fig.12.5b. The averaged stresses referred to nodes are calculated using Eqs.(7.34a).

The waves reflected from the bottom fixed edge are clearly seen. Reflections from the free lateral sides are also noticed but they are weaker in character. As the plate region is now bounded, steady undamped non-harmonic oscillations with period of $\bar{T} \approx 4$ are established.

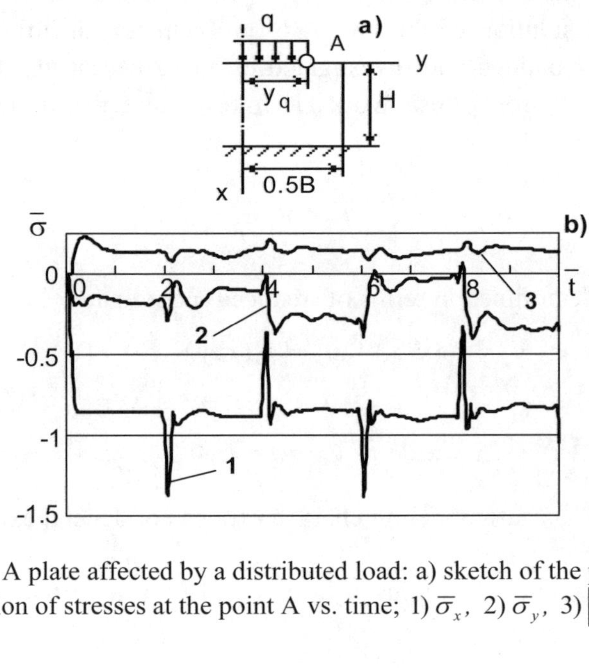

Fig.12.5. A plate affected by a distributed load: a) sketch of the problem, b) evolution of stresses at the point A vs. time; 1) $\bar{\sigma}_x$, 2) $\bar{\sigma}_y$, 3) $|\bar{\sigma}_{xy}|$

12.2 Varying Loads Affecting a Half-Space

Under the condition of a plane strain, a load (traction) $q(y,t)$ distributed over a free surface $x=0$ of a half-space can consist of normal (vertical) q_x and tangential (horizontal) q_y components arbitrarily varying in time. Any boundary conditions at bottom $x=H$ and lateral $y=\pm 0.5B$ faces of a half-space, infinite in the z direction, are possible. A load evenly distributed only along the z-axis will be conditionally called 'a point' force.

12.2.1 A Point Impulsive Force

12.2.1.1. **A. Problem 12.3. A half-space subjected to a point vertical impulsive load.** Both designations given in Fig.12.1 and determinations of nondimensional quantities of Eqs.(12.1,b) are generally valid; however, a plane strain with $\varepsilon_z = 0$ is assumed, and the force F_0 represents a load referred to unit length in the z direction. The displacements are scaled by a quantity

$$u^o = F_0 / E_r = F_0(1+\mu)(1-2\mu)/E(1-\mu),$$

and the speed of the dilatation wave is $c_r = \sqrt{E_r/\rho}$.

An analytical solution of this unsteady problem for an infinitesimally short pulse was obtained and investigated by Petrashen at al. (1950) and Kaplunov (1986). From those works it follows that the 'reduced' displacements

$$\widetilde{u}_x = u_x \frac{\pi G t}{F_0}, \quad \widetilde{u}_y = u_y \frac{\pi G t}{F_0} \tag{12.6}$$

are completely determined in terms of 'reduced' coordinates

$$\widetilde{u}_x = f_x(\widetilde{x},\widetilde{y}), \quad \widetilde{u}_y = f_y(\widetilde{x},\widetilde{y}), \tag{12.7a}$$

where

$$\widetilde{x} = x/c_g t, \ \widetilde{y} = y/c_g t, \tag{12.7b}$$

i.e., the solution has automodeling character (does not depend explicitly on time).

The varying semicircle radius $R_g = c_g t$, which is a distance that the shear wave travels with the speed $c_g = \sqrt{G/\rho}$ in time t, is taken for a characteristic linear size (Fig.12.6a).

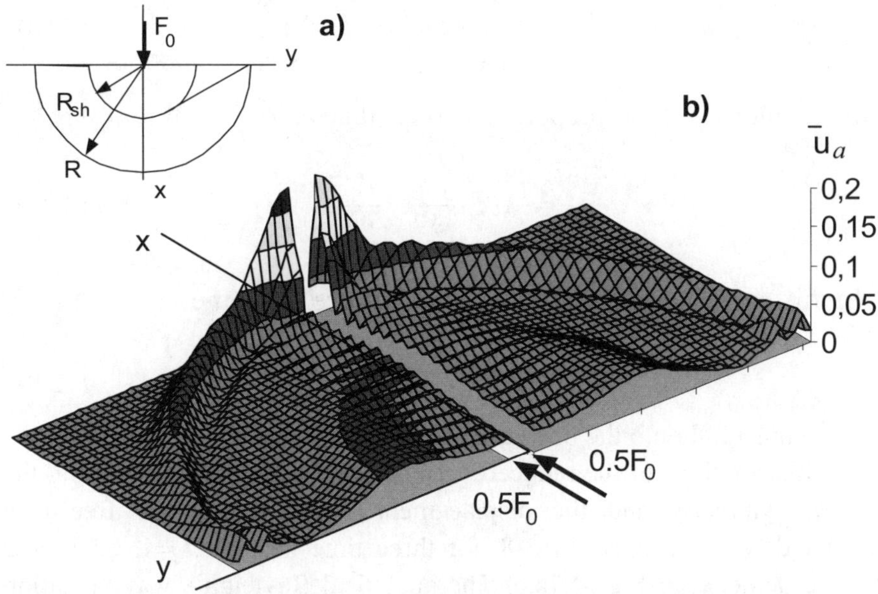

Fig.12.6. A half-space subjected to a point vertical impulsive load F_0 : a) theoretical map, b) calculated pattern of a full displacement

The leading front of the dilatation wave $R = c_r t$ advances beyond the shear front in the ratio of $R/R_g = c_r/c_g = 1/\bar{c}_g$. Interaction of the leading front and the free surface results in the rectilinear part of the shear front that connects the semicircles R_g and R. The point $\tilde{y}_R$ relates to the Rayleigh's surface wave.

With $\mu = 0.3$, the characteristic ratios are $R_g/R \approx 0.5345$ and $\tilde{y}_R/R_g \approx 0.9274$.

In Fig.12.6b, a common pattern of full displacement $\bar{u}_a = \sqrt{\bar{u}_x^2 + \bar{u}_y^2}$ within the region $L_x = L_y = R$, calculated using the WFEM program, is displayed. The mesh is 36×36 with the minimal impulse duration $\bar{t}_{imp} = 1/36$. The halves of the region are shown conditionally moved apart. Both the semicircles of the analytical wave fronts and the Rayleigh's surface wave are clearly seen.

B. It follows from Eqs.(12.6) and (12.7) that the displacements $u^{(1)}(x^{(1)}, y^{(1)}, t^{(1)})$ and $u^{(2)}(x^{(2)}, y^{(2)}, t^{(2)})$, relevant to different points

$x^{(1)}, y^{(1)}$ and $x^{(2)}, y^{(2)}$, will be connected to one another at two different time instants $t^{(1)}$ and $t^{(2)}$ by the equality

$$u^{(1)}(x^{(1)}, y^{(1)}, t^{(1)}) = u^{(2)}(x^{(2)}, y^{(2)}, t^{(2)}) \frac{t^{(2)}}{t^{(1)}} \tag{12.8a}$$

if the coordinate ratio is proportional to the time ratio

$$\frac{x^{(1)}}{x^{(2)}} = \frac{t^{(1)}}{t^{(2)}}, \quad \frac{y^{(1)}}{y^{(2)}} = \frac{t^{(1)}}{t^{(2)}}. \tag{12.8b}$$

In this case, the reduced displacements are the same

$$\widetilde{u}^{(1)}(\widetilde{x}^{(1)}, \widetilde{y}^{(1)}) = \widetilde{u}^{(2)}(\widetilde{x}^{(2)}, \widetilde{y}^{(2)}), \tag{12.9}$$

i.e. they must fall onto the one curve.

The distributions of the reduced vertical displacement $\widetilde{u}_x(\widetilde{x},0)$ along the axis of symmetry and the displacement $\widetilde{u}_x(0,\widetilde{y})$ along the free face calculated with the mesh 48×48 for three time instants $\bar{t} = 1,\ 0.75$, and 0.5 are depicted in Fig.12.7a,b. The analytical Rayleigh's wave position $\widetilde{y}_R$ at the free surface and distortion wave front $\widetilde{x}_g$ at the $\widetilde{x}$ - axis are also labeled in these Figures. The correlation between numerical and analytical results is sufficiently good. Theoretically, for impulse duration $t_{imp} = 0$, the displacement derivative at the dilatation wave front is $\partial u_y / \partial x \to \infty$. This leads to a sharp spike near the point $\widetilde{x} \approx 1$ in computations.

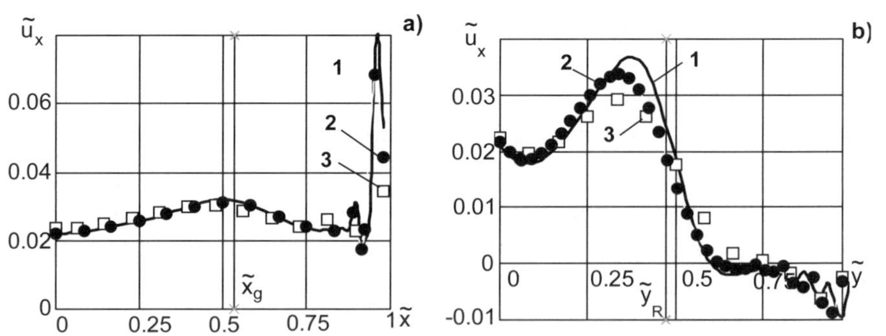

Fig.12.7. Distribution of reduced vertical displacement $\widetilde{u}_x$ along the reduced coordinates $\widetilde{x}$ or $\widetilde{y}$: a) for the axis of symmetry, b) for the free face; time instants $1)\bar{t} = 1,\ 2)\bar{t} = 0.75,\ 3)\bar{t} = 0.5$

12.2.1.2. **A.** Five points with coordinates $\bar{x}_j = \bar{y}_j$ plotted on the diagonal of the calculated domain, as shown in Fig.12.8a, are separated for further analysis. A mesh 48×48 with the minimal impulse duration $\bar{t}_{imp} = 1/48$ is taken. In Fig.12.8a, some node indexes for relevant axes are depicted. The time change of vertical displacements $\bar{u}_x$ at the points 2 to 5 is presented in Fig.12.8b. The instants $\bar{t}(\bar{x}_j)$ when the leading dilatation wave reaches the given points j approximate theoretical values of $\bar{t}(\bar{x}_j) = \bar{x}_j\sqrt{2}$. The second (shear) wave is also seen. After both fronts are transmitted, the displacements drop monotonically.

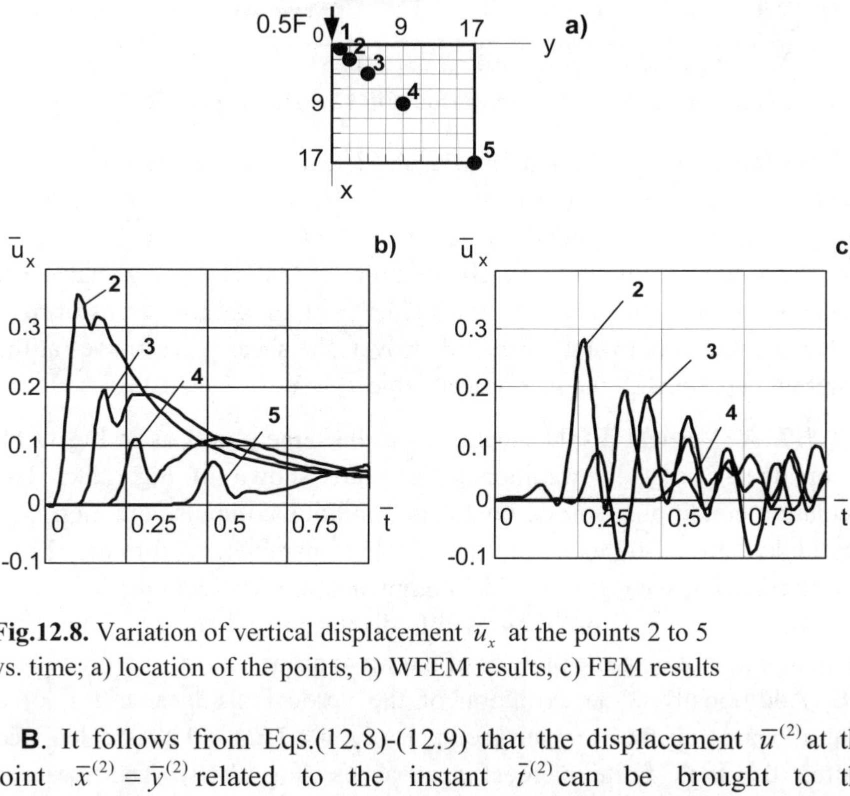

Fig.12.8. Variation of vertical displacement $\bar{u}_x$ at the points 2 to 5 vs. time; a) location of the points, b) WFEM results, c) FEM results

B. It follows from Eqs.(12.8)-(12.9) that the displacement $\bar{u}^{(2)}$ at the point $\bar{x}^{(2)} = \bar{y}^{(2)}$ related to the instant $\bar{t}^{(2)}$ can be brought to the displacement $\bar{u}^{(1)}$ at the other point $\bar{x}^{(1)} = \bar{y}^{(1)}$ for the instant $\bar{t}^{(1)}$ by displacement changing to $\bar{x}^{(2)}/\bar{x}^{(1)}$ times. The results of such a transformation of four points 1,3,4 and 5 to the point 2 are depicted in Fig.12.9. Once the time $\bar{t}$ significantly exceeds the impulse duration ($\bar{t}/\bar{t}_{imp} >> 1$, or $\bar{t} > 0.25$), all the 'transformed' displacements lie closely on the common curve. Within the time domain $\bar{t} < 0.25$ the curve are stratified. Two peaks referred to dilatation and shear wave fronts are detec-

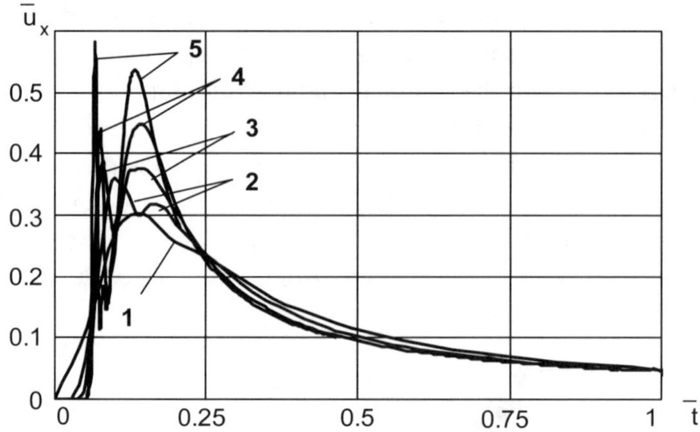

Fig.12.9. Transformation of the curves from Fig.12.8b to the point 2

ted here more clearly than in Fig.12.8a. The leading wave reaches the calculated point 2 with coordinates $\bar{x} = \bar{y} = 1/24$ at the time $\bar{t} \approx 0.06$ that is very close to the theoretical value $\bar{t} = \bar{x}\sqrt{2} \approx 0.059$. As a point recedes from the point of impulse, its effect more and more approximates the instantaneous one that leads to the increase of maximum 'transformed' displacements at both wave fronts. Moreover, the shear wave arrives at the instant that approaches the theoretical value $\bar{t}_g = \bar{x}\sqrt{2}/\bar{c}_g \approx 0.110$.

12.2.1.3. **A.** Vertical displacements $\bar{u}_x$ at the same points as in Fig.12.8b but obtained using the traditional FEM are shown in Fig.12.8c. The calculation conditions (mesh, boundary conditions, impulse duration, and magnitude) are completely identical. The parameters for the FEM algorithm are chosen due to guide recommendations (by default).

Visible significant oscillations of displacement curves with sign alternation do not map the physics of the wave process.

B. Additionally, time evolution of the vertical displacement $\bar{u}_x$ of a point allocated on the free surface at $\bar{x} = 0$, $\bar{y} = 7/24 \approx 0.29$ is calculated treating the both finite element approaches (Fig.12.10). The mesh is 24×24, impulse duration $\bar{t}_{imp} = 1/24$, and Poisson's factor $\mu = 0.1$. The calculations are prolonged to the time $\bar{t} = 1.67$ until a wave reflected from the free lateral side has returned to the given point. Curve 1 in Fig.12.10 relates to the WFEM calculation without smoothing, curves 2 and 3 are calculated using two FEM codes.

Notice that solutions of 'unwave' problems obtained by different FEM codes coincide, as a rule, quite well. The essential distinction of the calcu-

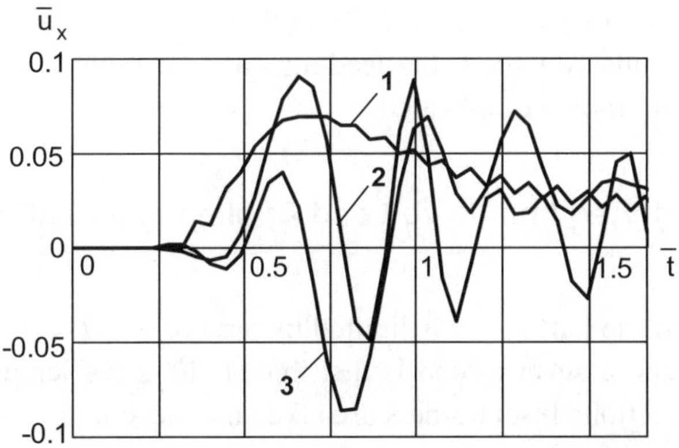

Fig.12.10. Variation of the vertical displacement at the point $\bar{x} = 0, \bar{y} = 7/24$ vs. time; 1) WFEM results, 2) and 3) results due to two different FEM codes

lated curves 2 and 3 and their large oscillations, which cannot be accounted for by wave reflections from domain boundaries, indicate the disadvantages of traditional FEM in application to problems where the wave processes are of fundamental importance.

12.2.1.4. Below, an example with a point rectangular impulse is treated.

Problem 12.4. A point vertical rectangular impulse. A mesh of 24×24 and impulse duration of $\bar{t}_{imp} = 1/6$ containing four time steps are taken below.

The total pattern of vertical displacement $\bar{u}_x(\bar{x}, \bar{y})$ at $\bar{t} = 0.75$, when the leading wave has not yet arrived at the edges of the given mesh, is presented in Fig.12.11.

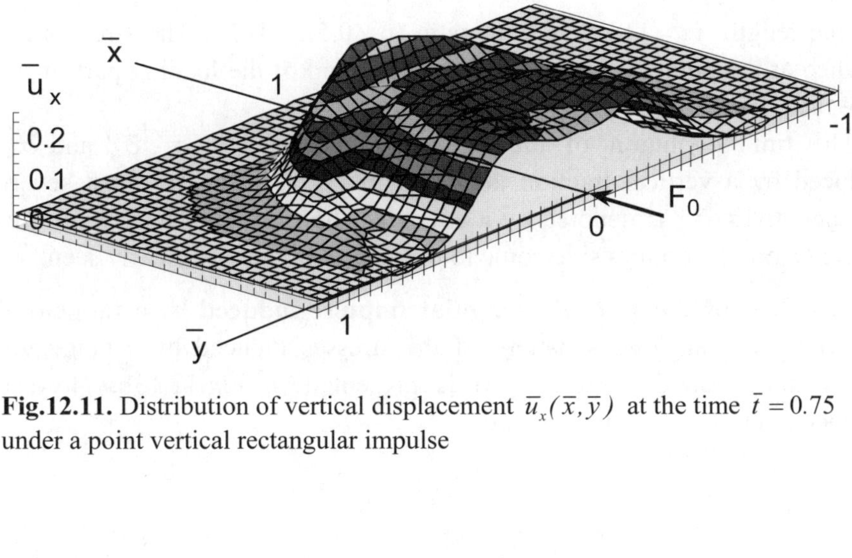

Fig.12.11. Distribution of vertical displacement $\bar{u}_x(\bar{x}, \bar{y})$ at the time $\bar{t} = 0.75$ under a point vertical rectangular impulse

Comparing the maps in Fig.12.6b and 12.11, we see that, with increasing of impulse duration, the leading wave becomes less sharp and the line of its front more complicated.

12.2.2 A Distributed Impulsive Load Applied to a Limited Domain

Now, a region of the half-space is limited by area of $B/H = 16/7 \approx 2.286$ with rigid borders, a surface load is distributed along the length $\bar{y}_q$, and the repeated reflections from borders are taken into account.

12.2.2.1. **Problem 12.5. Rectangular impulse induced by a normal traction.** A normal (vertical) surface traction $q_x = 1$ (Fig.12.12a) is applied

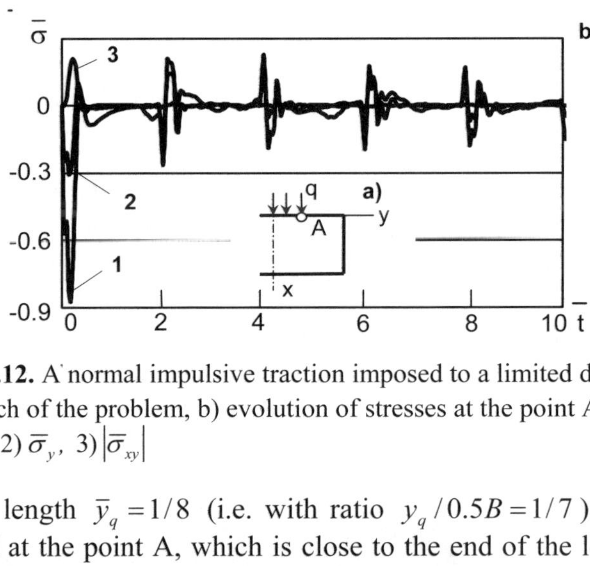

Fig.12.12. A normal impulsive traction imposed to a limited domain: a) sketch of the problem, b) evolution of stresses at the point A vs. time; 1) $\bar{\sigma}_x$, 2) $\bar{\sigma}_y$, 3) $|\bar{\sigma}_{xy}|$

on the length $\bar{y}_q = 1/8$ (i.e. with ratio $y_q / 0.5B = 1/7$). The stresses are studied at the point A, which is close to the end of the loading part of the free face.

The time evolution of the all stress components $\bar{\sigma}_x$, $\bar{\sigma}_y$ and $\bar{\sigma}_{xy}$ induced by a vertical traction is shown in Fig.12.12b. The most severe normal stress $\bar{\sigma}_x$ is denoted by a curve 1. The times at which waves-reflected from the bottom side come to the referred point are clearly seen.

12.2.2.2. **Problem 12.6. Rectangular impulse induced by a tangential traction.** The analogous pattern of the stresses induced by a tangential (horizontal) traction (Fig.12.13a) is presented in Fig.12.13b. Now, a surface traction $q_y = 1$ is assumed.

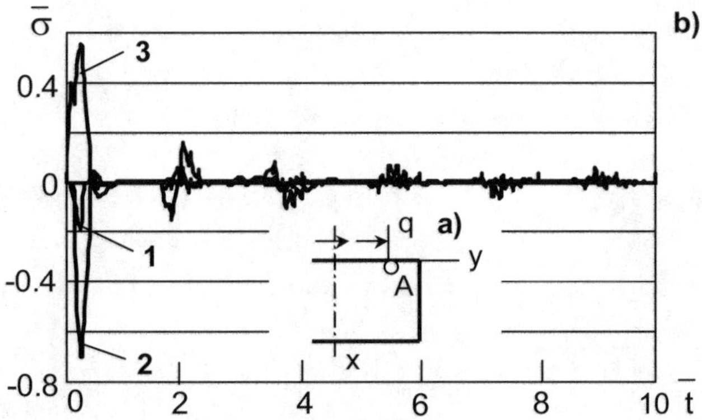

Fig.12.13. A tangential impulsive traction imposed to a limited domain: a) sketch of the problem, b) evolution of stresses at the point A vs. time; 1) $\bar{\sigma}_x$, 2) $\bar{\sigma}_y$, 3) $|\bar{\sigma}_{xy}|$

In this case, the problem becomes anti-symmetrical, with boundary conditions

$$v_x(x,0,t) = 0, \ F_y(x,0,t) = 0\,. \tag{12.9}$$

Under horizontal traction, the normal stress $\bar{\sigma}_y$ denoted by a curve 2 is seen to be the most significant. Attention is drawn to the large shear stress $\bar{\sigma}_{xy}$ (curve 3) arising soon after loading. The times when waves reflected from the nearest lateral side return to point A are also observed.

13 Some Special Problems of Solid Mechanics

13.1 Deformation of a Chain of a Varying Length

Among all the problems in solid mechanics a special place belongs to a problem of unsteady movement of rigid bodies with varying size and mass. General approaches to these problems are treated by Meshchersky and other authors. However, in doing so, one can obtain in some cases seemingly paradoxial results relevant to violation of the law of energy balance (see, e.g., Panovko 1985). To understand the nature of those paradoxes, the elastic properties of a solid need to be taken into account.

As an example, a problem, usually called the 'Kaly's problem' and analyzed by Mikhailov (1984) and Panovko (1985), is considered below.

13.1.1 Sliding Down of an Elastic Chain under Own Weight

13.1.1.1. **Problem 13.1 A flexible chain (string, cord, etc.) of unit cross-sectional area A=1, stacked at an edge of a smooth horizontal plane, slides down under the action of the own weight (Fig.13.1a).**

A. A chain is assumed to be originally folded in a coil, so its parts do not move simultaneously, but serially, during the process of unwinding the coil. Friction forces are neglected. These assumptions are, of course, only a conditional mathematical model of a real situation.

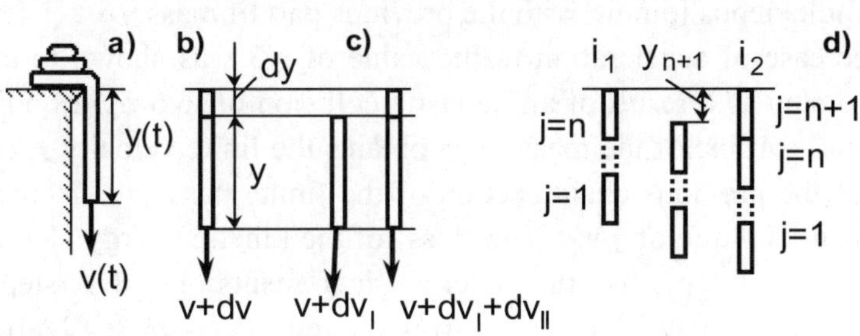

Fig.13.1. Sketches to Kaly's problem

Let initially the chain assume to be *inextensible* as was the case in the above cited papers. The length and the velocity of a vertically hanging part of the chain at time t are $y(t)$ and $v(t)$, respectively. As a new chain particle of the length $dy = vdt$ is included in the sliding branch, the law of momentum conservation yields (Fig.13.1b)

$$y\frac{d^2y}{dt^2} - gy + \left(\frac{dy}{dt}\right)^2 = 0, \tag{13.1}$$

where g is the accelaration due to gravity.

The solution of Eq.(13.1) with initial conditions $y(0) = 0$ and $v(0) = dy(0)/dt = 0$ is $y(t) = gt^2/6$, from which the velocity $v(t)$ and acceleration $a(t)$ are $v(t) = gt/3$, $a(t) = g/3$.

If the whole length of the chain is L, it begins to fall freely with acceleration $a_* = g$, starting at $t_* = \sqrt{6L/g}$ when $y_* = L$.

At this moment the velocity reaches a value of $v_* = \sqrt{2gL/3}$ and the work W_* done by the gravitation force $F_* = \rho gL$ is $W_* = \rho gL^2/2$, while the kinetic energy K_* of the chain is $K_* = 0.5\rho Lv_*^2 = \rho gL^2/3$. Thus, a part of the introduced work

$$\Delta W_* = W_* - K_* - \rho gL^2/6 \tag{13.2}$$

is 'lost' inspite of the absence of damping.

Moreover, the acceleration of the entire chain 'jumps' at $t = t_*$ to $\Delta a = a_* - a = 2g/3$; this seams to be phisically unprobable.

B. With a view of analyzing this situation, an inclusion of the new particle in the falling branch was represented by Shorr (1996) for infinitesimal time dt as two sequantial steps (Fig.13.1c): i) A free fall of the chain part of the given length $y(t)$ when it is dropped to $dy = v(t)dt$; and ii) A substitution of the released place by a new particle of mass ρdy and its simultaneous joining with the previous part of mass ρy.

The decrease of acceleration to the value of $g/3$ was shown to arise at the second step as a result of an inelastic collision of two rigid bodies: an infinitesimal particle of the mass ρdy obtains the finite velocity v, and the velocity of the previous chain section of the finite mass ρy decreases to an infinitesimal value of dv_{II}. The 'loss' of the kinetic energy also occurs at the second step, as the energy increments in the steps are $dK_I = \rho yvdv_I = \rho gydy$, $dK_{II} = -\rho gydy/3$, and $dK_I + dK_{II} = 2\rho gydy/3$. After integrating the last expression over the whole chain, we return to the quantity of $K_* = \rho g L^2 / 3 < W_*$. The role of an inelastic shock was described quantitively by Panovko (1985).

All given paradoxial phenomena are shown to result from the assumption of the chain inextensibility. However, any analytical or numerical solutions for the analogeous generalized Kaly's problem referred to an extensible elastic chain are not known to the author.

13.1.1.2. Conditional separation of the new particle joining to the sliding chain into two steps is convenient to numerical calculation by DMM.

In doing so, we separate an *extensible elastic* chain into n_0 elements of length $\Delta L = L / n_0$ and take the weight $0.5 \rho g \Delta L$ of each element half as an external force applied to its border. Hence, for an inner node *j* (taking into account the usual sign rule)

$$F_j^* = -\rho g \Delta L . \tag{13.3}$$

The invariable boundary condition for the first (lower) element $j = 1$ is

$$\sigma_1^- = -F_1^- = 0.5 \rho g \Delta L . \tag{13.4}$$

The equations controlling the inner boundary between elements $j-1$ and *j* are

$$\sigma_j^- - \sigma_{j-1}^+ - \rho g \Delta L = 0, \; v_{j-1}^+ = v_j^- , \tag{13.5}$$

from where

$$\left. \begin{aligned} v_j^- &= 0.5[v_{j,0} + v_{j-1,0} + (\sigma_{j,0} - \sigma_{j-1,0}) / \rho c - g \Delta L / c] \\ \sigma_j^- &= \sigma_{j,0} - (v_j^- - v_{j,0}) \rho c \end{aligned} \right\} . \tag{13.6}$$

Let a section of the chain with a number *n* of elements occur hanging down, beginning from some time step i_1. This section, including the current upper element *j=n*, is assumed to free falling under boundary conditions at the node $j = n + 1$

$$\left. \begin{aligned} \sigma_n^+ &= F_n^+ = -0.5 \rho g \Delta L, \\ v_n^+ &= v_{n,0} + (\sigma_n^+ - \sigma_{n,0}) / \rho c \end{aligned} \right\} . \tag{13.7}$$

The following element $j = n + 1$ will transmit from the silent horizontal branch to the vertical falling one after a step number $i_2 - i_1$, when the accomodated displacement of the node $j = n + 1$ reaches the value of element length, i.e.

$$\left|y_{n+1}\right| = \sum_{i=i_1}^{i=i_2} \left|\Delta y_{n+1}\right|_i \geq \Delta L \,. \tag{13.8}$$

From this moment, the element $j = n+1$ takes the position of the last upper element (see Fig.13.1d) with the starting state $\sigma_{n+1,0} = 0,\ v_{n+1,0} = 0.$ The previous node $j = n+1$ between the elements n and n+1 becomes the inner, and the boundary conditions of the type (13.5) allow us to determine the shock stress

$$\sigma_{n+1}^{-} = -\rho c v_{n+1}^{-} = 0.5[\sigma_{n,0} - \rho c v_{n,0} + \rho g \Delta L] \,. \tag{13.9}$$

Then, the calculation of the accomodated displacement of the following node $j = n+2$ begins again, and so forth.

After the last element $n = n_0$ be included in the vertical branch, the chain continues falling as a whole while the upper boundary conditions remain unchanged.

13.1.2 Numerical Example

13.1.2.1. For computation of a chain with the unit area of cross section A=1, we use the following nondimensional quantities:

$$\bar{\sigma} = \frac{\sigma}{\rho g L},\ \bar{v} = \frac{vc}{gL},\ \bar{x} = \frac{x}{L},\ \bar{t} = \frac{tc}{L},\ \bar{y} = \frac{yc^2}{gL^2},\ \bar{a} = \frac{a}{g} \tag{13.10a}$$

and also for energy characteristics

$$\overline{K}, \overline{P}, \overline{E}, \overline{W} = (K, P, E, W)c^2 / \rho g^2 L^3 \,. \tag{13.10b}$$

The condition (13.8) to inclusion of a new element in a falling branch of the chain may be expressed as

$$\left|\bar{y}_{n+1}\right| \geq \bar{y}_* / n_0 \,, \tag{13.11}$$

where $\bar{y}_* = c^2 / gL$.

As an example of a slipping elastic body, a rubber cord of length L=5m, for which $c = 37 m/c$ and $\rho = 1.25 * 10^3 kg/m^3$, was employed. In this case $\bar{y}_* = 27.9$, the complete dimensionless time of sliding down for non-deformable body of the same length L is $\bar{t}_* = \sqrt{6\bar{y}_*} = 12.94$, and the velocity is $\bar{v}_* = \sqrt{2\bar{y}_* / 3} = \bar{t}_* / 3 = 4.31$.

The time evolution of element velocities for the elastic cord is relatively complicated because of numerous reflections from borders of a body of varying length

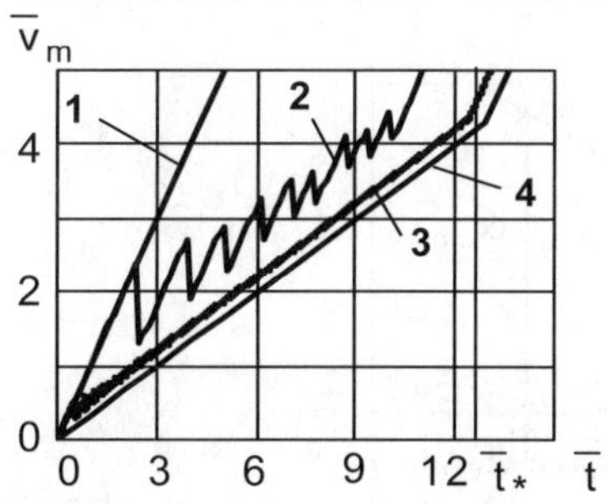

Fig.13.2. Averaged velocity of a slipping part of the falling cord vs. time; 1) rigid body; elastic cord: 2) $n_0 = 10$, 3) $n_0 = 100$; 4) inextensible cord

and finite number of elements. Therefore, in Fig.13.2 the change of average velocity $\bar{v}_m$ of the slipping part of the cord is shown, splitting it onto various total numbers n_0 of the chain elements. The velocity $\bar{v}_m$ is determined for varying number of the elements $n(\bar{t})$, which have been joined in fall to the moment $\bar{t}$, i.e.

$$\bar{v}_m(\bar{t}) = \frac{1}{n(\bar{t})} \sum_{j=1}^{n(\bar{t})} \bar{v}_j(\bar{t}) . \tag{13.12}$$

Line 1 corresponds to free fall of the whole cord as a rigid body and line 4 concerns a non-extensible cord, for which

$$\bar{v} = \bar{v}_m = \begin{cases} \bar{t}/3 & \text{with } \bar{t} \le \bar{t}_* \\ \bar{t} - 2\bar{t}_*/3 & \text{with } \bar{t} \ge \bar{t}_* \end{cases} , \tag{13.13}$$

and

$$\bar{a} = \bar{a}_m = \begin{cases} 1/3 & \text{with } \bar{t} \le \bar{t}_* \\ 1 & \text{with } \bar{t} \ge \bar{t}_* \end{cases} . \tag{13.14}$$

For a great number of elements, the average fall velocity and acceleration of the elastic cord approach the values for the non-extensible cord (cp. lines 3 and 4). However, the basic distinction of behavior of elastic and non-extensible bodies is the occurrence in the first case of elastic oscillations, for which part of the introduced work is spent.

13.1.2.2. In Fig.13.3, for the time interval $\bar{t}_2 - \bar{t}_1 = 4$, the curves of time evolution of the work $\overline{W}$ done by gravitation forces, kinetic energy $\overline{K}_m$ calculated with average velocity $\bar{v}_m$, potential energy $\overline{P}_e$, and full mechanical energy of elastic oscillation $\overline{E}_e$ are shown. The latter is

$$\overline{E}_e = \overline{K}_e + \overline{P}_e = 0.5\Delta\bar{x} \sum_{j=1}^{n} [(\bar{v}_j - \bar{v}_m)^2 + \bar{\sigma}_j^2] , \tag{13.15}$$

where the kinetic energy $\overline{K}_e$ of element oscillations is defined due to the difference $\bar{v}_j - \bar{v}_m$ of velocities.

The work $\overline{W}$ is strongly equal at any time to the complete mechanical energy $\overline{W} = \overline{E} = \overline{E}_e + \overline{K}_m$.

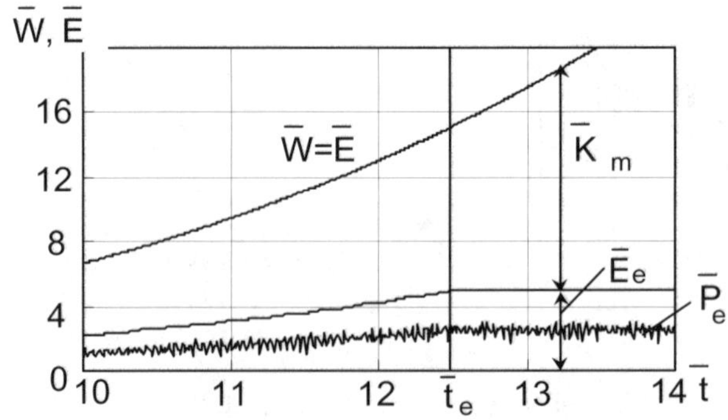

Fig.13.3. Energy components and work of gravitation forces for a sliding cord vs.time

After the time $\bar{t}_e$ when the fall of the cord becomes free, the energy $\overline{K}_m$ grows in connection with increase of work $\overline{W}$, while the complete energy of elastic oscillation $\overline{E}_e$ remains strongly constant, although the values of its potential and kinetic components vary in time (see Fig.13.3).

Thus, account in view of elasticity confirms that 'the loss of energy' at the slipping of a non-extensible cord (chain) in accuracy corresponds to energy going to internal elastic oscillations of a deformable cord. If inextensibility of a chain is considered as the limiting case for an elastic chain with very great energy dispersion resulted of internal friction in a material, the problem of energy loss does not arise.

The DMM equations allow us to determine the dynamic stresses in the cord or chain elements and at its borders for any time. It was shown by Shorr (1996) that shock stress in the last element of a metal chain with fixed end could sufficiently exceed a stress caused by its weight.

Making use the stated numerical approach, various problems on deformation of elastic cords of varying length can be easily solved, e.g., fall of a cord that has an initial hanging part and a gradual vertical stretching out a cord from a folded coil (see Panovko 1985).

13.2 Waves in Structures Interacting with 'Active' Media

In our context, a term 'active' implies the energy can be introduced from the medium (or from an 'active' foundation) to a mechanical system as a result of dynamic interaction. This leads to the possibility of shock waves arising, the development of self-induced oscillation, and other specific effects. The DMM approach allows us to study these phenomena numerically.

13.2.1 Strings on an 'Anti-Elastic' or 'Anti-Viscous' Foundation

13.2.1.1. The problem of string interaction with an 'anti-elastic' foundation was suggested to the author by Prof. Ju. Kaplunov motivated by application to wave propagation in pre-stressed and anisotropic structures. A similar problem can also arise when a mechanical system is in a magnetic field.

A. Problem 13.2. A taut string on an 'anti-elastic' foundation suddenly loaded by a constant force. Consider a long taut string suddenly loaded by a constant transverse force F_0 applied at $t=0$ to the left free end $x=0$.

Restricting the duration of force action to a short time, e.g. to one step $t_{imp}=\Delta t$, we simulate an impulsive force. The initial phase of wave propagation, until reflection from the opposite end of the string, will be studied here.

A distributed transverse force $q(x)$ of string/foundation interaction is assumed to be a linear function of a local string deflection $y(x)$

$$q(x,t)=ky(x,t), \tag{13.16}$$

where, in the case considered, the signs of the force and deflection coincide, i.e. $k>0$.

Applying the external forces F_j^* simulating the distributed load $q(x)$, as is usual in DMM, to nodes, we obtain

$$F_j^*=ky_{j,m}\Delta x, \tag{13.17}$$

where

$$y_{j,m}=y_{j,0}+0.5\Delta y_j=y_{j,0}+0.5v_{j,*}\Delta t \tag{13.18}$$

is the mean value of the node deflection in time Δt.

The nondimensional terms

$$\overline{Q}=Q/F_0,\ \overline{v}=v\rho cA/F_0,\ \overline{y}=yN/F_0L,\ \overline{x}=x/L,\ \overline{t}=tc/L,\ \overline{k}=kL^2/N, \tag{13.19}$$

with $c=\sqrt{N/\rho A}$, are used below where L is a characteristic linear size of a system (e.g., a maximum static string deflection on the same 'positive' elastic foundation under the unmoved force F_0, as in Subsect.11.2.1.).

Substituting Eqs.(13.17)-(13.18) into the general set of the equations for the string wave problem (see Subsect.2.3.1.), we obtain the node velocity

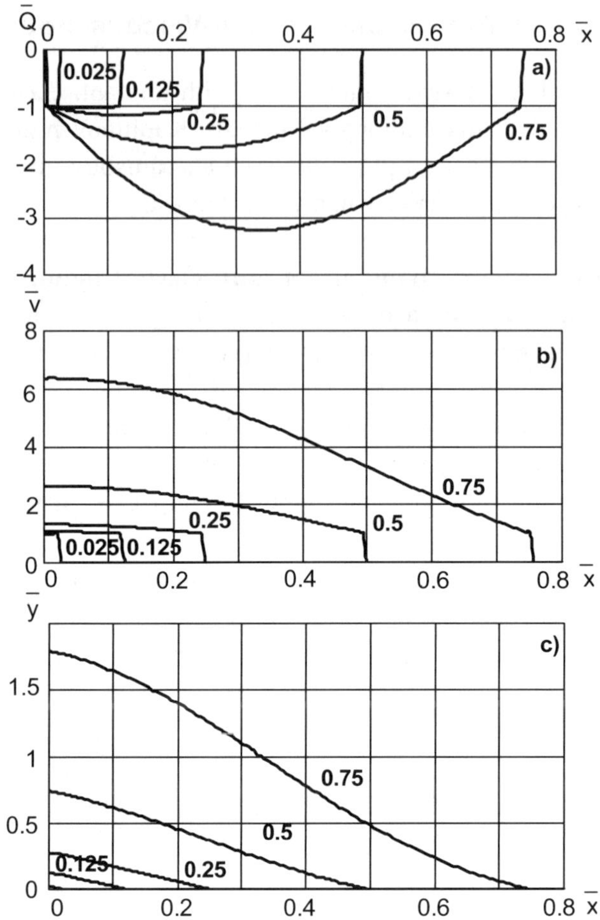

Fig.13.4. A string on an 'anti-elastic' foundation; a) inner force, b) transverse velocity, c) deflection

$$\overline{v}_{j,*} = \frac{\overline{v}_{j,0} + \overline{v}_{j-1,0} + \overline{Q}_{j,0} - \overline{Q}_{j-1,0} + \overline{k}\overline{y}_{j,0}\Delta}{2(1 - 0.25\overline{k}\Delta\overline{t}^2)}, \tag{13.20}$$

which is valid, since $\Delta\overline{t} = 1/n$, by the condition

$$n^2 >> 0.25\overline{k} \tag{13.21}$$

To provide a smooth time evolution of the calculated curves, it is also desirable to bond the value of $\overline{k}\Delta\overline{t} = \overline{k}/n$, so that the last term in the numerator of Eq.(13.20) will be significantly less than the others.

B. Results relevant to the boundary conditions at $j = 1$

$$\overline{Q}_1^- = -\overline{F}_0 = -1, \quad \overline{v}_1^- = \overline{v}_{1,0} + 1 + \overline{Q}_{1,0} \tag{13.22}$$

for $n = 200$ and $\overline{k} = 20$ are presented in Fig.13.4, where the inner force $\overline{Q}$, velocity $\overline{v}$, and deflection $\overline{y}$ are plotted against string length $\overline{x}$ for various $\overline{t}$ denoted by indexes affixed to the curves.

A subject of interest is the non-monotone behavior of the transverse force $\overline{Q}$ over the disturbed string domain, whereas the value of its leading wave remains constant for all time (Fig.13.4a). This effect was theoretically revealed by Kaplunov at al.(2002).

***13.2.1.2.* Problem 13.3. A taut string on an 'anti-viscous' foundation suddenly loaded by a constant force.** Continuing the attack on the previous problem, assume the distributed external force $q(x)$ is a linear function of the local transverse velocity $v(x)$, so

$$q(x,t) = \eta v(x,t), \tag{13.23}$$

where the signs of the force and velocity coincide, i.e. $\eta > 0$.

Such a phenomenon is possible under lateral oscillation of thin tubes in a heat exchanger.

We apply a similar procedure as above denoting

$$\overline{\eta} = \eta Lc / N \tag{13.24}$$

that leads to the governing equation for the node velocity

$$\overline{v}_{j,*} = \frac{\overline{v}_{j,0} + \overline{v}_{j-1,0} + \overline{Q}_{j,0} - \overline{Q}_{j-1,0}}{2(1 - 0.5\overline{\eta}\Delta\overline{x})}, \tag{13.25}$$

which is valid by the condition

$$n >> 0.5\overline{\eta}. \tag{13.26}$$

Below, it is assumed that $n = 200$, $\overline{\eta} = 3$.

The distribution of inner force $\overline{Q}$, transverse velocity $\overline{v}$, and deflection $\overline{y}$ over the string length $\overline{x}$ for some instants $\overline{t}$ are shown in Fig.13.5a,b,c, respectively.

Unlike the previous case, the leading front of the force is prominently shock-wave-like in character, for which the intensity increases as the disturbed domain spreads over the string.

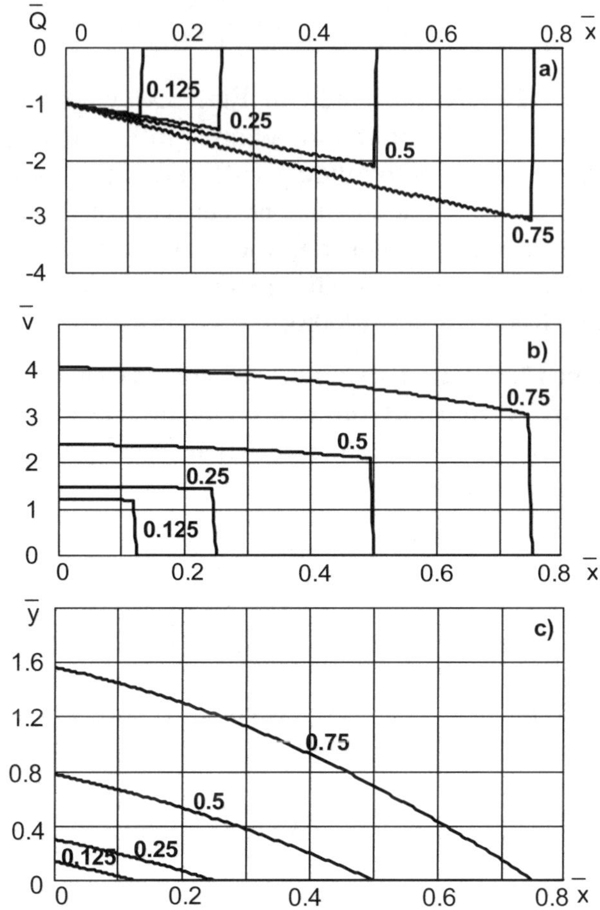

Fig.13.5. A string on an 'anti-viscous' foundation; a) inner force, b) transverse velocity, c) deflection

3.2.2 Auto-Oscillation of a String in Nonlinear Viscous Medium

12.3.2.1. **A.** Under unsteady oscillation of a deformable body in an active medium, taking account of damping, the establishment of a limited auto-oscillation cycle is possible.

Such a problem using the DMM approach was considered by Mel'nikova (2000) in respect of a taut string, which is affected from the medium by a distributed load $q(x)$ nonlinearly dependent on the local transverse string velocity $v(x)$ in such a way that

$$q(x,t) = \alpha v(x,t) - \beta [v(x,t)]^3 . \tag{13.27}$$

Here, the constants are $\alpha, \beta \geq 0$. The first term in Eq.(13.27) reflects an 'active' action of the medium, the second describing nonlinear damping forces.

Problem 13.4. Development and establishment of a limited auto-oscillation cycle of a string at the given initial speed. The initial conditions are: $y_{j,in} = 0$, $Q_{j,in} = 0$, and $v_{j,in} = v_0$. Boundary conditions of a string of a length L with both ends fixed in transversal direction are: $y_1 = 0$ and $y_{n+1} = 0$. We use the following dimensionless parameters scaled by the velocity v_0:

$$\overline{v} = v / v_0, \ \overline{Q} = Q / v_0 \rho c A, \overline{y} = y / 2 y_{\max}, \ \overline{\alpha} = \alpha L / \rho c A n, \overline{\beta} = \beta L v_0^2 / \rho c A n, \tag{13.28}$$

where $y_{\max} = v_0 L / 2c$ is the reference deflection of the string mid-point; the initial velocity v_0 induces this deflection under the free vibration.

Comparing Eqs.(13.28) and (13.25), we see $\overline{\alpha} = \overline{\eta} / n$.

In view of Eq.(13.27), the transverse node velocity is represented as

$$\overline{v}_{j,*} = \frac{\overline{v}_{j,**}}{1 - 0.5\overline{\alpha} + 0.5\overline{\beta}\overline{v}_{j,*}^2}, \tag{13.29}$$

where $\overline{v}_{j,**}$ is determined by Eq.(13.25) with $\overline{\eta} = 0$.

Taking into account condition (13.26) in the form $0.5\overline{\alpha} << 1$, Eq.(13.29) is readily solved by the method of successive approximation with a start value of $\overline{v}_{j,*} = \overline{v}_{j,**}$.

B. The distributions of string deflection $\overline{y}(\overline{x})$ along the string's length for various $\overline{t}$ that values are denoted near the curves, with two values of exciting factors $\overline{\alpha} = 0.065$ and $\overline{\alpha} = 0.25$, are shown in Fig.13.6a,c, respectively. The time evolution of string mid-point deflection $\overline{y}_{\overline{x}=0.5}(\overline{t})$ relevant to the above cases is presented in Fig.13.6b,d. It is assumed that $n = 100$ and $\overline{\beta} = 4 * 10^{-5}$. After some transient periods stable limited auto-oscillation cycles are established.

With a small value of exciting factor $\overline{\alpha} = 0.065$ (Fig.13.6a,b), the deflection amplitudes of the limited cycle take triangular form and the oscillation period becomes equal to $\overline{T} = 2$, as in the case of free string vibrations induced by the constant initial velocity $\overline{v}_0 = 1$. Such a dynamic pattern corresponds to the auto-oscillation velocity $\overline{v}_{j,*} = \sqrt{\overline{\alpha} / \overline{\beta}}$, which is

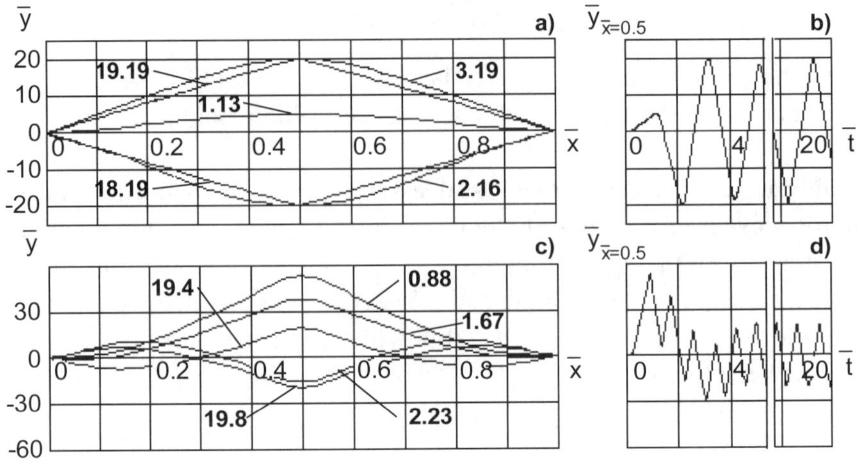

Fig.13.6. To auto-oscillation of a string; a) and c) distribution of deflections along the string; b) and d) time evolution of the string mid-point; a) and b) $\overline{\alpha} = 0.065$, c) and d) $\overline{\alpha} = 0.25$

constant for all nodes and results in the vanishing of the external force, $q(\overline{x},\overline{t}) = 0$. In our case $\overline{v}_{j,*} = 40.3$ and maximum of the mid-point deflection is $(\overline{y}_{\overline{x}=0.5})_{\max} = 0.25\overline{v}_{j,*}\overline{T} = 20.15$. This situation was studied analytically by Krupenin (1992).

With stronger excitation at $\overline{\alpha} = 0.25$, the auto-oscillation process changes in principle (Fig.13.6c,d). The distribution of steady deflection amplitudes becomes similar to the second symmetrical eigenmode of a string; however, the time period is $\overline{T} = 4/5$, while period of the second mode is $\overline{T}_2 = 2/3$. The auto-oscillation velocity varies along the string and the distributed external force $q(\overline{x},\overline{t}) \neq 0$. In spite of this, a stable auto-oscillation cycle arises since the total work

$$W = \int_T \int_L q(\overline{x},\overline{t}) d\overline{x} d\overline{t}$$

introduced to the string during the period $\overline{T} = 4/5$ vanishes.

13.2.2.2. **Problem 13.5. Development and establishment of a limited auto-oscillation cycle of a string, for which deflections are bonded by stopping devices.** The interaction conditions for a vibrating string and stopping devices (limiters), with constant values of initial clearances $\delta_{in}^{\pm}$ between those and the string, were considered in Subsect.10.2.1. They remain valid for string auto-oscillation in an active medium since at the contact points the velocity $\bar{v}_{j,*}$ and external force q both vanish. If the clearances alter along the string, the interaction conditions of Eqs.(10.24)-(10.26) must be checked at each node separately.

As an example, a distribution of deflection envelope for the steady auto-oscillation cycle, with single point limiter $\bar{\delta}_{in}^{+} = 5$ at the position $\bar{x} = 2/7$, is shown in Fig.13.7; as above, $\bar{\alpha} = 0.065$ and $\bar{\beta} = 4*10^{-5}$.

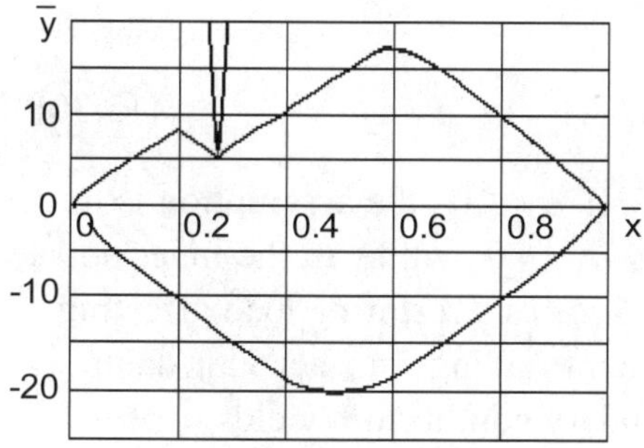

Fig.13.7. Steady auto-oscillation cycle of a string bounded by a point stopping device

Some other cases of auto-oscillation cycle development in a string were considered in detail by Mel'nikova (2000).

13.2.3 Auto-Oscillations in a System with Intermittent Contacts

13.2.3.1. In the two previous problems discussed in Sect.13.2 auto-oscillations are caused by a 'feedback' of external forces and displacements or velocities at the same points of the structure. Below, another situation where a feedback affects a system as a whole is considered.

Many systems of automatic control, electromagnetic relays, buzzers, and other similar sites content devices with interrupting contacts. When the contacts break, forces are generated that return the system to a status with closed contacts; but as soon as the contacts close, these forces disappear, resulting in the occurrence of an auto-oscillatory process.

Let's show the application of the DMM approach to the numerical simulation of such processes by considering an elementary example studied by Shorr and Mel'nikova (1988).

13.2.3.2. **Problem 13.6. Simulation of a 'buzzer' effect. A.** We consider a one-side fixed rod of unit cross-sectional area $A = 1$, with the free end $j = 1$, separated in an unloaded state from a contact device by a clearance δ_{in} (see below Fig.13.8a).

Under rod longitudinal vibration, the clearance changes within the range $0 \le \delta(t) \le \delta_{in}$. Until $\delta(t) > 0$, a uniformly distributed restoring load q affects the rod, and with $\delta(t) = 0$ the whole load vanishes.

Let the contact δ_0 at the beginning of given step be closed $\delta_0 = 0$. Assuming the contact will remain closed in the time Δt, we take the boundary velocity $v_1^- = 0$ and all the external nodal forces, including the force at the first node, zero.

As due to equations of Chap.1,

$$\sigma_1^- = \sigma_{1,0} - \rho c(v_1^- - v_{1,0}), \tag{13.30}$$

the boundary stress is $\sigma_1^- = \sigma_{1,0} + \rho c v_{1,0}$. If $\sigma_1^- \le 0$, the assumption is true. In contrast, we must put a contact stress $\sigma_{1,*}^- = 0$, while all the inner nodal forces become $F_j^* = -2F_0$, where $F_0 = 0.5q\Delta x$ is a restoring load affecting a half of each element. For the first element, taking into account damping force $F_c = -\eta\rho c v_1^-$, the condition of boundary equilibrium yields

$$\sigma_{1,*}^- - \sigma_1^- + F_0 - F_c = 0. \tag{13.31}$$

It follows from Eqs.(13.30)-(13.31) that

$$v_1^- = [v_{1,0} + (\sigma_{1,0} - F_0)/\rho c]/(1+\eta). \tag{13.32}$$

The clearance δ at the step termination is given by

$$\delta = \delta_0 + v_1^- \Delta t. \tag{13.33}$$

With $\delta \ge 0$, we go to the next step. However, an original situation can arise in the case of a great restoring force $F_0 = 0.5q\Delta x > \sigma_{1,0} + v_{1,0}\rho c$. It may occur that $v_1^- < 0$ and calculated value of the final clearance for $\delta_0 = 0$ becomes $\delta < 0$. This contradicts the condition of a gap occurrence over the step considered. To avoid this contradiction, one can decrease the force F_0 using a smaller time step Δt and element size $\Delta x = c\Delta t$. But it may be more convenient to assume that a contact over the step multiply breaks and an 'equivalent' force becomes $F_{0,eq} = \sigma_{1,0} + v_{1,0}\rho c < F_0$, with the gap conditions $v_{1,eq}^- = 0$, $\sigma_{1,*eq}^- = 0$, and $\sigma_{1,eq}^- = F_{0,eq}$ remaining valid.

B. If a contact at the beginning of a given step is broken ($\delta_0 > 0$), the boundary velocity v_1^- and final gap δ are determined by Eqs.(13.32)-(13.33). When $\delta \ge 0$, we pass to the next step. Obtaining a value of the gap $\delta < 0$, we assume that it exists only in the part of the step $\alpha\Delta t$, while during the remaining part $(1-\alpha)\Delta t$ the contact is closed. Here, $0 < \alpha < 1$.

The quantities averaged over the step are:

$$\left.\begin{aligned} & F^*_{1,m} = -\alpha F_0, \; F^*_{j,m} = 2F^*_{1,m}, \\ & v^-_{1,m} = \frac{\alpha}{1+\eta}[v_{1,0} + (\sigma_{1,0} - F_0)/\rho c, \\ & \sigma^-_{1,m} = \frac{(1-\alpha+\eta)(\sigma_{1,0} + v_{1,0}\rho c) + \alpha F_0}{1+\eta}, \\ & \sigma^-_{1,*m} = (1-\alpha)(\sigma_{1,0} + v_{1,0}\rho c) \end{aligned}\right\}, \tag{13.34}$$

where $\alpha = -\delta_0 / v_1^- \Delta t$ with a negative value of v_1^-.

The nodal forces have an electromagnetic origin and propagate with speed incommensurable greater, than the speed of mechanical waves. Hence, the contact at the end $j = 1$, which induces the boundary force F_1^*, must immediately cause the restoring forces $F_j^* = 2F_1^*$ in all other nodes.

Since in the given problem the external forces in the whole system depend on boundary conditions at the left border, the calculation on each step should begin from the first element. At the same time, the conditions of contact at the node $j = 1$ are completely determined by the stress-inertial status of only the first element.

C. The time evolution of the clearance $\overline{\delta}(\overline{t})$ for various values of restoring force $\overline{F}_0$ denoted near the curves, without and with damping are demonstrated in Fig.13.8b,c, respectively.

We use the nondimensional parameters: $\overline{\delta}(\overline{t}) = \delta(t)/\delta_{in}$, $\overline{F}_0 = F_0 / F_{0,st}$, and $\overline{t} = tc/L$, where $F_{0,st} = 0.5 q_{st}\Delta x = E\delta_{in}/Ln$ is a static force affecting a half of each element that calls under the distributed load q_{st} the rod displacement equal to initial clearance δ_{in}.

With a small restoring force until $\overline{F}_0 < 0.5$, the initial gap exceeds the rod dynamic displacement $2\overline{F}_0$ and a contact is impossible. Therefore, at $\overline{F}_0 \le 0.5$ we see harmonic steady oscillations, without damping, and fading oscillations to static value of $\overline{\delta}_{st}(\infty) = 1 - \overline{F}_0$, with damping. Within $0.5 < \overline{F}_0 < 1$, at first some intermittent contacts arise and then the damped oscillations also fade, so that the residual gap becomes $1 - \overline{F}_0$. The curves for $\overline{F}_0 = 0.8$ are equipped for clearness with white dots.

Under $\overline{F}_0 \ge 1$, auto-oscillations with intermittent contacts do not fade in spite of damping.

The curves $\overline{\delta}(\overline{t})$ for some restoring forces $\overline{F}_0 \ge 1$ are presented in Fig.13.9.

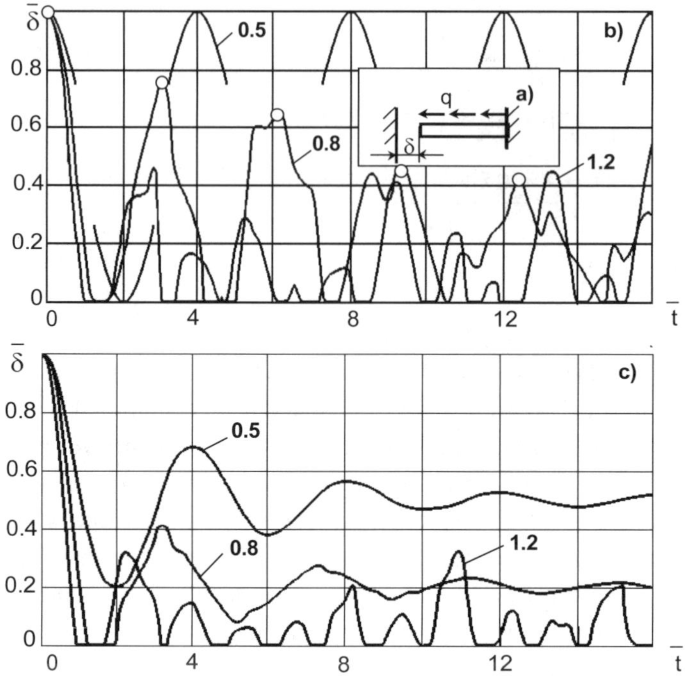

Fig.13.8. A system with intermittent contact; a) sketch of the problem, b) time evolution of the clearance without damping , c) the same, with damping factor $\overline{\eta} = 0.05$

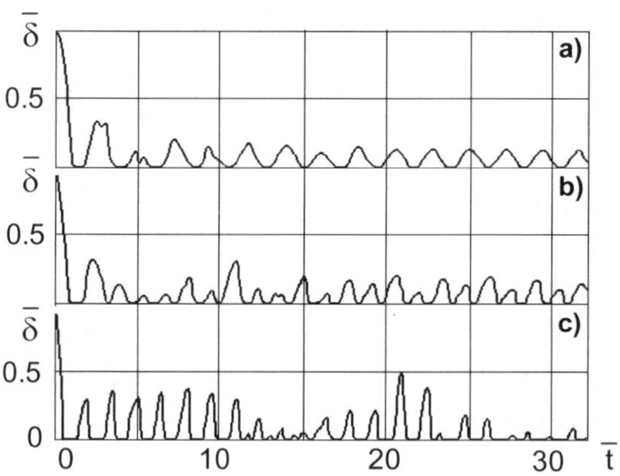

Fig.13.9. Time evolution of the clearance for restoring forces $\overline{F}_0 \geq 1$ and $\overline{\eta} = 0.05$; a) $\overline{F}_0 = 1.0$, b) $\overline{F}_0 = 1.2$, c) $\overline{F}_0 = 2.0$

One can observe that in this case the oscillation frequency increases as the value of restoring force grows.

14 Some Special Unsteady Problems in Engineering

14.1 Longitudinal Dynamics of a Train

Longitudinal dynamics of a train usually involves the tasks of calculated and experimental definition of dynamic longitudinal forces in coupling devices between carriages. The greatest importance has calculations of unsteady operation conditions of a train: starting, car collisions, braking, and so forth. Initial approaches for the calculation of longitudinal dynamic loads in a train were proposed by Zhukovsky (published in 1937) and later refined in the works of Lasar'an (1949), Blokhin and Manashkin (1982), Pershitz (1982), and others. A model of a train as a chain of discrete rigid masses connected by deformable links has got wide practical applications. The presence of a large number of nonlinear inter-car couplings with gaps complicates the application of more realistic discrete-continual models of a train including traditional FEM.

Use of the DMM approach allowed Kaplunova (1990a,b) to carry out a fuller analysis of the problem considered for passenger and cargo trains. Some of those results are presented below.

14.1.1 Setting of a Problem

***14.1.1.1.* A**. A model of a train with applied loads is presented in Fig.14.1. The train consists of n_c carriages, including one or several locomotives (1) that can be located arbitrarily, and cars of different types (2). A carriage is considered as an elastic rod of constant cross-sectional area A_j and length L_j. A conditional elastic modulus E_j and density ρ_j of the carriage are calculated using its stiffness β_j and mass m_j that are assumed to be known, through

$$E_j = \beta_j L_j / A_j, \; \rho_j = m_j / A_j L_j . \tag{14.1}$$

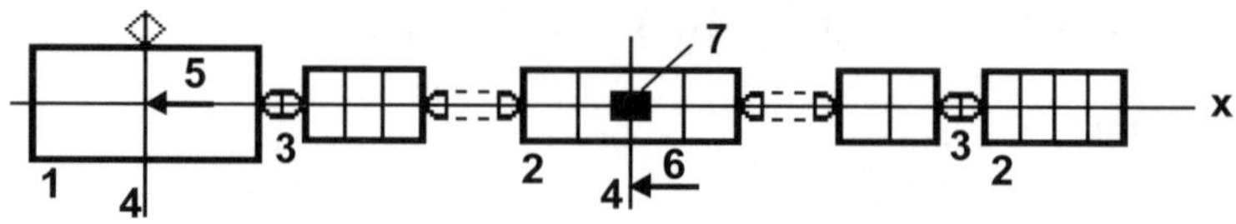

Fig.14.1. Model of a train

The carriages are connected to one another with non-inertial deformable couplings (3) that can have inner gaps.

Each carriage comprises a 'superelement' of n_j elements where $n_j \geq 2$. The total number of train elements is $n = \sum_{j=1}^{n_c} n_j$. The middle node of the carriage (or the nearest to it) or two border nodes are assumed to be 'loaded' (4): external forces as a locomotive traction (5), resistant mechanical and aerodynamic forces (6), and a car freight mass (7) are applied to them.

B. The carriage separation of elements is carried out in conformity with the procedure described in Subsect.1.2.2. We calculate the time t_j needed for an elastic wave to pass over the length of each carriage $t_j = L_j\sqrt{\rho_j / E_j}$ and find the carriage with minimum value of time $t_0 = (t_j)_{\min}$. Separating this carriage to $n_0 \geq 2$ elements, we obtain the necessary time step $\Delta t = t_0 / n_0$ for calculation; an integer $n_j = \mathrm{int}(t_j / \Delta t)$ is taken as a number of elements for the carriage *j*. To compensate the remainder $n_j - t_j / \Delta t$, we correct the density taking

$$\overset{\frown}{\rho}_j = \rho_j (n_j / n_0)^2 (t_0 / t_j)^2$$

and find a compensating mass $\Delta m_j = m_j (1 - \overset{\frown}{\rho}_j / \rho_j)$, which has to be added to the car freight mass at the 'loaded' nodes.

An appropriate calculation procedure including a point solid mass applied to a node was considered in Subsect.2.1.3.

14.1.1.2. **A**. Shock absorbers (dampers) of the inter-car coupling devices can be of different types. In the general case, a force F_* transmitted by an absorber nonlinearly depends on a relative displacement u_r and a relative velocity v_r of the adjacent cars, with different characteristics for extension and compression, and can reduce to zero at some moments.

A typical characteristic of a frictional absorber is shown in Fig.14.2.

Aside from the hysteresis loops, we see rigid sites, where the force F_* alternates under constant values of relative displacement $u_r = \pm\delta_1$ or $u_r = \pm\delta_2$ and a gap $2\delta_1$, within which the relative car displacement is pos-

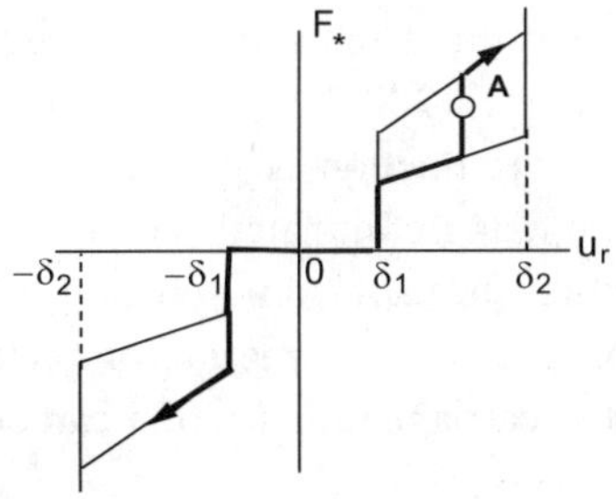

Fig.14.2. Characteristic of a frictional absorber

sible under $F_* = 0$. The magnitudes of δ_1 and δ_2 are determined by coupling construction. The sloping sites of the characteristic can be polygonal.

Due to the DMM assumption, a change of the displacement during a step Δt takes place with a permanent sign. Hence, a force alteration from any point A can run along one of the traces shown in Fig.14.2 by bold lines. The computation algorithm allows for all the possible traces.

B. The behavior of some absorbers can be described by a parallel connection of a dissipative unit of nonlinear viscous friction and a variant of a hysteretic-frictional unit. The last unit approximated by a polyhonal line is shown in Fig.14.3.

Sites AA and BB of this characteristic are elastic and a vertical line AB corresponds to rigid loading.

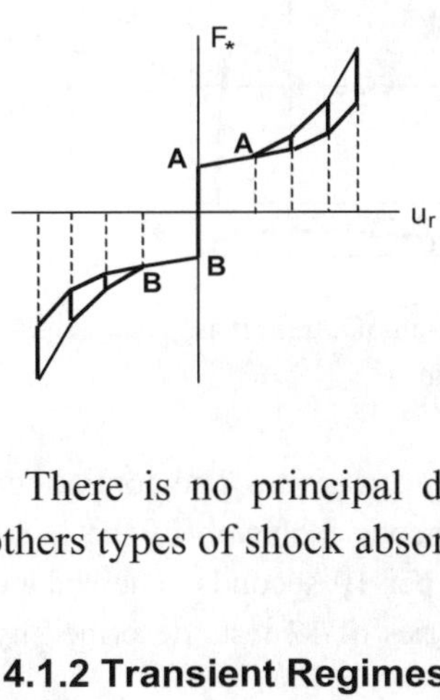

Fig.14.3. Characteristic of a hysteretic-frictional absorber's unit

There is no principal difficulties in extending the DMM approach to others types of shock absorbers.

14.1.2 Transient Regimes of a Train Motion

14.1.2.1. Start of a train. Below, a comparison of results of force calculation in inter-car couplings with data of measurements relevant to a heavy cargo train of mass 10000 tons is carried out. The train has two locomotives and 89 cars of different mass and rigidity. The locomotive tractive effort at the starting changes under exponential law $F_d = A[1-\exp(-\nu t)]$, where $A \approx 300$kN, $\nu \approx 2.46$, t in seconds. The cars are preliminarily 'snubbed', i.e., the traction is perceived by them consistently as the backlashes in couplings are being eliminated. Therefore, between the moments of inclusion in work of the first (head) locomotive and the second, located in the train middle, a delay is possible, which time at complete snubbing achieves 10c. The resistance force from the carriage/rails friction can be represented in the form

$$F_{j,fr} = -\text{sgn}\, v_j(A_0 + A_1 v_j^2) - A_2 v_j\,, \qquad (14.2)$$

where A_0, A_1, and A_2 are experimental coefficients.

The first term in Eq.(14.2) takes into account dry friction at $v=0$, while the others describe nonlinear viscous friction of motion, including aerodynamic resistance. A sketch of the locomotives and cars mass arrangement over the train length is displayed in Fig.14.4a.

In Fig.14.4b the length distribution of the maximal forces (in MN), which arise

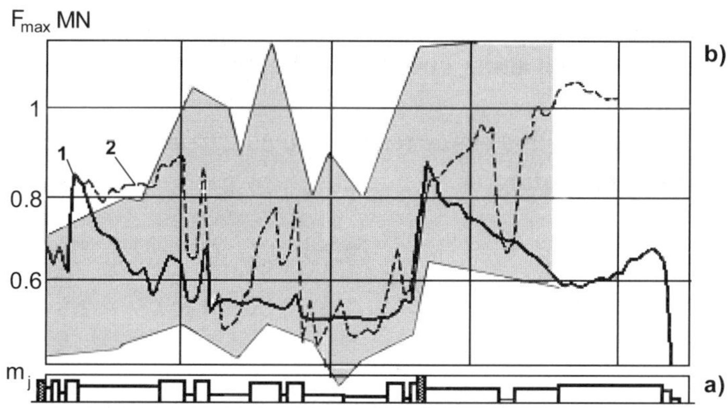

Fig.14.4. Inter-car coupling forces under a train start: a) sketch of a train mass, b) distribution of the maximal coupling forces along the train

in the couplings during the starting process of the train, is given. The continuous line 1 relates to the calculated forces under simultaneous inclusion of the locomotives, the dashed line 2 to inclusion after a delay per 10 seconds. The shaded area covers results of the force measurements in a series of 12 tests described by Blokhin (1972).

The computations provide acceptable accuracy for validation of the greatest quantity of coupling forces and describe reasonably the complex character of force distribution over the length of the train at its starting.

Sometimes, for a long stretched train, a locomotive tractive effort can be insufficient to overcome friction forces for all the cars. In this case, a part of the cars will come in movement, but a set of last cars will not be moved from a place. Along the train can arise intensive oscillations, at which inter-cars loads considerably exceed the locomotive traction.

14.1.2.2. Collision of cars. A situation, within which one car lowered from an inclined track impacts several motionless cars, can arise at the formation of a carriage rolling stock. In Fig.14.5, the load distribution over the length of a carriage chain consisting of 20 cars for consecutive times with an interval per 0.1s is given. The speed of the striking car was 2 m/s and the mass of each car was 100 tons. The carriage chain was previously assumed to be completely compressed; the amortization in absorbing devices was taken into account. The shock character of process, final speed of shock wave propagation over the structure, and fast attenuation of loads on chain length and time are well seen.

The use of DMM approach allows to be studied in details the role of the large number of factors influencing the dynamic loads in train coupling devices: forces under braking, heterogeneity of a train, optimal principles of its formation, arrangement of locomotives, magnitude and rate of tractive efforts, and many others.

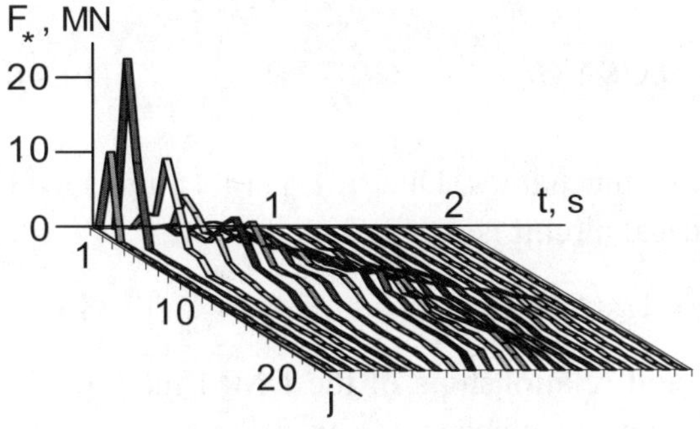

Fig.14.5. Inter-car coupling load distribution over a carriage chain

14.2 Wave Problems in Adjacent Areas of Engineering

Due to mathematical analogy, the DMM approach can be successively applied to simulation of some other 1-D problems of physics and engineering fields. Use of DMM for electric engineering and hydraulics is described in this Chapter. In Shorr and Mel'nikova (1988) the possibility of its applications to unsteady thermal conductivity, acoustics, aero-elasticity, and electro-magnetism were also briefly discussed.

14.2.1 A Transient Process in an Electrical Circuit

14.2.1.1. **A**. There is a well-known mathematical analogy between mechanical and electrical engineering systems. Analogous to the one-dimensional Eqs.(3.30) of mechanics, which were given in Chap.3, there correspond the equations of electrical engineering of a circuit

$$C\frac{\partial V}{\partial t} = -\frac{\partial I}{\partial x} - GV, \quad \frac{\partial V}{\partial x} = -L\frac{\partial I}{\partial t} - RI, \tag{14.3}$$

where V is a voltage, I is a current intensity, C is an electrical capacity, L is a self-induction, R is an active (ohmic) resistance, and G is a loss of a voltage because of a current outflow (outflow conductivity).

The quantities C, L, R, and G are referred to unit of a circuit length. There is a complete mathematical conformity between mechanical ($v, \sigma, \rho, E, \eta_c, \eta_v$) and electrical ($V, -I, C, 1/L, 1/R, G$) parameters. The amount (charge) of electricity $q = CV$ corresponds to momentum $M = \rho v$. Having excluded from Eqs.(14.3) the current intensity, we shall state the 'telegraphic equation'

$$\frac{\partial^2 V}{\partial x^2} - CL\frac{\partial^2 V}{\partial t^2} - (CR + GL)\frac{\partial V}{\partial t} - GRV - 0 \tag{14.4}$$

that is analogous to Eq.(3.30b) of mechanics. Due to Eq.(14.4), the speed of wave propagation in an electrical circuit is equal to

$$c = 1/\sqrt{CL}\,. \tag{14.5}$$

Using the specified analogy and relationships of the DMM method for mechanical processes, the equations of mechanics can be transformed to the appropriate equations for the electrical engineering. However, for simplification of treating the DMM method and its further development with reference to numerical calculation of transients in electrical circuits, the direct deduction of the method's equations using concepts and terms of electrical engineering is given below.

Note that the given form of mechanics/electricity analogy is not unique, see, e.g., Skudrzik (1968); however, it is most convenient for use of DMM.

B. Let us present a small finite element of an electrical circuit of a length Δx as a sequential connection of an internal continual part of realistic length Δx and two border links. The boundary between the link and the internal part is named 'inner'; the boundary coinciding with a node between adjacent elements – 'outer'. The internal part has distributed electrical capacity C, self-induction L, and is free from resistance. This part accounts for the wave character of transient electrical processes. The influence of the element active resistance $R\Delta x$ is referred to the border links, for which we take $R^{\pm} = 0.5R\Delta x$. Analogously, a current outflow $G\Delta x$ along the length of the element is referred, as usual in the DMM approach, to nodes where $G^{\pm} = 0.5G\Delta x$.

At a moment t^{-} the internal part is assumed to be entirely in a 'uniform' electrical state with a voltage V_0, current I_0, and amount of electricity $q_0 = CV_0\Delta x$. This is possible since the voltage does not drop along the element in the absence of resistance. Because of interaction with other elements, the voltage and current at the outer borders take at the infinitesimally close moment t^{+} values $V_*^{\pm}$ and $I_*^{\pm}$, respectively. These quantities are assumed permanent for the small time interval $\Delta t = \Delta x / c$, as long as an electrical wave travels along the inner part of the element with the speed c. Taking into account the resistance of the links, the voltages at the inner borders become

$$V^{\pm} = V_*^{\pm} \pm 0.5R\Delta x I^{\pm}. \tag{14.6}$$

Further, accounting for the current outflow referred to the nodes, the currents at the inner borders are

$$I^{\pm} = I_*^{\pm} \pm 0.5G\Delta x V_*^{\pm}. \tag{14.7}$$

Disturbances of the voltage $V^{\pm} - V_0$ and the current $I^{\pm} - I_0$ propagate over the entire element in a time interval Δt in accordance with the laws of an electrical circuit.

The current balance yields $q^{\pm} - q_0 = C(V^{\pm} - V_0)\Delta x = \mp(I^{\pm} - I_0)\Delta t$ or

$$I^{\pm} - I_0 = \mp Cc(V^{\pm} - V_0). \tag{14.8}$$

The voltage drop due to self-induction is $(V^{\pm} - V_0) = \mp L(I^{\pm} - I_0)\Delta x / \Delta t$ or

$$I^{\pm} - I_0 = \mp(V^{\pm} - V_0)/ Lc. \tag{14.9}$$

Equations (14.8) and (14.9) are satisfied by the wave speed c determined by the expression (14.5). They can be also obtained from Eqs.(14.3) with G=0 and R=0.

Notice that $Lc = 1/Cc = \sqrt{L/C}$.

New values of the voltage $V(t+\Delta t)$ and the current $I(t+\Delta t)$ at the given time step termination are

$$V = V^- + V^+ - V_0,\ I = I^- + I^+ - I_0. \tag{14.10}$$

It follows from Eqs.(14.6) and (14.9) that

$$I^\pm = \frac{I_0 Lc \pm (V_0 - V_*^\pm)}{Lc + 0.5R\Delta x}. \tag{14.11}$$

Inserting $I^\pm$ from Eq.(14.11) into (14.7) we obtain a correlation between the voltage and current at the outer borders

$$I_*^\pm (Lc + 0.5R\Delta x) \pm V_*^\pm [1 + 0.5G\Delta x(Lc + 0.5R\Delta x)] = I_0 Lc \pm V_0. \tag{14.12}$$

C. In the absence of electrical supplies, the connection conditions of the voltage and current for a node *j* between the elements $j-1$ and *j* are

$$V_{j-1,*}^+ = V_{j,*}^- = V_{j,*},\ I_{j-1,*}^+ = I_{j,*}^- = I_{j,*}\ , \tag{14.13}$$

where $V_{j,*}$ and $I_{j,*}$ are the node parameters.

Considering a homogeneous circuit with constant electrical characteristics and inserting the quantities $I_{j-1,*}^+$ and $I_{j,*}^-$ from Eqs.(14.12) into the second Eq.(14.13), we find

$$V_{j,*} = \frac{V_{j-1,0} + V_{j,0} + (I_{j-1,0} - I_{j,0})Lc}{2[1 + 0.5G\Delta x(Lc + 0,5R\Delta x)]}. \tag{14.14}$$

Making use of the voltages $V_{j-1,*}^-$ and $V_{j-1,*}^+$ for both nodes of the element $j-1$, we can calculate all other parameters of this element.

Equation (14.12) allows us to describe any boundary conditions for the current site, as this correlation determines a boundary current I^* for a given boundary voltage V^* and vice versa.

Using the DMM approach, it is easy to include several voltage sources, local resistances, and capacities in the calculation algorithm, and also to consider non-homogeneous and branching circuits with different boundary conditions. As an example, a problem with a local resistance and varying boundary condition is considered below.

14.2.1.2. **A. Problem 14.1. A transient in an electrical circuit with a varying boundary resistance.** A circuit site of length *l* is affected by a voltage source V^* suddenly applied at $t=0$ to the left end $x=0$

(Fig.14.6a). During the time interval $0 \le t < t_*$, the right end $x = l$ remains free (the circuit is broken and the boundary resistance must set as $R^* = \infty$). At the moment $t = t_*$ the path is closed and the resistance at $x = l$ takes a finite value R^*. Calculations are carried out using quantities scaled by the voltage V^* so that $\overline{V} = V / V^*$, $\overline{I} = ILc / V^*$ and

$$\overline{R} = 0.5Rl / nLc, \quad \overline{G} = 0.5GlLc / n, \quad \overline{R}^* = R^* / Lc, \ \overline{x} = x / l, \ \overline{t} = tc / l,$$

where n is a number of elements. The overbars for scaled quantities are omitted below. Equations (14.11), (14.12), and (14.14) become

$$I^{\pm} = [I_0 \pm (V_0 - V_*^{\pm})]/(1+R), \quad I_*^{\pm}(1+R) \pm V_*^{\pm}[1 + G(1+R)] = I_0 \pm V_0, \tag{14.15}$$

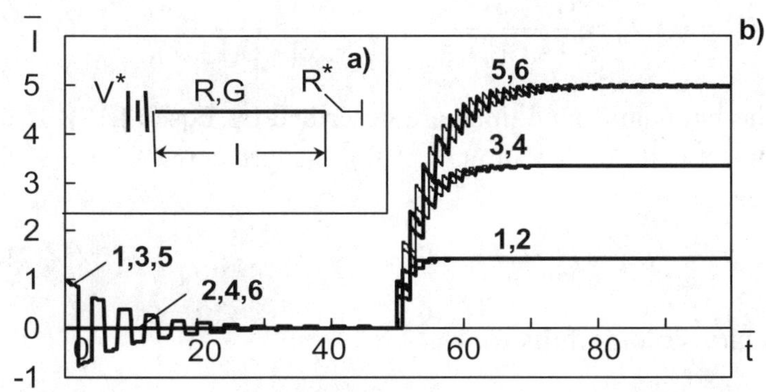

Fig.14.6. Transient in an electrical circuit; a) scheme of a circuit site, b) currents vs. time

and

$$V_{j,*} = \frac{V_{j-1,0} + V_{j,0} + I_{j-1,0} - I_{j,0}}{2[1 + G(1+R)]}. \tag{14.16}$$

For a permanent boundary condition at the left end $x = 0$ ($j = 1$), we obtain from Eqs.(14.15)

$$V_{1,*}^- = V^* = 1, \quad I_{1,*}^- = \frac{1 + I_{1,0} - V_{1,0} + G(1+R)}{1+R}, \quad I_1^- = \frac{1 + I_{1,0} - V_{1,0}}{1+R}. \tag{14.17}$$

At the right boundary $x = 1$ ($j = n$), where the resistance R^* is applied, the boundary condition is

$$V_{n,*}^+ = R^* I_{n,*}^+. \tag{14.18}$$

Employing Eq.(14.18), we obtain from Eqs.(14.15) and (14.10)

$$\left.\begin{aligned} I_{n,*}^{+} &= \frac{I_{n,0}+V_{n,0}}{1+R+R^{*}[1+G(1+R)]}, \\ I_{n}^{+} &= \frac{(I_{n,0}+V_{n,0})(1+GR^{*})}{1+R+R^{*}[1+G(1+R)]}, \\ V_{n,*}^{+} &= \frac{(I_{n,0}+V_{n,0})R^{*}}{1+R+R^{*}[1+G(1+R)]} \end{aligned}\right\}. \qquad (14.19)$$

As until the time $t < t_*$ the circuit is assumed to be broken, Eqs. (14.19) with $R^* = \infty$ yield

$$I_{n,*}^{+} = 0, \quad I_{n}^{+} = \frac{G(I_{n,0}+V_{n,0})}{1+G(1+R)}, \quad V_{n,*}^{+} = \frac{(I_{n,0}+V_{n,0})}{1+G(1+R)}. \qquad (14.20)$$

For $t \ge t_*$ the boundary conditions are described by Eqs.(14.19). If the resistance is too small (in the limit, $R^* = 0$) a short current occurs, the boundary current grows to

$$I_{n,*}^{+} = I_{n}^{+} = (I_{n,0} + V_{n,0})/(1+R)\ , \qquad (14.21a)$$

and the boundary voltage falls to

$$V_{n,*}^{+} = 0, \quad V_{n}^{+} = RI_{n}^{+}. \qquad (14.21b)$$

B. The calculations are carried out with R = 0.01, G = 0.001, n = 10, $t_* = 50$ and various values of R^*. In Fig.14.6b, time evolution of the boundary currents $I_{1,*}^{-}$ and $I_{n,*}^{+}$ for the resistances $R^* = 0.5$ (curves 1, 2), $R^* = 0.1$ (curves 3, 4), and $R^* = 0.001$ (curves 5, 6) is shown. The lines 1,3, and 5 are referred to the current $I_{1,*}^{-}$, the lines 2,4, and 6 to the current $I_{n,*}^{+}$. Maximum value $I_{\max} \approx 5$ corresponds to the short current.

A graph-analytic solution of similar problems, used by Bergeron (1962), requires very complicated derivations.

14.2.2 Unsteady Hydraulics Problems

14.2.2.1. **A.** Consider the occurrence and movement of waves under water flow in a horizontal channel filled with water to height H_0. The change in water level h is assumed small (so-called 'shallow' or 'fine' waves) with

$|h| << H_0$, and a flow velocity v is essentially smaller than the speed c of wave propagation, $|v| << c$. The water pressure p_m averaged over a channel section is $p_m = 0.5\rho g(H_0 + h)$ and the average horizontal force affecting a water stream in the channel is given by

$$F_m = p_m(H_0 + h) = 0.5\rho g(H_0 + h)^2 . \tag{14.22}$$

The variable water height h is usually called a 'water pressure'. The force F_m, the mass, and some other characteristics are referred to unit width of the channel.

In a short time interval Δt a wave travels a small distance $\Delta x = c\Delta t$ of the channel. Applying the law of momentum conservation to the water mass occupying the volume $(H_0 + h)\Delta x$, we obtain

$$0.5\rho g[(H_0 + h^{\pm})^2 - (H_0 + h_0)^2]\Delta t = \mp\rho[(H_0 + h^{\pm})v^{\pm} - (H_0 + h_0)v_0]\Delta x , \tag{14.23a}$$

where $h^{\pm}$ and $v^{\pm}$ are, respectively, a water pressure and velocity at element borders for the interval Δt, while h_0 and v_0 are the analogous element parameters at the beginning of a given step.

With accepted accuracy, we obtain

$$h^{\pm} - h_0 = \mp c(v^{\pm} - v_0)/g . \tag{14.23b}$$

Neglecting the influence of water compressibility in comparison with a varied height of water column on the change of the element mass, we obtain from the law of mass balance

$$\rho[(H_0 + h^{\pm}) - (H_0 + h_0)]\Delta x = \mp\rho[v^{\pm}(H_0 + h^{\pm}) - v_0(H_0 + h_0)]\Delta t \tag{14.24a}$$

or, with accepted accuracy,

$$h^{\pm} - h_0 = \mp H_0(v^{\pm} - v_0) . \tag{14.24b}$$

Comparing Eqs.(14.23b) and (14.24b), we see that $c = \sqrt{gH_0}$. The difference in the wave speeds relevant to the water and to the channel walls for $|v| << c$ is negligible.

The force of hydraulic resistance is assumed proportional to the square of the flow velocity. Hence, a node j between the elements $j-1$ and j is affected by the force

$$F_{j,*} = -\eta\Delta x|v_{j,*}|v_{j,*} , \tag{14.25}$$

where η is a loss factor of the water pressure for a unit channel length.

The conditions of the adjacent element interaction are

$$v_{j-1}^{+} = v_j^{-}, \quad h_{J-1}^{+} = h_j^{-} - F_{j,*}. \tag{14.26}$$

We introduce nondimensional quantities scaled by some water pressure h^o and the length L of a channel

$$\overline{h} = h / h^o, \ \overline{v} = vc / h^o g, \ \overline{\eta} = \eta h^o L(c/g)^2, \ \overline{x} = x / L, \ \overline{t} = tc / L, \tag{14.27}$$

with the overbars also omitted.

Inserting Eqs.(14.23b) with Eq.(14.25) for the neighboring elements $j-1$ and j into the interaction conditions (14.26), we obtain the node velocity $v_{j,*} = v_{j-1}^{+} = v_j^{-}$ in nondimensional terms as

$$v_{j,*} = \operatorname{sign}\widetilde{v}_{j,*}\left[\left(\sqrt{1 + 2\eta\Delta x|\widetilde{v}_{j,*}|} - 1\right) / \eta\Delta x\right], \tag{14.28}$$

where

$$\widetilde{v}_{j,*} = 0.5(v_{j-1,0} + v_{j,0} + h_{j-1,0} - h_{j,0}). \tag{14.29}$$

B. Problem 14.2. Change of water level in a channel by water filling. A channel site of the length *L*, which has water level of H_0, is separated at the left end $x = 0$ from an unlimited reservoir with constant water level of $H_0 + h_{in}$ by a closed gate (Fig.14.7a). The gate is suddenly opened at $t = 0$ and additional water begins to flow into the channel. Later, at $t = t_*$, the gate is closed again. We take for nondimensional terms $h^o = h_{in}$, so $\overline{h}_{in} = 1$.

The boundary conditions at the left end are:

$$\left.\begin{array}{ll} h_{1,*}^{-} = h_1^{-} - 0.5\eta\Delta x|v_1^{-}|v_1^{-} = 1 & \text{with} \quad 0 \le t < t_*, \\ v_1^{-} = 0 \quad \text{with} \quad t \ge t_* & \end{array}\right\}, \tag{14.30}$$

while at the right end $v_n^{+} = 0$. The solution for the boundary velocity $v_1^{-} = v_{1,*}$ within times $0 \le t < t_*$ has the form (14.28), as before, but the value of $\widetilde{v}_{1,*}$ is $\widetilde{v}_{1,*} = v_{1,0} - h_{1,0} + 1$.

The calculations are carried out with $n = 25$, $\eta = 2.5$, and $t_* = 0.72$. The patterns of the water surface at various times during the channel filling are shown in Fig.14.7b, c. Curves 1 ($t = 0.64$) and 2 ($t == 0.88$) illustrate the allocation of wave fronts directly before and after the moment of gate closes. After the first reflection from the right wall (curve 3, $t = 1.2$), the leading front moves towards the abated front, which have been arisen at the moment when the gate was closed down.

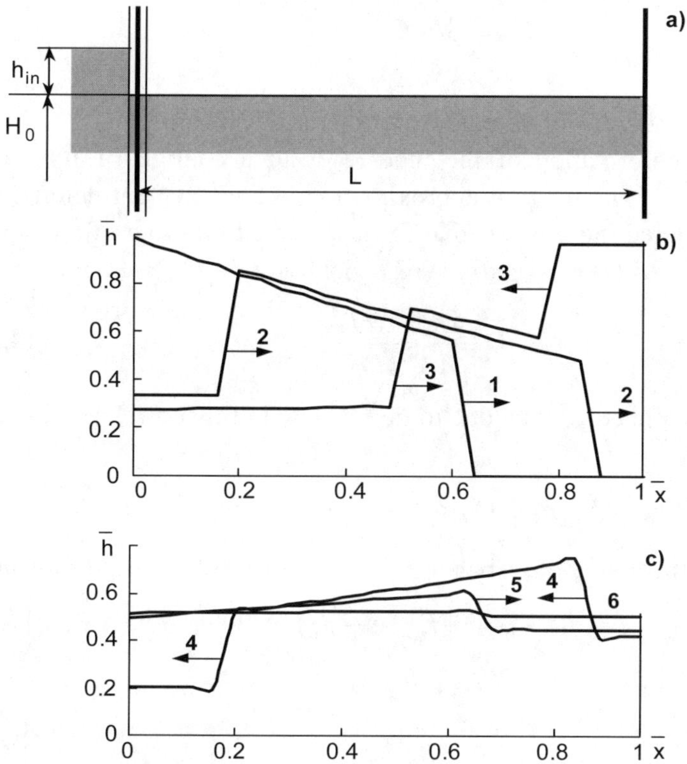

Fig.14.7. Additional filling of a channel by water; a) sketch of a channel, b) and c) water surface at various times

Thereupon (curve 4 in Fig.14.7c, $t = 1.8$), both fronts travel in the same direction, and so forth, till the waves fade (curve 5, t=4) and the final water level is established (curve 6, t=30).

14.2.2.2. Hydraulic shocks in stressed tubing. The DMM approach is very convenient for calculating the liquid current in stressed tubing, including the effects of hydraulic shocks. If a tube is completely filled with liquid, the law of moment conservation, Eq.(14.23b), takes the form

$$p^{\pm} - p_0 = \mp \rho c (v^{\pm} - v_0), \tag{14.31}$$

where p denotes the pressure.

A stream induces a change of the liquid mass $\Delta m = \rho A \Delta x$ in a volume of constant length Δx. For a rigid tube, this change results in a relative variation of liquid density $\Delta\rho$ and pressure Δp connected by the expression

$$\frac{\Delta\rho}{\rho}=\frac{\Delta p}{K_V}, \tag{14.32}$$

where K_V is a modulus of volume compression.

An elastic deformation of the tube leads to a change of its cross-section area A. For the first approximation, a tube element deformation may be considered the same as that for a separated thin ring of a diameter D and thickness δ (see Bergeron 1962), yielding

$$\frac{\Delta A}{A}\approx\frac{\Delta pD}{E\delta}. \tag{14.33}$$

The common mass change due to liquid flow in the tube element during the time Δt is

$$\Delta m^{\pm}=(\rho^{\pm}A^{\pm}-\rho_0A_0)\Delta x\approx[(\rho^{\pm}-\rho_0)A_0+\rho_0(A^{\pm}-A_0)]\Delta x.$$

Therefore, the law of mass balance, instead of Eq. (14.24b), results in

$$p^{\pm}-p_0=\mp K_{eq}(v^{\pm}-v_0)/c, \tag{14.34}$$

where

$$\frac{1}{K_{eq}}=\frac{1}{K_V}+\frac{D}{E\delta}. \tag{14.35}$$

Comparing Eqs.(14.31) and (14.35), we see that

$$c=\sqrt{K_{eq}/\rho}. \tag{14.36}$$

Thus, all the equations of Subsect.14.2.2.1 remain valid in scaled terms if the quantity h is changed to p and the wave speed c is determined by Eq.(14.36).

The DMM simulation can be developed to variable area of tubing and channel systems, accounting for the loss of pressure induced by filtration, etc, and also used for analysis of some 1-D biomechanics problems, for example, blood current in vessels.

Conclusion

In application to unsteady 1-D wave processes in solids, the wave finite element method (WFEM) in the form of the method of direct mathematical modeling (DMM), which begun to be developed in the late 1970's, is distinguished by simplicity and clearness of computing procedure, is unconditionally stable and yields enough exact results by increase of finite element number and appropriate reduction of a time step.

The method has passed multifold approbation by comparison to the known analytical solutions and some calculation results of other numerical methods. On retention of general principles of computing algorithm formation, the method DMM readily varies in conformity to concrete task features that has allowed it to be successfully used by researches in a wide range of the mechanics problems and in various engineering applications.

However, 1-D setting of problems and condition that a wave propagation speed has to be constant in time define restrictions of the DMM. A more general WFEM approach developed over the last few years is free from the specified restrictions.

The software for calculation of unsteady processes in a 2-D rectangular domain created on its basis has allowed solutions of a number of typical and some new problems of the elastic solid mechanics to be obtained. Their comparison with results of the known analytical and numerical solutions has shown that the WFEM gives a much more correct pattern of propagation and reflection of unsteady waves than the traditional FEM. The efficiency of the method for simulation of processes where waves of a various kind propagate simultaneously was also shown.

At the same time, the WFEM, as one of the approaches of the computing mechanics, is still far from completed.

A more thorough analysis of accuracy and dispersion characteristics, development of algorithms using finite elements of various kinds, including three-dimensional, account of inelastic deformations, and some other problems need further consideration.

The author hopes that among the readers of the book there will be young researchers, who will become interested in new computing opportunities of the wave finite element method and want to apply their efforts on solution of the mentioned problems.

References

Amerio L, Prouse G (1975) Study of the motion of a string vibrating against an obstacle. Rend di Mat 6, 8 (2): 563-585

Argyris JH, Scharpf DW (1969) Finite elements in space and time. J Roy Aeron Soc 73 №708: 1041-1044

Babitsky VI (1978) Theory of vibro-impact systems. Approximated methods (in Russian). Nauka, Moscow

Babitsky VI (1998) Theory of vibro-impact systems and applications. Springer, Berlin Heidelberg New York

Belytschko T (1976) Survey of numerical methods and computer programs for dynamic structural analysis. Nuclear Engineering and Design 37: 23-34

Belytschko T, Krongauz Y, Organ D, Fleming M, Krysl P (1996) Meshless methods: An overview and recent developments. Comput Meth Appl Mech Eng 139: 3-47

Bergeron L (1962) From hydraulic shock in pipes to discharge in an electrical circuit (in Russian). Mashgiz, Moscow

Biderman VL (1952) Vibrations of structure elements (in Russian). In: Ponomarev SD (ed) Foundations of contemporary strength computation methods in machinery. Mashgiz, Moscow, pp 247-326

Biderman VL, Maljukova RP (1964) Loads and deformations under a longitudinal impact (in Russian). In: Integrity Computations 10. Mashinostroenie, Moscow, pp 261-306

Birger IA at al. (1975) Thermal strength of machine details (in Russian). Birger IA, Shorr BF (eds) Mashinostroenie, Moscow

Blokhin EP (1972) Computations of forces arising at the starting of non uniform trains of 10-20 thousand tons weight (in Russian). Proc of Dnepropetrovsky Institute of Railway Transport 128, pp 31-35

Blokhin EP, Manashkin LA (1982) Train dynamics. Unsteady longitudinal vibrations (in Russian).Transport, Moscow

Boussinesq J (1883) Compt Rend 154

Boussinesq J (1885) Application des potentiels a l'etude l'equilibre et du mouve-ment des solides elastiques. Gautier-Villars, Paris

De S, Bathe KJ (2001) Towards an efficient meshless computational technique: the method of finite spheres. Engineering Computations 18: 170-192

Clebsch A (1862) Theorie der Elastizität fester Körper , Leipzig

Courant R, Friedrichs KO, Lewy H. (1928) Ueber die partiellen Differenzen-gleichungen der mathematishen Physik. Math Ann 100: 32-74

Flamant A (1892) Compt Rend 114: 1465

Flanagan DP, Belytschko T (1981) A uniform strain hexahedron and quadrilateral with orthogonal hourglass control. Intern J for Numerical Methods in Engineering 17: 679-706

Goldsmith W (1960) Impact. The theory and phisical behavior of colliding solids. Arnold, London

Goloskokov EG, Philippov AP (1997) Unsteady vibrations of deformable systems. Naukova Dumka, Kiev

Hopkins HG (1960) Dinamic expansion of spherical cavities in metals. In: Progress in Applied Mechanics 1, pp 84-164

Hopkinspn B (1905) Proc Roy So A 74: 498

Hopkinson B (1914) Phil Trans A 213: 437

Hopkinson J (1872) Collected Sci Papers II: 316

Hughes TJR, Hulbert GM (1988) Space-time finite element methods for elastodynamics: Formulations and error estimates. Comput Methods Appl Mech Engrg 66: 339-363

Ishlinsky AJu (1954) General theory of plasticity with linear hardening (in Russian). J Ukr Math Zh 6: 314

Iwan WD (1967) On a class of models for yielding behavior of continuous and composite systems. Trans ASME Ser E J Appl Mech 34: 612

Kadashevish JuI, Novozhilov VV (1958) The theory of plasticity which takes into account residual microstresses (in Russian). J Appl Math Mech 22: 104

Kaplunov JuD (1986) Non-stationary dynamics of an elastic half-plane under the action of a moving load (in Russian). Inst for Problems in Mechanics, AN SSSR Reprint 277, Moscow

Kaplunov JuD, Muravsky GB (1986) Oscillations of an infinite string on deformed foundation affected by evenly accelerated moving load. Transmission over critical speed (in Russian). Izv AN SSSR MTT 1: 155-160

Kaplunov JuD, Nolde EV, Rogerson GA (2002) Short wave motion in a pre-stressed incompressible elastic plate. IMA J of Appl Math 67: 383-399

Kaplunova OB (1990a) Unsteady longitudinal vibration in a train as in a system of elastic-inertial units with nonlinear links and gaps (in Russian). Ph.D.dissertation, Inst.of Railway Transport Engineers, Moscow

Kaplunova OB (1990b) Investigation of unsteady dynamic processes in a one-dimensional discrete-continual system using method of direct mathematical modeling (in Russian). In: Mechanics of solids, Saratov State University, Saratov, pp 47-53

Kirchhoff G (1859) Über das Gleichgewicht und die Bewegung eines unendlich dünnen elastischen Stabis, J f. Math 56

Knowles JK, Reissner E (1960) Torsion and extension of helicoidal shells. Quart Appl Math 17(4): 409

Kobrinsky AE, Kobrinsky AA (1973) Vibro-impact systems (in Russian). Nauka, Moscow

Kolsky H (1953) Stress waves in solids. Oxford University Press, Fair Lawn

Krupenin VL (1985) On vibration of a vibro-impact system with distributed impact units (in Russian). J Mashinostroenie 85 (4): 23-29

Krupenin VL (1992) To calculation of resonant and auto-resonant vibration of flexible filaments against rigid extended obstacles (in Russian). J of Machinery Manufacture and Reliability 4: 25-31 (Trans by Allerton Press Inc 1992)

Krupenin VL, Mel'nikova GV (1991) About modeling of vibro-impact processes in systems with distributed impact elements (in Russian). J of Machinery Manufacture and Reliability 3: 19-26

Krupenin VL, Veprick AM (1985) To calculation of systems with distributed impact units (in Russian). J Mashinostroenie 85 №6: 9

Lasar'an VA (1949) Investigation on unsteady motion regimes of trains (in Russian).Transzheldorizdat, Moscow

Lee EH, Kanter J (1953) Wave propagation in finite rods of viscoelastic material. J Appl Phys 24 9: 1115

Li XD, Wiberg NE (1996) Structural dynamic analysis by a time-discontinuous Galerkin finite element method. Int J Numer Methods Eng 39: 2131-2152

Li XD, Yao D (2002) A discontinous Galerkin finite element method for wave propagation analysis in elastoplastic saturwted porous media. In: 5th World Congress of Computational Mechanics, Book of Abstracts II. Vienna, p 43

Lippmann H, Winter W (1987) Elastisch-plastische Stabwerke mit kinematischer Verfestung als Modell für vielkristallines Werkstoffverhalten unter Wechselbeanspruchung. J Ing Arch 57: 431

Makushin VM (1952) Shock loading calculations (in Russian). In: Ponomarev SD (ed). Foundations of contemporary strength calculation methods in machinery. Mashgiz, Moscow, pp327-418

Mechta PK, Davids N (1966) A direct numerical analysis method for cylindrical and spherical plastic waves. AIAA J 4: 144-151

Mel'nikova GV (1985) Stress computation in rods of variable cross section under a longitudinal impact (in Russian). In: Integrity and Dynamic Problems in Aircraft Engine Engineering 3. CIAM Proc 1109, pp 46-53

Mel'nikova GV (1987) Mathematical modeling of unsteady mechanical processes in machine structures (in Russian). PhD dissertation, Inst of Aviation Technology, Moscow

Mel'nikova GV (2000) Mathematical modeling of a string auto-oscillation under nonlinear interaction with medium and stopping devices of arbitrary types (in Russia). J of Machinery Manufacture and Reliability 4: 12-18

Mikhailov GK (1984) The dynamics of mechanical systems with variable masses as developed at Cambridge during the second half of the Nineteenth century. Bul Inst of Mathematics and its Applications 20 №1/2: 13-19

Mitropol'sky JA (1955), Nonstationary processes in nonlinear oscillating systems (in Russian). AN UkSSR, Kiev

Morse PhM (1948) Vibration and sound. McGraw-Hill Inc, New York

Muravsky GB (1981) Oscillation of the Timoshenko type beam lying on the elastic-hereditary foundation (in Russian). Izv AN SSSR MTT 5: 167-169

Navier (1823) Rapport et memoire sur les ponts supendus

Nigul U (1965) On methods and results of investigations on transient bending waves in an elastic plate (in Russian). Izv AN ESSR XIY (3) Tallinn: 345-384

Oden JT (1969) A general theory of finite elements. II Applications. Int J Numer Methods Eng 1 (3): 247-259

Oden JT, Wellford LC, Reddy CT (1976) A study of convergence and stability of finite element approximation of shock and acceleration waves in nonlinear materials. US Army Research Office, P-11860-M/DAAG29-76-G-0022

Pal'mov VA (1998) Vibration of elasto-plastic bodies. Springer-Verlag, Berlin Heidelberg New York

Panovko JG (1985). Solid mechanics. Contemporary concepts, mistakes and paradoxes (in Russian). Nauka, Moscow

Petrashen GI, Marchuk GI, Ogurtzov KI (1950) On Lamb's problem in the case of a half-space (in Russian). Trans of Leningrad State University 21: 71-118

Pershitz JI (1982) Determined and stochastic problems of longitudinal dynamics of a freight train with inter-car coupling gaps under braking (in Russian). DSc's dissertation, Moscow

Philippov AP, Kokhman'uk SS, Vorob'ev YuS (1974) Dynamic loads action on structural elements (in Russian). Naukova Dumka, Kiev

Pierce J (1974) Almost all about waves. The MIT Press Cambridge, Massachusetts and London

Pupyrev VA, Pavlovskaya EE (1996) Longitudinal impact of a rigid body against a visco-elastic rod (in Russian). In: Pal'mov BA (ed) Proc of the XXIII Summer School "Nonlinear Oscillations in Mechanical Systems" Inst of Problems of Mechanical Engineering, Moscow, pp 241-250

Rao SS (1995) Mechanical vibrations, 3rd Ed. Addison-Wesley Publishing Company, New York

Ramsauer C (1909) Ann Phys 30: 416

Saint-Venant BD, Flamant (1883) Resistable vive on dynamique des solids. Representation graphique des lois du choc longitudinal. Compt Rend Acad Sci 97, 127,214,218,244, Paris

Sears JE (1908) Trans Cambridge Phil Soc 21: 49

Shorr BF (1954) Integrity designs of naturally twisted blades (in Russian). Proc of Central Institute of Aviation Motors 256

Shorr BF (1959) On experimental testing of the extension theory of pre-twisted rods (in Russian). Izv AN SSSR, Mekhanika i Mashinostroenie 4: 176-158

Shorr BF (1960) To theory of pre-twisted unevenly heated rods (in Russian). Izv AN SSSR, Mekhanika i Mashinostroenie 1: 102-112

Shorr BF (1968) Naturally pre-twisted rods (in Russian). In: Birger IA, Panovko YG (eds). Strength. Stability. Vibrations. Mashinostroenie, Moscow, pp. 440-465

Shorr BF (1975) To theory of non-isothermal plastic deformation under arbitrary loading laws (in Russian). In: Mekhanika 6, Kujbyshev Polytechnic Inst, Kujbyshev, pp 107-114

Shorr BF (1976a) Direct mathematical modelling of the process of mechanical perturbances propagation in dynamic problems of multiply colliding solids (in Russian). In: 4th All-Union Congress on Theoretical and Applied Mechanics, Book of Abstracts. Naukova Dumka, Kiev, p 37

Shorr BF (1976b) Direct mathematical modeling of the process of mechnical perturbances propagation in solds (in Russian) Design and Development of Aircraft Turbojet Engines, Kujbyshev's Aviation Institute 78, pp 70-75

Shorr BF (1979) Theory of non-isothermal elastic-plastic deformation of alternating-sign (in Russian). In: Fridman JaB (ed) Physics and mechanics of deformation and failure 7, Atomizdat, Moscow, pp 115-133

Shorr BF (1983) Mathematical modeling of dynamic processes under moving loads (in Russian). In: Vibro-strength and reliability of aircraft engines and systems. Proc of Ku jbyshev's Aviation Institute, Kujbyshev, pp 148-156

Shorr BF (1984) Mathematical modelling of wave processes in elastic-viscoplastic solids (in Russian). Izv AN SSSR, Mekhanika Tverdogo Tela 4:144-151 (Trans Allerton Press, 1984: 141)

Shorr BF (1985) Numerical simulations of bending waves in rods (in Russian). In: Birger IA (ed) Integrity and Dynamics Problems in Aircraft Engine Engineering 3. CIAM Proc 1109, Moscow, pp 103-123

Shorr BF (1989). To account of hysteretic energy loss in materials under non-stationary dynamic processes. In: Birger IA (ed) Integrity and Dynamics Problems in Aircraft Engine Engineering 4, CIAM Proc 1237, Moscow, pp 131-138

Shorr BF (1990) On harmonic linearization of forced vibration equations for systems with dry friction structures (in Russian). J Integrity Problems 6: 89

Shorr BF (1995) Analysis of wave propagation in elastic-plastic rod of a variable cross section using direct mathematical modeling. J Arch Appl Mech 65: 537-547

Shorr BF (1996) On movement of inextensible and elastic chains of varying length (in Russian). In: Proc of the XXIII Summer School "Nonlinear Oscillations in Mechanical Systems". Inst of Problems of Mechanical Engineering, St.Petersburg, pp 281-294

Shorr BF (1997) Finite element modelling of wave propagation in solids. 3rd Euromech Solid Mechanics Conference, Book of Abstracts. Stockholm, p 329

Shorr BF (1998) Mathematical modelling of wave propagation in a rod of time-dependent material. J Mech of Time-Dependent Materials 1(4): 397

Shorr BF (1999) A wave approach to finite element analysis of solids. J Mechanics Research Communications 26 (2): 191-196

Shorr BF, Kaplunova OB (1986) Mathematical modeling of bending oscillation of a beam on a viscoelastic foundation under moving loads (in Russian). In:Vibro-strength and reliability of aircraft engines and systems. Proc of Kujbyshev's Aviation Institute, Kujbyshev, pp 138-144

Shorr BF, Mel'nikova GV (1988) Calculation of mechanical systems using method of direct mathematical modelling (in Russian). Mashinostroenie, Moscow

Shorr BF, Mel'nikova GV (1996) Transient processes in a nonlinear system. In: Proc of the XXIII Summer School "Nonlinear Oscillation in Mechanical Systems". Inst of Mechanical Engineering Problems, St. Petersburg, pp 295-313

Shorr BF, Mel'nikova GV (2002) New approach to finite element modelling of transient wave processes in solids. In: 5th World Congress of Computational Mechanics, Book of Abstracts II. Vienna, p 42

Shorr BF, Tjulenev VN (1981) Methods of details vibration measurement in aviation gas turbine engines (in Russian). In: Birger IA, Shorr BF (eds) Dynamics of aviation gas turbine engines. Mashinostroenie, Moscow, pp 194-200

Skudrzyk E (1968) Simple and complex vibratory systems. Pennsylvania State University Press, London

Smirnov VI (1934) Course of advanced mathematics for engineers and physicists. Vol 2 (in Russian). Gostechteorisdat, Moscow

Srinivasann AV (1997) Flutter and resonant vibration characteristics of engine blades, IGTI Scholar Paper. Orlando, Florida

Steidel RF (1971) An introduction to mechanical vibrations 3rd Ed. John Wiley & Sons,

New York Chichester Brisbane Toronto Singapore

Stepanov GV (1978) Behavior of construction materials in elastic-plastic loading waves (in Russian). Naukova Dumka, Kiev

Strang G, Fix GJ (1973) An analysis of the finite element method. Prentice-Hall Inc, Englewood Cliffs, New York.

Taylor GI (1946) J Inst Civil Engrs 26: 486

Timoshenko SP (1955) Vibration problems in engineering. DVan Nostrand Company INC, Toronto New York London

Timoshenko SP, Goodier JN (1970) Theory of elasticity 3rd Ed. McGraw-Hill, New York

Tjulenev VN (1981) Vane rows with different steps (in Russian). In: Birger IA, Shorr BF (eds) Dynamics of aviation gas turbine engines. Mashinostroenie, Moscow, pp 126-130

Veklich NA, Malyshev BM (1972) Longitudinal impact of a rigid body against a fixed rod (in Russian). Izv AN SSSR, Mekhanika Tverdogo Tela 6: 140-146

Vorob'ev JS., Shorr BF (1983) Theory of pre-twisted rods (in Russian). Naukova Dumka, Kiev

Zhukovsky NE (1937) Complete connection of works (in Russian) 5. ONTI, Moscow

Zienkiewicz OC (1987) The finite element method, 4th Ed. McGraw-Hill Book Co, London

Zienkiewicz OC, Cheung YK (1967) The finite element method in structural and continuum mechanics. McGraw-Hill Book Co, New.York.

Appendix

The purpose of the DMM - FORTRAN- programs presented below is not to obtain final results but enable the readers to acquire a familiarity with typical structure of the programs and procedures of their design. Having got acquainted with the programs, the reader can independently them upgrade, changing loads, initial and boundary conditions, combining the programs among themselves, etc.

The programs are presented as illustrative, in which the subroutines are not used, the algorithms of results output and representation are almost not described; therefore, from the programming viewpoint, they could be improved.

Some needed comments are included in the Program texts. All the Programs employ dimensionless parameters. At the end of each program the benchmark tests are resulted.

The following common notations are used in the Programs:

N – number of elements
NT – number of time steps
S – stress
V – velocity
U – displacement
T – current time
X – nodal coordinate
I – index of time step (I=1,2,...,NT)
J – index of element (J=1,2,...,N) and node (J=1,2,...,N+1)
DT – time increment
DX – length of element
S1, V1 – parameters at left boundary of the Jth element (node J)
S2, V2 – parameters at right boundary of the Jth element (node J+1)

Program A1. Constant Compressive Force Suddenly Applied to the Free Boundary of a One-End Clamped Rod

Subsect.1.1.2.1; Problem 1.1. Sketch of the Problem, see Fig.1.1a; some results are shown in Fig.1.4.

```
      DIMENSION S(50),V(50)          ! Element stress and velocity
      DIMENSION U(51)                ! Nodal displacement
! Double arrays for tabular or graph representation of stress discontinuity
```

```
      DIMENSION X(102),SP(102)
      WRITE(*,*) 'Number of elements N<=50'         ! Imput data
      READ(*,*) N
      WRITE(*,*) 'Number of time steps NT'
      READ(*,*) NT
      NP=2*N
      DO 10 J=1, N                     ! Initial state of the system at T=0.
      S(J)=0.
      V(J)=0.
   10 U(J)=0.
      DX=1./N                          ! Length of element
      DT=DX                            ! Time increment
      DO 20 I=1, NT                    ! Beginning of time loop
      T=I*DT                           ! Current time
      S1=-1.                           ! Boundary conditions at free end, J=1
      V1=V(1)-S1+S(1)
      U(1)=U(1)+V1*DT                  ! Displacement at J=1
      DO 30 J=2, N                     ! Beginning of element loop
      V2=0.5*(V(J)+V(J-1)+S(J)-S(J-1))       ! V and S at right border
      S2=S(J-1)+V2-V(J-1)                    ! of the element J-1
      U(J)=U(J)+V2*DT                  ! Displacement at node J
      V(J-1)=V1+V2-V(J-1)              ! New values of V and S
      S(J-1)=S1+S2-S(J-1)              ! for element J-1
      V1=V2                            ! V and S at left border
      S1=S2                            ! of element J
   30 CONTINUE                         ! End of element loop
      V2=0.                            ! Boundary conditions at fixed
      S2=S(N)+V2-V(N)                  ! end, J=N+1
      V(N)=V1+V2-V(N)                  ! New values of V and S
      S(N)=S1+S2-S(N)                  ! for element J=N
   20 CONTINUE                         ! End of time loop
! To output of stress discontinuity along the rod length
      X(1)=0.
      X(2)=0.
      SP(1)=S(1)
      DO 40 JP=3, NP+2
      X(JP)=X(JP-2)+DX
   40 SP(JP-1)=S(JP/2)
      OPEN(5,FILE='STRESS')          ! Element stress vs. rod length at I=NT
      WRITE(5,*)'Element stress vs. rod length'
      WRITE(5,*)'         X           S(X)'
      WRITE(5,50)(X(JP+1),SP(JP),JP=1,NP)
   50 FORMAT(2X,2(E12.5,2X))
      OPEN(7,FILE='RESULTS')          ! Control results for NT=2*N
      WRITE(7,*) 'Control results for NT=2*N'
      WRITE(7,*) 'Input data: N=',N,' ','NT=',NT
      WRITE(7,*) 'Benchmark: T=2, U(1)=2, S(N)=-2, S2=-2'
      WRITE(7,*) 'Calculated: T=',T,' ','U(1)=',U(1)
      WRITE(7,*) 'S(N)=',S(N),' ','S2=',S2
      STOP
      END                             ! End of Program
```

Program A2. Interaction of Different Counter-Waves in a Free-Free Rod

Subsect. 1.1.2.3, Problem 1.3. Sketch of the Problem, see Fig.1.7a; some results for rectangular and triangular impulses are shown in Fig.1.7b.

```
    DIMENSION S(1000),V(1000)   ! Stress and velocity
    DIMENSION X(2002),SP(2002)  ! Double arrays for tabular or graph
                                ! representation of stress discontinuity
    REAL IR, NSTR
    WRITE(*,*) 'Even number of elements N<=1000'      ! Imput data
    READ(*,*) N
    WRITE(*,*) 'Number of time steps NT'
    READ(*,*) NT
    WRITE(*,*) 'Odd step number of impulse duration NIMP>>1'
    READ(*,*) NIMP
    NP=2.*N
    DX=1./N
    NST=(NIMP+1)/2
    NSTR=FLOAT(NST)
    IC=(N+NIMP+1)/2        ! To control
    JC=N/2+1
    DO 10 J=1, N           ! Initial state of the system
    S(J)=0.
 10 V(J)=0.
    DO 20 I=1, NT          ! Beginning of time loop
    IR=FLOAT(I)
! Boundary conditions at left end, node J=1
! Action of triangular impulse during NIMP steps
    IF(I.LE.NST) THEN
    S1=NIMP/NSTR/NSTR*IR
    ELSE
    S1=NIMP/NSTR/NSTR*(2.*NSTR-IR)
    ENDIF
    IF(I.GT.NIMP) S1=0.    ! End of the triangular impulse force
    V1=V(1)-S1+S(1)
    DO 30 J=2, N           ! Beginning of element loop
    S2=0.5*(S(J)+S(J-1)+V(J)-V(J-1))
    V2=V(J-1)+S2-S(J-1)
    S(J-1)=S1+S2-S(J-1)
    V(J-1)=V1+V2-V(J-1)
    V1=V2
    S1=S2
 30 CONTINUE               ! End of element loop
    S2=1                   ! Boundary conditions at right end, node J=N1+1
                           ! Action of rectangular impulse during NIMP steps
    IF(I.GT.NIMP) S2=0.    ! End of the rectangular impulse
    V2=V(N)+S2-S(N)
    S(N)=S1+S2-S(N)
    V(N)=V1+V2-V(N)
```

```
    IF(I.NE.IC) GOTO 20   ! To control
    S2C=0.5*(S(JC)+S(JC-1)+V(JC)-V(JC-1))
 20 CONTINUE                          ! End of time loop
! Distribution of stresses along the rod at I=NT with discontinuity tabulating
    X(1)=0.
    X(2)=0.
    SP(1)=S(1)
    DO 40 JP=3, NP+2
    X(JP)=X(JP-2)+DX
 40 SP(JP-1)=S(JP/2)
    OPEN(5,FILE='STRESS')    ! Element stress vs. rod length at I=NT
    WRITE(5,*) 'Element stress vs. rod length'
    WRITE(5,*) '              X              S(X)'
    WRITE(5,50) (X(JP+1),SP(JP),JP=1,NP)
 50 FORMAT(2X,2(E12.5,2X))
    OPEN(9,FILE='RESULTS')                  ! Control results
    WRITE(9,*) 'Imput data: N=',N,' ','NT=',NT,' ','NIMP=',NIMP
    WRITE(9,*) 'Control: with NIMP>>1 max.stress tends to S2C=3'
    WRITE(9,*)' Benchmark: N=1000, NT=625, NIMP=249, IC=625, S2C=2.992'
    WRITE(9,*) 'Calculated: IC=',IC,' ','S2C=',S2C
    STOP
    END
```

Program A3. Collision of Rods of a Different Length

Subsect. 1.1.2.5, Problem 1.5. Sketch of the Problem, see Fig.1.3d; some results are shown in Fig.1.10.

```
    DIMENSION S(200),V(200)        ! Stress and velocity
    REAl MOM0,MOM                  ! To control of momentum balance
    WRITE(*,*) 'Number of the 1st element N1<=100'  ! Imput data
    READ(*,*) N1
    WRITE(*,*) 'Number of the 2nd element N2<=100'
    READ(*,*) N2
    WRITE(*,*)'Velocity of the 1st element V10>0.'
    READ(*,*) V10
    WRITE(*,*) 'Velocity of the 2nd element V20<V10'  ! Impact condition
    READ(*,*) V20
    WRITE(*,*) 'Number of time steps NT'
    READ(*,*) NT
    N=N1+N2
    DT=1./N2
    DX=DT
    MOM0=(V10*N1+V20*N2)*DX                   ! Initial momentum
    EN0=0.5*(V10*V10*N1+V20*V20*N2)*DX        ! Initial energy
    DO 10 J=1, N1                  ! Initial state of the 1st rod
    S(J)=0.
 10 V(J)=V10
    DO 15 J=N1+1, N                ! Initial state of the 2nd rod
```

```
    S(J)=0.
 15 V(J)=V20
    U1=0.                          ! Initial displacements between rods
    U2=0.
    K=1                            ! Mark of rod interaction
    DO 20 I=1, NT                  ! Beginning of time loop
! To calculation of rods mean velocities and energy
    V1M=0.
    V2M=0.
    EN1=0.
    EN2=0.
! Free boundary conditions at left end of the 1st rod; node J=1
    S1=0.
    V1=V(1)-S1+S(1)
    DO 30 J=2, N1                  ! Element loop for the 1st rod
    S2=0.5*(S(J)+S(J-1)+V(J)-V(J-1))
    V2=V(J-1)+S2-S(J-1)
    S(J-1)=S1+S2-S(J-1)
    V(J-1)=V1+V2-V(J-1)
    V1M=V1M+V(J-1)
    EN1=EN1+0.5*(V(J-1)*V(J-1)+S(J-1)*S(J-1))*DX
    V1=V2
    S1=S2
 30 CONTINUE
    S2=0.5*(S(N1+1)+S(N1)+V(N1+1)-V(N1))     ! Rods move in contact
    IF(K.EQ.2) S2=0.                          ! Rod are separated
    IF(S2.GE.0.) THEN
    S2=0.
    K=2
    ELSE
    K=1
    ENDIF
    V2=V(N1)+S2-S(N1)
    U1=U1+V2*DT
    S(N1)=S1+S2-S(N1)
    V(N1)=V1+V2-V(N1)
    V1M=(V1M+V(N1))/N1            ! Mean velocity of the 1st rod at the step I
    EN1=EN1+0.5*(V(N1)*V(N1)+S(N1)*S(N1))*DX
    S1=S2                         ! Left boundary conditions of the 2nd rode
    V1=V(N1+1)-S1+S(N1+1)
    U2=U2+V1*DT
    DO 40 J=N1+2, N               ! Element loop for the 2nd rod
    S2=0.5*(S(J)+S(J-1)+V(J)-V(J-1))
    V2=V(J-1)+S2-S(J-1)
    S(J-1)=S1+S2-S(J-1)
    V(J-1)=V1+V2-V(J-1)
    V2M=V2M+V(J-1)
    EN2=EN2+0.5*(V(J-1)*V(J-1)+S(J-1)*S(J-1))*DX
    V1=V2
    S1=S2
 40 CONTINUE
```

```
! Free boundary conditions at right end of the 2nd rod; node J=N+1
      S2=0.
      V2=V(N)+S2-S(N)
      S(N)=S1+S2-S(N)
      V(N)=V1+V2-V(N)
      V2M=(V2M+V(N))/N2            ! Mean velocity of the 2nd rod at the step I
      MOM=(V1M*N1+V2M*N2)*DX       I Full momentum at the step I
      EN2=EN2+0.5*(V(N)*V(N)+S(N)*S(N))*DX
      EN=EN1+EN2                   ! Full energy at the step I
   20 CONTINUE                     ! End of time loop
! Control results
      OPEN(9,FILE='RESULTS')
      WRITE(9,*) 'Imput data: N1=',N1,' ','N2=',N2,' ','NT=',NT
      WRITE(9,*) 'Initial rod velocities: V10=',V10,' ','V20=',V20
      WRITE(9,*) 'Final rod mean velocities: V1M=',V1M,' ','V2M=',V2M
      WRITE(9,*) 'Momentum balance: MOM0=',MOM0,' ','MOM=',MOM
      WRITE(9,*) 'Energy balance: EN0=',EN0,' ','EN=',EN
      WRITE(9,*) 'Rod contact displacements U1=',U1,' ','U2=',U2
      WRITE(9,*) 'Control results:'
      WRITE(9,*) 'Benchmark1: N1=2, N2=1, V10=1, V20=-1, V1M=0, V20=1'
      WRITE(9,*) 'Benchmark2: N1=2, N2=1, V10=0, V20=-2, V1M=-1, V2M=0.'
      WRITE(9,*) 'Calculated:V1M=',V1M,' ','V2M=',V2M
      STOP
      END
```

Program A4. Impact of an 'Adhering' Body against an Elastic One-End Clamped Rod

Subsect.8.2.1.2, Problem 8.2; see also Subsects.8.2.2.1 – 8.2.2.3. Sketch of the Problem, see Fig.8.4a; some results are shown in Fig.8.6 and 8.7.

```
      DIMENSION S(400),V(400)                    ! Element stress and velocity
      REAL M
      WRITE(*,*) 'Number of elements N<=400'     ! Imput data
      READ(*,*) N
      WRITE(*,*) 'Number of time steps NT'
      READ(*,*) NT
      WRITE(*,*) 'Body/rod mass ratio M'
      READ(*,*) M
      WRITE(*,*) 'Time step for stress printing IP'
      READ(*,*) IP
      OPEN(8,FILE='Timerez')                     ! Time process
      G=1./M/N                                   ! G<<1
      DO 10 J=1, N                     ! Initial state of the system at T=0.
      S(J)=0
   10 V(J)=0.
      VM0=1.                           ! Initial body velocity
      DX=1./N                          ! Length of element
```

```
      DT=DX                        ! Time increment
      TP=float(IP)/N
      DO 20 I=1, NT                ! Beginning of time loop
      T=I*DT                       ! Current time
      V1=(VM0+0.5*G*(V(1)+S(1)))/(1.+0.5*G) ! Boundary conditions at the free end
      S1=(S(1)+V(1)-VM0)/(1.+0.5*G)
      VM0=VM0+G*S1                 ! New body velocity
      SPT1=S1
      IF(I.NE.IP) GOTO 15
      SP1=S1
   15 DO 30 J=2, N                 ! Beginning of element loop
      V2=0.5*(V(J)+V(J-1)+S(J)-S(J-1))
      S2=S(J-1)+V2-V(J-1)
      V(J-1)=V1+V2-V(J-1)
      S(J-1)=S1+S2-S(J-1)
      V1=V2
      S1=S2
   30 CONTINUE                     !  End of element loop
      V2=0.                        !  Boundary conditions at fixed
      S2=S(N)+V2-V(N)              ! end, J=N+1
      V(N)=V1+V2-V(N)
      S(N)=S1+S2-S(N)
      SPT2=S2
! Body velocity VM, stress S1 at J=1 and stress S2 at J=N+1 vs. time
      WRITE(8,*) 'I=',I,',','VM=',VM0,',','S1=',SPT1,',','S2=',SPT2
      IF(I.NE.IP) GOTO 20
      SP2=S2
      VMP=VM0
   20 CONTINUE                     ! End of time loop
      OPEN(7,FILE='RESULTS')       ! Control results
      WRITE(7,*) 'Input data: N=',N,' ','NT=',NT,' ','M=',M,' ','IP=',IP
      WRITE(7,*) 'Control results for M=1, N=400, and IP=2*N+1'
      WRITE(7,*) 'Benchmark: T=2.0025, S1=-2.1302, S2=-0.7348, VM=0.1300'
      WRITE(7,*) 'Control results for M=1, N=400, and IP=3*N+1'
      WRITE(7,*) 'Benchmark: T=3.0025, S1=-0.0488, S2=-2.2628, VM=-0.6861'
      WRITE(7,*) 'Calculated: T=',TP,' ','S1=',SP1,' ','S2=',SP2
      WRITE(7,*) 'Calculated: VM=',VMP
      STOP
      END                       ! End of Program
```

Program A5.Oscillation of a String under Impulse Loading

Subsect. 2.3.1.2, Problem 2.6. Sketch of the Problem, see Fig.2.9a; some results are shown in Fig.2.10

```
! Arrays of transverse force, velocity and deflection
      DIMENSION Q(200),V(200),Y(201)                    !
      DIMENSION X(200)                ! Point coordinate
```

```
      WRITE (*,*) 'Even number of elements N<=200'
      READ (*,*) N
      WRITE (*,*) 'Number of time steps NT'
      READ (*,*) NT
      WRITE (*,*) 'Time index for deflection printing I1'
      READ (*,*) I1
      DO 10 J=1,N                            ! Initial conditions
      V(J)=1.
      Q(J)=0.
   10 Y(0)=0.
      Y(N+1)=0.
      DX=1./N
      DT=DX
      TP=FLOAT(I1)/N
      OPEN(4,FILE='DEFLEC')
      WRITE(4,*) 'Deflection along the string at time T=',TP
      WRITE(4,*)'    X','          ','Y'
      DO 20 I=1,NT
      V1=0.                                  ! Fixed end at J=1
      Q1=-Q(1)+V1-V(1)
      Y(1)=0.
      X(1)=0.
      DO 30 J=2,N
      V2=0.5*(V(J)+V(J-1)+Q(J)-Q(J-1))
      Q2=Q(J-1)+V2-V(J-1)
      Q(J-1)=-Q1+Q2-Q(J-1)
      V(J-1)=V1+V2-V(J-1)
      Y(J)=Y(J)+V2*DT
      X(J)=X(J-1)+DX
      V1=V2
   30 Q1=-Q(J)+V1-V(J)
      V2=0.                                  ! Fixed end at J=N+1
      Q2=Q(N)+V2-V(N)
      Y(N+1)=0.
      X(N+1)=1.
      Q(N)=-Q1+Q2-Q(N)
      V(N)=V1+V2-V(N)
      IF(I.NE.I1) GO TO 20
      YP=Y(N/2+1)
      OPEN(4,FILE='DEFLEC')
      WRITE(4,40) (X(J),Y(J),J=1,N+1)
   40 FORMAT(2X,2(E12.5,2X))
   20 CONTINUE
! Control results
      OPEN(5,FILE='CONTROL')
      WRITE(5,*) 'Input data: N=',N,' ','NT=',NT,' ','I1=',I1
      WRITE(5,*) 'Benchmark: at X=N/2+1 deflection Y=1 for T=0.5'
      WRITE(5,*) 'Benchmark: at X=N/2+1 deflection Y=-1 for T=1.5'
      WRITE(5,*) 'Calculated:T=',TP,' ','Y=',YP
      STOP
      END
```

Program A6. An Initial Phase of Stress Development in a Rod under Harmonic Excitation

Subsect. 9.1.1.2, Problem 9.1. Sketch of the Problem, see Fig.9.1c; some results are shown in Fig.9.2b and 9.4

```
      DIMENSION S(400),V(400)                ! Element stress and velocity
      WRITE(*,*) 'Number of elements N<=400'  ! Imput data
      READ(*,*) N
      WRITE(*,*) 'Number of time steps NT'
      READ(*,*) NT
      WRITE(*,*) 'Relative exciting frequency F'
      READ(*,*) F
      PI=3.14159
      OPEN(8,FILE='Timerez')                  ! Time process
      WRITE(8,*) 'Stresses S1 at J=1 and S2 at J=N+1 vs. time'
      DO 10 J=1, N                            ! Initial state of the system
      S(J)=0.                                 ! at T=0.
   10 V(J)=0.
      DX=1./N                                 ! Length of element
      DT=DX                                   ! Time increment
      DO 20 I=1, NT                           ! Beginning of time loop
      I1=FLOAT(I)
      T=I1*DT                                 ! Current time
      S1=SIN(0.5*PI*F*(I1-0.5)*DT)            ! Harmonic exiting force
      V1=V(1)-S1+S(1)                         ! at the free end, J=1
      SP1=S1
   15 DO 30 J=2, N                            ! Beginning of element loop
      V2=0.5*(V(J)+V(J-1)+S(J)-S(J-1))
      S2=S(J-1)+V2-V(J-1)
      V(J-1)=V1+V2-V(J-1)
      S(J-1)=S1+S2-S(J-1)
      V1=V2
      S1=S2
   30 CONTINUE                                ! End of element loop
      V2=0.                                   ! Boundary conditions at fixed
      S2=S(N)+V2-V(N)                         ! end, J=N+1
      V(N)=V1+V2-V(N)
      S(N)=S1+S2-S(N)
      SP2=S2
! Output of stress S1 at J=1 and stress S2 at J=N+1 vs. time
      Write(8,*)' ',I,'    ',T,'    ',SP1,'    ',SP2
   20 CONTINUE                          ! End of time loop
      OPEN(7,FILE='RESULTS')            ! Control results
      WRITE(7,*) 'Input data:N=',N,' ','NT=',NT,' ','F=',F
      WRITE(7,*) 'Control results for F=1, N=100, and NT=2000'
      WRITE(7,*) 'Benchmark:I=2000, T=20, S1=-0.00788, S2=-20.'
      WRITE(7,*) 'Calculated:I=',I,' ','T=',T,' ','S1=',SP1,' ','S2=',SP2
      STOP
      END                          ! End of Program
```

Program A7.A Semi-Infinite Viscoelastic Rod of Maxwell's Material Affected by the Impact on the Free End

Subsect.3.2.2.1. Problem 3.1. Some results are shown in Fig.3.3

```
      DIMENSION S(500),V(500)              ! Element stress and velocity
      DIMENSION X(500)
      WRITE (*,*) 'Number of time steps NT'  ! Input data. Varying number of
      READ (*,*) NT                          ! elements is calculated)
      WRITE (*,*) 'Time increment scaled by relaxation time DT<<1'
      READ (*,*) DT
      WRITE (*,*) 'Step index IP to printing'
      READ (*,*) IP
      N0=NT                                  ! Maximal number of elements
      DX=DT
      TP=1.*IP*DT
      DO 10 J=1,N0                           ! Initial state
      S(J)=0.
      V(J)=0.
 10   X(J)=(1.*J-0.5)*DX
      OPEN(4,FILE='STRESS')
      WRITE(4,*) 'Stress vs. rod length at time TP'
      DO 20 I=1,NT                     ! Beginning  of time loop
      T=1.*I*DT
      N=I                              ! Current number of elements
      V1Z=1.                         ! Impact at J=1 with constant boundary velocity
      S1=(S(1)-1+V(1))/(1.+0.5*DT)
      V1=V(1)-S1+S(1)
      SP0=S1
      DO 30 J=2,N                      ! Element loop for N>=2
      S2=0.5*(S(J)+S(J-1)+V(J)-V(J-1))/(1.+0.5*DT)
      V2=V(J-1)+S2-S(J-1)
      S(J-1)=S1+S2-S(J-1)
      V(J-1)=V1+V2-V(J-1)
      S1=S2
 30   V1=V(J)-S1+S(J)
      S2=0.                            ! Silent boundary conditions
      V2=0.                            ! at moving end J=N+1
      S(N)=S1-S(N)
      V(N)=V1-V(N)
      IF(I.NE.IP) GO TO 20
      WRITE(4,*)' ','X',' ','S'        ! Output of stress vs. rod length for TP
      WRITE(4,40)(X(J),S(J),J=1,N0)
 40   FORMAT(2X,2(E12.5,2X))
      SP1=S(1)
      SP2=S(IP)
 20   CONTINUE
      OPEN(7,FILE='RESULTS')           ! Control results
      WRITE(7,*) 'Input data: NT=',NT,' ','DT=',DT,' ','IP=',IP
      WRITE(7,*) 'Control results for NT=400, DT=0.02, IP=100'
```

```
      WRITE(7,*) 'Benchmark:S(1)=-0.46575, S(100)=-0.36971'
      WRITE(7,*) 'Calculated: S(1)=',SP1,' ','S(100)=',SP2
      STOP
      END
```

Program A8. A Fixed-Free Rod with Inner Viscous Friction Excited by a Transient Quasi-Harmonic Load

Subsect. 9.1.3.2. Problem 9.3. Sketch of the Problem, Fig.9.1b; some results are shown in Fig.9.11 (curve 1)

```
      DIMENSION S(400),V(400)          ! Element stress and velocity
      DIMENSION SEN(400)               ! Stress envelope
      WRITE(*,*) 'Number of elements N<=400'  ! Input data for transient process
      READ(*,*) N                              ! with varying exciting frequency
      WRITE(*,*) 'Number of time steps NT'
      READ(*,*) NT
      WRITE(*,*) 'Initial exciting frequency FI'
      READ(*,*) FI
      WRITE(*,*) 'Final exciting frequency FF'
      READ(*,*) FF
      WRITE(*,*) 'Relaxation time TC'
      READ(*,*) TC
      PI=3.14159
      DX=1./N
      DT=DX
      FX=0.5*DT/TC              ! Relaxation parameter
      TK=NT*DT                  ! Process time
      AF=4*(FF-FI)/TK           ! Rate of exciting frequency
      DO 10 J=1,N               ! Initial state
      S(J)=0.
   10 V(J)=0.
      KEN=1                     ! Preparation of stress envelope printing
      KEN1=1
      EN1=0.
      EN2=0.
      SEN(1)=0.
      I1=0
      T=0.
      OPEN(19,FILE='ENVELS')
      WRITE(19,*) '     I        Time        Frequency         Stress'
      WRITE(19,*)I1,T,FI,SEN(1)
      DO 20 I=1,NT                 ! Beginning of time loop
      T=(1.*I-0.5)*DT              ! Running mean step time
      F=FI+0.25*AF*T               ! Running exciting frequency
      PH=FI+0.125*AF*T
      SS0=-SIN(0.5*PI*PH*T)        ! Running full harmonic force
      S12=SS0/N                    ! Distributed harmonic load referred to a node
```

```
      S1=-0.5*S12                  ! Boundary condition at J=1
      V1=V(1)-S1+S(1)
      DO 30 J=2,N                  ! Beginning of element loop
      S2=0.5*(S(J)+S(J-1)+V(J)-V(J-1))/(1.+FX)+0.5*S12
      V2=V(J-1)+S2-S(J-1)
      V(J-1)=V1+V2-V(J-1)
      S(J-1)=S1+S2-S(J-1)
      S1=S2-S12
      V1=V(J)-S1+S(J)
   30 CONTINUE
      V2X=0.                       ! Boundary condition at J=N+1
      S2=(S(N)-V(N))/(1.+FX)
      V2=V(N)+S2-S(N)
      V(N)=V1+V2-V(N)
      S(N)=S1+S2-S(N)
      SP=S2-0.5*S12                ! Stress at the fixed end
      IF(EN2.LE.EN1)THEN           ! Envelope formation for stress SP
      GO TO 50
      ELSE
      IF(ABS(SP).GT.EN2)THEN
      GO TO 50
      ELSE
      KEN=KEN+1
      SEN(KEN)=EN2
      ENDIF
      ENDIF
   50 EN1=EN2
      EN2=ABS(SP)
      TP=1.*I/N
      IF(KEN.LE.KEN1)GO TO 20
      OPEN(19,FILE='ENVELS')
      WRITE(19,*)I,TP,F,SEN(KEN)
      KEN1=KEN
   20 CONTINUE
      OPEN(9,FILE='RESULTS')
      WRITE(9,*) 'Imput data: N=',N,' ','NT=',NT
      WRITE(9,*) 'FI=',FI,' ','FF=',FF,' ','TC=',TC
      WRITE(9,*) 'Control for N=25,NT=6000,FI=0.9,FF=3.4,TC=15'
      WRITE(9,*) 'Benchmark: SP=9.006 at F=1.132; SP=3.164 at F=3.148'
      WRITE(9,*) 'Calculated results: see file "ENVELS" '
      STOP
      END
```

Program A9. Bending of a Beam Affected by a Stepped Transversal Force. Initial Phase (without Reflections)

Subsect. 5.3.1.1. Problem 5.1. Sketch of the Problem, see Fig.5.2a; some results are shown in Figs.5.2-5.3

```
! Arrays: element linear V and angular OM velocities, shear force F and bending
moment M, link 'spring' shear forces FQL and FQR, nodal deflection U, and
coordinate X
      DIMENSION V(400),OM(400),F(400),M(400),FQL(400),FQR(400)
      DIMENSION U(401),X(401)
      REAL M,M1,M2,M1X,M2X
      WRITE(*,*) 'Maximal number of elements NM<=400'   ! Imput data
      READ(*,*)NM
      WRITE(*,*) 'Number of time steps NT<=NM'
      READ(*,*)NT
      WRITE(*,*) 'Shear parameter BS>=1'
      READ(*,*)BS
      WRITE(*,*) 'Accuracy parameter AL>0, AL**2<<1'
      READ(*,*)AL
! Relative element length and time increment scaled by cross-sectional
! radius of inertia
      DX=2.*AL
      DT=DX
      N=NT   ! Number of element within which a wave propagates without reflection
      DO 10 J=1,NM              ! Initial conditions
      V(J)=0.
      OM(J)=0.
      F(J)=0.
      M(J)=0.
      FQL(J)=0.
   10 FQR(J)=0.
      DO 11 J=1, NM+1
   11 U(J)=0.
      T=0.
      DO 80 I=1,NT                   ! Beginning of time loop
      T=T+DT
      F1X=0.5                        ! Boundary conditions at J=1
      OM1X=0.                        ! accounting beam symmetry
      V1X=V(1)+F(1)+BS*F1X-(BS-1)*FQL(1)
      M1X=-M(1)-OM(1)+AL*F1X
      F1=F1X
      OM1=OM1X
      V1=V(1)+F1+F(1)
      M1=-M(1)+OM1-OM(1)
      U(1)=U(1)+V1X*DT
      X(1)=0.
      FQL(1)=2.*F1-FQL(1)
      DO 50 J=2,N                    ! Beginning of element loop
      X(J)=(J-1)*DX
      V2X=(V(J)+V(J-1)+F(J)-F(J-1)-(BS-1.)*(FQL(J)+FQR(J-1)))/2.
      OM2X=(BS*(OM(J)+OM(J-1)+M(J)-M(J-1))+AL*(F(J)+F(J-1)+
     *V(J)-V(J-1)-(BS-1.)*(FQL(J)-FQR(J-1))))/(2*(BS+AL*AL))
      F2X=(F(J-1)+(BS-1.)*FQR(J-1)+V2X-V(J-1)-AL*OM2X)/BS
      M2X=M(J-1)+OM2X*(1.+AL*AL/BS)-OM(J-1)-AL*(V2X-V(J-1)
     *+F(J-1)+(BS-1.)*FQR(J-1))/BS
      F2=F2X
```

```
      OM2=OM2X
      V2=V(J-1)+F2-F(J-1)
      M2=M(J-1)+OM2-OM(J-1)
      U(J)=U(J)+V2X*DT
      FQR(J-1)=2.*F2-FQR(J-1)
      V(J-1)=V1+V2-V(J-1)              ! New parameters of element J-1
      OM(J-1)=OM1+OM2-OM(J-1)
      F(J-1)=F2-F1-F(J-1)
      M(J-1)=M2-M1-M(J-1)
      V1X=V2X                          ! Transition to the next element
      OM1X=OM2X
      F1X=-F2X
      M1X=-M2X
      F1=F1X
      OM1=OM1X
      V1=V(J)+F1+F(J)
      M1=-M(J)+OM1-OM(J)
      FQL(J)=2.*F1-FQL(J)
 50   CONTINUE
      V2X=0.                           ! Boundary conditions at the node J=N+1
      OM2X=0.
      X(NX+1)=N*DX
      U(NX+1)=0.
      OM2=0.
      F2=(F(N)+(BS-1.)*FQR(N)-V(N))/BS
      V2=V(N)+F2-F(N)
      M2=M(N)-OM(N)
      M2X=M2-AL*F2
      V(N)=V1+V2-V(N)
      OM(N)=OM1-OM(N)
      F(N)=F2-F1-F(N)
      M(N)=M2-M1-M(N)
      FQR(N)=2.*F2-FQR(N)
 80   Continue
! To print moments M(J), forces F(J), and deflections U(J) along the beam at I=NT
      OPEN (7, FILE='FORCES')
      WRITE(7,*) 'Moments and forces vs. length of the beam at I=NT'
      WRITE(7,*) 'Time I=', NT
      WRITE(7,*) '          X           M           F'
      WRITE(7,60) (X(J),M(J),F(J),J=1,NM)
 60   FORMAT(2X,3(E12.4,2X))
      OPEN (8, FILE='DEFLECT')
      WRITE(8,*) 'Deflections vs. length of the beam at I=NT'
      WRITE(8,*) 'Time I=', NT
      WRITE(8,*) '          X           U'
      WRITE(8,70) (X(J),U(J),J=1,NX+1)
 70   FORMAT(2X,2(E12.4,2X))
      OPEN (9, FILE='RESULTS')
      WRITE(9,*) 'Input: NM=',NM,'.','N=',N,'.','BS=',BS,'.','AL=',AL
      WRITE(9,*) 'Control results for NM=NT=200, BS=3.078, AL=0.01'
      WRITE(9,*) 'Benchmark: M=Mmax=0.3594 at X=2.26 (J=114)'
```

```
      WRITE(9,*) 'Calculated: M=', M(114),'.','X=',X(114)
      STOP
      END
```

Program A10. Transient in an Electrical Circuit with Varying Boundary Resistance

Subsect. 14.2.1.2. Problem 14.1. Sketch of the Problem, see 14.6a; some results are shown in Fig.14.6b.

```
      DIMENSION V(400),C(400)              ! Element voltage V and current C
      WRITE(*,*) 'Number of elements N<=400'  ! Input data
      READ(*,*) N
      WRITE(*,*) 'Number of time steps NT'
      READ(*,*) NT
      WRITE(*,*) 'Relative circuit resistance R'
      READ(*,*) R
      WRITE(*,*) 'Relative circuit outflow G'
      READ(*,*) G
      WRITE(*,*) 'Step IR when a border resistance is connected up'
      READ(*,*) IR
      WRITE(*,*) 'Relative border resistance RB'
      READ(*,*) RB
      DO 10 J=1,N                          ! Initial conditions
      V(J)=0.
   10 C(J)=0.
      T=0.                                 ! Scaled time
      DT=1./N                              ! Time increment
      CP1=0.                               ! Current at J=1
      CP2=0.                               ! Current at J=N+1
      OPEN(3,FILE='CURRENT')
      WRITE(3,*) 'Current at the nodes J=1 and J=N+1 for instant T'
      WRITE(3,*) '          T             CP1             CP2'
      WRITE(3,80) T,CP1,CP2
   80 FORMAT(2X,3(E12.5,2X))
      DO 20 I=1,NT                   ! Beginning of time loop
      V1X=1.                         ! Voltage source suddenly applied to left
      C1=(C(1)+V1X-V(1))/(1.+R)      ! circuit boundary J=1 at T=0
      C1X=C1+G
      V1=V(1)+C1-C(1)
      VP1=V1X
      CP1=C1X
      DO 30 J=2,N                    ! Beginning of element loop
      V2X=0.5*(V(J-1)+V(J)+C(J-1)-C(J))/(1+G*(1.+R))
      C2=(C(J-1)+V(J-1)-V2X)/(1.+R)
      C2X=C2-G1
      V2=V(J-1)-C2+C(J-1)
      V(J-1)=V1+V2-V(J-1)
```

```
      C(J-1)=C1+C2-C(J-1)
      V1X=V2X
      C1=(C(J)+V1X-V(J))/(1.+R)
      C1X=C1+G
      V1=V(J)+C1-C(J)
 30 CONTINUE
! Varying boundary conditions at J=N+1: the circuit is broken with I<IR; it is closed
! with I=>IR through resistance RB
      IF(I.LT.IR) THEN
      C2X=0.
      V2X=(C(N)+V(N))/(1.+G*(1.+R))
      C2=V2X*G
      ELSE
      C2X=(C(N)+V(N))/(1.+R+RB*(1.+G*(1.+R)))
      C2=C2X*(1.+G*RB)
      V2X=C2X*RB
      ENDIF
      V2=V(N)-C2+C(N)
      V(N)=V1+V2-V(N)
      C(N)=C1+C2-C(N)
      CP2=C2X
      T=I*DT
      OPEN(3,FILE='CURRENT')              ! Currents C1 and C2 vs. time T
      WRITE(3,80)T,CP1,CP2
 20 CONTINUE
      OPEN(4,FILE='RESULTS')
      WRITE(4,*) 'Input data: N=',N,'.','NT–',NT,
      WRITE(4,*) 'R=',R,'.','G=',G,'.','IR=',IR,'.','RB=',RB
      WRITE(4,*) 'Control: N=10, NT=1000, R=0.01, G=0.001, IR=500, RB=0.1'
      WRITE(4,*) 'Benchmark: C1=3.334, C2=3.334 at T=100'
      WRITE(4,*) 'Calculated: T=',T,'.','C1=',CP1,'.','C2=',CP2
      STOP
      END
```

Foundations of Engineering Mechanics

***Series Editors*:** Vladimir I. Babitsky, Loughborough University
Jens Wittenburg, Karlsruhe University

Palmov	Vibrations of Elasto-Plastic Bodies (1998, ISBN 3-540-63724-9)
Babitsky	Theory of Vibro-Impact Systems and Applications (1998, ISBN 3-540-63723-0)
Skrzypek/ Ganczarski	Modeling of Material Damage and Failure of Structures Theory and Applications (1999, ISBN 3-540-63725-7)
Kovaleva	Optimal Control of Mechanical Oscillations (1999, ISBN 3-540-65442-9)
Kolovsky	Nonlinear Dynamics of Active and Passive Systems of Vibration Protection (1999, ISBN 3-540-65661-8)
Guz	Fundamentals of the Three-Dimensional Theory of Stability of Deformable Bodies (1999, ISBN 3-540-63721-4)
Alfutov	Stability of Elastic Structures (2000, ISBN 3-540-65700-2)
Morozov/ Petrov	Dynamics of Fracture (2000, ISBN 3-540-64274-9)
Astashev/ Babitsky/ Kolovsky	Dynamics and Control of Machines (2000, ISBN 3-540-63722-2)
Svetlitsky	Statics of Rods (2000, ISBN 3-540-67452-7)
Kolovsky/ Evgrafov/ Slousch/ Semenov	Advanced Theory of Mechanisms and Machines (2000, ISBN 3-540-67168-4)
Landa	Regular and Chaotic Oscillations (2001, ISBN 3-540-41001-5)

Foundations of Engineering Mechanics

Series Editors: Vladimir I. Babitsky, Loughborough University
Jens Wittenburg, Karlsruhe University

Muravskii	Mechanics of Non-Homogeneous and Anisotropic Foundations (2001, ISBN 3-540-41631-5)
Gorshkov/ Tarlakovsky	Transient Aerohydroelasticity of Spherical Bodies (2001, ISBN 3-540-42151-3)
Babitsky/ Krupenin	Vibration of Strongly Nonlinear Discontinuous Systems (2001, ISBN 3-540-41447-9
Manevitch/ Andrianov/ Oshmyan	Mechanics of Periodically Heterogeneous Structures (2002, ISBN 3-540-41630-7)
Lurie	Analytical Mechanics (2002, ISBN 3-540-42982-4)
Slepyan	Models and Phenomena in Fracture Mechanics (2002, ISBN 3-540-43767-3)
Nagaev	Dynamics of Synchronising Systems (2003, ISBN 3-540-44195-6)
Svetlitsky	Statistical Dynamics and Reliability Theory for Mechanical Structures (2003, ISBN 3-540-44297-9)
Neimark	Mathematical Models in Natural Science and Engineering (2003, ISBN 3-540-43680-4)
Babitsky/ Shipilov	Resonant Robotic Systems (2003, ISBN 3-540-00334-7)
Le xuan Anh	Dynamics of Mechanical Systems with Coulomb Friction (2003, ISBN 3-540-00654-0)
Perelmuter/ Slivker	Numerical Structural Analysis (2003, ISBN 3-540-00628-1)

Foundations of Engineering Mechanics

Series Editors: Vladimir I. Babitsky, Loughborough University
Jens Wittenburg, Karlsruhe University

Andrianov/ Awrejcewicz/ Manevitch	Asymptotical Mechanics of Thin-Walled Structures (2004, ISBN 3-540-40876-2)
Shorr	The Wave Finite Element Method (2004, ISBN 3-540-41638-2)

Printing: Saladruck Berlin
Binding: Stürtz AG, Würzburg